PRIMARY SOURCES
IN PSYCHOLOGY

Spencer A. Rathus
Montclair State University

ISBN: 0-15-507461-X

Address for Domestic Orders
Harcourt College Publishers, 6277 Sea Harbor Drive, Orlando, FL 32887-6777
800-782-4479

Address for International Orders
International Customer Service
Harcourt, Inc., 6277 Sea Harbor Drive, Orlando, FL 32887-6777
407-345-3800
(fax) 407-345-4060
(e-mail) hbintl@harcourtcollege.com

Address for Editorial Correspondence
Harcourt College Publishers, 301 Commerce Street, Suite 3700, Fort Worth, TX 76102

Web Site Address
http://www.harcourtcollege.com

Printed in the United States of America

9 0 1 2 3 4 5 6 7 8 202   9 8 7 6 5 4 3 2 1

Harcourt College Publishers

III LEARNING AND COGNITION 93

IV MOTIVATION AND EMOTION 191

V PERSONALITY AND PSYCHOTHERAPY
223

VI DEVELOPMENTAL PSYCHOLOGY
283

VII SOCIAL AND ENVIRONMENTAL PSYCHOLOGY 355

Harcourt, Inc.

hat is the difference between seeing a work of art in a museum or reading someone's description of it in a book? What is the difference between going to a live rock concert or reading a review of it in the newspaper the following morning? What is the difference between seeing a film and having a friend tell one about it? What does all of this have to do with the introduction to a collection of primary sources—original and undoctored theory and research from the discipline of psychology? When we visit a museum, go to a rock concert, or watch a film, or for that matter read primary sources, our encounter with the events is personal. We experience the work through our own intellectual, perceptual, or emotional lens. We form our own critical or ethical judgments rather than swallowing whole another's perspective.

The work of art is colorful; its description pales in comparison and details are lost. The review of the rock concert cannot capture its excitement or the immediate flesh and blood response of the crowd. The film is on the big screen, the audio surrounds the theater-goer, and there is tension as the plot unwinds. The best the friend can do is to say "It was great. You should see this for yourself."

Psychology students should see this—these primary sources—for themselves. Some of them are colorful. The details are present. The authors are of flesh and blood and there is often tension as the plots unwind. They loom large as life and demand to be experienced in their original form.

Intellectual Advantages

Psychology students, like students in any academic discipline, are also intellectually strengthened when they learn to read the psychological literature as it is, and need not rely on the cognitive filters of a textbook. Textbooks can provide summaries and shortcuts to learning, but they offer the author's interpretation of the primary sources and not the sources themselves. Thus they are always seen second-hand. The student may thus be encouraged to assume the viewpoint of the author rather than formulating one of his or her own. Giving students access to key primary sources, and encouraging students to think about them critically, creates the intellectual tools students need to stand on their own feet in a discipline.

The Excitement of Context

Regardless of when they were written, the primary sources often reflect the excitement of something that is very new. Darwin's theorizing on evolution occurred 150 years ago, during the middle of the 19th century, but you will catch his excitement at being on the cutting edge of the science of his day. Sigmund Freud's ideas are in a sense old hat a century after the fact, but in the beginning of the 20th century they broke new ground. The very language of the studies sometimes captures the cultural context in which they were written. Even the forward-looking Albert Bandura and his colleagues, for example, use the unwittingly sexist phrase "female appropriate activities, such as cooking" in their article on imitation of media aggression. We can imagine that the authors wince when they reflect on their writing of so many years ago.

The Personalities of the Authors

As you read these primary sources, you will also see that many of them provide insight into the personalities of the authors as well as into psychological theory, research, and practice. You will see, for example, that Harry Harlow was a "wag." He enjoyed verbally skewering people who held different points of view, even his fellow experimental psychologists. In an address he delivered to the convention of the American Psychological Association, "The Nature of Love," he quipped that experimental psychologists have a "peculiar propensity to discover facts that are not true." Carl Rogers, the originator of client-centered therapy, shows his humility when he writes that "Quite possibly all psychotherapy is basically similar, but . . . I am less sure of that than I once was." In their landmark study on sensory deprivation, Bexton and his colleagues also reveal their human side when they note that another scientist achieved isolation from sensory input by operating on the brains of laboratory animals; "College students, however, are reluctant to undergo brain operations for experimental purposes, so we had to be satisfied with less extreme isolation from the environment." You will see that John B. Watson, Colin Turnbull, and others also make many self-revealing remarks that comment on their roles as scientists or offer their personal opinions and outlooks. This is psychology in the raw—warts and all. It's good stuff. Fortunately or unfortunately, in more recent years journals have required more concise presentation, and have demanded that the "brushstrokes of the artist"—that is, the flourishes and personal touches of the author—be left out. The occasional key figure, like Albert Ellis, may escape such limitations, but in most cases the reading has become duller. What we may have gained in science, we have lost in art and pleasure.

The Sources

The primary sources included in this volume span the time of one and a half centuries. Some were written in the very year that this volume was collected. There are theoretical papers, book chapters, reports of empirical research, and even newspaper commentary.

To the sophisticated observer, any collection of primary sources must appear idiosyncratic at best and uninformed or biased at the worst. Nearly every instructor who reviews the table of contents will feel that there are serious omissions and that some of the sources chosen are foolish or superfluous. The only defense I can offer is that I have tried to achieve some sort of balance in terms of the fields of psychology covered and in terms of the kinds of writings selected to represent them. In some cases I have omitted major figures in favor of interesting studies. In other cases I have included the musings of key figures and neglected what some readers will consider to be key studies. But it is my hope that even the most critical observer will conclude that if students read and discuss the sources in this collection, they will become more sophisticated consumers of the psychological literature and better able to judge whether they might wish to further their education and training so that they might be able to add to that literature.

Let us now turn to some issues that will crop up as students read the sources.

Ethical Issues in Psychological Research

This collection contains many fascinating research studies with human and animal participants. You will notice that many of the studies could not have been carried out without deceiving the humans, and that many humans and animals were exposed to some degree of discomfort. Many of the animals, in fact, were "sacrificed" as a result of the research methods.

ETHICAL PRINCIPLES

Today psychologists tend to follow ethical principles such as those set forth by the American Psychological Association—the largest professional organization for psychologists—in December of 1992. Clause 1.14 of those principles, "Avoiding Harm," reads as follows:

> Psychologists take reasonable steps to avoid harming their patients or clients, research participants, students, and others with whom they work, and to minimize harm where it is foreseeable and unavoidable.

These principles are under review, and the American Psychological Society—the second largest body of psychologists—is participating in the review.

In any event, much of the classic research reported in this collection was carried out well before such a guiding principle was in effect. Even as written in 1992, the principle has some squiggle room built into it. For example, what exactly is the meaning of "harm"? Psychologists are expected to take "reasonable steps" to avoid harm. What exactly is a "reasonable step?" Then again, psychologists are expected to "minimize harm" that is "foreseeable" and "unavoidable"? These words and phrases are also less than crystal clear. I am not suggesting that the APA was seeking to weaken this principle even as it was being written. I am merely pointing out that the terms have a subjective quality that is open to interpretation.

Because of the lack of precision in the principle, books have been written on its interpretation and application in practice. You can hop over to www.apa.org to search for some of the discussion.

ETHICS REVIEW COMMITTEES

In order to help psychologists and other kinds of researchers function ethically, virtually all institutional settings, including colleges, hospitals, and research foundations, have established ethics review committees to help researchers weigh the potential harm to subjects in their proposals. When these committees find that proposals are unacceptably harmful to subjects, they may suggest less harmful alternative procedures. They may even withhold approval of a study until the proposal has been adequately modified.

INFORMED CONSENT

Today humans must also provide informed consent before they participate in research programs. Consent is "informed" when potential subjects are given a general overview of the research and the opportunity to choose not to participate. Well, of course! You may think, it's only fair. However, you will see that many of the studies with humans could not have been carried out if the true purpose of the research was explained at the beginning, so deception is sometimes an integral part of the research method.

DECEPTION

Deception means lying, or else withholding key information. The very concept of deception would seem to be at odds with ethical guidelines, but the guidelines, as put into practice, do not prevent psychologists from ever using deception. However, psychologists are advised to limit the use of deception to circumstances in which:

- they believe that the benefits of the research outweigh its potential harm,
- they believe that the individuals might have been willing to participate if they had understood the benefits of the research, and
- subjects receive an explanation afterward.

Consider the classic Milgram study on obedience in this collection. The subjects in the study (assigned the role of "teachers") were deceived into believing that they were shocking other people with electricity and that the purpose of the study was to determine the effects of punishment on learning. (It wasn't. The purpose was to see whether the subjects would obey the experimenter and shock innocent people.) Many psychologists have since debated the ethics of the Milgram study and the ethics of using deception in general.

DEBRIEFING

Psychological ethics require that research subjects who are deceived be debriefed afterward—that is, that they be informed of the actual purposes of the research and the effects of their behavior. For example, Milgram's subjects were informed that they had not actually shocked other people. Debriefing is intended to eliminate misconceptions and allay anxieties about the research and leave subjects with their dignity intact.

CONFIDENTIALITY

Psychologists treat the records of research subjects and clients as confidential. This is because they respect people's privacy and also because people are more likely to express their true thoughts and feelings when researchers or therapists keep their disclosures confidential. Thus you will not find the names or other identifying data of the participants in the studies presented here.

RESEARCH WITH ANIMALS

Ethics limit the types of research that psychologists may conduct. For example, how can we determine whether early separation from one's mother impairs social development? One way would be to observe the development of children who have been separated from their mothers at an early age. It is difficult to draw conclusions from such research, however, because of the selection factor. That is, the same factors that led to the separation—such as a family tragedy or irresponsible parents—and *not* the separation itself, may have led to the outcome. Scientifically, it would be more sound to run experiments in which researchers separate children from their mothers at an early age and compare their development with that of other children. But psychologists would not undertake such research because of the ethical issues they pose. Yet, they do run experiments with lower animals in which infants are separated from mothers. For example, the Harlow study on "The Nature of Love" used infant monkeys who had been separated from their mothers.

Psychologists and other scientists frequently use animals to conduct research that cannot be carried out with humans. In the following studies, for example, you will read that animals have been poisoned with curare in order to prevent them from using muscles voluntarily, that they have been operated on to prevent them from receiving sensory input from the environment, and that they have been "sacrificed" after experimental treatments have been completed. One article notes wryly that human subjects would probably object to such treatment, but animal rights activists do not find the treatment of animals to be a laughing matter.

Proponents of the use of animals in research argue that major advances in medicine and psychology could not have taken place without them. Nevertheless, the majority of psychologists disapprove of research in which animals are exposed to pain or killed. The ethical guidelines of the American Psychological Association suggest that animals may be harmed only when there is no alternative and when the researchers believe that the benefits of the research will justify the harm. Again, the language is imprecise, and different researchers may view the importance of a study or the amount of harm being done to animals differently.

Ethical guidelines are often inexact, but at the very least they show that someone is watching over research and making an effort to minimize the harm that is sometimes done.

Harcourt, Inc.

Types of Primary Sources

The types of sources included in this volume are mainly reports of empirical research studies and theoretical books and articles. The more recent research articles are written in "APA format." *APA* stands for American Psychological Association, and the format referred to is the standard for articles that are published in APA journals. Most psychology journals that are not published by the APA also require the APA format.

The APA format is somewhat rigid, but its purpose is to encourage researchers to report information clearly and concisely, so that readers may avail themselves of the information without obstacles. Put it another way: the APA format is designed to prevent writers from "getting in the way" of reporting their research findings or theoretical concepts. Conciseness is in fashion as we enter the new millennium; art is out.

REPORTS OF EMPIRICAL RESEARCH

These are reports of original research. The most recent studies in this volume are to the point (show economy in expression) and broken into standard sections. The older studies, such as those by Watson and Rayner and by Harlow, are a bit more free form, but even they follow a logical format. By paying attention to the dates in which studies were published you can observe the evolution of the style of reporting.

The usual sections or parts of reports of empirical research studies are:

- **Introduction** The introduction sets the stage for research by stating the problem, briefly reviewing previous research in the area, and showing how the current research will test or answer some of the issues in the area.
- **Method** The purpose of this section is to explain what the researchers did so clearly that people reading the report can replicate (duplicate) the work. It describes the subjects or participants, how they were selected for the study, how many actually participated and how many withdrew through the course of the study; the procedures that were used, including the treatments and the equipment; and the methods of assessment that were employed to measure the dependent variables (outcomes).
- **Results** This section reports the findings.
- **Discussion** The discussion section usually begins with a brief summary of the previous three sections. It then relates the findings to previous research in the area, discusses the implications of the findings for psychological theory, and may suggest directions for future research.

THEORETICAL WRITINGS

Theoretical papers evaluate scientific theory. In an introductory section, the author will usually state the theoretical problem and summarize much theoretical thinking up to the present day. There may then be a discussion of the shortcomings of current theoretical knowledge. Such shortcomings may involve theoretical contradictions or defects.

It may be argued, for example, that some tenets of psychodynamic theory are unscientific because they cannot be *disproved*. It may be argued that the behavior-therapy technique of systematic desensitization is not behavioral because it relies on mental imagery. Other shortcomings may involve inconsistencies between psychological theory and empirical evidence. The evidence, that is, may contradict the theory. The theory may suggest that increasing motivation enhances performance, but the evidence may show that increasing motivation helps up to a certain point, but then impairs performance. In a theoretical article, the concluding sections often suggest modifications to the theory that render the theory more logical or more consistent with empirical evidence.

Using This Volume

The organization of this volume is designed to help students locate or position the writings both in the history and the disciplines of psychology. There are seven broad areas of psychology or "parts" in the collection:

Part I	Biology and Behavior
Part II	Sensation, Perception, and Consciousness
Part III	Learning and Cognition
Part IV	Motivation and Emotion
Part V	Personality and Psychotherapy
Part VI	Developmental Psychology
Part VII	Social and Environmental Psychology

There is thus a flow of ideas and topics from the biological foundations of psychology to the psychology of the individual and then to the individual within the social or physical environment.

INTRODUCTIONS TO THE SOURCES

Each part begins with a "part opener" that describes the area of psychology and then briefly introduces the writings or primary sources contained within the part. Each individual source is prefaced with a broader introduction that will help set it in time and space and suggest some ideas that may help guide the reader through. In the case of major figures in psychology—the Darwins and Freuds and Watsons and Ellises—there is often a good deal of biographical information. In other cases, there may be more discussion of social issues or psychological questions that lie at the heart of the source.

QUESTIONS FOR REFLECTION AND DISCUSSION

Each source is then followed by questions for reflection and discussion that help the reader appreciate and evaluate the source. There are some repeated themes: questions that concern the personalities or personal views of the authors, questions that help students relate what they have read to their own experiences, questions that relate the source to broader issues in the field of psychology, questions for critical thinking and evaluation, and questions that refer to the ethics of research methods.

All in all, the reader should come away with a sense of the color of the originals, with a sense of the excitement of being there—of being at the cutting edge of discovery. It is more than hard science; it is also fun.

Acknowledgments

I gratefully acknowledge the help of the fine publishing professionals at Harcourt. Carol Wada provided guidance and a superb sounding board. Michele Tomiak converted a large carton of stuff into a book, and Carol Kincaid made it actually look like a book. I also want to thank my children for leaving me alone long enough to get this collection together and my wife for her excessive criticism of the first draft of the preface.

I

BIOLOGY AND BEHAVIOR

Many students who register for introductory psychology are surprised to find that there is much biology in the course—much on the nervous system and especially the brain, much on the endocrine system, and much on evolution and heredity. The reason for this is that our psychology is rooted in our biology. Our biology makes our behavior and mental processes possible and also sets limits on them. In the case of we humans, biology allows us to create and understand language, math, and music, but not to fly (without special equipment), live underwater (without special equipment), or go for a walk in outer space (without . . .). Therefore, one level of explanation of the human ability to do these things involves things that happen in the structures in our bodies, including those structures we can see, like the brain, and those that are microscopic, like individual brain cells and the myriad chemicals that flow from one brain cell to another.

The following primary sources are included in this section:

1. Olds, J., & Milner, P. (1954). Positive reinforcement produced by electrical stimulation of the septal area and other regions of rat brain. *Journal of Comparative and Physiological Psychology, 47,* 419–427.

This study describes one historic chapter in the ongoing enterprise of connecting biological structures with psychological functions. When it was reported, some psychologists and social commentators wondered whether human happiness might require little more than gaining control over the right area of the brain.

2. Gazzaniga, M. S. (1967). The split brain in man. *Scientific American, 217,* 24–29.

The brain looks something like a walnut (out of the shell), with its wrinkled surface and its division into hemispheres. These experiments were among the first to report on the effects of dividing that walnut (or brain) in twain. In some ways it seems that we wind up with two brains, not one.

3. Bouchard, T. J., Jr., Lykken, D. T., McGue, M., Segal, N. L., & Tellegen, A. (1990). Sources of human psychological differences: The Minnesota study of twins reared apart. *Science, 250,* 223–228.

It is no secret that people tend to look more like their parents and other relatives than strangers from the other side of the world. We readily attribute the similarity to our heredity. But what of our behavior and mental processes? Do we also tend to behave and think more like our parents? And if so, why? This study reports on ongoing research into the roles of heredity (nature) and environmental influences (nurture) on psychological similarities and differences.

4. I. Darwin, C. (1858/1993). Extract from an Unpublished Work on Species, by C. Darwin, Esq., Consisting of a Portion of a Chapter Entitled "On the Variation of Organic Beings in a State of Nature; on the Natural Means of Selection; on the Comparison of Domestic Races and True Species"; II. Darwin, C. (1858/1993). Abstract of a Letter from C. Darwin, Esq., to Prof. Asa Gray, Boston, U.S., dated Down, September 5, 1857; III. Wallace, A. R. (1858/1993). On the Tendency of Varieties to depart indefinitely from the Original Type, by Alfred Russel Wallace; IV. Darwin, C. (1959/1993). Sexual selection. From *On the origin of species by means of natural selection, or The preservation of favoured races in the struggle for life.* (1859/1993).

These historic sources were written nearly one and a half centuries ago, and they reflect ideas that are a generation older than that. Having said that, you may be amazed at how fresh and in tune they are with contemporary thought on evolution. Charles Darwin is one of the most celebrated figures in the history of science, and these readings will enable you to appreciate his genius—and that of a fellow theorist, Alfred Russel Wallace.

5. Buss, D. M. (1999, June 1). Evolutionary science ponders: Where is fancy bred? *The New York Times Online.*

Why do men have a roving eye? Why do women crave stable relationships? (Why have I just tossed two stereotypes in your path?) This source is taken from the popular media—*The New York Times*—and not from a professional journal or historic theoretical treatise. Its approach will provide a sometimes humorous counterpoint to the typical scientific article.

Many other articles will be found in this collection that also reflect the interfaces between biology and psychology. They include those by Dement (1960), Hobson & McCarley (1977), Miller (1969), and Bexton, Heron, & Scott (1954).

Olds, J., & Milner, P. (1954). Positive reinforcement produced by electrical stimulation of the septal area and other regions of rat brain. *Journal of Comparative and Physiological Psychology, 47*, 419–427.

Many scientific discoveries are made by accident. For example, McGill University psychologists James Olds and Peter Milner tried to implant an electrode in a rat's reticular formation to learn whether electrical stimulation of the area would have an effect on learning. However, Olds, whose training was in social psychology and not biological psychology, missed his target and hit a part of the hypothalamus instead. Although Olds made a mistake, the rat did not complain. Instead, it appeared to savor the error. It did whatever it could to receive more electrical stimulation, such as press a lever or remain in the part of its cage where it had been stimulated. Because the animal sought out this stimulation, to the point where it would exhaust itself by pressing a lever hundreds of times without pausing, this area of the brain has been referred to as a "pleasure center."

As you will see, the article itself makes no reference to a term like "pleasure center." To be frank, the article is as dry as can be. There is hardly any inkling in it of its importance to the field of biological psychology or of its possible implications for humans. Even the brief introduction to the article, which speaks of the eliciting and reinforcing functions of stimuli, provides little insight into the excitement that this line of research has stirred.

Positive Reinforcement Produced by Electrical Stimulation of Septal Area and Other Regions of Rat Brain

JAMES OLDS AND PETER MILNER
MCGILL UNIVERSITY

Stimuli have eliciting and reinforcing functions. In studying the former, one concentrates on the responses which come after the stimulus. In studying the latter, one looks mainly at the responses which precede it. In its reinforcing capacity, a stimulus increases, decreases, or leaves unchanged the frequency of preceding responses, and accordingly it is called a reward, a punishment, or a neutral stimulus (cf. 16).

Previous studies using chronic implantation of electrodes have tended to focus on the eliciting functions of electrical stimuli delivered to the brain (2, 3, 4, 5, 7, 10, 12, 14). The present study, on the other hand, has been concerned with the reinforcing function of the electrical stimulation.

Method

GENERAL

Stimulation was carried out by means of chronically implanted electrodes which did not interfere with the health or free behavior of *S*s to any appreciable extent. The *S*s were 15 male hooded rats, weighing approximately 250 gm. at the start of the experiment. Each *S* was tested in a Skinner box which delivered alternating current to the brain so long as a lever was depressed. The current was delivered over a loose lead, suspended from the ceiling, which connected the stimulator to the rat's electrode. The Ss were given a total of 6 to 12 hr. of acquisition testing, and 1 to 2 hr. of extinction testing. During acquisition, the stimulator was turned on so that a response produced electrical stimulation; during extinction, the stimulator was turned off so that a response produced no electrical stimulation. Each S was given a percentage score denoting the proportion of his total acquisition time given to responding. This score could be compared with the animal's extinction score to determine whether the stimulation had a positive, negative, or neutral reinforcing effect. After testing, the animal was sacrificed. Its brain was frozen, sectioned, stained, and examined microscopically to determine which structure of the brain had been stimulated. This permitted correlation of acquisition scores with anatomical structures.

ELECTRODE IMPLANTATION

Electrodes are constructed by cementing a pair of enameled silver wires of 0.010-in. diameter into a Lucite block, as shown in Figure 1.01. The parts of the wires which penetrate the brain are cemented together to form a needle, and this is cut to the correct length to reach the desired structure in the brain. This length is determined from Krieg's rat brain atlas (11) with slight modifications as found necessary by experience. The exposed cross section of the wire is the only part of the needle not insu-

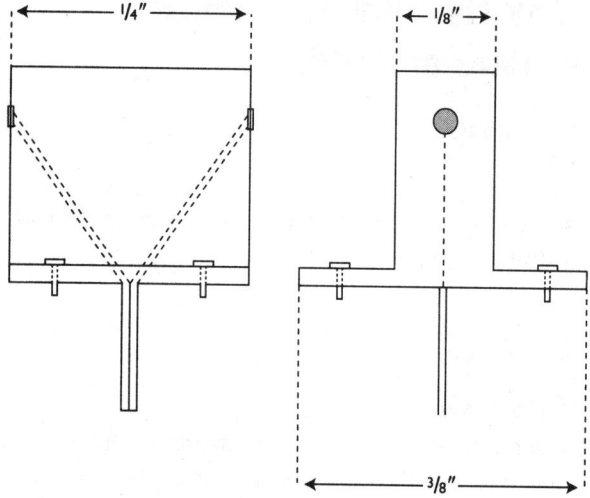

FIGURE 1.01

Electrode design (see text for detailed description).

lated from the brain by enamel; stimulation therefore occurs only at the tip. Contact with the lead from the stimulator is made through two blobs of solder on the upper ends of the electrode wires; these blobs make contact with the jaws of an alligator clip which has been modified to insulate the two jaws from one another. A light, flexible hearing-aid lead connects the clip to the voltage source.

The operation of implantation is performed with the rat under Nembutal anesthesia (0.88 cc/Kg) and held in a Johnson-Krieg stereotaxic instrument (11). A mid-line incision is made in the scalp and the skin held out of the way by muscle retractors. A small hole is drilled in the skull with a dental burr at the point indicated by the stereotaxic instrument for the structure it is desired to stimulate. The electrode, which is clamped into the needle carrier of the instrument, is lowered until the flange of the Lucite block rests firmly on the skull. Four screw holes are then drilled in the skull through four fixing holes in the flange, and the electrode, still clamped firmly in the instrument, is fastened to the skull with jeweler's screws which exceed the diameter of the screw holes in the skull by 0.006 in. The electrode is then released from the clamp and the scalp wound closed with silk sutures. The skin is pulled tightly around the base of the Lucite block and kept well away from the contact plates. A recovery period of three days is allowed after the operation before testing.

TESTING

The testing apparatus consisted of a large-levered Skinner box 11 in. long, 5 in. wide, and 12 in. high. The top was open to allow passage for the stimulating lead. The lever actuated a microswitch in the stimulating circuit so that when it was depressed, the rat received electrical stimulation. The current was obtained from the 60-cycle power line, through a step-down transformer, and was adjustable between 0 and 10 v. r.m.s. by means of a variable potentiometer. In the experiments described here the stimulation continued as long as the lever was pressed, though for some tests a time delay switch was incorporated which cut the current off after a predetermined interval if the rat continued to hold the lever down. Responses were recorded automatically on paper strip.

On the fourth day after the operation rats were given a pretesting session of about an hour in the boxes. Each rat was placed in the box and on the lever by E with the stimulus set at 0.5 v. During the hour, stimulation voltage was varied to determine the threshold of a "just noticeable" effect on the rat's behavior. If the animal did not respond regularly from the start, it was placed on the lever periodically (at about 5-min. intervals). Data collected on the first day were not used in later calculations. On subsequent days, Ss were placed in the box for about $3\frac{1}{2}$ hr. a day; these were 3 hr. of acquisition and $\frac{1}{2}$ hr. of extinction. During the former, the rats were allowed to stimulate themselves with a voltage which was just high enough to produce some noticeable response in the resting animal. As this threshold voltage fluctuated with the passage of time, E would make a determination of it every half hour, unless S was responding regularly. At the beginning of each acquisition period, and after each voltage test, the animal was placed on the lever once by E. During extinction periods, conditions were precisely the same except that a bar press produced no electrical stimulation. At the beginning of each extinction period, animals which were not responding regularly were placed on the lever once by E. At first, rats were tested in this way for four days, but as there appeared to be little difference between the results on different days, this period was reduced to three and then to two days for subsequent animals. Thus, the first rats had about 12 hr. of acquisition after pretesting whereas later rats had about 6 hr. However, in computing the scores in our table, we have used only the first 6 hr. of acquisition for all animals, so the scores are strictly comparable. In behavioral curves, we have shown the full 12 hr. of acquisition on the earlier animals so as to illustrate the stability of the behavior over time.

At no time during the experiment were the rats deprived of food or water, and no reinforcement was used except the electrical stimulus.

Animals were scored on the percentage of time which they spent bar pressing regularly during acquisition. In order to find how much time the animal would spend in the absence of reward or punishment, a similar score was computed for periods of extinction. This extinction score provided a base line. When the acquisition score is above the extinction score, we have reward; when it is below the extinction score, we have punishment.

In order to determine percentage scores, periods when the animal was responding regularly (at least one response every 30 sec.) were counted as periods of responding; i.e., *intervals of 30 sec. or longer without a response were counted as periods of no responding.* The percentage scores were computed as the proportion of total acquisition or extinction time given to periods of responding.

DETERMINATION OF LOCUS

On completion of testing, animals were perfused with physiological saline, followed by 10 per cent formalin. The brains were removed, and after further fixation in formalin for about a week, frozen sections 40 microns thick were cut through the region of the electrode track. These were stained with cresyl violet and the position of the electrode tip determined.

Results

LOCUS

In Table 1.01, acquisition and extinction scores are correlated with electrode placements. Figure 1.02 presents the acquisition scores again, this time on three cross-sectional maps of the rat brain, one at the forebrain level, one at the thalamic level, and one at the mid-brain level. The position of a score on the map indicates the electrode placement from which this acquisition score was obtained.

The highest scores are found together in the central portion of the forebrain. Beneath the *corpus callosum* and between the two lateral ventricles in section I of Figure 1.02, we find four acquisition scores ranging from 75 to 92 per cent. This is the septal area. The Ss which produced these scores are numbered 32, 34, M-1, and M-4 in Table 1.01. It will be noticed that while all of them spent more than 75 per cent of their acquisition time responding, they all spent less than 22 per cent of their extinction time responding. Thus the electrical stimulus in the septal area has an effect which is apparently equivalent to that of a conventional primary reward as far as the maintenance of a lever-pressing response is concerned.

If we move outside the septal area, either in the direction of the caudate nucleus (across the lateral ventricle) or in the direction of the *corpus callosum,* we find acquisition scores drop abruptly to levels of from 4 to 6 per cent. These are definitely indications of neutral (neither rewarding nor punishing) effects.

However, above the *corpus callosum* in the cingulate cortex we find an acquisition score of 37 per cent. As the extinction score in this case was 9 per cent, we may say that stimulation was rewarding.

At the thalamic level (section II of Fig. 1.02) we find a 36 per cent acquisition score produced by an electrode placed again in the cingulate cortex, an 11 per cent score produced by an electrode placed in the hippocampus, a 71 per cent score produced by an electrode placed exactly in the mammillothala-

TABLE 1.01

ACQUISITION AND EXTINCTION SCORE FOR ALL ANIMALS TOGETHER WITH ELECTRODE PLACEMENTS AND THRESHOLD VOLTAGES USED DURING ACQUISITION TESTS

ANIMAL'S NO.	LOCUS OF ELECTRODE	STIMULATION VOLTAGE R.M.S.	PERCENTAGE OF ACQUISITION TIME SPENT RESPONDING	PERCENTAGE OF EXTINCTION TIME SPENT RESPONDING
32	septal	2.2–2.8	75	18
34	septal	1.4	92	6
M-1	septal	1.7–4.8	85	21
M-4	septal	2.3–4.8	88	13
40	c.c.	.7–1.1	6	3
41	caudate	.9–1.2	4	4
31	cingulate	1.8	37	9
82	cingulate	.5–1.8	36	10
36	hip.	.8–2.8	11	14
3	m.l.	.5	0	4
A-5	m.t.	1.4	71	9
6	m.g.	.5	0	31
11	m.g.	.5	0	21
17	teg.	.7	2	1
9	teg.	.5	77	81

KEY: c.c., corpus callosum; hip., *hippocampus;* m.l., *medial lemniscus;* m.t., *Mammillothalamic tract;* m.g., *medial geniculate;* teg., *tegmentum.*

mic tract, and a zero per cent score produced by an electrode placed in the medial lemniscus. The zero denotes negative reinforcement.

At the mid-brain level (section III of Fig. 1.02) there are two zero scores produced by electrodes which are in the posterior portion of the medial geniculate bodies; here again, the scores indicate a negative effect, as the corresponding extinction scores are 31 and 21 per cent. There is an electrode deep in the medial, posterior tegmentum which produces a 2 per cent score; this seems quite neutral, as the extinction score in this case is 1 per cent. Finally, there is an electrode shown on this section which actually stands $1\frac{1}{2}$ mm. anterior to the point where it is shown; it was between the red nucleus and the posterior commissure. It produced an acquisition score of 77 per cent, but an extinction score of 81 per cent. This must be a rewarding placement, but the high extinction score makes it difficult to interpret.

BEHAVIOR

We turn our attention briefly to the behavioral data produced by the more rewarding electrode placements.

The graph in Figure 1.03 is a smoothed cumulative response curve illustrating the rate of responding of rat No. 32 (the lowest-scoring septal area rat) during acquisition and extinction. The animal gave a total of slightly over 3000 responses in the 12 hr. of acquisition. When the current was turned on, the animal responded at a rate of 285 responses an hour; when the current was turned off, the rate fell close to zero.

The graph in Figure 1.04 gives similar data on rat No. 34 (the highest-scoring septal rat). The animal stimulated itself over 7500 times in 12 hr. Its average response rate during acquisition was 742 responses an hour; during extinction, practically zero.

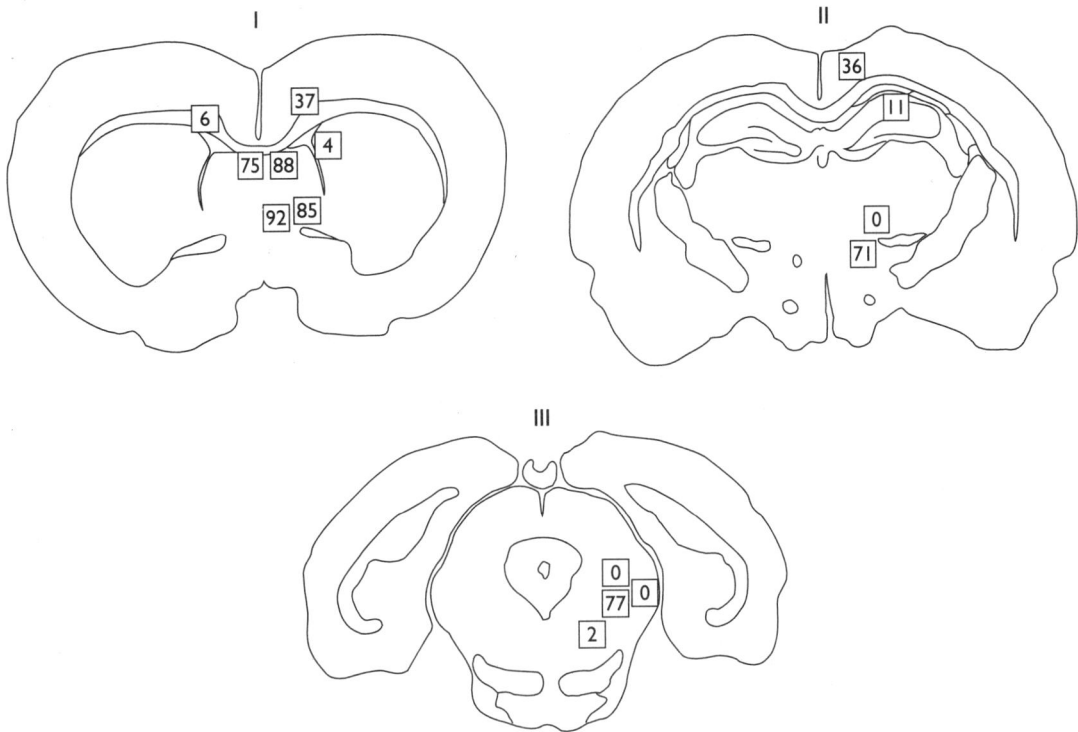

FIGURE 1.02

Maps of three sections, (I) through the forebrain, (II) through the thalamus, (III) through the mid-brain of the rat. Boxed numbers give acquisition percentage scores produced by animals with electrodes stimulating at these points. On section I the acquisition scores 75, 88, 92, 85 fall in the septal forebrain area. On the same section there is a score of 4 in the caudate nucleus, a score of 6 in the white matter below the cortex, and a score of 37 in the medial (cingulate) cortex. On section II the acquisition score of 36 is in the medial (cingulate) cortex, II is in the hippocampus, 71 is in the mammillothalamic tract, and 0 is in the medial lemniscus. On section III the two zeroes are in the medial geniculate, 2 is in the tegmental reticular substance, 77 falls 2 mm. anterior to the section shown—it is between the posterior commissure and the red nucleus.

Figure 1.05 presents an unsmoothed cumulative response curve for one day of responding for rat No. A-5. This is to illustrate in detail the degree of control exercised by the electrical reward stimulus. While this rat was actually bar pressing, it did so at 1920 responses an hour; that is, about one response for every 2 sec. During the first period of the day it responded regularly while on acquisition, extinguished very rapidly when the current was turned off, and reconditioned readily when the current was turned on again. At reconditioning points, *E* gave *S* one stimulus to show that the current was turned on again, but *E* did not place *S* on the lever. During longer periods of acquisition, *S* occasionally stopped responding for short periods, but in the long run *S* spent almost three-quarters of its acquisition time responding. During the long period of extinction at the end of the day, there was very little responding, but *S* could be brought back to the lever quite quickly if a stimulus was delivered to show that the current had been turned on again.

Discussion

It is clear that electrical stimulation in certain parts of the brain, particularly the septal area, produces acquisition and extinction curves which compare favorably with those produced by a conventional primary reward. With other electrode placements, the stimulation appears to be neutral or punishing.

Because the rewarding effect has been produced maximally by electrical stimulation in the septal area, but also in lesser degrees in the mammillothalamic tract and cingulate cortex, we are led to speculate that a system of structures previously attributed to the rhinencephalon may provide the locus for the reward phenomenon. However, as localization studies which will map the whole brain with respect to the reward and punishment dimension are continuing, we will not discuss in detail the problem of locus. We will use the term "reinforcing structures" in further discussion as a general name for the septal

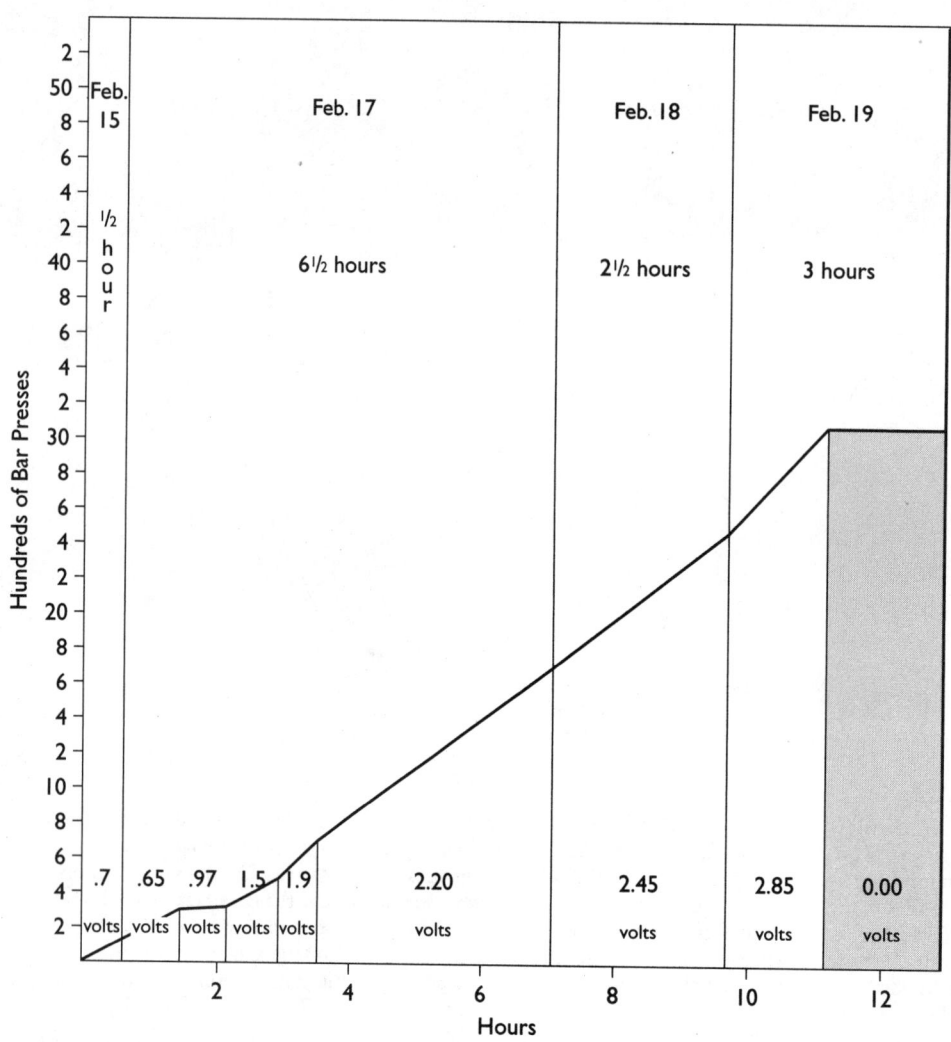

FIGURE 1.03

Smoothed cumulative response curve for rat No. 32. Cumulative response totals are given along the ordinate, and hours along the abscissa. The steepness of the slope indicates the response rate. Stimulating voltages are given between black lines. Shading indicates extinction.

area and other structures which produce the reward phenomenon.

To provide an adequate canvass of the possible explanations for the rewarding effect would require considerably more argument than could possibly fit within the confines of a research paper. We have decided, therefore, to rule out briefly the possibility that the implantation produces pain which is reduced by electrical stimulation of reinforcing structures, and to confine further discussion to suggestions of ways the phenomenon may provide a methodological basis for study of physiological mechanisms of reward.

The possibility that the implantation produces some painful "drive stimulus" which is alleviated by electrical stimulation of reinforcing structures does not comport with the facts which we have observed. If there were some chronic, painful drive state, it would be indicated by emotional signs in the animal's daily behavior. Our Ss, from the first day after the operation, are normally quiet, nonaggressive; they eat regularly, sleep regularly, gain weight. There is no evidence in their behavior to support the postulation of chronic pain. Septal preparations which have lived healthy and normal lives for months after the operation have given excellent response rates.

As there is no evidence of a painful condition preceding the electrical stimulation, and as the animals are given free access to food and water at all times except while actually in the Skinner boxes,

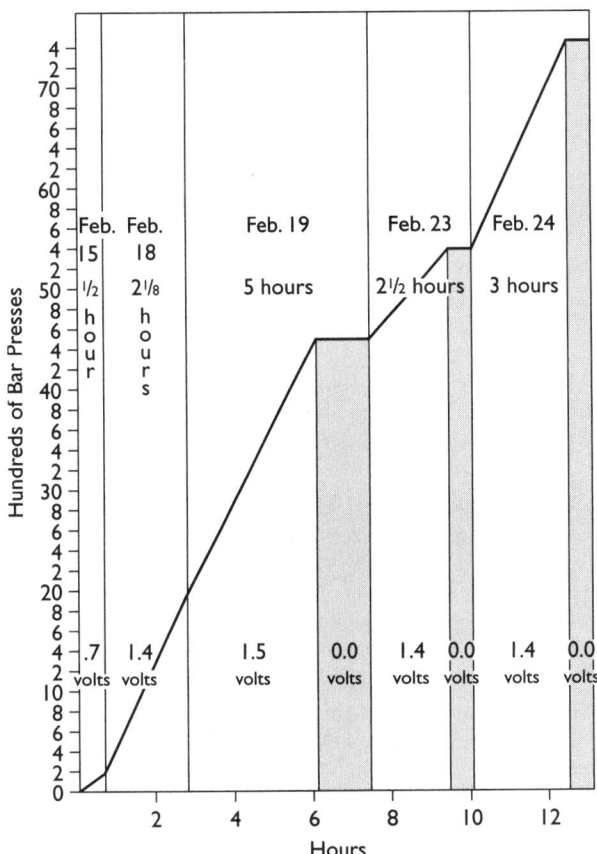

FIGURE 1.04

Smoothed cumulative response curve for rat No. 34.

there is no explicitly manipulated drive to be reduced by electrical stimulation. Barring the possibility that stimulation of a reinforcing structure specifically inhibits the "residual drive" state of the animal, or the alternative possibility that the first

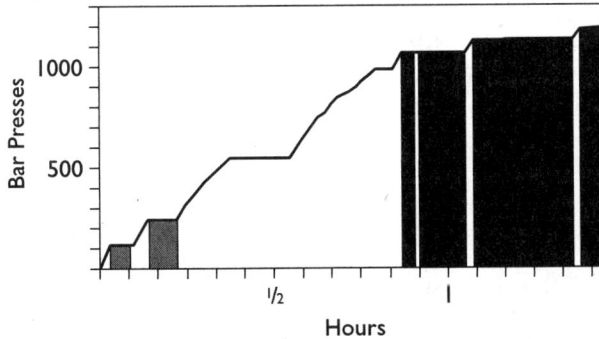

FIGURE 1.05

Unsmoothed cumulative response curve showing about $\frac{3}{4}$ hr. of acquisition and $\frac{3}{4}$ hr. extinction for rat No. A-5. Shading indicates extinction.

electrical stimulus has noxious after-effects which are reduced by a second one, we have some evidence here for a primary rewarding effect which is not associated with the reduction of a primary drive state. It is perhaps fair in a discussion to report the "clinical impression" of the *E*s that the phenomenon represents strong pursuit of a positive stimulus rather than escape from some negative condition.

Should the latter interpretation prove correct, we have perhaps located a system within the brain whose peculiar function is to produce a rewarding effect on behavior. The location of such a system puts us in a position to collect information that may lead to a decision among conflicting theories of reward. By physiological studies, for example, we may find that the reinforcing structures act selectively on sensory or motor areas of the cortex. This would have relevance to current S-S versus S-R controversies (8, 9, 13, 16).

Similarly, extirpation studies may show whether reinforcing structures have primarily a quieting or an activating effect on behavior; this would be relevant to activation versus negative feedback theories of reward (6, 13, 15, 17). A recent study by Brady and Nauta (1) already suggests that the septal area is a quieting system, for its surgical removal produced an extremely active animal.

Such examples, we believe, make it reasonable to hope that the methodology reported here should have important consequences for physiological studies of mechanisms of reward.

Summary

A preliminary study was made of rewarding effects produced by electrical stimulation of certain areas of the brain. In all cases rats were used and stimulation was by 60-cycle alternating current with voltages ranging from $\frac{1}{2}$ to 5 v. Bipolar needle electrodes were permanently implanted at various points in the brain. Animals were tested in Skinner boxes where they could stimulate themselves by pressing a lever. They received no other reward than the electrical stimulus in the course of the experiments. The primary findings may be listed as follows: (*a*) There are numerous places in the lower centers of the brain where electrical stimulation is rewarding in the sense that the experimental animal will stimulate itself in these places frequently and regularly for long periods of time if permitted to do so. (*b*) It is possible to obtain these results from as far back as the tegmentum, and as far forward as the septal area; from as far down as the subthalamus, and as far up as the cingulate gyrus of the cortex. (*c*) There are also sites in the lower centers where the effect is just the opposite: animals do everything possible to avoid stimulation. And there are neutral sites: animals do nothing to obtain or to avoid stimulation. (*d*) The reward results are obtained more dependably with electrode placements in some areas than others, the septal area being the most dependable to date. (*e*) In septal area preparations, the control exercised over the animal's behavior by means of this reward is extreme, possibly exceeding that exercised by any other reward previously used in animal experimentation.

The possibility that the reward results depended on some chronic painful consequences of the implantation operation was ruled out on the evidence that no physiological or behavioral signs of such pain could be found. The phenomenon was discussed as possibly laying a methodological foundation for a physiological study of the mechanisms of reward.

References

1. Brady, J. V., & Nauta, W. J. H. Subcortical mechanisms in emotional behavior: affective changes following septal forebrain lesions in the albino rat. *J. Comp. Physiol. Psychol.*, 1953, **46**, 339–346.
2. Delgado, J. M. R. Permanent implantation of multilead electrodes in the brain. *Yale J. Biol. Med.*, 1952, **24**, 351–358.
3. Delgado, J. M. R. Responses evoked in waking cat by electrical stimulation of motor cortex. *Amer. J. Physiol.*, 1952, **171**, 436–446.
4. Delgado, J. M. R., & Anand, B. K. Increase of food intake induced by electrical stimulation of the lateral hypothalamus. *Amer. J. Physiol.*, 1953, **172**, 162–168.
5. Dell, P. Correlations entre le système vegetatif et le système de la vie relation: mesencephale, diencephale, et cortex cerebral. *J. Physiol.* (Paris), 1952, **44**, 471–557.
6. Deutsch, J. A. A new type of behavior theory. *Brit. J. Psychol.*, 1953, **44**, 304–317.
7. Gastaut, H. Correlations entre le système nerveux vegetatif et le système de la vie de relation dans le rhinencephale. *J. Physiol.* (Paris), 1952, **44**, 431–470.
8. Hebb, D. O. *The organization of behavior.* New York: Wiley, 1949.
9. Hull, C. L. *Principles of behavior.* New York: D. Appleton-Century, 1943.
10. Hunter, J., & Jasper, H. H. Effects of thalamic stimulation in unanaesthetized animals. *EEG Clin. Neurophysiol.*, 1949, **1**, 305–324.
11. Krieg, W. J. S. Accurate placement of minute lesions in the brain of the albino rat. *Quart. Bull., Northwestern Univer. Med. School*, 1946, **20**, 199–208.
12. MacLean, P. D., & Delgado, J. M. R. Electrical and chemical stimulation of frontotemporal portion of limbic system in the waking animal. *EEG Clin. Neurophysiol.*, 1953, **5**, 91–100.
13. Olds, J. A neural model for sign-gestalt theory. *Psychol. Rev.*, 1954, **61**, 59–72.
14. Rosvold, H. E., & Delgado, J. M. R. The effect on the behavior of monkeys of electrically stimulating or destroying small areas within the frontal lobes. *Amer. Psychologist*, 1953, **8**, 425–426. (Abstract)
15. Seward, J. P. Introduction to a theory of motivation in learning. *Psychol. Rev.*, 1952, **59**, 405–413.
16. Skinner, B. F. *The behavior of organisms.* New York: D. Appleton-Century, 1938.
17. Wiener, N. *Cybernetics.* New York: Wiley, 1949. *Received July 15, 1954.*

QUESTIONS FOR REFLECTION AND DISCUSSION:

1. Why do you think that the tone or style of the authors is so dry and matter-of-fact?

2. What ethical considerations are involved in the treatment of the animals in this study? What does it mean to say that the rats were "sacrificed" after testing so that the placement of the electrodes could be better determined?

3. What evidence do the authors present that the animals were not in pain during testing?

4. Why do you think some scientists object to use of the term *pleasure center* in discussions of the behavior of rats? Why do behaviorists prefer to stick to terms like *reinforcement*? (Hint: In your answer, you may wish to refer to the term *anthropomorphizing.*)

5. People who refer to this study usually speak of the discovery of a pleasure center in the brain. What else did the researchers discover?

6. Humans have brain areas like those of the rats in this study, but stimulation of these areas has not been shown to have the same dramatic effects. Nevertheless, what are the implications of this line of research for control of the behavior of humans? (Why have some social commentators been frightened by this sort of discovery?)

7. Assume that people have pleasure centers (or reinforcement centers) in the brain and that it is possible to stimulate them as with the rats in the Olds and Milner study. Do you think that legislators might try to make such self-stimulation illegal? Why or why not?

SOURCE

Gazzaniga, M. S. (1967). The split brain in man. *Scientific American, 217,* 24—29. Reprinted with permission of Eric Mose, Jr. Copyright © 1967 by Scientific American, Inc. All rights reserved.

Psychologists look in many directions in the effort to understand and explain human behavior and mental processes. Some look to processes of learning and consider the roles of educational experiences and cultural expectations. Some study the ways in which people reason and solve problems. Some look to our bodies, and within our bodies to the functioning of the nervous system. It is widely accepted today that for every mental process—for every decision, for every judgment, for every memory, delicious or vile—there are underlying biological processes. The mind, that is, is based on substance, the substance of the nervous system, and particularly that most important part of the central nervous system, the brain.

Terrible and glorious accidents and coincidences have fueled the human quest for knowledge of the workings of the brain. In the year 1848, for example, a promising young railroad worker named Phineas Gage was the victim of an explosion that shot a metal rod through his cheek and brain and out the top of his head. Miraculously, Gage survived, but months later, after his external wounds had healed, it became obvious that his wound had changed his personality. The once dependable, mild-mannered Gage had become unreliable, foul-mouthed, and ill-mannered. We now recognize that the trajectory of the rod had spared parts of the frontal lobes that were involved in language and movement but damaged the parts connected with personality.

Also in the 19th century, French surgeon Paul Broca was the first to observe a behavior problem and then locate the area of the brain that caused it. In 1861, Leborgne, a patient at the Paris asylum called La Bicêtre, came down with gangrene in the leg and was admitted to the surgical ward. Leborgne could understand what people said to him, but he could only utter the meaningless sound "tan" and sometimes, when feeling frustrated, blurt out "Sacred name of God!" After Leborgne died, Broca performed an autopsy and discovered that an egg-sized area on the left side of the brain had deteriorated. Broca concluded that this part of the brain was the seat of speech. We now call it Broca's area.

In the 20th century, surgeons began severing much of the corpus callosum, the thick bundle of fibers that connects the left and right hemispheres of the brain, in an effort to control severe cases of epilepsy. In epilepsy, neural discharges can occur rapidly, bouncing messages back and forth between the hemispheres like ping pong balls, creating an electrochemical tempest. As described by Michael Gazzaniga in the classic "The Split Brain in Man," these operations may be helpful with epilepsy, but they also give rise to some very unexpected psychological effects.

Harcourt, Inc.

The Split Brain in Man

The human brain is actually two brains, each capable of advanced mental functions. When the cerebrum is divided surgically, it is as if the cranium contained two separate spheres of consciousness.

MICHAEL S. GAZZANIGA

The brain of the higher animals, including man, is a double organ, consisting of right and left hemispheres connected by an isthmus of nerve tissue called the corpus callosum. Some 15 years ago Ronald E. Myers and R. W. Sperry, then at the University of Chicago, made a surprising discovery: When this connection between the two halves of the cerebrum was cut, each hemisphere functioned independently as if it were a complete brain. The phenomenon was first investigated in a cat in which not only the brain but also the optic chiasm, the crossover of the optic nerves, was divided, so that visual information from the left eye was dispatched only to the left brain and information from the right eye only to the right brain. Working on a problem with one eye, the animal could respond normally and learn to perform a task; when that eye was covered and the same problem was presented to the other eye, the animal evinced no recognition of the problem and had to learn it again from the beginning with the other half of the brain.

The finding introduced entirely new questions in the study of brain mechanisms. Was the corpus callosum responsible for integration of the operations of the two cerebral hemispheres in the intact brain? Did it serve to keep each hemisphere informed about what was going on in the other? To put the question another way, would cutting the corpus callosum literally result in the right hand not knowing what the left was doing? To what extent were the two half-brains actually independent when they were separated? Could they have separate thoughts, even separate emotions?

Such questions have been pursued by Sperry and his co-workers in a wide-ranging series of animal studies at the California Institute of Technology over the past decade [see "The Great Cerebral Commissure," by R. W. Sperry; SCIENTIFIC AMERICAN, January, 1964]. Recently these questions have been investigated in human patients who underwent the brain-splitting operation for medical reasons. The demonstration in experimental animals that sectioning of the corpus callosum did not seriously impair mental faculties had encouraged surgeons to resort to this operation for people afflicted with uncontrollable epilepsy. The hope was to confine a seizure to one hemisphere. The operation proved to be re-

markably successful; curiously there is an almost total elimination of all attacks, including unilateral ones. It is as if the intact callosum had served in these patients to facilitate seizure activity.

This article is a brief survey of investigations Sperry and I have carried out at Cal Tech over the past five years with some of these patients. The operations were performed by P. J. Vogel and J. E. Bogen of the California College of Medicine. Our studies date back to 1961, when the first patient, a 48-year-old war veteran, underwent the operation: cutting of the corpus callosum and other commissure structures connecting the two halves of the cerebral cortex [see Fig. 2.02]. As of today 10 patients have had the operation, and we have examined four thoroughly over a long period with many tests.

From the beginning one of the most striking observations was that the operation produced no noticeable change in the patients' temperament, personality or general intelligence. In the first case the patient could not speak for 30 days after the operation, but he then recovered his speech. More typical was the third case: on awaking from the surgery the patient quipped that he had a "splitting headache," and in his still drowsy state he was able to repeat the tongue twister "Peter Piper picked a peck of pickled peppers."

Close observation, however, soon revealed some changes in the patients' everyday behavior. For example, it could be seen that in moving about and responding to sensory stimuli the patients favored the right side of the body, which is controlled by the dominant left half of the brain. For a considerable period after the operation the left side of the body rarely showed spontaneous activity, and the patient generally did not respond to stimulation of that side: when he brushed against something with his left side he did not notice that he had done so, and when an object was placed in his left hand he generally denied its presence.

More specific tests identified the main features of the bisected-brain syndrome. One of these tests examined responses to visual stimulation. While the patient fixed his gaze on a central point on a board, spots of light were flashed (for a tenth of a second) in a row across the board that spanned both the left

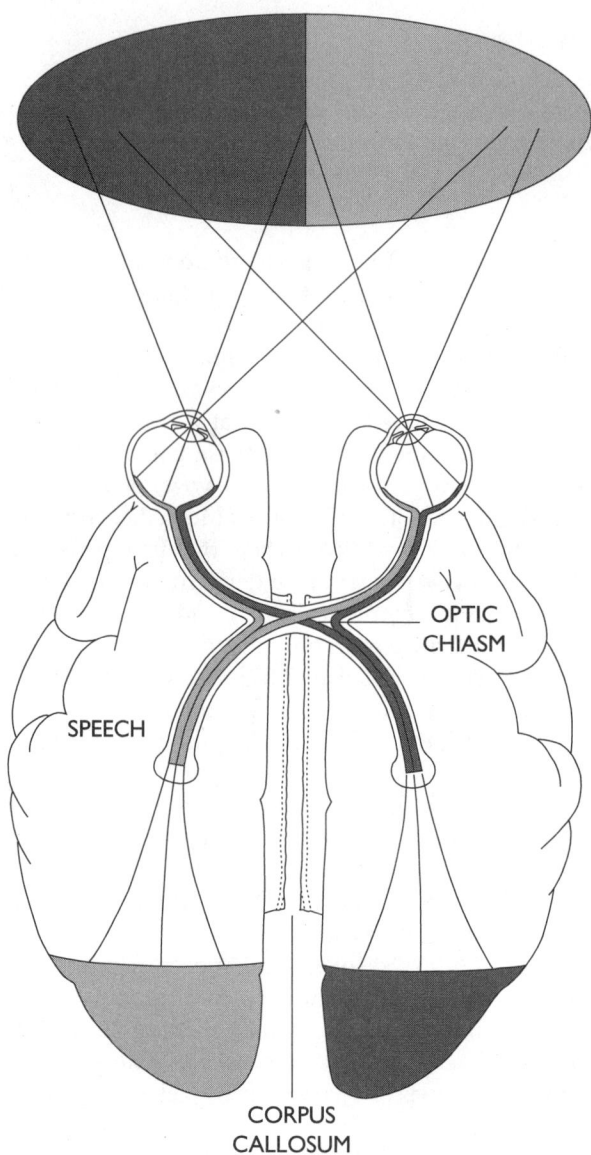

OPTIC
CHIASM

SPEECH

CORPUS
CALLOSUM

FIGURE 2.01

Visual input to bisected brain was limited to one hemisphere by presenting information only in one visual field. The right and left fields of view are projected, via the optic chiasm, to the left and right hemispheres of the brain respectively. If a person fixes his gaze on a point, therefore, information to the left of the point goes only to the right hemisphere and information to the right of the point goes to the left hemisphere. Stimuli in the left visual field cannot be described by a split-brain patient because of the disconnection between the right hemisphere and the speech center, which is in the left hemisphere.

and the right half of his visual field. The patient was asked to tell what he had seen. Each patient reported that lights had been flashed in the right half of the visual field. When lights were flashed only in the left half of the field, however, the patients generally denied having seen any lights. Since the right

side of the visual field is normally projected to the left hemisphere of the brain and the left field to the right hemisphere, one might have concluded that in these patients with divided brains the right hemisphere was in effect blind. We found, however, that this was not the case when the patients were directed to point to the lights that had flashed instead of giving a verbal report. With this manual response they were able to indicate when lights had been flashed in the left visual field, and perception with the brain's right hemisphere proved to be almost equal to perception with the left. Clearly, then, the patients' failure to report the right hemisphere's perception verbally was due to the fact that the speech centers of the brain are located in the left hemisphere.

Our tests of the patients' ability to recognize objects by touch at first resulted in the same general finding. When the object was held in the right hand, from which sensory information is sent to the left hemisphere, the patient was able to name and describe the object. When it was held in the left hand (from which information goes primarily to the right hemisphere), the patient could not describe the object verbally but was able to identify it in a nonverbal test—matching it, for example, to the same object in a varied collection of things. We soon realized, however, that each hemisphere receives, in addition to the main input from the opposite side of the body, some input from the same side. This "ipsilateral" input is crude; it is apparently good mainly for "cuing in" the hemisphere as to the presence or absence of stimulation and relaying fairly gross information about the location of a stimulus on the surface of the body. It is unable, as a rule, to relay information concerning the qualitative nature of an object.

Tests of motor control in these split-brain patients revealed that the left hemisphere of the brain exercised normal control over the right hand but had less than full control of the left hand (for instance, it was poor at directing individual movements of the fingers). Similarly, the right hemisphere had full control of the left hand but not of the right hand. When the two hemispheres were in conflict, dictating different movements for the same hand, the hemisphere on the side opposite the hand generally took charge and overruled the orders of the side of the brain with the weaker control. In general the motor findings in the human patients were much the same as those in split-brain monkeys.

We come now to the main question on which we centered our studies, namely how the separation of the hemispheres affects the mental capacities of the human brain. For these psychological tests we used

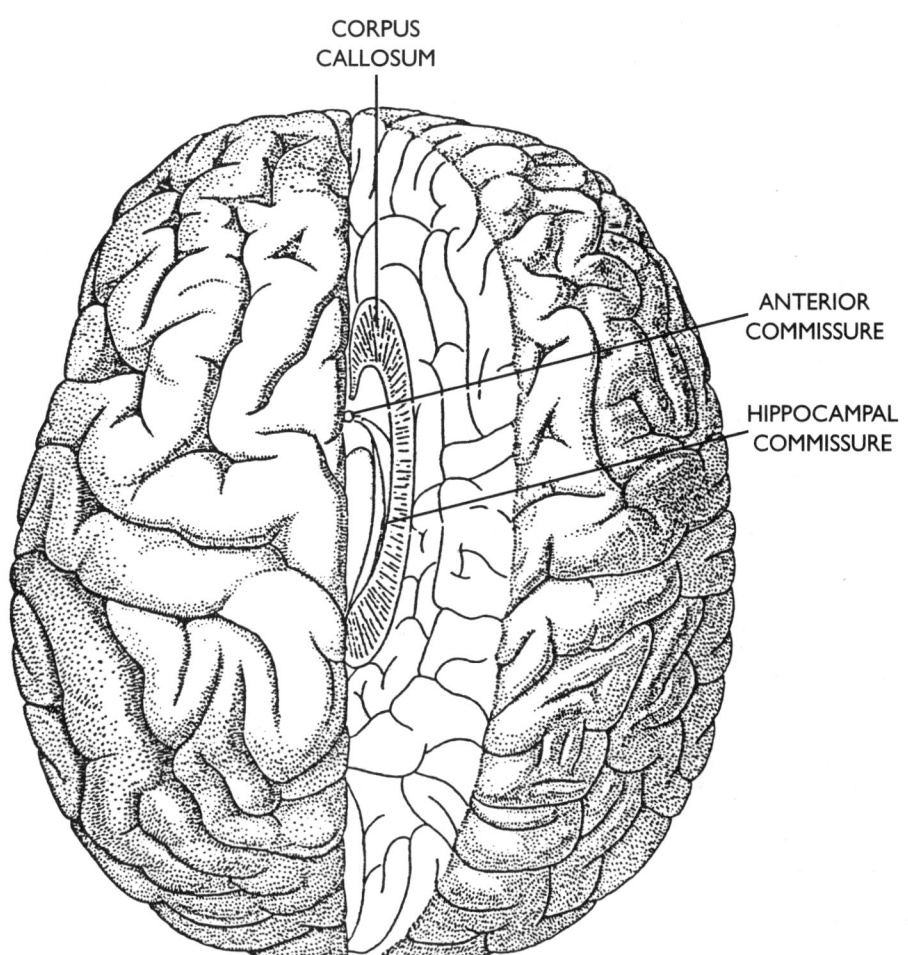

CORPUS
CALLOSUM

ANTERIOR
COMMISSURE

HIPPOCAMPAL
COMMISSURE

FIGURE 2.02

Two hemispheres of the human brain are divided by neurosurgeons to control epileptic seizures. In this top view of the brain the right hemisphere is retracted and the corpus callosum and other commissures, or connectors, that are generally cut are shown in color.

two different devices. One was visual: a picture or written information was flashed (for a tenth of a second) in either the right or the left visual field, so that the information was transmitted only to the left or to the right brain hemisphere [*see* Fig. 2.03]. The other type of test was tactile: an object was placed out of view in the patient's right or left hand, again for the purpose of conveying the information to just one hemisphere—the hemisphere on the side opposite the hand.

When the information (visual or tactile) was presented to the dominant left hemisphere, the patients were able to deal with and describe it quite normally, both orally and in writing. For example, when a picture of a spoon was shown in the right visual field or a spoon was placed in the right hand, all the patients readily identified and described it. They were able to read out written messages and to perform problems in calculation that were presented to the left hemisphere.

In contrast, when the same information was presented to the right hemisphere, it failed to elicit such spoken or written responses. A picture transmitted to the right hemisphere evoked either a haphazard guess or no verbal response at all. Similarly, a pencil placed in the left hand (behind a screen that cut off vision) might be called a can opener or a cigarette lighter, or the patient might not even attempt to describe it. The verbal guesses presumably came not from the right hemisphere but from the left, which had no perception of the object but might attempt to identify it from indirect clues.

Did this impotence of the right hemisphere mean that its surgical separation from the left had reduced its mental powers to an imbecilic level? The earlier tests of its nonverbal capacities suggested that this was almost certainly not so. Indeed, when we switched to asking for nonverbal answers to the visual and tactile information presented in our new psychological tests, the right hemisphere in several patients showed considerable capacity for accurate performance. For example, when a picture of a spoon was presented to the right hemisphere, the patients were able to feel around with the left hand among a varied group of objects (screened from sight) and select a spoon as a match for the picture.

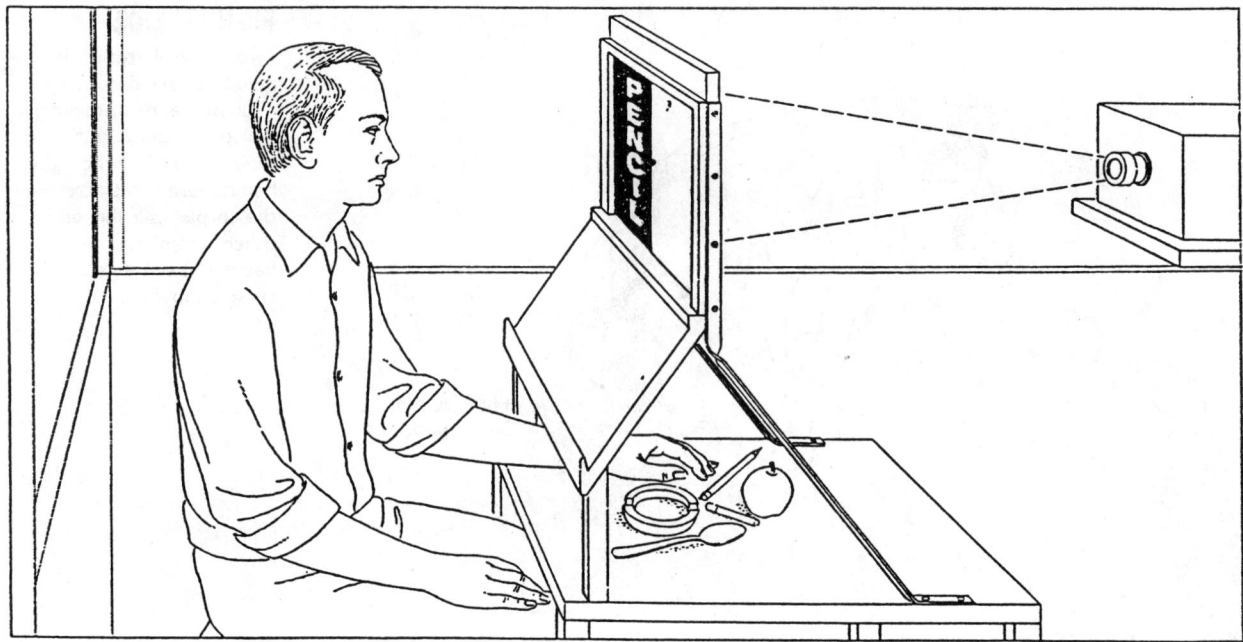

FIGURE 2.03

Response to visual stimulus is tested by flashing a word or a picture of an object on a translucent screen. The examiner first checks the subject's gaze to be sure it is fixed on a dot that marks the center of the visual field. The examiner may call for a verbal response—reading the flashed word, for example—or for a nonverbal one, such as picking up the object that is named from among a number of things spread on the table. The objects are hidden from the subject's view so that they can be identified only by touch.

Furthermore, when they were shown a picture of a cigarette they succeeded in selecting an ashtray, from a group of 10 objects that did not include a cigarette, as the article most closely related to the picture. Oddly enough, however, even after their correct response, and while they were holding the spoon or the ashtray in their left hand, they were unable to name or describe the object or the picture. Evidently the left hemisphere was completely divorced, in perception and knowledge, from the right.

Other tests showed that the right hemisphere did possess a certain amount of language comprehension. For example, when the word "pencil" was flashed to the right hemisphere, the patients were able to pick out a pencil from a group of unseen objects with the left hand. And when a patient held an object in the left hand (out of view), although he could not say its name or describe it, he was later able to point to a card on which the name of the object was written.

In one particularly interesting test the word "heart" was flashed across the center of the visual field, with the "he" portion to the left of the center and "art" to the right. Asked to tell what the word was, the patients would say they had seen "art"—

the portion projected to the left brain hemisphere (which is responsible for speech). Curiously when, after "heart" had been flashed in the same way, the patients were asked to point with the left hand to one of two cards—"art" or "he"—to identify the word they had seen, they invariably pointed to "he." The experiment showed clearly that both hemispheres had simultaneously observed the portions of the word available to them and that in this particular case the right hemisphere, when it had had the opportunity to express itself, had prevailed over the left.

Because an auditory input to one ear goes to both sides of the brain, we conducted tests for the comprehension of words presented audibly to the right hemisphere not by trying to limit the original input but by limiting the ability to answer to the right hemisphere. This was done most easily by having a patient use his left hand to retrieve, from a grab bag held out of view, an object named by the examiner. We found that the patients could easily retrieve such objects as a watch, comb, marble or coin. The object to be retrieved did not even have to be named; it might simply be described or alluded to. For example, the command "Retrieve the fruit monkeys like best" results in the patients' pulling

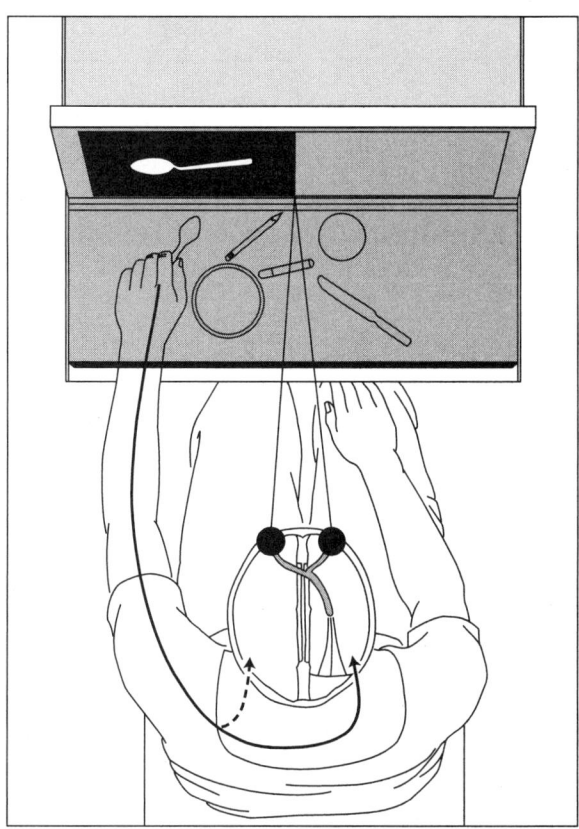

FIGURE 2.04

Visual-tactile association is performed by a split-brain patient. A picture of a spoon is flashed to the right hemisphere; with the left hand he retrieves a spoon from behind the screen. The touch information from the left hand projects (*color*) mainly to the right hemisphere, but a weak "ipsilateral" component goes to the left hemisphere. This is usually not enough to enable him to say (using the left hemisphere) what he has picked up.

out a banana from a grab bag full of plastic fruit; at the command "Sunkist sells a lot of them" the patients retrieve an orange. We knew that touch information from the left hand was going exclusively to the right hemisphere because moments later, when the patients were asked to name various pieces of fruit placed in the left hand, they were unable to score above a chance level.

The upper limit of linguistic abilities in each hemisphere varies from subject to subject. In one case there was little or no evidence for language abilities in the right hemisphere, whereas in the other three the amount and extent of the capacities varied. The most adept patient showed some evidence of even being able to spell simple words by placing plastic letters on a table with his left hand. The subject was told to spell a word such as "pie," and the examiner then placed the three appropriate letters, one at a time in a random order, in his left hand to be arranged on the table. The patient was able to spell even more abstract words such as "how," "what" and "the." In another test three or four letters were placed in a pile, again out of view, to be felt with the left hand. The letters available in each trial would spell only one word, and the instructions to the subject were "Spell a word." The patient was able to spell such words as "cup" and "love." Yet after he had completed this task, the patient was unable to name the word he had just spelled!

The possibility that the right hemisphere has not only some language but even some speech capabilities cannot be ruled out, although at present there is no firm evidence for this. It would not be surprising to discover that the patients are capable of a few simple exclamatory remarks, particularly when under emotional stress. The possibility also remains, of course, that speech of some type could be trained into the right hemisphere. Tests aimed at this question, however, would have to be closely scrutinized and controlled.

The reason is that here, as in many of the tests, "cross-cuing" from one hemisphere to the other could be held responsible for any positive findings. We had a case of such cross-cuing during a series of tests of whether the right hemisphere could respond verbally to simple red or green stimuli. At first, after either a red or a green light was flashed to the right hemisphere, the patient would guess the color at a chance level, as might be expected if the speech mechanism is solely represented in the left hemisphere. After a few trials, however, the score improved whenever the examiner allowed a second guess.

We soon caught on to the strategy the patient used. If a red light was flashed and the patient by chance guessed red, he would stick with that answer. If the flashed light was red and the patient by chance guessed green, he would frown, shake his head and then say, "Oh no, I meant red." What was happening was that the right hemisphere saw the red light and heard the left hemisphere make the guess "green." Knowing that the answer was wrong, the right hemisphere precipitated a frown and a shake of the head, which in turn cued in the left hemisphere to the fact that the answer was wrong and that it had better correct itself! We have learned that this cross-cuing mechanism can become extremely refined. The realization that the neurological patient has various strategies at his command emphasizes how difficult it is to obtain a clear neurological description of a human being with brain damage.

Is the language comprehension by the right hemisphere that the patients exhibited in these tests

FIGURE 2.05

"Visual constructional" tasks are handled better by the right hemisphere. This was seen most clearly in the first patient, who had poor ipsilateral control of his right hand. Although right-handed, he could copy the examples only with this left hand.

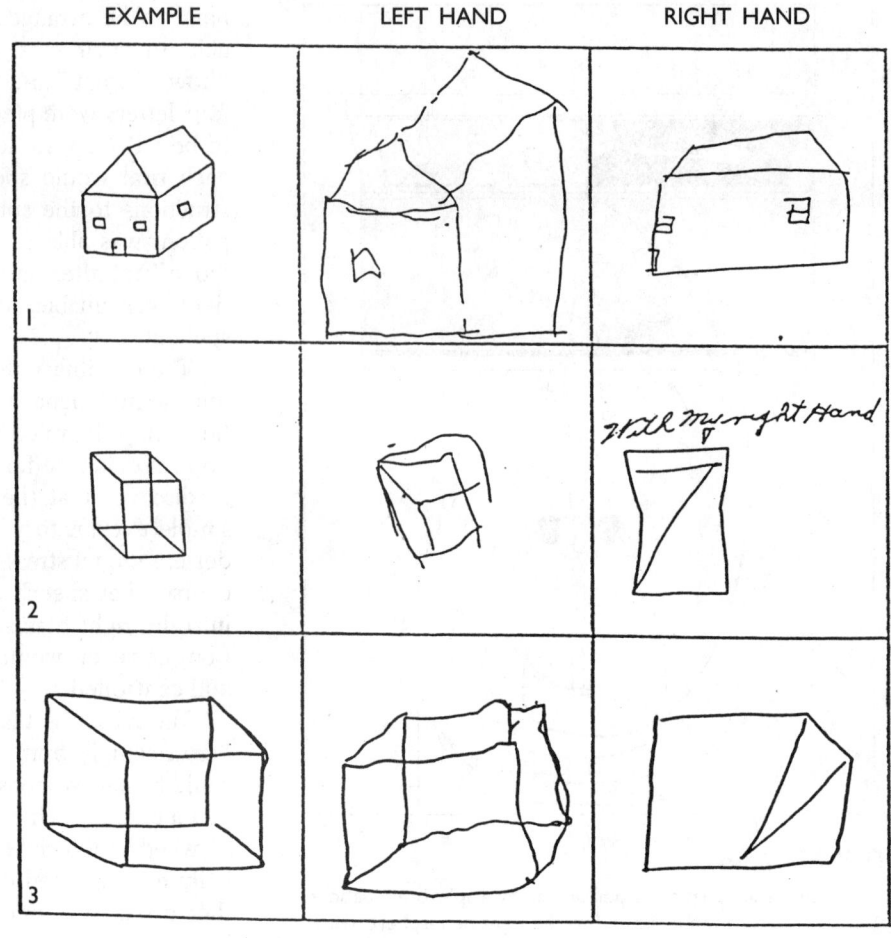

EXAMPLE   LEFT HAND   RIGHT HAND

a normal capability of that hemisphere or was it acquired by learning after their operation, perhaps during the course of the experiments themselves? The issue is difficult to decide. We must remember that we are examining a half of the human brain, a system easily capable of learning from a single trial in a test. We do know that the right hemisphere is decidedly inferior to the left in its overall command of language. We have established, for instance, that although the right hemisphere can respond to a concrete noun such as "pencil," it cannot do as well with verbs; patients are unable to respond appropriately to simple printed instructions, such as "smile" or "frown," when these words are flashed to the right hemisphere, nor can they point to a picture that corresponds to a flashed verb. Some of our recent studies at the University of California at Santa Barbara also indicate that the right hemisphere has a very poorly developed grammar; it seems to be incapable of forming the plural of a given word, for example.

In general, then, the extent of language present in the adult right hemisphere in no way compares with that present in the left hemisphere or, for that matter, with the extent of language present in the child's right hemisphere. Up to the age of four or so, it would appear from a variety of neurological observations, the right hemisphere is about as proficient in handling language as the left. Moreover, studies of the child's development of language, particularly with respect to grammar, strongly suggest that the foundations of grammar—a ground plan for language, so to speak—are somehow inherent in the human organism and are fully realized between the ages of two and three. In other words, in the young child each hemisphere is about equally developed with respect to language and speech function. We are thus faced with the interesting question of why the right hemisphere at an early age and stage of development possesses substantial language capacity whereas at a more adult stage it possesses a rather poor capacity. It is difficult indeed to conceive of the underlying neurological mechanism that would allow for the establishment of a capacity of a high order in a particular hemisphere on a temporary basis. The implication is that during maturation the processes and systems active in making this capacity manifest are somehow inhibited and dismantled in the right hemisphere and allowed to reside only in the dominant left hemisphere.

Yet the right hemisphere is not in all respects inferior or subordinate to the left. Tests have demonstrated that it excels the left in some specialized functions. As an example, tests by us and by Bogen have shown that in these patients the left hand is capable of arranging blocks to match a pictured design and of drawing a cube in three dimensions, whereas the right hand, deprived of instructions from the right hemisphere, could not perform either of these tasks.

It is of interest to note, however, that although the patients (our first subject in particular) could not execute such tasks with the right hand, they were capable of matching a test stimulus to the correct design when it appeared among five related patterns presented in their right visual field. This showed that the dominant left hemisphere is capable of discriminating between correct and incorrect stimuli. Since it is also true that the patients have no motor problems with their right hand, the patients' inability to perform these tasks must reflect a breakdown of an integrative process somewhere between the sensory system and the motor system.

We found that in certain other mental processes the right hemisphere is on a par with the left. In particular, it can independently generate an emotional reaction. In one of our experiments exploring the matter we would present a series of ordinary objects and then suddenly flash a picture of a nude woman. This evoked an amused reaction regardless of whether the picture was presented to the left

hemisphere or to the right. When the picture was flashed to the left hemisphere of a female patient, she laughed and verbally identified the picture as a nude. When it was later presented to the right hemisphere, she said in reply to a question that she saw nothing, but almost immediately a sly smile spread over her face and she began to chuckle. Asked what she was laughing at, she said: "I don't know . . . nothing . . . oh—that funny machine." Although the right hemisphere could not describe what it had seen, the sight nevertheless elicited an emotional response like the one evoked from the left hemisphere.

Taken together, our studies seem to demonstrate conclusively that in a split-brain situation we are really dealing with two brains, each separately capable of mental functions of a high order. This implies that the two brains should have twice as large a span of attention—that is, should be able to handle twice as much information—as a normal whole brain. We have not yet tested this precisely in human patients, but E. D. Young and I have found that a split-brain monkey can indeed deal with nearly twice as much information as a normal animal [*see illustration below*]. We have so far determined also that brain-bisected patients can carry out two tasks as fast as a normal person can do one.

Just how does the corpus callosum of the intact brain combine and integrate the perceptions and knowledge of the two cerebral hemispheres? This has been investigated recently by Giovanni Berlucchi, Giacomo Rizzolati and me at the Istituto di Fisiologia Umana in Pisa. We made recordings of

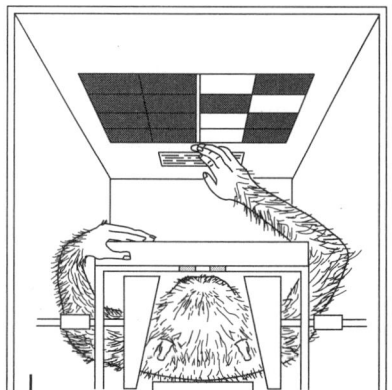 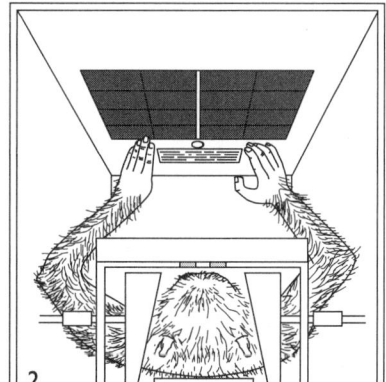 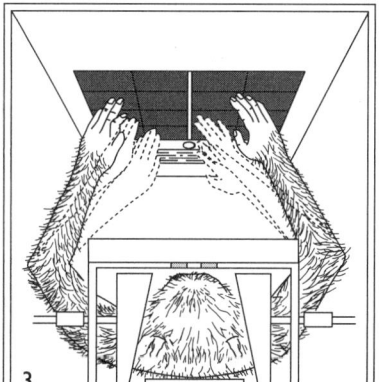

FIGURE 2.06

Split-brain monkeys can handle more visual information than normal animals. When the monkey pulls a knob (*1*), eight of the 16 panels light momentarily. The monkey must then start at the bottom and punch the lights that were lit and no others (*2*). With the panels lit for 600 milliseconds normal monkeys get up to the third row from the bottom before forgetting which panels were lit (*3*). Split-brain monkeys complete the entire task with the panels lit only 200 milliseconds. The monkeys look at the panels through filters; since the optic chiasm is cut in these animals, the filters allow each hemisphere to see the colored panels on one side only.

neural activity in the posterior part of the callosum of the cat with the hope of relating the responses of that structure to stimulation of the animal's visual fields. The kinds of responses recorded turned out to be similar to those observed in the visual cortex of the cat. In other words, the results suggest that visual pattern information can be transmitted through the callosum. This finding militates against the notion that learning and memory are transferred across the callosum, as has usually been suggested. Instead, it looks as though in animals with an intact callosum a copy of the visual world as seen in one hemisphere is sent over to the other, with the result that both hemispheres can learn together a discrimination presented to just one hemisphere. In the split-brain animal this extension of the visual pathway is cut off; this would explain rather simply why no learning proceeds in the visually isolated hemisphere and why it has to learn the discrimination from scratch.

Curiously, however, the neural activity in the callosum came only in response to stimuli at the midline of the visual field. This finding raises difficult questions. How can it be reconciled with the well-established observation that the left hemisphere of a normal person can give a running description of all the visual information presented throughout the entire half-field projected to the right hemisphere? For this reason alone one is wearily driven back to the conclusion that somewhere and somehow all or part of the callosum transmits not only a visual scene but also a complicated neural code of a higher order.

All the evidence indicates that separation of the hemispheres creates two independent spheres of consciousness within a single cranium, that is to say, within a single organism. This conclusion is disturbing to some people who view consciousness as an indivisible property of the human brain. It seems premature to others, who insist that the capacities revealed thus far for the right hemisphere are at the level of an automaton. There is, to be sure, hemispheric inequality in the present cases, but it may well be a characteristic of the individuals we have studied. It is entirely possible that if a human brain were divided in a very young person, both hemispheres could as a result separately and independently develop mental functions of a high order at the level attained only in the left hemisphere of normal individuals.

QUESTIONS FOR REFLECTION AND DISCUSSION:

1. In "The Split Brain in Man," Gazzaniga writes, "The human brain is actually two brains, each capable of advanced mental functions." Does this conclusion appear to be justified by the findings reported in his article? Explain.

2. It has become popular to speak of "left-brain" functions and "right-brain" functions. Do the findings of Gazzaniga suggest that the left hemisphere of the cerebral cortex differs in its functions from the right hemisphere? How so?

3. What is the corpus callosum? What appear to be some of the functions of the corpus callosum?

4. Psychology is the study of behavior and mental processes, so why are psychologists interested in the functioning of the brain?

SOURCE

Reprinted with permission from Bouchard, T. J., Jr., Lykken, D. T., McGue, M., Segal, N. L., & Tellegen, A. (1990). Sources of human psychological differences: The Minnesota study of twins reared apart. *Science, 250,* 223–228. Copyright © 1990 American Association for the Advancement of Science.

Psychologists are interested in sorting out the relative influences of nature (heredity) and nurture (environmental influences) on behavior and mental processes, especially in the cases of intelligence, aggression, and psychological disorders. Humans and other animals inherit biological structures that allow certain behaviors. But environmental factors like nutrition, schooling, cultural beliefs, and accidents figure into whether the individual will actually develop behavior patterns that are genetically possible. Psychologists undertake various kinds of research studies, including kinship studies, to try to determine whether behavior patterns are affected by heredity.

Because their genetic makeup (their nature) is the same, it is assumed that differences between identical (monozygotic) twins reflect their nurture (that is, environmental influences). Identical twins are more likely to develop the same features and even health problems (such as high cholesterol levels) than fraternal (dizygotic) twins. In terms of behavior and mental processes, it has been shown that identical twins are more likely than fraternal twins to share traits such as sociability and activity levels, and psychological disorders such as schizophrenia. Twin studies even suggest that people inherit a tendency toward being happy or unhappy. Despite the roller-coaster ride of daily experience, people tend to maintain or return to characteristic levels of cheer or sadness.

The following report by Thomas Bouchard and his colleagues summarizes the ongoing results of a well-known longitudinal study that compares twins who have been reared together with those reared apart.

Sources of Human Psychological Differences: The Minnesota Study of Twins Reared Apart

THOMAS J. BOUCHARD, JR., DAVID T. LYKKEN, MATTHEW MCGUE, NANCY L. SEGAL, AUKE TELLEGEN

Since 1979, a continuing study of monozygotic and dizygotic twins, separated in infancy and reared apart, has subjected more than 100 sets of reared-apart twins or triplets to a week of intensive psychological and physiological assessment. Like the prior, smaller studies of monozygotic twins reared apart, about 70% of the variance in IQ was found to be associated with genetic variation. On multiple measures of personality and temperament, occupational and leisure-time interests, and social attitudes, monozygotic twins reared apart are about as similar as are monozygotic twins reared together. These findings extend and support those from numerous other twin, family, and adoption studies. It is a plausible hypothesis that genetic differences affect psychological differences largely indirectly, by influencing the effective environment of the developing child.

This evidence for the strong heritability of most psychological traits, sensibly construed, does not detract from the value or importance of parenting, education, and other propaedeutic interventions.

Monozygotic and dizygotic twins who were separated early in life and reared apart (MZA and DZA twin pairs) are a fascinating experiment of nature. They also provide the simplest and most powerful method for disentangling the influence of environmental and genetic factors on human characteristics. The rarity of twins reared apart explains why only three previous studies of modest scope are available in the literature (*1–4*).

More than 100 sets of reared-apart twins or triplets from across the United States and the United Kingdom have participated in the Minnesota Study of Twins Reared Apart since it began in 1979. Participants have also come from Australia, Canada, China, New Zealand, Sweden, and West Germany. The study of these reared-apart twins has led to two general and seemingly remarkable conclusions concerning the sources of the psychological differences—behavioral variation—between people: (i) genetic factors exert a pronounced and pervasive influence on behavioral variability, and (ii) the effect of being reared in the same home is negligible for many psychological traits. These conclusions will not come as revelations to the many behavioral geneticists who have observed similar results and drawn similar conclusions (*5*). This study and the broader behavioral genetic literature, nevertheless, challenge prevailing psychological theories on the origins of individual differences in ability, personality, interests, and social attitudes (*6*). Here we summarize our procedures and review our results and interpretations of them.

Participants complete approximately 50 hours of medical and psychological assessment. Two or more test instruments are used in each major domain of psychological assessment to ensure adequate coverage (for example, four personality trait inventories, three occupational interest inventories, and two mental ability batteries). A systematic assessment of aspects of the twins' rearing environments that might have had causal roles in their psychological development is also carried out. Separate examiners administer the IQ test, life history interview, psychiatric interview, and sexual life history interview. A comprehensive mental ability battery is administered as a group test. The twins also complete questionnaires independently, under the constant supervision of a staff member.

Reared-apart twins have been ascertained in several ways, such as: (i) friends, relatives, or the reunited twins themselves, having learned of the project, contact the Minnesota Center for Twin and Adoption Research (MICTAR); (ii) members of the adoption movement, social workers, and other professionals who encounter reared-apart twins serve as intermediaries; (iii) twins who are, or become aware of, a separated co-twin solicit assistance from the MICTAR staff in locating this individual. Selection on the basis of similarity is minimized by vigorously recruiting all reared-apart twins, regardless of known or presumed zygosity and similarity. We have been unable to recruit to the study six pairs of twins reared apart whom we believe to be monozygotic.

Zygosity diagnosis is based on extensive serological comparisons, fingerprint ridge count, and anthropometric measurements. The probability of misclassification is less than 0.001 (*7*). Where appropriate, our data are corrected for age and sex effects (*8*). Due to space limitations and the smaller size of the DZA sample (30 sets), in this article we focus on the MZA data (56 sets). The results reported here are, for the most part, based on previously reported findings, so that the sample sizes do not include the most recently assessed pairs and vary depending on when in the course of this ongoing study the analyses were conducted.

As shown in Table 3.01, the sample consists of adult twins, separated very early in life, reared apart during their formative years, and reunited as adults. Circumstances of adoption were sometimes informal, and the adoptive parents, in comparison to parents who volunteer to participate in most adoption studies, have a lower level of education (mean equals 2 years of high school), and are quite heterogeneous in educational attainment and socioeconomic status (SES). Because our sample includes no subjects with IQs in the retardate range (≤70), the mean IQ is higher and the standard deviation lower than for the general population.

Components of Phenotypic Variance

If genetic and environmental factors are uncorrelated and combine additively (points we return to later), the total observed variance, V_t, of a trait within a population can be expressed as

$$V_t = V_g + V_e + V_m \qquad (1)$$

where V_g is variance due to genetic differences among people, V_e is variance due to environmental

TABLE 3.01

MEANS, STANDARD DEVIATIONS (SD), AND RANGES FOR AGE, MEASURES OF CONTACT, IQ, AND PARENTAL EDUCATIONAL LEVEL FOR MZA TWINS. TWO MZA MALE TRIPLET SETS WERE EACH ENTERED AS ONE SET. DATA ARE BASED ON THE FIRST 56 SETS OF MZAS RECRUITED, ALTHOUGH THE SAMPLE SIZE VARIES SLIGHTLY FROM MEASURE TO MEASURE, AS DATA ARE NOT ALWAYS AVAILABLE OR RELEVANT (FOR EXAMPLE, REARING MOTHER DIED VERY EARLY IN TWINS' LIFE OR TWINS COULD NOT BE TESTED WITH AN ENGLISH LANGUAGE WAIS).

STATISTIC	AGE (YEARS)	TIME TOGETHER PRIOR TO SEPARATION (MONTHS)	TIME APART TO FIRST REUNION (YEARS)	TOTAL CONTACT TIME (WEEKS)	IQ (WAIS)	REARING FATHER'S EDUCATION LEVEL (YEARS)	REARING MOTHER'S EDUCATION LEVEL (YEARS)
Mean	41.0	5.1	30.0	112.5	108.1	10.7	10.3
SD	12.0	8.5	14.3	230.7	10.8	4.5	3.7
Range	19.0–68.0	0–48.7	0.5–64.7	1–1233	79–133	0–20	0–19

or experiential factors, and V_m is variance due to measurement error and unsystematic temporal fluctuations. For measures of psychological traits, V_m ranges from approximately 10% (of V_t) for the most reliably measured and stable of traits (for example, IQ) to as high as 50 to 60% for traits that are less reliable or that show considerable secular instability (for example, some social attitudes). The environmental component, V_e, can be divided into variance due to experiences that are shared, V_{es}, and experiences that are unshared, V_{eu}. Shared events may be experienced differently by two siblings (for example, a roller coaster ride or a family vacation), in which case they contribute to the V_{eu} component. If the total variance, V_t, is set at unity, the correlation between MZ twins, R_{mz}, equals $V_g + V_{es}$. The heritability of a trait equals V_g; the heritability of the stable component of a trait (for example, the mean value around which one's aggressiveness varies) equals $V_g/(V_t - V_m)$. V_t and V_m can be estimated from studies of singletons, but V_g is more elusive: for monozygotic twins reared together (MZT), some of the within-pair correlation might be due to effects of shared experience, V_{es}. The power of the MZA design is that for twins reared apart from early infancy and randomly placed for adoption, V_{es} is negligible, so that V_g can be directly estimated from the MZA correlation.

Similarity in the IQ of MZA Twins

The study of IQ is paradigmatic of human behavior genetic research. There are more than 100 relevant twin, adoptee, and family studies of IQ, and IQ has been at the center of the nature-nurture debate (9). The analysis of IQ is also paradigmatic of the approach taken by this study. It illustrates our use of replicated measures, evaluation of rearing environmental effects, and analysis of environmental similarity. We obtain three independent measures of IQ: (i) the Wechsler Adult Intelligence Scale (WAIS); (ii) a Raven, Mill-Hill composite; and (iii) the first principal component (PC) of two multiple abilities batteries.

The WAIS consists of a set of six verbal and five performance subtests that are individually administered, requiring about 1.5 hours, and that yield an age-corrected estimate of IQ (10). To avoid examiner bias, we administer the WAIS simultaneously to the twins in different rooms by professional psychometrists. The Raven Progressive Matrices (Standard Set) is a widely used nonverbal measure of problem-solving ability often paired with the Mill-Hill Vocabulary Test, a multiple-choice word knowledge test (11). In this study, the Raven and Mill-Hill are both administered and scored by computer. The two age- and sex-corrected scores are transformed to have a mean equal to 50 and a standard deviation of 10. The sum of these transformed scores (which intercorrelate about 0.57) provides a separate estimate of IQ. The first major ability battery included in our assessment is an expanded version of the battery used in the Hawaii Family Study of Cognition (12). The second major ability battery is the Comprehensive Ability Battery (13). Detailed results from analysis of both tests are reported elsewhere (14).

In each of the three prior studies of MZA twins, two independent estimates of intelligence

TABLE 3.02

SAMPLE SIZES AND INTRACLASS CORRELATIONS (± STANDARD ERROR) FOR ALL IQ MEASURES AND WEIGHTED AVERAGES FOR FOUR STUDIES OF MZA TWINS.					
STUDY AND TEST USED (PRIMARY/SECONDARY/TERTIARY)	N FOR EACH TEST	PRIMARY TEST	SECONDARY TEST	TERTIARY TEST	MEAN OF MULTIPLE TEST (43)
Newman et al. (1) (Stanford-Binet/Otis)	19/19	0.68 ± 0.12	0.74 ± 0.10		0.71
Juel-Nielsen (1) (Wechsler-Bellevue/Raven)	12/12	0.64 ± 0.17	0.73 ± 0.13		0.69
Shields (1) (Mill-Hill/Dominoes)	38/37	0.74 ± 0.07	0.76 ± 0.07		0.75
Bouchard et al. (42) (WAIS/Raven, Mill-Hill/ first principal component)	48/42/43	0.69 ± 0.07	0.78 ± 0.07	0.78 ± 0.07	0.75

were obtained. The sample sizes and intraclass correlations for all four studies are compared in Table 3.02. The table illustrates the remarkable consistency of the MZA correlations on IQ across measurement instrument, country of origin, and time period. These correlations vary within a narrow range (0.64 to 0.74) and suggest, under the assumption of no environmental similarity, that genetic factors account for approximately 70% of the variance in IQ.

This estimate of the broad heritability of IQ is higher than the recent estimates (0.47 to 0.58) based on a review of the literature that includes all kinship pairings (9, 15). Virtually the entire literature on IQ similarity in twins and siblings is limited, however, to studies of children and adolescents. It has been demonstrated (16) that heritability of cognitive ability increases with age. A heritability estimate of approximately 70% from these four studies of mainly middle-aged adults is not inconsistent with the previous literature.

Do Environmental Similarities in Rearing Environments Explain MZA IQ Similarity?

Such marked behavioral similarities between reared-apart MZ twins raise the question of correlated placement: were the twins' adoptive homes selected to be similar in trait-relevant features which, in turn, induced psychological similarity? If so, given that the total variance equals 1.0, then V_{es} will equal at least $R_{ff} \times r^2_{ft}$, where R_{ff} is the within-pair correlation for a given feature, f, of the adoptive homes (the placement coefficient), and r_{ft} is the product-moment correlation between the feature and the trait in question, t.

A checklist of available household facilities (for example, power tools, sailboat, telescope, unabridged dictionary, and original artwork) provides an index of the cultural and intellectual resources in the adoptive home (17). Each twin completes the Moos Family Environment Scale (FES), a widely used instrument with scales describing the individual's retrospective impression of treatment and rearing provided by the adoptive parents during childhood and adolescence (18). The age- and sex-corrected placement coefficients for these and other measures are shown in Table 3.03, together with the correlations between twins' IQ and the environmental measure (r_{ft}) and the total estimated contribution to MZA twin similarity. The maximum contribution to MZA trait correlations that could be explained by measured similarity of the adoptive rearing environments on a single variable is about 0.03 (19). The absence of any significant effect due to SES or other environmental measures on the IQ scores of these adult adopted twins is consistent with the findings of other investigators (20). Rearing SES effects on IQ in adoption studies have been found for young children but not in adult samples (21), suggesting that although parents may be able to affect their children's rate of cognitive skill acquisition, they may have relatively little influence on the ultimate level attained.

TABLE 3.03

PLACEMENT COEFFICIENTS FOR ENVIRONMENTAL VARIABLES, CORRELATIONS
BETWEEN IQ AND THE ENVIRONMENTAL VARIABLES, AND ESTIMATES OF THE
CONTRIBUTION OF PLACEMENT TO TWIN SIMILARITY IN WAIS IQ.

PLACEMENT VARIABLE	MZA SIMILARITY (R_{ff})	CORRELATION BETWEEN IQ AND PLACEMENT VARIABLE (r_{ft})	CONTRIBUTION OF PLACEMENT TO THE MZA CORRELATION $(R_{ff} \times r^2_{ft})$
SES indicators			
Father's education	0.134	0.100	0.001
Mother's education	0.412	−0.001	0.000
Father's SES	0.267	0.174	0.008
Physical facilities			
Material possessions	0.402	0.279**	0.032
Scientific/technical	0.151	−0.090	0.001
Cultural	−0.085	−0.279**	−0.007
Mechanical	0.303	0.077	0.002
Relevant FES scales			
Achievement	0.11	−0.103	0.001
Intellectual orientation	0.27	0.106	0.003

**r_{ft} significantly different from zero at $P < 0.01$.

Has Pre- and Post-Reunion Contact Contributed to MZA Twin Similarity in IQ?

MZA twins share prenatal and perinatal environments, but except for effects of actual trauma, such as fetal alcohol syndrome, there is little evidence that early shared environment significantly contributes to the variance of psychological traits. Twins are especially vulnerable to prenatal and perinatal trauma, but these effects are most likely to decrease, rather than increase, within-pair similarity (22). There is evidence that twins who maintain closer contact with each other later in life tend to be more similar in some respects than twins who engage in infrequent contact (23). It appears, however, that it is the similarity that leads to increased contact, rather than the other way around (24). MZA twins in this study vary widely in the amount of contact they have had prior to assessment. All twin pairs spent their formative years apart. Some had their first adult reunion at the time of assessment, whereas others met as much as 20 years earlier and had experienced varying degrees of contact. A small number of the pairs actually met at intervals during childhood. As shown in Table 3.01, total contact

time for the MZA twins ranges from 1 to 1233 weeks. In the one case of 1233 weeks of contact, the twins met as teenagers and lived near each other until assessment when they were adults. Since they met on a regular basis, most of this time was coded as contact time. Degree of social contact between two members of a reared-apart twin pair accounts for virtually none of their similarity. The correlations with the within-pair absolute WAIS IQ difference are 0.06 ± 0.15 for time together prior to separation, 0.08 ± 0.15 for time apart to first reunion, -0.14 ± 0.15 for total contact time, and 0.17 ± 0.15 for percentage of lifetime spent apart (25).

The absolute within-pair difference in WAIS IQ of co-twins as a function of degree of contact are plotted in Fig. 3.01. Also shown are the expected absolute IQ differences between randomly paired individuals and between two testings of the same individual (26). Although the MZA average difference approximates the absolute difference expected between two testings of a single individual, we do observe a wide range of differences. It is not that we have found no evidence of environmental influence; in individual cases environmental factors have been highly significant (for example, the 29 IQ point difference in Fig. 3.01). Rather, we find

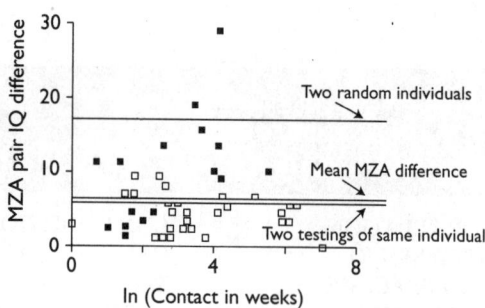

FIGURE 3.01

The absolute value of the MZA within-pair IQ difference as function of the natural logarithm of pair contact in weeks. The horizontal lines are the expected absolute IQ difference between two randomly selected individuals, the observed average MZA absolute difference, and the expected IQ difference between two testings of the same individual.

little support for the types of environmental influences on which psychologists have traditionally focused (27).

Similarity of MZA Twins on a Variety of Dimensions

Table 3.04 (28) gives the MZA correlations, most previously published, on variables ranging from anthropometry and psychophysiology, to aptitudes, personality and temperament, leisure-time and vocational interests, to social attitudes. Correlations for MZT twins and retest stability coefficients are also provided for comparison. Stable, reliably measured variables like fingerprint ridge count and stature show the highest correlations. Brain wave spectra are highly reproducible (29) and are strongly correlated in both MZA and MZT twins. Most other psychophysiological variables (for example, blood pressure and electrodermal response) vary considerably across time so that the retest correlations between repeated measurements on the same persons range from 0.5 to 0.8 (30). These retest correlations set the upper limit of similarity that might be found between MZ co-twins. The retest stability of aptitude measures, such as IQ, is rather better, ranging from 0.8 to 0.9 (10), whereas stability of personality and interest measures ranges from 0.6 to 0.7.

With these upper limits in mind, the findings in Table 3.04 demonstrate remarkable similarity between MZA twins. In terms of standardized tests and measures, the MZA twin similarities are often nearly equal to those for MZT twins (last column)

and constitute a substantial portion of the reliable variance (column 5) of each trait.

The Minimal Effect of Being Reared Together

Some of the MZA twins have had considerable contact as adults, but all of them were reared apart throughout the formative periods of childhood and adolescence. If being reared together enhances similarity in twins, within-pair correlations for MZA twins are expected to be smaller than those for MZT twins. For example, the mean MZT correlation for IQ, based on 34 studies of primarily children or adolescents, is 0.86 (9) as compared to 0.72 for all, primarily adult, MZA twins. If the mean MZT correlation were maintained into adulthood, its difference from the MZA correlation would suggest that common rearing increases the similarity of IQ in twins (and siblings). However, the MZT correlation apparently declines with age (for example, as a result of the accumulation of nonshared environmental effects) (16), in which event the small MZT-MZA correlation difference would suggest little influence of common rearing on adult IQ. In any case, a significant contribution of shared environment is found for the personality trait of social closeness (31), and possibly religious interests and values (32).

As illustrated in Table 3.04, however, adult MZ twins are about equally similar on most physiological and psychological traits, regardless of rearing status. This finding and the failure to find significant r_{ft} effects for cognitive abilities (17) or personality (31), together with findings from numerous studies of MZT and DZT twins, sibs, and foster sibs, implies that common rearing enhances familial resemblance during adulthood only slightly and on relatively few behavioral dimensions. This conclusion is given detailed discussion by Plomin and Daniels (5).

Why Are MZA Twins So Similar?

It is well known to naturalists and to animal breeders that there are wide and heritable differences in behavior within other species, but there is a curious reluctance among some scientists (33) to acknowledge the contribution of genetic variation to psychological differences within the human species. Our findings support and extend those from many family, twin, and adoption studies (15), a broad consilience of findings leading to the following generalization: For almost every behavioral trait so far

TABLE 3.04

INTERCLASS CORRELATIONS (R), SAMPLE SIZES, AND MZA/MZT RATIO FOR MONOZYGOTIC TWINS REARED APART AND TOGETHER FOR NINE CLASSES OF VARIABLES. NA, NOT AVAILABLE.

VARIABLES (REFERENCE)	MINNESOTA MZAs		MZTs			
	R	PAIRS (NO.)	R	PAIRS (NO.)	RELIA- BILITY*	R_{MZA}/R_{MZT}
Anthropometric variables (28)						
Fingerprint ridge count	0.97	54	0.96	274	0.99	1.01
Height	0.86	56	0.93	274	0.98	0.925
Weight	0.73	56	0.83	274	NA	0.880
Electroencephalographic (brainwave) variables (28)						
Amount of 8- to 12-Hz (alpha) activity	0.80	35	0.81	42	NA	0.987
Midfrequency of alpha activity	0.80	35	0.82	42	NA	0.975
Psychophysiologic variables (29)						
Systolic blood pressure	0.64	56	0.70	34	0.70	0.914
Heart rate	0.49	49	0.54	160	0.58–0.80	0.907
Electrodermal response (EDR) amplitude†						
Males	0.82	20	0.70	17	NA	1.17
Females	0.30	23	0.54	19	NA	0.555
Trials to habituation EDR	0.43	43	0.42	36	NA	1.02
Information processing ability factors (17)						
Speed of response	0.56	40	0.73	50	NA	0.767
Acquisition speed	0.20	40	NA	NA	NA	NA
Speed of spatial processing	0.36	40	NA	NA	NA	NA
Mental ability—general factor (44)						
WAIS IQ—full scale	0.69	48	0.88	40	0.90	0.784
WAIS IQ—verbal	0.64	48	0.88	40	0.84	0.727
WAIS IQ—performance	0.71	48	0.79	40	0.86	0.899
Raven, Mill-Hill composite	0.78	42	0.76	37	NA	1.03
First principal component of special mental abilities	0.78	43	NA	NA	NA	NA
Special mental abilities (14)						
Mean of 15 Hawaii-battery scales	0.45	45	NA	NA	0.80	NA
Mean of 13 Comprehensive Ability Battery scales	0.48	41	NA	NA	0.78	NA
Personality variables (31)						
Mean of 11 Multidimensional Personality Questionnaire (MPQ) scales	0.50	44	0.49	217	0.88	1.02
Mean of 18 California Psychological Inventory (CPI) scales	0.48	38	0.49	99	0.65	0.979
Psychological interests (45)						
Mean of 23 Strong Campbell Interest Inventory scales (SCII)	0.39	52	0.48	116‡	0.82	0.813
Mean of 34 Jackson Vocational Interest Survey scales (JVIS)	0.43	45	NA	NA	0.84	NA
Mean of 17 Minnesota Occupational Interest scales	0.40	40	0.49	376	0.75	0.816
Social attitudes (32)						
Mean of 2 religiosity scales	0.49	31	0.51	458	0.80	0.961
Mean of 14 nonreligious social attitude items	0.34	42	0.28	421	0.48	1.21
MPQ traditionalism scale	0.53	44	0.50	217	0.49	1.06

*The correlation between two testings of the same individual. These estimates of the stable component of the observed trait variance also estimate the upper limit for R_{MZ}.
†The marked difference in EDR amplitude between males and females is discussed in Lykken et al. (29).
‡This value is for 116 studies, not pairs.

investigated, from reaction time to religiosity, an important fraction of the variation among people turns out to be associated with genetic variation. This fact need no longer be subject to debate (34); rather, it is time instead to consider its implications. We suggest the following:

1) *General intelligence or IQ is strongly affected by genetic factors.* The IQs of the adult MZA twins assessed with various instruments in four independent studies correlate about 0.70, indicating that about 70% of the observed variation in IQ in this population can be attributed to genetic variation. Since only a few of these MZA twins were reared in real poverty or by illiterate parents and none were retarded, this heritability estimate should not be extrapolated to the extremes of environmental disadvantage still encountered in society. Moreover, these findings do not imply that traits like IQ cannot be enhanced. Flynn (35), in a survey covering 14 countries, has shown that the average IQ test score has significantly increased in recent years. This increase may be limited to that part of the population with low IQs (36). The present findings, therefore, do not define or limit what might be conceivably achieved in an optimal environment. They do indicate that, in the current environments of the broad middle-class, in industrialized societies, two-thirds of the observed variance of IQ can be traced to genetic variation.

2) *The institutions and practices of modern Western society do not greatly constrain the development of individual differences in psychological traits.* The heritability of a psychological trait reveals as much about the culture as it does about human nature. Heritability must increase as V_e, the variance affected by the environment, decreases. Where the culture's influence is relatively homogeneous and efficacious, V_e will decrease and heritability will increase; most American boys, for example, have similar opportunities to play baseball, so that one expects heritability of baseball skill in American young men to be high. Where culture is efficacious, but heterogeneous, V_e (and total phenotypic variance) will increase; thus, one would expect the heritability of specific linguistic or religious behaviors in the United States or in the Soviet Union to be low. Individuals in Western societies are heterogeneous with respect to personality traits, interests, and attitudes, yet the heritabilities of these traits are relatively high. We infer that the diverse cultural agents of our society, in particular most parents, are less effective in imprinting their distinctive stamp on the children developing within their spheres of influence—or are less inclined to do so—than has been supposed.

Psychologists have been surprised by the evidence that being reared by the same parents in the same physical environment does not, on average, make siblings more alike as adults than they would have been if reared separately in adoptive homes. It is obvious that parents can produce shared effects if they grossly deprive or mistreat all their children. It seems reasonable that charismatic, dedicated parents, determined to make all their children share certain personal qualities, interests, or values, may sometimes succeed. Our findings and those of others (37), do not imply that parenting is without lasting effects. The remarkable similarity in MZA twins in social attitudes (for example, traditionalism and religiosity) does not show that parents cannot influence those traits, but simply that this does not tend to happen in most families.

3) *MZA twins are so similar in psychological traits because the identical genomes make it probable that their effective environments are similar.* Specific mechanisms by which genetic differences in human behavior are expressed in phenotypic differences are largely unknown. It is a plausible conjecture that a key mechanism by which the genes affect the mind is indirect, and that genetic differences have an important role in determining the effective psychological environment of the developing child (38).

Infants with different temperaments elicit different parenting responses. Toddlers who are active and adventurous undergo different experiences than their more sedentary or timid siblings. In addition, children and adolescents seek out environments that they find congenial. These are forms of gene-environment covariance, C_{ge}. Moreover, different individuals pay different attention to or respond differently to the same objective experience, or both. These are forms of gene-environment interaction, V_{ge}. From infancy onwards, genetic individuality helps to steer the developing organism through the multitude of possible experiences and choices. That is, Eq. 1 must be elaborated to include these indirect and modifiable ways in which the genome exerts its influence

$$V_t = V_g + V_e + C_{ge} + V_{ge} + V_m \qquad (2)$$

The proximal cause of most psychological variance probably involves learning through experience, just as radical environmentalists have always believed. The effective experiences, however, to an important extent are self-selected, and that selection is guided by the steady pressure of the genome (a more distal cause). We agree with Martin *et al.* (39) who see "humans as exploring organisms whose innate abilities and predispositions help them select what is relevant and adaptive from the range of opportunities and stimuli presented in the environment. The effects of mobility and learning, therefore, augment rather than eradicate the effects of the genotype on behavior" (p. 4368).

If this view is correct, the developmental experiences of MZ twins are more similar than those of DZ twins, again as environmentalist critics of twin research have contended. However, even MZA twins tend to elicit, select, seek out, or create very similar effective environments and, to that extent, the impact of these experiences is counted as a genetic influence. Finally, if the genome impresses itself on the psyche largely by influencing the character, selection, and impact of experiences during development—if the correct formula is nature via nurture—then intervention is not precluded even for highly heritable traits, but should be the more effective when tailored to each specific child's talents and inclinations.

Relevance to Evolutionary Psychology and Sociobiology

This research focuses on individual differences, but like other animals we share certain species-specific tendencies by virtue of our being human. Whereas behavioral geneticists study variations within a species, evolutionary psychologists or sociobiologists attempt to delineate species-typical proclivities or instincts and to understand the relevant evolutionary developments that took place in the Pleistocene epoch and were adaptive in the lives of tribal hunter-gatherers. The genes sing a prehistoric song that today should sometimes be resisted but which it would be foolish to ignore.

At the interface of behavioral genetics and sociobiology is the question of the origin and function, if any, of the within-species variability we have been discussing. One view is that it represents evolutionary debris (40), unimportant to fitness and perhaps not expressed in prehistoric environments. Another view is that variability has an adaptive function and has been selected for. Whether sociobiologists can make evolutionary sense of the varieties of human genetic variation we have discussed here remains to be seen (41).

Whatever the ancient origins and functions of genetic variability, its repercussions in contemporary society are pervasive and important. A human species whose members did not vary genetically with respect to significant cognitive and motivational attributes, and who were uniformly average

by current standards, would have created a very different society than the one we know. Modern society not only augments the influence of genotype on behavioral variability, as we have suggested, but permits this variability to reciprocally contribute to the rapid pace of cultural change. If genetic variation was evolutionary debris at the end of the Pleistocene, it is now a salient and essential feature of the human condition.

References and Notes

1. H. H. Newman, F. N. Freeman, K. J. Holzinger, *Twins: A Study of Heredity and Environment* (Univ. of Chicago Press, Chicago, 1937); N. Juel-Nielsen, *Acta Psychiatr. Neurol. Scand. Suppl.* **183**, (1965); J. Shields, *Monozygotic Twins: Brought up Apart and Brought up Together* (Oxford Univ. Press, London, 1962). There are two other ongoing studies of twins reared apart, one in Sweden (2) and one in Finland (3). The questionable study by Burt (4) has been omitted.
2. N. Pedersen, G. E. McClearn, R. Plomin, L. Friberg, *Behav. Genet.* **15**, 407 (1985); R. Plomin, P. Lichtenstein, N. L. Pedersen, G. E. McClearn, J. R. Nesselroade, *Psychol. Aging* **5**, 25 (1990).
3. H. Langainvainio, J. Kaprio, M. Koskenvuo, J. Lönnqvist, *Acta Genet. Med. Gemellol.* **33**, 259 (1984).
4. L. Hearnshaw, *Cyril Burt: Psychologist* (Hodder & Stoughten, London, 1979); but see R. B. Joynson, *The Burt Affair* (Routledge, London, 1990).
5. R. Plomin and D. Daniels, *Behav. Brain Sci.* **10**, 1 (1987); L. J. Eaves, H. J. Eysenck, N. G. Martin, *Genes Culture and Personality: An Empirical Approach* (Academic Press, New York, 1989).
6. T. J. Bouchard, Jr., in *The Chemical and Biological Bases of Individuality*, S. Fox, Ed. (Plenum, New York, 1984), p. 147; N. L. Segal, W. M. Grove, T. J. Bouchard, Jr., in *Genetic Issues in Psychosocial Epidemiology*, M. Tsuang, K. Kendler, M. Lyons, Eds. (Rutgers Univ. Press, New Brunswick, NJ, in press).
7. D. T. Lykken, *Behav. Genet.* **8**, 437 (1978).
8. M. McGue and T. J. Bouchard, Jr., *ibid.* **14**, 325 (1984).
9. T. J. Bouchard, Jr., and M. McGue, *Science* **212**, 1055 (1981).
10. J. D. Matarazzo, *Wechsler's Measurement and Appraisal of Adult Intelligence* (Williams and Wilkins, Baltimore, ed. 5, 1972).
11. J. Raven, *Manual for Raven's Progressive Matrices and Vocabulary Scales* (Lewis, London, 1986).
12. J. C. DeFries *et al.*, *Behav. Genet.* **9**, 23 (1979).
13. A. R. Hakstian and R. B. Cattell, *J. Educ. Psychol.* **70**, 657 (1978).
14. T. J. Bouchard, Jr., N. L. Segal, D. T. Lykken, *Acta Genet. Med. Gemellol.* **39**, 193 (1990).

15. J. C. Loehlin, *Am. Psychol.* **44**, 1285 (1989); R. Plomin and J. C. Loehlin, *Behav. Genet.* **19**, 331 (1989).

16. K. McCartney, M. J. Harris, F. Bernieri, *Psychol. Bull.* **107**, 26 (1990).

17. M. McGue and T. J. Bouchard, Jr., in *Advances in the Psychology of Human Intelligence*, R. J. Sternberg, Ed. (Erlbaum, New York, 1989), vol. 5, p. 7. This checklist yields four relatively independent scales: scientific or technical, cultural, mechanical, and material possessions.

18. R. H. Moos and B. S. Moos, *Manual: Family Environment Scale* (Consulting Psychologists Press, Palo Alto, CA, 1986).

19. Formally, this is the maximum linear contribution; nonlinear effects are, of course, possible. For these data, however, investigation of higher-ordered relationships (quadratic and cubic) showed no associations that did not exist at the linear level, and there was no discernible nonlinearity detected in visual inspection of the scatterplots.

20. T. J. Bouchard, Jr., *Intelligence* **7**, 175 (1983).

21. C. Capron and M. Duyme [*Nature* **340**, 552 (1989)] have shown an SES effect in an adoption study of young children; S. Scarr and R. Weinberg [*Amer. Sociol. Rev.* **43**, 674 (1978)] did not find an SES effect in a study of young adult adoptees.

22. B. Price, *Am J. Hum. Genet.* **2**, 293 (1950).

23. R. J. Rose and J. Kaprio, *Behav. Genet.* **18**, 309 (1988).

24. D. T. Lykken, T. J. Bouchard, Jr., M. McGue, A. Tellegen, *Behav. Genet.*, in press.

25. As in our earlier analysis, nonlinear relationships were tested for and found not to exist. Additionally, deletion of a single outlier (IQ difference of 29 points) did not appreciably change the correlation estimates.

26. Expected difference (D) can be expressed as a function of the correlation (r) and standard deviation as $D = 1.13 \sigma \sqrt{1 - r}$ [R. Plomin and J. C. DeFries, *Intelligence* **4**, 15 (1980)].

27. K. R. White, *Psychol. Bull.* **86**, 461 (1982).

28. D. T. Lykken, T. J. Bouchard, Jr., M. McGue, A. Tellegen, *Acta Genet. Med. Gemellol.* **39**, 35 (1990); and (6).

29. H. H. Stassen, D. T. Lykken, G. Bomben, *Eur. Arch. Psychiatry Neurol. Sci.* **237**, 244 (1988).

30. Systolic blood pressure from Minnesota twin studies. Heart rate from B. Hanson *et al., Am. J. Cardiol.* **63**, 606 (1989). Electrodermal and habituation data from D. T. Lykken, W. G. Iacono, K. Haroian, M. McGue, T. J. Bouchard, Jr., *Psychophysiology* **25**, 4 (1988). Reliability data from K. Matthews, C. Rakczky, C. Stoney, S. Manuck, *ibid.* **24**, 464 (1987); M. Llabre *et al., ibid.* **25**, 97 (1988).

31. MPQ data from A. Tellegen *et al., J. Pers. Soc. Psychol.* **54**, 1031 (1988); CPI data from T. J. Bouchard, Jr., and M. McGue, *J. Pers.* **58**, 263 (1990). Reliability data from test manuals.

32. MZA and MZT Religiosity data from N. G. Waller, B. A. Kojetin, T. J. Bouchard, Jr., D. T. Lykken, A. Tellegen, *Psychol. Sci.* **1**, 138 (1990). Reliability of religious leisure time interests and religious occupational interests and mean of 14 nonreligious social attitude items from Minnesota twin study data base (28). Reliability of other scales from test manuals. For a general discussion of the reliability of traits such as those measured in this study, see K. C. H. Parker, R. K. Hanson, J. Hunsley [*Psychol. Bull.* **103**, 367 (1988)] and J. J. Conley [*Pers. Individ. Differ.* **5**, 11 (1984)].

33. R. C. Lewontin, S. Rose, L. J. Kamin, *Not in Our Genes; Biology, Ideology, and Human Nature* (Pantheon, New York, 1984).

34. S. Scarr, *Behav. Genet.* **17**, 219 (1987).

35. J. R. Flynn, *Psychol. Bull.* **101**, 171 (1987).

36. R. Lynn, *Pers. Individ. Differ.* **11**, 273 (1990); T. W. Teasedale and D. R. Owen, *Intelligence* **13**, 255 (1989).

37. R. Wilson, *Child Dev.* **54**, 298 (1983).

38. K. J. Hayes, *Psychol. Rep.* **10**, 299 (1962); C. J. Lumsden and E. O. Wilson, *Genes, Mind and Culture* (Harvard Univ. Press, Cambridge, MA, 1981); S. Scarr and K. McCartney, *Child Dev.* **54**, 424 (1983).

39. N. G. Martin *et al., Proc. Nat. Acad. Sci. U.S.A.* **83**, 4364 (1986).

40. M. W. Feldman and R. C. Lewontin, *Science* **190**, 1163 (1975); D. Symonds, *The Evolution of Human Sexuality* (Oxford Univ. Press, New York, 1979).

41. D. M. Buss, *J. Pers.* **58**, 1 (1990).

42. T. J. Bouchard, Jr., D. T. Lykken, M. McGue, N. L. Segal, A. Tellegen, this article.

43. The MZA correlation of 0.771 reported by the late Sir Cyril Burt and questioned for its authenticity after his death (4) falls within the range of findings reviewed here.

44. WAIS data for MZTs from K. Tambs, J. M. Sundet, P. Magnus, *Intelligence* **8**, 283 (1984). Reliabilities from (10). Raven, Mill-Hill, and composite data from Minnesota twin studies (6, 42).

45. MZA data on SCII and JVIS from D. Moloney, unpublished thesis (University of Minnesota, Minneapolis, 1990). Minnesota Occupational Interest Scale data from N. Waller, D. T. Lykken, A. Tellegen, in *Wise Counsel: Essays in Honor of Lloyd Lofquist*, R. Dawis and D. Lubinski, Eds. (Univ. of Minnesota Press, Minneapolis, in press). SCII MZT data from Nichols [*Homo* **29**, 158 (1978)]. Reliability data from test manuals.

46. We thank our colleagues E. D. Eckert, L. L. Heston, and I. I. Gottesman for their help on the medical and psychiatric portions of the study and H. Polesky, director, for the blood testing. This research has been supported by grants from The Pioneer Fund, The Seaver Institute, The University of Minnesota Graduate School, The Koch Charitable Foundation, The Spencer Foundation, The National Science Foundation (BNS-7926654), The National Institute of Mental Health (MH37860), The National Institute on Aging (AG06886), and the Harcourt Brace Jovanovich Publishing Company.

QUESTIONS FOR REFLECTION AND DISCUSSION:

1. How do monozygotic and dizygotic twins who are separated early and reared apart provide a means for distinguishing the effects of nature and nurture on human characteristics?

2. What does it mean to say that there is a "heritability estimate of 70%" in the heritability of IQ?

3. The research sample included no individuals whose IQ was intellectually deficient (equal to or less than 70). How might this restricted range of IQ scores affect the results of the study?

4. The authors say that there is evidence of strong heritability for most psychological traits, including intelligence. Yet, they also say, "This evidence . . . does not detract from the value or importance of parenting, education," and other childhood experiences. Is it truly possible that such strong evidence of heritability does not "detract from" the value of education and parenting? If so, how?

5. Your authors suggest that one reason that monozygotic twins who are reared apart are so similar in IQ is that the "institutions and practices of modern Western society" are widespread and encouraging enough that they allow individual differences in psychological traits to develop. Do you share this view of "institutions and practices of modern Western society"? Why or why not?

6. The authors write, "It is well known to naturalists and to animal breeders that there are wide and heritable differences in behavior within other species, but there is a curious reluctance among some scientists to acknowledge the contribution of genetic variation to psychological differences within the human species." Why do you believe there is this "curious reluctance"? (Hint: In your answer, you may wish to consider implications for education and for the possibility of eugenics.)

7. In the discussion of the relevance of their findings to evolutionary psychology, your authors write, poetically, that "The genes sing a prehistoric song that today should sometimes be resisted but which it would be foolish to ignore." What is this prehistoric song? Why should it sometimes be resisted today? Why would it be foolish to ignore the "song"?

SOURCE

I. Darwin, C. (1858/1993). Extract from an Unpublished Work on Species, by C. Darwin, Esq., Consisting of a Portion of a Chapter Entitled "On the Variation of Organic Beings in a State of Nature; on the Natural Means of Selection; on the Comparison of Domestic Races and True Species"; II. Darwin, C. (1858/1993). Abstract of a Letter from C. Darwin, Esq., to Prof. Asa Gray, Boston, U.S., dated Down, September 5, 1857; III. Wallace, A. R. (1858/1993). On the Tendency of Varieties to depart indefinitely from the Original Type, by Alfred Russel Wallace; IV. Darwin, C. IV. (1959/1993). Sexual selection. From *On the origin of species by means of natural selection, or The preservation of favoured races in the struggle for life.* (1859/1993). In Porter, D. M., & Graham, P. W. (Eds.), *The portable Darwin.* New York: Penguin, pp. 89–166.

The following sources are from letters and brief papers by Charles Darwin and Alfred Russel Wallace, and from Darwin's monumental work, The Origin of Species by Means of Natural Selection, which was published in 1859. Darwin is certainly the better known of the two scientists, although they both worked on evolutionary theory, sometimes sharing notes and cooperating, sometimes—at least in the case of Darwin—competing.

Darwin is considered by some to be the greatest scientist of the 19th century. He was born in England in 1809, on the same day that Abraham Lincoln was born in the United States, and spent most of his life in England. The notable exception is his 5-year scientific expedition, begun in 1831, on the HMS Beagle, whose main mission was to map the coasts of Tierra del Fuego and Patagonia. Darwin was the naturalist (natural scientist) on board, and his observations of the development of species in various locations fueled his ideas on evolution. His innovations included the observations that animals produce more offspring than can survive (i.e., there is a struggle for survival); that these offspring vary in traits; and that those offspring that possess traits that enable them to survive are most likely to live to reproductive age and transmit these traits to future generations. This process is referred to as natural selection.

Darwin was reluctant to publish his views at first because they countered the religious view of the creation, and because he feared that their appearance might endanger his family. Prior to the appearance of The Origin of Species, however, he shared his ideas with a small number of fellow scientists, including Wallace. In 1858, Wallace sent Darwin a letter asking him to forward an enclosed paper on evolution to the Linnean Society (a scientific society). Darwin experienced great conflict because the paper expressed ideas that Wallace had probably gleaned from Darwin and because Wallace's name could be forever attached to those ideas. After much to do, the society presented a "joint paper" by Darwin and Wallace. The first two parts are by Darwin and the third by Wallace. Darwin was given the primary role and Wallace, rather than resent Darwin, appears to have been honored to be associated with Darwin. The three papers present ideas that are developed more fully in Darwin's larger work.

The fourth source presented here is on sexual selection and comes directly from The Origin of Species by Means of Natural Selection. Sexual selection does not refer to the broader struggle for survival, but to "a struggle between the males for the possession of the females." That concept may sound sexist today, but Darwin is referring to many species, not particularly humans—although we can note that during most of human history women were literally given by fathers to husbands and were considered the property of men. But the extract shown here refers specifically to deer, birds, alligators, beetles, and some other kinds of animals.

Harcourt, Inc.

The Portable Darwin

DUNCAN M. PORTER AND PETER W. GRAHAM, EDS.

J. J. Bennett, Esq.,

Secretary of the Linnean Society

I. Extract from an Unpublished Work on Species, by C. Darwin, Esq., Consisting of a Portion of a Chapter Entitled, "On the Variation of Organic Beings in a State of Nature; on the Natural Means of Selection; on the Comparison of Domestic Races and True Species"

De Candolle, in an eloquent passage, has declared that all nature is at war, one organism with another, or with external nature. Seeing the contented face of nature, this may at first well be doubted; but reflection will inevitably prove it to be true. The war, however, is not constant, but recurrent in a slight degree at short periods, and more severely at occasional more distant periods; and hence its effects are easily overlooked. It is the doctrine of Malthus applied in most cases with tenfold force. As in every climate there are seasons, for each of its inhabitants, of greater and less abundance, so all annually breed; and the moral restraint which in some small degree checks the increase of mankind is entirely lost. Even slow-breeding mankind has doubled in twenty-five years; and if he could increase his food with greater ease, he would double in less time. But for animals without artificial means, the amount of food for each species must, on an average, be constant, whereas the increase of all organisms tends to be geometrical, and in a vast majority of cases at an enormous ratio. Suppose in a certain spot there are eight pairs of birds, and that *only* four pairs of them annually (including double hatches) rear only four young, and that these go on rearing their young at the same rate, then at the end of seven years (a short life, excluding violent deaths, for any bird) there will be 2048 birds, instead of the original sixteen. As this increase is quite impossible, we must conclude either that birds do not rear nearly half their young, or that the average life of a bird is, from accident, not nearly seven years. Both checks proba-

bly concur. The same kind of calculation applied to all plants and animals affords results more or less striking, but in very few instances more striking than in man.

Many practical illustrations of this rapid tendency to increase are on record, among which, during peculiar seasons, are the extraordinary numbers of certain animals; for instance, during the years 1826 to 1828, in La Plata, when from drought some millions of cattle perished, the whole country actually *swarmed* with mice. Now I think it cannot be doubted that during the breeding-season all the mice (with the exception of a few males or females in excess) ordinarily pair, and therefore that this astounding increase during three years must be attributed to a greater number than usual surviving the first year, and then breeding, and so on till the third year, when their numbers were brought down to their usual limits on the return of wet weather. Where man has introduced plants and animals into a new and favourable country, there are many accounts in how surprisingly few years the whole country has become stocked with them. This increase would necessarily stop as soon as the country was fully stocked; and yet we have every reason to believe, from what is known of wild animals, that *all* would pair in the spring. In the majority of cases it is most difficult to imagine where the checks fall— though generally, no doubt, on the seeds, eggs, and young; but when we remember how impossible, even in mankind (so much better known than any other animal), it is to infer from repeated casual observations what the average duration of life is, or to discover the different percentage of deaths to births in different countries, we ought to feel no surprise at our being unable to discover where the check falls in any animal or plant. It should always be remembered, that in most cases the checks are recurrent yearly in a small, regular degree, and in an extreme degree during unusually cold, hot, dry, or wet years, according to the constitution of the being in question. Lighten any check in the least degree, and the geometrical powers of increase in every organism will almost instantly increase the average number of the favoured species. Nature may be compared to a surface on which rest ten thousand sharp wedges touching each other and driven inwards by incessant blows. Fully to realize these views much reflection is requisite. Malthus on man should be studied; and all such cases as those of the mice in

La Plata, of the cattle and horses when first turned out in South America, of the birds by our calculation, &c., should be well considered. Reflect on the enormous multiplying power *inherent and annually in action* in all animals; reflect on the countless seeds scattered by a hundred ingenious contrivances, year after year, over the whole face of the land; and yet we have every reason to suppose that the average percentage of each of the inhabitants of a country usually remains constant. Finally, let it be borne in mind that this average number of individuals (the external conditions remaining the same) in each country is kept up by recurrent struggles against other species or against external nature (as on the borders of the Arctic regions, where the cold checks life), and that ordinarily each individual of every species holds its place, either by its own struggle and capacity of acquiring nourishment in some period of its life, from the egg upwards; or by the struggle of its parents (in short-lived organisms, when the main check occurs at longer intervals) with other individuals of the *same* or *different* species.

But let the external conditions of a country alter. If in a small degree, the relative proportions of the inhabitants will in most cases simply be slightly changed; but let the number of inhabitants be small, as on an island, and free access to it from other countries be circumscribed, and let the change of conditions continue progressing (forming new stations), in such a case the original inhabitants must cease to be as perfectly adapted to the changed conditions as they were originally. It has been shown in a former part of this work, that such changes of external conditions would, from their acting on the reproductive system, probably cause the organization of those beings which were most affected to become, as under domestication, plastic. Now, can it be doubted, from the struggle each individual has to obtain subsistence, that any minute variation in structure, habits, or instincts, adapting that individual better to the new conditions, would tell upon its vigour and health? In the struggle it would have a better *chance* of surviving; and those of its offspring which inherited the variation, be it ever so slight, would also have a better *chance*. Yearly more are bred than can survive; the smallest grain in the balance, in the long run, must tell on which death shall fall, and which shall survive. Let this work of selection on the one hand, and death on the other, go on for a thousand generations, who will pretend to affirm that it would produce no effect, when we remember what, in a few years, Bakewell effected in cattle, and Western in sheep, by this identical principle of selection?

To give an imaginary example from changes in progress on an island:—let the organization of a canine animal which preyed chiefly on rabbits, but sometimes on hares, become slightly plastic; let these same changes cause the number of rabbits very slowly to decrease, and the number of hares to increase; the effect of this would be that the fox or dog would be driven to try to catch more hares: his organization, however, being slightly plastic, those individuals with the lightest forms, longest limbs, and best eyesight, let the difference be ever so small, would be slightly favoured, and would tend to live longer, and to survive during that time of the year when food was scarcest; they would also rear more young, which would tend to inherit these slight peculiarities. The less fleet ones would be rigidly destroyed. I can see no more reason to doubt that these causes in a thousand generations would produce a marked effect, and adapt the form of the fox or dog to the catching of hares instead of rabbits, than that greyhounds can be improved by selection and careful breeding. So would it be with plants under similar circumstances. If the number of individuals of a species with plumed seeds could be increased by greater powers of dissemination within its own area (that is, if the check to increase fell chiefly on the seeds), those seeds which were provided with ever so little more down, would in the long run be most disseminated; hence a greater number of seeds thus formed would germinate, and would tend to produce plants inheriting the slightly better-adapted down.

Besides this natural means of selection, by which those individuals are preserved, whether in their egg, or larval, or mature state, which are best adapted to the place they fill in nature, there is a second agency at work in most unisexual [misprint for "bisexual"—editors] animals, tending to produce the same effect, namely, the struggle of the males for the females. These struggles are generally decided by the law of battle, but in the case of birds, apparently, by the charms of their song, by their beauty or their power of courtship, as in the dancing rock-thrush of Guiana. The most vigorous and healthy males, implying perfect adaptation, must generally gain the victory in their contests. This kind of selection, however, is less rigorous than the other; it does not require the death of the less successful, but gives to them fewer descendants. The struggle falls, moreover, at a time of year when food is generally abundant, and perhaps the effect chiefly produced would be the modification of the secondary sexual characters, which are not related to the power of obtaining food, or to defence from enemies, but to fighting with or rivalling other males.

The result of this struggle amongst the males may be compared in some respects to that produced by those agriculturists who pay less attention to the careful selection of all their young animals, and more to the occasional use of a choice mate [misprint for "male"—editors].

II. Abstract of a Letter from C. Darwin, Esq., to Prof. Asa Gray, Boston, U.S., dated Down, September 5th, 1857

1. It is wonderful what the principle of selection by man, that is the picking out of individuals with any desired quality, and breeding from them, and again picking out, can do. Even breeders have been astounded at their own results. They can act on differences inappreciable to an uneducated eye. Selection has been *methodically* followed in *Europe* for only the last half century; but it was occasionally, and even in some degree methodically, followed in most ancient times. There must have been also a kind of unconscious selection from a remote period, namely in the preservation of the individual animals (without any thought of their offspring) most useful to each race of man in his particular circumstances. The "roguing," as nurserymen call the destroying of varieties which depart from their type, is a kind of selection. I am convinced that intentional and occasional selection has been the main agent in the production of our domestic races; but however this may be, its great power of modification has been indisputably shown in later times. Selection acts only by the accumulation of slight or greater variations, caused by external conditions, or by the mere fact that in generation the child is not absolutely similar to its parent. Man, by this power of accumulating variations, adapts living beings to his wants—may be said to make the wool of one sheep good for carpets, of another for cloth, &c.

2. Now suppose there were a being who did not judge by mere external appearances, but who could study the whole internal organization, who was never capricious, and should go on selecting for one object during millions of generations; who will say what he might not effect? In nature we have some *slight* variation occasionally in all parts; and I think it can be shown that changed conditions of existence is the main cause of the child not exactly resembling its parents; and in nature geology shows us what changes have taken place, and are taking place. We have almost unlimited time; no one but a practical geologist can fully appreciate this. Think of the Glacial period, during the whole of which the same species at least of shells have existed; there must have been during this period millions on millions of generations.

3. I think it can be shown that there is such an unerring power at work in *Natural Selection* (the title of my book), which selects exclusively for the good of each organic being. The elder Dr. Candolle, W. Herbert, and Lyell have written excellently on the struggle for life; but even they have not written strongly enough. Reflect that every being (even the elephant) breeds at such a rate, that in a few years, or at most a few centuries, the surface of the earth would not hold the progeny of one pair. I have found it hard constantly to bear in mind that the increase of every single species is checked during some part of its life, or during some shortly recurrent generation. Only a few of those annually born can live to propagate their kind. What a trifling difference must often determine which shall survive, and which perish!

4. Now take the case of a country undergoing some change. This will tend to cause some of its inhabitants to vary slightly—not but that I believe most beings vary at all times enough for selection to act on them. Some of its inhabitants will be exterminated; and the remainder will be exposed to the mutual action of a different set of inhabitants, which I believe to be far more important to the life of each being than mere climate. Considering the infinitely various methods which living beings follow to obtain food by struggling with other organisms, to escape danger at various times of life, to have their eggs or seeds disseminated, &c. &c., I cannot doubt that during millions of generations individuals of a species will be occasionally born with some slight variation, profitable to some part of their economy. Such individuals will have a better chance of surviving, and of propagating their new and slightly different structure; and the modification may be slowly increased by the accumulative action of natural selection to any profitable extent. The variety thus formed will either coexist with, or, more commonly, will exterminate its parent form. An organic being, like the woodpecker or misseltoe, may thus come to be adapted to a score of contingencies—natural selection accumulating those slight variations in all parts of its structure, which are in any way useful to it during any part of its life.

5. Multiform difficulties will occur to every one, with respect to this theory. Many can, I think, be satisfactorily answered. *Natura non facit saltum* ["Nature does not move by jumps."—editors] answers some of the most obvious. The slowness of the change, and only a very few individuals undergoing

change at any one time, answers others. The extreme imperfection of our geological records answers others.

6. Another principle, which may be called the principle of divergence, plays, I believe, an important part in the origin of species. The same spot will support more life if occupied by very diverse forms. We see this in the many generic forms in a square yard of turf, and in the plants or insects on any little uniform islet, belonging almost invariably to as many genera and families as species. We can understand the meaning of this fact amongst the higher animals, whose habits we understand. We know that it has been experimentally shown that a plot of land will yield a greater weight if sown with several species and genera of grasses, than if sown with only two or three species. Now, every organic being, by propagating so rapidly, may be said to be striving its utmost to increase in numbers. So it will be with the offspring of any species after it has become diversified into varieties, or sub-species, or true species. And it follows, I think, from the foregoing facts, that the varying offspring of each species will try (only few will succeed) to seize on as many and as diverse places in the economy of nature as possible. Each new variety or species, when formed, will generally take the place of, and thus exterminate its less well-fitted parent. This I believe to be the origin of the classification and affinities of organic beings at all times; for organic beings always *seem* to branch and sub-branch like the limbs of a tree from a common trunk, the flourishing and diverging twigs destroying the less vigorous—the dead and lost branches rudely representing extinct genera and families.

This sketch is *most* imperfect; but in so short a space I cannot make it better. Your imagination must fill up very wide blanks.

III. On the Tendency of Varieties to depart indefinitely from the Original Type, by Alfred Russel Wallace

One of the strongest arguments which have been adduced to prove the original and permanent distinctness of species is, that *varieties* produced in a state of domesticity are more or less unstable, and often have a tendency, if left to themselves, to return to the normal form of the parent species; and this instability is considered to be a distinctive peculiarity of all varieties, even of those occurring among wild animals in a state of nature, and to constitute a provision for preserving unchanged the originally created distinct species.

In the absence or scarcity of facts and observations as to *varieties* occurring among wild animals, this argument has had great weight with naturalists, and has led to a very general and somewhat prejudiced belief in the stability of species. Equally general, however, is the belief in what are called "permanent or true varieties,"—races of animals which continually propagate their like, but which differ so slightly (although constantly) from some other race, that the one is considered to be a *variety* of the other. Which is the *variety* and which the original *species,* there is generally no means of determining, except in those rare cases in which the one race has been known to produce an offspring unlike itself and resembling the other. This, however, would seem quite incompatible with the "permanent invariability of species," but the difficulty is overcome by assuming that such varieties have strict limits, and can never again vary further from the original types, although they may return to it, which, from the analogy of the domesticated animals, is considered to be highly probable, if not certainly proved.

It will be observed that this argument rests entirely on the assumption, that *varieties* occurring in a state of nature are in all respects analogous to or even identical with those of domestic animals, and are governed by the same laws as regards their permanence or further variation. But it is the object of the present paper to show that this assumption is altogether false, that there is a general principle in nature which will cause many *varieties* to survive the parent species, and to give rise to successive variations departing further and further from the original type, and which also produces, in domesticated animals, the tendency of varieties to return to the parent form.

The life of wild animals is a struggle for existence. The full exertion of all their faculties and all their energies is required to preserve their own existence and provide for that of their infant offspring. The possibility of procuring food during the least favourable seasons, and of escaping the attacks of their most dangerous enemies, are the primary conditions which determine the existence both of individuals and of entire species. These conditions will also determine the population of a species; and by a careful consideration of all the circumstances we may be enabled to comprehend, and in some degree to explain, what at first sight appears so inexplicable—the excessive abundance of some species, while others closely allied to them are very rare.

The general proportion that must obtain between certain groups of animals is readily seen.

Harcourt, Inc.

Large animals cannot be so abundant as small ones; the carnivora must be less numerous than the herbivora; eagles and lions can never be so plentiful as pigeons and antelopes; the wild asses of the Tartarian deserts cannot equal in numbers the horses of the more luxuriant prairies and pampas of America. The greater or less fecundity of an animal is often considered to be one of the chief causes of its abundance or scarcity; but a consideration of the facts will show us that it really has little or nothing to do with the matter. Even the least prolific of animals would increase rapidly if unchecked, whereas it is evident that the animal population of the globe must be stationary, or perhaps, through the influence of man, decreasing. Fluctuations there may be; but permanent increase, except in restricted localities, is almost impossible. For example, our own observation must convince us that birds do not go on increasing every year in a geometrical ratio, as they would do, were there not some powerful check to their natural increase. Very few birds produce less than two young ones each year, while many have six, eight, or ten; four will certainly be below the average; and if we suppose that each pair produce young only four times in their life, that will also be below the average, supposing them not to die either by violence or want of food. Yet at this rate how tremendous would be the increase in a few years from a single pair! A simple calculation will show that in fifteen years each pair of birds would have increased to nearly ten millions! whereas we have no reason to believe that the number of the birds of any country increases at all in fifteen or in one hundred and fifty years. With such powers of increase the population must have reached its limits, and have become stationary, in a very few years after the origin of each species. It is evident, therefore, that each year an immense number of birds must perish—as many in fact as are born; and as on the lowest calculation the progeny are each year twice as numerous as their parents, it follows that, whatever be the average number of individuals existing in any given country, *twice that number must perish annually,*—a striking result, but one which seems at least highly probable, and is perhaps under rather than over the truth. It would therefore appear that, as far as the continuance of the species and the keeping up the average number of individuals are concerned, large broods are superfluous. On the average all above *one* become food for hawks and kites, wild cats and weasels, or perish of cold and hunger as winter comes on. This is strikingly proved by the case of particular species; for we find that their abundance in individuals bears no relation whatever to their fertility in producing offspring.

Perhaps the most remarkable instance of an immense bird population is that of the passenger pigeon of the United States, which lays only one, or at the most two eggs, and is said to rear generally but one young one. Why is this bird so extraordinarily abundant, while others producing two or three times as many young are much less plentiful? The explanation is not difficult. The food most congenial to this species, and on which it thrives best, is abundantly distributed over a very extensive region, offering such differences of soil and climate, that in one part or another of the area the supply never fails. The bird is capable of a very rapid and long-continued flight, so that it can pass without fatigue over the whole of the district it inhabits, and as soon as the supply of food begins to fail in one place is able to discover a fresh feeding-ground. This example strikingly shows us that the procuring a constant supply of wholesome food is almost the sole condition requisite for ensuring the rapid increase of a given species, since neither the limited fecundity, nor the unrestrained attacks of birds of prey and of man are here sufficient to check it. In no other birds are these peculiar circumstances so strikingly combined. Either their food is more liable to failure, or they have not sufficient power of wing to search for it over an extensive area, or during some season of the year it becomes very scarce, and less wholesome substitutes have to be found; and thus, though more fertile in offspring, they can never increase beyond the supply of food in the least favourable seasons. Many birds can only exist by migrating, when their food becomes scarce, to regions possessing a milder, or at least a different climate, though, as these migrating birds are seldom excessively abundant, it is evident that the countries they visit are still deficient in a constant and abundant supply of wholesome food. Those whose organization does not permit them to migrate when their food becomes periodically scarce, can never attain a large population. This is probably the reason why woodpeckers are scarce with us, while in the tropics they are among the most abundant of solitary birds. Thus the house sparrow is more abundant than the redbreast, because its food is more constant and plentiful,—seeds of grasses being preserved during the winter, and our farm-yards and stubble-fields furnishing an almost inexhaustible supply. Why, as a general rule, are aquatic, and especially sea birds, very numerous in individuals? Not because they are more prolific than others, generally the contrary; but because their food never fails, the sea-shores and river-banks daily swarming with a fresh supply of small mollusca and crustacea. Exactly the same laws will apply to mammals. Wild cats are prolific and have few enemies; why then are they never as abundant as rabbits? The only intelligible answer is, that their supply of food is more precarious. It appears evident, therefore, that so long as a country remains physically unchanged, the numbers of its animal population cannot materially increase. If one species does so, some others requiring the same kind of food must diminish in proportion. The numbers that die annually must be immense; and as the individual existence of each animal depends upon itself, those that die must be the weakest—the very young, the aged, and the diseased,—while those that prolong their existence can only be the most perfect in health and vigour— those who are best able to obtain food regularly, and avoid their numerous enemies. It is, as we commenced by remarking, "a struggle for existence," in which the weakest and least perfectly organized must always succumb.

Now it is clear that what takes place among the individuals of a species must also occur among the several allied species of a group,—viz. that those which are best adapted to obtain a regular supply of food, and to defend themselves against the attacks of their enemies and the vicissitudes of the seasons, must necessarily obtain and preserve a superiority in population; while those species which from some defect of power or organization are the least capable of counteracting the vicissitudes of food, supply, &c., must diminish in numbers, and, in extreme cases, become altogether extinct. Between these extremes the species will present various degrees of capacity for ensuring the means of preserving life; and it is thus we account for the abundance or rarity of species. Our ignorance will generally prevent us from accurately tracing the effects to their causes; but could we become perfectly acquainted with the organization and habits of the various species of animals, and could we measure the capacity of each for performing the different acts necessary to its safety and existence under all the varying circumstances by which it is surrounded, we might be able even to calculate the proportionate abundance of individuals which is the necessary result.

If now we have succeeded in establishing these two points—1st, *that the animal population of a country is generally stationary, being kept down by a periodical deficiency of food, and other checks;* and, 2nd, *that the comparative abundance or scarcity of the individuals of the several species is entirely due to their organization and resulting habits, which, rendering it more difficult to procure a regular supply of food and to provide for their personal safety in some cases than in others, can only be balanced by a difference in the population which have to exist in a given area*—we shall be in a condition to proceed to the consideration of *varieties*, to which the preceding remarks have a direct and very important application.

Most or perhaps all the variations from the typical form of a species must have some definite effect, however slight, on the habits or capacities of the individuals. Even a change of colour might, by rendering them more or less distinguishable, affect their safety; a greater or less development of hair might modify their habits. More important changes, such as an increase in the power or dimensions of the limbs or any of the external organs, would more or less affect their mode of procuring food or the range of country which they inhabit. It is also evident that most changes would affect, either favourably or adversely, the powers of prolonging existence. An antelope with shorter or weaker legs must necessarily suffer more from the attacks of the feline carnivora; the passenger pigeon with less powerful wings would sooner or later be affected in its powers of procuring a regular supply of food; and in both cases the result must necessarily be a diminution of the population of the modified species. If, on the other hand, any species should produce a variety having slightly increased powers of preserving existence, that variety must inevitably in time acquire a superiority in numbers. These results must follow as surely as old age, intemperance, or scarcity of food produce an increased mortality. In both cases there may be many individual exceptions; but on the average the rule will invariably be found to hold good. All varieties will therefore fall into two classes—those which under the same conditions would never reach the population of the parent species, and those which would in time obtain and keep a numerical superiority. Now, let some alternation of physical conditions occur in the district—a long period of drought, a destruction of vegetation by locusts, the irruption of some new carnivorous animal seeking "pastures new"—any change in fact tending to render existence more difficult to the species in question, and tasking its utmost powers to avoid complete extermination; it is evident that, of all the individuals composing the species, those forming the least numerous and most feebly organized variety would suffer first, and, were the pressure severe, must soon become extinct. The same causes continuing in action, the parent species would next suffer, would gradually diminish in numbers, and with a recurrence of similar unfavourable conditions might also become extinct. The superior variety would then alone remain, and on a return to favourable circumstances would rapidly increase in numbers and occupy the place of the extinct species and variety.

The *variety* would now have replaced the *species,* of which it would be a more perfectly developed and more highly organized form. It would be in all respects better adapted to secure its safety, and to prolong its individual existence and that of the race. Such a variety *could not* return to the original form; for that form is an inferior one, and could never compete with it for existence. Granted, therefore, a "tendency" to reproduce the original type of the species, still the variety must ever remain preponderant in numbers, and under adverse physical conditions *again alone survive.* But this new, improved, and populous race might itself, in course of time, give rise to new varieties, exhibiting several diverging modifications of form, any of which, tending to increase the facilities for preserving existence, must, by the same general law, in their turn become predominant. Here, then, we have *progression and continued divergence* deduced from the general laws which regulate the existence of animals in a state of nature, and from the undisputed fact that varieties do frequently occur. It is not, however, contended that this result would be invariable; a change of physical conditions in the district might at times materially modify it, rendering the race which had been the most capable of supporting existence under the former conditions now the least so, and even causing the extinction of the newer and, for a time, superior race, while the old or parent species and its first inferior varieties continued to flourish. Variations in unimportant parts might also occur, having no perceptible effect on the life-preserving powers; and the varieties so furnished might run a course parallel with the parent species, either giving rise to further variations or returning to the former type. All we argue for is, that certain varieties have a tendency to maintain their existence longer than the original species, and this tendency must make itself felt; for though the doctrine of chances or averages can never be trusted to on a limited scale, yet, if applied to high numbers, the results come nearer to what theory demands, and, as we approach to an infinity of examples, becomes strictly accurate. Now the scale on which nature works is so vast—the numbers of individuals and periods of time with which she deals approach so near to infinity, that any cause, however slight, and however liable to be veiled and counteracted by accidental circumstances, must in the end produce its full legitimate results.

Let us now turn to domesticated animals, and inquire how varieties produced among them are affected by the principles here enunciated. The essential difference in the condition of wild and domestic animals is this,—that among the former, their well-being and very existence depend upon the full exercise and healthy condition of all their senses and physical powers, whereas, among the latter, these are only partially exercised, and in some cases are absolutely unused. A wild animal has to search, and often to labour, for every mouthful of food—to exercise sight, hearing, and smell in seeking it, and in avoiding dangers, in procuring shelter from the inclemency of the seasons, and in providing for the subsistence and safety of its offspring. There is no muscle of its body that is not called into daily and hourly activity; there is not sense or faculty that is not strengthened by continual exercise. The domestic animal, on the other hand, has food provided for it, is sheltered, and often confined, to guard it against the vicissitudes of the seasons, is carefully secured from the attacks of its natural enemies, and seldom even rears its young without human assistance. Half of its senses and faculties are quite useless; and the other half are but occasionally called into feeble exercise, while even its muscular system is only irregularly called into action.

Now when a variety of such an animal occurs, having increased power or capacity in any organ or sense, such increase is totally useless, is never called into action, and may even exist without the animal ever becoming aware of it. In the wild animal, on the contrary, all its faculties and powers being brought into full action for the necessities of existence, any increase becomes immediately available, is strengthened by exercise, and must even slightly modify the food, the habits, and the whole economy of the race. It creates as it were a new animal, one of the superior powers, and which will necessarily increase in numbers and outlive those inferior to it.

Again, in the domesticated animal all variations have an equal chance of continuance; and those which would decidedly render a wild animal unable to compete with its fellows and continue its existence are no disadvantage whatever in a state of domesticity. Our quickly fattening pigs, short-legged sheep, pouter pigeons, and poodle dogs could never have come into existence in a state of nature, because the very first step towards such inferior forms would have led to the rapid extinction of the race; still less could they now exist in competition with their wild allies. The great speed but slight endurance of the race horse, the unwieldy strength of the ploughman's team, would both be useless in a state of nature. If turned wild [in] the pampas, such animals would probably soon become extinct, or under favourable circumstances might each lose those extreme qualities which would never be called into action, and in a few generations would revert to a common type, which must be that in which the various powers and faculties are so proportioned to each other as to be best adapted to procure food and secure safety,—that in which by the full exercise of every part of his organization the animal can alone continue to live. Domestic varieties, when turned wild, *must* return to something near the type of the original wild stock, or *become altogether extinct.*

We see, then, that no inferences as to varieties in a state of nature can be deduced from the observation of those occurring among domestic animals. The two are so much opposed to each other in every circumstance of their existence, that what applies to the one is almost sure not to apply to the other. Domestic animals are abnormal, irregular, artificial; they are subject to varieties which never occur and never can occur in a state of nature: their very existence depends altogether on human care; so far are many of them removed from that just proportion of faculties, that true balance of organization, by means of which alone an animal left to its own resources can preserve its existence and continue its race.

The hypothesis of Lamarck—that progressive changes in species have been produced by the attempts of animals to increase the development of their own organs, and thus modify their structure and habits—has been repeatedly and easily refuted by all writers on the subject of varieties and species, and it seems to have been considered that when this was done the whole question has been finally settled; but the view here developed renders such an hypothesis quite unnecessary, by showing that similar results must be produced by the action of principles constantly at work in nature. The powerful retractile talons of the falcon- and the cat-tribes have not been produced or increased by the volition of those animals; but among the different varieties which occurred in the earlier and less highly organized forms of these groups, *those always survived longest which had the greatest facilities for seizing their prey.* Neither did the giraffe acquire its long neck by desiring to reach the foliage of the more lofty shrubs, and constantly stretching its neck for the purpose, but because any varieties which occurred among its antitypes with a longer neck than usual *at once secured a fresh range of pasture over the same ground as their shorter-necked companions, and on the first scarcity of food were thereby enabled to outlive them.* Even the peculiar colours of many animals, especially insects, so closely resembling the soil or the leaves or the trunks on which they habitually reside, are explained on the same principle; for though in the course of ages varieties of many tints may have occurred, *yet those races having colours best adapted to concealment from their enemies would inevitably survive the longest.* We have also here an acting cause to account for that balance so often observed in nature,—a deficiency in one set of organs always being compensated by an increased development of some others—powerful wings accompanying weak feet, or great velocity making up for the absence of defensive weapons; for it has been shown that all varieties in which an unbalanced deficiency occurred could not long continue their existence. The action of this principle is exactly like that of the centrifugal governor of the steam engine, which checks and corrects any irregularities almost before they become evident; and in like manner no unbalanced deficiency in the animal kingdom can ever reach any conspicuous magnitude, because it would make itself felt at the very first step, by rendering existence difficult and extinction almost sure soon to follow. An origin such as is here advocated will also agree with the peculiar character of the modifications of form and structure which obtain in organized beings—the many lines of divergence from a central type, the increasing efficiency and power of a particular organ through a succession of allied species, and the remarkable persistence of unimportant parts such as colour, texture of plumage and hair, form of horns or crests, through a series of species differing considerably in more essential characters. It also furnishes us with a reason for that "more specialized structure" which Professor Owen states to be a characteristic of recent compared with extinct forms, and which would evidently be the result of the progressive modification of any organ applied to a special purpose in the animal economy.

We believe we have now shown that there is a tendency in nature to the continued progression of certain classes of *varieties* further and further from the original type—a progression to which there appears no reason to assign any definite limits—and that the same principle which produces this result in a state of nature will also explain why domestic varieties have a tendency to refer to the original type. This progression, by minute steps, in various directions, but always checked and balanced by the necessary conditions, subject to which alone existence can be preserved, may, it is believed, be followed out so as to agree with all the phenomena presented by organized beings, their extinction and succession in past ages, and all the extraordinary modifications of form, instinct, and habits which they exhibit.

IV. Sexual Selection

Inasmuch as peculiarities often appear under domestication in one sex and become hereditarily attached to that sex, the same fact probably occurs under nature, and if so, natural selection will be able to modify one sex in its functional relations to the other sex, or in relation to wholly different habits of life in the two sexes, as is sometimes the case with insects. And this leads me to say a few words on what I call Sexual Selection. This depends, not on a struggle for existence, but on a struggle between the males for possession of the females; the result is not death to the unsuccessful competitor, but few or no offspring. Sexual selection is, therefore, less rigorous than natural selection. Generally, the most vigorous males, those which are best fitted for their places in nature, will leave most progeny. But in many cases, victory will depend not on general vigour, but on having special weapons, confined to the male sex. A hornless stag or spurless cock would have a poor chance of leaving offspring. Sexual selection by always allowing the victor to breed might surely give indomitable courage, length to the spur, and strength to the wing to strike in the spurred leg, as well as the brutal cock-fighter, who knows well that he can improve his breed by careful selection of the best cocks. How low in the scale of nature this law of battle descends, I know not; male alligators have been described as fighting, bellowing, and whirling round, like Indians in a war-dance, for the possession of the females; male salmons have been seen fighting all day long; male stag-beetles often bear wounds from the huge mandibles of other males. The war is, perhaps, severest between the males of polygamous animals, and these seem oftenest provided with special weapons. The males of carnivorous animals are already well armed; though to them and to others, special means of defence may be given through means of sexual selection, as the mane to the lion, the shoulder-pad to the boar, and the hooked jaw to the male salmon; for the shield may be as important for victory, as the sword or spear.

Amongst birds, the contest is often of a more peaceful character. All those who have attended to the subject, believe that there is the severest rivalry between the males of many species to attract by singing the females. The rock-thrush of Guiana, birds of Paradise, and some others, congregate; and successive males display their gorgeous plumage and perform strange antics before the females, which standing by as spectators, at last choose the most attractive partner. Those who have closely attended to birds in confinement well know that they often take individual preferences and dislikes: thus Sir R. Heron has described how one pied peacock was eminently attractive to all his hen birds. It may appear childish to attribute any effect to such apparently weak means: I cannot here enter on the details necessary to support this view; but if man can in a short time give elegant carriage and beauty to his bantams, according to his standard of beauty, I can see no good reason to doubt that female birds, by selecting, during thousands of generations, the most melodious or beautiful males, according to their standard of beauty, might produce a marked effect. I strongly suspect that some well-known laws with respect to the plumage of male and female birds, in comparison with the plumage of the young, can be explained on the view of plumage having been chiefly modified by sexual selection, acting when the birds have come to the breeding age or during the breeding season; the modifications thus produced being inherited at corresponding ages or seasons, either by the males alone, or by the males and females; but I have not space here to enter on this subject.

Thus it is, as I believe, that when the males and females of any animal have the same general habits of life, but differ in structure, colour, or ornament, such differences have been mainly caused by sexual selection; that is, individual males have had, in successive generations, some slight advantage over other males, in their weapons, means of defence, or charms; and have transmitted these advantages to their male offspring. Yet, I would not wish to attribute all such sexual differences to this agency: for we see peculiarities arising and becoming attached to the male sex in our domestic animals (as the wattle in male carriers, horn-like protuberances in the cocks of certain fowls, &c.), which we cannot believe to be either useful to the males in battle, or attractive to the females. We see analogous cases under nature, for instance, the tuft of hair on the breast of the turkey-cock, which can hardly be either useful or ornamental to this bird;—indeed, had the tuft appeared under domestication, it would have been called a monstrosity.

QUESTIONS FOR REFLECTION AND DISCUSSION:

1. Darwin quotes another scientist who wrote that "all nature is at war." What does the quote mean? Do you agree or disagree? Why?

2. Darwin refers to the doctrine of Malthus. Who was Malthus? How is his doctrine relevant to Darwin's views?

3. What traits in humans do you believe would be most useful in the "struggle for survival"? Why?

4. What kinds of traits do women find attractive in men, and what kinds of traits do men find attractive in women? How might these gender differences fit in with Darwin's ideas on sexual selection?

5. Do you see the theory of evolution as inconsistent with religious views? Why or why not?

6. Darwin's views have been attacked on many grounds over the years. A scientific argument is that evolution might occur in leaps and bounds, whereas Darwin was suggesting that evolution occurs gradually and piecemeal. But others have attacked Darwin's views on moral and ethical grounds, suggesting, for example, that the implications of evolutionary theory do not speak well of "human nature." Why do you think that this criticism has been made?

7. If people were to evolve to become yet more adaptive, what directions do you think such evolution might take? Why?

SOURCE

Buss, D. M. (1999, June 1). Evolutionary science ponders: Where is fancy bred? *The New York Times Online.* Copyright © 1999 by the New York Times Co. Reprinted by permission.

How important is your partner's physical appearance to you? Studies on the selection of dates and mates find that women are usually more concerned than men about their partner's professional status and income and psychological traits like consideration, dependability, and fondness for children. Men tend to be relatively more concerned about physical attractiveness.

Evolutionary psychologists like David M. Buss believe that evolutionary forces favor the survival of women who desire mates with status and men who desire physically alluring mates because these preferences provide reproductive advantages. The value of men as reproducers is intertwined with factors that contribute to a stable environment for child rearing—such as social status and reliability. A woman's appeal is more strongly connected with her age and health, both of which are markers of reproductive capacity.

Some primary sources are found in media such as magazines and newspapers. The following essay by Buss appeared in The New York Times. *Thus its character differs from that of the other readings found in this collection.*

In the 19th century, Charles Darwin did not want his theory of evolution published until after his death. He feared that it would be reviled because it contradicted religious views, which are today often referred to as creationism, and that his family might even be in danger from the public backlash. As pointed out in this essay by evolutionary psychologist David M. Buss, there are many more reasons that the evolutionary perspective on gender differences in preferences for mates has been met with scorn.

Evolutionary Science Ponders: Where is Fancy Bred?

DAVID M. BUSS

"Men are slime."

That's how a woman graduate student summarized my conclusions about the things men will do to have sex. Though this reaction stings, as an evolutionary psychologist I've grown accustomed to it.

The theories of evolutionary psychology—the idea that the ways we think and act now arose through the process of natural selection and that men, for example, evolved a strong desire for a variety of sex partners—disturbs so many people that the field swirls with controversy. Goldie Hawn's publicist said she wanted to slap me. One male colleague once called me a "semenhead."

According to evolutionary psychology, evolution by natural selection has fashioned specific psychological inclinations in response to adaptive problems repeatedly encountered over thousands of generations. Because mating lies at the center of so much of life, it is a particularly important area of study for evolutionary psychologists.

Sociologically, mating affects the distribution of wealth, and can create patterns of inequality.

Psychologically, it influences everything from depression to social success. Mate preferences—how we pick partners, attract them, conflict with them, keep them, lose them, and then start all over again—determine who is selected and shunned, altering our species' evolution.

And men and women differ more in mating than in any other area of life. A man can produce a child in as little as a few minutes of sex, but women tie up their bodies for nine months in pregnancy. Furthermore, women have always been 100 percent certain that they are mothers of their children. Men can never be sure.

As the saying goes, "Mama's baby, papa's maybe."

Evolutionary psychologists believe it would be extraordinarily unlikely for such spectacular differences in reproductive biology, recurring over millions of years of evolutionary history, to result in a sexual psychology identical in men and women.

Men and women all want mates who are kind, understanding, dependable, intelligent and healthy. But men and women differ in three clusters of preferences. Women place a greater premium on a mate's financial capacity, as well as the qualities that lead to resources, such as ambition, industriousness and social status; these likely aided the survival and reproduction of ancestral women and their children. Men, in contrast, place a greater premium on cues to fertility, such as a woman's youth and physical appearance, as well as desiring a greater variety of sex partners.

The idea that people's love lives are influenced by human evolution is shocking. When I first presented my findings on mate preferences in 37 cultures at a professional meeting, for example, a woman approached me and suggested that I suppress the work.

Her sentiment reminded me of Lady Ashley, a contemporary of Darwin, who said upon hearing his theory: "Let's hope that it's not true; but if it is true, let's hope that it doesn't become widely known."

But the theories of evolutionary psychology did become widely known and a robust reaction set in. Some argued that God, not evolution, created the human mind. Others fretted that anything forged in the furnace of evolution would be unchangeable. And mainstream social scientists argued that society molded the mind.

But for me, theories that people are blank slates on which culture writes the script could neither predict nor explain sex differences that research tells us are universal.

The most common concern now is that the findings will be misused.

Men, for example, might justify sexual infidelity—"I couldn't help it; my evolved psychology made me do it." But I have also heard men say that knowledge of evolutionary psychology helps them remain faithful. One told me, "When I find myself attracted to another woman, I realize that it's just my evolved desire for sexual variety; it doesn't mean I don't love my wife." He added, "Knowing this helps me to stay faithful."

Another worry is that discoveries of sex differences will justify discrimination. If evolution has made women and men different, this reasoning goes, it might justify keeping women out of certain jobs or at home barefoot and pregnant.

But the findings of evolutionary psychology provide no justification for these inferences.

Men and women may have different reproductive strategies, but neither can be considered inferior or superior to the other, any more than a bird's wings can be considered superior or inferior to a fish's fins.

And besides, there remains the issue of female infidelity, a phenomenon common among species from birds to people. Perhaps it is an adaptive sexual strategy that secures women the best of both worlds: long-term investment from one man and higher quality genes from another.

Some ancestral mothers had affairs with men who were stronger, healthier, more attractive or more powerful than their husbands.

Some of us are their descendants.

Men fidget nervously when I describe this theory.

As much as evolutionary psychology can explain sexual treachery, it also illuminates the importance of long-term love.

In the 37-cultures study, I found that both women and men prize mutual love, judging it more indispensable than any other quality.

As one Botswana woman said in the book "Nisa," by Marjorie Shostak: "When two people are first together, their hearts are on fire and their passion is very great. After a while . . . they continue to love each other, but in a different way—warm and dependable."

According to one evolutionary hypothesis, love emerged along with the evolution of helpless offspring needing care from both parents, with consequent commitment and pair-bonding. People cherish a spouse because that spouse is the one person on a planet of billions who has as much of an interest in the fate of their children as they do.

QUESTIONS FOR REFLECTION AND DISCUSSION:

1. Why are so many people opposed to the ideas about gender differences in sexual interests and behavior which are suggested by evolutionary psychologists?

2. How do evolutionary psychologists explain gender differences in sexual interests and behavior?

3. If it is "natural" for men to be interested in multiple sex partners, as suggested by evolutionary psychologists, is it then right or moral for married men to "stray"?

4. What kinds of differences do you notice between the writing in this *New York Times* article and the writing found in articles that are published in scientific journals?

5. What kinds of clues can you find as to whether as essay like this essay is backed by scholarship and evidence?

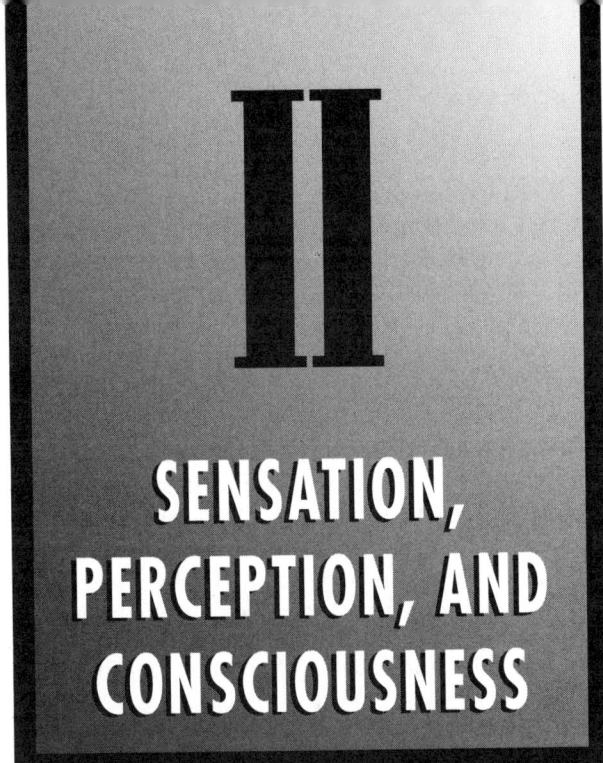

II

SENSATION, PERCEPTION, AND CONSCIOUSNESS

Think of your brain as your central processing unit (CPU). Your brain, like the CPU of a computer, learns about the world outside by means of peripheral devices that feed it with information. These peripheral devices include your keyboard, mouse, disks, modem, and so on. Your sensory organs are the peripheral devices that feed your brain with information and make it conscious of the world outside. Your computer's peripheral devices are connected to the CPU by means of cables that may carry many thousands of pieces of information per second. Your sensory organs are connected to your brain by nerves that may carry many millions of pieces of information each second.

Three of the following readings are about the ways in which the brain processes information about the world outside. Two of them are about sensory processes that are stirred when we are in an altered state of consciousness—sleep; these processes are connected with dreaming. Dreams are some of the most fascinating topics in psychology, and humans have tried to make "sense" of them for thousands of years.

The following primary sources are included in this section:

6. Gibson, E. J., & Walk, R. D. (1960). The "visual cliff." *Scientific American, 202,* 67–71.

This study and the one by Fantz could as easily have been placed in the part on developmental psychology. They concern perceptual development. This first one, on the classic visual cliff experiments, shows that most of us have the sense not to go off the deep end—even before we reach our first birthday.

7. Fantz, R. L. (1961). The origin of form perception. *Scientific American, 204*(5), 66–72.

This classic experiment uses some innovative technology to measure the visual preferences of newborn infants. Why bother, you wonder? One answer is that this line of research may help us understand whether we are born with an interest in other people, or whether that interest develops through experience. Then again, isn't it fun to try to find out what babies like to look at? Or put it this way: Just what about your face is so interesting to babies?

8. Turnbull, C. M. (1961). Some observations regarding the experiences and behavior of the BaMbuti Pygmies. *American Journal of Psychology, 74,* 304–308.

Here is a classic cross-cultural study based on field observations of a Pygmy who has become very well known in the literature on sensation and perception. In psychology textbooks we often learn that Kenge, the Pygmy, mistook buffalo for insects when he viewed them from a distance. But there are many more details here about the Pygmies, including some that are relevant to the psychology of language development.

9. Dement, W. (1960). The effect of dream deprivation. *Science, 131,* 1705–1707.

Here's an interesting classic experiment on the possible functions of dreams. If you wanted to study the effect of dream deprivation, how would you go about preventing people from dreaming? What effects would you look for? How would you measure them?

10. Hobson, J. A., & McCarley, R. W. (1977). The brain as a dream state generator: An activation-synthesis hypothesis of the dream process. *American Journal of Psychiatry, 134,* 1335–1348.

How many friends do you have who are ready to interpret your dreams for you? After all, Freud wrote that dreams are the "royal road to the unconscious," so they must be filled with meaning, right? Perhaps, perhaps not. This study suggests that dreams may simply be a byproduct of brain activity.

SOURCE

Gibson, E. J., & Walk, R. D. (1960). The "visual cliff." *Scientific American, 202,* 67–71. Reprinted with permission. Copyright © 1960 by Scientific American, Inc. All rights reserved.

Developmental psychologists have been fascinated by the ways in which infants perceive the world. In classic research, they have found that infants generally respond to cues for depth by the time they are able to crawl about, that is, by about 6 to 8 months of age. It thus appears that we can say that most infants will avoid "going off the deep end." They won't crawl off ledges and tabletops into open space. In one of the most important studies of this type, Eleanor Gibson and Richard Walk placed infants of various ages on a fabric-covered runway that ran across the center of a clever device called a visual cliff. The visual cliff consists of a sheet of plexiglas that covers a cloth with a high-contrast checkerboard pattern. On one side the cloth is placed immediately beneath the plexiglas, and on the other, it is dropped about 4 feet below. Since the plexiglas alone would easily support the infant, this is a visual cliff rather than an actual cliff. In the Gibson and Walk study, the majority of infants who had begun to crawl refused to venture onto the seemingly unsupported surface, even when their mothers beckoned encouragingly from the other side. Gibson and Walk also report on depth perception and locomotion in other species.

The "Visual Cliff"

ELEANOR J. GIBSON AND RICHARD D. WALK

This simple apparatus is used to investigate depth perception in different animals. All species thus far tested seem able to perceive and avoid a sharp drop as soon as they can move about.

Human infants at the creeping and toddling stage are notoriously prone to falls from more or less high places. They must be kept from going over the brink by side panels on their cribs, gates on stairways and the vigilance of adults. As their muscular coordination matures they begin to avoid such accidents on their own. Common sense might suggest that the child learns to recognize falling-off places by experience—that is, by falling and hurting himself. But is experience really the teacher? Or is the ability to perceive and avoid a brink part of the child's original endowment?

Answers to these questions will throw light on the genesis of space perception in general. Height perception is a special case of distance perception: information in the light reaching the eye provides stimuli that can be utilized for the discrimination both of depth and of receding distance on the level. At what stage of development can an animal respond effectively to these stimuli? Does the onset of such response vary with animals of different species and habitats?

At Cornell University we have been investigating these problems by means of a simple experimental setup that we call a visual cliff. The cliff is a simulated one and hence makes it possible not only to control the optical and other stimuli (auditory and tactual, for instance) but also to protect the experimental subjects. It consists of a board laid across a large sheet of heavy glass which is supported a foot or more above the floor. On one side of the board a sheet of patterned material is placed flush against the undersurface of the glass, giving the glass the appearance as well as the substance of solidity. On the other side a sheet of the same material is laid upon the floor; this side of the board thus becomes the visual cliff (Fig. 6.01).

We tested 36 infants ranging in age from six months to 14 months on the visual cliff. Each child was placed upon the center board, and his mother called him to her from the cliff side and the shallow side successively. All of the 27 infants who moved off the board crawled out on the shallow side at least once; only three of them crept off the brink onto the glass suspended above the pattern on the floor. Many of the infants crawled away from the mother when she called to them from the cliff side; others cried when she stood there, because they could not come to her without crossing an apparent chasm. The experiment thus demonstrated that most human infants can discriminate depth as soon as they can crawl.

The behavior of the children in this situation gave clear evidence of their dependence on vision. Often they would peer down through the glass on the deep side and then back away. Others would pat the glass with their hands, yet despite this tactual assurance of solidity would refuse to cross. It was equally clear that their perception of depth had matured more rapidly than had their locomotor abilities. Many supported themselves on the glass over the deep side as they maneuvered awkwardly on the board; some even backed out onto the glass as they started toward the mother on the shallow side. Were it not for the glass some of the children would have fallen off the board. Evidently infants should not be left close to a brink, no matter how well they may discriminate depth.

FIGURE 6.01

THE CLASSIC VISUAL CLIFF EXPERIMENT

This young explorer has the good sense not to crawl out onto an apparently unsupported surface, even when Mother beckons from the other side. Rats, pups, kittens, and chicks also will not try to walk across to the other side. (So don't bother asking why the chicken crossed the visual cliff.)

Harcourt, Inc.

This experiment does not prove that the human infant's perception and avoidance of the cliff are innate. Such an interpretation is supported, however, by the experiments with nonhuman infants. On the visual cliff we have observed the behavior of chicks, turtles, rats, lambs, kids, pigs, kittens and dogs. These animals showed various reactions, each of which proved to be characteristic of their species. In each case the reaction is plainly related to the role of vision in the survival of the species, and the varied patterns of behavior suggest something about the role of vision in evolution.

In the chick, for example, depth perception manifests itself with special rapidity. At an age of less than 24 hours the chick can be tested on the visual cliff. It never makes a "mistake" and always hops off the board on the shallow side. Without doubt this finding is related to the fact that the chick, unlike many other young birds, must scratch for itself a few hours after it is hatched.

Kids and lambs, like chicks, can be tested on the visual cliff as soon as they can stand. The response of these animals is equally predictable. No goat or lamb ever stepped onto the glass of the deep side, even at one day of age. When one of these animals was placed upon the glass on the deep side, it displayed characteristic stereotyped behavior. It would refuse to put its feet down and would back up into a posture of defense, its front legs rigid and its hind legs limp. In this state of immobility it could be pushed forward across the glass until its head and field of vision crossed the edge of the surrounding solid surface, whereupon it would relax and spring forward upon the surface.

At the Cornell Behavior Farm a group of experimenters has carried these experiments with kids and goats a step further. They fixed the patterned material to a sheet of plywood and were thus able to adjust the "depth" of the deep side. With the pattern held immediately beneath the glass, the animal would move about the glass freely. With the optical floor dropped more than a foot below the glass, the animal would immediately freeze into its defensive posture. Despite repeated experience of the tactual solidity of the glass, the animals never learned to function without optical support. Their sense of security or danger continued to depend upon the visual cues that give them their perception of depth.

The rat, in contrast, does not depend predominantly upon visual cues. Its nocturnal habits lead it to seek food largely by smell, when moving about in the dark, it responds to tactual cues from the stiff whiskers (vibrissae) on its snout. Hooded rats tested on the visual cliff show little preference for the shallow side so long as they can feel the glass with their vibrissae. Placed upon the glass over the deep side, they move about normally. But when we raise the center board several inches, so that the glass is out of reach of their whiskers, they evince good visual depth-discrimination: 95 to 100 per cent of them descend on the shallow side.

Cats, like rats, are nocturnal animals, sensitive to tactual cues from their vibrissae. But the cat, as a predator, must rely more strongly on its sight. Kittens proved to have excellent depth-discrimination. At four weeks—about the earliest age that a kitten can move about with any facility—they invariably choose the shallow side of the cliff. On the glass over the deep side, they either freeze or circle aimlessly backward until they reach the center board.

The animals that showed the poorest performance in our series were the turtles. The late Robert M. Yerkes of Harvard University found in 1904 that aquatic turtles have somewhat poorer depth-discrimination than land turtles. On the visual cliff one might expect an aquatic turtle to respond to the reflections from the glass as it might to water and so prefer the deep side. They showed no such preference: 76 per cent of the aquatic turtles crawled off the board on the shallow side. The relatively large minority that choose the deep side suggests either that this turtle has poorer depth-discrimination than other animals, or that its natural habitat gives it less occasion to "fear" a fall.

All of these observations square with what is known about the life history and ecological niche of each of the animals tested. The survival of a species requires that its members develop discrimination of depth by the time they take up independent locomotion, whether at one day (the chick and the goat), three to four weeks (the rat and the cat) or six to 10 months (the human infant). That such a vital capacity does not depend on possibly fatal accidents of learning in the lives of individuals is consistent with evolutionary theory.

To make sure that no hidden bias was concealed in the design of the visual cliff we conducted a number of control experiments. In one of them we eliminated reflections from the glass by lighting the patterned surfaces from below the glass (to accomplish this we dropped the pattern below the glass on both sides, but more on one side than on the other). The animals—hooded rats—still consistently chose the shallow side. As a test of the role of the patterned surface we replaced it on either side of the center-board with a homogeneous gray surface. Confronted with this choice, the rats showed no preference for either the shallow or the deep side. We also eliminated the optical difference between the two sides of the board by placing the patterned surface directly against the undersurface of the glass on each side. The rats then descended without preference to either side. When we lowered the pattern 10 inches below the glass on each side, they stayed on the board.

We set out next to determine which of two visual cues plays the decisive role in depth perception. To an eye above the center board the optical pattern on the two sides differs in at least two important respects. On the deep side distance decreases the size and spacing of the pattern elements projected on the retina. "Motion parallax," on the other hand, causes the pattern elements on the shallow side to move more rapidly across the field of vision when the animal moves its position on the board or moves its head, just as nearby objects seen from a moving car appear to pass by more quickly than distant ones (Fig. 6.02). To eliminate the potential distance cue provided by pattern density we increased the size and spacing of the pattern elements on the deep side in proportion to its distance from the eye (Fig. 6.03, top). With only the cue of motion parallax to guide them, adult rats still preferred the shallow side, though not so strongly as in the standard experiment. Infant rats chose the shallow side nearly 100 per cent of the time under both conditions, as did day-old chicks. Evidently both species can discriminate depth by differential motion alone, with no aid from texture density and probably little help from other cues. The perception of distance by binocular parallax, which doubtless plays an important part in human behavior, would not seem to have a significant role, for example, in the depth perception of chicks and rats.

To eliminate the cue of motion parallax we placed the patterned material directly against the glass on either side of the board but used smaller and more densely spaced pattern-elements on the cliff side. Both young and adult hooded rats preferred the side with the larger pattern, which evidently "signified" a nearer surface. Day-old chicks, however, showed no preference for the larger pattern. It may be that learning plays some part in the preference exhibited by the rats, since the young rats were tested at a somewhat older age than the chicks. This supposition is supported by the results of our experiments with animals reared in the dark.

The effects of early experience and of such deprivations as dark-rearing represent important clues to the relative roles of maturation and learning in animal behavior. The first experiments along this line were performed by K. S. Lashley and James T. Russell at the University of Chicago in 1934. They tested light-reared and dark-reared rats on a "jump-ing stand" from which they induced animals to leap toward a platform placed at varying distances. Upon finding that both groups of animals jumped with a force closely correlated with distance, they concluded that depth perception in rats is innate. Other investigators have pointed out, however, that the dark-reared rats required a certain amount of "pretraining" in the light before they could be made to jump. Since the visual-cliff technique requires no pretraining, we employed it to test groups of light-reared and dark-reared hooded rats. At the age of 90 days both groups showed the same preference for the shallow side of the apparatus, confirming Lashley's and Russell's conclusion.

Recalling our findings in the young rat, we then took up the question of whether the dark-reared rats relied upon motion parallax or upon contrast in texture density to discriminate depth. When the animals were confronted with the visual cliff, cued only by motion parallax, they preferred the shallow side, as had the light-reared animals. When the choice was cued by pattern density, however, they departed from the pattern of the normal animals and showed no significant preference (Fig. 6.05). The behavior of dark-reared rats thus resembles that of the day-old chicks, which also lack visual experience. It seems likely, therefore, that of the two cues only motion parallax is an innate cue for depth discrimination. Responses to differential pattern-density may be learned later.

One cannot automatically extrapolate these results to other species. But experiments with dark-reared kittens indicate that in these animals, too, depth perception matures independently of trial and error learning. In the kitten, however, light is necessary for normal visual maturation. Kittens reared in the dark to the age of 27 days at first crawled or fell off the center board equally often on the deep and shallow sides. Placed upon the glass over the deep side, they did not back in a circle like normal kittens but showed the same behavior that they had exhibited on the shallow side. Other investigators have observed equivalent behavior in dark-reared kittens; they bump into obstacles, lack normal eye movement and appear to "stare" straight ahead. These difficulties pass after a few days in the light. We accordingly tested the kittens every day. By the end of a week they were performing in every respect like normal kittens. They showed the same unanimous preference for the shallow side. Placed upon the glass over the deep side, they balked and circled backward to a visually secure surface. Repeated descents to the deep side, and placement upon the glass during their "blind" period, had not taught them that the

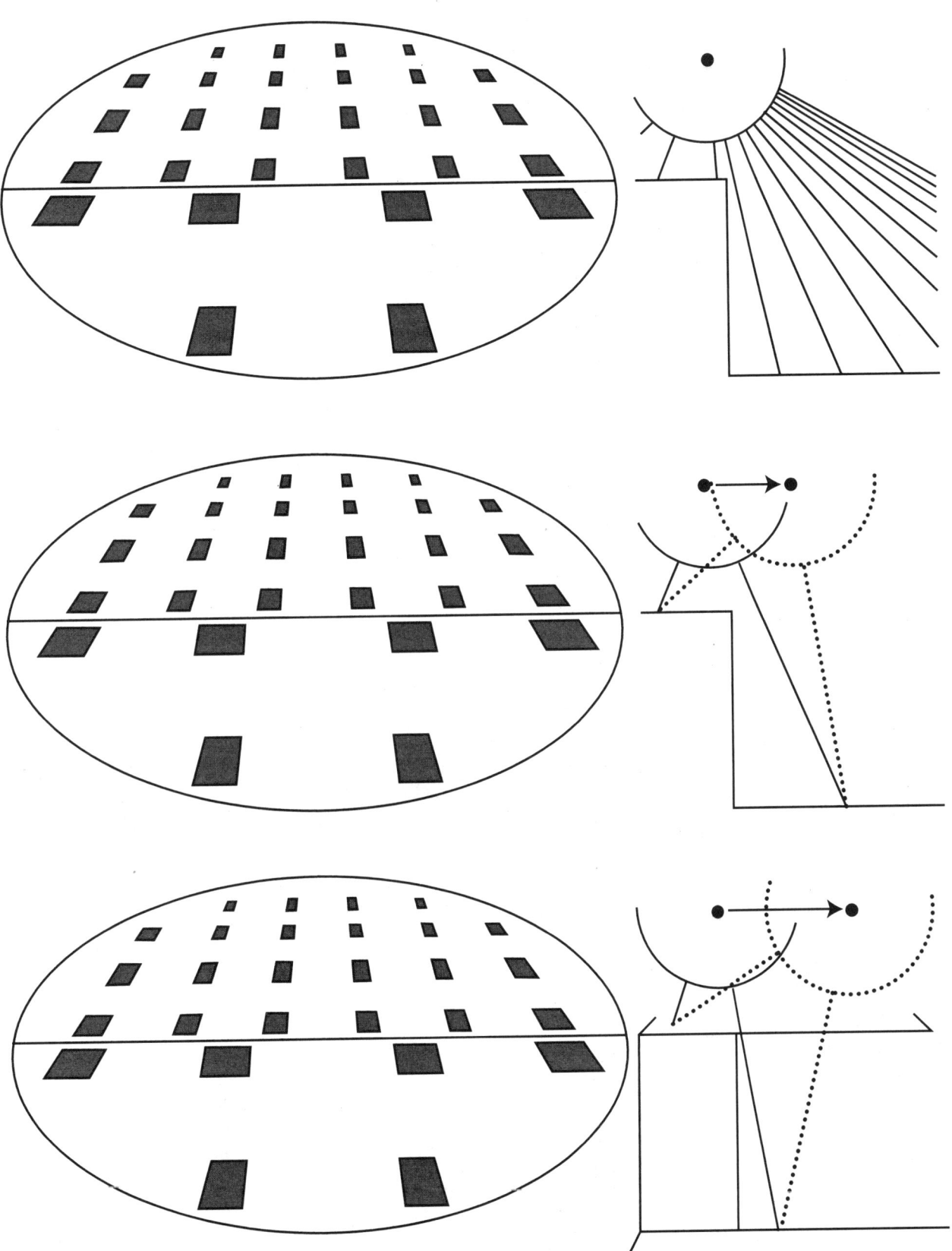

FIGURE 6.02

Two types of visual depth-cue are diagrammed schematically on this page. Ellipses approximate the visual field of an animal standing near the edge of the cliff and looking toward it; diagrams at right give the geometrical explanation of differences in the fields. The spacing of the pattern elements (*solid color*) decreases sharply beyond the edge of the cliff (*top*). The optical motion (*shaded color*) of the elements as the animal moves forward (*center*) or sideways (*bottom*) shows a similar drop-off.

Harcourt, Inc.

FIGURE 6.03

Separation of visual cues is shown in these diagrams. Pattern density is held constant (*top*) by using a larger pattern on the low side of the cliff; the drop in optical motion (motion parallax) remains. Motion parallax is equalized (*bottom*) by placing patterns at same level; the smaller pattern on one side preserves difference in spacing.

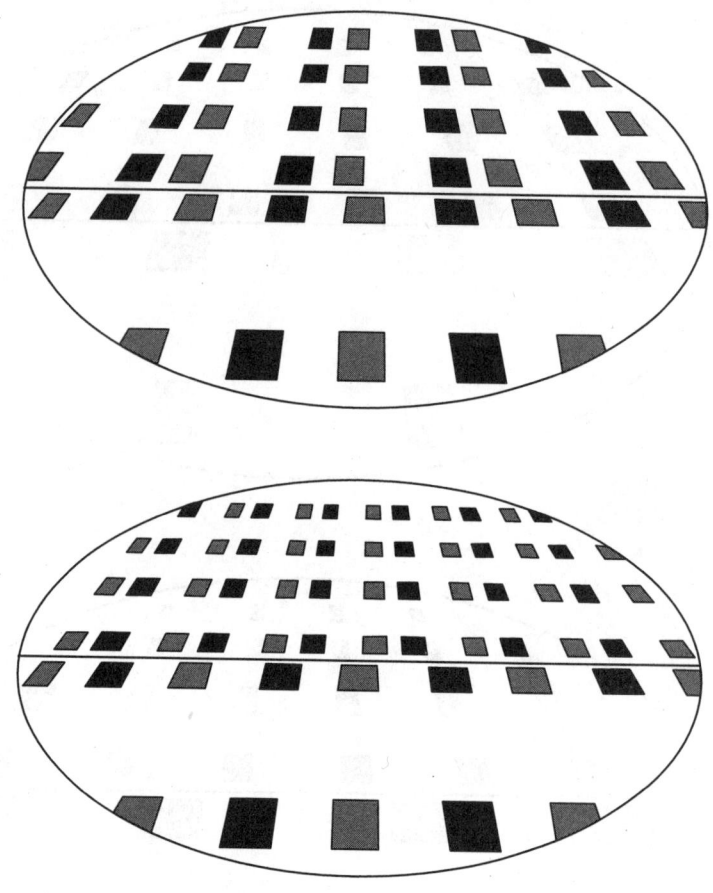

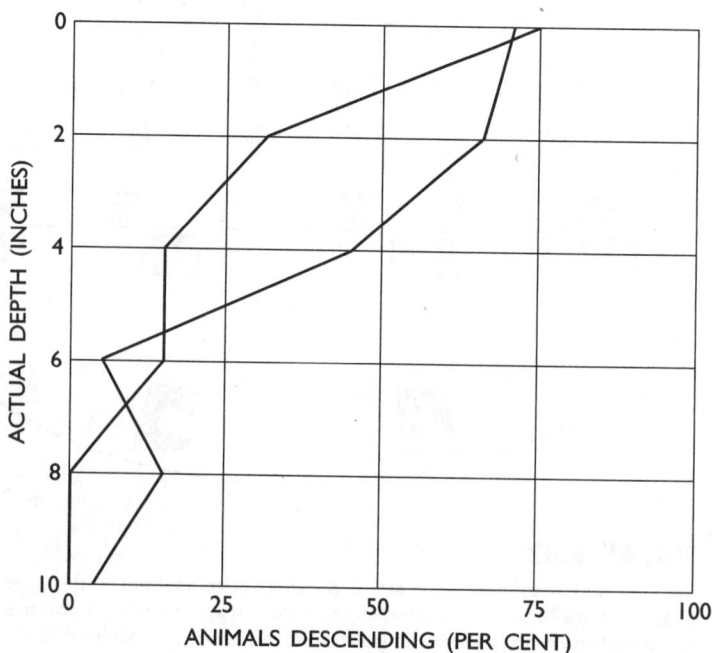

deep side was "safe." Instead they avoided it more and more consistently. The initial blindness of dark-reared kittens makes them ideal subjects for studying the maturation of depth perception. With further study it should be possible to determine which cues they respond to first and what kinds of visual experience accelerate or retard the process of maturation.

FIGURE 6.04

Control experiment measured the effect on rats of reflections on the glass of the apparatus. The percentage of animals leaving the center board decreased with increasing depth in much the same way, whether glass was present (*black curve*) or not (*colored curve*).

FIGURE 6.05

Dark-rearing experiments reveal the order in which different depth-cues are utilized as animals mature. Animals reared in the light (*open bars*) all strongly preferred the shallow side (*color*) to the deep side (*gray*). Dark-reared rats (*solid bars*), utilizing motion parallax alone, still preferred the shallow side; pattern density alone elicited no preference. Dark-reared kittens also showed no preference, because of temporary blindness. After seven days in the light all of them chose the shallow side (*hatched bar*).

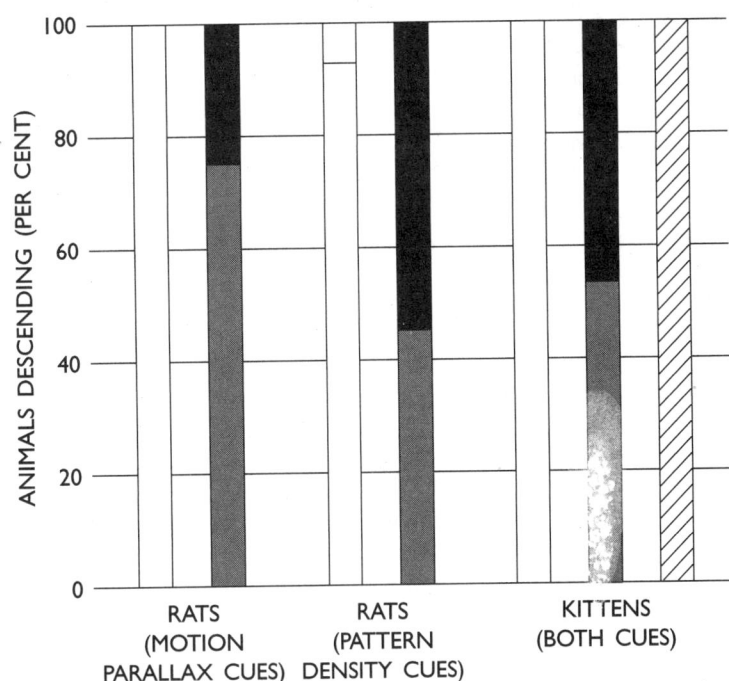

From our first few years of work with the visual cliff we are ready to venture the rather broad conclusion that a seeing animal will be able to discriminate depth when its locomotion is adequate, even when locomotion begins at birth. But many experiments remain to be done, especially on the role of different cues and on the effects of different kinds of early visual experience.

QUESTIONS FOR REFLECTION AND DISCUSSION:

1. Many of the studies reported in this collection have complicated statistics, including *F* values and levels of confidence. The study by Gibson and Walk reports simple numbers and percentages. However, there seems to be what one statistics professor of mine called a strong "wow!" effect. Do the numbers and percentages "wow" you, or do you believe that there should have been a more complex statistical analysis? Explain.

2. Psychologists, and particularly developmental psychologists, are vitally concerned about the so-called nature-nurture controversy. That is, they seek to determine the influences of our nature (heredity and maturation) and our nurture (learning experiences, nutrition, etc.) on our behavior and mental processes. Does the study by Gibson and Walk appear to offer more support for nature or nurture in the perceptual development of the infant?

3. Gibson and Walk report on the behavior of kittens, chicks, and even turtles on the visual cliff. Do their findings seem to hold from one species to another? Are there implications for humans in their cross-species data?

4. Imagine that you are a behaviorist and that a maturational theorist argues that the results of studies with the visual cliff prove that nature is more important than nurture in perceptual development. How might you counter this argument?

SOURCE

Fantz, R. L. (1961). The origin of
form perception. *Scientific American,
204*(5), 66–72. Reprinted with
permission. Copyright © 1961 by
Scientific American, Inc. All rights
reserved.

What are the things that capture the attention of babies? How do visual preferences develop? Researchers have typically equated infants' interest in objects with the amount of time they spend looking at them or whether they turn toward them. For example, infants attend longer to stripes than blobs, and most babies show distinct preferences for curved lines over straight ones.

Robert Fantz also wondered whether there was something intrinsically interesting about the human face that drew the attention of babies. To investigate this question, he showed 2-month-old infants a variety of test objects. As you will see in this classic study, one object contained a caricature of human features, another newsprint, and still another a bull's-eye. The remaining three were featureless but colored red, white, and yellow.

The Origin of Form Perception

ROBERT L. FANTZ

Is man's ability to perceive the form of objects inborn or must it be learned? Experiments indicate that it is innate but that maturation and learning play important roles in its development.

Long before an infant can explore his surroundings with hands and feet he is busy exploring it with his eyes. What goes on in the infant's mind as he stares, blinks, looks this way and that? Does he sense only a chaotic patchwork of color and brightness or does he perceive and differentiate among distinctive forms? The question has always fascinated philosophers and scientists, for it bears on the nature and origin of knowledge. At issue is the perennial question of nature *v.* nurture. On one side is the nativist, who believes that the infant has a wide range of innate visual capacities and predilections, which have evolved in animals over millions of years, and that these give a primitive order and meaning to the world from the "first look." On the other side is the extreme empiricist, who holds that the infant learns

to see and to use what he sees only by trial and error or association, starting, as John Locke put it, with a mind like a blank slate.

It has long been known that very young infants can see light, color and movement. But it is often argued that they cannot respond to such stimuli as shape, pattern, size or solidity; in short, that they cannot perceive form. This position is the last stronghold of the empiricist, and it has been a hard one to attack. How is one to know what an infant sees? My colleagues and I have recently developed an experimental method of finding out. We have already disposed of the basic question, that of whether babies can perceive form at all. They can, at least to some degree, although it appears that neither the view of the simple nativist nor that of the simple empiricist tells the whole story. Now we are investigating the further question of how and when infants use their capacity to perceive form to confer order and meaning on their environment.

The technique grew out of studies with lower animals, which are of importance in themselves. They

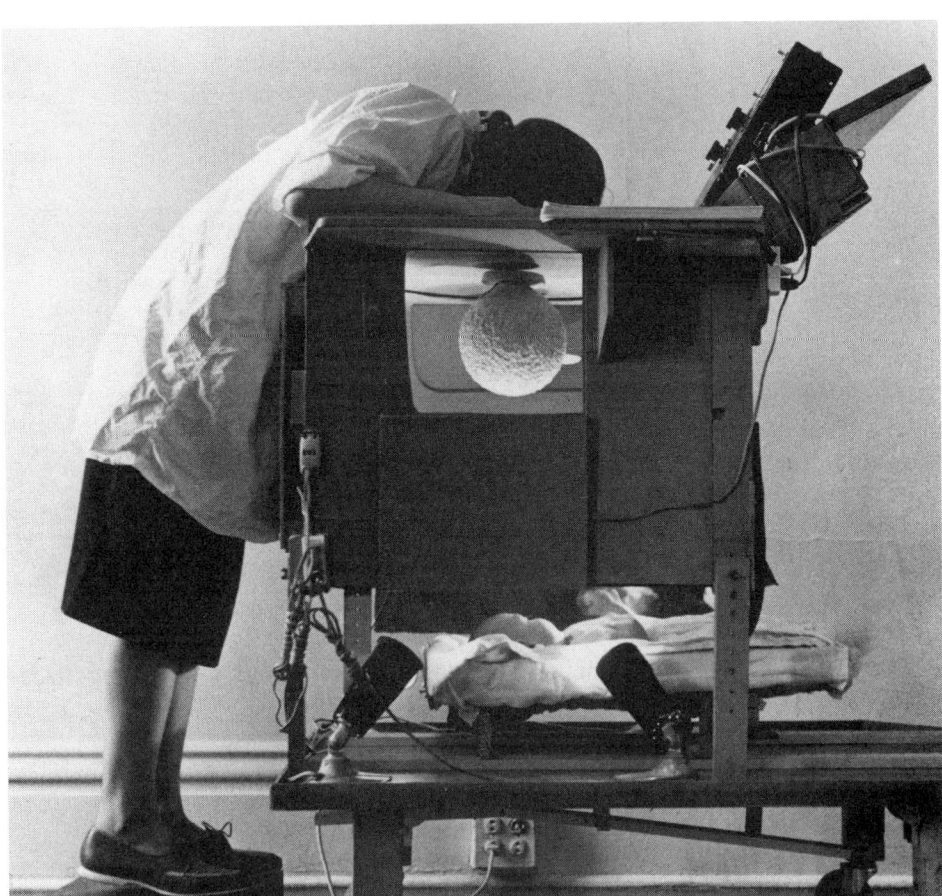

FIGURE 7.01

"Looking chamber" was used to test the visual interests of chimpanzee and human infants. Here a human infant lies on a crib in the chamber, looking at objects hung from the ceiling. The observer, watching through a peephole, records the attention given each object.

were undertaken in 1951 at the University of Chicago with newly hatched chicks. Paradoxically, chicks can "tell" more directly what they see than higher animals can. Soon after they break out of the shell they go about the business of finding things to peck at and eat. Their purposeful, visually dominated behavior is ideally suited for observation and experiment.

We presented the chicks with a number of small objects of different shapes. Each object was enclosed in a clear plastic container to eliminate the possible influence of touch, smell or taste, but this did not prevent the chicks from pecking at preferred forms for hours on end. An electrical circuit attached to each container recorded the number of pecks at it.

More than 1,000 chicks were tested on some 100 objects. To exclude any opportunity for learning, the chicks were hatched in darkness and tested on their first exposure to light, before they had had any experience with real food. Presented with eight objects of graded angularity, from a sphere to a pyramid, the subjects pecked 10 times oftener at the sphere than they did at the pyramid. Among the flat forms, circles were preferred to triangles regardless

of comparative size; among circles, those of $\frac{1}{8}$-inch diameter drew the most attention. In a test of the effect of three-dimensionality the chicks consistently selected a sphere over a flat disk.

The results provided conclusive evidence that the chick has an innate ability to perceive shape, three-dimensionality and size. Furthermore, the chick uses the ability in a "meaningful" way by selecting, without learning, those objects most likely to be edible: round, three-dimensional shapes about the size of grain or seeds. Other birds exhibit similar visual capacity. For example, N. Tinbergen of the University of Oxford found selective pecking by newly hatched herring gulls. These chicks prefer shapes resembling that of the bill of the parent bird, from which they are fed [see "The Evolution of Behavior in Gulls," by N. Tinbergen; SCIENTIFIC AMERICAN," December, 1960].

Of course, what holds true for birds does not necessarily apply to human beings. The inherent capacity for form perception that has developed in birds may have been lost somewhere along the evolutionary branch leading to the primates, unlikely as it seems. Or, more plausibly, the primate infant may require a period of postnatal development to reach

FIGURE 7.02

Visual interest in various shapes was determined by noting reflections in the subject's eyes. In this case, with the reflection over the center of the infant's eye, the reflected object is being fixated, or looked at directly. (Because this young infant's binocular coordination is poor, only the right eye is fixating the object.) The length of each such fixation was recorded electrically.

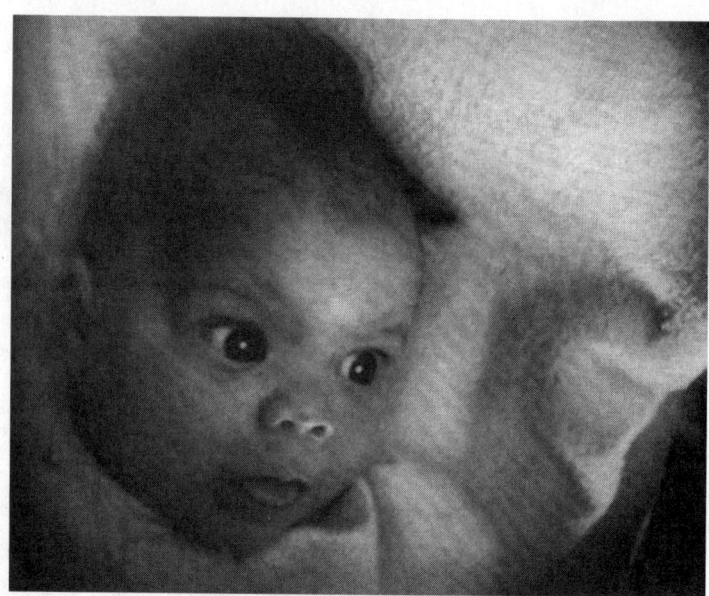

the level of function of the comparatively precocious chick.

When we set out to determine the visual abilities of helpless infants, the only indicator we could find was the activity of the eyes themselves. If an infant consistently turns its gaze toward some forms more often than toward others, it must be able to perceive form. Working on this premise, we developed a visual-interest test, using as our first subjects infant chimpanzees at the Yerkes Laboratories of Primate Biology in Orange Park, Fla.

A young chimpanzee lay on its back in a comfortable crib inside a "looking chamber" of uniform color and illumination. We attached to the ceiling of the chamber pairs of test objects, slightly separated from each other. They were exposed to view, alternately at right and left, in a series of short periods. Through a peephole in the ceiling we could see tiny images of the objects mirrored in the subjects' eyes. When the image of one of the objects was at the center of the eye, over the pupil, we knew the chimpanzee was looking directly at it. The experimenter recorded on an electric timer the amount of attention given each target. The results were then analyzed to determine their statistical significance. Our first subject was a five-month-old chimpanzee. Later we followed a chimpanzee from birth, keeping it in darkness except during the tests. In both cases we found a definite preference for certain objects, indicating an inborn ability to distinguish among them.

Turning to human infants, we made no major change in our procedure except that we did not tamper with their everyday environment. The experiments did not disturb the infants but they did demand great patience of the investigators. Human infants are more rapidly bored than chimpanzees and they tend to go to sleep.

In the first experiment we tested 30 infants, aged one to 15 weeks, at weekly intervals. Four pairs of test patterns were presented in random sequence. In decreasing order of complexity they were: horizontal stripes and a bull's-eye design, a checkerboard and two sizes of plain square, a cross and a circle, and two identical triangles. The total time spent looking at the various pairs differed sharply, the more complex pairs drawing the greater attention. Moreover, the relative attractiveness of the two members of a pair depended on the presence of a pattern difference. There were strong preferences between stripes and bull's-eye and between checkerboard and square. Neither the cross and circle nor the two triangles aroused a significant differential interest. The differential response to pattern was shown at all ages tested, indicating that it was not the result of a learning process. The direction of preference between stripes and bull's-eye, on the other hand, changed at two months of age, due either to learning or to maturation.

Later we learned that a Swiss pediatrician, F. Stirnimann, had obtained similar results with still younger infants. He held cards up to the eyes of infants one to 14 days old and found that patterned cards were of more interest than those with plain colors.

Clearly some degree of form perception is innate. This, however, does not dispose of the role of physiological growth or of learning in the further development of visual behavior. Accordingly we turned our attention to the influence of these factors.

FIGURE 7.03

Pattern preference of newly hatched chicks is studied by recording their pecks at each of a number of different shapes in plastic containers set into the wall of a test box.

By demonstrating the existence of form perception in very young infants we had already disproved the widely held notion that they are anatomically incapable of seeing anything but blobs of light and dark. Nevertheless, it seems to be true that the eye, the visual nerve-pathways and the visual part of the brain are poorly developed at birth. If this is so, then the acuteness of vision—the ability to distinguish detail in patterns—should increase as the infant matures.

To measure the change in visual acuity we presented infants in the looking chamber with a series of patterns composed of black and white stripes, each pattern paired with a gray square of equal brightness. The width of the stripes was decreased in graded steps from one pattern to the next. Since we already knew that infants tend to look longer and more frequently at a patterned object than at a plain one, the width of the stripes of the finest pattern that was preferred to gray would provide an index to visual acuity. In this modified version the visual-interest test again solved the difficulties involved in getting infants to reveal what they see.

The width of the finest stripes that could be distinguished turned out to decrease steadily with increasing age during the first half-year of life. By six months babies could see stripes 1/64 inch wide at a distance of 10 inches—a visual angle of five minutes of arc, or 1/12 degree. (The adult standard is one minute of arc.) Even when still less than a month old, infants were able to perceive $\frac{1}{8}$-inch stripes at 10 inches, corresponding to a visual angle of a little less than one degree. This is poor performance compared to that of an adult, but it is a far cry from a complete lack of ability to perceive pattern.

The effects of maturation on visual acuity are relatively clear and not too hard to measure. The problem of learning is more subtle. Other investigators have shown that depriving animals of patterned

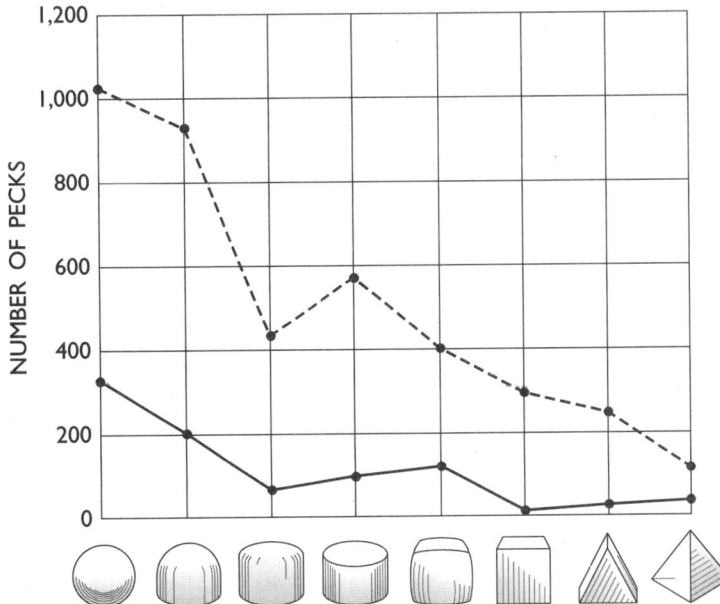

FIGURE 7.04

Preference for roundness is shown by this record of total pecks by 112 chicks at the eight test objects shown across the bottom of the chart. The results are for the chicks' first 10 minutes (*black line*) and first 40 minutes (*dashed line*) of visual experience.

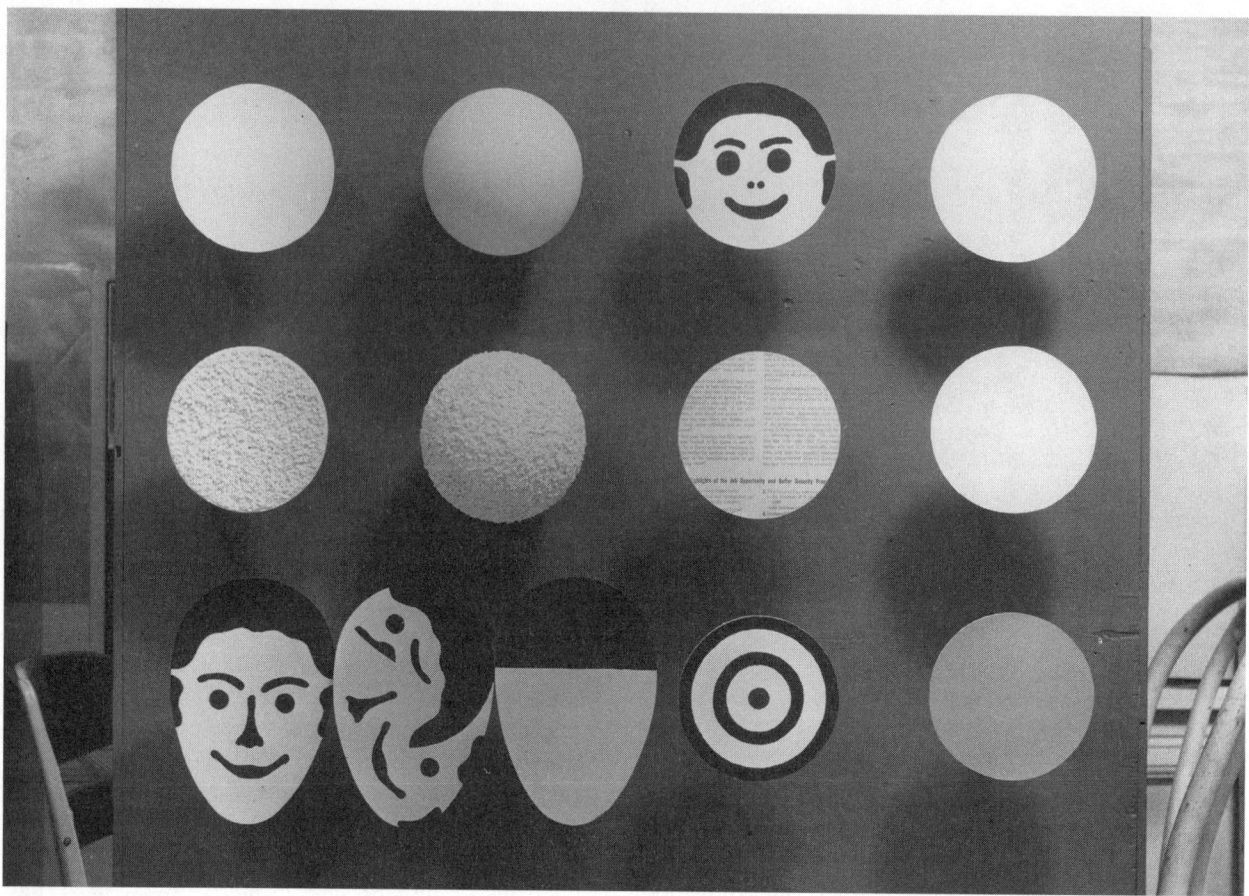

FIGURE 7.05

Test objects included smooth and textured disks and spheres (*upper left*) to check interest in solidity. Attention to faces was tested with three patterns at lower left. The six round patterns at the right included (*top to bottom, left to right*) a face, a piece of printed matter, a bull's-eye, yellow, white and red disks. Round objects are six inches in diameter; "faces," nine inches long.

visual stimuli for a period after birth impairs their later visual performance, especially in form perception [see "Arrested Vision," by Austin H. Riesen; SCIENTIFIC AMERICAN, July, 1950]. Learned behavior is particularly vulnerable, but even innate responses are affected. For example, chicks kept in darkness for several weeks after hatching lose the ability to peck at food.

Research is now under way at Western Reserve University on this perplexing problem. We have raised monkeys in darkness for periods varying from one to 11 weeks. In general, the longer the period of deprivation, the poorer the performance when the animals were finally exposed to light and the more time they required to achieve normal responses. When first brought into the light, the older infant monkeys bumped into things, fell off tables, could not locate objects visually—for all practical purposes they were blind. It sometimes took weeks for them to "learn to see."

Monkeys kept a shorter time in the dark usually showed good spatial orientation in a few hours or days. Moreover, they showed normal interest in patterned objects, whereas the animals deprived of light for longer periods seemed more interested in color, brightness and size.

These results cannot be explained by innate capacity, maturation or learning alone. If form perception were wholly innate, it would be evident without experience at any age, and visual deprivation would have no effect. If maturation were the controlling factor, younger infant animals would be inferior rather than superior to older ones with or without visual experience. If form perception were entirely learned, the same period of experience would be required regardless of age and length of deprivation.

Instead there appears to be a complex interplay of innate ability, maturation and learning in the molding of visual behavior, operating in this manner: there is a critical age for the development of a given visual response when the visual, mental and motor capacities are ready to be used and under normal circumstances will be used together. At that

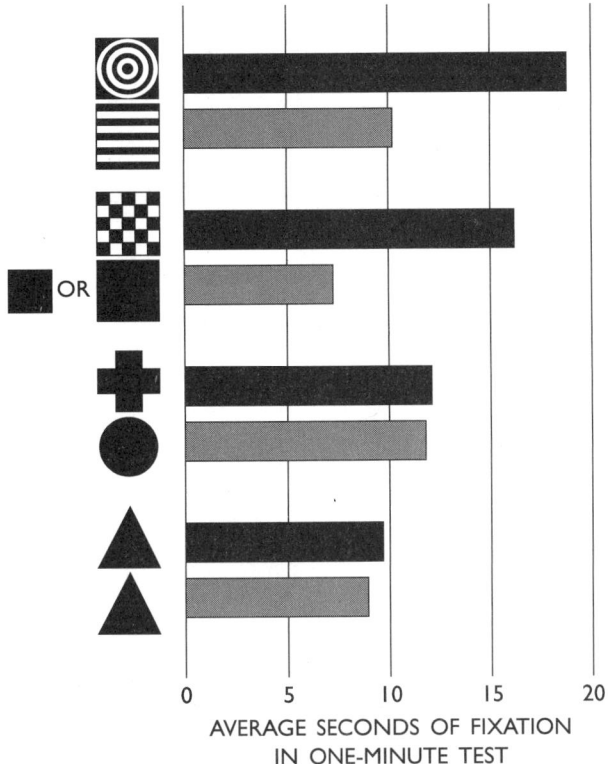

FIGURE 7.06

Interest in form was proved by infants' reactions to various pairs of patterns (*left*) presented together. (The small and large plain squares were used alternately.) The more complex pairs received the most attention, and within each of these pairs differential interest was based on pattern differences. These results are for 22 infants in 10 weekly tests.

time the animal will either show the response without experience or will learn it readily. If the response is not "imprinted" at the critical age for want of visual stimulus, development proceeds abnormally, without the visual component. Presented with the stimulus later on, the animal learns to respond, if it responds at all, only with extensive experience and training. This explanation, if verified by further studies, would help to reconcile the conflicting claims of the nativist and the empiricist on the origin of visual perception.

To return to human infants, the work described so far does not answer the second question posed earlier in this article: whether or not the infant's innate capacity for form perception introduces a measure of order and meaning into what would otherwise be a chaotic jumble of sensations. An active selection process is necessary to sort out these sensations and make use of them in behavior. In the case of chicks such a process is apparent in the selection of forms likely to be edible.

In the world of the infant, people have an importance that is perhaps comparable to the importance of grain in the chick's world. Facial pattern is the most distinctive aspect of a person, the most reliable for distinguishing a human being from other objects and for identifying him. So a facelike pattern might be expected to bring out selective perception in an infant if anything could.

We tested infants with three flat objects the size and shape of a head. On one we painted a stylized face in black on a pink background, on the second

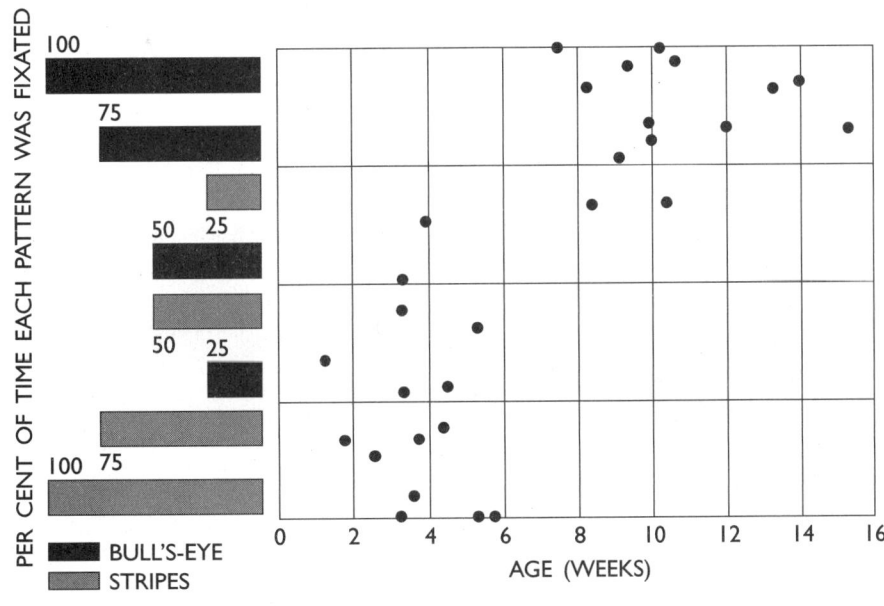

FIGURE 7.07

Reversal of interest from the striped pattern to the bull's-eye was apparent at two months of age. Each dot is for a single infant's first test session. It shows the time spent looking at the bull's-eye and at the stripes as a per cent of the time spent looking at both.

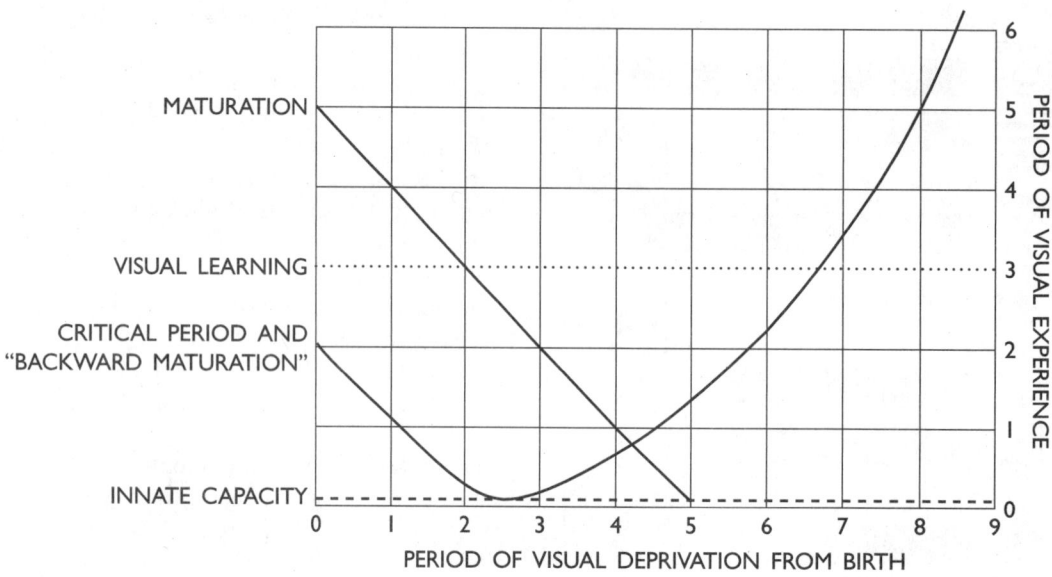

FIGURE 7.08

Hypothetical results that might be expected if any one developmental factor operated alone are plotted. The horizontal axis shows the period of rearing without visual experience; the vertical axis, the time subsequently required in the light until a given response is shown. Units of time are arbitrary. If innate capacity alone were effective, the response would always come without any experience (*dashed line*). If maturation were necessary, the response would not be shown before a certain age, in this case five units, regardless of deprivation (*solid line*). If learning alone were operative, the required amount of experience would be constant (*dotted line*). Actually tests with chicks and monkey infants suggest the result shown by the solid black curve: after a short period of maturation, a "critical period" is reached when innate capacity can be manifested; more deprivation brings on "backward maturation," in which more and more experience is required before a response is shown.

we rearranged the features in a scrambled pattern, and on the third we painted a solid patch of black at one end with an area equal to that covered by all the features. We made the features large enough to be perceived by the youngest baby, so acuity of vision was not a factor. The three objects, paired in all possible combinations, were shown to 49 infants from four days to six months old.

The results were about the same for all age levels: the infants looked mostly at the "real" face, somewhat less often at the scrambled face, and largely ignored the control pattern. The degree of preference for the "real" face to the other one was not large, but it was consistent among individual infants, especially the younger ones. The experiment suggested that there is an unlearned, primitive

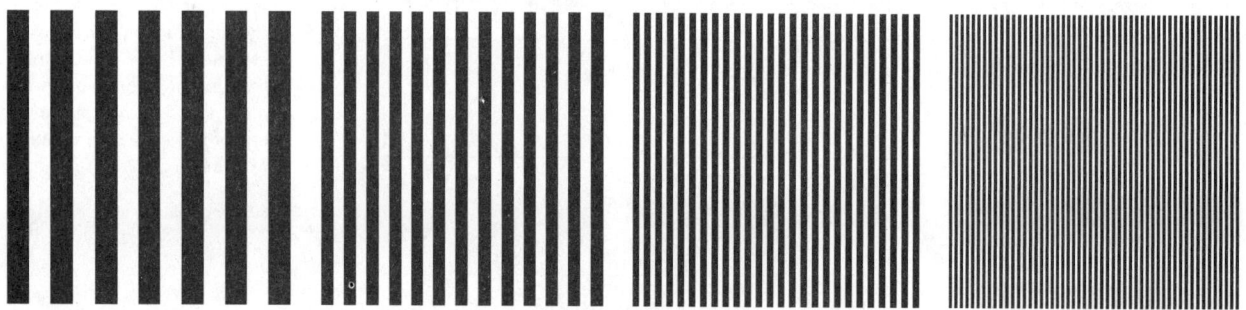

FIGURE 7.09

Visual acuity was tested with these stripes: 1/8, 1/16, 1/32 and 1/64 inch wide. Each pattern was displayed with a gray square of equal brightness 10 inches from the infants' eyes. The finest pattern consistently preferred to gray showed how narrow a stripe the infant could perceive. Infants under a month old could see the 1/8-inch stripes and the six-month-old could see 1/64-inch stripes.

meaning in the form perception of infants as well as of chicks.

Further support for the idea was obtained when we offered our infant subjects a choice between a solid sphere and a flat circle of the same diameter. When the texture and shading clearly differentiated the sphere from the circle—in other words, when there was a noticeable difference in pattern—the solid form was the more interesting to infants from one to six months old. This unlearned selection of a pattern associated with a solid object gives the infant a basis for perceiving depth.

The last experiment to be considered is a dramatic demonstration of the interest in pattern in comparison to color and brightness. This time there were six test objects: flat disks six inches in diameter. Three were patterned—a face, a bull's-eye and a patch of printed matter. Three were plain— red, fluorescent yellow and white. We presented them, against a blue background, one at a time in varied sequence and timed the length of the first glance at each.

The face pattern was overwhelmingly the most interesting, followed by the printing and the bull's-eye. The three brightly colored plain circles trailed far behind and received no first choices. There was no indication that the interest in pattern was secondary or acquired.

What makes pattern so intrinsically interesting to young infants? It seems to me that the answer must lie in the uses of vision for the child and adult.

One of these functions is the recognition of objects under various conditions. The color and brightness of objects change with illumination; apparent changes with distance; outline changes with point of view; binocular depth perception is helpful only at short range. But the pattern of an object—the texture, the arrangement of details, the complexity of contours—can be relied on for identification under diverse conditions.

A good example is social perception. As noted earlier, the general confirmation of a face identifies a human being to an infant. At a later age a specific person is recognized primarily by the precise perception of facial patterns, and later, subtle details of facial expression tell the child whether a person is happy or sad, pleased or displeased, friendly or unfriendly.

Another important function of vision is to provide orientation in space. To this purpose James J. Gibson of Cornell University has shown clearly the importance of a specific type of pattern in face texture. For example, texture indicates a solid surface, whereas untextured light usually indicates air or water. Gradual changes in texture show whenever a surface is vertical or horizontally oblique, flat or

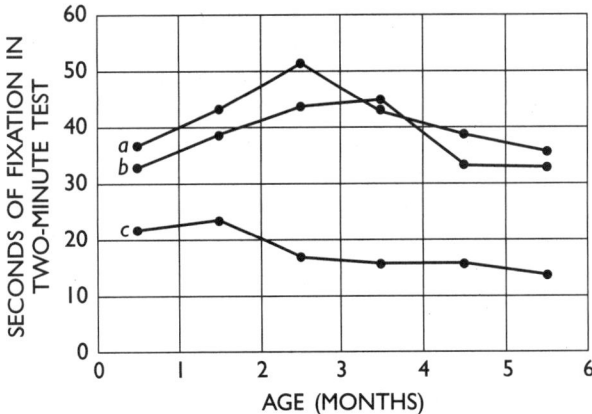

FIGURE 7.10

Adaptive significance of form perception was indicated by the preference that infants showed for a "real" face (*a*) over a scrambled face (*b*), and for both over a control (*c*). The results charted here show the average time scores for infants at various ages when presented with the three face-shaped objects paired in all the possible combinations.

curved or angular therefore indicate whether it can be walked on, walked around or climbed over. Discontinuities in texture mark the edges of objects and abrupt changes to surfaces.

From these few examples there can be no question of the importance of visual pattern in everyday life. It is therefore reasonable to suppose that the

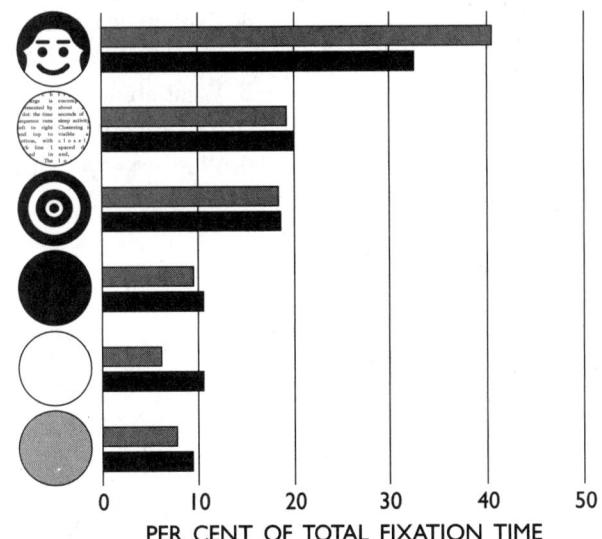

FIGURE 7.11

Importance of pattern rather than color or brightness was illustrated by the response of infants to a face, a piece of printed matter, a bull's-eye and plain red, white and yellow disks. Even the youngest infants preferred patterns. Black bars show the results for infants from two to three months old; gray bars, for infants more than three months old.

early interest of infants in forming pattern in general, as well as in particular kinds of pattern, play an important role in the development of behavior by focusing attention on stimuli that will later have adaptive significance.

Further research is necessary to nail down this and other implications concretely, but the results to date do require the rejection of the view that the newborn infant or animal must start from scratch to learn to see and organize patterned stimulation. Lowly chicks as well as lofty primates perceive and respond to form without experience if given the oportunity at the appropriate stage of development. Innate knowledge of the environment is demonstrated by the preference of newly hatched chicks for forms likely to be edible and by the interest of young infants for the kinds of form that will later aid in subject recognition, social response, and spatial orientation. This primary knowledge provides a foundation for the vast accumulation of knowledge through experience.

QUESTIONS FOR REFLECTION AND DISCUSSION:

1. What method did Fantz and his colleagues devise to determine whether infants can perceive form?

2. In this study, the infants attended to the human face longer than they did to some other test stimuli. Does this finding suggest that there is an inborn perceptual tendency to prefer people to other objects in the environment? (Note that subsequent studies suggest that the babies in the Fantz study may not have preferred the human face so much because it was a face as because it had a complex, intriguing pattern of dots [eyes] within an outline.)

3. At the beginning of the article, Fantz asks "Is man's ability to perceive the form of objects inborn or must it be learned?" He answers, "Experiments indicate that it is innate but that maturation and learning play important roles in its development." Does the research evidence reported in his study support this conclusion? Explain.

4. Explain what is meant by the terms "maturation," "critical period," and "backward maturation."

5. What stimuli did Fantz use to measure visual acuity in infants? How were they used to assess acuity?

6. Why are psychologists interested in the perceptual processes of infants?

SOURCE

Turnbull, C. M. (1961). Some observations regarding the experiences and behavior of the BaMbuti Pygmies. *American Journal of Psychology, 74,* 304–308. Copyright 1961 by the Board of Trustees of the University of Illinois. Used with permission of the University of Illinois.

The nature-nurture issue is found in perceptual development, just as it is in other dimensions of development. In the area of perception, the issue can be traced to the philosophers of the 17th and 18th centuries. Rene Descartes and Immanuel Kant took the nativist view that children are born with predispositions to perceive the world in certain ways. Kant, for example, believed that our innate makeup causes us to sense and organize the objects of the world according to certain "categories." We perceive some things and are oblivious to others because of our inborn ways of organizing the world outside.

George Berkeley and John Locke took the empiricist view that experience determines our ways of perceiving the world. Locke, for example, argued that mental representations reflect the impact of the world on the sense organs. There is no particular inborn way of organizing sensations of the world. The world, instead, impresses the mind with its own stamp.

Today, few developmentalists subscribe to either extreme. Most would agree that nature (the nativist view) and nurture (the empiricist view) interact to give shape to perceptual development.

Turnbull's classic observations of the BaMbuti Pygmies—particularly of a young man named Kenge—have implications for these views of perceptual development. Although they are recorded in a psychology journal, they also read like the writings of the anthropologist who studies various cultures. As you read the article, you will find many facts of interest to students of psychology, such as those concerning size constancy ("distance and size perception") and those involving names of colors.

Some Observations Regarding the Experiences and Behavior of the BaMbuti Pygmies

COLIN M. TURNBULL
AMERICAN MUSEUM OF NATURAL HISTORY

The identity of the BaMbuti Pygmies of the Ituri Forest in the Congo with the forest itself goes beyond their social life; they are also psychologically conditioned by their environment. This can best be illustrated by some observations that I made during a recent field trip in their country.

Distance- and Size-Perception

At the end of a particularly long and tiring period of trekking through the forest from one hunting group to another, I found myself on the eastern edge, on a high hill which had been cleared of trees by a missionary station. There was a distant view over the last few miles of forest to the Ruwenzori Mountains: in the middle of the Ituri Forest such views are seldom if ever encountered. With me was a Pygmy youth, named Kenge, who always accompanied me and served, amongst other capacities, as a valid introduction to BaMbuti groups where I was not known. Kenge was then about 22 yr. old, and had never before seen a view such as this. He asked me what the "things" before us were (referring to the mountains). "Were they hills? Were they clouds? Just what were they?" I said that they were hills bigger than any in his forest, and that if he liked we would leave the forest and go and see them and have a rest there. He was not too sure about this, but the BaMbuti are an incorrigibly curious people and he finally agreed. We drove by automobile in a violent thunderstorm which did not clear until we entered the Chango National Park at the foot of the mountains and on the edge of Lake Edward. Up to that moment from the time we had left the edge of the forest, near Beni, visibility had been about 100 yd.

As we drove through the park the rain stopped and the sky cleared, and that rare moment came when the Ruwenzori Mountains were completely free of cloud and stood up in the late afternoon sky, their snow-capped peaks shining in the sun. I stopped the car and Kenge very unwillingly got out. His first remark was to reiterate, what he had been saying ever since the rain stopped and we could see around us, that this was a very bad country, there were no trees. Then he looked up at the mountains and was completely unable to express any ideas—quite possibly because his language had no suitable terms, being limited to the experience of a strictly forest people. The snow fascinated him, he thought it must be some kind of rock. More important, however, was the next observation.

As we turned to get back in the car, Kenge looked over the plains and down to where a herd of about a hundred buffalo were grazing some miles away. He asked me what kind of insects they were, and I told him they were buffalo, twice as big as the forest buffalo known to him. He laughed loudly and told me not to tell such stupid stories, and asked me again what kind of insects they were. He then talked to himself, for want of more intelligent company, and tried to liken the buffalo to the various beetles and ants with which he was familiar.

He was still doing this when we got into the car and drove down to where the animals were grazing. He watched them getting larger and larger, and though he was as courageous as any Pygmy, he moved over and sat close to me and muttered that it

was witchcraft. (Witchcraft, incidentally, is known to the BaMbuti only through association with the Bantu. They have no similar concept of the supernormal.) Finally when he realized that they were real buffalo he was no longer afraid, but what puzzled him still was why they had been so small, and whether they *really* had been small and had suddenly grown larger, or whether it had been some kind of trickery.

As we came over the crest of the last low hill, Lake Edward stretched out into the distance beyond, losing itself in a hazy horizon. Kenge had never seen any expanse of water wider than the Ituri river, a few hundred yards across. This was another new experience difficult for him to comprehend. He again had the same difficulty of believing that a fishing boat a couple of miles out contained several human beings. "But, it's just a piece of wood," he protested. I reminded him of the buffalo, and he nodded unbelievingly.

Later we went all over the National Park with one of the African guides. He and Kenge conversed in KiNgwana, the *lingua franca* of the area, and Kenge was constantly looking out for animals and trying to guess at what they were. He was no longer afraid or unbelieving; he was trying to adapt himself, and succeeding, to a totally new environment and new experience.

The next day he asked to be taken back to the forest. He reverted to his original argument. "This is bad country, there are no trees."

The inability of the BaMbuti to correlate size-constancy and distance had never even struck me as a possibility. In the forest, vision is strictly limited to a matter of yards, the greatest distance one can see, when up a tree looking down onto a camp, being a hundred feet or more below. Kenge was, however, a sophisticated and well travelled Pygmy. He had been with me a long time, had travelled along roads where he could see for as much as a quarter of a mile, and had seen aircraft and knew that they contained people. Such instances, however, were rare, and on the whole his experience of visual distance was limited to the relatively slight diminution of size in seeing a person or people walking along a road a quarter of a mile away. He had seldom seen any animal from further away than a few yards, he had never seen any boat bigger than a dug-out canoe, and that no further away than a few hundred feet.

Number-Perception

Size-perception is, however, only one of many phenomena of interest to the psychologist. The Pygmy, unless he is one who has constant dealings with the Bantu, is unable to count above four. He has, however, such an eye for patterns that, for example, if several arrows are taken from a bunch, he can detect the reduction and can usually replace the correct number withdrawn to bring the bunch to its original size. In a gambling game *(panda)* common in the region, up to 40 or so pebbles, seeds, or beans are thrown onto a mat. In a single glance the Pygmy can tell you if they form a multiple of four, or how many—one, two, or three—have to be added to make it into such a multiple. The game is a test of skill in number perception and manipulation. Spare beans are concealed between the fingers and toes, and as a player makes his throw, while the beans are still rolling on the mat, he has already made his calculation and added the requisite number from his concealed reserve to bring the total to the winning multiple.

Art

(1) VISUAL

Another phenomenon worthy of study, and again associated with environmental influence, is the almost total lack of any form of physical art. The BaMbuti refer to white, black and red by color names, for other colors they make comparisons—"like leaves," "like leopards," instead of "green" or "yellow." They use red or blue-black dyes in the crude decoration of their bark cloths, smearing the dye on with their fingers. More complicated are the designs painted on the bodies of the girls and women, using the black stain obtained from the gardenia fruit. Except for these decorations, visual art is lacking. Wooden implements are never carved or decorated or even polished. Perhaps the world of the BaMbuti is too close around him, too confined and colorless, too much lacking in variety, to produce a visual art.

(2) AUDITORY

In contrast to this lack the Pygmy has the most complex music in the whole of Africa. It is complex not only in terms of rhythm, melody, and harmony (the latter surprising enough in Africa), but also in terms of technique. The BaMbuti can improvise a 15 part liturgy or canon, with melodies frequently running in parallel seconds, and hold it without the slightest difficulty. When this gets too tame, they divide the melodic line up, note by note, among the performers, each of whom will hoot his note at the appropriate moment. The melody then travels counterclockwise around the group who may be sitting about a central fire or even in the natural circle formed by their huts, each at his own hearth. There

is obvious material here for anyone interested in esthetics, as well as for those who might be more interested in the relatively small part that vision plays in the life of these forest nomads. (Even when hunting a great deal is done by hearing rather than seeing, and perhaps even smell is more important as a sense. Vision is used by the hunters in the examination of tracks, but the firing of the arrow is often done by sound rather than sight.) I should mention again that music permeates their whole life.

Historical Records

The earliest historical records of the BaMbuti, found in a tomb dating from the sixth dynasty in Egypt, places this tribe where it is today, refers to it as forest dwellers, and indicates that song and dance played a great part in the life of its people then just as it does today, over four thousand years later. In the forest there are few forces that stimulate change, and it is probable that the BaMbuti remained for most of this time living much the same kind of life. As recently as three or four hundred years ago, however, the great Bantu migrations forced certain Bantu and Sudanic tribes into the forest. For a number of highly significant reasons the resultant contact has had relatively little effect on the life of the BaMbuti, who consciously and forcefully reject the values of the plains and savannah, and unite in common opposition to the village world of the invaders.

It is a pity that such an exceptional opportunity for the study of a truly primitive people should be missed. In a few years the opportunity will be gone. There is little literature of scientific value available on these people. The references that I give here are those of the greatest interest, but even so are for the most part of general rather than specific value.[1] The

---

[1] Martin Gusinde, Die Kongo Pygmäen in Geschichte and Gegenwart, *Acta Nova Leopoldina,* 76, 1942; *Urwaldmenschen am Ituri,* 1948; *Die Twiden, Pygmäen und Pygmoida im Tropischen Afrika,* 1956, P. E. Joset, Buda Efeba, *Zaïre,* 1, 1948, 137–157; Paul Schebesta, *Among Congo Pygmies,* 1933; *My Pygmy and Negro Hosts,* 1936; *Revisiting by Pygmy Hosts,* 1937; *Les Pygmé es du Congo Belge,* 1952; George Schweinfurth, *The Heart of Africa,* 1874; C. T. Turnbull, Initiation among the BaMbuti Pygmies of the Central Ituri, *J. roy. Anthropol. Instit.,* 87, 1957, 191–216; Legends of the BaMbuti, *ibid.,* 89, 1959, 45–60; Some recent developments in the sociology of the BaMbuti Pygmies, *Trans. N.Y. Acad. Sci.,* Ser. II, 22, 1960, 275–284; The *elima.* A pre-marital festival among the BaMbuti Pygmies, *Zaïre,* 2–3, 1960, 175–192; Field work among the BaMbuti Pygmies, *Man,* 60, 1960; *The Forest People,* 1961.

work of Schebesta was undertaken a number of years ago, and his later findings, as well as my own, indicate that particularly with regard to his analysis of the Pygmy-Negro relationship he was observing more from the point of view of the village than of the forest. This was due to the fact that it was impossible for him at that time to have access to the BaMbuti except through the offices of the local Negro chiefs. The presence of the Negroes changed the situation, even when in the forest, from a truly forest to a village environment, and the Pygmies reacted accordingly.

True hunters, particularly those who are as heavily conditioned by their environment as are the Ba-Mbuti, are rare. The fact that they are surrounded by so many different cultures, yet have managed to maintain their own cultural integrity is an indication of the depth and vitality of their way of life and thought, however simple and static it may seem on the surface. If they lose their integrity in the next few years, it will not be because of any process of acculturation, but because the forest is no longer theirs and it will have been physically impossible for them to maintain their forest way of life. They are aware of the future that faces them, and while some say, "We shall just have to live like the *savages* and plant bananas," the majority say, "When the forest is no more, we shall die." I am afraid it will be the latter.

QUESTIONS FOR REFLECTION AND DISCUSSION:

1. How can observations of Kenge be said to provide evidence that nurture can play an important role in perceptual development?

2. What kinds of experiences led Kenge to misperceive the buffalo and the boat?

3. What are the implications of the BaMbuti methods of referring to colors for the linguistic relativity hypothesis?

4. Do you notice any signs of condescension toward the BaMbuti or toward other African groups on the part of the author?

5. Many of Turnbull's observations are made on the basis of his experiences with one person, Kenge. Do you believe that he can generalize his observations to other Pygmies? Why or why not?

SOURCE

Reprinted with permission from Dement, W. (1960). The effect of dream deprivation. *Science, 131*, 1705–1707. Copyright 1960 American Association for the Advancement of Science.

For something that is so familiar, much about sleep remains mysterious. For example, sleep appears to rejuvenate a fatigued body, but nobody is exactly sure how. People seem to seek a characteristic amount of sleep, even though they can usually get by on somewhat less. The functions of dreams, if any, are also less than clear. The psychoanalyst Sigmund Freud suggested that dreams reflect unconscious wishes and "protect sleep" by providing imagery that helps keep disturbing, repressed thoughts out of consciousness. According to the activation-synthesis model, dreams reflect neural activity in the parts of the cortex involved in memory, and the synthesis of this activity into story lines. Or it could simply be that with the brain cut off from the world outside, memories are replayed and altered during sleep. Still another possibility is that the REM activity connected with dreams is a way of testing whether the individual has benefitted from the restorative functions of sleep and is ready to awaken.

Although theories abound concerning the "meaning" of dreams, classic research by dream researcher William Dement and others suggests that preventing people from dreaming is connected with unpleasant psychological consequences.

The Effect of Dream Deprivation

WILLIAM DEMENT
MOUNT SINAI HOSPITAL

The need for a certain amount of dreaming each night is suggested by recent experiments.

About a year ago, a research program was initiated at the Mount Sinai Hospital which aimed at assessing the basic function and significance of dreaming. The experiments have been arduous and time-consuming and are still in progress. However, the results of the first series have been quite uniform, and because of the length of the program, it has been decided to issue this preliminary report.

In recent years, a body of evidence has accumulated which demonstrates that dreaming occurs in association with periods of rapid, binocularly synchronous eye movements (1–3). Furthermore, the amount and directional patterning of these eye movements and the associated dream *content* are related in such a way as to strongly suggest that the eye movements represent scanning movements made by the dreamer as he watches the events of the dream (3). In a study of undisturbed sleep (4), the eye-movement periods were observed to occur regularly throughout the night in association with the lightest phases of a cyclic variation in depth of sleep, as measured by the electroencephalograph. The length of individual cycles averaged about 90 minutes, and the mean duration of single periods of eye movement was about 20 minutes. Thus, a typical night's sleep includes four or five periods of dreaming, which account for about 20 percent of the total sleep time.

One of the most striking facts apparent in all the works cited above was that a very much greater amount of dreaming occurs normally than had heretofore been realized—greater both from the standpoint of frequency and duration in a single night of sleep and in the invariability of its occurrence from night to night. In other words, dreaming appears to be an intrinsic part of normal sleep and, as such, although the dreams are not usually recalled, occurs every night in every sleeping person.

A consideration of this aspect of dreaming leads more or less inevitably to the formulation of certain rather fundamental questions. Since there appear to be no exceptions to the nightly occurrence of a substantial amount of dreaming in every sleeping person, it might be asked whether or not this amount of dreaming is in some way a necessary and vital part of our existence. Would it be possible for human beings to continue functioning normally if their dream life were completely or partially suppressed? Should dreaming be considered necessary in a psychological sense or a physiological sense or both?

The obvious attack on these problems was to study subjects who had somehow been deprived of the opportunity to dream. After a few unsuccessful preliminary trials with depressant drugs, it was decided to use the somewhat drastic method of awakening sleeping subjects immediately after the onset of dreaming and to continue this procedure throughout the night, so that each dream period would be artificially terminated right at its beginning.

Subjects and Method

The data in this article are from the first eight subjects in the research program, all males, ranging in age from 23 to 32. Eye movements and accompanying low-voltage, nonspindling electroencephalographic patterns (4) were used as the objective criteria of dreaming. The technique by which these variables are recorded, and their precise relationship to dreaming, have been extensively discussed elsewhere (2, 4). Briefly, the subjects came to the laboratory at about their usual bedtime. Small silver-disk electrodes were carefully attached near their eyes and on their scalps; then the subjects went to sleep in a quiet, dark room in the laboratory. Lead wires ran from the electrodes to apparatus in an adjacent room upon which the electrical potentials of eye movements and brain waves were recorded continuously throughout the night.

Eye movements and brain waves of each subject were recorded throughout a series of undisturbed night of sleep, to evaluate his base-line total nightly dream time and over-all sleep pattern. After this, recordings were made throughout a number of nights in which the subject was awakened by the experimenter every time the eye-movement and electroencephalographic recordings indicated that he had begun to dream. These "dream-deprivation" nights were always consecutive. Furthermore, the subjects were requested not to sleep at any other time. Obviously, if subjects were allowed to nap, or to sleep at home on any night in the dream-deprivation period, an unknown amount of dreaming would take place, offsetting the effects of the deprivation. On the first night immediately after the period of dream deprivation, and for several consecutive nights thereafter, the subject was allowed to sleep without disturbance. These nights were designated "recovery nights." The subject then had a varying number of nights off, after which he returned for another series of interrupted nights which exactly duplicated the dream-deprivation series in number of nights and number of awakenings per night. The only difference was that the subject was awakened in the intervals between eye-movement (dream) periods. Whenever a dream period began, the subject was allowed to sleep on without interruption, and was awakened only after the dream had ended spontaneously. Next, the subject had a number of recovery nights of undisturbed sleep equal to the number of recovery nights in his original dream-deprivation series. Altogether, as many as 20 to 30 all-night recordings were made for each subject, most of them on consecutive nights. Since, for the most part, tests could be made on only one subject at a time, and since a minute-by-minute all-night vigil was required of the experimenter to catch each dream episode immediately at its onset, it can be understood why the experiments have been called arduous and time-consuming.

Table 9.01 summarizes most of the pertinent data. As can be seen, the total number of base-line nights for the eight subjects was 40. The mean sleep time for the 40 nights was 7 hours and 2 minutes, the mean total nightly dream time was 82 minutes, and the mean percentage of dream time (total dream time to total sleep time $\times$ 100) was 19.4. Since total sleep time was not held absolutely constant, percentage figures were routinely calculated as a check on the possibility that differences in total nightly dream time were due to differences in total sleep time. Actually, this is not a plausible explanation for any but quite small differences in dream time, because the range of values for total sleep time for each subject turned out to be very narrow throughout the entire study. When averaged in terms of individuals rather than nights, the means were:

TABLE 9.01

SUMMARY OF EXPERIMENTAL RESULTS. *TST*, TOTAL SLEEP TIME; *TDT*, TOTAL DREAM TIME.

	MEAN AND RANGE, BASE-LINE NIGHTS			DREAM-DEPRIVATION NIGHTS (NO.)	AWAKENINGS (NO.)		DREAM-DEPRIVATION RECOVERY NIGHTS FIRST NIGHT				FIRST CONTROL RECOVERY NIGHT		
	TST	TDT	PERCENT		FIRST NIGHT	LAST NIGHT	NO.	TST	TDT	PERCENT	TST	TDT	PERCENT
Subject W.T. (4 base-line nights)													
	6^{h}36^m	1^{h}17^m	19.5	5	8	14	1	6^{h}43^m	2^{h}17^m	34.0	6^{h}50^m	1^{h}04^m	15.6
	6^{h}24^m–6^{h}48^m	1^{h}10^m–1^{h}21^m	17.0–21.3										
Subject H.S. (5 base-line nights)													
	7^{h}27^m	1^{h}24^m	18.8	7	7	24	2	8^{h}02^m	2^{h}45^m	34.2	8^{h}00^m	1^{h}49^m	22.7
	7^{h}07^m–7^{h}58^m	1^{h}07^m–1^{h}38^m	15.4–21.8										
Subject N.W. (7 base-line nights)													
	6^{h}39^m	1^{h}18^m	19.5	5	11	30	5	6^{h}46^m	1^{h}12^m	17.8	7^{h}10^m	1^{h}28^m	20.2
	5^{h}50^m–7^{h}10^m	1^{h}11^m–1^{h}27^m	17.4–22.4										
Subject B.M. (6 base-line nights)													
	6^{h}59^m	1^{h}18^m	18.6	5	7	23	5	7^{h}25^m	1^{h}58^m	26.3	7^{h}48^m	1^{h}28^m	18.8
	6^{h}28^m–7^{h}38^m	0^{h}58^m–1^{h}35^m	14.8–22.2										
Subject R.G. (10 base-line nights)													
	7^{h}26^m	1^{h}26^m	19.3	5	10	20	5	7^{h}14^m	2^{h}08^m	29.5	7^{h}18^m	1^{h}55^m	26.3
	7^{h}00^m–7^{h}57^m	1^{h}13^m–1^{h}46^m	16.9–22.7										
Subject W.D. (4 base-line nights)													
	6^{h}29^m	1^{h}21^m	20.8	4	13	20	3	8^{h}53^m	2^{h}35^m	29.0			
	5^{h}38^m–7^{h}22^m	1^{h}08^m–1^{h}32^m	17.8–23.4										
Subject S.M. (2 base-line nights)													
	6^{h}41^m	1^{h}12^m	17.9	4	22	30	6	5^{h}08^m	1^{h}01^m	19.8	6^{h}40^m	1^{h}07^m	16.8
	6^{h}18^m–7^{h}04^m	1^{h}01^m–1^{h}23^m	16.2–19.3						6^{h}32^m*	1^{h}50^m*	28.1*			
Subject W.G. (2 base-line nights)													
	6^{h}16^m	1^{h}22^m	20.8	3	9	13							
	6^{h}08^m–6^{h}24^m	1^{h}17^m–1^{h}27^m	20.7–20.9										

*Second recovery night (see text).

total sleep time, 6 hours 50 minutes; total dream time, 80 minutes; percentage of dream time, 19.5; this indicates that the figures were not skewed by the disparate number of base-line nights per subject. The remarkable uniformity of the findings for individual nights is demonstrated by the fact that the standard deviation of the total nightly dream time was only plus or minus 7 minutes.

Progressive Increase in Dream "Attempts"

The number of consecutive nights of dream deprivation arbitrarily selected as a condition of the study was five. However, one subject left the study in a flurry of obviously contrived excuses after only three nights, and two subjects insisted on stopping after four nights but consented to continue with the recovery nights and the remainder of the schedule. One subject was pushed to seven nights. During each awakening the subjects were required to sit up in bed and remain fully awake for several minutes. On the first nights of dream deprivation, the return to sleep generally initiated a new sleep cycle, and the next dream period was postponed for the expected amount of time. However, on subsequent nights the number of forced awakenings required to suppress dreaming steadily mounted. Or, to put it another way, there was a progressive increase in the number of attempts to dream. The number of awakenings required on the first and last nights of deprivation are listed in Table 9.01. *All* the subjects showed this progressive increase, although there was considerable variation in the starting number and the amount of the increase. An important point is that each awakening was preceded by a minute or two of dreaming. This represented the time required for the experimenter to judge the emerging record and make the decision to awaken the subject after he first noticed the beginning of eye movements. In some cases the time was a little longer, as when an eye-movement period started while the experimenter was looking away from the recording apparatus. It is apparent from this that the method employed did not constitute absolute dream deprivation but, rather, about a 65- to 75-percent deprivation, as it turned out.

Nightly Dream Time Elevated after Deprivation

The data on the first night of the dream deprivation recovery period are summarized for each subject in Table 9.01. As was mentioned, one subject had quit the study. The mean total dream time on the first recovery night was 112 minutes, or 26.6 percent of the total mean sleep time. If the results for two subjects who did not show marked increases on the first recovery night are excluded, the mean dream time is 127 minutes or 29 percent, which represents a 50-percent increase over the group base-line mean. For all seven subjects together, on the first recovery night the increase in percentage of dream time over the base-line mean (Table 9.01, col. 3, mean percentage figures; col. 10, first recovery night percentages) was significant at the $p < .05$ level in a one-tail Wilcoxin matched-pairs signed-ranks test (5).

It is important to mention, however, that one (S.M. in Table 9.01) of the two subjects alluded to above as exceptions was not really an exception because, although he had only 1 hour 1 minute of dreaming on his first recovery night, he showed a marked increase on *four* subsequent nights. His failure to show a rise on the first recovery night was in all likelihood due to the fact that he had imbibed several cocktails at a party before coming to the laboratory so that the expected increase in dream time was offset by the depressing effect of the alcohol. The other one of the two subjects (N.W. in Table 9.01) failed to show a significant increase in dream time on any of five consecutive recovery nights and therefore must be considered the single exception to the over-all results. Even so, it is hard to reconcile his lack of increase in dream time on recovery nights with the fact that during the actual period of dream deprivation he showed the largest build-up in number of awakenings required to suppress dreaming (11 to 30) of any subject in this group. One may only suggest that, although he was strongly affected by the dream loss, he could not increase his dream time on recovery nights because of an unusually stable basic sleep cycle that resisted modification.

The number of consecutive recovery nights for each subject in this series of tests was too small in some cases, mainly because it was naively supposed at the beginning of the study that an increase in dream time, if it occurred, would last only one or two nights. One subject had only one recovery night, another two, and another three. The dream time was markedly elevated above the base-line on all these nights. For how many additional nights each of these three subjects would have maintained an elevation in dream time can only be surmised in the absence of objective data. All of the remaining four subjects had five consecutive recovery nights. One was the single subject who showed no increase, two were nearing the base-line dream time by the fifth night, and one still showed marked elevation in dream time. From this admittedly incomplete sample it appears that about five nights of increased dreaming usually follow four or five nights of dream suppression achieved by the method of this study.

Effect Not Due to Awakening

Six of the subjects underwent the series of control awakenings—that is, awakenings during non-dream periods. This series exactly duplicated the dream-deprivation series for each subject in number of nights, total number of awakenings, and total number of awakenings per successive night. The dream time on these nights was slightly below base-line levels as a rule. The purpose of this series was, of course, to see if the findings following dream deprivation were solely an effect of the multiple awakenings. Data for the first recovery nights after nights of control awakenings are included in Table 9.01. There was no significant increase for the group. The mean dream time was 88 minutes, and the mean percentage was 20.1. Subsequent recovery nights in this series also failed to show the marked rise in dream time that was observed after nights of dream deprivation. A moderate increase found on four out of a total of 24 recovery nights for the individuals in the control-awakening group was felt to be a response to the slight reduction in dream time on control-awakening nights.

Behavioral Changes

Psychological disturbances such as anxiety, irritability, and difficulty in concentrating developed during the period of dream deprivation, but these were not catastrophic. One subject, as was mentioned above, quit the study in an apparent panic, and two subjects insisted on stopping one night short of the goal of five nights of dream deprivation, presumably because the stress was too great. At least one subject exhibited serious anxiety and agitation. Five subjects developed a marked increase in appetite during the period of dream deprivation; this observation was supported by daily weight measurements which showed a gain in weight of 3 to 5 pounds in three of the subjects. The psychological changes disappeared as soon as the subjects were allowed to dream. The most important fact was that *none* of the observed changes were seen during the period of control awakenings.

The results have been tentatively interpreted as indicating that a certain amount of dreaming each night is a necessity. It is as though a pressure to dream builds up with the accruing dream deficit during successive dream-deprivation nights—a pressure which is first evident in the increasing frequency of attempts to dream and then, during the recovery period, in the marked increase in total dream time and percentage of dream time. The fact that this increase may be maintained over four or more successive recovery nights suggests that there is a more or less quantitative compensation for the deficit. It is possible that if the dream suppression were carried on long enough, a serious disruption of the personality would result (6).

References and Notes

1. E. Aserinsky and N. Kleitman, *J. Appl. Physiol.* **8**, 1 (1955); W. Dement and E. Wolpert, *J. Nervous Mental Disease* **126**, 568 (1958); D. Goodenough, A. Shapiro, M. Holden, L. Steinschriber, *J. Abnormal Social Psychol.* **59**, 295 (1959); E. Wolpert and H. Trosman, *A.M.A. Arch. Neurol. Psychiat.* **79**, 603 (1958).
2. W. Dement, *J. Nervous Mental Disease,* **122**, 263 (1955).
3. —— and N. Kleitman, *J. Exptl. Psychol.* **53**, 339 (1957); W. Dement and E. Wolpert, *ibid.* **55**, 543 (1958).
4. W. Dement and N. Kleitman, *Electroencephalog. and Clin. Neurophysiol.* **9**, 673 (1957).
5. S. Siegel, *Nonparametric Statistics for the Behavioral Sciences* (McGraw-Hill, New York, 1956).
6. The research reported in this paper was aided by a grant from the Foundations' Fund for Research in Psychiatry.

QUESTIONS FOR REFLECTION AND DISCUSSION:

1. How did Dement determine cyclic variation in sleep? What are the physiological signs of dreaming?

2. How did Dement prevent subjects from dreaming?

3. Is dreaming statistically normal? About what percentage of the time asleep is spent in dreaming?

4. Why were subjects awakened more frequently during the night as the study progressed from day to day?

5. What were the effects of dream deprivation?

6. Are you satisfied that the effects reported by Dement resulted from the deprivation of dreams? Can you think of a rival explanation? (Hint: How did Dement know when subjects were dreaming?)

SOURCE

Hobson, J. A., & McCarley, R. W. (1977). The brain as a dream state generator: An activation-synthesis hypothesis of the dream process. *American Journal of Psychiatry, 134,* 1335–1348. Copyright 1977, the American Psychiatric Association. Reprinted by permission.

Dreams are psychological events, but as noted by Sigmund Freud and the authors of the current article, J. Allan Hobson and Robert McCarley, there is assumed to be a mind-body isomorphism; that is, psychological events are assumed to have a biological basis in the body, and in particular in the brain.

Biology is usually considered the "reducing science" for psychology. That is, when psychologists look to other disciplines for explanations of psychological events, they most often turn to biology, and particularly to neuroscience. Many students wonder why there is "so much biology" in psychology. It happens that psychological events such as dreams, problem solving, and the emotional life occur within our flesh and blood being. Psychological events are accompanied by changes in the body, and very often, changes in the body give rise to psychological events. For example, arousal of the sympathetic branch of the autonomic nervous system is often connected with feelings of anxiety or fear. Similarly, in the classic study presented here, Hobson and McCarley theorize that arousal of the reticular activating system—a part of the brain—is connected with dreaming.

The Brain as a Dream State Generator: An Activation-Synthesis Hypothesis of the Dream Process

J. ALLAN HOBSON, M.D., & ROBERT W. MCCARLEY, M.D.

Recent research in the neurobiology of dreaming sleep provides new evidence for possible structural and functional substrates of formal aspects of the dream process. The data suggest that dreaming sleep is physiologically determined and shaped by a brain stem neuronal mechanism that can be modeled physiologically and mathematically. Formal features of the generator processes with strong implications for dream theory include periodicity and automaticity of forebrain activation, suggesting a preprogrammed neural basis for dream mentation in sleep; intense and sporadic activation of brain stem sensorimotor circuits including reticular, oculomotor, and vestibular neurons, possibly determining spatiotemporal aspects of dream imagery; and shifts in transmitter ratios, possibly accounting for dream amnesia. The authors suggest that the automatically activated forebrain synthesizes the dream by comparing information generated in specific brain stem circuits with information stored in memory.

Since the turn of the century, dream theory has been dominated by the psychoanalytic hypothesis that dreaming is a reactive process designed to protect consciousness and sleep from the disruptive effect of unconscious wishes that are released in sleep (1). Thus dreaming has been viewed as a psychodynamically determined state, and the distinctive formal features of dream content have been interpreted as manifestations of a defensive transformation of the unconscious wishes found unacceptable to consciousness by a hypothetical censor. A critical tenet of this wish fulfillment-disguise theory is that the transformation of the unconscious wish by the censor disguises or degrades the ideational information in forming the dream imagery. We were surprised to discover the origins of the major tenets of psychoanalytic dream theory in the neurophysiology of 1890 and have specified the transformations made by Freud in an earlier, related article (2). In detailing the neurophysiological origins of psychoanalytic dream theory, the concept of mind-body isomorphism, denoting similarity of form between psychological and physiological events, was seen as an explicit premise of Freud's thought.

Sharing Freud's conviction that mind-body isomorphism is a valid approach, we will now review modern neurophysiological evidence that we believe permits and necessitates important revisions in psychoanalytic dream theory. The activation-synthesis hypothesis that we will begin to develop in this paper asserts that many formal aspects of the dream experience may be the obligatory and relatively undistorted psychological concomitant of the regularly recurring and physiologically determined brain state called "dreaming sleep." It ascribes particular formal features of the dream experience to the particular organizational features of the brain during that state of sleep. More specifically, the theory details the mechanisms by which the brain becomes periodically activated during sleep and specifies the means by which both sensory input and motor output are simultaneously blocked, so as to account for the maintenance of sleep in the face of strong central activation of the brain. The occurrence and character of dreaming are seen as both determined and shaped by these physiological processes.

The most important tenet of the activation-synthesis hypothesis is that during dreaming the activated brain generates its own information by a pontine brain stem neuronal mechanism, which will be described in detail. We hypothesize that this internally generated sensorimotor information, which is partially random and partially specific, is then compared with stored sensorimotor data in the synthesis of dream content. The functional significance of the brain activation and the synthesis of endogenous information in dreaming sleep is not known, but we suggest that state-dependent learning is at least as likely a result of dreaming as is tension reduction or sleep maintenance.

While we believe that the two processes emphasized in this paper—activation and synthesis—are major and important advances in dream theory, we wish to state explicitly and comment on some of the things that our theory does not attempt to do. The ac-tivation-synthesis hypothesis does not exclude possible defensive distortions of the value-free sensorimotor dream stimuli, but it does deny the primacy of any such process in attempting to explain *formal* aspects of dream content or the fundamental impetus to dreaming itself. The idea that dreams reveal wishes is also beyond the direct reach of our new theory, but some specific alternatives to this interpretation of several classic dream situations can be advanced.

The new theory cannot yet account for the emotional aspects of the dream experience, but we assume that they are produced by the activation of brain regions subserving affect in parallel with the activation of the better known sensorimotor pathways. Finally, the new theory does not deny meaning to dreams, but it does suggest 1) a more direct route to their acquisition than anamnesis via free association, since dream origins are in basic physiological processes and not in disguised wishes, 2) a less complex approach to their interpretation than conversion from manifest to latent content, since unusual aspects of dreams are not seen as disguises but as results of the way the brain and mind function during sleep, and 3) a broader view of their use in therapy than that provided by the transference frame of reference, since dreams are not to be interpreted as the product of disguised unconscious (transference) wishes. Dreams offer a royal road to the mind and brain in a behavioral state, with different operating rules and principles than during waking and with the possibility of clinically useful insights from the product of these differences. These points are discussed in the last section of this paper and elsewhere (3).

What Is a Dream?

A dream may be defined as a mental experience, occurring in sleep, which is characterized by hallucinoid imagery, predominantly visual and often vivid; by bizarre elements due to such spatiotemporal distortions as condensation, discontinuity, and acceleration; and by a delusional acceptance of these phenomena as "real" at the time that they occur. Strong emotion may or may not be associated with these distinctive formal properties of the dream, and subsequent recall of these mental events is almost invariably poor unless an immediate arousal from sleep occurs.

That this technical jargon describes a universal human experience seems certain, since the five key points in this definition are easily elicited from both naïve and sophisticated individuals when they are asked to characterize their dreams. We leave aside

ELECTROGRAPHIC CRITERIA FOR BEHAVIORAL STATE DETERMINATION			
STATE	ELECTROMYOGRAM	EEG	ELECTROOCULOGRAM
Waking	+	Low voltage, fast	+
Sleep			
Synchronized	+	High voltage, slow	−
Desynchronized	−	Low voltage, fast	+

the question of whether other less vivid and non-perceptual forms of mental activity during sleep should also be called "dreams" and confine ourselves here to the psychophysiology of the hallucinoid type of dream. In doing so, we not only simplify the immediate task at hand but may also gain insight into the mechanisms underlying the most florid symptoms of psychopathology. We mean, of course, the hallucinations and delusions of the psychotic experience, which have so often invited comparison with the dream as we have defined it here.

What Is the State of the Brain during Dreaming Sleep?

The physiological substrate of the dream experience is the CNS in one of its three principal operating states: waking (W), synchronized sleep (S), and desynchronized sleep (D). These states can be reliably and objectively differentiated by recording the EEG, the electromyogram (EMG), and the electrooculogram (Table 10.01). Hallucinoid dreaming in man occurs predominantly during the periodically recurrent phase of sleep characterized by EEG desynchronization, EMG suppression, and REMs (4). We call this kind of sleep "D" (meaning desynchronized, but also conveniently denoting dreaming).

In the systems analysis terms used in Figure 10.01, this D brain state is characterized by the following "sensorimotor" properties: activation of the brain; relative exclusion of external input; generation of some internal input, which the activated forebrain then processes as information; and blocking of motor output, except for the oculomotor pathway. In this model the substrate of emotion is considered to be a part of the forebrain; it will not be further distinguished here because we have no specific physiological evidence as to how this part of the system might work in any brain state. Memory is not shown but is considered to be a differentiated function of the brain that operates during the D

state, such that output from long-term storage is facilitated but input to long-term storage is blocked. A highly specific hypothesis about dream amnesia has previously been derived (5) from the same evidence that we will now review in our attempt to account for the general sensorimotor aspects of the dream process.

Electrophysiology of the Brain during the Dream State

The three major electrographic features of the D state are of obvious relevance to our attempt to

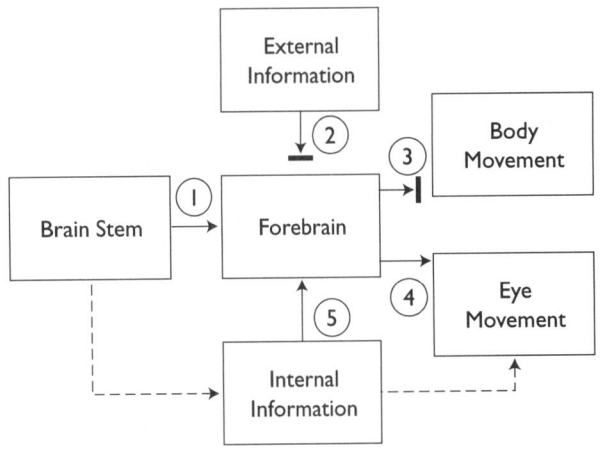

Processes Accounted for:

1. Activation of forebrain
2. Blockade of exteroceptive input
3. Blockade of motor output
4. Oculomotor activation
5. Provision of forebrain with internally generated information

FIGURE 10.01

Systems Model of Dream State Generation

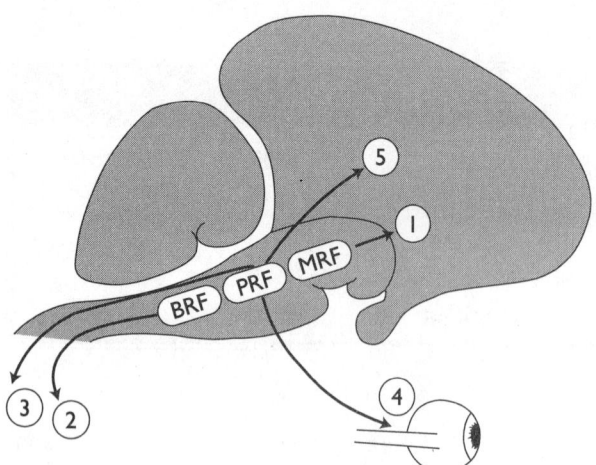

Processes Accounted for:

1. Activation of forebrain

2. Blockade of exteroceptive input

3. Blockade of motor output

4. Oculomotor activation

5. Provision of forebrain with internally generated information

FIGURE 10.02

Physiological Model of Dream State Generation Using the Sagittal Section of the Cat Brain and Showing the Bulbar (BRF), Pontine (PRF), and Midbrain (MRF) Divisions of the Reticular Formation

answer the following three questions about the organization of the brain in the dream state.

How is the forebrain activated in the D state? Since EEG desynchronization also characterizes waking, similar mechanisms of "activation" may be involved in both instances. Physiological evidence suggests that this is so: the reticular formation of the anterior brain stem is at least as active in D sleep as it is in the waking state (Fig. 10.02).

How is motor output blocked in the D state? Physiological evidence clearly shows that the profound EMG suppression of D sleep is a consequence of the direct inhibition of spinal cord motoneurons (6). As a consequence, any organized motor patterns that might be generated during the intense brain activation of D sleep cannot be expressed.

That organized movement patterns are in fact generated, but not expressed, in normal D sleep is dramatically demonstrated by cats with lesions of the anterodorsal pontine brain stem (7). The animals show all of the major manifestations of D sleep except the atonia; instead of the fine twitches of the digits and the limb jerks that are normally present in D, these cats display complex motor behaviors in-

cluding repetitive paw movements and well-coordinated attack and defense sequences that have no apparent relationship to the environment.

How is sensory imagery generated in the D state? In waking, a corollary discharge of the oculomotor system has been shown to suppress visual transmission during saccadic eye movements, possibly contributing to the stability of the visual field during that state (8). The same mechanisms might underlie the hallucinoid dream imagery by inhibiting and exciting neurons of the lateral geniculate body (9) and the visual cortex (10) during D sleep, when retinal input is reduced and unformed.

The possibility that oculomotor impulses trigger visual imagery is particularly intriguing in view of the demonstrated quantitative correlation between eye movement intensity and dream intensity (11). More specific correlations have also been reported to relate eye movement direction to orientation of the hallucinated gaze in dreams (12). This finding has been interpreted as indicative of "scanning" the visual field—implying cortical control of the eye movements in dreaming sleep. An alternative, although not exclusive, hypothesis is that the oculomotor activity is generated at the brain stem level and that the cortex is then provided with feedforward information about the eye movements. According to this view, we are not so much scanning dream imagery with our D sleep eye movements as we are synthesizing the visual imagery appropriate to them. We will return to the implications of this intriguing possibility in discussing the generation of eye movements in dreaming sleep, but we wish to stress here the general significance of this clue to the identity of an "internal information generator" operating at the brain stem level in the dreaming sleep state.

The eye-movement-related inhibition of sensory relays (13), as well as the possible occlusion of exogenous inputs by internally generated excitation, may also contribute to the maintenance of sleep in the face of strong central activation of the brain. In this sense the dream process is seen as having a sleep maintenance mechanism built into its physiological substrate rather than a sleep guardian function operating at the psychological level.

A firm general conclusion can be reached at this point: the desynchronized phase of sleep is the physiological substrate of hallucinoid dreaming, as defined. This conclusion is of profound significance to psychophysiology, since we can now reliably and objectively characterize and measure many aspects of the brain when it is in the dream state. For example, one feature that emerges from the psychophysiological study of dreaming and one that was not at all evident from introspective, psychoanalytically oriented research, is that the brain enters the dream state at regular intervals during sleep and stays in that state for appreciable and predictable lengths of time. One clear implication of this finding is that dreaming is an automatically preprogrammed brain event and not a response to exogenous (day residue) or endogenous (visceral) stimuli. A second implication is that the dream state generator mechanism is periodic, that is, the dream state generator is a neurobiological clock (14). Since the length of the sleep cycle and, by inference, the frequency of dreaming, is a function of body size within and across mammalian species (15), the system controlling the length of the period must have a structural substrate. Thus we must account for size-related periodicity with our model of the dream state generator.

An Animal Model of the Brain during the Dream State

We said that the length of the sleep cycle varies "across species." Does that mean that nonhuman animals dream? Unfortunately we cannot know, but we are willing to assert that if they do so, it is when their brains are in the D sleep state. Because we have no direct evidence of any significant difference between the brain state of man and the brain state of other mammals in D sleep, we therefore feel justified in asserting that the brain state of our experimental animal, the cat, constitutes a reasonable subject for our study of the brain as a dream process generator, whether or not cats dream. This assertion seems justified since we are restricting our attention here to formal aspects of the dream experience; our experimental model need not dream or even possess "consciousness" to be useful as a source of physiological information. If we accept this argument and use the definition of dreaming offered above, then the presence of D sleep in cats (16) offers nothing less than an animal model in which to study the neurophysiological basis of a hallucinoid mental process in man. Such a model is as important in experimental psychiatry as it is rare. Let us now turn to the biological data upon which our sketches of the brain as a dream state generator are based.

Localization of the Power Supply or Trigger Zone of the Dream State Generator

Lesion, stimulation, and recording studies pioneered by Jouvet (17) have strongly implicated the pontine

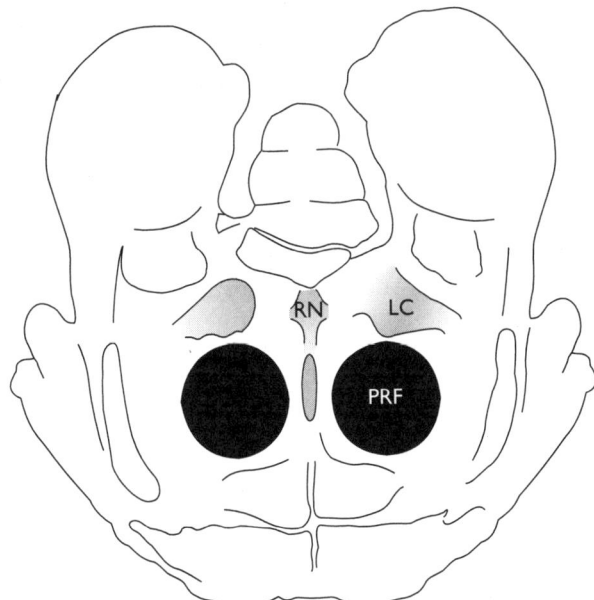

FIGURE 10.03

The Anatomy of the Pontine Brain Stem*

---

* On this frontal section of the cat brain stem, the cells that are selectively activated are in the paramedian reticular formation (PRF) (giganto cellular tegmental field), while the cells that are selectively inactivated lie more dorsally (in the region of the locus coeruleus [LC]) and medially (in the region of the raphe nuclei [RN]). Compare this with Figure 10.05, which summarizes the neurophysiology and shows the anatomy in a sagittal section.

brain stem as critical to the generation of the desynchronized sleep phase (see Fig. 10.03 for a summary of the neuroanatomy of this region). Important findings supporting this hypothesis include the following.

Large lesions of the pontine reticular formation prevent the occurrence of desynchronized sleep for several weeks in cats (17). This suggests that the pontine reticular formation may be the site of an executive or triggering mechanism for desynchronized sleep. Prepontine transections and forebrain ablation have no effect upon periodicity or duration of the skeletal, muscular, and oculomotor manifestations of D sleep (17). The data indicate that the trigger, the power supply, and the clock are pontine.

The pontine brain stem is thus implicated as the site of both the trigger and the clock. The periodicity of the D sleep clock in poikilothermic pontine cats lengthens as temperature declines, indicating orthodox metabolic mediation of the cycle, in contrast to the temperature independence of circadian rhythms. If we assume that the physiological substrate of consciousness is in the forebrain, these facts completely eliminate any possible contribution of ideas (or their neural substrate) to the primary driving force of the dream process.

Small lesions of the dorsal pontine brain stem, in the region of the locus coeruleus (LC), may eliminate the atonia but no other aspects of desynchronized sleep (7). This suggests that inhibition of muscle tone is somehow dependent upon the integrity of the LC. The elaborate motor behavior that characterizes the D sleep of cats with LC lesions has been described as "pseudo-hallucinatory" (7). Whether or not one accepts the sensory implications of that designation, the importance of motor inhibition in quelling the effects of central excitation during the dream state is clear.

This finding has an important bearing on mechanisms of dream paralysis and suggests that in the classic chase dream, the dreamer who has trouble fleeing from a pursuer is as much accurately reading the activated state of his motor pattern generator and the paralyzed state of his spinal neurons as he is "wishing" to be caught. This dream experience is so universal and the feeling of constrained motor action so impressive as to make its physiological basis in the descending inhibition of motoneurons seem to us inescapable. Conversely, this reasonable and adequate explanation of the paradox of the chase dream makes its interpretation as wish fulfillment less compelling. Other implications of the D sleep activation of various motor system pattern generators for movements and dream plots have been discussed elsewhere (3).

The vestibular system, as classically established, integrates head position and movement with eye position and posture. Pompeiano and Morrison (18) showed that lesions of the vestibular nuclei interfered with the bursts of REM but not with the isolated eye movements of D. This finding suggested that the vestibular system contributed to the elaboration and rhythmicity of the eye movements but that the eye movement generator was extravestibular. Magherini and associates (19) found that systemic injections of the anticholinesterase agent physostigmine produced rhythmic eye movements in decerebrate cats, suggesting that the eye movement generator may be cholinergic. Thus the central, automatic activation during sleep of the vestibular system may provide a substrate for endogenously generated, specific information about body position and movement. Flying dreams may thus be a logical, direct, and unsymbolic way of synthesizing information generated endogenously by the vestibular system in D sleep. In view of this reasonable and direct explanation, it seems gratuitous to "interpret" the sensual flying dream as sexual.

In accord with the isomorphism principle, the degree of neuronal activation in brain systems should parallel the frequency and intensity of dreams to these systems (3), and the predominance of visual sensorimotor activity in both brain and mind supports this notion. Symbol formation and the often bizarre juxtaposition of sensations in the dream may be a reflection of the heightened degree of simultaneous activation of multiple sensory channels in dreaming as compared with waking (3).

Long-term electrical stimulation of the pontine brain stem results in the earlier appearance of sleep episodes and in increases in the absolute amounts of desynchronized sleep, but it does not affect the periodicity of its occurrence (20). By implication, the delivery of electrical energy accomplishes what most psychological and behavioral treatments fail to achieve: an increase in the duration of dreaming sleep. Testing the assumption that the generator neurons are cholinoceptive, our laboratory team has recently established that injection of the cholinergic agent carbachol into the pontine reticular formation produces prolonged enhancement of D-like sleep behavior (21). In man the parenteral injection of the anticholinesterase agent physostigmine potentiates D sleep, and the pharmacologically induced episodes are associated with hallucinoid dreaming (22). The time of occurrence and duration of dreams may thus be chemically determined.

In summary, these results support the hypothesis that the pontine brain stem is the generator zone for the D sleep state. The trigger mechanism for the whole system, including the eye movement generator, may be cholinoceptive and the executive zones are probably in the reticular formation. The LC is involved, possibly in a permissive or reciprocal way, and is especially important in mediating spinal reflex inhibition. Together, these two regions may constitute the clock. We will have more to say about the hypothesis of reciprocal interaction between them later in this paper.

Although the brain stem mechanisms mediating atonia remain obscure, it is clear from the work of Pompeiano (6) that both monosynaptic and polysynaptic spinal reflexes are tonically inhibited during D sleep (Fig. 10.04). In addition, during the bursts of REM, there is a descending presynaptic inhibition of the most rapidly conducting (group 1*a*) spinal afferent endings. Both presynaptic and postsynaptic inhibition appear to be of brain stem origin. Phasic presynaptic inhibition has also been shown to occur in sensory relays elsewhere in the brain during D sleep (6). Thus motor output is tonically damped throughout D and sensory input is phasically damped in concert with the REM bursts. In other words, we are not only paralyzed during our dreams, but the degree to which we are paralyzed fluctuates in concert with the intensity of the

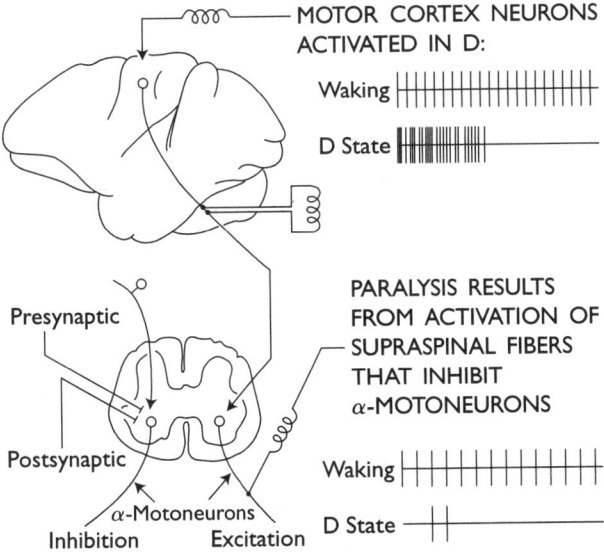

MOTOR CORTEX NEURONS
ACTIVATED IN D:

Waking

D State

PARALYSIS RESULTS
FROM ACTIVATION OF
SUPRASPINAL FIBERS
THAT INHIBIT
α-MOTONEURONS

Waking

D State

Presynaptic

Postsynaptic

α-Motoneurons
Inhibition   Excitation

FIGURE 10.04

Mechanisms of Sleep Paralysis*

---

* The upper part of the figure illustrates the intense activation in D sleep of antidromically identified pyramidal tract neurons of the motor cortex. Note the relatively regular discharge in waking (W) and the clustering of discharges in D sleep in these models of 3-second epochs of microelectrode recordings (vertical lines indicate discharges). The lower portion of the figure shows the inhibitory events of D at the spinal cord level that largely prevent alpha motoneuron discharge and consequent muscle excitation, despite the activation of excitatory (arrow) pyramidal tract fibers. Both presynaptic and postsynaptic inhibition (bars) are present in D (sketched on the left side of the cord section). Absence of this inhibition in W allows alpha motoneuron discharge in response to excitation from pyramidal tract

internally generated information and the degree to which we suppress exogenous input.

On the basis of this evidence, the systems terminology used earlier (see Fig. 10.01) can be tentatively translated into the anatomical and physiological terms of Figure 10.02; and the activation-synthesis hypothesis of dreaming can be stated as follows: during D sleep, a cholinergic mechanism in the reticular formation of the pontine brain stem is periodically activated. The consequences of this activation are as follows:

1. The forebrain is tonically activated, probably via the midbrain reticular formation that is also responsible for its activation during waking. Thus the forebrain is made ready to process information.

2. The spinal reflexes are tonically inhibited, possibly via the bulbar reticular formation

and LC; thus motor outflow is blocked despite high levels of activity in the brain, including the motor cortex.

3. The oculomotor and vestibular systems are phasically activated by the pontine reticular formation so as to produce eye movements. This circuitry, in its entirety, is an internal information source or generator that provides the forebrain with spatially specific but temporally disorganized information about eye velocity, relative position, and direction of movement. Information may similarly be derived from the brain stem generators of patterned motor activity.

4. At the same time that internal information feedback is being generated by the activation of various motor systems, exteroceptive input to sensory systems is phasically blocked. This may intensify the relative impact of the endogenous inputs to the brain, accounting for the intensity of dream imagery and preventing sleep disruption by the externally generated excitation.

This working sketch of the dream state generator, based on the classical localizing methods of experimental neurology, is intriguing but unsatisfying in that it fails to specify the mechanisms by which the pontine generator is turned on, kept active for a time, and then shut off. Further, it does not say anything about the mechanism of periodicity. To provide details about the anatomy and physiology of the periodic trigger mechanisms of the generator process, we will now turn our attention to the neuronal level of analysis. In doing so, we also come full circle in our reaffirmation of isomorphism since it was the neuron that Freud recognized as the physical unit of the nervous system on which he based his dream theory (2).

Histological Features of Relevance to the Periodic Triggering of the Dreaming Sleep State Generator

Several structural details of the pontine brain stem are notable as possible elements of a D sleep control device with rhythmic properties (see Fig. 10.03 for an illustration of the anatomy discussed).

In his discussion of the histology of the pontine brain stem, Cajal (23) emphasized three points:

1. The paramedian reticular giant cells, with their rostral and caudal axonal projections, are admirably suited to serve as output elements of the generator; when excited they could

influence many other cells. The work of Brodal (24) and the Scheibels (25) shows that the spinal cord and thalamus receive projections from these elements. Although they are relatively few in number, conservative estimates of their postsynaptic domain indicate that each directly projects to nine million (9×10^6) postsynaptic neurons. Thus the 3,000 pontine reticular giant cells in the cat might make many billions of synapses (2.9×10^{10}). Since the giant cells also project to other brain stem nuclei and have recurrent axons to themselves, mutual interaction with raphe-type elements (see below) and self-reexcitation are both possible. These two features could be used to create excitability variability, with powerful consequences for the whole nervous system.

2. The raphe neurons of the midline are ideally situated and connected to regulate excitability of paramedian elements, and they also have extensive projections to other brain regions. The discovery that these cells concentrate the biogenic amine serotonin (26) gives this regulatory hypothesis an attractive corollary: these cells might regulate excitability of their postsynaptic neurons via specific transmitter substances. Another brain stem cell group, in the locus coeruleus, has been shown to concentrate the amine norepinephrine (26). There are thus at least two neuronal candidates for a level setting role, and both are probably inhibitory. Since the giant cells are excitatory (and probably cholinergic; see below), a substrate for reciprocal interaction is established.

3. Cajal (23) suggested that input to the central reticular core might be via small stellate cells in the lateral zone. This input channel, which we now know to be more diffuse than was originally suspected, could be used to abort or damp the core oscillator at critical ambient stimulus levels. This is an important feature, since adaptation depends on the capacity to interrupt the cycle and not to incorporate all exogenous stimuli into the dream plot.

Cellular Activity in the Pontine Brain Stem during the Sleep Cycle

A direct experimental approach to the question of D state control has been made with cats by recording from individual neurons in many parts of the brain as the sleep cycle normally evolved. In this experimental paradigm, the frequency and pattern of extracellular action potentials, which are the signal units of nerve cells, are taken as indices of a cell's excitability; the influence of a recorded neuron upon other cells and that neuron's own control mechanism may also be inferred from the data. This method has the advantage of being relatively physiological since it does little to alter or damage the properties of the system under study. When cats are kept active at night, they will sleep under the necessary conditions of restraint during the daytime. The microelectrodes can then be stereotaxically directed at the brain stem and individual cell activity recorded for as long as 20 hours, allowing many successive sleep cycles to be studied (Fig. 10.05).

The pontine brain stem control hypothesis has been tested in three ways at the level of single cells.

Selectivity criterion: which cells change rate most in D? We assumed that cells which showed pronounced alterations in discharge rate over the sleep cycle were more likely to be playing a controlling role than those showing minimal change. We further assumed that those cells having peaks of activity in phase with the D phase of the cycle were more likely to be specifically and actively involved in dreaming sleep state control than those with multiple peaks. We found that the giant cells of the pontine tegmentum concentrated their discharge in the D phase of sleep to a greater extent than any other group of neurons (27). They became our prime candidate for a generator function.

Tonic latency criterion: which cells change rate first in D onset? If the cells with positive discharge selectivity were driving the dreaming sleep phase of the sleep cycle, then their rates would be expected to increase in advance of the behavioral state change. Such phase leads might well be longer than those of the follower neurons under the control of the giant cells. The giant cells, when recorded over entire sleep cycles and through repeated sleep cycles, were found to change rate continuously (28). Significant rate increases occurred *as long as 5 minutes* before a desynchronized sleep phase. When the 2 minutes just prior to desynchronized sleep onset were studied, a rate increase in a pool of giant cells was observed 10 seconds before a similar increase in a pool of cerebral cortical neurons.

The rapidly accelerating limb of the giant cell activity curves at D sleep phase onset indicated that this was a time of maximal excitability change in this pool of neurons. The goodness of fit of the data by an exponential curve indicated that reexcitation within the pool might be superimposed upon disin-

CELL RECORDING

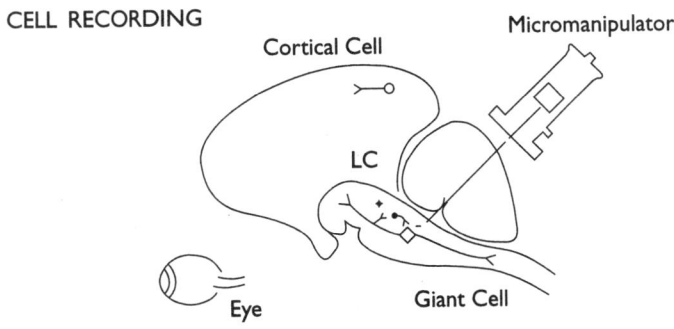

SELECTIVITY

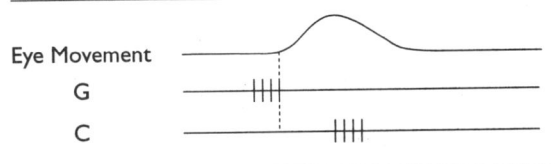

TONIC LATENCY

Cell	Synchronized $\longrightarrow$ Desynchronized
G	++++++++++++++++++++++++++++++
C	+++++++++++++++++++++++++++

PHASIC LATENCY

Eye Movement
G
C

PERIODICITY

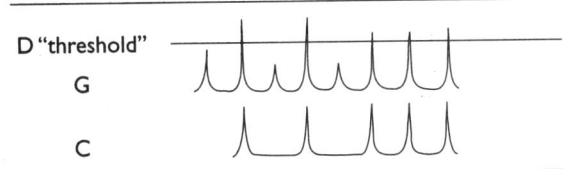

PHASIC PATTERN

Cell	Pattern in D	
G	++++ + +++++ + ++ ++++	Phasic
Other	+++++++++++++++++++++++++	Tonic

RECIPROCAL INTERACTION

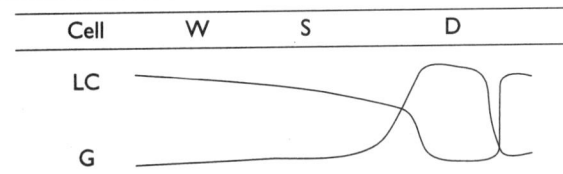

Cell	W	S	D
LC			
G			

FIGURE 10.05

Cellular Neurophysiology of Dream State Generation*

---

* The cell recordings are made from hydraulically driven microelectrodes that can be stereotaxically directed at neurons in the cat brain during natural sleep. Two classes of brain stem neurons are represented by the reticular giant cell (G in the physiological models) and the LC cell; the synaptic interactions suggested are detailed in Figure 10.08. A cortical cell is also shown.

The results of the cell recording experiments are shown in six models representing the criteria used to quantify discharge properties: selectivity—giant cells concentrate their discharge in D to a greater extent than cerebral cortical or other brain stem neurons; tonic latency—giant cells show rate increases that precede those of cortical neurons during the S to D transition; phasic latency—giant cells fire before the REMs of D, while cortical neurons fire after them; periodicity— peaks in the giant cell activation curves are periodic and the higher peaks are associated with D sleep episodes and peaks of cortical activity; phasic pattern—giant cells show a higher degree of clustered firing in D than do other neurons; and reciprocal interaction—the rate curves of giant cells and LC cells are reciprocal over the sleep cycle.

---

hibition from without. The positive tonic latency indicated that the activation of the forebrain might be a consequence of activation of the brain stem but that the converse could not be the case.

Phasic latency criterion: which cells fire before eye movements of D? Because of the proximity and

direct projections to oculomotor neurons from giant cells, we tested the possibility that they might be generating the REMs so characteristic of the desynchronized phase of sleep by determining the time of occurrence of short-term rate increases by the giant cells in relation to eye movement onset. On the average, such rate increases were more prominent and anticipated eye movement by longer intervals than other brain stem neurons (29). Rate increases by presumed follower elements (in the posterolateral cerebral cortex) *followed* the eye movements by many milliseconds. It could therefore be concluded that the eye movements might be initiated by giant cells but could not be generated by cortical neurons. This finding practically wrecks the scanning hypothesis and strongly favors the idea that visual cortical events are determined by events in the oculomotor brain stem.

At this point we felt justified in concluding that the giant cells of the pontine tegmentum were critical output elements in a sleep cycle control mechanism. More particularly, we proposed that they might be generator elements for some of the tonic and phasic excitatory events in the desynchronized sleep phase of the cycles: most important to the activation-synthesis hypothesis of dreaming are the determination of EEG desynchronization (activation of the forebrain) and REMs (provision of forebrain with internally generated information). At the very least, we felt that we had found an important avenue to understanding sleep cycle control, since we could now examine the properties and possible mechanisms of giant cell excitability regulation. In this regard there are three additional points worthy of emphasis.

Periodicity criterion. Long-term recordings of giant cells revealed peaks of activity in phase with each full-blown desynchronized sleep episode (30) (Fig. 10.06). Less prominent peaks were associated with abortive episodes and were rarely seen with no electrographic evidence of desynchronized sleep. Spectral analysis of these long-term data confirmed the impression of powerful periodicity in the discharge peaks, indicating that 1) sleep cycles are periodic, 2) underlying cell activity is probably even more so, and by definition, 3) cell excitability is under the control of a neurobiological clock. The possible mechanisms of excitability control are thus of great interest.

Phasic pattern criterion. The pattern of giant cell discharge within each D sleep episode indicated that classical pacemaker mechanisms are *not* involved in giant cell excitability regulation (31). Regular interspike intervals were exceptional, indicating that the rate increases were not caused by endogenous membrane depolarizations. The tendency, rather, was for giant cells to discharge in intermittent, prolonged clusters of irregularly distributed spikes as if the cells were responding to excitatory postsynaptic potentials from other neurons (Fig. 10.07). In our view, a likely source of much of this input, especially as the longer clusters developed, was other giant cells. Once other neurons were excited, feedback from them is to be expected. It also seemed likely that the clusters of giant cell discharge were causally related to the eye movement bursts of the D sleep phase.

Reciprocal interaction criterion. If giant cell excitability change is not an intrinsic property of the giant cells, what other cell group might regulate it and in what way might that regulation be effected? Since all indices showed giant cells to discharge first in relation to both the tonic and phasic events of desynchronized sleep, we considered the possible contribution of inhibitory neurons. Since interneurons do not appear to exist in the giant cell fields, such cells should be discrete from but proximal to the giant cell. To be effective, projections should be abundant and should have inhibitory transmitter action upon the giant cells. Reciprocal rate changes during the sleep cycle are to be expected if such cells exist. We have discovered just such changes in a small number of unidentified cells in the region of the posterior locus coeruleus and the nucleus subcoeruleus (32). Not only is discharge concentration of these elements quantitatively inverse to those of the giant cells in the phases of the cycle, but their decelerating rate curve is the approximate mirror image of that of the giant cells at desynchronized sleep onset as seen in part C. We called such cells "D-off" cells to contrast their activity curves with those of the giant cells, prototypes of the "D-on" species of neurons. We do not know if the "D-off" cells are catecholaminergic but their location and discharge properties make this possible.

McGinty and associates (33) have found similar reciprocal rate changes in the dorsal raphe nucleus (DRN) neurons and we have recently confirmed this finding. The low regular rates of discharge by these cells in waking suggest a level-setting or pacemaker function. Their location and discharge properties are the same as those cells thought to be serotonergic on the basis of pharmacological experiments (34). Since both the LC and DRN are adjacent to and project to giant cells, and since giant cells receive abundant serotonergic and catecholaminergic endings, we thought that the mutual interconnections of these D-on and D-off cells could form a substrate for reciprocal interaction which regulated sleep cycle oscillation (30).

A Model for a Brain Stem Sleep Cycle Oscillator

Restricting attention to within-sleep changes, we constructed a physiological model that bears a strik-

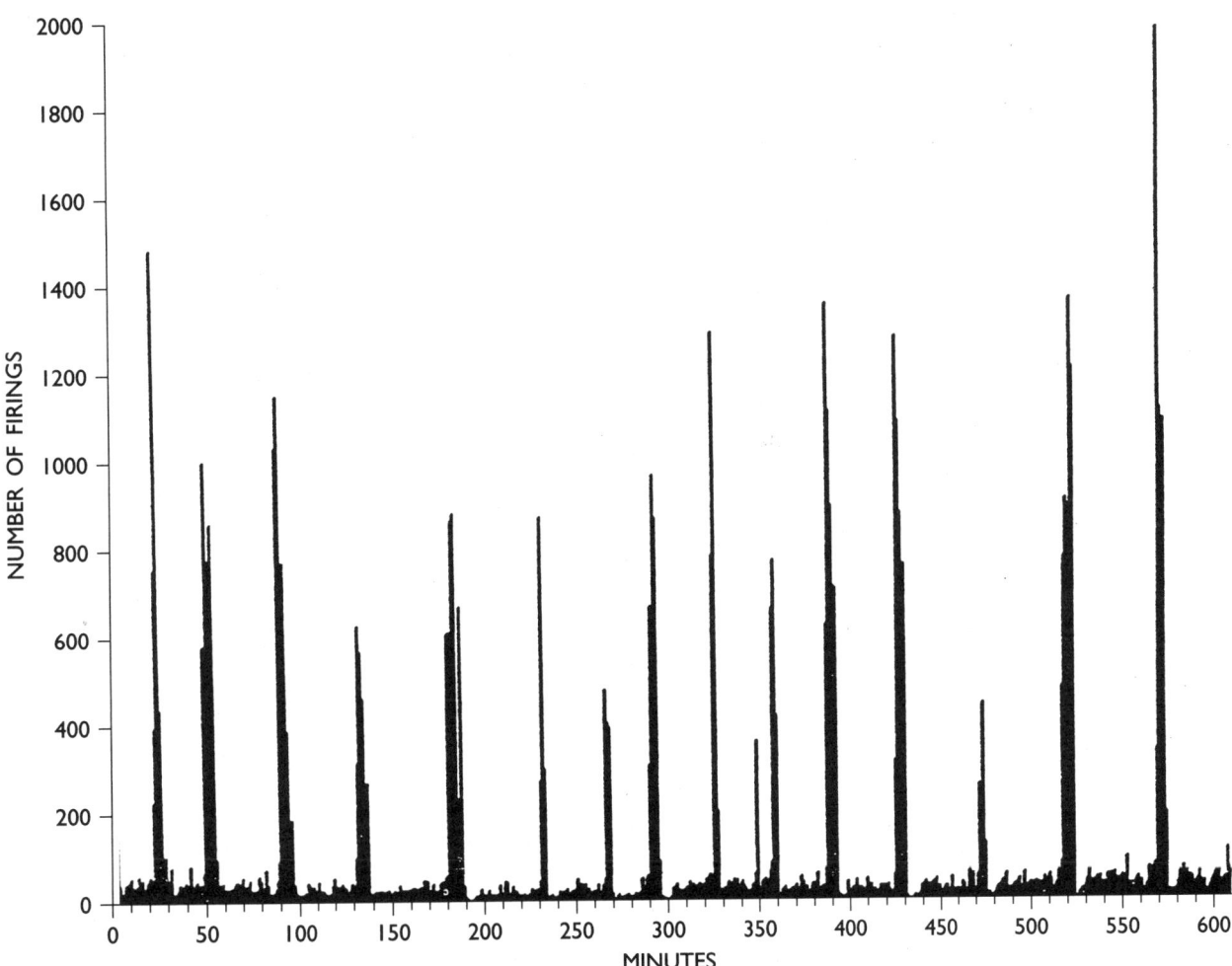

FIGURE 10.06

Discharge Activity of a Giant Cell Neuron Recorded over Multiple Sleep-Waking Cycles*

* Each peak corresponds to a desynchronized sleep episode, and a regular trend of discharge activity over a cycle is observable; a peak in desynchronized sleep; a rapid decline at the end of the desynchronized sleep episode; a trough, often associated with waking; a slow rise (in synchronized sleep and preceding all electrographic signs of desynchronized sleep); and an explosive acceleration at the onset of desynchronized sleep. Note also the extreme modulation of activity and the periodicity (30).
Reprinted by permission from *Science,* volume 189, pages 58–60, July 4, 1975. Copyright 1975 by the American Association for the Advancement of Science.

ing resemblance to the a priori schema derived from Cajal (Fig. 10.08, top portion). Most of the connections have been demonstrated but many of the synaptic assumptions are as yet unproven physiologically. In addition to being explanatory, the model suggests experiments, particularly those employing pharmacological methods, the results of which will lead to its future modification. Since the LC, DRN, and giant cell groups are chemically differentiated, we deduced that their action and interaction may involve specific neurotransmitters.

In preliminary tests of the model, we have found that microinjection of the cholinomimetic substance carbachol into the giant cell zone not only gives more potent desynchronized sleep phase enhancement than injections into the adjacent tegmental fields but simultaneously activates giant cells. The results also indicate that an opposite effect is obtained at locus coeruleus sites (as if an inhibitory cell group were being activated). We have not yet tested this last hypothesis directly, but the LC cells do resume firing before the end of

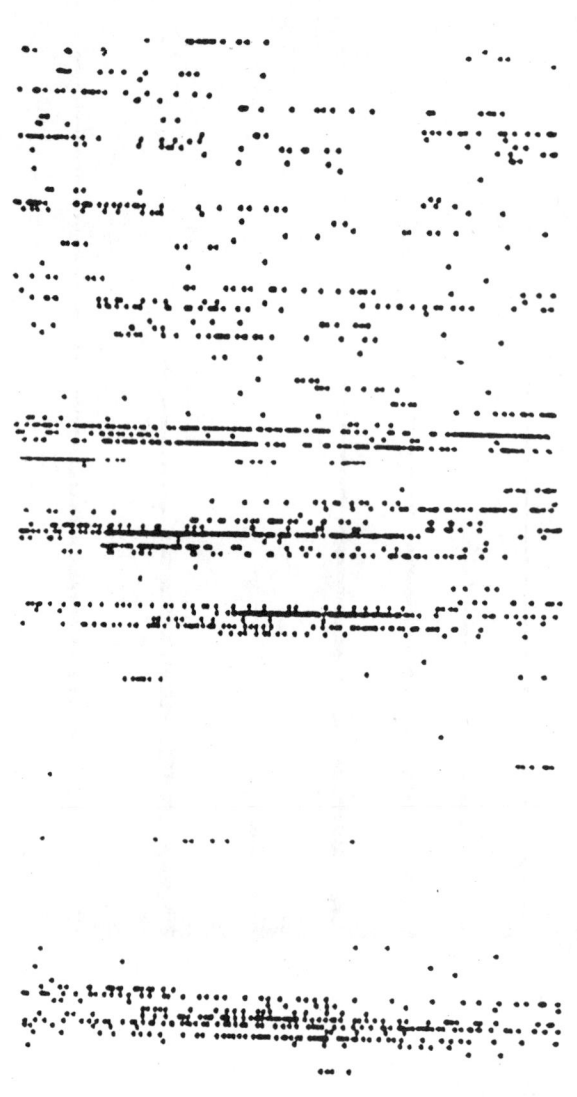

FIGURE 10.07

Temporal Clustering of Extracellularly Recorded Discharges of Cat Giant Cell Neurons During D Sleep*

---

* Each discharge is represented by a dot; the time sequence runs left to right and top to bottom, with each line 1 second in duration. The figure encompasses about 200 seconds of D sleep activity. Clustering is visible as closely spaced dots and, over longer durations, as "bands" of activity, some of which appear to occur rhythmically. Note the various durations of clusters and the presence of shorter duration clusters of activity within longer duration clusters. Clusters are delimited by periods of relative inactivity. Such sequences of giant cell neuronal activity are temporally associated with runs of eye movements and ponto-geniculo-occipital waves, and similar sequences of executive neuron discharges may represent the neuronal substrate of dream sequences in man (Hobson and Mc-Carley, unpublished data).

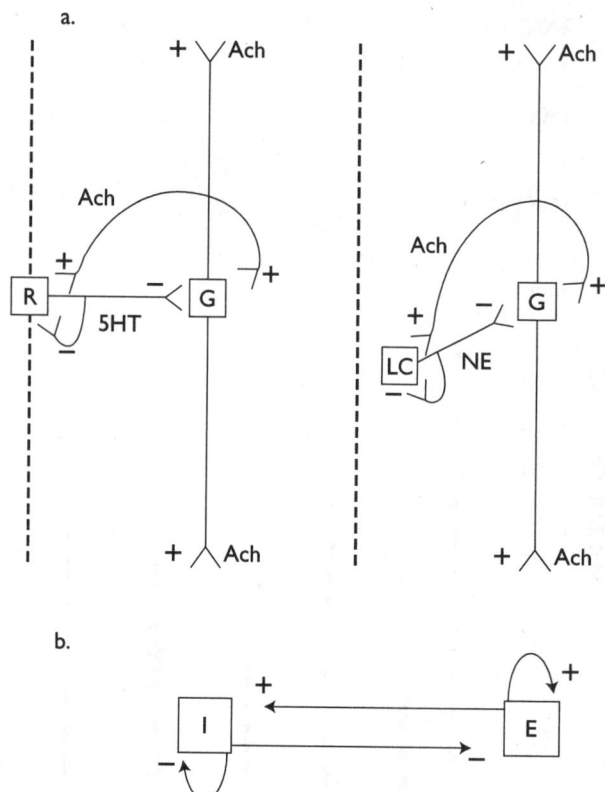

FIGURE 10.08

Reciprocal Interaction Model of Generator Process*

---

* Physiological models used to organize and interpret results of pharmacological experiments on desynchronized sleep. The G cells are seen as executive elements; they excite with and are excited by acetylcholine (Ach). They interact reciprocally with two aminergic cell groups, the LC and raphe (R), which utilize norepinephrine (NE) and serotonin (5HT) respectively. Both amines are hypothesized to be inhibitory to the G cells. D sleep will therefore be enhanced by increasing G cell excitability, and this can occur by either adding cholinergic drive or subtracting aminergic inhibition. Conversely, D sleep will be suppressed by subtracting cholinergic drive or by adding aminergic inhibition.

Formal reduction of the elements in the top portion of the figure yields the general model of reciprocal interaction, of inhibitory (I,−) and excitatory (E,+) populations, each of which contains a self-loop as well as a projection to the other set. The resulting oscillation of activity in the two sets can be mathematically described by the Lotka-Volterra equations.

D sleep. We assume that as FTG excitation declines and LC inhibition grows, the cycle ends. In the decerebrate cat, physostigmine-induced D episodes are associated with activation of neurons in the giant cell and suppression of firing by cells in the LC and DRN (35).

The physiological model can be reduced to a simple unit susceptible to mathematical analysis (see Figure 10.08, bottom portion). Cell group E (giant cell) and cell group I (raphe and/or LC) are assumed to be mutually interconnected; cell group E is excitatory to itself and to group I, which inhibits itself and group E. Growth of activity in one group occurs at the expense of growth in the other, and vice versa. As such the cell groups are analogous to two populations, prey and predator, whose interaction can be described by a set of nonlinear differential equations, the Lotka-Volterra equations (30). As shown in Figure 10.09, the time course of activity of cell group E closely resembles that predicted by these equations. It is now possible to plot the activity curves of cell group I and compare the actual data with the curves predicted by the model. The phase lag between the reciprocal cycles remains to be explained and the previously noted fact that cycle length is proportional to brain size

suggests that a distance factor may be at work. The distance between the two cell fields could be such a factor through its determination of protein transport time. Assuming an average LC-FTG internuclear distance of 2.5 mm and a fast protein transport time of 96 mm/day, a period length of about 35 minutes is predicted for the cat. This figure is within limits normal for that species. Another possible substrate for the long, size-dependent time constant of the cycle is the recently discovered class of long-duration postsynaptic transmitter actions (36) that may be mediated by second messengers such as cyclic AMP (37). Since the cyclic nucleotides activate protein kinases, the metabolic activity of the neuron, including the synthesis of neurotransmitters, can be linked to and entrained by membrane events.

An important point is that the mathematical model parallels, but is not identical to, the physiological model. This means that even if the specific assumptions about physiological interaction are incorrect, the mathematical model may be viable and useful in another system—for example, the coupling of the circadian and ultradian oscillators (14) or, at another level of analysis, in a molecular system. This is particularly important to keep in mind since it is also at the molecular level that time constant elements necessary to explain the long periodicity of the sleep-dream cycle may be found.

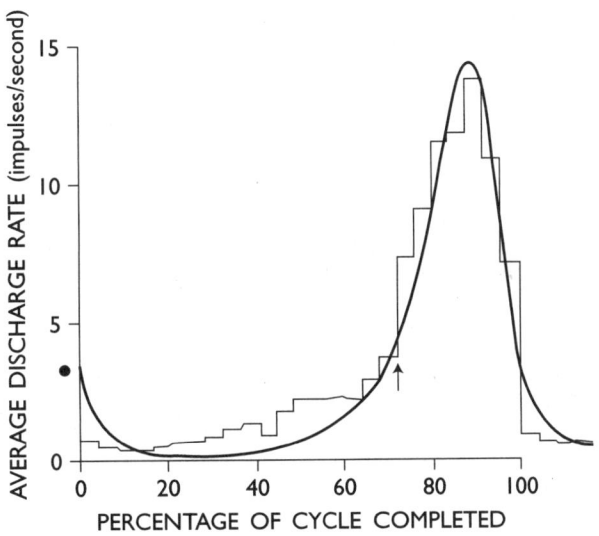

FIGURE 10.09

Time Course of Giant Cell Activity over the Sleep Cycle*

---

* The histogram shows the average discharge level (impulses/second) of a giant cell neuron over 12 sleep-waking cycles, each normalized to constant duration. The cycle begins and ends with the end of a desynchronized sleep period. The arrow indicates the average time of D sleep onset. The smooth curve is derived from a mathematical model of sleep cycle control and shows a good fit to the experimental data. The probability of obtaining dream-like mentation reports might be expected to show the same trajectory as these curves (30). Reprinted by permission from *Science*, volume 189, pages 58–60, July 4, 1975. Copyright 1975 by the American Association for the Advancement of Science.

Psychological Implications of the Cellular Neurophysiology of Dream Sleep Generation

Hallucinoid dreaming is regarded as the psychological concomitant of D sleep. Brain activity in the D state has been analyzed to account for activation of the forebrain, occlusion of sensory input, blockade of motor output at the spinal cord level, and the generation of information within the system. The evidence that the pontine brain stem contains a clock-trigger mechanism that contributes to activation of the forebrain, occlusion of sensory input, and the generation of internal information has been reviewed. The periodicity of the triggering mechanism is hypothesized to be a function of reciprocal interaction of reciprocally connected, chemically coded cell groups in the pontine brain stem.

The psychological implications of this model, which we call the activation-synthesis hypothesis of the dream process (schematically represented in Fig. 10.10), contrast sharply with many tenets of the

PSYCHOANALYTIC MODEL

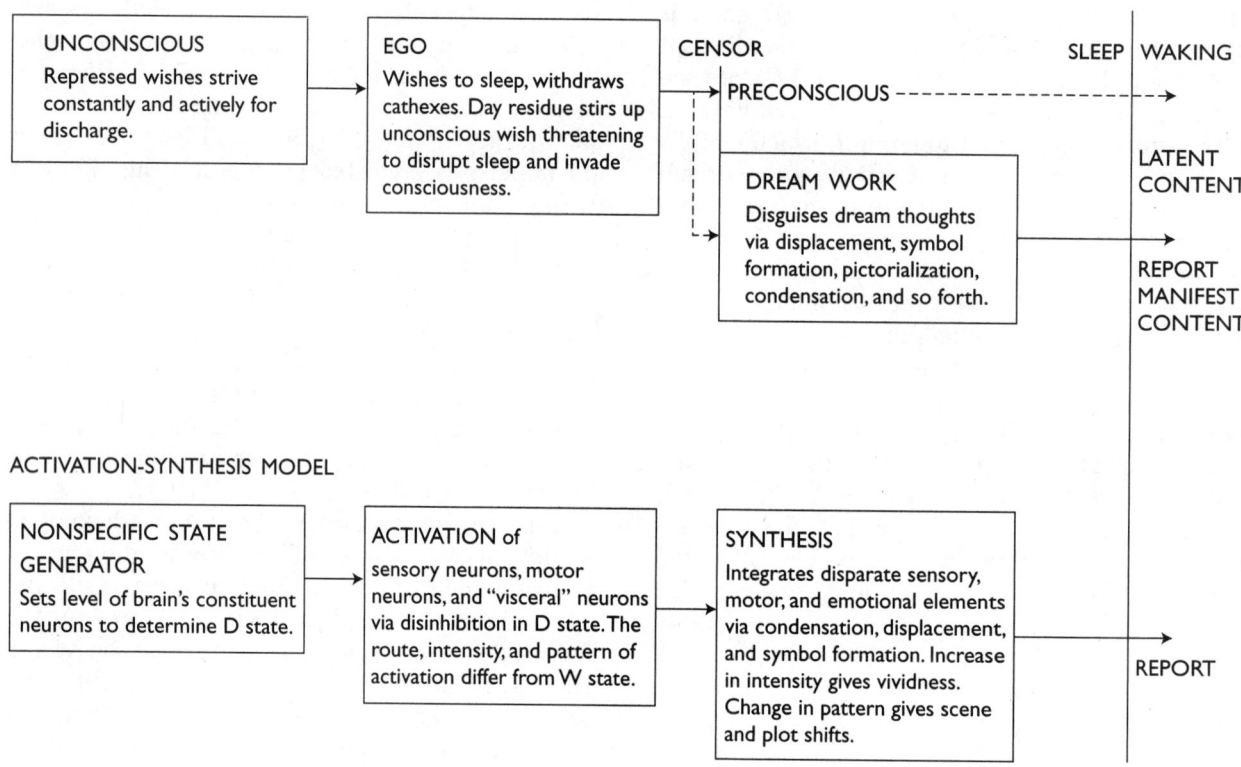

FIGURE 10.10

Two Models of the Dream Process*

---

* In the psychoanalytic model the motive force of the process is the dynamically repressed unconscious wish that is released from control in sleep. The dream thoughts that emerge threaten consciousness and sleep; they are deterred by the censor. The "dream work" transforms the unconscious wish by the processes that are listed. The product, or manifest content, that becomes conscious thus contains only disguised elements of the original (latent) dream thoughts. The activation-synthesis model is designed to contrast activation-synthesis theory with the guardian-censorship theory illustrated in the top portion of this figure. The motive force of the process is seen to be nonspecific neural energy or excitation hypothesized to arise from a nonspecific generator. This excitation affects the component systems of the forebrain represented in the upper box: sensory systems generate scene frames, structural fragments, and qualitative features; cognitive systems generate ideas that may be conscious (day residue thoughts) or unconscious (instinctually determined); emotion is also generated at this first stage. The dream report, easily obtainable if a state change to waking occurs, is seen as an accurate reflection of the integrated product of disparate, internally generated elements.

dream theory provided by psychoanalysis (also represented in Fig. 10.10) in the following ways:

1. *The primary motivating force for dreaming* is not psychological but physiological since the time of occurrence and duration of dreaming sleep are quite constant, suggesting a preprogrammed, neurally determined genesis. In fact, the neural mechanisms involved can now be precisely specified. This conclusion does not, of course, mean that dreams are not also psychological events; nor does it imply that they are without psychological meaning or function. But it does imply that the process is

much more basic than the psychodynamically determined, evanescent, "guardian of sleep" process that Freud had imagined it to be; and it casts serious doubt upon the exclusively psychological significance attached to both the occurrence and quality of dreams.

2. *Specific stimuli for the dream imagery* appear to arise intracerebrally but from the pontine brain stem and not in cognitive areas of the cerebrum. These stimuli, whose generation appears to depend upon a largely random or reflex process, may provide spatially specific information which can be used in constructing

Harcourt, Inc.

dream imagery; but the unusual intensity, intermittency, and velocity of the eye movements may also contribute to features of the dream experience which are formally bizarre and have been interpreted as defensive by psychoanalysis. Thus such features as scene shifts, time compression, personal condensations, splitting, and symbol formation may be directly isomorphic with the state of the nervous system during dreaming sleep. In other words, the forebrain may be making the best of a bad job in producing even partially coherent dream imagery from the relatively noisy signals sent up to it from the brain stem.

The dream process is thus seen as having its origin in sensorimotor systems, with little or no primary ideational, volitional, or emotional content. This concept is markedly different from that of the "dream thoughts" or wishes seen by Freud as the primary stimulus for the dream. The sensorimotor stimuli are viewed as possibly providing a frame into which ideational, volitional, or emotional content may be projected to form the integrated dream image, but this frame is itself conflict free. Thus both the major energetic drive for the dream process and the specific primary stimulus of the dream content are genotypically determined and therefore conflict free in the specifically psychodynamic sense of the term.

3. *The elaboration of the brain stem stimulus* by the perceptual, conceptual, and emotional structures of the forebrain is viewed as primarily a synthetic constructive process, rather than a distorting one as Freud presumed. Best fits to the relative inchoate and incomplete data provided by the primary stimuli are called up from memory, the access to which is facilitated during dreaming sleep. The brain, in the dreaming sleep state, is thus likened to a computer searching its addresses for key words. Rather than indicating a need for disguise, this fitting of phenotypic experiential data to genotypic stimuli is seen as the major basis of the "bizarre" formal qualities of dream mentation. There is, therefore, no need to postulate either a censor or an information degrading process working at the censor's behest. The dream content elaborated by the forebrain may include conflictually charged memories, but even this aspect of dream construction is seen as synthetic and transparent rather than degradative and opaque.

4. *With respect to the forgetting of dreams,* the normally poor recall is seen principally to reflect a state-dependent amnesia, since a carefully effected state change, to waking, may produce abundant recall even of highly charged dream material. There is thus no need to invoke repression to account for the forgetting of dreams. This hypothesis is appealingly economical, and in the light of the reciprocal interaction hypothesis dream amnesia can now be modeled in a testable way as the result of a different balance between cholinergic and aminergic neuronal activity and the resulting effects on second messengers and macromolecules (5). Among its other surprising gifts to psychophysiology, dreaming sleep may thus also provide a biological model for the study of memory, and a functional role for dreaming sleep in promoting some aspect of the learning process is suggested.

Summary and Conclusions

Assuming that isomorphism, or identity of form, must characterize the simultaneous physiological and psychological events during dreaming, we have reviewed the general and cellular neurophysiology of dreaming sleep in search of new ways of accounting for some of the formal aspects of dream psychology. We have noted that the occurrence of dreaming depends upon the periodic activation of the forebrain during sleep. We have hypothesized that the activated forebrain synthesizes the dreams by fitting experiential data to information endogenously and automatically generated by reticular, vestibular, and oculomotor neurons in the pontine brain stem. A specific physiological and mathematical model of the pontine generator, based upon single cell recording studies in cats, is described: the model posits reciprocal interaction between inhibitory aminergic (level-setting) and excitatory cholinergic (generator) neurons.

Some of the "bizarre" formal features of the dream may directly reflect the properties of the brain stem neuronal generator mechanism. The physiological features of the generator mechanisms and their corresponding psychological implications include the following: the automaticity and periodicity of activation indicate a metabolically determined, conflict-free energetics of the dream process; the random but specific nature of the generator signals could provide abnormally sequenced and shaped, but spatiotemporally specific, frames for dream imagery; and the clustering of runs of generator signals might constitute time-marks for dream subplots and scene changes. Further, the activation by generator neurons of diffuse post-synaptic forebrain elements in multiple parallel channels might account for the disparate sensory, motor, and emotional elements that contribute to the "bizarreness" of dreams; the suppression of motor output and sensory input simultaneous with central activation of both sensory and motor patterns could assure the maintenance of sleep in the face of massive central excitation of the brain; and the change in the ratio of neurotransmitters affecting forebrain neurons might account for dream amnesia and indicate a state-dependent alteration of neural plasticity, with implications for the learning process.

References

1. Freud S: The interpretation of dreams (1900), in The Complete Psychological Works, standard ed, vols 4 and 5. Translated and edited by Strachey J. London, Hogarth Press, 1966

2. McCarley RW, Hobson JA: The neurobiological origins of psychoanalytic dream theory. Am J Psychiatry 134:1211–1221, 1977

3. McCarley RW: Mind-body isomorphism and the study of dreams, in Advances in Sleep Research, vol 6. Edited by Fishbein W. New York, Spectrum (in press)

4. Dement W, Kleitman N: The relation of eye movements during sleep to dream activity: an objective method for the study of dreaming. J Exp Psychol 53:89–97, 1957

5. Hobson JA: The reciprocal interaction model of sleep cycle control: implication for PGO wave generation and dream amnesia, in Sleep and Memory. Edited by Drucker-Colin R, McGaugh J. New York, Academic Press, 1977, pp. 159–183

6. Pompeiano O: The neurophysiological mechanisms of the postural and motor events during desynchronized sleep. Res Publ Assoc Res Nerv Ment Dis 45:351–423, 1967

7. Jouvet M, Delorme F: Locus coeruleus et sommeil paradoxol. Soc Biol 159:895, 1965

8. Volkman F: Vision during voluntary saccadic eye movements. J Opt Soc Am 52:571–578, 1962

9. Bizzi E: Discharge pattern of single geniculate neurons during the rapid eye movements of sleep. J Neurophysiol 29:1087–1095, 1966

10. Evarts EV: Activity of individual cerebral neurons during sleep and arousal. Res Publ Assoc Res Nerv Ment Dis 45:319–337, 1967

11. Hobson JA, Goldfrank F, Snyder F: Sleep and respiration. J Psychiatr Res 3:79–90, 1965

12. Roffwarg HP, Dement WC, Muzio JN, et al: Dream imagery: relationship to rapid eye movements of sleep. Arch Gen Psychiatry 7:235–258, 1962

13. Pompeiano O: Sensory inhibition during motor activity in sleep, in Neurophysiological Basis of Normal and Abnormal Motor Activities. Edited by Yahr MD, Purpura DP. New York, Raven Press, 1967, pp. 323–375

14. Hobson JA: The sleep-dream cycle, a neurobiological rhythm, in Pathobiology Annual. Edited by Ioachim H. New York, Appleton-Century Crofts, 1975, pp 369–403

15. Zepelin H, Rechtschaffen A: Mammalian sleep, longevity and energy metabolism. Brain Behav Evol 10:425–470, 1974

16. Dement W: The occurrence of low-voltage fast electroencephalogram patterns during behavioral sleep in the cat. Electroencephalogr Clin Neurophysiol 10:291–296, 1958

17. Jouvet M: Recherches sur les structures nerveuses et les mecanismes responsables des differentes phases du sommeil physiologique. Arch Ital Biol 100:125–206, 1962

18. Pompeiano O, Morrison AR: Vestibular influences during sleep. I. Abolition of the rapid eye movements of desynchronized sleep following vestibular lesions. Arch Ital Biol 103:569–595, 1965

19. Magherini PC, Pompeiano O, Thoden U: Cholinergic mechanisms related to REM sleep. I. Rhythmic activity of the vestibulo-oculomotor system induced by an anticholinesterase in the decerebrate cat. Arch Ital Biol 110:234–259, 1972

20. Frederickson CJ, Hobson JA: Electrical stimulation of the brain stem and subsequent sleep. Arch Ital Biol 108:564–576, 1970

21. Amatruda TT, Black DA, McKenna TM, et al: Sleep cycle control and cholinergic mechanisms: differential effects of carbachol at pontine brain stem sites. Brain Res 98:501–515, 1975

22. Sitaram N, Wyatt RJ, Dawson S, et al: REM sleep induction by physostigmine infusion during sleep. Science 191:1281–1283, 1976

23. Cajal R: Histologie du System Nerveux, vol 1. Madrid, Consejo Superior de Investigaciones Cientificas, 1952

24. Brodal A: The Reticular Formation of the Brain Stem. Anatomical Aspects and Functional Correlations. Edinburgh, Oliver and Boyd, 1957

25. Scheibel ME, Scheibel AB: Anatomical basis of attention mechanisms in vertebrate brains, in The Neurosciences: A Study Program. Edited by Quarton GC, Melnechuk T, Schmitt FO. New York, Rockefeller University Press, 1967, pp 577–602

26. Dahlstrom A, Fuxe K: Evidence for the existence of monoamine-containing neurons in the central nervous system. I. Demonstration of monoamines in the cell bodies of brain stem neurons. Acta Physiol Scand 62:1–55, 1964

27. Hobson JA, McCarley RW, Pivik RT, et al: Selective firing by cat pontine brain stem neurons in desynchronized sleep. J Neurophysiol 37:497–511, 1974

28. Hobson JA, McCarley RW, Freedman R, et al: Time course of discharge rate changes by cat pontine brain

stem neurons during the sleep cycle. J Neurophysiol 37:1297–1309, 1974

29. Pivik RT, McCarley RW, Hobson JA: Eye movement-associated discharge in brain stem neurons during desynchronized sleep. Brain Res 121:59–76, 1977
30. McCarley RW, Hobson JA: Neuronal excitability modulation over the sleep cycle: a structural and mathematical model. Science 189:58–60, 1975
31. McCarley RW, Hobson JA: Discharge patterns of cat pontine brain stem neurons during desynchronized sleep. J Neurophysiol 38:751–766, 1975
32. Hobson JA, McCarley RW, Wyzinski PW: Sleep cycle oscillation: reciprocal discharge by two brainstem neuronal groups. Science 189:55–58, 1975
33. McGinty DJ, Harper RM, Fairbanks MK: 5 HT-containing neurons: unit activity in behaving cats, in Serotonin and Behavior. Edited by Barchas J, Usdin E. New York, Academic Press, 1973, pp 267–279
34. Aghajanian GK, Foote WE, and Sheard MH: Action of psychogenic drugs on single midbrain raphe neurons. J Pharmacol Exp Ther 171:178–187, 1970
35. Pompeiano O, Hoshino K: Central control of posture: reciprocal discharge by two pontine neuronal groups leading to suppression of decerebrate rigidity. Brain Res 116:131–138, 1976
36. Libet B: Generation of slow inhibitory and excitatory postsynaptic potentials. Fed Proc 29:1945–1955, 1970
37. Bloom FE: Role of cyclic nucleotides in central synaptic function. Rev Physiol Biochem Pharmacol 74:1–103, 1975

QUESTIONS FOR REFLECTION AND DISCUSSION:

1. What is the psychoanalytic theory of dreams, according to the authors?

2. How do the authors define a dream? What do they mean by a "hallucinoid" type of dream?

3. The activation-synthesis model allows that dreams might reflect "defensive distortions" of dream stimuli. What do they mean by defensive distortion? (Hint: You may wish to relate your answer to the psychoanalytic theory of dreams.)

4. What is meant by the terms *CNS, EEG, EMG, REM, oculomotor activity,* and *pontine brain stem*?

5. Part of the authors' theory is that spinal reflexes are inhibited when people are dreaming. Why would it be a "good idea," biologically or behaviorally speaking, if this were so?

6. How did the authors use microelectrodes with cats to test their hypotheses?

7. The Hobson and McCarley article contains a great deal of physiological detail. How much of this information should be understood and remembered by psychology students? (Hint: Your answer may depend on the field within psychology of interest to that student.)

8. What do the authors say is the "primary motivating force" for dreaming?

9. What do the authors mean when they write that the forebrain's elaboration of the brain stem stimulus a "synthetic" process rather than a "distorting" one?

10. What do the authors suggest may be the origins of some of the bizarre content of dreams?

III

LEARNING AND COGNITION

In lower organisms, much behavior is instinctive, or inborn. Salmon instinctively return to spawn in the stream where they were born, even after they have spent years roaming the seas. Robins instinctively sing the song of their species and build nests. But the variety and complexity of human behavior is largely learned. Experience is essential to learning to walk and acquiring the language of our parents and community. Humans learn to read, to compute numbers, and to surf the net. Humans learn right from wrong.

There would be no point to discussing learning if learning could not be remembered from second to second or from day to day. Learning is therefore intricately entwined with memory. Other related topics include thinking and intelligence. Thinking allows us to manipulate the information in memory so that we can make use of it. Intelligence has to do with our capacities to learn, remember, and think. These topics for many psychologists provide the core of psychology as a science.

This part contains the following primary sources:

11. Watson, J. B., & Rayner, R. (1920). Conditioned emotional reactions. *Journal of Experimental Psychology, 3,* 1–14.

Here is the classic experiment with "Little Albert," who has become something of an actor in a starring role in psychology. Reading it will tell you much about conditioning, something about ethics, and even more about the personal opinions of its authors.

12. Skinner, B. F. (1948). 'Superstition' in the pigeon. *Journal of Experimental Psychology, 38,* 168–172.

Why do some baseball pitchers touch their caps or rub their gloves across their noses before delivering every pitch? Why does a colleague of mine continue to meditate for ten minutes before every speech even though he has not had stagefright for years? The answers may not be simple, but in this classic experiment, B. F. Skinner relates them to behavior in a pigeon.

Wait a minute! How can a pigeon be superstitious, you ask? Skinner was a behaviorist, so the answer is that superstition is as superstition does. Read all about it.

13. Lang, P. J., & Melamed, B. B. (1969). Case report: Avoidance conditioning therapy of an infant with chronic ruminative vomiting. *Journal of Abnormal Psychology, 74,* 1–8.

   This case study speaks to the innovations in therapy made possible by learning theory. It also hints at why behavior modification may have obtained a questionable reputation in some quarters. In any event, this is one case in which behavior modification may very well have saved an infant's life. Read it and judge the ethics for yourself.

14. Miller, N. E. (1969). Learning of visceral and glandular responses. *Science, 163,* 434–445.

   Miller's research broke new ground, showing how animals (and presumably people) could learn to gain conscious control over bodily functions such as their heart rates and the emission of particular brain waves. If that sounds remarkable, perhaps it should; it is rather remarkable.

15. Bandura, A., Ross, D., & Ross, S. A. (1961). Transmission of aggression through imitation of aggressive models. *Journal of Abnormal and Social Psychology, 63,* 575–582.

   It should come as no surprise that one of the ways in which people learn is by watching other people. Why else would we ask others to demonstrate how to hit a gold ball or use new software? What was of value in Bandura's research is the evidence that children learn to imitate the violence they observe in the media—and will then use it.

16. Tolman, E. C. (1948). Cognitive maps in rats and men. *Psychological Review, 55,* 189–208.

   At mid-20th century, many behaviorists argued that organisms only learned to do things when they are rewarded or reinforced for doing so. Tolman had a suspicion that there can be a difference between learning and doing. His classic experiments show that even rats form mental maps of the environment which they can store away for future reference—and to obtain future rewards.

17. Craik, F. I. M., & Watkins, M. J. (1973). The role of rehearsal in short-term memory. *Journal of Verbal Learning and Verbal Behavior, 12,* 599–607.

   What's the best way to learn something? By repeating it endlessly? Not necessarily. Craik and Watson's research suggests that it may be more useful to make what we are trying to learn meaningful.

18. Loftus, E. F., & Palmer, J. C. (1973). Reconstruction of automobile destruction. *Journal of Verbal Learning and Verbal Behavior, 13,* 585–589, 599–607.

   Just what happened when that accident occurred? Were one or both cars going too fast? Are you sure? This classic experiment in the reconstruction of memory shows that memories are not perfect snapshots of experience. Rather, memories are altered by our biases, even by our language. Put it another way: our choice of words can "lead us" as witnesses to supply incorrect testimony.

19. Steele, C. M., & Aronson, J. (1995). Stereotype threat and the intellectual test performance of African Americans. *Journal of Personality and Social Psychology, 69,* 797–811.

As a group, African Americans do not perform as well as European Americans on standard intelligence tests. This important experiment by Claude Steele and Joshua Aronson suggests that many African Americans have an attitude that causes them to "self destruct" during tests, even when they are every bit as capable as European Americans.

The article by Thomas Bouchard and his colleagues found in Part I, "Sources of human psychological differences: The Minnesota study of twins reared apart," also addresses the thorny issue of contributors to intelligence.

Harcourt, Inc.

SOURCE

Watson, J. B., & Rayner, R. (1920).
Conditioned emotional reactions.
Journal of Experimental Psychology,
3, 1–14.

John B. Watson (1878–1958) was the son of a Southern farmer and beat up African Americans in his youth. He taught rats to find their way through a miniature maze that replicated the maze at King Henry VIII's retreat in the London suburbs. He had an affair with a student, Rosalie Rayner, which led the president of Johns Hopkins University to demand his resignation as chair of the Psychology Department. He helped make the "coffee break" a custom in the United States. Watson also popularized behaviorism and became president of the American Psychological Association in 1915.

Watson's aim was to show how most human behavior and emotional reactions—other than a few inborn reflexes—were the result of conditioning. Perhaps his most renowned experiment was with "Little Albert," who was conditioned by Watson and Rayner to fear a rat. Watson became passionate about Rosalie, who was more than 20 years younger than he. He was fired when their affair was discovered and left the academic world for New York, where he worked as a psychologist for the J. Walter Thompson advertising agency. He grew wealthy through successful ad campaigns for products such as Camel cigarettes, Johnson & Johnson Baby Powder, and Maxwell House Coffee—in which he used the idea of the coffee break.

He married Rosalie and the couple had two sons. Rosalie died from dysentery in her 30s and Watson, 58, never married again. He let himself go, dressed carelessly, and put on weight. A year before he died, the APA awarded him a gold medal for his contributions to psychology.

Watson's article with Rayner, "Conditioned Emotional Reactions," is a classic in the history of psychology.

Conditioned Emotional Reactions

JOHN B. WATSON & ROSALIE RAYNER

In recent literature various speculations have been entered into concerning the possibility of conditioning various types of emotional response, but direct experimental evidence in support of such a view has been lacking. If the theory advanced by Watson and Morgan[1] to the effect that in infancy the original emotional reaction patterns are few, consisting so far as observed of fear, rage and love, then there must be some simple method by means of which the range of stimuli which can call out these emotions and their compounds is greatly increased. Otherwise, complexity in adult response could not be accounted for. These authors without adequate experimental evidence advanced the view that this range was increased by means of conditioned reflex factors. It was suggested there that the early home life

---

[1] 'Emotional Reactions and Psychological Experimentation,' *American Journal of Psychology,* April, 1917, Vol. 28, pp. 163–174.

of the child furnishes a laboratory situation for establishing conditioned emotional responses. The present authors have recently put the whole matter to an experimental test.

Experimental work has been done so far on only one child, Albert B. This infant was reared almost from birth in a hospital environment; his mother was a wet nurse in the Harriet Lane Home for Invalid Children. Albert's life was normal: he was healthy from birth and one of the best developed youngsters ever brought to the hospital, weighing twenty-one pounds at nine months of age. He was on the whole stolid and unemotional. His stability was one of the principal reasons for using him as a subject in this test. We felt that we could do him relatively little harm by carrying out such experiments as those outlined below.

At approximately nine months of age we ran him through the emotional tests that have become a part of our regular routine in determining whether fear reactions can be called out by other stimuli than sharp noises and the sudden removal of support. Tests of this type have been described by the senior author in another place.[2] In brief, the infant was confronted suddenly and for the first time successively with a white rat, a rabbit, a dog, a monkey, with masks with and without hair, cotton wool, burning newspapers, etc. A permanent record of Albert's reactions to these objects and situations has been preserved in a motion picture study. Manipulation was the most usual reaction called out. *At no time did this infant ever show fear in any situation.* These experimental records were confirmed by the casual observations of the mother and hospital attendants. No one had ever seen him in a state of fear and rage. The infant practically never cried.

Up to approximately nine months of age we had not tested him with loud sounds. The test to determine whether a fear reaction could be called out by a loud sound was made when he was eight months, twenty-six days of age. The sound was that made by striking a hammer upon a suspended steel bar four feet in length and three-fourths of an inch in diameter. The laboratory notes are as follows:

> One of the two experimenters caused the child to turn its head and fixate her moving hand; the other, stationed back of the child, struck the steel bar a sharp blow. The child started violently, his breathing was checked and the arms were raised in a characteristic manner. On the second stimulation the same

thing occurred, and in addition the lips began to pucker and tremble. On the third stimulation the child broke into a sudden crying fit. This is the first time an emotional situation in the laboratory has produced any fear or even crying in Albert.

We had expected just these results on account of our work with other infants brought up under similar conditions. It is worth while to call attention to the fact that removal of support (dropping and jerking the blanket upon which the infant was lying) was tried exhaustively upon this infant on the same occasion. It was not effective in producing the fear response. This stimulus is effective in younger children. At what age such stimuli lose their potency in producing fear is not known. Nor is it known whether less placid children ever lose their fear of them. This probably depends upon the training the child gets. It is well known that children eagerly run to be tossed into the air and caught. On the other hand it is equally well known that in the adult fear responses are called out quite clearly by the sudden removal of support, if the individual is walking across a bridge, walking out upon a beam, etc. There is a wide field of study here which is aside from our present point.

The sound stimulus, thus, at nine months of age, gives us the means of testing several important factors. I. Can we condition fear of an animal, *e.g.,* a white rat, by visually presenting it and simultaneously striking a steel bar? II. If such a conditioned emotional response can be established, will there be a transfer to other animals or other objects? III. What is the effect of time upon such conditioned emotional responses? IV. If after a reasonable period such emotional responses have not died out, what laboratory methods can be devised for their removal?

I. The establishment of conditioned emotional responses. At first there was considerable hesitation upon our part in making the attempt to set up fear reactions experimentally. A certain responsibility attaches to such a procedure. We decided finally to make the attempt, comforting ourselves by the reflection that such attachments would arise anyway as soon as the child left the sheltered environment of the nursery for the rough and tumble of the home. We did not begin this work until Albert was eleven months, three days of age. Before attempting to set up a conditioned response we, as before, put him through all of the regular emotional tests. *Not the slightest sign of a fear response was obtained in any situation.*

The steps taken to condition emotional responses are shown in our laboratory notes.

---

[2] 'Psychology from the Standpoint of a Behaviorist,' p. 202.

11 Months 3 Days

1. White rat suddenly taken from the basket and presented to Albert. He began to reach for rat with left hand. Just as his hand touched the animal the bar was struck immediately behind his head. The infant jumped violently and fell forward, burying his face in the mattress. He did not cry, however.

2. Just as the right hand touched the rat the bar was again struck. Again the infant jumped violently, fell forward and began to whimper.

In order not to disturb the child too seriously no further tests were given for one week.

11 Months 10 Days

1. Rat presented suddenly without sound. There was steady fixation but no tendency at first to reach for it. The rat was then placed nearer, whereupon tentative reaching movements began with the right hand. When the rat nosed the infant's left hand, the hand was immediately withdrawn. He started to reach for the head of the animal with the forefinger of the left hand, but withdrew it suddenly before contact. It is thus seen that the two joint stimulations given the previous week were not without effect. He was tested with his blocks immediately afterwards to see if they shared in the process of conditioning. He began immediately to pick them up, dropping them, pounding them, etc. In the remainder of the tests the blocks were given frequently to quiet him and to test his general emotional state. They were always removed from sight when the process of conditioning was under way.

2. Joint stimulation with rat and sound. Started, then fell over immediately to right side. No crying.

3. Joint stimulation. Fell to right side and rested upon hands, with head turned away from rat. No crying.

4. Joint stimulation. Same reaction.

5. Rat suddenly presented alone. Puckered face, whimpered and withdrew body sharply to the left.

6. Joint stimulation. Fell over immediately to right side and began to whimper.

7. Joint stimulation. Started violently and cried, but did not fall over.

8. Rat alone. *The instant the rat was shown the baby began to cry. Almost instantly he turned sharply to the left, fell over on left side, raised himself on all fours and began to crawl away so rapidly that he was caught with difficulty before reaching the edge of the table.*

This was as convincing a case of a completely conditioned fear response as could have been theoretically pictured. In all seven joint stimulations were given to bring about the complete reaction. It is not unlikely had the sound been of greater intensity or of a more complex clang character that the number of joint stimulations might have been materially reduced. Experiments designed to define the nature of the sounds that will serve best as emotional stimuli are under way.

II. When a conditioned emotional response has been established for one object, is there a transfer? Five days later Albert was again brought back into the laboratory and tested as follows:

11 Months 15 Days

1. Tested first with blocks. He reached readily for them, playing with them as usual. This shows that there has been no general transfer to the room, table, blocks, etc.

2. Rat alone. Whimpered immediately, withdrew right hand and turned head and trunk away.

3. Blocks again offered. Played readily with them, smiling and gurgling.

4. Rat alone. Leaned over to the left side as far away from the rat as possible, then fell over, getting up on all fours and scurrying away as rapidly as possible.

5. Blocks again offered. Reached immediately for them, smiling and laughing as before.

The above preliminary test shows that the conditioned response to the rat had carried over completely for the five days in which no tests were given. The question as to whether or not there is a transfer was next taken up.

6. Rabbit alone. The rabbit was suddenly placed on the mattress in front of him. The reaction was pronounced. Negative responses began at once. He leaned as far away from the animal as possible, whimpered, then burst into tears. When the rabbit was placed in contact with him he buried his face in the mattress, then got up on all fours and crawled away, crying as he went. This was a most convincing test.

7. The blocks were next given him, after an interval. He played with them as before. It was observed by four people that he played

far more energetically with them than ever before. The blocks were raised high over his head and slammed down with a great deal of force.

8. Dog alone. The dog did not produce as violent a reaction as the rabbit. The moment fixation occurred the child shrank back and as the animal came nearer he attempted to get on all fours but did not cry at first. As soon as the dog passed out of his range of vision he became quiet. The dog was then made to approach the infant's head (he was lying down at the moment). Albert straightened up immediately, fell over to the opposite side and turned his head away. He then began to cry.

9. The blocks were again presented. He began immediately to play with them.

10. Fur coat (seal). Withdrew immediately to the left side and began to fret. Coat put close to him on the left side, he turned immediately, began to cry and tried to crawl away on all fours.

11. Cotton wool. The wool was presented in a paper package. At the end the cotton was not covered by the paper. It was placed first on his feet. He kicked it away but did not touch it with his hands. When his hand was laid on the wool he immediately withdrew it but did not show the shock that the animals or fur coat produced in him. He then began to play with the paper, avoiding contact with the wool itself. He finally, under the impulse of the manipulative instinct, lost some of his negativism to the wool.

12. Just in play W. put his head down to see if Albert would play with his hair. Albert was completely negative. Two other observers did the same thing. He began immediately to play with their hair. W. then brought the Santa Claus mask and presented it to Albert. He was again pronouncedly negative.

11 Months 20 Days

1. Blocks alone. Played with them as usual.

2. Rat alone. Withdrawal of the whole body, bending over to left side, no crying. Fixation and following with eyes. The response was much less marked than on first presentation the previous week. It was thought best to freshen up the reaction by another joint stimulation.

3. Just as the rat was placed on his hand the rod was struck. Reaction violent.

4. Rat alone. Fell over at once to left side. Reaction, practically as strong as on former occasion but no crying.

5. Rat alone. Fell over to left side, got up on all fours and started to crawl away. On this occasion there was no crying, but strange to say, as he started away he began to gurgle and coo, even while leaning far over to the left side to avoid the rat.

6. Rabbit alone. Leaned over to left side as far as possible. Did not fall over. Began to whimper but reaction not so violent as on former occasions.

7. Blocks again offered. He reached for them immediately and began to play.

All of the tests so far discussed were carried out upon a table supplied with a mattress, located in a small, well-lighted dark-room. We wished to test next whether conditioned fear responses so set up would appear if the situation were markedly altered. We thought it best before making this test to freshen the reaction both to the rabbit and to the dog by showing them at the moment the steel bar was struck. It will be recalled that this was the first time any effort had been made to directly condition response to the dog and rabbit. The experimental notes are as follows:

8. The rabbit at first was given alone. The reaction was exactly as given in test (6) above. When the rabbit was left on Albert's knees for a long time he began tentatively to reach out and manipulate its fur with forefingers. While doing this the steel rod was struck. A violent fear reaction resulted.

9. Rabbit alone. Reaction wholly similar to that on trial (6) above.

10. Rabbit alone. Started immediately to whimper, holding hands far up, but did not cry. Conflicting tendency to manipulate very evident.

11. Dog alone. Began to whimper, shaking head from side to side, holding hands as far away from the animal as possible.

12. Dog and sound. The rod was struck just as the animal touched him: A violent negative reaction appeared. He began to whimper, turned to one side, fell over and started to get up on all fours.

13. Blocks. Played with them immediately and readily.

On this same day and immediately after the above experiment Albert was taken into the large well-lighted lecture room belonging to the laboratory. He was placed on a table in the center of the room immediately under the skylight. Four people were present. The situation was thus very different from that which obtained in the small dark room.

1. Rat alone. No sudden fear reaction appeared at first. The hands, however, were held up and away from the animal. No positive manipulatory reactions appeared.

2. Rabbit alone. Fear reaction slight. Turned to left and kept face away from the animal but the reaction was never pronounced.

3. Dog alone. Turned away but did not fall over. Cried. Hands moved as far away from the animal as possible. Whimpered as long as the dog was present.

4. Rat alone. Slight negative reaction.

5. Rat and sound. It was thought best to freshen the reaction to the rat. The sound was given just as the rat was presented. Albert jumped violently but did not cry.

6. Rat alone. At first he did not show any negative reaction. When rat was placed nearer he began to show negative reaction by drawing back his body, raising his hands, whimpering, etc.

7. Blocks. Played with them immediately.

8. Rat alone. Pronounced withdrawal of body and whimpering.

9. Blocks. Played with them as before.

10. Rabbit alone. Pronounced reaction. Whimpered with arms held high, fell over backward and had to be caught.

11. Dog alone. At first the dog did not produce the pronounced reaction. The hands were held high over the head, breathing was checked, but there was no crying. Just at this moment the dog, which had not barked before, barked three times loudly when only about six inches from the baby's face. Albert immediately fell over and broke into a wail that continued until the dog was removed. The sudden barking of the hitherto quiet dog produced a marked fear response in the adult observers!

From the above results it would seem that emotional transfers do take place. Furthermore it would seem that the number of transfers resulting from an experimentally produced conditioned emotional reaction may be very large. In our observations we had no means of testing the complete number of transfers which may have resulted.

III. The effect of time upon conditioned emotional responses. We have already shown that the conditioned emotional response will continue for a period of one week. It was desired to make the time

test longer. In view of the imminence of Albert's departure from the hospital we could not make the interval longer than one month. Accordingly no further emotional experimentation was entered into for thirty-one days after the above test. During the month, however, Albert was brought weekly to the laboratory for tests upon right and left-handedness, imitation, general development, etc. No emotional tests whatever were given and during the whole month his regular nursery routine was maintained in the Harriet Lane Home. The notes on the test given at the end of this period are as follows:

1 Year 21 Days

1. Santa Claus mask. Withdrawal, gurgling, then slapped at it without touching. When his hand was forced to touch it, he whimpered and cried. His hand was forced to touch it two more times. He whimpered and cried on both tests. He finally cried at the mere visual stimulus of the mask.

2. Fur coat. Wrinkled his nose and withdrew both hands, drew back his whole body and began to whimper as the coat was put nearer. Again there was the strife between withdrawal and the tendency to manipulate. Reached tentatively with left hand but drew back before contact had been made. In moving his body to one side, his hand accidentally touched the coat. He began to cry at once, nodding his head in a very peculiar manner (this reaction was an entirely new one). Both hands were withdrawn as far as possible from the coat. The coat was then laid on his lap and he continued nodding his head and whimpering, withdrawing his body as far as possible, pushing the while at the coat with his feet but never touching it with his hands.

3. Fur coat. The coat was taken out of his sight and presented again at the end of a minute. He began immediately to fret, withdrawing his body and nodding his head as before.

4. Blocks. He began to play with them as usual.

5. The rat. He allowed the rat to crawl towards him without withdrawing. He sat very still and fixated it intently. Rat then touched his hand. Albert withdrew it immediately, then leaned back as far as possible but did not cry. When the rat was placed on his arm he withdrew his body and began to fret, nodding his head. The rat was then allowed to crawl against his chest. He first began to fret and then covered his eyes with both hands.

Harcourt, Inc.

6. Blocks. Reaction normal.

7. The rabbit. The animal was placed directly in front of him. It was very quiet. Albert showed no avoiding reactions at first. After a few seconds he puckered up his face, began to nod his head and to look intently at the experimenter. He next began to push the rabbit away with his feet, withdrawing his body at the same time. Then as the rabbit came nearer he began pulling his feet away, nodding his head, and wailing "da da." After about a minute he reached out tentatively and slowly and touched the rabbit's ear with his right hand, finally manipulating it. The rabbit was again placed in his lap. Again he began to fret and withdrew his hands. He reached out tentatively with his left hand and touched the animal, shuddered and withdrew the whole body. The experimenter then took hold of his left hand and laid it on the rabbit's back. Albert immediately withdrew his hand and began to suck his thumb. Again the rabbit was laid in his lap. He began to cry, covering his face with both hands.

8. Dog. The dog was very active. Albert fixated it intensely for a few seconds, sitting very still. He began to cry but did not fall over backwards as on his last contact with the dog. When the dog was pushed closer to him he at first sat motionless, then began to cry, putting both hands over his face.

These experiments would seem to show conclusively that directly conditioned emotional responses as well as those conditioned by transfer persist, although with a certain loss in the intensity of the reaction, for a longer period than one month. Our view is that they persist and modify personality throughout life. It should be recalled again that Albert was of an extremely phlegmatic type. Had he been emotionally unstable probably both the directly conditioned response and those transferred would have persisted throughout the month unchanged in form.

IV. "Detachment" or removal of conditioned emotional responses. Unfortunately Albert was taken from the hospital the day the above tests were made. Hence the opportunity of building up an experimental technique by means of which we could remove the conditioned emotional responses was denied us. Our own view, expressed above, which is possibly not very well grounded, is that these responses in the home environment are likely to persist indefinitely, unless an accidental method for removing them is hit upon. The importance of establishing some method must be apparent to all.

Had the opportunity been at hand we should have tried out several methods, some of which we may mention. (1) Constantly confronting the child with those stimuli which called out the responses in the hopes that habituation would come in corresponding to "fatigue" of reflex when differential reactions are to be set up. (2) By trying to "recondition" by showing objects calling out fear responses (visual) and simultaneously stimulating the erogenous zones (tactual). We should try first the lips, then the nipples and as a final resort the sex organs. (3) By trying to "recondition" by feeding the subject candy or other food just as the animal is shown. This method calls for the food control of the subject. (4) By building up "constructive" activities around the object by imitation and by putting the hand through the motions of manipulation. At this age imitation of overt motor activity is strong, as our present but unpublished experimentation has shown.

Incidental Observations

(a) Thumb sucking as a compensatory device for blocking fear and noxious stimuli. During the course of these experiments, especially in the final test, it was noticed that whenever Albert was on the verge of tears or emotionally upset generally he would continually thrust his thumb into his mouth. The moment the hand reached the mouth he became impervious to the stimuli producing fear. Again and again while the motion pictures were being made at the end of the thirty-day rest period, we had to remove the thumb from his mouth before the conditioned response could be obtained. This method of blocking noxious and emotional stimuli (fear and rage) through erogenous stimulation seems to persist from birth onward. Very often in our experiments upon the work adders with infants under ten days of age the same reaction appeared. When at work upon the adders both of the infants arms are under slight restraint. Often rage appears. They begin to cry, thrashing their arms and legs about. If the finger gets into the mouth crying ceases at once. The organism thus apparently from birth, when under the influence of love stimuli is blocked to all others.[3] This resort to sex stimulation when under

---

[3] The stimulus to love in infants according to our view is stroking of the skin, lips, nipples and sex organs, patting and rocking, picking up, etc. Patting and rocking (when not conditioned) are probably equivalent to actual stimulation of the sex organs. In adults of course, as every lover knows, vision, audition and olfaction soon become conditioned by joint stimulation with contact and kinaesthetic stimuli.

the influence of noxious and emotional situations, or when the individual is restless and idle, persists throughout adolescent and adult life. Albert, at any rate, did not resort to thumb sucking except in the presence of such stimuli. Thumb sucking could immediately be checked by offering him his blocks. These invariably called out active manipulation instincts. It is worth while here to call attention to the fact that Freud's conception of the stimulation of erogenous zones as being the expression of an original "pleasure" seeking principle may be turned about and possibly better described as a compensatory (and often conditioned) device for the blockage of noxious and fear and rage producing stimuli.

(b) Equal primacy of fear, love and possibly rage. While in general the results of our experiment offer no particular points of conflict with Freudian concepts, one fact out of harmony with them should be emphasized. According to proper Freudians sex (or in our terminology, love) is the principal emotion in which conditioned responses arise which later limit and distort personality. We wish to take sharp issue with this view on the basis of the experimental evidence we have gathered. Fear is as primal a factor as love in influencing personality. Fear does not gather its potency in any derived manner from love. It belongs to the original and inherited nature of man. Probably the same may be true of rage although at present we are not so sure of this.

The Freudians twenty years from now, unless their hypotheses change, when they come to analyze Albert's fear of a seal skin coat—assuming that he comes to analysis at that age—will probably tease from him the recital of a dream which upon their analysis will show that Albert at three years of age attempted to play with the pubic hair of the mother and was scolded violently for it. (We are by no means denying that this might in some other case condition it.) If the analyst has sufficiently prepared Albert to accept such a dream when found as an explanation of his avoiding tendencies, and if the analyst has the authority and personality to put it over, Albert may be fully convinced that the dream was a true revealer of the factors which brought about the fear.

It is probable that many of the phobias in psychopathology are true conditioned emotional reactions either of the direct or the transferred type. One may possibly have to believe that such persistence of early conditioned responses will be found only in persons who are constitutionally inferior. Our argument is meant to be constructive. Emotional disturbances in adults cannot be traced back to sex alone. They must be retraced along at least three collateral lines—to conditioned and transferred responses set up in infancy and early youth in all three of the fundamental human emotions.

QUESTIONS FOR REFLECTION AND DISCUSSION:

1. Why do you think that this article has such a prominent place in the history of psychology and is still referred to frequently by behavior therapists?

2. What are the roles of generalization and discrimination in this study? (Under what circumstances do they each occur?)

3. This article is a case study with one subject. Do you believe that the findings can be extended or generalized to other people? Why or why not?

4. What four methods does Watson recommend for the removal of conditioned emotional responses? Which method might land Watson in jail for child abuse if he were to try it today? Which method relies on the principle of extinction? Which method relies on what is referred to today as observational learning? Which methods are referred to today as counterconditioning?

5. Many ethical questions have been raised about Watson and Rayner's experiment with Albert. One is simply whether the treatment (the clanging of the steel and hammer) was too aversive and should not have been undertaken. What do you think?

6. Another ethical question raised about the experiment is why Watson and Rayner did not make every effort to "detach" or "remove" the conditioned emotional response in Albert. Watson clearly had ideas as to how to do so.

What reason does Watson offer as to why this was not done? Do you find the explanation credible? Why or why not?

7. In their final paragraph, the authors suggest that many adult phobias reflect childhood conditioning. They go on to write, "One may possibly have to believe that such persistence of early conditioned responses will be found only in persons who are constitutionally inferior." Do you have any thoughts on the attitudes displayed by the authors?

SOURCE

Skinner, B. F. (1948). 'Superstition'
in the pigeon. *Journal of
Experimental Psychology, 38,*
168–172.

During his first TV appearance Burrhus Frederic (B. F.) Skinner (1904–1990) was asked, "Would you, if you had to choose, burn your children or your books?" He said he would choose to burn his children, since his contribution to the future lay more in his writings than in his genes. Skinner delighted in controversy, and his response earned him additional TV appearances.

Skinner was born into a middle-class Pennsylvania family. As a youth he was always building things, always tinkering—scooters, sleds, wagons, rafts, slides, and merry-go-rounds. Later he would build the so-called Skinner box, which improved on Thorndike's puzzle box, as a way of studying operant behavior. He earned an undergraduate degree in English and turned to psychology only after failing to make his mark as a writer in New York's Greenwich Village.

A great popularizer of his own views, Skinner used reinforcement to teach pigeons to play basketball and the piano—sort of. On a visit to his daughter's grammar school class, it occurred to him that similar techniques might work with children. He therefore invented programmed learning. *Although he had earlier failed at writing, he gathered a cultish following when he published his novel* Walden II, *in which children were socialized from infancy into* wanting *to engage in prosocial behavior.*

Skinner and his followers have applied his principles not only to programmed learning but also to behavior modification programs for helping people with disorders ranging from substance abuse to phobias to sexual dysfunctions. He died eight days after receiving an unprecedented Lifetime Contribution to Psychology award from the American Psychological Association.

"'Superstition' in the Pigeon" is a classic in the psychology of learning, describing the power of reinforcement.

'Superstition' in the Pigeon

B. F. SKINNER
INDIANA UNIVERSITY

To say that a reinforcement is contingent upon a response may mean nothing more than that it follows the response. It may follow because of some mechanical connection or because of the mediation of another organism; but conditioning takes place presumably because of the temporal relation only, expressed in terms of the order and proximity of response and reinforcement. Whenever we present a state of affairs which is known to be reinforcing at a given drive, we must suppose that conditioning takes place, even though we have paid no attention to the behavior of the organism in making the presentation. A simple experiment demonstrates this to be the case.

A pigeon is brought to a stable state of hunger by reducing it to 75 percent of its weight when well fed. It is put into an experimental cage for a few minutes each day. A food hopper attached to the cage may be swung into place so that the pigeon can eat from it. A solenoid and a timing relay hold the hopper in place for five sec. at each reinforcement.

If a clock is now arranged to present the food hopper at regular intervals *with no reference whatsoever to the bird's behavior,* operant conditioning usually takes place. In six out of eight cases the resulting responses were so clearly defined that two observers could agree perfectly in counting instances. One bird was conditioned to turn counterclockwise about the cage, making two or three turns between reinforcements. Another repeatedly thrust its head into one of the upper corners of the cage. A third developed a 'tossing' response, as if placing its head beneath an invisible bar and lifting it repeatedly. Two birds developed a pendulum motion of the head and body, in which the head was extended forward and swung from right to left with a sharp movement followed by a somewhat slower return. The body generally followed the movement and a few steps might be taken when it was extensive. Another bird was conditioned to make incomplete pecking or brushing movements directed toward but not touching the floor. None of these responses appeared in any noticeable strength during adaptation to the cage or until the food hopper was periodically presented. In the remaining two cases, conditioned responses were not clearly marked.

The conditioning process is usually obvious. The bird happens to be executing some response as the hopper appears; as a result it tends to repeat this response. If the interval before the next presentation is not so great that extinction takes place, a second 'contingency' is probable. This strengthens the response still further and subsequent reinforcement becomes more probable. It is true that some responses go unreinforced and some reinforcements appear when the response has not just been made, but the net result is the development of a considerable state of strength.

With the exception of the counter-clockwise turn, each response was almost always repeated in the same part of the cage, and it generally involved an orientation toward some feature of the cage. The effect of the reinforcement was to condition the bird to respond to some aspect of the environment rather than merely to execute a series of movements. All responses came to be repeated rapidly between reinforcements—typically five or six times in 15 sec.

The effect appears to depend upon the rate of reinforcement. In general, we should expect that the shorter the intervening interval, the speedier and more marked the conditioning. One reason is that the pigeon's behavior becomes more diverse as time passes after reinforcement. A hundred photographs, each taken two sec. after withdrawal of the hopper, would show fairly uniform behavior. The bird would be in the same part of the cage, near the hopper, and probably oriented toward the wall where the hopper has disappeared or turning to one side or the other. A hundred photographs taken after 10 sec., on the other hand, would find the bird in various parts of the cage responding to many different aspects of the environment. The sooner a second reinforcement appears, therefore, the more likely it is that the second reinforced response will be similar to the first, and also that they will both have one of a few standard forms. In the limiting case of a very brief interval the behavior to be expected would be holding the head toward the opening through which the magazine has disappeared.

Another reason for the greater effectiveness of short intervals is that the longer the interval, the greater the number of intervening responses emitted without reinforcement. The resulting extinction cancels the effect of an occasional reinforcement.

According to this interpretation the effective interval will depend upon the rate of conditioning and the rate of extinction, and will therefore vary with the drive and also presumably between species. Fifteen sec. is a very effective interval at the drive level indicated above. One min. is much less so. When a response has once been set up, however, the interval can be lengthened. In one case it was extended to two min., and a high rate of responding was maintained with no sign of weakening. In another case, many hours of responding were observed with an interval of one min. between reinforcements.

In the latter case, the response showed a noticeable drift in topography. It began as a sharp movement of the head from the middle position to the left. This movement became more energetic, and eventually the whole body of the bird turned in the same direction, and a step or two would be taken. After many hours, the stepping response became the predominant feature. The bird made a well defined hopping step from the right to the left foot, meanwhile turning its head and body to the left as before.

When the stepping response became strong, it was possible to obtain a mechanical record by putting the bird on a large tambour directly connected with a small tambour which made a delicate electric contact each time stepping took place. By

Harcourt, Inc.

watching the bird and listening to the sound of the recorder it was possible to confirm the fact that a fairly authentic record was being made. It was possible for the bird to hear the recorder at each step, but this was, of course, in no way correlated with feeding. The record obtained when the magazine was presented once every min. resembles in every respect the characteristic curve for the pigeon under periodic reinforcement of a standard selected response. A well marked temporal discrimination develops. The bird does not respond immediately after eating, but when 10 or 15 or even 20 sec. have elapsed it begins to respond rapidly and continues until the reinforcement is received.

In this case it was possible to record the 'extinction' of the response when the clock was turned off and the magazine was no longer presented at any time. The bird continued to respond with its characteristic side to side hop. More than 10,000 responses were recorded before 'extinction' had reached the point at which few if any responses were made during a 10 or 15 min. interval. When the clock was again started, the periodic presentation of the magazine (still without any connection whatsoever with the bird's behavior) brought out a typical curve for reconditioning after periodic reinforcement, shown in Figure 12.01. The record had been essentially horizontal for 20 min. prior to the beginning of this curve. The first reinforcement had some slight effect and the second a greater effect. There is a smooth positive acceleration in rate as the bird returns to the rate of responding which prevailed when it was reinforced every min.

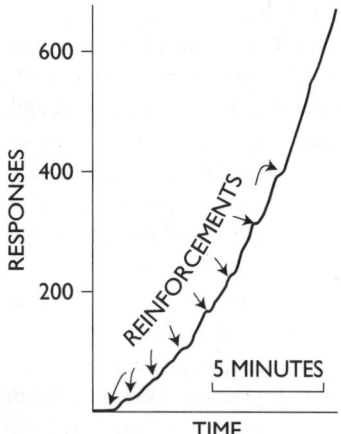

FIGURE 12.01

'Reconditioning' of a superstitious response after extinction. The response of hopping from right to left had been thoroughly extinguished just before the record was taken. The arrows indicate the automatic presentation of food at one-min. intervals without reference to the pigeon's behavior.

When the response was again extinguished and the periodic presentation of food then resumed, a different response was picked up. This consisted of a progressive walking response in which the bird moved about the cage. The response of hopping from side to side never reappeared and could not, of course, be obtained deliberately without making the reinforcement contingent upon the behavior.

The experiment might be said to demonstrate a sort of superstition. The bird behaves as if there were a causal relation between its behavior and the presentation of food, although such a relation is lacking. There are many analogies in human behavior. Rituals for changing one's luck at cards are good examples. A few accidental connections between a ritual and favorable consequences suffice to set up and maintain the behavior in spite of many unreinforced instances. The bowler who has released a ball down the alley but continues to behave as if he were controlling it by twisting and turning his arm and shoulder is another case in point. These behaviors have, of course, no real effect upon one's luck or upon a ball half way down an alley, just as in the present case the food would appear as often if the pigeon did nothing—or, more strictly speaking, did something else.

It is perhaps not quite correct to say that conditioned behavior has been set up without any previously determined contingency whatsoever. We have appealed to a uniform sequence of responses in the behavior of the pigeon to obtain an over-all net contingency. When we arrange a clock to present food every 15 sec., we are in effect basing our reinforcement upon a limited set of responses which frequently occur 15 sec. after reinforcement. When a response has been strengthened (and this may result from one reinforcement), the setting of the clock implies an even more restricted contingency. Something of the same sort is true of the bowler. It is not quite correct to say that there is no connection between his twisting and turning and the course taken by the ball at the far end of the alley. The connection was established before the ball left the bowler's hand, but since both the path of the ball and the behavior of the bowler are determined, some relation survives. The subsequent behavior of the bowler may have no effect upon the ball, but the behavior of the ball has an effect upon the bowler. The contingency, though not perfect, is enough to maintain the behavior in strength. The particular form of the behavior adopted by the bowler is due to induction from responses in which there is actual contact with the ball. It is clearly a movement appropriate to changing the ball's direction. But this does not invalidate the comparison, since we are not concerned with what response is selected but with why it persists in strength. In rituals for changing luck the inductive strengthening of a particular form of behavior is generally absent. The behavior of the pigeon in this experiment is of the latter sort, as the variety of responses obtained from different pigeons indicates. Whether there is any unconditioned behavior in the pigeon appropriate to a given effect upon the environment is under investigation.

The results throws some light on incidental behavior observed in experiments in which a discriminative stimulus is frequently presented. Such a stimulus has reinforcing value and can set up superstitious behavior. A pigeon will often develop some response such as turning, twisting, pecking near the locus of the discriminative stimulus, flapping its wings, etc. In much of the work to date in this field the interval between presentations of the discriminative stimulus has been one min. and many of these superstitious responses are short-lived. Their appearance as the result of accidental correlations with the presentation of the stimulus is unmistakable.

QUESTIONS FOR REFLECTION AND DISCUSSION:

1. Skinner was a great tinkerer as well as a psychologist. What methodology did he use in this study?

2. Why should reinforcement be delivered rapidly after a response occurs if it (the reinforcement) is to increase the frequency of that response?

3. What is a discriminative stimulus?

4. Why did the pigeons in Skinner's study learn to do different things?

5. Why is the word *superstition* used to describe the behavior of the pigeons in the study?

6. Baseball players, especially pitchers, are often said to be superstitious. Some pitchers always touch their caps before letting the ball go, or look to a certain part of the field or stands. How did they become superstitious? Can their superstition be considered similar to "superstition" in the pigeon? Explain.

7. Have you known anyone who became "superstitious" after experiencing good fortune of some kind? Describe.

8. Can you think of experiences that can lead to superstition in humans but not in pigeons?

SOURCE

Lang, P. J., & Melamed, B. B. (1969). Case report: Avoidance conditioning therapy of an infant with chronic ruminative vomiting. *Journal of Abnormal Psychology, 74*, 1–8.
Copyright © 1969 by the American Psychological Association. Reprinted with permission.

One of the strengths of learning theory and of the therapy techniques derived from learning theory—called behavior therapy *or* behavior modification *techniques—is that they have been helpful with serious human problems and might not have been thought of from the vantage point of other theories. For example, learning theory has led to the innovation of techniques for the management of psychiatric wards (e.g., selective reinforcement and the token economy), for reducing maladaptive behavior (e.g., smoking and child molestation), and as shown in the current primary source, chronic vomiting by an infant. So-called insight-oriented therapies like psychoanalysis and client-centered therapy have not been of reliable benefit in such cases.*

The infant in the study was 9 months old. He was throwing up his food and his health was deteriorating. How does one do "therapy" with a child like this? The child is unlikely to follow suggestions or commands, even if he understands them. You certainly cannot interview the child to try to understand whether deep-seated, unconscious conflicts lie at the roots of his problems. Yet Peter Lang and Barbara Melamed were able to use principles of learning to devise a method of therapy that may well have saved the child's life.

Case Report: Avoidance Conditioning Therapy of an Infant with Chronic Ruminative Vomiting

PETER J. LANG & BARBARA G. MELAMED
UNIVERSITY OF WISCONSIN

This paper reports the treatment of a 9-mo.-old male infant whose life was seriously endangered by persistent vomiting and chronic rumination. An aversive conditioning paradigm, employing electric shock, significantly reduced the frequency of this maladaptive response pattern in a few, brief treatment sessions. Electromyographic records were used in assessing response characteristics of the emesis, and in determining the shock contingencies used in therapy. Cessation of vomiting and rumination was accompanied by weight gains, increased activity level, and general responsiveness to people.

A variety of techniques have been used in the treatment of persistent vomiting in infants and children. In general these therapies are tailored to the known or hypothesized causes of the disorder. Thus, the presence of functional disturbance in the intestinal tract would encourage the use of pharmacologic agents—"tranquilizers," antinauseants, or antiemetics. If gastric, anatomical anomalies can be diagnosed, their surgical removal often proves to be the most effective treatment. Animal studies suggest that surgical manipulation of the central nervous system may also become a vehicle for emesis control (Borison, 1959).

When diagnosis excludes obvious, organic antecedents, both the etiology and treatment of the disorder appear less certain. However, clinical workers have described an apparently "psychosomatic" vomiting in children which is generally accompanied by a ruminative rechewing of the vomitus. In reviewing the syndrome, Richmond, Eddy, and Green (1958) adhere to the widely held psychoanalytic hypothesis that it results from a disruption in the mother-infant relationship. They suggest that the condition is brought about by the inability of the mother to fulfill an adult psychosexual role which is reflected in marital inadequacy. She is unable to give up her own dependent needs and is incapable of providing warm, comfortable, and intimate physical care for the infant. This lack of comfort from without causes the infant to seek and recreate such gratification from within. Thus, in attempting to regain some satisfaction from the feeding situation, he regurgitates his food and retains it in his mouth. The recommended treatment is the interruption in the mother-infant relationship by hospitalization and the provision of a stimulating, warm environment with a substitute mother figure. This method achieved success in the four cases reviewed. Berlin, McCullough, Lisha, and Szurek (1957) offer a similar psychoanalytic interpretation in reporting a case study of a 4-yr.-old child hospitalized for 8 mo. at Langley-Porter Clinic. Psychotherapy, involving concomitant counseling to improve the relationship between the parents, led to an alleviation of the child's vomiting reaction.

From the point of view espoused by learning theorists, emesis and rumination may be learned habits. In point of fact, vomiting has been clearly demonstrated as a conditioned response in at least three independent studies (Collins & Tatum, 1925; Kleitman & Crisler, 1927; Pavlov, 1927). This prompts the corollary hypothesis that such behavior could be eliminated directly by counterconditioning procedures.

A number of case reports indicate that considerable success may be achieved in modifying alimentary habits in the clinic setting. Both Bachrach, Erwin, and Mohr (1965) and Meyer[1] successfully treated adult anorexic patients by making various

social and physical reinforcers contingent on eating behavior or weight gain. Lang (1965) described the therapy of a young adult patient who became nauseous and vomited under social stress. In this case, counterconditioning methods increased the patient's tolerance of formerly aversive social situations, and thus markedly reduced the frequency of nausea and emesis.

The only study reviewed, attempting to apply conditioning methods specifically in the treatment of ruminative vomiting was reported by White and Taylor (1967). Electric shock was applied to two mentally retarded patients (23-yr.-old female, 14-yr.-old male) whenever throat, eye, or coughing gestures signaled rumination. They suggest that the shock served to distract the patient and he engaged in other activities rather than ruminating. Significant improvement occurred after 1 wk. of treatment, and gains were maintained at a 1-mo. follow-up.

The following case report illustrates the efficacy of aversive conditioning in reversing the vomiting and rumination of a 9-mo.-old infant whose life was endangered by this behavior. The case is of general interest because of the extreme youth of the patient, the speed of treatment, and the fact that conditioning procedures were undertaken only after other treatments had been either ruled out by diagnostic procedures, or had been given a reasonable trial without success. These data also have further implications for the understanding of aversive conditioning procedures in clinical practice.

History of Problem and Family Background

A. T. at the age of 9 mo. was admitted to the University Hospital for failure to retain food and chronic rumination. This infant had undergone three prior hospitalizations for his persistent vomiting after eating and failure to gain weight. Born in an eastern state after an uneventful 39-wk. pregnancy, the patient was bottle fed and gained steadily from a birth weight of 9 lb. 4 oz. to 17 lb. at 6 mo. of age. Vomiting was first noted during the fifth month, and increased in severity to the point where the patient vomited 10–15 min. after each meal. This activity was often associated with vigorous thumbsucking, placing fingers in his mouth, blotchiness of the face, and ruminating behavior. The mother remarked that the start of vomiting may have coincided with her indisposition due to a broken ankle which forced the family to live with maternal grandparents for several weeks. Some friction was reported between

---

[1] Meyer, V. Personal communication, 1964.

the patient's mother and her own adoptive mother concerning care of the child. The patient's father is a part-time college student and the family received financial assistance from the paternal grandfather, a successful dentist. At the time of the most recent hospitalization, the social worker's report suggested that the parents were making a marginal marital adjustment.

Three brief periods of hospitalization which included medical tests (gastrointestinal fluoroscopy, EEG, and neuropsychological testing) failed to find an organic basis for this persistent regurgitation. An exploratory operation was performed and a cyst on the right kidney removed, with no discernible effect on his condition. The patient had no history of head trauma. One previous incident of persistent vomiting in a paternal uncle was noted to be of very short duration. The paternal grandfather and two uncles are reported to suffer ulcers.

Several treatment approaches were applied without success. Dietary changes (Pro-Sobee, skim milk), the administration of antinauseants, and various mechanical maneuvers to improve the feeding situation (different positions, small amounts at each feeding, burping) gave short-lived, if any, relief. As thumbsucking often preceded the response, restraints were tried. However, this did little to reduce the frequency of emesis. An attempt had been made to initiate intensive nursing care "to establish and maintain a one-to-one relationship and to provide the child with warm, friendly, and secure feelings [nurse's chart]." This had to be abandoned because it was not inhibiting the vomiting and some observers felt that it increased the child's anxiety and restlessness.

At the time the present investigators were called in, the infant was in critical condition, down to a weight of 12 lb., and being fed through a nasogastric pump. The attending physician's clinical notes attest that conditioning procedures were applied as a last attempt, "in view of the fact that therapy until now has been unsuccessful and the life of the child is threatened by continuation of this behavior."

Therapeutic Procedure and Results

The patient was given a private room, continuous nursing care, and assigned a special graduate nurse to assist in the conditioning procedures. The authors closely observed the infant for 2 days during and after normal feeding periods. He reliably regurgitated most of his food intake within 10 min. of each feeding and continued to bring up small amounts

throughout the day. Observers on the hospital staff suggested that vomiting was originally induced by thumb pressure at the back of the throat. However, at this stage thumb manipulations were not a necessary part of the vomiting sequence. He did protest, however, if hand restraint was enforced. His frail appearance and general unresponsiveness, made him a pathetic looking child as seen from a photograph taken just prior to treatment (Fig. 13.01).

In an attempt to obtain a clearer picture of the patterning of his response, electromyograph (EMG) activity at three sites was monitored on a Gilson Polygraph. Responses leading up to and into the vomiting sequence reliably coincided with the nurse's concurrent description of the sequence of behavior. Figure 13.02 illustrates the typical response pattern. The uppermost channel of information represents muscle potentials recorded just under the chin, and shows the sucking behavior which usually preceded vomiting; the lowest channel is an integrated record taken from the throat muscles of the neck; the center channel which monitors the upper chest region is largely EKG artifact. It can be noted from this segment that the onset of vomiting is clearly accompanied by vigorous throat movements indicated by rhythmic, high-frequency, high-amplitude activity, in contrast with quiescent periods and periods where crying predominated.

The authors were concerned with eliminating the inappropriate vomiting, without causing any fundamental disturbance in the feeding behavior of the child. Fortunately, the child did not vomit during feeding, and the sucking and vomiting could be distinguished readily on the EMG. After 2 days of monitoring, conditioning procedures were initiated. The aversive conditioning paradigm called for brief and repeated shock (approximately 1 sec. long with a 1-sec. interpulse interval) as soon as vomiting occurred, continuing until the response was terminated and an effort was made to initiate shock at the first sign of reverse peristalsis, but not during the preceding sucking behavior. The contingency was determined from the nurse's observations of the patient and the concurrent EMG records. In general, the nurse would signal as soon as she thought an emesis was beginning. If EMG confirmed the judgment, shock was delivered. Occasionally, the EMG would initiate this sequence, with the observational judgment following.[2] Shock was delivered by means of a Harvard Inductorium to electrodes placed on the calf of the patient's leg. A 3,000-cps tone was

---

[2] Particular thanks are due to Mary Kachoy, the nurse who assisted at all the therapy sessions.

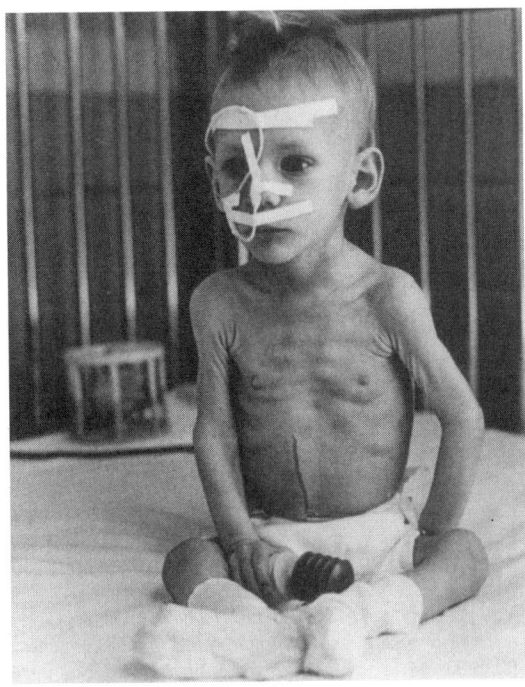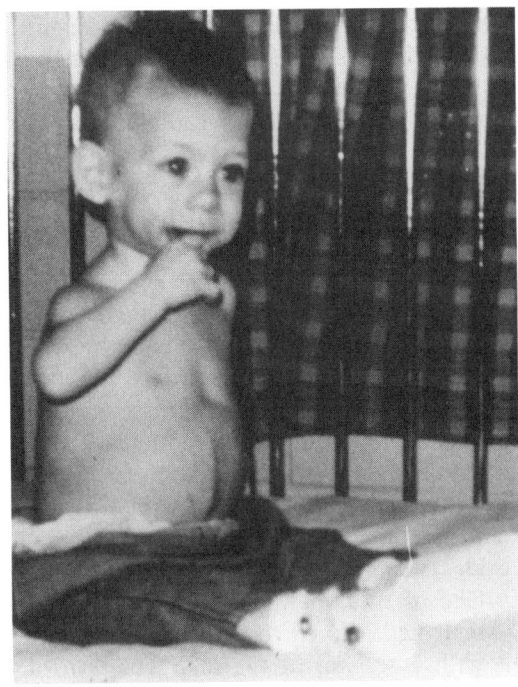

FIGURE 13.01

The photograph at the left was taken during the observation period just prior to treatment. (It clearly illustrates the patient's debilitated condition—the lack of body fat, skin hanging in loose folds. The tape around the face holds tubing for the nasogastric pump. The photograph at the right was taken on the day of discharge from the hospital, 13 days after the first photo. The 26% increase in body weight already attained is easily seen in the full, more infantlike face, the rounded arms, and more substantial trunk.)

temporally coincident with each shock presentation.[3] Sessions were chosen following feeding to insure some frequency of response. Each session lasted less than 1 hour.

After two sessions shock was rarely required. The infant would react to the shock by crying and cessation of vomiting. By the third session only one or two brief presentations of shock were necessary

[3] Shock level was first determined by applying the electrodes to the *E*s, who judged it to be quite painful and unpleasant. Intensity was incremented slightly during the first and second sessions on the basis of the patient's response, but was subsequently unchanged. This inductorium does not permit for exact or wholly reliable measures of current level. However, under the conditions of treatment described here, the average current was within a range of from .10 to .30 ma., with a cycle frequency of approximately 50 cps. It should be borne in mind that pulses from an inductorium vary widely in amplitude, and the authors' instrument produced some spikes over 10 ma. Electrodes were first applied to the ball of the foot and then moved to the calf for reasons stated in the text. The accompanying tone was generated by a Hewlett-Packard signal generator and administered by a small oval speaker in a free field. The intensity was loud but not harmful (approximately 80–95 db.), and varied considerably because of spontaneous changes in the infant's position. It was employed in order to increase the density of the reinforcer and on the possibility that the therapists might employ it alone if shock proved to have negative side effects.

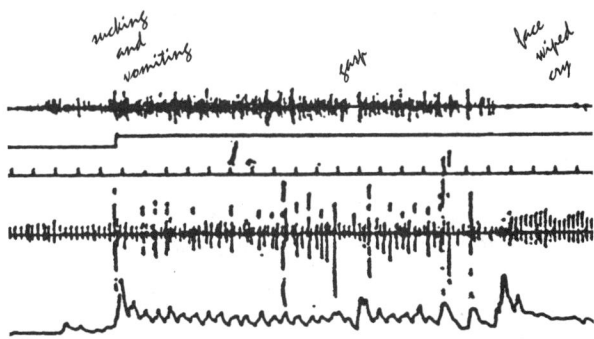

FIGURE 13.02

Three channels of EMG activity are presented. (The nurse observer's comments are written just above the first channel. The intense muscle activity on this line is associated with sucking behavior, recorded from electrodes on the underside of the chin. The second channel is just below the one pulse per second, timing line, and was taken from electrodes on the upper chest, at the base of the throat. The EKG dominates this channel, with some local muscle activity. Electrodes straddling the esophagus yielded the lowest line, which in this integrated record clearly shows the rhythmic pulsing of the vomiting response.)

to cause cessation of any vomiting sequence. Figure 13.03 illustrates the typical sequence of a conditioning trial.

The course of therapy is indicated in Figure 13.04. Few shocks were administered over the first day of treatment, and both the time spent vomiting and the average length of each vomiting period were abruptly reduced. After only two sessions it seemed that the infant was anticipating the unpleasant consequences of his behavior. He would begin to suck vigorously using his thumb, and then he would remove his thumb and cry loudly.

The data graphed (Figure 13.04) for the second treatment session represent those reinforcers that the authors are certain were delivered. Early in this session, it became obvious that the infant was not receiving the majority of the administered shocks. The electrodes were at that time attached to the plantar surface of the foot. Observation suggested that the patient had learned to curl his foot, either coincident with emesis or at the first sensation of shock, so as to lift the electrodes off the skin and thus avoid the painful stimulus. At this point, the electrodes were relocated on the calf, and conditioning proceeded normally. If the shock administrations prior to this procedural change are added to those on the graph, Day 3, afternoon figures for emesis period, percentage of emesis, and shock, respectively, are 11 sec., 21.6% and 77.

By the sixth session the infant no longer vomited during the testing procedures. He would usually fall asleep toward the middle of the hour. Figure 13.05 indicates the sequence of response demonstrating the replacement of vigorous sucking with

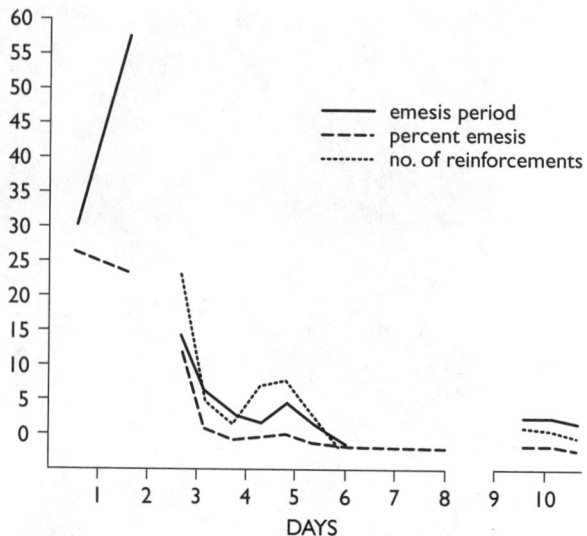

FIGURE 13.04

The abscissa describes successive days (morning and afternoon) on which observation or treatment was accomplished. ("Emesis period" is the length of any continuous period of vomiting. "Percentage of emesis" is the total time spent vomiting divided by the time observed. Sessions varied from 16 min. to 60 min. Treatment began on Day 3 which included two unshocked emesis periods. In Session 10 tone alone was presented on one trial. It is of interest to note that following therapy, nursing staff reported that they could now block the very rare vomiting periods with a sharp handclap.)

what the nursing observers described as a "pacifier" use of the thumb.

To vary the conditions under which learning would take place, thereby providing for transfer of effects, the sessions were scheduled at different hours of the day, and while the infant was being held, playing on the floor, as well as lying in bed. Nursing staff reported a progressive decrease in his

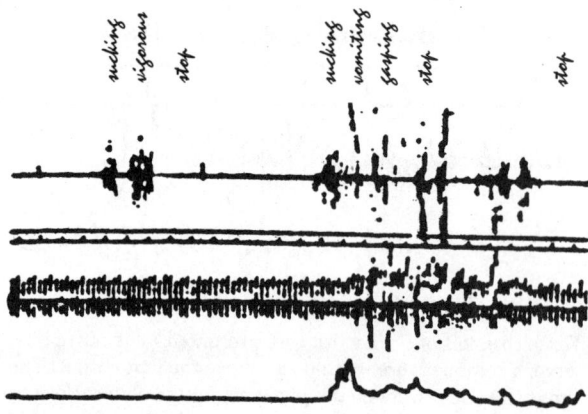

FIGURE 13.03

The electrode positions are the same as in Figure 13.02. (The top line shows the point at which two brief shocks were administered. It may be noted that they follow closely on the first pulse of the vomiting response and that the rhythmic regurgitation observed in Figure 13.02 never gets underway.)

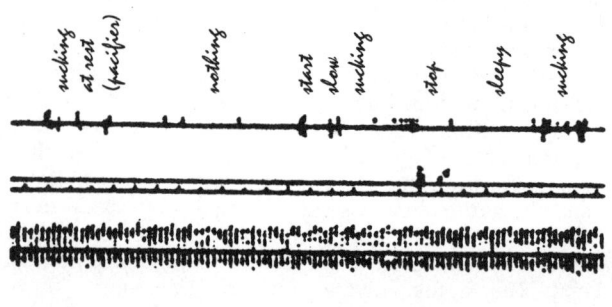

FIGURE 13.05

The above segment is representative of behavior near the end of a conditioning session. (Only mild sucking activity is apparent in the upper EMG channel. The electrode positions are the same as in Figure 13.02.)

ruminating and vomiting behavior during the rest of the day and night, which paralleled the reduction observed across therapy sessions.

After three sessions in which there was no occurrence of vomiting, the procedure was discontinued. Two days later there was some spontaneous recovery, which included some vigorous sucking, with a little vomiting and rumination. Three additional sessions were initiated to maintain the reduced frequency of the response (see Fig. 13.04). Except for a brief slackening prior to these trials, there was a steady, monotonic increase in his weight as shown in Figure 13.06. In general, his activity level increased, he became more interested in his environment, enjoyed playroom experience, and smiled and reached out to be held by the nurse and other visitors.

The mother was reintroduced the day following the last conditioning trial. She took over some of the patient's caretaking needs, including feedings. There was no marked change in his ruminating behavior at this time. The mother responded well and her child reciprocated her attention. He was discharged from the hospital 5 days later, after exhibiting almost no ruminating behavior. The remarkable contrast in his physical appearance is noted in a photograph taken on the day of discharge (Fig. 13.01).

Follow-up

Correspondence with the mother indicated that there was no further need for treatment. A. T. was eating well and gaining weight regularly. She reported that any thumbsucking or rumination was easily arrested by providing him with other forms of stimulation. He was beginning to seek attention from other people and enjoyed the company of other children. One month following discharge from the hospital, he was seen for a physical check-up. He appeared as a healthy looking 21-lb. child and, aside from a slight anemic condition, was found fully recovered by the attending physician. His local physician reported on a visit 5 mo. later when his weight was 26 lb., 1 oz. "His examinations were negative for any problems. . . . He was eating quite well . . . no vomiting had recurred. He was alert, active and attentive. A snapshot taken by the mother a few weeks before this examination is reproduced in Figure 13.07. One year after treatment

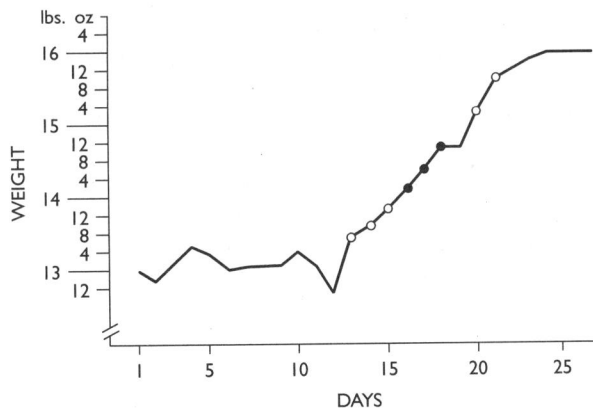

FIGURE 13.06

The infant's body weight as determined from the nursing notes is plotted over time, from well before conditioning therapy was instituted to the day of discharge from the hospital. (Days on which conditioning sessions occurred are marked by circles on the curve. Reinforcers were delivered only on days marked by open circles. The decline in body weight in the few days just prior to therapy was probably occasioned by the discontinuance of the nasogastric pump, in favor of normal feeding procedures. The marked weight gain from Day 13 to 18 is coincident with the first 6 days of therapy. The temporary reduction in weight increase, associated with a resumption of emesis, is apparent at Day 19. The additional conditioning trials appear to have acted immediately to reinstate weight gain.)

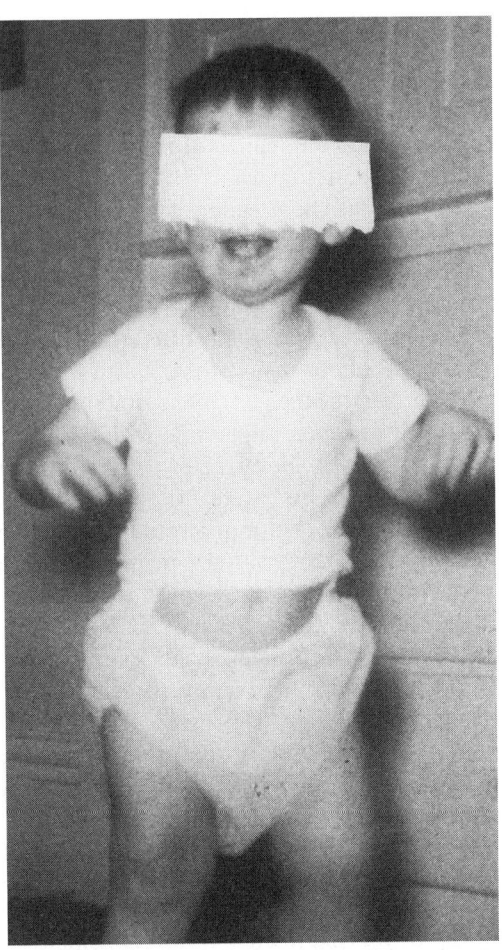

FIGURE 13.07

The patient 5 mo. after treatment.

he continues to thrive. Mother and father are both pleased with his development, and no further treatment is indicated.

Discussion

The rapid recovery of this 9-mo.-old male infant following brief aversive conditioning therapy, argues for the effectiveness of behavioral modification in the treatment of this type of psychosomatic disorder. The vomiting and ruminating were treated as maladaptive behavior patterns, and electric shock was used to inhibit a previously well-established response sequence. Elimination of the response was accompanied by increase in the infant's responsiveness to people, as well as substantial weight gains, and physiological improvement.

Treatment was undertaken without analysis of the disorder's antecedents. Nevertheless, the family history of the infant could be construed as consistent with other cases in the literature. One clinical worker suggested that a feeling of hostility dominated this infant's home. It is true that the parents' wedding was attended by difficulties and the subsequent birth of the patient occurred before the parents were fully prepared for this responsibility. Furthermore, the mother later expressed anxiety about her marriage and complained of the problem of balancing the separate demands of father and child. She also reported her feeling that her own stepmother had not provided a good maternal model. As a consequence she felt inadequate herself and uncertain in the role.

The caseworker's notes are thus rich in "dynamics," and while one is unable to establish the relative accuracy or significance of these statements, it is clear that this case is interpretable within traditional personality theories. Nevertheless, therapies generated by this orientation were not successful in the present case. In deference, it should also be noted that "one-to-one" care was not maintained as long or as consistently as in many cases reported in the literature, and despite evidence of some marital discord, no extensive counseling of the parents was undertaken. However, like many psychiatric treatments, the above are expensive of professional personnel and prolonged in duration. The aversive conditioning procedures used here achieved success in little more than a week, and considering the developing danger to the child's life, speed was of more than usual importance.

No evidence of "symptom substitution" was observed following treatment. On the other hand, positive social behavior increased coincident with the successful conditioning therapy. The infant became more responsive to adults, smiled more frequently, and seemed to be more interested in toys and games than he had been previously. An analogous improvement in social behavior was noticed in the defective adults treated by White and Taylor (1967). Lovaas, Freitag, Gold, and Kassorla (1965) and Lovaas, Schaeffer, and Simmons (1965) have cited similar effects following the avoidance conditioning of tantrum behavior in autistic children. The latter investigators suggest that the *E*s attained secondary reinforcing value because of their association with shock reduction. This provides the basis for training the children to exhibit affectionate patterns toward adults. In the present case this contingency was very imprecise, and it is not clear that the above mechanism mediated change. What could be called normal infant behavior increased regularly, as the emesis decreased. The social environment appeared simply to replace ruminating as the infant's focus of attention.

Aversive conditioning has been applied widely in adult therapy as well as with autistic children. Eysenck and Rachman (1965) and Feldman (1966) describe its use in treating alcoholic and sexual disorders. However, one hesitates to interpret these findings in a straightforward manner. Adult patients may submit to aversive conditioning procedures from a variety of motives, and cognitive factors may blunt the impact or distort the meaning of aversive stimuli. The present case is of particular interest because these procedures were successful in treating an apparently normal child. Furthermore, the absence of language and the limited cognitive development achieved at this age permit one to interpret this change as avoidance conditioning, unmitigated by the above factors.

Finally, it should be noted that the present case represents a productive use of psychophysiologic recording in therapy. Not only did the EMG provide extensive documentation of the response, but concurrent recording was of considerable help in guiding the treatment effort. Specifically, these records confirmed in an objective manner external observations of mouth and throat movements which seemed to precede emesis. Furthermore, they extended these observations, helping the authors to specify those aspects of the response which were unique to the vomiting sequence, thus assuring that shock was never delivered following noncontingent behavior. Finally, observation of the recordings during therapy probably reduced the latency of reinforcement, particularly during the early trials when the validity of external signs seemed less certain, and provided the clearest indicator of the end of the response when shock was promptly terminated. While the importance of this information to the results obtained cannot be unequivocally established, it certainly increased the confidence of the therapists in their method, and, in turn, the speed and precision with which they proceeded. The further exploration of physiological analysis in the therapeutic setting is encouraged.

References

1. Bachrach, A. J., Erwin, W. J., & Mohr, J. P. The control of eating behavior in an anorexic by operant conditioning techniques. In L. P. Ullman & L. Krasner (Eds.), *Case studies in behavior modification.* New York: Holt, Rinehart & Winston, 1965.
2. Berlin, I. N., McCullough, G., Lisha, E. S., & Szurek, S. Intractable episodic vomiting in a three-year old child. *Psychiatric Quarterly,* 1957, **31,** 228–249.
3. Borison, H. L. Effect of ablation of medullary emetic chemoreceptor trigger zone on vomiting response to cerebral intra-ventricular injection of adrenaline, apomorphine and pilocarpine in the cat. *Journal of Physiology,* 1959, **147,** 172–177.
4. Collins, K. H., & Tatum, A. L. A conditioned salivary reflex established by chronic morphine poisoning. *American Journal of Physiology,* 1925, **74,** 14–15.
5. Eysenck, H. J., & Rachman, S. *The causes and cures of neurosis.* San Diego, Calif.: Knapp, 1965.
6. Feldman, M. P. Aversion therapy for sexual deviations: A critical review. *Psychological Bulletin,* 1966, **65,** 65–79.
7. Kleitman, N., & Crisler, G. A quantitative study of the conditioned salivary reflex. *American Journal of Physiology,* 1927, **79,** 571–614.
8. Lang, P. J. Behavior therapy with a case of nervous anorexia. In L. P. Ullmann & L. Krasner (Eds.), *Case studies in behavior modification.* New York: Holt, Rinehart & Winston, 1965.
9. Lovaas, O. I., Freitag, G., Gold, V., & Kassorla, I. Experimental studies in childhood schizophrenia: Analysis of self-destructive behavior. *Journal of Experimental Child Psychology,* 1965, **2,** 67–84.
10. Lovaas, O. I., Schaeffer, B., & Simmons, J. Building social behavior in autistic children by use of electric shock. *Journal of Experimental Research in Personality,* 1965, **1,** 99–109.
11. Pavlov, I. P. *Conditioned reflexes: An investigation of the physiological activity of the cerebral cortex.* Lecture III, Oxford, England; Oxford University Press, 1927.
12. Richmond, J. B., Eddy, E., & Green, M. Rumination: A psychosomatic syndrome of infancy. *Pediatrics,* 1958, **22,** 49–55.
13. White, J. D., & Taylor, D. Noxious conditioning as a treatment for rumination. *Mental Retardation,* 1967, **5,** 30–33.

QUESTIONS FOR REFLECTION AND DISCUSSION:

1. What do the authors report to be the psychoanalytic interpretation of "psychosomatic" ruminative vomiting in children?

2. What treatments had been tried before Lang and Melamed used avoidance conditioning?

3. What aversive stimulus did the researchers use to inhibit the vomiting? What ethical considerations are involved in using such a treatment with a sickly, 9-month-old infant? Do you think that the treatment was justified? Why or why not?

4. What is "spontaneous recovery"? What instance of spontaneous recovery occurred during treatment?

5. The authors note, "Treatment was undertaken without analysis of the disorder's antecedents," and they admit that the family history can be seen as consistent with psychoanalytic theory. Do the possible "dynamics" of the case matter as long as the treatment method worked? What do you think?

6. What is the "symptom-substitution hypothesis" as expressed by psychoanalytic theorists who are critical of behavior modification? Did symptom substitution occur in this case?

7. Was it necessary for the infant to "understand" what was happening during aversive conditioning in order for learning to occur? Explain.

8. Why is this case important in the history of psychology and in the literature concerning behavior modification?

Neal E. Miller's early career in psychology was highlighted by books such as Frustration and Aggression *(1939),* Social Learning and Imitation *(1941), and* Personality and Psychotherapy *(1950), which he wrote with John Dollard and other authors. The works were based on learning theory. The thesis of* Social Learning and Imitation *was that people discover that they can obtain rewards by imitating other people. As a result, they acquire a drive to imitate.* Personality and Psychotherapy *is a fascinating translation of psychoanalytic therapy into learning theory. It explained the value of free association, the central method of psychoanalysis, by theorizing that talking about troubling events and ideas under safe circumstances—that is, in the office of the accepting psychoanalyst—leads to the extinction of the fear associated with the events.*

One of the tenets of learning theory is that people and lower animals can learn many responses mechanically—that is, without thinking about them or fully understanding them. B. F. Skinner showed that pigeons will learn to do . . . whatever they are doing . . . at the time that they are given food. Babies can learn to stop crying when they hear a door opening, because the sound of a door opening is associated with the arrival of a parent and a reduction of distress. Pigeons and babies do not think deeply about either event, however.

"Learning of Visceral and Glandular Responses" was written some 30 years after Frustration and Aggression *and lays the groundwork for the therapy method of biofeedback training (BFT). BFT is a behavior therapy technique that is based on principles of operant conditioning. That is, organisms learn to increase the frequency of behaviors that are reinforced. Miller's great contribution is his research in the learning of automatic, autonomic responses, such as salivation, heart rate, and brain waves. These behaviors were not supposed to be subject to conscious control, but Miller showed that organisms can indeed learn to modify them in a desired direction.*

Learning of Visceral and Glandular Responses

NEAL E. MILLER

Recent experiments on animals show the fallacy of an ancient view of the autonomic nervous system.

There is a strong traditional belief in the inferiority of the autonomic nervous system and the visceral responses that it controls. The recent experiments disproving this belief have deep implications for theories of learning, for individual differences in autonomic responses, for the cause and the cure of abnormal psychosomatic symptoms, and possibly also for the understanding of normal homeostasis. Their

Harcourt, Inc.

success encourages investigators to try other unconventional types of training. Before describing these experiments, let me briefly sketch some elements in the history of the deeply entrenched, false belief in the gross inferiority of one major part of the nervous system.

Historical Roots and Modern Ramifications

Since ancient times, reason and the voluntary responses of the skeletal muscles have been considered to be superior, while emotions and the presumably involuntary glandular and visceral responses have been considered to be inferior. This invidious dichotomy appears in the philosophy of Plato (*1*), with his superior rational soul in the head above and inferior souls in the body below. Much later, the great French neuroanatomist Bichat (*2*) distinguished between the cerebrospinal nervous system of the great brain and spinal cord, controlling skeletal responses, and the dual chain of ganglia (which he called "little brains") running down on either side of the spinal cord in the body below and controlling emotional and visceral responses. He indicated his low opinion of the ganglionic system by calling it "vegetative"; he also believed it to be largely independent of the cerebrospinal system, an opinion which is still reflected in our modern name for it, the autonomic nervous system. Considerably later, Cannon (*3*) studied the sympathetic part of the autonomic nervous system and concluded that the different nerves in it all fire simultaneously and are incapable of the finely differentiated individual responses possible for the cerebrospinal system, a conclusion which is enshrined in modern textbooks.

Many, though not all, psychiatrists have made an invidious distinction between the hysterical and other symptoms that are mediated by the cerebrospinal nervous system and the psychosomatic symptoms that are mediated by the autonomic nervous system. Whereas the former are supposed to be subject to a higher type of control that is symbolic, the latter are presumed to be only the direct physiological consequences of the type and intensity of the patient's emotions (see, for example, *4*).

Similarly, students of learning have made a distinction between a lower form, called classical conditioning and thought to be involuntary, and a superior form variously called trial-and-error learning, operant conditioning, type II conditioning, or instrumental learning and believed to be responsible for voluntary behavior. In classical conditioning, the reinforcement must be by an unconditioned stimulus that already elicits the specific response to be learned; therefore, the possibilities are quite limited. In instrumental learning, the reinforcement, called a reward, has the property of strengthening any immediately preceding response. Therefore, the possibilities for reinforcement are much greater; a given reward may reinforce any one of a number of different responses, and a given response may be reinforced by any one of a number of different rewards.

Finally, the foregoing invidious distinctions have coalesced into the strong traditional belief that the superior type of instrumental learning involved in the superior voluntary behavior is possible only for skeletal responses mediated by the superior cerebrospinal nervous system, while, conversely, the inferior classical conditioning is the only kind possible for the inferior, presumably involuntary, visceral and emotional responses mediated by the inferior autonomic nervous system. Thus, in a recent summary generally considered authoritative, Kimble (*5*) states the almost universal belief that "for autonomically mediated behavior, the evidence points unequivocally to the conclusion that such responses can be modified by classical, but not instrumental, training methods." Upon examining the evidence, however, one finds that it consists only of failure to secure instrumental learning in two incompletely reported exploratory experiments and a vague allusion to the Russian literature (*6*). It is only against a cultural background of great prejudice that such weak evidence could lead to such a strong conviction.

The belief that instrumental learning is possible only for the cerebrospinal system and, conversely, that the autonomic nervous system can be modified only by classical conditioning has been used as one of the strongest arguments for the notion that instrumental learning and classical conditioning are two basically different phenomena rather than different manifestations of the same phenomenon under different conditions. But for many years I have been impressed with the similarity between the laws of classical conditioning and those of instrumental learning, and with the fact that, in each of these two situations, some of the specific details of learning vary with the specific conditions of learning. Failing to see any clear-cut dichotomy, I have assumed that there is only one kind of learning (*7*). This assumption has logically demanded that instrumental training procedures be able to produce the learning of any visceral responses that could be acquired through classical conditioning procedures. Yet it was only a little over a dozen years ago that I began some experimental work on this problem and a somewhat shorter time ago that I first, in published articles (*8*), made specific sharp challenges to the traditional view that the instrumental learning of visceral responses is impossible.

Some Difficulties

One of the difficulties of investigating the instrumental learning of visceral responses stems from the fact that the responses that are the easiest to measure—namely, heart rate, vasomotor responses, and the galvanic skin response—are known to be affected by skeletal responses, such as exercise, breathing, and even tensing of certain muscles, such as those in the diaphragm. Thus, it is hard to rule out the possibility that, instead of directly learning a visceral response, the subject has learned a skeletal response the performance of which causes the visceral change being recorded.

One of the controls I planned to use was the paralysis of all skeletal responses through administration of curare, a drug which selectively blocks the motor end plates of skeletal muscles without eliminating consciousness in human subjects or the neural control of visceral responses, such as the beating of the heart. The muscles involved in breathing are paralyzed, so the subject's breathing must be maintained through artificial respiration. Since it seemed unlikely that curarization and other rigorous control techniques would be easy to use with human subjects, I decided to concentrate first on experiments with animals.

Originally I thought that learning would be more difficult when the animal was paralyzed, under the influence of curare, and therefore I decided to postpone such experiments until ones on nonparalyzed animals had yielded some definitely promising results. This turned out to be a mistake because, as I found out much later, paralyzing the animal with curare not only greatly simplifies the problem of recording visceral responses without artifacts introduced by movement but also apparently makes it easier for the animal to learn, perhaps because paralysis of the skeletal muscles removes sources of variability and distraction. Also, in certain experiments I made the mistake of using rewards that induced strong unconditioned responses that interfered with instrumental learning.

One of the greatest difficulties, however, was the strength of the belief that instrumental learning of glandular and visceral responses is impossible. It was extremely difficult to get students to work on this problem, and when paid assistants were assigned to it, their attempts were so half-hearted that it soon became more economical to let them work on some other problem which they could attack

with greater faith and enthusiasm. These difficulties and a few preliminary encouraging but inconclusive early results have been described elsewhere (9).

Success with Salivation

The first clear-cut results were secured by Alfredo Carmona and me in an experiment on the salivation of dogs. Initial attempts to use food as a reward for hungry dogs were unsuccessful, partly because of strong and persistent unconditioned salivation elicited by the food. Therefore, we decided to use water as a reward for thirsty dogs. Preliminary observations showed that the water had no appreciable effects one way or the other on the bursts of spontaneous salivation. As an additional precaution, however, we used the experimental design of rewarding dogs in one group whenever they showed a burst of spontaneous salivation, so that they would be trained to increase salivation, and rewarding dogs in another group whenever there was a long interval between spontaneous bursts, so that they would be trained to decrease salivation. If the reward had any unconditioned effect, this effect might be classically conditioned to the experimental situation and therefore produce a change in salivation that was not a true instance of instrumental learning. But in classical conditioning the reinforcement must elicit the response that is to be acquired. Therefore, conditioning of a response elicited by the reward could produce either an increase or a decrease in salivation, depending upon the direction of the unconditioned response elicited by the reward, but it could not produce a change in one direction for one group and in the opposite direction for the other group. The same type of logic applies for any unlearned cumulative aftereffects of the reward; they could not be in opposite directions for the two groups. With instrumental learning, however, the reward can reinforce any response that immediately precedes it; therefore, the same reward can be used to produce either increases or decreases.

The results are presented in Fig. 14.01, which summarizes the effects of 40 days of training with one 45-minute training session per day. It may be seen that in this experiment the learning proceeded slowly. However, statistical analysis showed that each of the trends in the predicted rewarded direction was highly reliable (10).

Since the changes in salivation for the two groups were in opposite directions, they cannot be attributed to classical conditioning. It was noted, however, that the group rewarded for increases seemed to be more aroused and active than the one

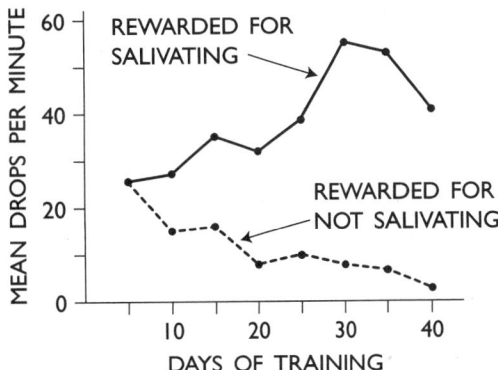

FIGURE 14.01

Learning curves for groups of thirsty dogs rewarded with water for either increases or decreases in spontaneous salivation. [From Miller and Carmona (*10*)]

rewarded for decreases. Conceivably, all we were doing was to change the level of activation of the dogs, and this change was, in turn, affecting the salivation. Although we did not observe any specific skeletal responses, such as chewing movements or panting, which might be expected to elicit salivation, it was difficult to be absolutely certain that such movements did not occur. Therefore, we decided to rule out such movements by paralyzing the dogs with curare, but we immediately found that curare had two effects which were disastrous for this experiment: it elicited such copious and continuous salivation that there were no changes in salivation to reward, and the salivation was so viscous that it almost immediately gummed up the recording apparatus.

Heart Rate

In the meantime, Jay Trowill, working with me on this problem, was displaying great ingenuity, courage, and persistence in trying to produce instrumental learning of heart rate in rats that had been paralyzed by curare to prevent them from "cheating" by muscular exertion to speed up the heart or by relaxation to slow it down. As a result of preliminary testing, he selected a dose of curare (3.6 milligrams of *d*-tubocurarine chloride per kilogram, injected intraperitoneally) which produced deep paralysis for at least 3 hours, and a rate of artificial respiration (inspiration-expiration ratio 1:1; 70 breaths per minute; peak pressure reading, 20 cm-H_2O) which maintained the heart at a constant and normal rate throughout this time.

In subsequent experiments, DiCara and I have obtained similar effects by starting with a smaller dose (1.2 milligrams per kilogram) and constantly infusing additional amounts of the drug, through intraperitoneal injection, at the rate of 1.2 milligrams per kilogram per hour, for the duration of the experiment. We have recorded, electromyographically, the response of the muscles, to determine that this dose does indeed produce a complete block of the action potentials, lasting for at least an hour after the end of infusion. We have found that if parameters of respiration and the face mask are adjusted carefully, the procedure not only maintains the heart rate of a 500-gram control animal constant but also maintains the vital signs of temperature, peripheral vasomotor responses, and the $p\mathrm{CO}_2$ of the blood constant.

Since there are not very many ways to reward an animal completely paralyzed by curare, Trowill and I decided to use direct electrical stimulation of rewarding areas of the brain. There were other technical difficulties to overcome, such as devising the automatic system for rewarding small changes in heart rate as recorded by the electrocardiogram. Nevertheless, Trowill at last succeeded in training his rats (*11*). Those rewarded for an increase in heart rate showed a statistically reliable increase, and those rewarded for a decrease in heart rate showed a statistically reliable decrease. The changes, however, were disappointingly small, averaging only 5 percent in each direction.

The next question was whether larger changes could be achieved by improving the technique of training. DiCara and I used the technique of shaping—in other words, of immediately rewarding first very small, and hence frequently occurring, changes in the correct direction and, as soon as these had been learned, requiring progressively larger changes as the criterion for reward. In this way, we were able to produce in 90 minutes of training changes averaging 20 percent in either direction (*12*).

Key Properties of Learning: Discrimination and Retention

Does the learning of visceral responses have the same properties as the learning of skeletal responses? One of the important characteristics of the instrumental learning of skeletal responses is that a discrimination can be learned, so that the responses are more likely to be made in the stimulus situations in which they are rewarded than in those in which they are not. After the training of the first few rats had convinced us that we could produce large changes in heart rate, DiCara and I gave all the rest of the rats in the experiment described above 45 minutes of additional training with the most difficult criterion. We did this in order to see whether they could learn to give a greater response during a "time-in" stimulus (the presence of a flashing light and a tone) which indicated that a response in the proper direction would be rewarded than during a "time-out" stimulus (absence of light and tone) which indicated that a correct response would not be rewarded.

Figure 14.02 shows the record of one of the rats given such training. Before the beginning of the special discrimination training it had slowed its heart from an initial rate of 350 beats per minute to a rate of 230 beats per minute. From the top record of Figure 14.02 one can see that, at the beginning of the special discrimination training, there was no appreciable reduction in heart rate that was specifically associated with the time-in stimulus. Thus it took the rat considerable time after the onset of this stimulus to meet the criterion and get the reward. At the end of the discrimination training the heart rate during time-out remained approximately the same, but when the time-in light and tone came on, the heart slowed down and the criterion was promptly met. Although the other rats showed less change than this, by the end of the relatively short period of discrimination training their heart rate did change reliably ($P < .001$) in the predicted direction when the time-in stimulus came on. Thus, it is clear that instrumental visceral learning has at least one of the important properties of instrumental skeletal learning—namely, the ability to be brought under the control of a discriminative stimulus.

Another of the important properties of the instrumental learning of skeletal responses is that it is

remembered. DiCara and I performed a special experiment to test the retention of learned changes in heart rate (*13*). Rats that had been given a single training session were returned to their home cages for 3 months without further training. When curarized again and returned to the experimental situation for nonreinforced test trials, rats in both the "increase" and the "decrease" groups showed good retention by exhibiting reliable changes in the direction rewarded in the earlier training.

Escape and Avoidance Learning

Is visceral learning by any chance peculiarly limited to reinforcement by the unusual reward of direct electrical stimulation of the brain, or can it be reinforced by other rewards in the same way that skeletal learning can be? In order to answer this question, DiCara and I (*14*) performed an experiment using the other of the two forms of thoroughly studied reward that can be conveniently used with rats which are paralyzed by curare—namely, the chance to avoid, or escape from, mild electric shock. A shock signal was turned on; after it had been on for 10 seconds it was accompanied by brief pulses of mild electric shock delivered to the rat's tail. During the first 10 seconds the rat could turn off the shock signal and avoid the shock by making the correct response of changing its heart rate in the required direction by the required amount. If it did not make the correct response in time, the shocks continued to be delivered until the rat escaped them by making the correct response, which immediately turned off both the shock and the shock signal.

For one group of curarized rats, the correct response was an increase in heart rate; for the other

FIGURE 14.02

Electrocardiograms at the beginning and at the end of discrimination training of curarized rat rewarded for slow heart rate. Slowing of heart rate is rewarded only during a "time-in" stimulus (tone and light). [From Miller and DiCara (*12*)]

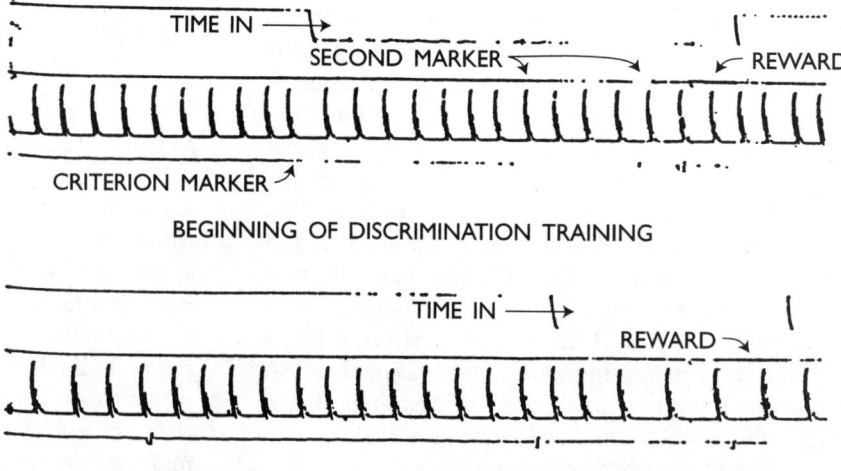

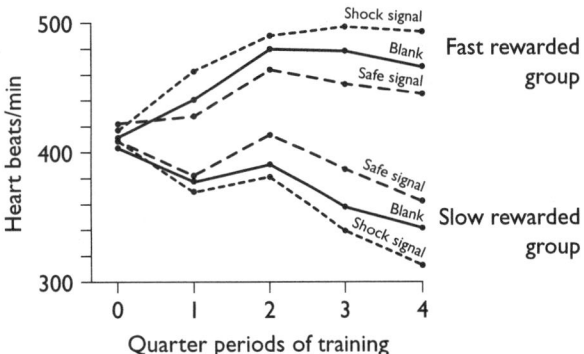

FIGURE 14.03

Changes in heart rate during avoidance training. [From DiCara and Miller (*14*)]

group it was a decrease. After the rats had learned to make small responses in the proper direction, they were required to make larger ones. During this training the shock signals were randomly interspersed with an equal number of "safe" signals that were not followed by shock; the heart rate was also recorded during so-called blank trials—trials without any signals or shocks. For half of the rats the shock signal was a tone and the "safe" signal was a flashing light; for the other half the roles of these cues were reversed.

The results are shown in Figure 14.03. Each of the 12 rats in this experiment changed its heart rate in the rewarded direction. As training progressed, the shock signal began to elicit a progressively greater change in the rewarded direction than the change recorded during the blank trials; this was a statistically reliable trend. Conversely, as training progressed, the "safe" signal came to elicit a statistically reliable change in the opposite direction, toward the initial base line. These results show learning when escape and avoidance are the rewards; this means that visceral responses in curarized rats can be reinforced by rewards other than direct electrical stimulation of the brain. These rats also discriminate between the shock and the "safe" signals. You will remember that, with noncurarized thirsty dogs, we were able to use yet another kind of reward, water, to produce learned changes in salivation.

Transfer to Noncurarized State: More Evidence against Mediation

In the experiments discussed above, paralysis of the skeletal muscles by curare ruled out the possibility that the subjects were learning the overt performance of skeletal responses which were indirectly

eliciting the changes in the heart rate. It is barely conceivable, however, that the rats were learning to send out from the motor cortex central impulses which would have activated the muscles had they not been paralyzed. And it is barely conceivable that these central impulses affected heart rate by means either of inborn connections or of classically conditioned ones that had been acquired when previous exercise had been accompanied by an increase in heart rate and relaxation had been accompanied by a decrease. But, if the changes in heart rate were produced in this indirect way, we would expect that, during a subsequent test without curare, any rat that showed learned changes in heart rate would show the movements in the muscles that were no longer paralyzed. Furthermore, the problem of whether or not visceral responses learned under curarization carry over to the noncurarized state is of interest in its own right.

In order to answer this question, DiCara and I (*15*) trained two groups of curarized rats to increase or decrease, respectively, their heart rate in order to avoid, or escape from, brief pulses of mild electric shock. When these rats were tested 2 weeks later in the noncurarized state, the habit was remembered. Statistically reliable increases in heart rate averaging 5 percent and decreases averaging 16 percent occurred. Immediately subsequent retraining without curare produced additional significant changes of heart rate in the rewarded direction, bringing the total overall increase to 11 percent and the decrease to 22 percent. While, at the beginning of the test in the noncurarized state, the two groups showed some differences in respiration and activity, these differences decreased until, by the end of the retraining, they were small and far from statistically reliable ($t = 0.3$ and 1.3, respectively). At the same time, the difference between the two groups with respect to heart rate was increasing, until it became large and thus extremely reliable ($t = 8.6$, d.f. $= 12$, $P < .001$).

In short, while greater changes in heart rate were being learned, the response was becoming more specific, involving smaller changes in respiration and muscular activity. This increase in specificity with additional training is another point of similarity with the instrumental learning of skeletal responses. Early in skeletal learning, the rewarded correct response is likely to be accompanied by many unnecessary movements. With additional training during which extraneous movements are not rewarded, they tend to drop out.

It is difficult to reconcile the foregoing results with the hypothesis that the differences in heart rate were mediated primarily by a difference in either respiration or amount of general activity. This is especially true in view of the research, summarized by Ehrlich and Malmo (*16*), which shows that muscular activity, to affect heart rate in the rat, must be rather vigorous.

While it is difficult to rule out completely the possibility that changes in heart rate are mediated by central impulses to skeletal muscles, the possibility of such mediation is much less attractive for other responses, such as intestinal contractions and the formation of urine by the kidney. Furthermore, if the learning of these different responses can be shown to be specific in enough visceral responses, one runs out of different skeletal movements each eliciting a specific different visceral response (*17*). Therefore, experiments were performed on the learning of a variety of different visceral responses and on the specificity of that learning. Each of these experiments was, of course, interesting in its own right, quite apart from any bearing on the problem of mediation.

Specificity: Intestinal versus Cardiac

The purpose of our next experiment was to determine the specificity of visceral learning. If such learning has the same properties as the instrumental learning of skeletal responses, it should be possible to learn a specific visceral response independently of other ones. Furthermore, as we have just seen, we might expect to find that, the better the rewarded response is learned, the more specific is the

learning. Banuazizi and I worked on this problem (*18*). First we had to discover another visceral response that could be conveniently recorded and rewarded. We decided on intestinal contractions, and recorded them in the curarized rat with a little balloon filled with water thrust approximately 4 centimeters beyond the anal sphincter. Changes of pressure in the balloon were transduced into electric voltages which produced a record on a polygraph and also activated an automatic mechanism for delivering the reward, which was electrical stimulation of the brain.

The results for the first rat trained, which was a typical one, are shown in Figure 14.04. From the top record it may be seen that, during habituation, there were some spontaneous contractions. When the rat was rewarded by brain stimulation for keeping contractions below a certain amplitude for a certain time, the number of contractions was reduced and the base line was lowered. After the record showed a highly reliable change indicating that relaxation had been learned (Figure 14.04, second record from the top), the conditions of training were reversed and the reward was delivered whenever the amplitude of contractions rose above a certain level. From the next record (Figure 14.04, middle) it may be seen that this type of training increased the number of contractions and raised the base line. Finally (Fig. 14.04, two bottom records) the reward was discontinued and, as would be expected, the response continued for a while but gradually became extinguished, so that the activity eventually returned to approximately its original base-line level.

FIGURE 14.04

Typical samples of a record of instrumental learning of an intestinal response by a curarized rat. (From top to bottom) Record of spontaneous contraction before training; record after training with reward for relaxation; record after training with reward for contractions; records during nonrewarded extinction trials. [From Miller and Banuazizi (*18*)]

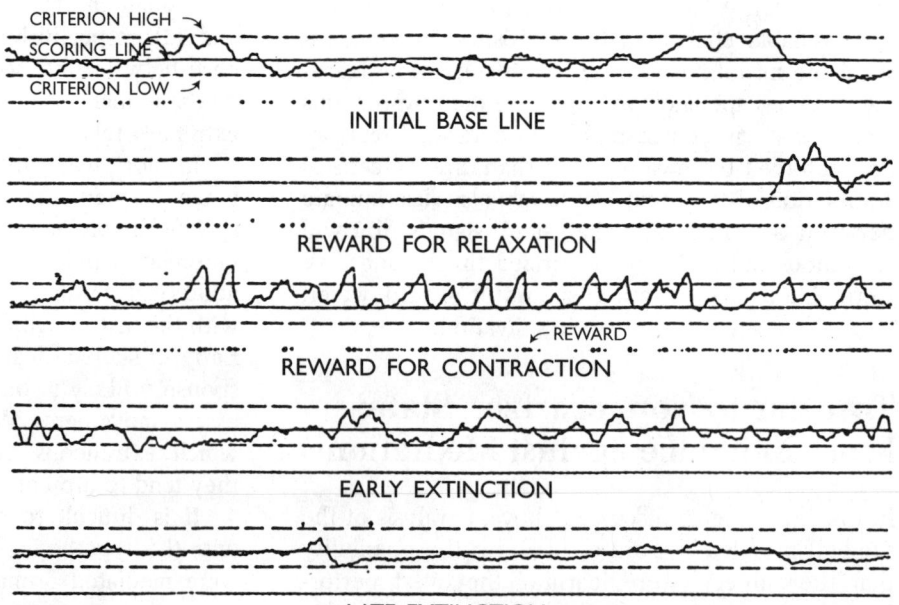

CRITERION HIGH
SCORING LINE
CRITERION LOW
INITIAL BASE LINE

REWARD FOR RELAXATION

REWARD
REWARD FOR CONTRACTION

EARLY EXTINCTION

LATE EXTINCTION

After studying a number of other rats in this way and convincing ourselves that the instrumental learning of intestinal responses was a possibility, we designed an experiment to test specificity. For all the rats of the experiment, both intestinal contractions and heart rate were recorded, but half the rats were rewarded for one of these responses and half were rewarded for the other response. Each of these two groups of rats was divided into two subgroups, rewarded, respectively, for increased and decreased response. The rats were completely paralyzed by curare, maintained on artificial respiration, and rewarded by electrical stimulation of the brain.

The results are shown in Figs. 14.05 and 14.06. In Fig. 14.05 it may be seen that the group rewarded for increases in intestinal contractions learned an increase, the group rewarded for decreases learned a decrease, but neither of these groups showed an appreciable change in heart rate. Conversely (Fig. 14.06), the group rewarded for increases in heart rate showed an increase, the group rewarded for decreases showed a decrease, but neither of these groups showed a change in intestinal contractions.

The fact that each type of response changed when it was rewarded rules out the interpretation that the failure to secure a change when that change was not rewarded could have been due to either a strong and stable homeostatic regulation of that response or an inability of our techniques to measure changes reliably under the particular conditions of our experiment.

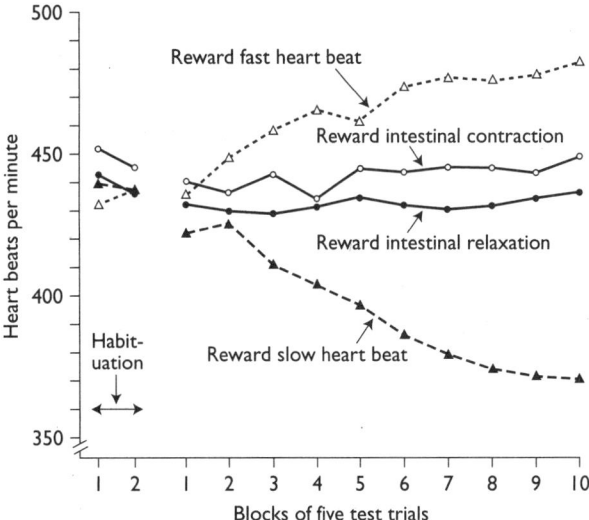

FIGURE 14.06

Graph showing that the heart rate is changed by rewarding either increases or decreases in heart rate but is unaffected by rewarding changes in intestinal contractions. Comparison with Fig. 14.05 demonstrates the specificity of visceral learning. [From Miller and Banuazizi (18)]

Each of the 12 rats in the experiment showed statistically reliable changes in the rewarded direction; for 11 the changes were reliable beyond the $P < .001$ level, while for the 12th the changes were reliable only beyond the .05 level. A statistically reliable negative correlation showed that the better the rewarded visceral response was learned, the less change occurred in the other, nonrewarded response. This greater specificity with better learning is what we had expected. The results showed that visceral learning can be specific to an organ system, and they clearly ruled out the possibility of mediation by any single general factor, such as level of activation or central commands for either general activity or relaxation.

In an additional experiment, Banuazizi (19) showed that either increases or decreases in intestinal contractions can be rewarded by avoidance of, or escape from, mild electric shocks, and that the intestinal responses can be discriminatively elicited by a specific stimulus associated with reinforcement.

Kidney Function

Encouraged by these successes, DiCara and I decided to see whether or not the rate of urine formation by the kidney could be changed in the curarized rat rewarded by electrical stimulation of the brain (20). A catheter, permanently inserted, was used to prevent accumulation of urine by the blad-

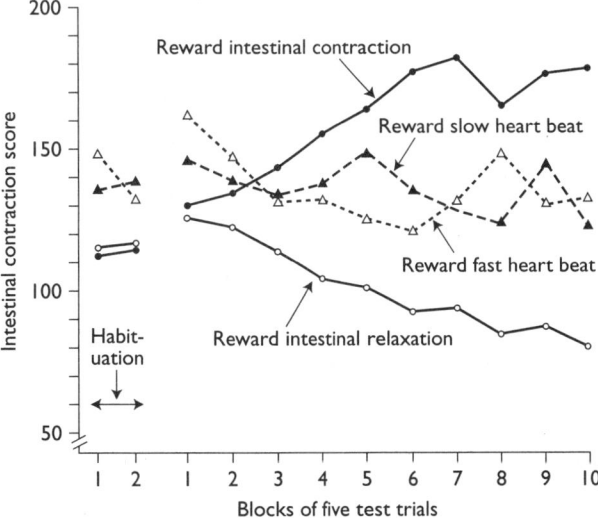

FIGURE 14.05

Graph showing that the intestinal contraction score is changed by rewarding either increases or decreases in intestinal contractions but is unaffected by rewarding changes in heart rate. [From Miller and Banuazizi (18)]

dcr, and the rate of urine formation was measured by an electronic device for counting minute drops. In order to secure a rate of urine formation fast enough so that small changes could be promptly detected and rewarded, the rats were kept constantly loaded with water through infusion by way of a catheter permanently inserted in the jugular vein.

All of the seven rats rewarded when the intervals between times of urine-drop formation lengthened showed decreases in the rate of urine formation, and all of the seven rats rewarded when these intervals shortened showed increases in the rate of urine formation. For both groups the changes were highly reliable ($P < .001$).

In order to determine how the change in rate of urine formation was achieved, certain additional measures were taken. As the set of bars at left in Fig. 14.07 shows, the rate of filtration, measured by means of ^{14}C-labeled insulin, increased when increases in the rate of urine formation were rewarded and decreased when decreases in the rate were rewarded. Plots of the correlations showed that the changes in the rates of filtration and urine formation were not related to changes in either blood pressure or heart rate.

The middle set of bars in Fig. 14.07 shows that the rats rewarded for increases in the rate of urine formation had an increased rate of renal blood flow, as measured by [3]H-*p*-aminohippuric acid, and that those rewarded for decreases had a decreased rate of renal blood flow. Since these changes in blood flow were not accompanied by changes in general blood pressure or in heart rate, they must have been achieved by vasomotor changes of the renal arteries. That these vasomotor changes were at least somewhat specific is shown by the fact that vasomotor responses of the tail, as measured by a photoelectric plethysmograph, did not differ for the two groups of rats.

The set of bars at right in Fig. 14.07 shows that when decreases in rate of urine formation were rewarded, a more concentrated urine, having higher osmolarity, was formed. Since the slower passage of urine through the tubules would afford more opportunity for reabsorption of water, this higher concentration does not necessarily mean an increase in the secretion of antidiuretic hormone. When an increased rate of urine formation was rewarded, the urine did not become more diluted—that is, it showed no decrease in osmolarity; therefore, the increase in rate of urine formation observed in this experiment cannot be accounted for in terms of an inhibition of the secretion of antidiuretic hormone.

From the foregoing results it appears that the learned changes in urine formation in this experiment were produced primarily by changes in the rate of filtration, which, in turn, were produced primarily by changes in the rate of blood flow through the kidneys.

Gastric Changes

In the next experiment, Carmona, Demierre, and I used a photoelectric plethysmograph to measure changes, presumably in the amount of blood, in the

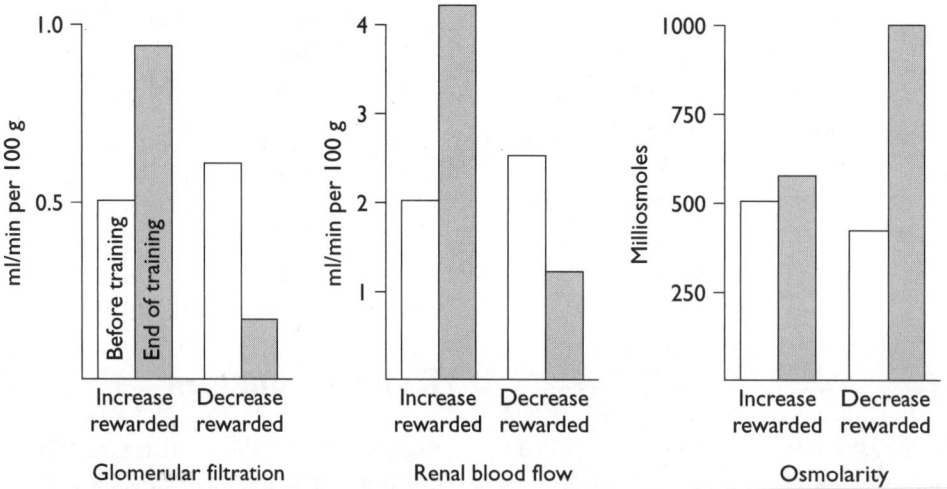

FIGURE 14.07

Effects of rewarding increased rate of urine formation in one group and decreased rate in another on measures of glomerular filtration, renal blood flow, and osmolarity. [From data in Miller and DiCara (20)]

stomach wall (*21*). In an operation performed under anesthesia, a small glass tube, painted black except for a small spot, was inserted into the rat's stomach. The same tube was used to hold the stomach wall against a small glass window inserted through the body wall. The tube was left in that position. After the animal had recovered, a bundle of optical fibers could be slipped snugly into the glass tube so that the light beamed through it would shine out through the unpainted spot in the tube inside the stomach, pass through the stomach wall, and be recorded by a photocell on the other side of the glass window. Preliminary tests indicated that, as would be expected, when the amount of blood in the stomach wall increased, less light would pass through. Other tests showed that stomach contractions elicited by injections of insulin did not affect the amount of light transmitted.

In the main experiment we rewarded curarized rats by enabling them to avoid or escape from mild electric shocks. Some were rewarded when the amount of light that passed through the stomach wall increased, while others were rewarded when the amount decreased. Fourteen of the 15 rats showed changes in the rewarded direction. Thus, we demonstrated that the stomach wall, under the control of the autonomic nervous system, can be modified by instrumental learning. There is strong reason to believe that the learned changes were achieved by vasomotor responses affecting the amount of blood in the stomach wall or mucosa, or in both.

In another experiment, Carmona (*22*) showed that stomach contractions can be either increased or decreased by instrumental learning.

It is obvious that learned changes in the blood supply of internal organs can affect their functioning—as, for example, the rate at which urine was formed by the kidneys was affected by changes in the amount of blood that flowed through them. Thus, such changes can produce psychosomatic symptoms. And if the learned changes in blood supply can be specific to a given organ, the symptom will occur in that organ rather than in another one.

Peripheral Vasomotor Responses

Having investigated the instrumental learning of internal vasomotor responses, we next studied the learning of peripheral ones. In the first experiment, the amount of blood in the tail of a curarized rat was measured by a photoelectric plethysmograph, and changes were rewarded by electrical stimulation of the brain (*23*). All of the four rats rewarded for

vasoconstriction showed that response, and, at the same time, their average core temperature, measured rectally, decreased from 98.9° to 97.9°F. All of the four rats rewarded for vasodilatation showed that response and, at the same time, their average core temperature increased from 99.9° to 101°F. The vasomotor change for each individual rat was reliable beyond the $P < .01$ level, and the difference in change in temperature between the groups was reliable beyond the .01 level. The direction of the change in temperature was opposite to that which would be expected from the heat conservation caused by peripheral vasoconstriction or the heat loss caused by peripheral vasodilatation. The changes are in the direction which would be expected if the training had altered the rate of heat production, causing a change in temperature which, in turn, elicited the vasomotor response.

The next experiment was designed to try to determine the limits of the specificity of vasomotor learning. The pinnae of the rat's ears were chosen because the blood vessels in them are believed to be innervated primarily, and perhaps exclusively, by the sympathetic branch of the autonomic nervous system, the branch that Cannon believed always fired nonspecifically as a unit (*3*). But Cannon's experiments involved exposing cats to extremely strong emotion-evoking stimuli, such as barking dogs, and such stimuli will also evoke generalized activity throughout the skeletal musculature. Perhaps his results reflected the way in which sympathetic activity was elicited, rather than demonstrating any inherent inferiority of the sympathetic nervous system.

In order to test this interpretation, DiCara and I (*24*) put photocells on both ears of the curarized rat and connected them to a bridge circuit so that only differences in the vasomotor responses of the two ears were rewarded by brain stimulation. We were somewhat surprised and greatly delighted to find that this experiment actually worked. The results are summarized in Fig. 14.08. Each of the six rats rewarded for relative vasodilatation of the left ear showed that response, while each of the six rats rewarded for relative vasodilatation of the right ear showed that response. Recordings from the right and left forepaws showed little if any change in vasomotor response.

It is clear that these results cannot be by-products of changes in either heart rate or blood pressure, as these would be expected to affect both ears equally. They show either that vasomotor responses mediated by the sympathetic nervous system are capable of much greater specificity than has previously been believed, or that the innervation of the

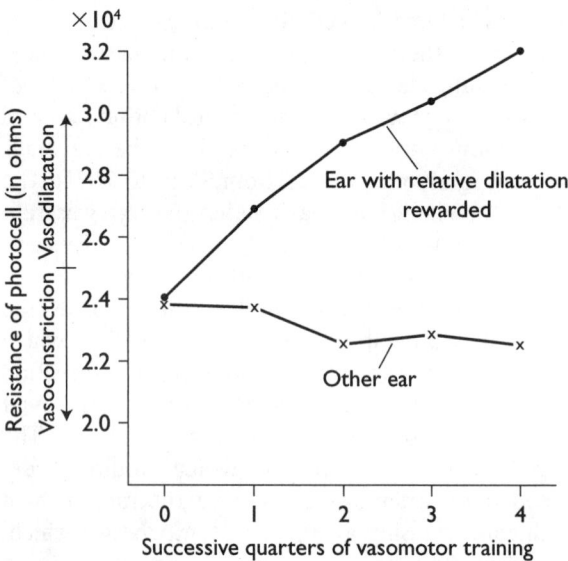

FIGURE 14.08

Learning a difference in the vasomotor responses of the two ears in the curarized rat. [From data in DiCara and Miller (24)]

blood vessels in the pinnae of the ears is not restricted almost exclusively to sympathetic-nervous-system components, as has been believed, and involves functionally significant parasympathetic components. In any event, the changes in the blood flow certainly were surprisingly specific. Such changes in blood flow could account for specific psychosomatic symptoms.

Blood Pressure Independent of Heart Rate

Although changes in blood pressure were not induced as by-products of rewarded changes in the rate of urine formation, another experiment on curarized rats showed that, when changes in systolic blood pressure are specifically reinforced, they can be learned (25). Blood pressure was recorded by means of a catheter permanently inserted into the aorta, and the reward was avoidance of, or escape from, mild electric shock. All seven rats rewarded for increases in blood pressure showed further increases, while all seven rewarded for decreases showed decreases, each of the changes, which were in opposite directions, being reliable beyond the $P < .01$ level. The increase was from 139 mm-Hg, which happens to be roughly comparable to the normal systolic blood pressure of an adult man, to 170 mm-Hg, which is on the borderline of abnormally high blood pressure in man.

Each experimental animal was "yoked" with a curarized partner maintained on artificial respiration and having shock electrodes on its tail wired in series with electrodes on the tail of the experimental animal, so that it received exactly the same electric shock and could do nothing to escape or avoid them. The yoked controls for both the increase-rewarded and the decrease-rewarded groups showed some elevation in blood pressure as an unconditioned effect of the shocks. By the end of training, in contrast to the large difference in the blood pressures of the two groups specifically rewarded for changes in opposite directions, there was no difference in blood pressure between the yoked control partners for these two groups. Furthermore, the increase in blood pressure in these control groups was reliably less ($P < .01$) than that in the group specifically rewarded for increases. Thus, it is clear that the reward for an increase in blood pressure produced an additional increase over and above the effects of the shocks per se while the reward for a decrease was able to overcome the unconditioned increase elicited by the shocks.

For none of the four groups was there a significant change in heart rate or in temperature during training; there were no significant differences in these measures among the groups. Thus, the learned change was relatively specific to blood pressure.

Transfer from Heart Rate to Skeletal Avoidance

Although visceral learning can be quite specific, especially if only a specific response is rewarded, as was the case in the experiment on the two ears, under some circumstances it can involve a more generalized effect.

In handling the rats that had just recovered from curarization, DiCara noticed that those that had been trained, through the avoidance or escape reward, to increase their heart rate were more likely to squirm, squeal, defecate, and show other responses indicating emotionality than were those that had been trained to reduce their heart rate. Could instrumental learning of heart-rate changes have some generalized effects, perhaps on the level of emotionality, which might affect the behavior in a different avoidance-learning situation? In order to look for such an effect, DiCara and Weiss (26) used a modified shuttle avoidance apparatus. In this apparatus, when a danger signal is given, the rat must run from compartment A to compartment B. If he runs fast enough, he avoids the shock; if not, he must run to escape it. The next time the danger signal is given, the rat must run in the opposite direction, from B to A.

Other work had shown that learning in this apparatus is an inverted U-shaped function of the strength of the shocks, with shocks that are too strong eliciting emotional behavior instead of running. DiCara and Weiss trained their rats in this apparatus with a level of shock that is approximately optimum for naive rats of this strain. They found that the rats that had been rewarded for decreasing their heart rate learned well, but that those that had been rewarded for increasing their heart rate learned less well, as if their emotionality had been increased. The difference was statistically reliable ($P < .001$). This experiment clearly demonstrates that training a visceral response can affect the subsequent learning of a skeletal one, but additional work will be required to prove the hypothesis that training to increase heart rate increases emotionality.

Visceral Learning without Curare

Thus far, in all of the experiments except the one on teaching thirsty dogs to salivate, the initial training was given when the animal was under the influence of curare. All of the experiments, except the one on salivation, have produced surprisingly rapid learning—definitive results within 1 or 2 hours. Will learning in the normal, noncurarized state be easier, as we originally thought it should be, or will it be harder, as the experiment on the noncurarized dogs suggests? DiCara and I have started to get additional evidence on this problem. We have obtained clear-cut evidence that rewarding (with the avoidance or escape reward) one group of freely moving rats for reducing heart rate and rewarding another group for increasing heart rate produces a difference between the two groups (27). That this difference was not due to the indirect effects of the overt performance of skeletal responses is shown by the fact that it persisted in subsequent tests during which the rats were paralyzed by curare. And, on subsequent retraining without curare, such differences in activity and respiration as were present earlier in training continued to decrease, while the differences in heart rate continued to increase. It seems extremely unlikely that, at the end of training, the highly reliable differences in heart rate ($t = 7.2$; $P < .0001$) can be explained by the highly unreliable differences in activity and respiration ($t = .07$ and 0.2, respectively).

Although the rats in this experiment showed some learning when they were trained initially in the noncurarized state, this learning was much poorer than that which we have seen in our other experiments on curarized rats. This is exactly the opposite of my original expectation, but seems plausible in the light of hindsight. My hunch is that paralysis by curare improved learning by eliminating sources of distraction and variability. The stimulus situation was kept more constant, and confusing visceral fluctuations induced indirectly by skeletal movements were eliminated.

Learned Changes in Brain Waves

Encouraged by success in the experiments on the instrumental learning of visceral responses, my colleagues and I have attempted to produce other unconventional types of learning. Electrodes placed on the skull or, better yet, touching the surface of the brain record summative effects of electrical activity over a considerable area of the brain. Such electrical effects are called brain waves, and the record of them is called an electroencephalogram. When the animal is aroused, the electroencephalogram consists of fast, low-voltage activity; when the animal is drowsy or sleeping normally, the electroencephalogram consists of considerably slower, higher-voltage activity. Carmona attempted to see whether this type of brain activity, and the state of arousal accompanying it, can be modified by direct reward of changes in the brain activity (28, 29).

The subjects of the first experiment were freely moving cats. In order to have a reward that was under complete control and that did not require the cat to move, Carmona used direct electrical stimulation of the medial forebrain bundle, which is a rewarding area of the brain. Such stimulation produced a slight lowering in the average voltage of the electroencephalogram and an increase in behavioral arousal. In order to provide a control for these and any other unlearned effects, he rewarded one group for changes in the direction of high-voltage activity and another group for changes in the direction of low-voltage activity.

Both groups learned. The cats rewarded for high-voltage activity showed more high-voltage slow waves and tended to sit like sphinxes, staring out into space. The cats rewarded for low-voltage activity showed much more low-voltage fast activity, and appeared to be aroused, pacing restlessly about, sniffing, and looking here and there. It was clear that this type of training had modified both the character of the electrical brain waves and the general level of the behavioral activity. It was not clear, however, whether the level of arousal of the brain

FIGURE 14.09

Instrumental learning by cu-rarized rats rewarded for high-voltage or for low-volt-age electroencephalograms recorded from the cerebral cortex. After a period of nonrewarded extinction, which produced some drowsiness as indicated by an increase in voltage, the rats in the two groups were then rewarded for voltage changes opposite in direction to the changes for which they were rewarded earlier. [From Car-mona (29)]

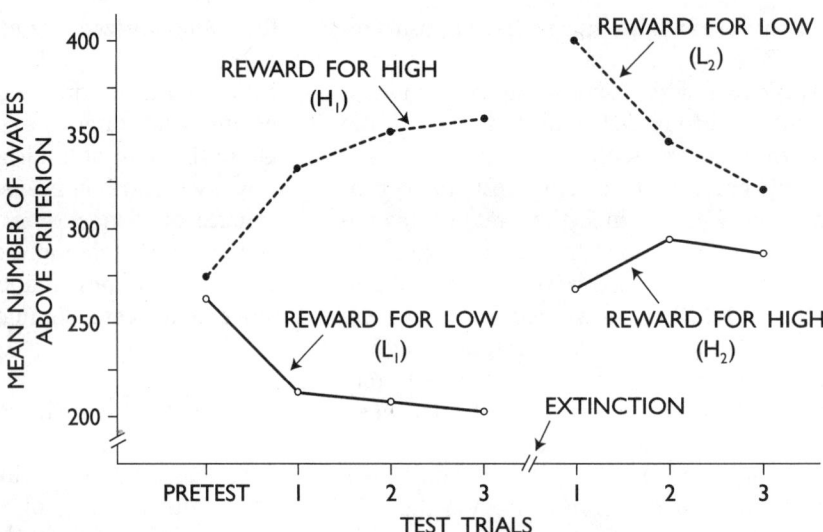

was directly modified and hence modified the be-havior; whether the animals learned specific items of behavior which, in turn, modified the arousal of the brain as reflected in the electroencephalogram; or whether both types of learning were occurring si-multaneously.

In order to rule out the direct sensory conse-quences of changes in muscular tension, movement, and posture, Carmona performed the next experi-ment on rats that had been paralyzed by means of curare. The results, given in Fig. 14.09, show that both rewarded groups showed changes in the re-warded direction; that a subsequent nonrewarded rest increased the number of high-voltage responses in both groups; and that, when the conditions of re-ward were reversed, the direction of change in volt-age was reversed.

At present we are trying to use similar tech-niques to modify the functions of a specific part of the vagal nucleus, by recording and specifically re-warding changes in the electrical activity there. Pre-liminary results suggest that this is possible. The next step is to investigate the visceral consequences of such modification. This kind of work may open up possibilities for modifying the activity of specific parts of the brain and the functions that they con-trol. In some cases, directly rewarding brain activity may be a more convenient or more powerful tech-nique than rewarding skeletal or visceral behavior. It also may be a new way to throw light on the func-tions of specific parts of the brain (30).

Human Visceral Learning

Another question is that of whether people are ca-pable of instrumental learning of visceral responses.

I believe that in this respect they are as smart as rats. But, as a recent critical review by Katkin and Murray (31) points out, this has not yet been com-pletely proved. These authors have comprehensively summarized the recent studies reporting successful use of instrumental training to modify human heart rate, vasomotor responses, and the galvanic skin re-sponse. Because of the difficulties in subjecting hu-man subjects to the same rigorous controls, includ-ing deep paralysis by means of curare, that can be used with animal subjects, one of the most serious questions about the results of the human studies is whether the changes recorded represent the true in-strumental learning of visceral responses or the un-conscious learning of those skeletal responses that can produce visceral reactions. However, the able investigators who have courageously challenged the strong traditional belief in the inferiority of the au-tonomic nervous system with experiments at the more difficult but especially significant human level are developing ingenious controls, including demon-strations of the specificity of the visceral change, so that their cumulative results are becoming increas-ingly impressive.

Possible Role in Homeostasis

The functional utility of instrumental learning by the cerebrospinal nervous system under the condi-tions that existed during mammalian evolution is obvious. The skeletal responses mediated by the cerebrospinal nervous system operate on the exter-nal environment, so that there is survival value in the ability to learn responses that bring rewards such as food, water, or escape from pain. The fact that the responses mediated by the autonomic nervous system do not have such direct action on the external environment was one of the reasons for believing that they are not subject to instrumental learning. Is the learning ability of the autonomic nervous system something that has no normal function other than that of providing my students with subject matter for publications? Is it a mere accidental by-product of the survival value of cerebrospinal learning, or does the instrumental learning of autonomically mediated responses have some adaptive function, such as helping to maintain that constancy of the internal environment called homeostasis?

In order for instrumental learning to function homeostatically, a deviation away from the optimum level will have to function as a drive to motivate learning, and a change toward the optimum level will have to function as a reward to reinforce the learning of the particular visceral response that produced the corrective change.

When a mammal has less than the optimum amount of water in his body, this deficiency serves as a drive of thirst to motivate learning; the overt consummatory response of drinking functions as a reward to reinforce the learning of the particular skeletal responses that were successful in securing the water that restored the optimum level. But is the consummatory response essential? Can restoration of an optimum level by a glandular response function as a reward?

In order to test for the possible rewarding effects of a glandular response, DiCara, Wolf, and I (*32*) injected albino rats with antidiuretic hormone (ADH) if they chose one arm of a T-maze and with the isotonic saline vehicle if they chose the other, distinctively different, arm. The ADH permitted water to be reabsorbed in the kidney, so that a smaller volume of more concentrated urine was formed. Thus, for normal rats loaded in advance with H_2O, the ADH interfered with the excess-water excretion required for the restoration of homeostasis, while the control injection of isotonic saline allowed the excess water to be excreted. And, indeed, such rats learned to select the side of the maze that assured them an injection of saline so that their glandular response could restore homeostasis.

Conversely, for rats with diabetes insipidus, loaded in advance with hypertonic NaCl, the homeostatic effects of the same two injections were reversed; the ADH, causing the urine to be more concentrated, helped the rats to get rid of the excess NaCl, while the isotonic saline vehicle did not. And, indeed, a group of rats of this kind learned the opposite choice of selecting the ADH side of the maze. As a further control on the effects of the ADH per se, normal rats which had not been given H_2O or

NaCl exhibited no learning. This experiment showed that an excess of either H_2O or NaCl functions as a drive and that the return to the normal concentration produced by the appropriate response of a gland, the kidney, functions as a reward.

When we consider the results of this experiment together with those of our experiments showing that glandular and visceral responses can be instrumentally learned, we will expect the animal to learn those glandular and visceral responses mediated by the central nervous system that promptly restore homeostasis after any considerable deviation. Whether or not this theoretically possible learning has any practical significance will depend on whether or not the innate homeostatic mechanisms control the levels closely enough to prevent any deviations large enough to function as a drive from occurring. Even if the innate control should be accurate enough to preclude learning in most cases, there remains the intriguing possibility that, when pathology interferes with innate control, visceral learning is available as a supplementary mechanism.

Implications and Speculations

We have seen how the instrumental learning of visceral responses suggests a new possible homeostatic mechanism worthy of further investigation. Such learning also shows that the autonomic nervous system is not as inferior as has been so widely and firmly believed. It removes one of the strongest arguments for the hypothesis that there are two fundamentally different mechanisms of learning, involving different parts of the nervous system.

CAUSE OF PSYCHOSOMATIC SYMPTOMS

Similarly, evidence of the instrumental learning of visceral responses removes the main basis for assuming that the psychosomatic symptoms that involve the autonomic nervous system are fundamentally different from those functional symptoms, such as hysterical ones, that involve the cerebrospinal nervous system. Such evidence allows us to extend to psychosomatic symptoms the type of learning-theory analysis that Dollard and I (*7, 33*) have applied to other symptoms.

For example, suppose a child is terror-stricken at the thought of going to school in the morning because he is completely unprepared for an important examination. The strong fear elicits a variety of fluctuating autonomic symptoms, such as a queasy stomach at one time and pallor and faintness at another; at this point his mother, who is particularly concerned about cardiovascular symptoms, says, "You are sick and must stay home." The child feels a great relief from fear, and this reward should reinforce the cardiovascular responses producing pallor and faintness. If such experiences are repeated frequently enough, the child, theoretically, should learn to respond with that kind of symptom. Similarly, another child whose mother ignored the vasomotor responses but was particularly concerned by signs of gastric distress would learn the latter type of symptom. I want to emphasize, however, that we need careful clinical research to determine how frequently, if at all, the social conditions sufficient for such theoretically possible learning of visceral symptoms actually occur. Since a given instrumental response can be reinforced by a considerable variety of rewards, and by one reward on one occasion and a different reward on another, the fact that glandular and visceral responses can be instrumentally learned opens up many new theoretical possibilities for the reinforcement of psychosomatic symptoms.

Furthermore, we do not yet know how severe a psychosomatic effect can be produced by learning. While none of the 40 rats rewarded for speeding up their heart rates have died in the course of training under curarization, 7 of the 40 rats rewarded for slowing down their heart rates have died. This statistically reliable difference (chi square = 5.6, $P < .02$) is highly suggestive, but it could mean that training to speed up the heart helped the rats resist the stress of curare rather than that the reward for slowing down the heart was strong enough to overcome innate regulatory mechanisms and induce sudden death. In either event the visceral learning had a vital effect. At present, DiCara and I are trying to see whether or not the learning of visceral responses can be carried far enough in the noncurarized animal to produce physical damage. We are also investigating the possibility that there may be a critical period in early infancy during which visceral learning has particularly intense and long-lasting effects.

INDIVIDUAL AND CULTURAL DIFFERENCES

It is possible that, in addition to producing psychosomatic symptoms in extreme cases, visceral learning can account for certain more benign individual and cultural differences. Lacey and Lacey (34) have shown that a given individual may have a tendency, which is stable over a number of years, to respond to a variety of different stresses with the same profile of autonomic responses, while other individuals may have statistically reliable tendencies to respond with different profiles. It now seems possible that

differential conditions of learning may account for at least some of these individual differences in patterns of autonomic response.

Conversely, such learning may account also for certain instances in which the same individual responds to the same stress in different ways. For example, a small boy who receives a severe bump in rough-and-tumble play may learn to inhibit the secretion of tears in this situation since his peer group will punish crying by calling it "sissy." But the same small boy may burst into tears when he gets home to his mother, who will not punish weeping and may even reward tears with sympathy.

Similarly, it seems conceivable that different conditions of reward by a culture different from our own may be responsible for the fact that Homer's adult heroes so often "let the big tears fall." Indeed, a former colleague of mine, Herbert Barry III, has analyzed cross-cultural data and found that the amount of crying reported for children seems to be related to the way in which the society reacts to their tears (35).

I have emphasized the possible role of learning in producing the observed individual differences in visceral responses to stress, which in extreme cases may result in one type of psychosomatic symptom in one person and a different type in another. Such learning does not, of course, exclude innate individual differences in the susceptibility of different organs. In fact, given social conditions under which any form of illness will be rewarded, the symptoms of the most susceptible organ will be the most likely ones to be learned. Furthermore, some types of stress may be so strong that the innate reactions to them produce damage without any learning. My colleagues and I are currently investigating the psychological variables involved in such types of stress (36).

THERAPEUTIC TRAINING

The experimental work on animals has developed a powerful technique for using instrumental learning to modify glandular and visceral responses. The improved training technique consists of moment-to-moment recording of the visceral function and immediate reward, at first, of very small changes in the desired direction and then of progressively larger ones. The success of this technique suggests that it should be able to produce therapeutic changes. If the patient who is highly motivated to get rid of a symptom understands that a signal, such as a tone, indicates a change in the desired direction, that tone could serve as a powerful reward. Instruction to try to turn the tone on as often as possible and praise for success should increase the reward. As patients find that they can secure some control of the symptom, their motivation should be strengthened. Such a procedure should be well worth trying on any symptom, functional or organic, that is under neural control, that can be continuously monitored by modern instrumentation, and for which a given direction of change is clearly indicated medically—for example, cardiac arrhythmias, spastic colitis, asthma, and those cases of high blood pressure that are not essential compensation for kidney damage (*37*). The obvious cases to begin with are those in which drugs are ineffective or contraindicated. In the light of the fact that our animals learned so much better when under the influence of curare and transferred their training so well to the normal, non-drugged state, it should be worth while to try to use hypnotic suggestion to achieve similar results by enhancing the reward effect of the signal indicating a change in the desired direction, by producing relaxation and regular breathing, and by removing interference from skeletal responses and distraction by irrelevant cues.

Engel and Melmon (*38*) have reported encouraging results in the use of instrumental training to treat cardiac arrhythmias of organic origin. Randt, Korein, Carmona, and I have had some success in using the method described above to train epileptic patients in the laboratory to suppress, in one way or another, the abnormal paroxysmal spikes in their electroencephalogram. My colleagues and I are hoping to try learning therapy for other symptoms—for example, the rewarding of high-voltage electroencephalograms as a treatment for insomnia. While it is far too early to promise any cures, it certainly will be worth while to investigate thoroughly the therapeutic possibilities of improved instrumental training techniques.

References and Notes

1. *The Dialogues of Plato*, B. Jowett, Transl., (Univ. of Oxford Press, London, ed. 2, 1875), vol. 3, "Timaeus."
2. X. Bichat, *Recherches Physiologiques sur la Vie et le Mort* (Brosson, Gabon, Paris, 1800).
3. W. B. Cannon, *The Wisdom of the Body* (Norton, New York, 1932).
4. F. Alexander, *Psychosomatic Medicine: Its Principles and Applications* (Norton, New York, 1950), pp. 40–41.
5. G. A. Kimble, *Hilgard and Marquis' Conditioning and Learning* (Appleton-Century-Crofts, New York, ed. 2, 1961), p. 100.
6. B. F. Skinner, *The Behavior of Organisms* (Appleton-Century, New York, 1938); O. H. Mowrer, *Harvard Educ. Rev.* **17**, 102 (1947).
7. N. E. Miller and J. Dollard, *Social Learning and Imitation* (Yale Univ. Press, New Haven, 1941); J. Dollard and N. E. Miller, *Personality and Psychotherapy* (McGraw-Hill, New York, 1950); N. E. Miller, *Psychol. Rev.* **58**, 375 (1951).
8. N. E. Miller, *Ann. N.Y. Acad. Sci.* **92**, 830 (1961); ——, in *Nebraska Symposium on Motivation*, M. R. Jones, Ed. (Univ. of Nebraska Press, Lincoln, 1963); ——, in *Proc. 3rd World Congr. Psychiat., Montreal, 1961* (1963), vol. 3, p. 213.
9. ——, in "Proceedings, 18th International Congress of Psychology, Moscow, 1966," in press.
10. —— and A. Carmona, *J. Comp. Physiol. Psychol.* **63**, 1 (1967).
11. J. A. Trowill, *ibid.*, p. 7.
12. N. E. Miller and L. V. DiCara, *ibid.*, p. 12.
13. L. V. DiCara and N. E. Miller, *Commun. Behav. Biol.* **2**, 19 (1968).
14. ——, *J. Comp. Physiol. Psychol.* **65**, 8 (1968).
15. ——, *ibid.*, in press.
16. D. J. Ehrlich and R. B. Malmo, *Neuropsychologia* **5**, 219 (1967).
17. "It even becomes difficult to postulate enough different thoughts each arousing a different emotion, each of which in turn innately elicits a specific visceral response. And if one assumes a more direct specific connection between different thoughts and different visceral responses, the notion becomes indistinguishable from the ideo-motor hypothesis of the voluntary movement of skeletal muscles." [W. James, *Principles of Psychology* (Dover, New York, new ed., 1950), vol. 2, chap. 26].
18. N. E. Miller and A. Banuazizi, *J. Comp. Physiol. Psychol.* **65**, 1 (1968).
19. A. Banuazizi, thesis, Yale University (1968).
20. N. E. Miller and L. V. DiCara, *Amer. J. Physiol.* **215**, 677 (1968).
21. A. Carmona, N. E. Miller, T. Demierre, in preparation.
22. A. Carmona, in preparation.
23. L. V. DiCara and N. E. Miller, *Commun. Behav. Biol.* **1**, 209 (1968).
24. ——, *Science* **159**, 1485 (1968).
25. ——, *Psychosom. Med.* **30**, 489 (1968).
26. L. V. DiCara and J. M. Weiss, *J. Comp. Physiol. Psychol.*, in press.
27. L. V. DiCara and N. E. Miller, *Physiol. Behav.*, in press.
28. N. E. Miller, *Science* **152**, 676 (1966).
29. A. Carmona, thesis, Yale University (1967).
30. For somewhat similar work on the single-cell level, see J. Olds and M. E. Olds, *in Brain Mechanisms and Learning*, J. Delafresnaye, A. Fessard, J. Konorski, Eds. (Blackwell, London, 1961).
31. E. S. Katkin and N. E. Murray, *Psychol. Bull.* **70**, 52 (1968); for a reply to their criticisms, see A. Crider, G. Schwartz, S. Shnidman, *ibid.*, in press.

32. N. E. Miller, L. V. DiCara, G. Wolf, *Amer. J. Physiol.* **215**, 684 (1968).
33. N. E. Miller, in *Personality Change,* D. Byrne and P. Worchel, Eds. (Wiley, New York, 1964), p. 149.
34. J. I. Lacey and B. C. Lacey, *Amer. J. Psychol.* **71**, 50 (1958); *Ann. N.Y. Acad. Sci.* **98**, 1257 (1962).
35. H. Barry III, personal communication.
36. N. E. Miller, *Proc. N.Y. Acad. Sci.*, in press.
37. Objective recording of such symptoms might be useful also in monitoring the effects of quite different types of psychotherapy.
38. B. T. Engel and K. T. Melmon, personal communication.
39. The work described is supported by U.S. Public Health Service grant MH 13189.

QUESTIONS FOR REFLECTION AND DISCUSSION:

1. What is the autonomic nervous system? What behaviors (bodily responses) are affected by the autonomic nervous system? What kinds of autonomic responses were conditioned by Miller?

2. What is the difference between voluntary and involuntary behavior?

3. How did you respond when you read that Miller had paralyzed animals with curare? Why did he use it? (How did use of curare prevent rats from "cheating" to alter their heart rates?)

4. What is meant by escape and avoidance learning? How did DiCara and Miller use escape and avoidance learning in the conditioning of rats?

5. What problems does Miller refer to in discussing the difficulty of replicating his studies with animals with humans?

6. What kinds of "therapeutic (biofeedback) training" does Miller suggest for humans?

SOURCE

Bandura, A., Ross, D., & Ross, S. A. (1961). Transmission of aggression through imitation of aggressive models. *Journal of Abnormal and Social Psychology, 63,* 575–582.

Psychologists, educators, social commentators, and parents are vitally concerned about the epidemic of violence in the media. Nearly all of our children are routinely exposed to murder, beatings, and sexual assault—that is, when they turn on the TV set. It has been estimated that if a child watches two to four hours of TV a day, she or he will have seen 8,000 murders and another 100,000 acts of violence by the time she or he has finished elementary school. Moreover, violence tends to be glamorized on TV. In the typical Saturday morning cartoon show, superheroes battle villains who are trying to take over the world. Violence is also often shown to have only temporary or minimal effects. (How often has Wily Coyote fallen from a cliff and been pounded into the ground by a boulder, only to bounce back and pursue the Road Runner again?) In most TV shows, there is no remorse, criticism, or penalty for violent behavior.

What do viewers learn? Does exposure to this orgy of violence encourage young (and older) viewers to be violent themselves? In the early days of TV, answers were somewhat speculative. Some observers argued with sincerity—if not with knowledge—that children could easily distinguish between the scenes they watched on TV and their own lives, and that TV violence was merely entertaining. Then researchers such as psychologist Albert Bandura and others conducted experiments that began to make the overwhelming case that continual exposure to mayhem in the media could well encourage children to commit mayhem in their own lives. Here is one of the classic early studies on the effects of media violence, courtesy of Bandura and his colleagues.

Transmission of Aggression Through Imitation of Aggressive Models

ALBERT BANDURA, DOROTHEA ROSS, AND SHEILA A. ROSS
STANFORD UNIVERSITY

A previous study, designed to account for the phenomenon of identification in terms of incidental learning, demonstrated that children readily imitated behavior exhibited by an adult model in the presence of the model (Bandura & Huston, 1961). A series of experiments by Blake (1958) and others (Grosser, Polansky, & Lippitt, 1951; Rosenblith, 1959; Schachter & Hall, 1952) have likewise shown that mere observation of responses of a model has a facilitating effect on subjects' reactions in the immediate social influence setting.

While these studies provide convincing evidence for the influence and control exerted on others by the behavior of a model, a more crucial test of imitative learning involves the generalization of imitative response patterns to new settings in which the model is absent.

In the experiment reported in this paper children were exposed to aggressive and nonaggressive adult models and were then tested for amount of imitative learning in a new situation in the absence of the model. According to the prediction, subjects exposed to aggressive models would reproduce aggressive acts resembling those of their models and would differ in this respect both from subjects who observed nonaggressive models and from those who had no prior exposure to any models. This hypothesis assumed that subjects had learned imitative habits as a result of prior reinforcement, and these tendencies would generalize to some extent to adult experimenters (Miller & Dollard, 1941).

It was further predicted that observation of subdued nonaggressive models would have a generalized inhibiting effect on the subjects' subsequent behavior, and this effect would be reflected in a difference between the nonaggressive and the control groups, with subjects in the latter group displaying significantly more aggression.

Hypotheses were also advanced concerning the influence of the sex of model and sex of subjects on imitation. Fauls and Smith (1956) have shown that preschool children perceive their parents as having distinct preferences regarding sex appropriate modes of behavior for their children. Their findings, as well as informal observation, suggest that parents reward imitation of sex appropriate behavior and discourage or punish sex inappropriate imitative responses, e.g., a male child is unlikely to receive much reward for performing female appropriate activities, such as cooking, or for adopting other aspects of the maternal role, but these same behaviors are typically welcomed if performed by females. As a result of differing reinforcement histories, tendencies to imitate male and female models thus acquire differential habit strength. One would expect, on this basis, subjects to imitate the behavior of a same-sex model to a greater degree than a model of the opposite sex.

Since aggression, however, is a highly masculine-typed behavior, boys should be more predisposed than girls toward imitating aggression, the difference being most marked for subjects exposed to the male aggressive model.

Method

SUBJECTS

The subjects were 36 boys and 36 girls enrolled in the Stanford University Nursery School. They ranged in age from 37 to 69 months, with a mean age of 52 months.

Two adults, a male and a female, served in the role of model, and one female experimenter conducted the study for all 72 children.

EXPERIMENTAL DESIGN

Subjects were divided into eight experimental groups of six subjects each and a control group consisting of 24 subjects. Half the experimental subjects were exposed to aggressive models and half were exposed to models that were subdued and nonaggressive in their behavior. These groups were further subdivided into male and female subjects. Half the subjects in the aggressive and nonaggressive conditions observed same-sex models, while the remaining subjects in each group viewed models of the opposite sex. The control group had no prior exposure to the adult models and was tested only in the generalization situation.

It seemed reasonable to expect that the subjects' level of aggressiveness would be positively related to the readiness with which they imitated aggressive modes of behavior. Therefore, in order to increase the precision of treatment comparisons, subjects in the experimental and control groups were matched individually on the basis of ratings of their aggressive behavior in social interactions in the nursery school.

The subjects were rated on four five-point rating scales by the experimenter and a nursery school teacher, both of whom were well acquainted with the children. These scales measured the extent in which subjects displayed physical aggression, verbal aggression, aggression toward inanimate objects, and aggressive inhibition. The latter scale, which dealt with the subjects' tendency to inhibit aggressive reactions in the face of high instigation, provided a measure of aggression anxiety.

Fifty-one subjects were rated independently by both judges so as to permit an assessment of interrater agreement. The reliability of the composite aggression score, estimated by means of the Pearson product-moment correlation, was .89.

The composite score was obtained by summing the ratings on the four aggression scales; on the basis of these scores, subjects were arranged in triplets and assigned at random to one of two treatment conditions or to the control group.

EXPERIMENTAL CONDITIONS

In the first step in the procedure subjects were brought individually by the experimenter to the experimental room and the model who was in the hallway outside the room, was invited by the experimenter to come and join in the game. The experimenter then escorted the subject to one corner of the room, which was structured as the subject's play area. After seating the child at a small table, the experimenter demonstrated how the subject could design pictures with potato prints and picture stickers provided. The potato prints included a variety of geometrical forms; the stickers were attractive multicolor pictures of animals, flowers, and western figures to be pasted on a pastoral scene. These activities were selected since they had been established, by previous studies in the nursery school, as having high interest value for the children.

After having settled the subject in his corner, the experimenter escorted the model to the opposite corner of the room which contained a small table and chair, a tinker toy set, a mallet, and a 5-foot inflated Bobo doll. The experimenter explained that these were the materials provided for the model to play with and, after the model was seated, the experimenter left the experimental room.

With subjects in the *nonaggressive condition*, the model assembled the tinker toys in a quiet subdued manner totally ignoring the Bobo doll.

In contrast, with subjects in the *aggressive condition*, the model began by assembling the tinker toys but after approximately a minute had elapsed, the model turned to the Bobo doll and spent the remainder of the period aggressing toward it.

Imitative learning can be clearly demonstrated if a model performs sufficiently novel patterns of responses which are unlikely to occur independently of the observation of the behavior of a model and if a subject reproduces these behaviors in substantially identical form. For this reason, in addition to punching the Bobo doll, a response that is likely to be performed by children independently of a demonstration, the model exhibited distinctive aggressive acts which were to be scored as imitative responses. The model laid Bobo on its side, sat on it and punched it repeatedly in the nose. The model then raised the Bobo doll, picked up the mallet and struck the doll on the head. Following the mallet aggression, the model tossed the doll up in the air aggressively and kicked it about the room. This sequence of physically aggressive acts was repeated approximately three times, interspersed with verbally aggressive responses such as, "Sock him in the nose . . . ," "Hit him down . . . ," "Throw him in the air . . . ," "Kick him . . . ," "Pow . . . ," and two nonaggressive comments, "He keeps coming back for more" and "He sure is a tough fella."

Thus in the exposure situation, subjects were provided with a diverting task which occupied their attention while at the same time insured observation of the model's behavior in the absence of any instructions to observe or to learn the responses in question. Since subjects could not perform the model's aggressive behavior, any learning that occurred was purely on an observational or covert basis.

At the end of 10 minutes, the experimenter entered the room, informed the subject that he would now go to another game room, and bid the model goodbye.

AGGRESSION AROUSAL

Subjects were tested for the amount of imitative learning in a different experimental room that was set off from the main nursery school building. The two experimental situations were thus clearly differentiated; in fact, many subjects were under the impression that they were no longer on the nursery school grounds.

Prior to the test for imitation, however, all subjects, experimental and control, were subjected to mild aggression arousal to insure that they were under some degree of instigation to aggression. The arousal experience was included for two main reasons. In the first place, observation of aggressive behavior exhibited by others tends to reduce the probability of aggression on the part of the observer (Rosenbaum & deCharms, 1960). Consequently, subjects in the aggressive condition, in relation both to the nonaggressive and control groups, would be under weaker instigation following exposure to the models. Second, if subjects in the nonaggressive condition expressed little aggression in the face of appropriate instigation, the presence of an inhibitory process would seem to be indicated.

Following the exposure experience, therefore, the experimenter brought the subject to an anteroom that contained these relatively attractive toys: a fire engine, a locomotive, a jet fighter plane, a cable car, a colorful spinning top, and a doll set complete with wardrobe, doll carriage, and baby crib. The experimenter explained that the toys were for the subject to play with but, as soon as the subject became sufficiently involved with the play material (usually in about 2 minutes), the experimenter remarked that these were her very best toys, that she did not let just anyone play with them, and that she had decided to reserve these toys for the other children. However, the subject could play with any of the toys that were in the next room. The experimenter and the subject then entered the adjoining experimental room.

It was necessary for the experimenter to remain in the room during the experimental session; otherwise a number of the children would either refuse to remain alone or would leave before the termination of the session. However, in order to minimize any influence her presence might have on the subject's behavior, the experimenter remained as inconspicuous as possible by busying herself with paper work at a desk in the far corner of the room and avoiding any interaction with the child.

TEST FOR DELAYED IMITATION

The experimental room contained a variety of toys including some that could be used in imitative or nonimitative aggression, and others that tended to elicit predominantly nonaggressive forms of behavior. The aggressive toys included a 3-foot Bobo doll, a mallet and peg board, two dart guns, and a tether ball with a face painted on it which hung from the ceiling. The nonaggressive toys, on the other hand, included a tea set, crayons and coloring paper, a ball, two dolls, three bears, cars and trucks, and plastic farm animals.

In order to eliminate any variation in behavior due to mere placement of the toys in the room, the play material was arranged in a fixed order for each of the sessions.

The subject spent 20 minutes in this experimental room during which time his behavior was rated in terms of predetermined response categories by judges who observed the session through a one-way mirror in an adjoining observation room. The 20-minute session was divided into 5-second intervals by means of an electric interval timer, thus yielding a total number of 240 response units for each subject.

The male model scored the experimental sessions for all 72 children. Except for the cases in which he served as model, he did not have knowledge of the subjects' group assignments. In order to provide an estimate of interscorer agreement, the performances of half the subjects were also scored independently by a second observer. Thus one or the other of the two observers usually had no knowledge of the conditions to which the subjects were assigned. Since, however, all but two of the subjects in the aggressive condition performed the models' novel aggressive responses while subjects in the other conditions only rarely exhibited such reactions, subjects who were exposed to the aggressive models could be readily identified through their distinctive behavior.

The responses scored involved highly specific concrete classes of behavior and yielded high interscorer reliabilities, the product-moment coefficients being in the .90s.

RESPONSE MEASURES

Three measures of imitation were obtained:

Imitation of physical aggression: This category included acts of striking the Bobo doll with the mallet, sitting on the doll and punching it in the nose, kicking the doll, and tossing it in the air.

Imitative verbal aggression: Subject repeats the phrases, "Sock him," "Hit him down," "Kick him," "Throw him in the air," or "Pow."

Imitative nonaggressive verbal responses: Subject repeats, "He keeps coming back for more," or "He sure is a tough fella."

During the pretest, a number of the subjects imitated the essential components of the model's behavior but did not perform the complete act, or they directed the imitative aggressive response to some object other than the Bobo doll. Two responses of this type were therefore scored and were interpreted as partially imitative behavior.

Mallet aggression: Subject strikes objects other than the Bobo doll aggressively with the mallet.

Sits on Bobo doll: Subject lays the Bobo doll on its side and sits on it, but does not aggress toward it.

The following additional nonimitative aggressive responses were scored:

Punches Bobo doll: Subject strikes, slaps, or pushes the doll aggressively.

Nonimitative physical and verbal aggression: This category included physically aggressive acts directed toward objects other than the Bobo doll and any hostile remarks except for those in the verbal imitation category; e.g., "Shoot the Bobo," "Cut him," "Stupid ball," "Knock over people," "Horses fighting, biting."

Aggressive gun play: Subject shoots darts or aims the guns and fires imaginary shots at objects in the room.

Ratings were also made of the number of behavior units in which subjects played nonaggressively or sat quietly and did not play with any of the material at all.

Results

COMPLETE IMITATION OF MODELS' BEHAVIOR

Subjects in the aggression condition reproduced a good deal of physical and verbal aggressive behavior resembling that of the models, and their mean scores differed markedly from those of subjects in the nonaggressive and control groups who exhibited virtually no imitative aggression (see Table 15.01).

TABLE 15.01

	MEAN AGGRESSION SCORES FOR EXPERIMENTAL AND CONTROL SUBJECTS				
	EXPERIMENTAL GROUPS				
	AGGRESSIVE		NONAGGRESSIVE		
RESPONSE CATEGORY	F MODEL	M MODEL	F MODEL	M MODEL	CONTROL GROUPS
Imitative physical aggression					
Female subjects	5.5	7.2	2.5	0.0	1.2
Male subjects	12.4	25.8	0.2	1.5	2.0
Imitative verbal aggression					
Female subjects	13.7	2.0	0.3	0.0	0.7
Male subjects	4.3	12.7	1.1	0.0	1.7
Mallet aggression					
Female subjects	17.2	18.7	0.5	0.5	13.1
Male subjects	15.5	28.8	18.7	6.7	13.5
Punches Bobo doll					
Female subjects	6.3	16.5	5.8	4.3	11.7
Male subjects	18.9	11.9	15.6	14.8	15.7
Nonimitative aggression					
Female subjects	21.3	8.4	7.2	1.4	6.1
Male subjects	16.2	36.7	26.1	22.3	24.6
Aggressive gun play					
Female subjects	1.8	4.5	2.6	2.5	3.7
Male subjects	7.3	15.9	8.9	16.7	14.3

Since there were only a few scores for subjects in the nonaggressive and control conditions (approximately 70% of the subjects had zero scores), and the assumption of homogeneity of variance could not be made, the Friedman two-way analysis of variance by ranks was employed to test the significance of the obtained differences.

The prediction that exposure of subjects to aggressive models increases the probability of aggressive behavior is clearly confirmed (see Table 15.02). The main effect of treatment conditions is highly significant both for physical and verbal imitative aggression. Comparison of pairs of scores by the sign test shows that the obtained over-all differences were due almost entirely to the aggression displayed by subjects who had been exposed to the aggressive models. Their scores were significantly higher than those of either the nonaggressive or control groups, which did not differ from each other (Table 15.02).

Imitation was not confined to the model's aggressive responses. Approximately one-third of the subjects in the aggressive condition also repeated the model's nonaggressive verbal responses while none of the subjects in either the nonaggressive or control groups made such remarks. This difference, tested by means of the Cochran Q test, was significant well beyond the .001 level (Table 15.02).

PARTIAL IMITATION OF MODELS' BEHAVIOR

Differences in the predicted direction were also obtained on the two measures of partial imitation.

Analysis of variance of scores based on the subjects' use of the mallet aggressively toward objects other than the Bobo doll reveals that treatment conditions are a statistically significant source of variation (Table 15.02). In addition, individual sign tests show that both the aggressive and the control groups, relative to subjects in the nonaggressive condition, produced significantly more mallet aggression, the difference being particularly marked with

TABLE 15.02

| | | | | COMPARISON OF PAIRS OF TREATMENT CONDITIONS | | |
| | | | | AGGRESSIVE VS. NON-AGGRESSIVE | AGGRESSIVE VS. CONTROL | NONAG-GRESSIVE VS. CONTROL |
RESPONSE CATEGORY	$\chi^2 r$	Q	p	p	p	p
Imitative responses						
Physical aggression	27.17		<.001	<.001	<.001	.09
Verbal aggression	9.17		<.02	.004	.048	.09
Nonaggressive verbal responses		17.50	<.001	.004	.004	ns
Partial imitation						
Mallet aggression	11.06		<.01	.026	ns	.005
Sits on Bobo		13.44	<.01	.018	.059	ns
Nonimitative aggression						
Punches Bobo doll	2.87		ns			
Physical and verbal	8.96		<.02	.026	ns	ns
Aggressive gun play	2.75		ns			

Table caption: SIGNIFICANCE OF THE DIFFERENCES BETWEEN EXPERIMENTAL AND CONTROL GROUPS IN THE EXPRESSION OF AGGRESSION

regard to female subjects. Girls who observed nonaggressive models performed a mean number of 0.5 mallet aggression responses as compared to mean values of 18.0 and 13.1 for girls in the aggressive and control groups, respectively.

Although subjects who observed aggressive models performed more mallet aggression ($M = 20.0$) than their controls ($M = 13.3$), the difference was not statistically significant.

With respect to the partially imitative response of sitting on the Bobo doll, the over-all group differences were significant beyond the .01 level (Table 15.02). Comparison of pairs of scores by the sign test procedure reveals that subjects in the aggressive group reproduced this aspect of the models' behavior to a greater extent than did the nonaggressive ($p = .018$) or the control ($p = .059$) subjects. The latter two groups, on the other hand, did not differ from each other.

NONIMITATIVE AGGRESSION

Analyses of variance of the remaining aggression measures (Table 15.02) show that treatment conditions did not influence the extent to which subjects engaged in aggressive gun play or punched the Bobo doll. The effect of conditions is highly significant ($\chi^2_r = 8.96$, $p < .02$), however, in the case of the subjects' expression of nonimitative physical

and verbal aggression. Further comparison of treatment pairs reveals that the main source of the overall difference was the aggressive and nonaggressive groups which differed significantly from each other (Table 15.02), with subjects exposed to the aggressive models displaying the greater amount of aggression.

INFLUENCE OF SEX OF MODEL AND SEX OF SUBJECTS ON IMITATION

The hypothesis that boys are more prone than girls to imitate aggression exhibited by a model was only partially confirmed. *t* tests computed for subjects in the aggressive condition reveal that boys reproduced more imitative physical aggression than girls ($t = 2.50$, $p < .01$). The groups do not differ, however, in their imitation of verbal aggression.

The use of nonparametric tests, necessitated by the extremely skewed distributions of scores for subjects in the nonaggressive and control conditions, preclude an over-all test of the influence of sex of model per se, and of the various interactions between the main effects. Inspection of the means presented in Table 15.01 for subjects in the aggression condition, however, clearly suggests the possibility of a Sex × Model interaction. This interaction effect is much more consistent and pronounced for the male model than for the female model. Male subjects, for example, exhibited more physical ($t = 2.07$, $p < .05$) and verbal imitative aggression ($t = 2.51$, $p < .05$), more nonimitative aggression ($t = 3.15$, $p < .025$), and engaged in significantly more aggressive gun play ($t = 2.12$, $p < .05$) following exposure to the aggressive male model than the female subjects. In contrast, girls exposed to the female model performed considerably more imitative verbal aggression and more nonimitative aggression than did the boys (Table 15.01). The variances, however, were equally large and with only a small N in each cell the mean differences did not reach statistical significance.

Data for the nonaggressive and control subjects provide additional suggestive evidence that the behavior of the male model exerted a greater influence than the female model on the subjects' behavior in the generalization situation.

It will be recalled that, except for the greater amount of mallet aggression exhibited by the control subjects, no significant differences were obtained between the nonaggressive and control groups. The data indicate, however, that the absence of significant differences between these two groups was due primarily to the fact that subjects exposed to the nonaggressive female model did not differ from the controls on any of the measures of aggression. With respect to the male model, on the other hand, the differences between the groups are striking. Comparison of the sets of scores by means of the sign test reveals that, in relation to the control group, subjects exposed to the nonaggressive male model performed significantly less imitative physical aggression ($p = .06$), less imitative verbal aggression ($p = .002$), less mallet aggression ($p = .003$), less nonimitative physical and verbal aggression ($p = .03$), and they were less inclined to punch the Bobo doll ($p = .07$).

While the comparison of subgroups, when some of the over-all tests do not reach statistical significance, is likely to capitalize on chance differences, nevertheless the consistency of the findings adds support to the interpretation in terms of influence by the model.

NONAGGRESSIVE BEHAVIOR

With the exception of expected sex differences, Lindquist (1956) Type III analyses of variance of the nonaggressive response scores yielded few significant differences.

Female subjects spent more time than boys playing with dolls ($p < .001$), with the tea set ($p < .001$), and coloring ($p < .05$). The boys, on the other hand, devoted significantly more time than the girls to exploratory play with the guns ($p <$ .01). No sex differences were found in respect to the subjects use of the other stimulus objects, i.e., farm animals, cars, or tether ball.

Treatment conditions did produce significant differences on two measures of nonaggressive behavior that are worth mentioning. Subjects in the nonaggressive condition engaged in significantly more nonaggressive play with dolls than either subjects in the aggressive group ($t = 2.67$, $p < .02$), or in the control group ($t = 2.57$, $p < .02$).

Even more noteworthy is the finding that subjects who observed nonaggressive models spent more than twice as much time as subjects in aggressive condition ($t = 3.07$, $p < .01$) in simply sitting quietly without handling any of the play material.

Discussion

Much current research on social learning is focused on the shaping of new behavior through rewarding and punishing consequences. Unless responses are emitted, however, they cannot be influenced. The results of this study provide strong evidence that observation of cues produced by the behavior of others is one effective means of eliciting certain forms of responses for which the original probability is very low or zero. Indeed, social imitation may hasten or short-cut the acquisition of new behaviors without the necessity of reinforcing successive approximations as suggested by Skinner (1953).

Thus subjects given an opportunity to observe aggressive models later reproduced a good deal of physical and verbal aggression (as well as nonaggressive responses) substantially identical with that of the model. In contrast, subjects who were exposed to nonaggressive models and those who had no previous exposure to any models only rarely performed such responses.

To the extent that observation of adult models displaying aggression communicates permissiveness for aggressive behavior, such exposure may serve to weaken inhibitory responses and thereby to increase the probability of aggressive reactions to subsequent frustrations. The fact, however, that subjects expressed their aggression in ways that clearly resembled the novel patterns exhibited by the models provides striking evidence for the occurrence of learning by imitation.

In the procedure employed by Miller and Dollard (1941) for establishing imitative behavior, adult or peer models performed discrimination responses following which they were consistently rewarded, and the subjects were similarly reinforced whenever they matched the leaders' choice responses. While these experiments have been widely accepted as demonstrations of learning by means of imitation, in fact, they simply involve a special case of discrimination learning in which the behavior of others serves as discriminative stimuli for responses that are already part of the subject's repertoire. Auditory or visual environmental cues could easily have been substituted for the social stimuli to facilitate the discrimination learning. In contrast, the process of imitation studied in the present experiment differed in several important respects from the one investigated by Miller and Dollard in that subjects learned to combine fractional responses into relatively complex novel patterns solely by observing the performance of social models without any opportunity to perform the models' behavior in the exposure setting, and without any reinforcers delivered either to the models or to the observers.

An adequate theory of the mechanisms underlying imitative learning is lacking. The explanations that have been offered (Logan, Olmsted, Rosner, Schwartz, & Stevens, 1955; Maccoby, 1959) assume that the imitator performs the model's responses covertly. If it can be assumed additionally that rewards and punishments are self-administered in conjunction with the covert responses, the process of imitative learning could be accounted for in terms of the same principles that govern instrumental trial-and-error learning. In the early stages of the developmental process, however, the range of component responses in the organism's repertoire is probably increased through a process of classical conditioning (Bandura & Huston, 1961; Mowrer, 1950).

The data provide some evidence that the male model influenced the subjects' behavior outside the exposure setting to a greater extent than was true for the female model. In the analyses of the Sex × Model interactions, for example, only the comparisons involving the male model yielded significant differences. Similarly, subjects exposed to the nonaggressive male model performed less aggressive behavior than the controls, whereas comparisons, involving the female model were consistently nonsignificant.

In a study of learning by imitation, Rosenblith (1959) has likewise found male experimenters more effective than females in influencing childrens' behavior. Rosenblith advanced the tentative explanation that the school setting may involve some social deprivation in respect to adult males which, in turn, enhance the male's reward value.

The trends in the data yielded by the present study suggest an alternative explanation. In the case of a highly masculine-typed behavior such as physical aggression, there is a tendency for both male and female subjects to imitate the male model to a greater degree than the female model. On the other hand, in the case of verbal aggression, which is less clearly sex linked, the greatest amount of imitation occurs in relation to the same-sex model. These trends together with the finding that boys in relation to girls are in general more imitative of physical aggression but do not differ in imitation of verbal aggression, suggest that subjects may be differentially affected by the sex of the model but that predictions must take into account the degree to which the behavior in question is sex-typed.

The preceding discussion has assumed that maleness-femaleness rather than some other personal characteristics of the particular models involved, is the significant variable—an assumption that cannot be tested directly with the data at hand. It was clearly evident, however, particularly from boys' spontaneous remarks about the display of aggression by the female model, that some subjects at least were responding in terms of a sex discrimination and their prior learning about what is sex appropriate behavior (e.g., "Who is that lady. That's not the way for a lady to behave. Ladies are supposed to act like ladies. . . ." "You should have seen what that girl did in there. She was just acting like a man. I never saw a girl act like that before. She was punching and fighting but no swearing."). Aggression by the male model, on the other hand, was more likely to be seen as appropriate and approved by both the boys ("Al's a good socker, he beat up Bobo. I want to sock like Al.") and the girls ("That man is a strong fighter, he punched and punched and he could hit Bobo right down to the floor and if Bobo got up he said, 'Punch your nose.' He's a good fighter like Daddy.").

The finding that subjects exposed to the quiet models were more inhibited and unresponsive than subjects in the aggressive condition, together with the obtained difference on the aggression measures, suggests that exposure to inhibited models not only decreases the probability of occurrence of aggressive behavior but also generally restricts the range of behavior emitted by the subjects.

"Identification with aggressor" (Freud, 1946) or "defensive identification" (Mowrer, 1950), whereby a person presumably transforms himself from object to agent of aggression by adopting the attributes of an aggressive threatening model so as to allay anxiety, is widely accepted as an explanation of the imitative learning of aggression.

The development of aggressive modes of response by children of aggressively punitive adults, however, may simply reflect object displacement without involving any such mechanism of defensive identification. In studies of child training antecedents of aggressively antisocial adolescents (Bandura & Walters, 1959) and of young hyperaggressive boys (Bandura, 1960), the parents were found to be nonpermissive and punitive of aggression directed toward themselves. On the other hand, they actively encouraged and reinforced their sons' aggression toward persons outside the home. This pattern of differential reinforcement of aggressive behavior served to inhibit the boys' aggression toward the original instigators and fostered the displacement of aggression toward objects and situations eliciting much weaker inhibitory responses.

Moreover, the findings from an earlier study (Bandura & Huston, 1961), in which children imitated to an equal degree aggression exhibited by a nurturant and a nonnurturant model, together with the results of the present experiment in which subjects readily imitated aggressive models who were more or less neutral figures suggest that mere observation of aggression, regardless of the quality of the model-subject relationship, is a sufficient condition for producing imitative aggression in children. A comparative study of the subjects' imitation of aggressive models who are feared, who are linked and esteemed, or who are essentially neutral figures would throw some light on whether or not a more parsimonious theory than the one involved in "identification with the aggressor" can explain the modeling process.

Summary

Twenty-four preschool children were assigned to each of three conditions. One experimental group observed aggressive adult models; a second observed inhibited nonaggressive models; while subjects in a control group had no prior exposure to the models. Half the subjects in the experimental conditions observed same-sex models and half viewed models of the opposite sex. Subjects were then tested for the amount of imitative as well as nonimitative aggression performed in a new situation in the absence of the models.

Comparison of the subjects' behavior in the generalization situation revealed that subjects exposed to aggressive models reproduced a good deal of aggression resembling that of the models, and that their mean scores differed markedly from those of subjects in the nonaggressive and control groups. Subjects in the aggressive condition also exhibited significantly more partially imitative and nonimitative aggressive behavior and were generally less inhibited in their behavior than subjects in the nonaggressive condition.

Imitation was found to be differentially influenced by the sex of the model with boys showing more aggression than girls following exposure to the male model, the difference being particularly marked on highly masculine-typed behavior.

Subjects who observed the nonaggressive models, especially the subdued male model, were generally less aggressive than their controls.

The implications of the findings based on this experiment and related studies for the psychoanalytic theory of identification with the aggressor were discussed.

References

1. Bandura, A. Relationship of family patterns to child behavior disorders. Progress Report, 1960, Stanford University, Project No. M-1734, United States Public Health Service.
2. Bandura, A., & Huston, Aletha C. Identification as a process of incidental learning. *J. Abnorm. Soc. Psychol.,* 1961, **63**, 311–318.
3. Bandura, A., & Walters, R. H. *Adolescent aggression.* New York: Ronald, 1959.
4. Blake, R. R. The other person in the situation. In R. Tagiuri & L. Petrullo (Eds.), *Person perception and interpersonal behavior.* Stanford, Calif: Stanford Univer. Press, 1958. Pp. 229–242.
5. Fauls, Lydia B., & Smith, W. D. Sex-role learning of five-year olds. *J. Genet. Psychol.,* 1956, **89**, 105–117.
6. Freud, Anna. *The ego and the mechanisms of defense.* New York: International Univer. Press, 1946.
7. Grosser, D., Polansky, N., & Lippitt, R. A laboratory study of behavior contagion. *Hum. Relat.,* 1951, **4**, 115–142.
8. Lindquist, E. F. *Design and analysis of experiments.* Boston: Houghton Mifflin, 1956.
9. Logan, F., Olmsted, O. L., Rosner, B. S., Schwartz, R. D., & Stevens, C. M. *Behavior theory and social science.* New Haven: Yale Univer. Press, 1955.
10. Maccoby, Eleanor E. Role-taking in childhood and its consequences for social learning. *Child Developm.,* 1959, **30**, 239–252.
11. Miller, N. E., & Dollard, J. *Social learning and imitation.* New Haven: Yale Univer. Press, 1941.
12. Mowrer, O. H. (Ed.) Identification: A link between learning theory and psychotherapy. In, *Learning theory and personality dynamics.* New York: Ronald, 1950. Pp. 69–94.
13. Rosenbaum, M. E., & deCharms, R. Direct and vicarious reduction of hostility. *J. Abnorm. Soc. Psychol.,* 1960, **60**, 105–111.
14. Rosenblith, Judy F. Learning by imitation in kindergarten children. *Child Developm.,* 1959, **30**, 69–80.
15. Schachter, S., & Hall, R. Group-derived restraints and audience persuasion. *Hum. Relat.,* 1952, **5**, 397–406.
16. Skinner, B. F. *Science and human behavior.* New York: Macmillan, 1953.

QUESTIONS FOR REFLECTION AND DISCUSSION:

1. In their introduction, which was published in 1961, the authors speak of "female appropriate activities, such as cooking." If the authors were writing today, do you think that their choice of wording would be different? How would it differ? Why?

2. Why do the researchers predict that boys will be more likely than girls to imitate aggressive behavior?

3. What was the aggressive behavior displayed by the model in the experiment?

4. What kinds of behaviors by subjects were interpreted as indicative of imitation and aggression?

5. Are you satisfied that the kinds of aggressive behavior shown by the subjects is the equivalent of criminal aggression in society at large? Why or why not?

6. Your authors write that exposure to an aggressive model "may serve to weaken inhibitory responses." What does that mean?

7. Your authors write that "An adequate theory of the mechanisms underlying imitative learning is lacking"? Why do some learning theorists think that it is important to suggest that "the imitator performs the model's responses covertly"? (Hint: Refer to the concepts of vicarious conditioning and rewards.) Which theory suggests that the explanation might be "identification with the aggressor"? Why would people be motivated to identify with an aggressor?

8. Males and females were not equally effective as aggressive models for boys and girls. What reasons do your authors offer for the difference?

9. What studies have been carried out on the effects of media violence since the current study? Are the findings consistent with current findings?

SOURCE

Tolman, E. C. (1948). Cognitive maps in rats and men. *Psychological Review, 55,* 189–208.

Many learning theorists, particularly behaviorists, see the processes of learning as largely mechanical. When asked why finding a tray of food may lead a rat to learn to turn right or turn left at a choice point in a maze, they may answer, "Because it is reinforced for doing so." That is, they explain learning in terms of the environmental conditions or situation that rat is in, not in terms of what might be going on inside the rat.

Behavioral explanations of learning are scientific in that they enable us to avoid speculating about things we cannot directly observe or measure. (Who can observe or measure the events occurring in the mind of a human, much less than in the "mind" of a rat?) In fact, one of the motivating forces on John Watson, the founder of American behaviorism, is that he was asked to speculate on what a rat might be thinking at choice points in mazes. He saw the question as absurd and argued that we must focus on public events such as what organisms do, and not on private events such as thinking. What was going on inside the organism as it learned became referred to as a "black box"—meaning that one could not see within—and most laboratory researchers at the time agreed that it was most scientific to leave the black box alone.

There is no question that behaviorism is scientific, but one hallmark of a useful theory is the range of events that it can describe, explain, predict, and control. Behaviorism argued that organisms learn to expect things on the basis of association (classical conditioning), but that they learn to do things—such as turn in a certain direction in a maze on the basis of operant conditioning. Reinforcement is at the heart of operant conditioning; the learning of operants is not supposed to occur in the absence of reinforcement. However, in a classic paper published at about mid-20th century, University of California psychologist presented evidence that organisms can indeed learn to do things in the absence of reinforcement. In fact, Tolman dared to venture within the black box to declare that organisms— even the lowly rat—form cognitive (mental) maps of their environment and then call upon their knowledge, as needed, to obtain reinforcers.

Cognitive Maps in Rats and Men

EDWARD C. TOLMAN
UNIVERSITY OF CALIFORNIA

I shall devote the body of this paper to a description of experiments with rats. But I shall also attempt in a few words at the close to indicate the significance of these findings on rats for the clinical behavior of men. Most of the rat investigations, which I shall report, were carried out in the Berkeley laboratory. But I shall also include, occasionally, accounts of the behavior of non-Berkeley rats who obviously have misspent their lives in out-of-State laboratories. Furthermore, in reporting our Berkeley experiments I shall have to omit a very great many. The ones I *shall* talk about were carried out by graduate students (or underpaid research assistants) who, supposedly, got some of their ideas from me. And a few, though a very few, were even carried out by me myself.

Let me begin by presenting diagrams for a couple of typical mazes, an alley maze and an elevated maze. In the typical experiment a hungry rat is put at the entrance of the maze (alley or elevated), and wanders about through the various true path segments and blind alleys until he finally comes to the food box and eats. This is repeated (again in the typical experiment) one trial every 24 hours and the animal tends to make fewer and fewer errors (that is, blind-alley entrances) and to take less and less time between start and goal-box until finally he is entering no blinds at all and running in a very few seconds from start to goal. The results are usually presented in the form of average curves of blind-entrances, or of seconds from start to finish, for groups of rats.

All students agree as to the facts. They disagree, however, on theory and explanation.

(1) First, there is a school of animal psychologists which believes that the maze behavior of rats is a matter of mere simple stimulus-response connections. Learning, according to them, consists in the strengthening of some of these connections and in the weakening of others. According to this 'stimulus-

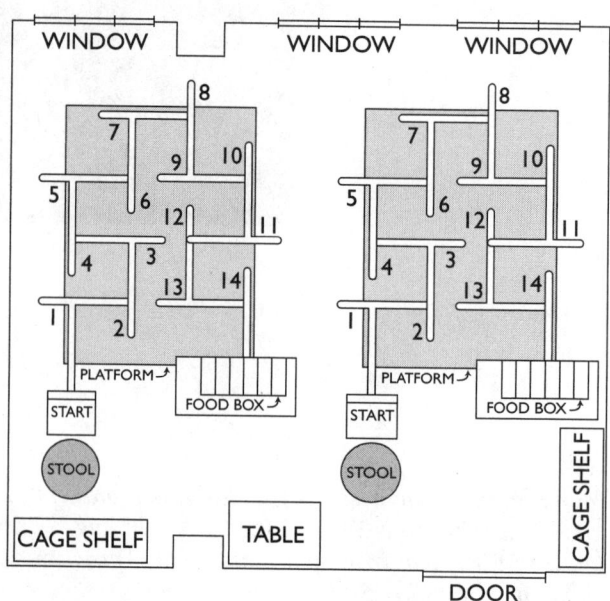

FIGURE 16.02

14-Unit T-Elevated Mazes. (From C. H. Honzik, The sensory basis of maze learning in rats. *Compar. Psychol. Monogr.,* 1936, 13, No. 4, p. 4. These were two identical mazes placed side by side in the same room.)

response' school the rat in progressing down the maze is helplessly responding to a succession of external stimuli—sights, sounds, smells, pressures, etc. impinging upon his external sense organs—plus internal stimuli coming from the viscera and from the skeletal muscles. These external and internal stimuli call out the walkings, runnings, turnings, retracings, smellings, rearings, and the like which appear. The rat's central nervous system, according to this view, may be likened to a complicated telephone switchboard. There are the incoming calls from sense-organs and there are the outgoing messages to muscles. Before the learning of a specific maze, the connecting switches (synapses according to the physiologist) are closed in one set of ways and produce the primarily exploratory responses which appear in the early trials. *Learning,* according to this view, consists in the respective strengthening and weakening of various of these connections; those connections which result in the animal's going down the true path become relatively more open to the passage of nervous impulses, whereas those which lead him into the blinds become relatively less open.

It must be noted in addition, however, that this stimulus-response school divides further into two subgroups.

(a) There is a subgroup which holds that the mere mechanics involved in the running of a maze

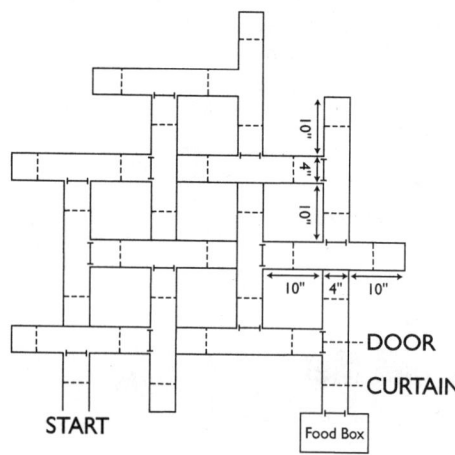

FIGURE 16.01

Plan of maze; 14-Unit T-Alley Maze. (From M. H. Elliott, The effect of change of reward on the maze performance of rats. *Univ. Calif. Publ. Psychol.,* 1928, 4, p. 20.)

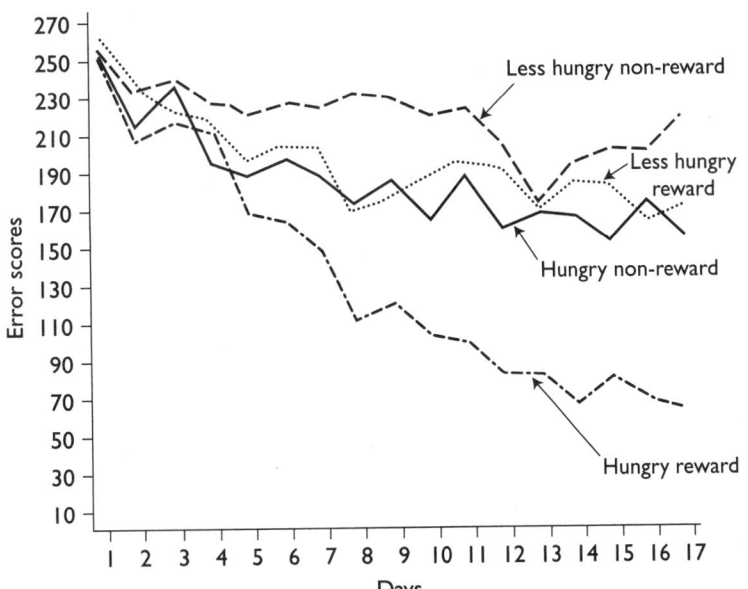

FIGURE 16.03

Error curves for four groups, 36 rats. (From E. C. Tolman and C. H. Honzik, Degrees of hunger, reward and non-reward, and maze learning in rats. *Univ. Calif. Publ. Psychol.,* 1930, 4, No. 16, p. 246. A maze identical with the alley maze shown in Fig. 16.01 was used.)

is such that the crucial stimuli from the maze get presented simultaneously with the correct responses more frequently than they do with any of the incorrect responses. Hence, just on a basis of this greater frequency, the neural connections between the crucial stimuli and the correct responses will tend, it is said, to get strengthened at the expense of the incorrect connections.

(b) There is a second subgroup in this stimulus-response school which holds that the reason the appropriate connections get strengthened relatively to the inappropriate ones is, rather, the fact that the responses resulting from the correct connections are followed more closely in time by need-reductions. Thus a hungry rat in a maze tends to get to food and have his hunger reduced *sooner* as a result of the true path responses than as a result of the blind alley responses. And such immediately following need-reductions or, to use another term, such 'positive reinforcements' tend somehow, it is said, to strengthen the connections which have most closely preceded them. Thus it is as if—although this is certainly not the way this subgroup would themselves state it—the satisfaction-receiving part of the rat telephoned back to Central and said to the girl: "Hold that connection; it was good; and see to it that you blankety-blank well use it again the next time these same stimuli come in." These theorists also assume (at least some of them do some of the time) that, if bad results—'annoyances,' 'negative reinforcements'—follow, then this same satisfaction-and-annoyance-receiving part of the rat will telephone back and say, "Break that connection and don't you dare use it next time either."

So much for a brief summary of the two subvarieties of the 'stimulus-response,' or telephone switchboard school.

(2) Let us turn now to the second main school. This group (and I belong to them) may be called the field theorists. We believe that in the course of learning something like a field map of the environment gets established in the rat's brain. We agree with the other school that the rat in running a maze is exposed to stimuli and is finally led as a result of these stimuli to the responses which actually occur. We feel, however, that the intervening brain processes are more complicated, more patterned and often, pragmatically speaking, more autonomous than do the stimulus-response psychologists. Although we admit that the rat is bombarded by stimuli, we hold that his nervous system is surprisingly selective as to which of these stimuli it will let in at any given time.

Secondly, we assert that the central office itself is far more like a map control room than it is like an old-fashioned telephone exchange. The stimuli, which are allowed in, are not connected by just simple one-to-one switches to the outgoing responses. Rather, the incoming impulses are usually worked over and elaborated in the central control room into a tentative, cognitive-like map of the environment. And it is this tentative map, indicating routes and paths and environmental relationships, which finally determines what responses, if any, the animal will finally release.

Finally, I, personally, would hold further that it is also important to discover in how far these maps are relatively narrow and strip-like or relatively broad

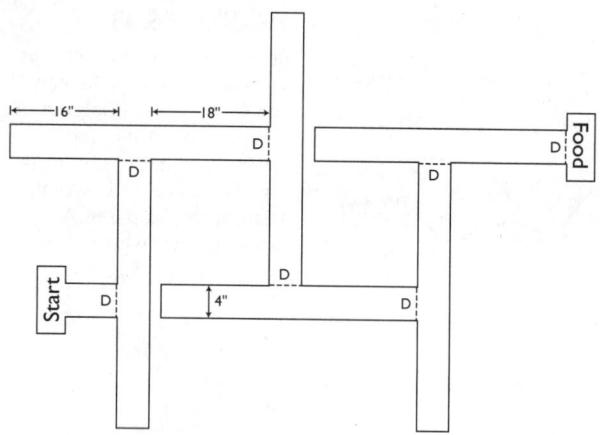

FIGURE 16.04

6-Unit Alley T-Maze. (From H. C. Blodgett, The effect of the introduction of reward upon the maze performance of rats. *Univ. Calif. Publ. Psychol.*, 1929, 4, No. 8, p. 117.)

and comprehensive. Both strip-maps and comprehensive-maps may be either correct or incorrect in the sense that they may (or may not), when acted upon, lead successfully to the animal's goal. The differences between such strip maps and such comprehensive maps will appear only when the rat is later presented with some change within the given environment. Then, the narrower and more strip-like the original map, the less will it carry over successfully to the new problem; whereas, the wider and the more comprehensive it was, the more adequately it will serve in the new set-up. In a strip-map the given position of the animal is connected by only a relatively simple and single path to the position of the goal. In a comprehensive-map a wider arc of the environment is represented, so that, if the starting position of the animal be changed or variations in the specific routes be introduced, this wider map will allow the animal still to behave relatively correctly and to choose the appropriate new route.

But let us turn, now, to the actual experiments. The ones, out of many, which I have selected to report are simply ones which seem especially important in reinforcing the theoretical position I have been presenting. This position, I repeat, contains two assumptions: First, that learning consists not in stimulus-response connections but in the building up in the nervous system of sets which function like cognitive maps, and second, that such cognitive maps may be usefully characterized as varying from a narrow strip variety to a broader comprehensive variety.

The experiments fall under five heads: (1) "latent learning," (2) "vicarious trial and error" or "VTE," (3) "searching for the stimulus," (4) "hypotheses" and (5) "spatial orientation."

(1) *"Latent Learning" Experiments.* The first of the latent learning experiments was performed at Berkeley by Blodgett. It was published in 1929. Blodgett not only performed the experiments, he also originated the concept. He ran three groups of rats through a six-unit alley maze, shown in Fig. 16.04. He had a control group and two experimental groups. The error curves for these groups appear in Fig. 16.05. The solid line shows the error curve for Group I, the control group. These animals were run in orthodox fashion. That is, they were run one trial a day and found food in the goal-box at the

FIGURE 16.05

(From H. C. Blodgett, The effect of the introduction of reward upon the maze performance of rats. *Univ. Calif. Publ. Psychol.*, 1929, 4, No. 8, p. 120.)

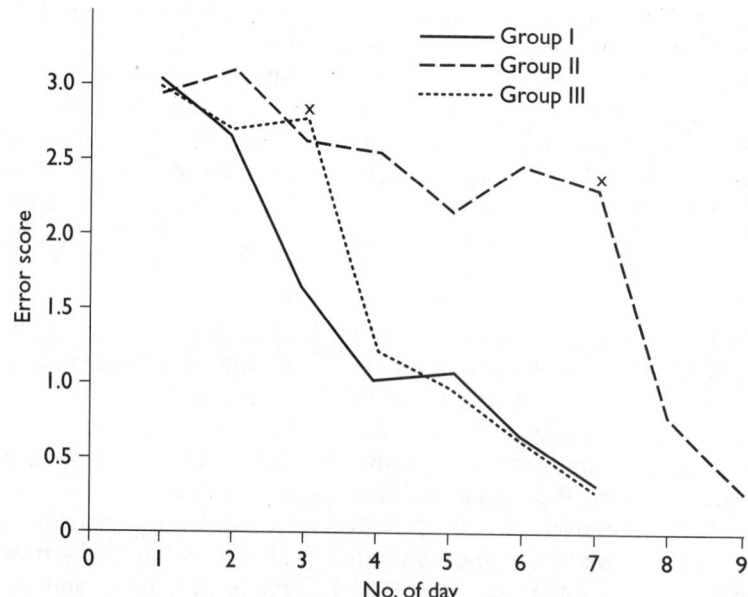

end of each trial. Groups II and III were the experimental groups. The animals of Group II, the dash line, were not fed in the maze for the first six days but only in their home cages some two hours later. On the seventh day (indicated by the small cross) the rats found food at the end of the maze for the first time and continued to find it on subsequent days. The animals of Group III were treated similarly except that they first found food at the end of the maze on the third day and continued to find it there on subsequent days. It will be observed that the experimental groups as long as they were not finding food did not appear to learn much. (Their error curves did not drop.) But on the days immediately succeeding their first finding of the food their error curves did drop astoundingly. It appeared, in short, that during the non-rewarded trials these animals had been learning much more than they had exhibited. This learning, which did not manifest itself until after the food had been introduced, Blodgett called "latent learning." Interpreting these results anthropomorphically, we would say that as long as the animals were not getting any food at the end of the maze they continued to take their time in going through it, they continued to enter many blinds. Once, however, they knew they were to get food, they demonstrated that during these preceding non-rewarded trials they had learned where many of the blinds were. They had been building up a 'map,' and could utilize the latter as soon as they were motivated to do so.

Honzik and myself repeated the experiments (or rather he did and I got some of the credit) with the 14-unit T-mazes shown in Fig. 16.01, and with larger groups of animals, and got similar results. The resulting curves are shown in Fig. 16.06. We used two control groups—one that never found food in the maze (HNR) and one that found it throughout (HR). The experimental group (HNR-R) found food at the end of the maze from the 11th day on and showed the same sort of a sudden drop.

But probably the best experiment demonstrating latent learning was, unfortunately, done not in Berkeley but at the University of Iowa, by Spence and Lippitt. Only an abstract of this experiment has as yet been published. However, Spence has sent a preliminary manuscript from which the following account is summarized. A simple Y-maze (see Fig. 16.07) with two goal-boxes was used. Water was at the end of the right arm of the Y and food at the end of the left arm. During the training period the rats were run neither hungry nor thirsty. They were satiated for both food and water before each day's trials. However, they were willing to run because after each run they were taken out of whichever end box they had got to and put into a living cage, with other animals in it. They were given four trials a day in this fashion for seven days, two trials to the right and two to the left.

In the crucial test the animals were divided into two subgroups one made solely hungry and one solely thirsty. It was then found that on the first trial the hungry group went at once to the left, where the food had been, statistically more frequently than to the right; and the thirsty group went to the right, where the water had been, statistically more frequently than to the left. These results indicated that under the previous non-differential and very mild

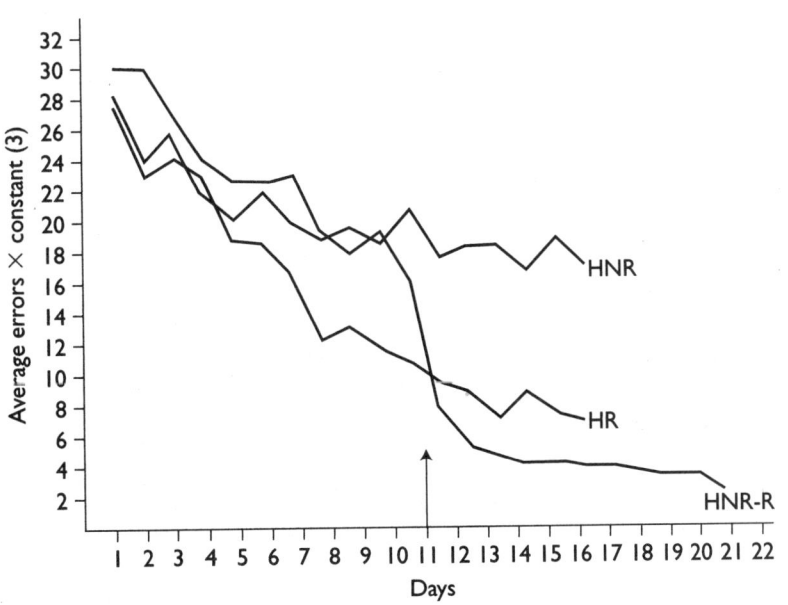

FIGURE 16.06

Error curves for HR, HNR, and HNR-R. (From E. C. Tolman and C. H. Honzik, Introduction and removal of reward, and maze performance in rats. *Univ. Calif. Publ. Psychol.*, 1930, 4, No. 19, p. 267.)

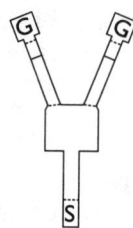

FIGURE 16.07

Ground plan of the apparatus. (Taken from K. W. Spence and R. Lippitt, An experimental test of the sign-gestalt theory of trial and error learning. *J. Exper. Psychol.,* 1946, 36, p. 494. In this article they were describing another experiment but used the same maze.)

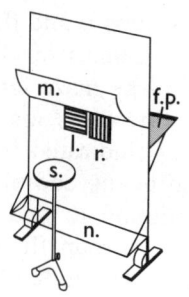

FIGURE 16.08

Apparatus Used for Testing Discrimination of Visual Patterns. (From K. S. Lashley, The mechanism of vision. I. A method for rapid analyses of pattern-vision in the rat. *J. Genet. Psychol.,* 1930, 37, p. 454.)

rewarding conditions of merely being returned to the home cages the animals had nevertheless been learning where the water was and where the food was. In short, they had acquired a cognitive map to the effect that food was to the left and water to the right, although during the acquisition of this map they had not exhibited any stimulus-response propensities to go more to the side which became later the side of the appropriate goal.

There have been numerous other latent learning experiments done in the Berkeley laboratory and elsewhere. In general, they have for the most part all confirmed the above sort of findings.

Let us turn now to the second group of experiments.

(2) *"Vicarious Trial and Error" or "VTE."* The term Vicarious Trial and Error (abbreviated as VTE) was invented by Prof. Muenzinger at Colorado[1] to designate the hesitating, looking-back-and-forth, sort of behavior which rats can often be observed to indulge in at a choice-point before actually going one way or the other.

Quite a number of experiments upon VTEing have been carried out in our laboratory. I shall report only a few. In most of them what is called a discrimination set-up has been used. In one characteristic type of visual discrimination apparatus designed by Lashley (shown in Fig. 16.08) the animal is put on a jumping stand and faced with two doors which differ in some visual property say, as here shown, vertical stripes vs. horizontal stripes.

One of each such pair of visual stimuli is made always correct and the other wrong; and the two are interchanged from side to side in random fashion. The animal is required to learn, say, that the verti-

cally striped door is always the correct one. If he jumps to it, the door falls open and he gets to food on a platform behind. If, on the other hand, he jumps incorrectly, he finds the door locked and falls into a net some two feet below from which he is picked up and started over again.

Using a similar set-up (see Fig. 16.09), but with landing platforms in front of the doors so that if the rat chose incorrectly he could jump back again and start over, I found that when the choice was an easy one, say between a white door and a black door, the animals not only learned sooner but also did more VTEing than when the choice was difficult, say between a white door and a gray door (see Fig. 16.10). It appeared further (see Fig. 16.11) that the VTEing began to appear just as (or just before) the rats began to learn. After the learning had become estab-

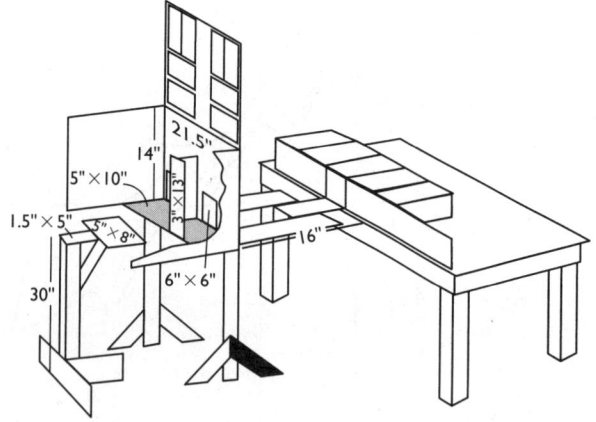

FIGURE 16.09

(From E. C. Tolman, Prediction of vicarious trial and error by means of the schematic sowbug. *Psychol. Rev.,* 1939, 46, p. 319.)

<hr />

[1] *Vide:* K. F. Muenzinger, Vicarious trial and error at a point of choice: I. A general survey of its relation to learning efficiency. *J. Genet. Psychol.,* 1938, 53, 75–86.

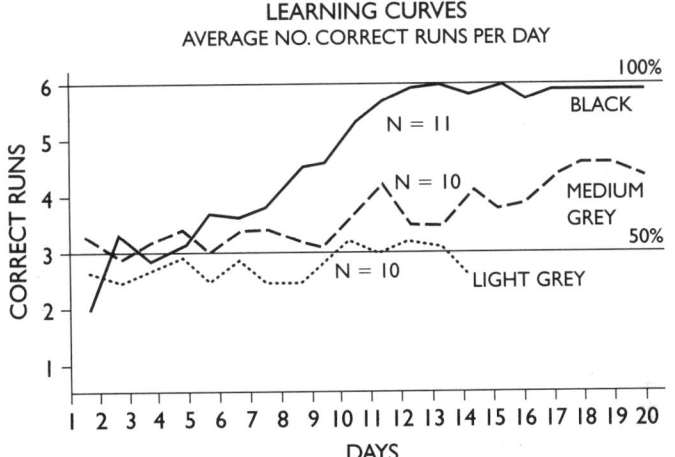

LEARNING CURVES
AVERAGE NO. CORRECT RUNS PER DAY

FIGURE 16.10

(From E. C. Tolman, Prediction of vicarious trial and error by means of the schematic sowbug. *Psychol. Rev.*, 1939, 46, p. 319.)

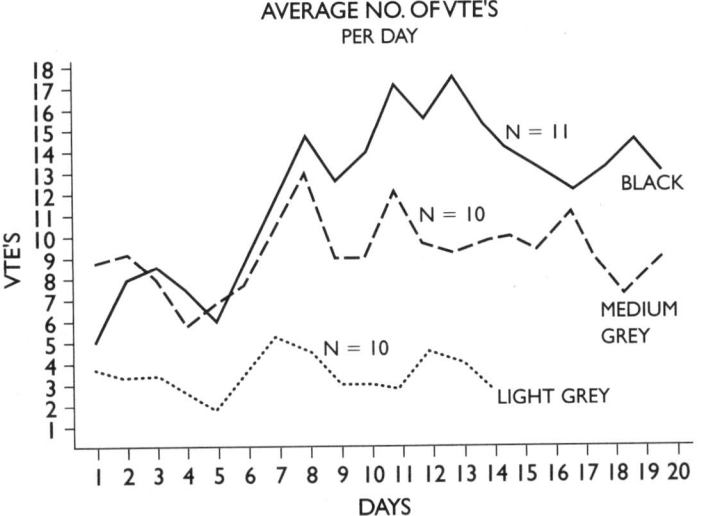

AVERAGE NO. OF VTE'S
PER DAY

FIGURE 16.11

(From E. C. Tolman, Prediction of vicarious trial and error by means of the schematic sowbug. *Psychol. Rev.*, 1939, 46, p. 320.)

lished, however, the VTE's began to go down. Further, in a study of individual differences by myself, Geier and Levin[2] (actually done by Geier and Levin) using this same visual discrimination apparatus, it was found that with one and the same difficulty of problem the smarter animal did the more VTEing.

To sum up, in *visual discrimination* experiments the better the learning, the more the VTE's. But this seems contrary to what we would perhaps have expected. We ourselves would expect to do more VTEing, more sampling of the two stimuli, when it is difficult to choose between them than when it is easy.

What is the explanation? The answer lies, I believe, in the fact that the manner in which we set the visual discrimination problems for the rats and the manner in which we set similar problems for ourselves are different. *We* already have our 'instructions.' We know beforehand what it is we are to do. We are told, or we tell ourselves, that it is the lighter of the two grays, the heavier of the two weights, or the like, which is to be chosen. In such a setting we do more sampling, more VTEing, when the stimulus-difference is small. But for the rats the usual problem in a discrimination apparatus is quite different. They do not know what is wanted of them. The major part of their learning in most such experiments seems to consist in their discovering the instructions. The rats have to discover that it is the differences in visual brightness, not the differences between left and right, which they are to pay attention to. Their VTEing appears when they begin to 'catch on.' The greater the difference between the

---

[2] F. M. Geier, M. Levin & E. C. Tolman, Individual differences in emotionality, hypothesis formation, vicarious trial and error and visual discrimination learning in rats. *Compar. Psychol. Monogr.*, 1941, 17, No. 3.

FIGURE 16.12

(From E. C. Tolman and E. Minium, VTE in rats: over-learning and difficulty of discrimination. *J. Comp. Psychol.,* 1942, 34, p. 303.)

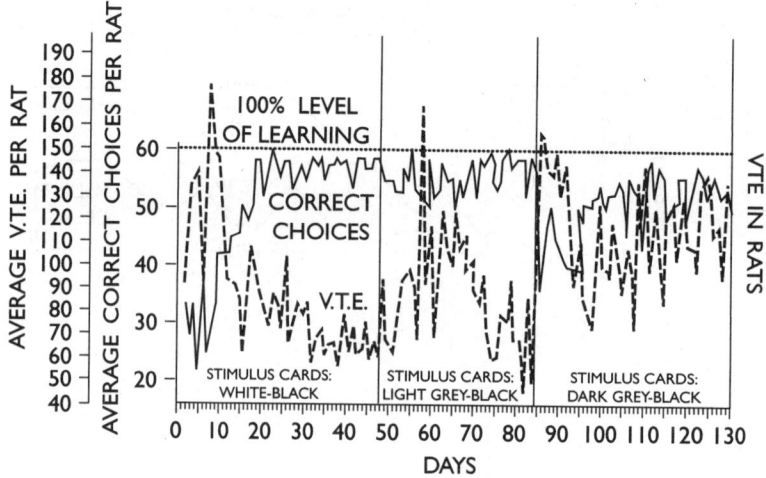

two stimuli the more the animals are attracted by this difference. Hence the sooner they catch on, and during this catching on, the more they VTE.

That this is a reasonable interpretation appeared further, from an experiment by myself and Minium (the actual work done, of course, by Minium) in which a group of six rats was first taught a white vs. black discrimination, then two successively more difficult gray vs. black discriminations. For each difficulty the rats were given a long series of further trials beyond the points at which they had learned. Comparing the beginning of each of these three difficulties the results were that the rats did more VTEing for the easy discriminations than for the more difficult ones. When, however, it came to a comparison of amounts of VTEing during the final performance after each learning had reached a plateau, the opposite results were obtained. In other words, after the rats had finally divined their instructions, then they, like human beings, did more VTEing, more sampling, the more difficult the discrimination.

Finally, now let us note that it was also found at Berkeley by Jackson[3] that in a maze the difficult maze units produce more VTEing and also that the more stupid rats do the more VTEing. The explanation, as I see it, is that, in the case of mazes, rats know their instructions. For them it is natural to expect that the same spatial path will always lead to the same outcome. Rats in mazes don't have to be told.

But what, now, is the final significance of all this VTEing? How do these facts about VTEing affect

our theoretical argument? My answer is that these facts lend further support to the doctrine of a building up of maps. VTEing, as I see it, is evidence that in the critical stages—whether in the first picking up of the instructions or in the later making sure of which stimulus is which—the animal's activity is not just one of responding passively to discrete stimuli, but rather one of the active selecting and comparing of stimuli. This brings me then to the third type of experiment.

(3) *"Searching for the Stimulus."* I refer to a recent, and it seems to me extremely important experiment, done for a Ph.D. dissertation by Hudson. Hudson was first interested in the question of whether or not rats could learn an avoidance reaction in one trial. His animals were tested one at a time in a living cage (see Fig. 16.13) with a small striped visual pattern at the end, on which was

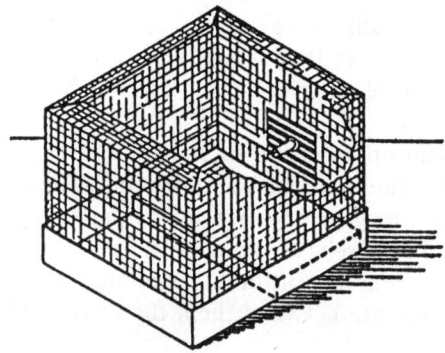

FIGURE 16.13

(From Bradford Hudson, Ph.D. Thesis: 'One trial learning: A study of the avoidance behavior of the rat.' On deposit in the Library of the University of California, Berkeley, California.)

---

[3] L. L. Jackson, V. T. E. on an elevated maze. *J. Comp. Psychol.,* 1943, 36, 99–107.

mounted a food cup. The hungry rat approached this food cup and ate. An electrical arrangement was provided so that when the rat touched the cup he could be given an electric shock. And one such shock did appear to be enough. For when the rat was replaced in this same cage days or even weeks afterwards, he usually demonstrated immediately strong avoidance reactions to the visual pattern. The animal withdrew from that end of the cage, or piled up sawdust and covered the pattern, or showed various other amusing responses all of which were in the nature of withdrawing from the pattern or making it disappear.

But the particular finding which I am interested in now appeared as a result of a modification of this standard procedure. Hudson noticed that the animals, anthropomorphically speaking, often seemed to look around *after* the shock to see what it was that had hit them. Hence it occurred to him that, if the pattern were made to disappear the instant the shock occurred, the rats might not establish the association. And this indeed is what happened in the case of many individuals. Hudson added further electrical connections so that when the shock was received during the eating, the lights went out, the pattern and the food cup dropped out of sight, and the lights came on again all within the matter of a second. When such animals were again put in the cage 24 hours later, a large percentage showed no avoidance of the pattern. Or to quote Hudson's own words:

> "Learning what object to avoid . . . may occur exclusively during the period after the shock. For if the object from which the shock was actually received is removed at the moment of the shock, a significant number of animals fail to learn to avoid it, some selecting other features in the environment for avoidance, and others avoiding nothing."

In other words, I feel that this experiment reinforces the notion of the largely active selective character in the rat's building up of his cognitive map. He often has to look actively for the significant stimuli in order to form his map and does not merely passively receive and react to all the stimuli which are physically present.

Turn now to the fourth type of experiment.

(4) *The "Hypothesis" Experiments.* Both the notion of hypotheses in rats and the design of the experiments to demonstrate such hypotheses are to be credited to Krech. Krech used a four-compartment discrimination-box. In such a four-choice box the correct door at each choice-point may be determined by the experimenter in terms of its being lighted or dark, left or right, or various combinations of these. If all possibilities are randomized for the 40 choices made in 10 runs of each day's test, the problem could be made insoluble.

When this was done, Krech found that the individual rat went through a succession of systematic choices. That is, the individual animal might perhaps begin by choosing practically all right-hand doors, then he might give this up for choosing practically all left-hand doors, and then, for choosing all dark doors, and so on. These relatively persistent, and well-above-chance systematic types of choice Krech called "hypotheses." In using this term he obviously did not mean to imply verbal processes in the rat but merely referred to what I have been calling cognitive maps which, it appears from his experiments, get set up in a tentative fashion to be tried out first one and then another until, if possible, one is found which works.

Finally, it is to be noted that these hypothesis experiments, like the latent learning, VTE, and "looking for the stimulus" experiments, do not, as such, throw light upon the widths of the maps which are picked up but do indicate the generally map-like and self-initiated character of learning.

For the beginning of an attack upon the problem of the width of the maps let me turn to the last group of experiments.

(5) *"Spatial Orientation" Experiments.* As early as 1929, Lashley reported incidentally the case of a couple of his rats who, after having learned an alley maze, pushed back the cover near the starting box, climbed out and ran directly across the top of the goal-box where they climbed down in again and ate. Other investigators have reported related findings. All such observations suggest that rats really develop wider spatial maps which include more than the mere trained-on specific paths. In the experiments now to be reported this possibility has been subjected to further examination.

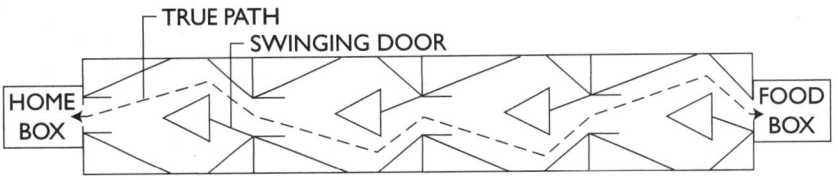

TRUE PATH
SWINGING DOOR
HOME BOX
FOOD BOX

FIGURE 16.14

(From I. Krechevsky (Now D. Krech), The genesis of "hypotheses" in rats. *Univ. Calif. Publ. Psychol.*, 1932, 6, No. 4, p. 46.)

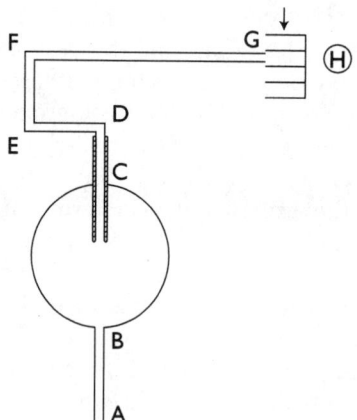

Apparatus used in preliminary training

FIGURE 16.15

(From E. C. Tolman, B. F. Ritchie and D. Kalish, Studies in spatial learning. I. Orientation and the short-cut. *J. Exp. Psychol.,* 1946, 36, p. 16.)

In the first experiment, Tolman, Ritchie and Kalish (actually Ritchie and Kalish) used the set-up shown in Fig. 16.15.

This was an elevated maze. The animals ran from A across the open circular table through CD (which had alley walls) and finally to G, the food box. H was a light which shone directly down the path from G to F. After four nights, three trials per night, in which the rats learned to run directly and without hesitation from A to G, the apparatus was changed to the sun-burst shown in Fig. 16.16. The starting path and the table remained the same but a series of radiating paths was added.

The animals were again started at A and ran across the circular table into the alley and found themselves blocked. They then returned onto the table and began exploring practically all the radiating paths. After going out a few inches only on any one path, each rat finally chose to run all the way out on one. The percentages of rats finally choosing each of the long paths from 1 to 12 are shown in Fig. 16.17. It appears that there was a preponderant tendency to choose path No. 6 which ran to a point some four inches in front of where the entrance to the food-box had been. The only other path chosen with any appreciable frequency was No. 1—that is, the path which pointed perpendicularly to the food-side of the room.

These results seem to indicate that the rats in this experiment had learned not only to run rapidly down the original roundabout route but also, when this was blocked and radiating paths presented, to select one pointing rather directly towards the point where the food had been or else at least to select a path running perpendicularly to the food-side of the room.

As a result of their original training, the rats had, it would seem, acquired not merely a strip-map to the effect that the original specifically trained-on path led to food but, rather, a wider comprehensive map to the effect that food was located in such and such a direction in the room.

Consider now a further experiment done by Ritchie alone. This experiment tested still further the breadth of the spatial map which is acquired. In this further experiment the rats were again run

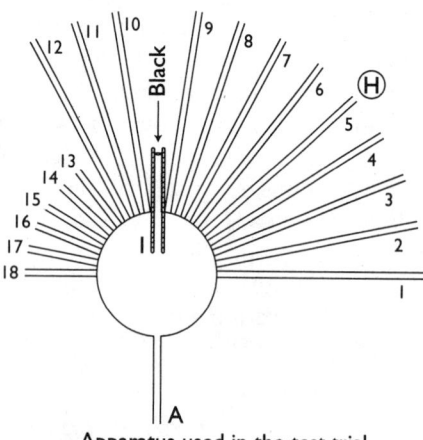

Apparatus used in the test trial

FIGURE 16.16

(From E. C. Tolman, B. F. Ritchie and D. Kalish, Studies in spatial learning. I. Orientation and short-cut. *J. Exp. Psychol.,* 1946, 36, p. 17.)

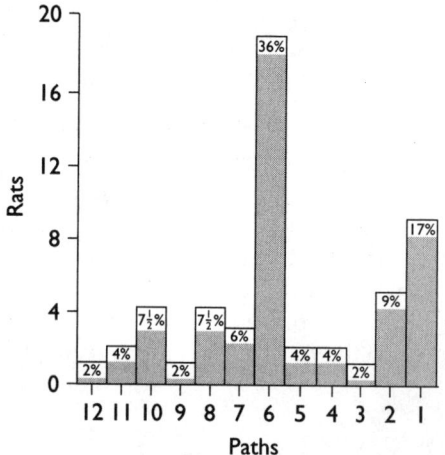

Number of rats which chose each of the paths

FIGURE 16.17

(From E. C. Tolman, B. F. Ritchie and D. Kalish, Studies in spatial learning. I. Orientation and the short-cut. *J. Exp. Psychol.,* 1946, 36, p. 19.)

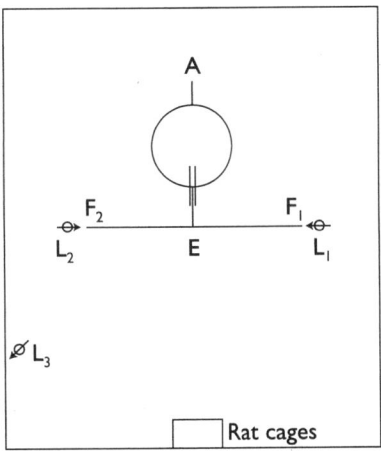

FIGURE 16.18
(From B. F. Ritchie, Ph.D. Thesis: 'Spatial learning in rats.' On deposit in the Library of the University of California, Berkeley, California.)

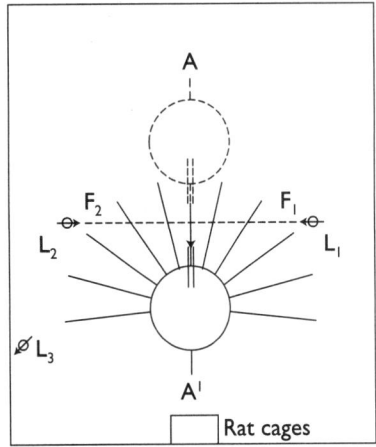

FIGURE 16.19
(From B. F. Ritchie, Ph.D. Thesis: 'Spatial learning in rats.' On deposit in the Library of the University of California, Berkeley, California.)

across the table—this time to the arms of a simple T. (See Fig. 16.18.)

Twenty-five animals were trained for seven days, 20 trials in all, to find food at F_1; and twenty-five animals were trained to find it at F_2. The L's in the diagram indicate lights. On the eighth day the starting path and table top were rotated through 180 degrees so that they were now in the position shown in Fig. 16.19. The dotted lines represent the old position. And a series of radiating paths was added. What happened? Again the rats ran across the table into the central alley. When, however, they found themselves blocked, they turned back onto the table and this time also spent many seconds touching and trying out for only a few steps practically all the paths. Finally, however, within seven minutes, 42 of the 50 rats chose one path and ran all the way out on it. The paths finally chosen by the 19 of these an-

imals that had been fed at F_1 and by the 23 that had been fed at F_2 are shown in Fig. 16.20.

This time the rats tended to choose, not the paths which pointed directly to the spots where the food had been, but rather paths which ran perpendicularly to the corresponding sides of the room. The spatial maps of these rats, when the animals were started from the opposite side of the room, were thus not completely adequate to the precise goal positions but were adequate as to the correct sides of the room. The maps of these animals were, in short, not altogether strip-like and narrow.

This completes my report of experiments. There were the *latent learning experiments,* the *VTE experiments,* the *searching for the stimulus experiment,* the *hypothesis experiments,* and these last *spatial orientation experiments.*

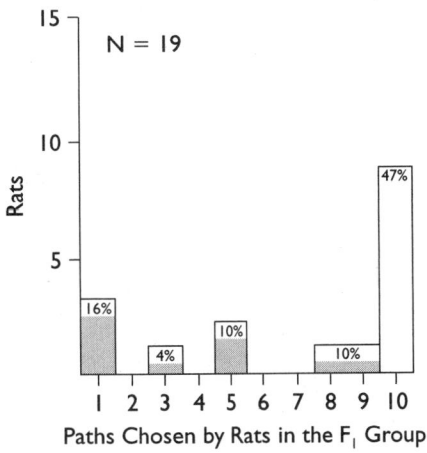

Paths Chosen by Rats in the F_1 Group

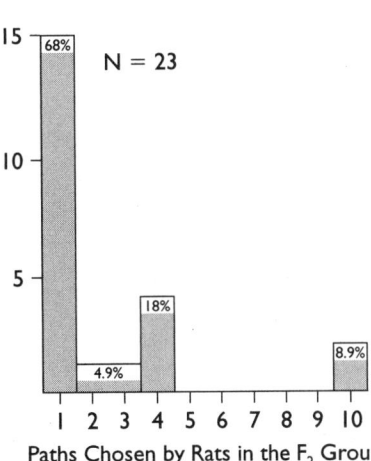

Paths Chosen by Rats in the F_2 Group

FIGURE 16.20
(From B. F. Ritchie, Ph.D. Thesis: 'Spatial learning in rats.' On deposit in the Library of the University of California, Berkeley, California.)

And now, at last, I come to the humanly significant and exciting problem: namely, what are the conditions which favor narrow strip-maps and what are those which tend to favor broad comprehensive maps not only in rats but also in men?

There is considerable evidence scattered throughout the literature bearing on this question both for rats and for men. Some of this evidence was obtained in Berkeley and some of it elsewhere. I have not time to present it in any detail. I can merely summarize it by saying that narrow strip maps rather than broad comprehensive maps seem to be induced: (1) by a damaged brain, (2) by an inadequate array of environmentally presented cues, (3) by an overdose of repetitions on the original trained-on path and (4) by the presence of too strongly motivational or of too strongly frustrating conditions.

It is this fourth factor which I wish to elaborate upon briefly in my concluding remarks. For it is going to be my contention that some, at least, of the so-called 'psychological mechanisms' which the clinical psychologists and the other students of personality have uncovered as the devils underlying many of our individual and social maladjustments can be interpreted as narrowings of our cognitive maps due to too strong motivations or to too intense frustration.

My argument will be brief, cavalier, and dogmatic. For I am not myself a clinician or a social psychologist. What I am going to say must be considered, therefore, simply as in the nature of a *rat* psychologist's *rat*iocinations offered free.

By way of illustration, let me suggest that at least the three dynamisms called, respectively, "regression," "fixation," and "displacement of aggression onto outgroups" are expressions of cognitive maps which are too narrow and which get built up in us as a result of too violent motivation or of too intense frustration.

(a) Consider *regression*. This is the term used for those cases in which an individual, in the face of too difficult a problem, returns to earlier more childish ways of behaving. Thus, to take an example, the overprotected middle-aged woman (reported a couple of years ago in *Time Magazine*) who, after losing her husband, regressed (much to the distress of her growing daughters) into dressing in too youthful a fashion and into competing for their beaux and then finally into behaving like a child requiring continuous care, would be an illustration of regression. I would not wish you to put too much confidence in the reportorial accuracy of *Time,* but such an extreme case is not too different from many actually to be found in our mental hospitals or even sometimes in ourselves. In all such instances my argument would be (1) that such regression results from too strong a present emotional situation and (2) that it consists in going back to too narrow an earlier map, itself due to too much frustration or motivation in early childhood. *Time*'s middle-aged woman was presented by too frustrating an emotional situation at her husband's death and she regressed, I would wager, to too narrow adolescent and childhood maps since these latter had been originally excessively impressed because of overstressful experiences at the time she was growing up.

(b) Consider *fixation*. Regression and fixation tend to go hand in hand. For another way of stating the fact of the undue persistence of early maps is to say that they were fixated. This has even been demonstrated in rats. If rats are too strongly motivated in their original learning, they find it very difficult to relearn when the original path is no longer correct. Also after they have relearned, if they are given an electric shock they, like *Time*'s woman, tend to regress back again to choosing the earlier path.

(c) Finally, consider the *"displacement of aggressions onto outgroups."* Adherence to one's own group is an ever-present tendency among primates. It is found in chimpanzees and monkeys as strongly as in men. We primates operate in groups. And each individual in such a group tends to identify with his whole group in the sense that the group's goals become his goals, the group's life and immortality, his life and immortality. Furthermore, each individual soon learns that, when as an individual he is frustrated, he must not take out his aggressions on the other members of his own group. He learns instead to displace his aggressions onto outgroups. Such a displacement of aggression I would claim is also a narrowing of the cognitive map. The individual comes no longer to distinguish the true locus of the cause of his frustration. The poor Southern whites, who take it out on the Negroes, are displacing their aggressions from the landlords, the southern economic system, the northern capitalists, or wherever the true cause of their frustration may lie, onto a mere convenient outgroup. The physicists on the Faculty who criticize the humanities, or we psychologists who criticize all the other departments, or the University as a whole which criticizes the Secondary School system or, vice versa, the Secondary School system which criticizes the University—or, on a still larger and far more dangerous scene—we Americans who criticize the Russians and the Russians who criticize us, are also engaging, at least in part, in nothing more than such irrational displacements of our aggressions onto outgroups.

I do not mean to imply that there may not be some true interferences by the one group with the goals of the other and hence that the aggressions of the members of the one group against the members of the other are necessarily *wholly* and *merely* displaced aggressions. But I do assert that often and in large part they are such mere displacements.

Over and over again men are blinded by too violent motivations and too intense frustrations into blind and unintelligent and in the end desperately dangerous hates of outsiders. And the expression of these their displaced hates ranges all the way from discrimination against minorities to world conflagrations.

What in the name of Heaven and Psychology can we do about it? My only answer is to preach again the virtues of reason—of, that is, broad cognitive maps. And to suggest that the child-trainers and the world-planners of the future can only, if at all, bring about the presence of the required rationality (*i.e.*, comprehensive maps) if they see to it that nobody's children are too over-motivated or too frustrated. Only then can these children learn to look before and after, learn to see that there are often round-about and safer paths to their quite proper goals—learn, that is, to realize that the well-beings of White and of Negro, of Catholic and of Protestant, of Christian and of Jew, of American and of Russian (and even of males and females) are mutually interdependent.

We dare not let ourselves or others become so over-emotional, so hungry, so ill-clad, so over-motivated that only narrow strip-maps will be developed. All of us in Europe as well as in America, in the Orient as well as in the Occident, must be made calm enough and well-fed enough to be able to develop truly comprehensive maps, or, as Freud would have put it, to be able to learn to live according to the Reality Principle rather than according to the too narrow and too immediate Pleasure Principle.

We must, in short, subject our children and ourselves (as the kindly experimenter would his rats) to the optimal conditions of moderate motivation and of an absence of unnecessary frustrations, whenever we put them and ourselves before that great God-given maze which is our human world. I cannot predict whether or not we will be able, or be allowed, to do this; but I *can* say that, only insofar as we *are* able and *are* allowed, have we cause for hope.

QUESTIONS FOR REFLECTION AND DISCUSSION:

1. Do you believe that you can know what another person is thinking or imagining? What is the evidence for such a belief? (Hint: Are you assessing what the person is thinking or what he or she is saying?)

2. What arguments are used by cognitive psychologists who assert that the richness of experience and behavior cannot be understood without reference to cognition (events occurring within the black box)?

3. How do the behaviorists (or "animal psychologists") to whom Tolman refers explain a rat's progressing through a maze?

4. Tolman refers to himself as a "field theorist." How does the field-theory view of a rat's behavior in a maze differ from that of the "animal psychologist"?

5. What is meant by the terms *latent learning* and *vicarious trial and error (VTE)*? What evidence did Tolman find for latent learning?

6. What evidence did Hudson find of rats' "searching for the stimulus"? How does such searching counter behaviorist explanation of behavior?

7. What evidence is there that rats generate hypotheses as to what to do?

8. Does it seem that Tolman digresses from his study's scientific points in his discussions of displaced aggression? Explain.

SOURCE

Craik, F. I. M., & Watkins, M. J. (1973). The role of rehearsal in short-term memory. *Journal of Verbal Learning and Verbal Behavior, 12,* 599–607. Reprinted by permission of Academic Press.

Memory is one of the time-honored topics in psychology. The German psychologist Herrmann Ebbinghaus studied memory in the latter half of the 19th century. He read through lists of nonsense syllables repeatedly until he had memorized them. Then he would test himself. He noted that his memory deteriorated as time passed. Ebbinghaus was so dedicated to his research that on one occasion he rehearsed 420 lists of 16 nonsense syllables 34 times each. His immense labors led to the commonly used concepts of savings *and the forgetting curve.*

By repeating the lists of nonsense syllables, Ebbinghaus was engaging in rote learning or what is now called maintenance rehearsal. *But maintenance rehearsal does not give meaning to information by linking it to past learning. In the latter half of the 20th century, Francis Craik and Michael Watkins showed that it is not the best way to permanently store information. They showed that a more effective method is to make information more meaningful—to elaborate it, as in applying it in many situations. For example, language arts teachers encourage students to use new vocabulary words in sentences to help remember them. Each new usage is an instance of* elaborative rehearsal. *Math teachers have us apply formulas and procedures to solve many algebra and geometry problems. As a consequence, we are more likely to remember the procedures and when to use them.*

The Role of Rehearsal in Short-Term Memory

FERGUS I. M. CRAIK
UNIVERSITY OF TORONTO
AND
MICHAEL J. WATKINS
YALE UNIVERSITY

Several widely accepted models of memory postulate that the adequacy of an item's registration in long-term storage is a positive function of its length of stay in the short-term store. However, when short-term storage times were measured, these times did not predict long-term recall or recognition. Two further experiments showed that neither the length of an item's stay in short-term storage nor the number of overt rehearsals it received was related to subsequent recall. It is concluded that the "maintenance" and "elaborative" aspects of rehearsal can be clearly separated, and that the duration of rehearsal is related to long-term memory and learning only in the latter case. Maintenance rehearsal does not lead to an improvement in memory performance.

Rehearsal must play a major part in any complete theory of memory, yet its function is still poorly understood. Waugh and Norman (1965) postulated that rehearsal serves the dual purpose of maintaining items in a short-term store and transferring information about the items to a more permanent long-term store. This view was endorsed, in general, by Atkinson and Shiffrin (1968). They argued that the principal function of rehearsal was to maintain a small set of items in short-term store by repetition, but also that "any information in short-term store is transferred to long-term store to some degree throughout its stay in the short-term store" (p. 115).

The principle that an item's strength in long-term store is a direct function of its length of stay in the short-term store has been stated explicitly by Atkinson and Shiffrin (1968), Waugh (1970), and Norman and Rumelhart (1970). The notion has received good support from studies involving an overt rehearsal procedure (Rundus & Atkinson, 1970; Rundus, 1971). In these studies, the probability of an item's retrieval from long-term store varied directly with the number of rehearsals the item received. This finding also seems to provide a good explanation for the negative recency effect in free recall (Craik, 1970); that is, items at the end of a list are not rehearsed as often as prerecency items, and are thus poorly retrieved in a subsequent recall test. The adequacy of this explanation is examined in Experiment II of the present paper.

Initially, however, we were concerned with examining the notion that time in short-term store predicted later memory performance. The technique adopted involved measuring the time intervals between the presentation and recall of those items retrieved from short-term storage in an immediate free recall test, and then relating these intervals to the probability of recalling the item from long-term storage in a second, delayed recall test. Although input–output intervals will accurately measure short-term storage durations only if destructive readout is postulated, it seems reasonable to assume that these intervals will be at least highly correlated with short-term storage times. The measurements were carried out in an experiment reported by Craik, Gardiner, and Watkins (1970, Experiment 3); the study will be described only briefly here. Twenty subjects were given ten 20-word lists for free recall. The words were presented auditorily at a 2-sec rate; recall was spoken and recorded on tape. Two minutes after recall of the last list, the subject was given an unexpected final recall test in which he wrote down as many words as possible from all ten lists. Finally, the subject was read a list of 200 words at a 3-sec rate. This list contained a randomly selected 100 words from the presentation list, plus 100 new words. The subject's task was to rate each word on a 5-point scale of recognition confidence, ranging from "certain old" (5) to "certain new" (1). It was assumed that the final recall and recognition tasks reflected retrieval from long-term storage only.

In immediate recall, a word was considered a short-term store item if no more than six words (either stimuli or responses) intervened between its presentation and recall (Tulving & Colotla, 1970). For each subject, the interval between the input and retrieval of each short-term store item was measured with the aid of an event recorder and used as an index of time "in store." The mean short-term storage times for items which were retrieved and not retrieved in final recall, were 13.2 and 12.8 sec, respectively. While this difference is in the predicted direction, it is very small and not statistically reliable, $p > .25$. In the recognition analysis, mean durations in short-term store were 6.7, 5.7, 5.5, 5.9, and 4.2 sec for the confidence ratings 5 to 1, respectively. That is, there was some tendency for longer times in short-term storage to be associated with higher subsequent recognition ratings. However, a linear trend analysis revealed that the relationship was nonsignificant, $F(1, 252) = 2.28$, $p > .10$.

Thus, in the study under consideration at least, neither final recall nor recognition performance was significantly related to short-term storage time. The clear inference is that information was not in fact being transferred to long-term storage during the items' stay in the short-term store. Since this conclusion is directly opposed to the prediction from the Waugh and Norman (1965) and the Atkinson and Shiffrin (1968) models, further information was sought from an experiment in which short-term storage time was manipulated directly.

Experiment I

A paradigm was designed in which subjects were induced to hold single words in short-term storage for varying lengths of time. The subjects were instructed to listen to a series of word lists, and to report after each list just the last word beginning with a particular letter. The subject was informed of the "critical letter" before list presentation, and he could therefore ignore words from the start of the list until the first critical word was presented. He then held that word in mind until a further critical word was presented at which time he dropped the first word and replaced it with the second. This procedure continued until the list ended, when he wrote down the latest critical word. Three rates of presentation were used. Thus the time for which a critical word was held in short-term storage varied both as a function of presentation rate, and of the number of noncritical words monitored between presentation and replacement (or report). For example, where "G" is the critical letter and the list begins DAUGHTER OIL RIFLE GARDEN GRAIN TABLE FOOTBALL ANCHOR GIRAFFE . . . , the subject would first hold GARDEN, replace it by GRAIN and then by GIRAFFE; if the remaining words were noncritical (that is, did not begin with G), GIRAFFE would be reported at the end of the list.

After presentation of all the lists, the subjects were unexpectedly asked to recall as many words as possible from all lists. For each rate of presentation, the delayed recall of both the "replaced" and "reported" critical words was examined as a function of the number of noncritical presentations during which the words were held. Presumably if time in short-term store predicts long-term store retrieval, then final recall performance should increase directly with the number of items monitored during the retention of the critical words, and inversely with presentation rate.

METHOD

Design The experiment was carried out in three sessions with 18 subjects participating in each session. All 54 subjects heard the same 27 lists of 21 words. Within each session the 18 subjects were randomly allocated into three groups of six subjects, and each group was given a different set of critical words. That is, on any one list, the three groups received different critical initial letters. Three rates of presentation were used: slow, 1 word every 2 sec; medium, 1 word every sec; and fast, 1 word every half sec. Lists presented at one speed in the first session were presented at the other two speeds over the remaining sessions. In each session, nine lists were presented at each speed, with order of list presentation randomized separately for each session.

Two further within-subject variables were involved in the design. The first is i-value, which refers to the number of intervening (noncritical) words which were monitored during the retention of the critical words. There were nine i values: 0, 1, 2, 3, 4, 5, 6, 8, and 12. The second variable concerns the critical words, and whether they were "replaced" by further critical words during the list or whether they were "reported" as the last critical word in the list. Thus if a list contained two critical words, presented at serial positions 6 and 12, the first would be a "replace" word with an i value of 5, and the second a "report" word having an i value of 9. Construction of the lists ensured that all subjects received 81 critical words, equally distributed over i value and presentation rate. Hence the nine lists shown at a given

rate included three critical words at each i value; of these two were "replace" words and one a "report" word. Order of i values was essentially random, so that when a critical word was presented, the subject knew neither its i value nor whether it would have to be replaced or reported. On the other hand, order of i value was not entirely random, in that an effort was made to avoid confounding serial position and i value of the "replace" words. In addition, the first three serial positions were not used. Apart from the 27 experimental lists, three practice lists were presented, one at each rate. All subjects were given a final free recall test following the 27 lists.

The words were one- and two-syllable concrete nouns. The lists were recorded on tape, and each list was preceded by a reference to the list number and the speed of presentation. A tone, presented at the same rate as the list words, signaled the end of the list. Separate randomizations and recordings were made for each session.

The subjects were 54 introductory psychology students from the North East London Polytechnic.

Procedure The subjects in each session were randomly assigned to three groups of six. The subjects were informed that they formed the control group of a perception-memory experiment; whereas other subjects had a task with a substantial memory load, they merely had to keep track of the latest word beginning with a particular letter. Thus, they were to carefully monitor the lists and write down the last word in each list which began with the critical letter. It was stressed that their performance should be virtually perfect before any useful conclusions could be drawn from the other conditions. Before the presentation of each list, each subject turned over a card which contained the number of the list and the critical letter for that list (the critical letter changed from list to list). After the list ended, subjects wrote down on the card the last word beginning with the critical letter, and immediately placed the card into an envelope which had been provided for each subject. Lists were presented with an intertrial interval of 15 seconds.

Immediately following the last list, subjects engaged in a 1-min arithmetic task, during which time paper was distributed for the final recall test. A 10-min period was then allowed for the free recall of any of the words presented (both critical and noncritical).

RESULTS

An average of 26.2 of a possible 27 "report" words were correctly identified and reported, with no subject making more than two errors. It was therefore assumed that the critical words were correctly perceived and retained over their respective intervals.

The recall data for the critical items were pooled over sessions and groups of subjects. The percentages of words recalled under each condition are shown in Table 17.01. An analysis of variance revealed significant effects of reporting, $F(1, 36) = 24.10$, $p < .001$, and presentation rate, $F(2, 72) = 7.00$, $p < .005$. The findings reflect the advantages of reported over replaced words, and of slower presentation. The only other significant effect was the second order interaction between rate, i value and replaced-reported, the implications of which are not obvious. The most important finding for the present purpose is the nonsignificance of the i value variable, $F(8, 36) = 1.14$, $p > .10$. It could be argued that an overall test of the main effect is not the most sensitive method of assessing a potentially monotonic relationship between i value and recall. Accordingly, a linear test of trend was performed, with due allowance made for the fact that the i values represented were not evenly spaced. This also failed to achieve significance, $F(1, 36) = 1.70$, $p > .10$. For reported words, i value is necessarily confounded with serial position: Those reported words which had a small i value were at the end of the list. However, since the same pattern of results was obtained with replaced words (Table 17.01) and since i value was not confounded with serial position for replaced words, it is tentatively concluded that the confounding had no crucial effect on the recall of reported words.

DISCUSSION

The most interesting finding of Experiment I was that the probability of recalling an item from long-term store remained essentially independent of its i value. This result is clearly contrary to the idea that recall probability necessarily increases in direct proportion to the total amount of time an item has been thought about or attended to (Waugh, 1970); a view which is implicit in most of the two-process models of short-term memory.

On the other hand, recall was inversely related to presentation rate. Apparently, the beneficial effect of slower input occurred during the interval before the next item was presented. It is speculatively suggested that the subject uses the interitem interval to process or analyze the last presented word, and that the level of analysis achieved increases with available time. The lack of an i value effect implies the use of a rehearsal process which was sufficient to retain a critical item in a highly accessible state (that is, in short-term storage) during the presentation of subsequent noncritical items, but did not have any long-term effects.

A first sight, the present results seem inconsistent with evidence indicating that retention varies directly with amount of rehearsal (Rundus, 1971; Rundus & Atkinson, 1970) and with repetition (Bjork, 1970; Waugh, 1963). It is suggested that this discrepancy can be reconciled by postulating two distinct modes of rehearsal—the one being a simple maintaining process, and the other an elaborative process (Craik & Lockhart, 1972). Time in short-term store will only predict later long-term store performance when the subject has used the time to encode the items elaboratively. Contrary to the models of Atkinson and Shiffrin (1968) and Waugh and Norman (1965), time in short-term store does not by itself lead to long-term retention. Experiment II reports further evidence on this issue.

TABLE 17.01

PERCENTAGE RECALL AS A FUNCTION OF EXPERIMENTAL CONDITION, i VALUE, AND PRESENTATION RATE

CONDITION	PRESENTATION RATE	0	1	2	3	4	5	6	8	12	MEAN
Replaced	Slow	12	13	22	10	21	19	19	18	19	17
	Medium	10	15	22	12	14	19	09	12	11	14
	Fast	14	07	11	06	06	14	09	16	15	11
	Mean	12	12	19	10	14	17	13	15	15	14
Reported	Slow	19	20	20	20	31	39	22	26	28	25
	Medium	20	22	19	19	31	26	20	28	20	23
	Fast	26	15	22	26	20	31	19	11	20	21
	Mean	22	19	20	22	28	32	20	22	23	23

Experiment II

Craik (1970) reported an experiment in which ten lists of words for immediate free recall were followed by a final free recall test, in which subjects attempted to recall all previously presented words. It was found that while the immediate recall data showed the typical large recency effect, the final recall data showed no such effect. In fact, terminal items were the least well recalled in the final recall test. Two possible explanations of this negative recency effect will be considered here. The first says simply that terminal items receive fewest rehearsals in immediate recall and are thus poorly registered in long-term store. This explanation obtains good support from the overt rehearsal experiments of Rundus (Rundus & Atkinson, 1970; Rundus, 1971), since he showed directly that the last items in a list are indeed rehearsed least often.

An alternative explanation of negative recency is that it is the type of rehearsal, not the amount of rehearsal, which is critical for later recall. Experiment I demonstrated that time in short-term store did not by itself enhance subsequent recall and it was suggested that the subject must rehearse in an associative or elaborative fashion for efficient later performance. It is possible that, if the subject knows the end of the list is near, he relies on highly effective, but transient, phonemic information for recall of terminal items. Earlier items have been encoded in a more semantic-associative fashion. Thus the last few items in the list are the best recalled in immediate recall but the least well recalled in final recall.

In the present experiment, subjects were induced to rehearse the last few items in the list at least as many times as they rehearsed the first few. If number of rehearsals is the critical factor, then negative recency in final recall should disappear and a slight positive recency effect, analogous to primacy, should appear. On the other hand, if type of rehearsal is critical, and the extra rehearsals are of a "maintaining" type, then these rehearsals should merely prolong the recency effect in immediate recall and should not lead to a strengthened trace. Thus if it is the quality, not the quantity, of rehearsal activity which is important, the recency positions in final recall should not be affected by the extra rehearsal period in immediate recall.

In summary, subjects were given several lists of words for free recall. They were allowed to recall some lists at the end of presentation, but for other lists, a 20-sec unfilled delay was interpolated between presentation and recall. In all cases, subjects were informed that they must recall the last four words of each list, rehearsing where necessary. The subjects were asked to rehearse aloud and their spoken rehearsals were tape-recorded and later counted. In this way it was hoped that subjects would rehearse terminal items a great deal in the delay condition. After all lists had been presented and recalled, the subjects were unexpectedly asked to recall all previous words in a final free recall test.

METHOD

Sixteen University of Toronto undergraduates were used as subjects. They were paid for their services. Each subject was tested individually. He was told that the experiment concerned the effect of rehearsal on immediate retention and that all his rehearsal must be spoken aloud. Each trial consisted of the visual presentation of a 12-word list at a 3-sec rate. On half of the trials, recall was immediate—signaled by a loud tap just after presentation of the last word. On the remaining trials, recall was delayed for 20 sec after the last word. The recall signal was again a loud tap, and in this case the subject was encouraged to rehearse aloud during the unfilled 20-sec interval. In all cases instructions were for free recall but with the additional strongly emphasized instruction that recall of the last four words was particularly important. These words were printed in block capitals to distinguish them from the first eight words in each list which were typed in lower case letters. By this means, the subject was encouraged to recall the last four words first of all and to rehearse them in particular, during the delay condition. Thus it was hoped that, in the delayed condition, subjects would rehearse the last four words as often as the first few.

The words used were common nouns. Twelve lists were presented—six under immediate recall and six under delayed recall conditions. The order of immediate and delayed trials was randomized independently for each subject. Also, the subject did not know until the end of each list whether it was an immediate or a delayed trial. The subject was given 1 min for written recall on each trial. The 12 scored lists were preceded by three practice lists using letters as material since subjects required some practice and encouragement to keep them rehearsing aloud during presentation and during the delay interval. After the 12 lists had been presented and recalled, the subject was engaged in conversation for 2 min and was then asked to recall as many of the words as he could, in a final free recall test. No subject anticipated that he would be asked to recall the words a second time. Ten minutes were allowed for the final recall test.

RESULTS

The results, shown in Figure 17.01, are clear cut. Even in the immediate condition the strong instructions regarding the last four words resulted in a boost in rehearsals for these words. Otherwise, the pattern of rehearsal is similar to that obtained by Rundus (1971). In the delayed condition, rehearsal of the first eight words was increased slightly, and rehearsal of the last four increased substantially by an average of six extra rehearsals per word. The initial free recall results were essentially identical for the two conditions, showing that subjects were able to maintain the words over the 20-sec interval. Of greater interest is the finding that the final recall scores for the immediate and delayed initial recall conditions were also identical. Despite the great increase in rehearsal for the last four words under the delayed condition, the mean final recall level for the last four words is less in the delayed condition (9.1%) than in the immediate condition (9.8%). Since the mean final recall score was less for the condition in which more rehearsal was demonstrated, no statistical test of the hypothesis that rehearsal leads inevitably to a stronger long-term trace was deemed necessary.

DISCUSSION

Experiment II gives strong support to the position that time in short-term store does not by itself lead to good long-term retention. When subjects were forced to maintain items in short-term storage over a 20-sec interval, such maintenance rehearsal had no effect on later recall from the long-term store. It is important to note that in the present study subjects were probably encouraged to adopt a purely maintenance rehearsal strategy for the last four list items for the following reasons: (*a*) Since they were not expecting a final recall test there was no reason for them to indulge in complex semantic-associative coding. (*b*) They were very well aware that the list was nearly ended, since the last four words were printed in capital letters. (*c*) It is likely that phonemic encoding was encouraged by the necessity to rehearse aloud. To the extent that experimental procedures preclude these factors, some semantic encoding and some positive recency in final recall might be expected.

Although it is not easy to determine whether genuine negative recency effects have been obtained with list-length as short as 12 items, the present results clearly imply that negative recency is not due to fewer rehearsals of the last few items. In Experiment II, recency items were rehearsed at least as often as primacy items, yet the recall of recency items in final recall remained poor. It seems probable that it is the type of rehearsal rather than the amount of rehearsal which is critical for good long-term retention. If the last few items are encoded and maintained at the phonemic level only, final recall performance will be poor; performance should

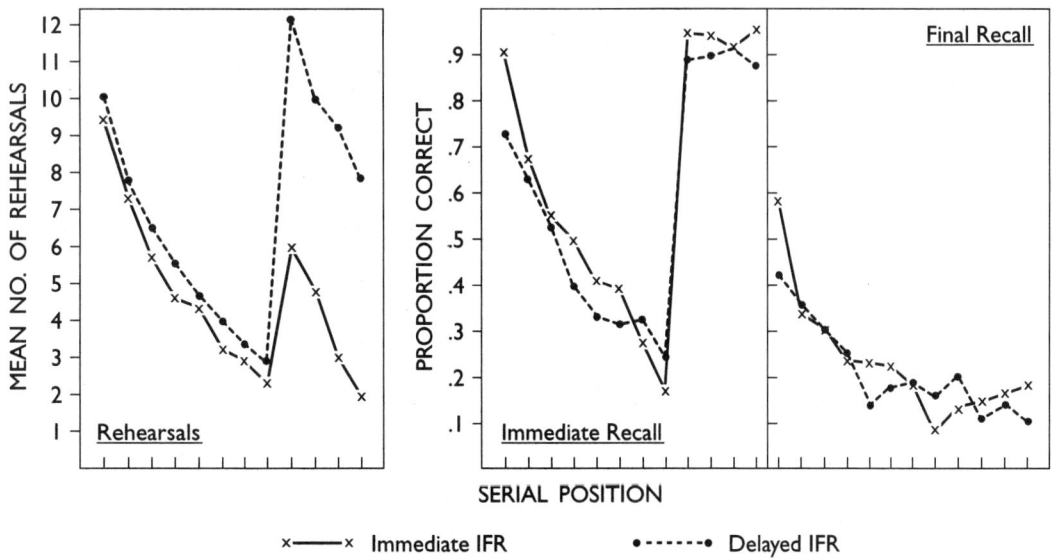

FIGURE 17.01
Number of rehearsals, immediate free recall, and final free recall, with and without an unfilled 20-sec delay between presentation and immediate free recall (IFR).

be enhanced if the subject encodes the words in a richer semantic-associative fashion.

General Discussion

At first sight the results reported in this paper are surprising. They show that neither the prolonged maintenance of an item in short-term storage (Experiment I) nor a substantial increase in the number of overt rehearsals (Experiment II) increased final free recall performance. It is assumed that final recall performance depends only on the long-term store; thus the results imply that maintenance of an item in short-term storage does not necessarily lead to better registration in the long-term store. This finding is opposed to the conclusions of Waugh and Norman (1965), Atkinson and Shiffrin (1968), and Rundus (1971), since all these workers postulated that longer residence in short-term storage, or a greater number of rehearsals, led to better long-term performance.

On the other hand, there is evidence from a number of recent studies giving strong support to the notion that rehearsal will not enhance final recall performance when a simple maintenance type of rehearsal is sufficient to meet the immediate task requirements. Jacoby and Bartz (1972) showed that, relative to a silent delay, an interpolated filled delay reduced immediate recall of five-word lists and reduced recall from the recency portion of 20-word lists, but that the filled delay condition yielded better recall performance in a final recall test. The results were interpreted as showing that subjects encoded the words semantically in order to survive the filled delays. Watkins and Watkins (1974) varied the list lengths of a series of free recall lists, and then in a subsequent recall test found negative recency only when subjects were informed of list length; it was also found that knowledge of list length gave rise to a larger recency effect in immediate free recall. Watkins and Watkins concluded that when subjects can identify during input which items are terminal ones, they will process them in a fashion which on the one hand enhances their immediate recall, but on the other hand gives rise to poor long-term retention. Jacoby (1973) has reported an experiment in which subjects recalled five-word lists either immediately after presentation, or following 15 sec of overt rehearsal. Despite their greater amount of rehearsal, final recall performance for the second group was no higher than that of the "immediate recall" group. Meunier, Ritz, and Meunier (1972) had subjects recall CVC trigrams in the Brown-Peterson paradigm. One group was given the orthodox counting backwards task as an interpolated activity while a second group was free to rehearse during the retention interval. Not surprisingly, the rehearsal group performed better in the immediate recall test, but the groups performed equally well in an unexpected final recall test. The authors concluded that rehearsal had maintained the items in short-term storage without increasing their strength in the long-term store. Glanzer and Meinzer (1967) showed that while silent and overt rehearsal gave rise to equal performance in the recency portion of free recall lists, overt rehearsal actually led to poorer recall from early list positions. Finally, Tulving (1966) demonstrated that word-list learning was no better for subjects who had previously read aloud the words in the list six times.

The present results, in conjunction with these past findings, demonstrate beyond all reasonable doubt that neither overt rehearsal nor maintenance in short-term storage is by itself sufficient to enhance long-term memory performance. This conclusion opposes the models of Waugh and Norman (1965), Atkinson and Shiffrin (1968), and the "total time hypothesis" (see Cooper & Pantle, 1967). Obviously there are situations in which more rehearsal, longer residence in the short-term store, a greater amount of learning time, and more repetitions do lead to better memory performance. Following Craik and Lockhart (1972), it is suggested that rehearsal can be usefully broken down into its "maintaining" function and its "elaborating" function. To the extent that the subject uses the rehearsal time to enrich and elaborate the memory trace, subsequent retention will be enhanced. If the time is used merely to maintain the trace in some simple form (a phonemic representation, for example), then further repetitions or a prolonged stay in the short-term store will not lead to better learning and long-term retention.

More sophisticated models of human memory must be devised which show how the time devoted to learning interacts with the qualitative nature of the processing carried out during that time.

References

1. Atkinson, R. C., & Shiffrin, R. M. Human memory. A proposed system and its control processes. In K. W. Spence & J. T. Spence (Eds.) *The psychology of learning and motivation.* New York: Academic Press, 1968. Vol. 2, pp. 89–195.
2. Bjork, R. A. Repetition and rehearsal mechanisms in models for short-term memory. In D. A. Norman (Ed.) *Models of human memory.* New York: Academic Press, 1970. Pp. 307–330.

3. Cooper, E. H., & Pantle, A. J. The total-time hypothesis in verbal learning. *Psychological Bulletin*, 1967, **68**, 221–234.

4. Craik, F. I. M. The fate of primary memory items in free recall. *Journal of Verbal Learning and Verbal Behavior*, 1970, **9**, 143–148.

5. Craik, F. I. M., Gardiner, J. M., & Watkins, M. J. Further evidence for a negative recency effect in free recall. *Journal of Verbal Learning and Verbal Behavior*, 1970, **9**, 554–560.

6. Craik, F. I. M., & Lockhart, R. S. Levels of processing: A framework for memory research. *Journal of Verbal Learning and Verbal Behavior*, 1972, **11**, 671–684.

7. Glanzer, M., & Meinzer, A. The effects of intralist activity on free recall. *Journal of Verbal Learning and Verbal Behavior*, 1967, **6**, 928–935.

8. Jacoby, L. L. Encoding processes, rehearsal, and recall requirements. *Journal of Verbal Learning and Verbal Behavior*, 1973, **12**, 302–310.

9. Jacoby, L. L., & Bartz, W. H. Rehearsal and transfer to LTM. *Journal of Verbal Learning and Verbal Behavior*, 1972, **11**, 561–565.

10. Meunier, G. F., Ritz, D., & Meunier, J. A. Rehearsal of individual items in short-term memory. *Journal of Experimental Psychology*, 1972, **95**, 465–467.

11. Norman, D. A., & Rumelhart, D. E. A system for perception and memory. D. A. Norman (Ed.) *Models of human memory*. New York: Academic Press, 1970. Pp. 21–64.

12. Rundus, D. Analysis of rehearsal processes in free recall. *Journal of Experimental Psychology*, 1971, **89**, 63–77.

13. Rundus, D., & Atkinson, R. C. Rehearsal processes in free recall: A procedure for direct observation. *Journal of Verbal Learning and Verbal Behavior*, 1970, **9**, 99–105.

14. Tulving, E. Subjective organization and effects of repetition in multitrial free-recall learning. *Journal of Verbal Learning and Verbal Behavior*, 1966, **5**, 193–197.

15. Tulving, E., & Colotla, V. Free recall of trilingual lists. *Cognitive Psychology*, 1970, **1**, 86–98.

16. Waugh, N. C. Immediate memory as a function of repetition. *Journal of Verbal Learning and Verbal Behavior*, 1963, **2**, 107–112.

17. Waugh, N. C. On the effective duration of a repeated word. *Journal of Verbal Learning and Verbal Behavior*, 1970, **9**, 587–595.

18. Waugh, N. C., & Norman, D. A. Primary memory. *Psychological Review*, 1965, **72**, 89–104.

19. Watkins, M. J., & Watkins, O. C. Processing of recency items for free recall. *Journal of Experimental Psychology*, 1974, (in press).

QUESTIONS FOR REFLECTION AND DISCUSSION:

1. How does the PQ4R method of studying apply the findings of Craik and Watson?

2. What kinds of memory tasks are addressed by the Craik and Watson study? Does it address episodic, semantic, or procedural memory? Explain.

3. Can you relate the findings of Craik and Watkins to the Atkinson and Shiffrin model of memory, which includes roles for short-term memory and long-term memory?

4. Craik and Watkins propose the concept of level of analysis as opposed to stages of memory. What is meant by *level of analysis* (also termed *level of processing*)?

5. How did the researchers induce subjects to engage in maintenance rehearsal but not elaborative rehearsal?

6. How do Craik and Watkins account for the finding that "longer residence in short-term store" sometimes leads to better learning and long-term retention?

7. What are the implications of the findings in this study for teaching young children the alphabet and for teaching adults about the science of psychology?

SOURCE

Loftus, E. F., & Palmer, J. C. (1973). Reconstruction of automobile destruction. *Journal of Verbal Learning and Verbal Behavior, 13,* 585–589, 599–607. Reprinted by permission of Academic Press.

A number of psychologists have held that memories are stored much like photographs. If you can find or retrieve the memory from its proper storage bin, you will have an exact record of the experience. This view of memory was reinforced by experiments with patients in brain surgery. When the surgeon, Wilder Penfield, electrically stimulated parts of their brain, they reported re-experiencing past events with what seems to be precision. It was as if the charge of electricity opened the proper door in the brain and the memory was found whole within.

Yet memory researcher Elizabeth Loftus notes that the memory-like experiences stimulated by Penfield's probes were actually vague and sometimes wrong. Her own research suggests that memories are far from exact replicas of the past. Memories are distorted by our schemas—that is by the ways in which we mentally represent our worlds. Sometimes our schemas are our concepts or words for things. Sometimes our schemas reflect our prejudices.

Reconstruction of Automobile Destruction:
An Example of the Interaction Between Language and Memory

ELIZABETH F. LOFTUS AND JOHN C. PALMER
UNIVERSITY OF WASHINGTON

Two experiments are reported in which subjects viewed films of automobile accidents and then answered questions about events occurring in the films. The question, "About how fast were the cars going when they smashed into each other?" elicited higher estimates of speed than questions which used the verbs *collided, bumped, contacted,* or *hit* in place of *smashed.* On a retest one week later, those subjects who received the verb *smashed* were more likely to say "yes" to the question, "Did you see any broken glass?", even though broken glass was not present in the film. These results are consistent with the view that the questions asked subsequent to an event can cause a reconstruction in one's memory of that event.

How accurately do we remember the details of a complex event, like a traffic accident, that has happened in our presence? More specifically, how well do we do when asked to estimate some numerical quantity such as how long the accident took, how fast the cars were traveling, or how much time elapsed between the sounding of a horn and the moment of collision?

It is well documented that most people are markedly inaccurate in reporting such numerical details as time, speed, and distance (Bird, 1927; Whipple, 1909). For example, most people have difficulty estimating the duration of an event, with some research indicating that the tendency is to overestimate the duration of events which are complex (Block, 1974; Marshall, 1969; Ornstein, 1969). The judgment of speed is especially difficult, and practically every automobile accident results in huge variations from one witness to another as to how fast a vehicle was actually traveling (Gardner, 1933). In one test administered to Air Force personnel who knew in advance that they would be questioned about the speed of a moving automobile, estimates ranged from 10 to 50 mph. The car they watched was actually going only 12 mph (Marshall, 1969, p. 23).

Given the inaccuracies in estimates of speed, it seems likely that there are variables which are potentially powerful in terms of influencing these estimates. The present research was conducted to investigate one such variable, namely, the phrasing of the question used to elicit the speed judgment. Some questions are clearly more suggestive than others. This fact of life has resulted in the legal concept of a leading question and in legal rules indicating when leading questions are allowed (*Supreme Court Reporter*, 1973). A leading question is simply one that, either by its form or content, suggests to the witness what answer is desired or leads him to the desired answer.

In the present study, subjects were shown films of traffic accidents and then they answered questions about the accident. The subjects were interrogated about the speed of the vehicles in one of several ways. For example, some subjects were asked, "About how fast were the cars going when they hit each other?" while others were asked, "About how fast were the cars going when they smashed into each other?" As Fillmore (1971) and Bransford and McCarrell (in press) have noted, *hit* and *smashed* may involve specification of differential rates of movement. Furthermore, the two verbs may also involve differential specification of the likely consequences of the events to which they are referring. The impact of the accident is apparently gentler for *hit* than for *smashed*.

Experiment I

METHOD

Forty-five students participated in groups of various sizes. Seven films were shown, each depicting a traffic accident. These films were segments from longer driver's education films borrowed from the Evergreen Safety Council and the Seattle Police Department. The length of the film segments ranged from 5 to 30 sec. Following each film, the subjects received a questionnaire asking them first to, "give an account of the accident you have just seen," and then to answer a series of specific questions about the accident. The critical question was the one that interrogated the subject about the speed of the vehicles involved in the collision. Nine subjects were asked, "About how fast were the cars going when they hit each other?" Equal numbers of the remaining subjects were interrogated with the verbs *smashed, collided, bumped,* and *contacted* in place of *hit*. The entire experiment lasted about an hour and a half. A different ordering of the films was presented to each group of subjects.

RESULTS

Table 18.01 presents the mean speed estimates for the various verbs. Following the procedures outlined by Clark (1973), an analysis of variance was performed with verbs as a fixed effect, and subjects and films as random effects, yielding a significant quasi F ratio, $F'(5, 55) = 4.65, p < .005$.

Some information about the accuracy of subjects' estimates can be obtained from our data. Four of the seven films were staged crashes; the original purpose of these films was to illustrate what can happen to human beings when cars collide at various speeds. One collision took place at 20 mph, one at 30, and two at 40. The mean estimates of speed for these four films were: 37.7, 36.2, 39.7, and 36.1 mph, respectively. In agreement with previous work, people are not very good at judging how fast a vehicle was actually traveling.

DISCUSSION

The results of this experiment indicate that the form of a question (in this case, changes in a single word) can markedly and systematically affect a witness's answer to that question. The actual speed of the vehicles controlled little variance in subject reporting, while the phrasing of the question controlled considerable variance.

Two interpretations of this finding are possible. First, it is possible that the differential speed esti-

TABLE 18.01

SPEED ESTIMATES FOR THE VERBS USED IN EXPERIMENT I	
VERB	**MEAN SPEED ESTIMATE**
Smashed	40.8
Collided	39.3
Bumped	38.1
Hit	34.0
Contacted	31.8

mates result merely from response-bias factors. A subject is uncertain whether to say 30 mph or 40 mph, for example, and the verb *smashed* biases his response towards the higher estimate. A second interpretation is that the question form causes a change in the subject's memory representation of the accident. The verb *smashed* may change a subject's memory such that he "sees" the accident as being more severe than it actually was. If this is the case, we might expect subjects to "remember" other details that did not actually occur, but are commensurate with an accident occurring at higher speeds. The second experiment was designed to provide additional insights into the origin of the differential speed estimates.

Experiment II

METHOD

One hundred and fifty students participated in this experiment, in groups of various sizes. A film depicting a multiple car accident was shown, followed by a questionnaire. The film lasted less than 1 min; the accident in the film lasted 4 sec. At the end of the film, the subjects received a questionnaire asking them first to describe the accident in their own words, and then to answer a series of questions about the accident. The critical question was the one that interrogated the subject about the speed of the vehicles. Fifty subjects were asked, "About how fast were the cars going when they smashed into each other?" Fifty subjects were asked, "About how fast were the cars going when they hit each other?" Fifty subjects were not interrogated about vehicular speed.

One week later, the subjects returned and without viewing the film again they answered a series of questions about the accident. The critical question here was, "Did you see any broken glass?" which the subjects answered by checking "yes" or "no." This question was embedded in a list totalling 10 questions, and it appeared in a random position in the list. There was no broken glass in the accident, but, since broken glass is commensurate with accidents occurring at high speed, we expected that the subjects who had been asked the *smashed* question might more often say "yes" to this critical question.

RESULTS

The mean estimate of speed for subjects interrogated with *smashed* was 10.46 mph; with *hit* the estimate was 8.00 mph. These means are significantly different, $t(98) = 2.00$, $p < .05$.

TABLE 18.02

DISTRIBUTION OF "YES" AND "NO" RESPONSES TO THE QUESTION, "DID YOU SEE ANY BROKEN GLASS?"			
	VERB CONDITION		
RESPONSE	**SMASHED**	**HIT**	**CONTROL**
Yes	16	7	6
No	34	43	44

Table 18.02 presents the distribution of "yes" and "no" responses for the *smashed, hit,* and control subjects. An independence chi-square test on these responses was significant beyond the .025 level, $\chi^2(2) = 7.76$. The important result in Table 18.02 is that the probability of saying "yes," P(Y), to the question about broken glass is .32 when the verb *smashed* is used, and .14 with *hit*. Thus *smashed* leads both to more "yes" responses and to higher speed estimates. It appears to be the case that the effect of the verb is mediated at least in part by the speed estimate. The question now arises: Is *smashed* doing anything else besides increasing the estimate of speed? To answer this, the function relating P(Y) to speed estimate was calculated separately for *smashed* and *hit*. If the speed estimate is the only way in which effect of verb is mediated, then for a given speed estimate, P(Y) should be independent of verb. Table 18.03 shows that this is not the case. P(Y) is lower for *hit* than for *smashed;* the difference between the two verbs ranges from .03 for estimates of 1–5 mph to .18 for estimates of 6–10 mph. The average difference between the two curves is about .12. Whereas the unconditional difference of .18 between the *smashed* and *hit* con-

TABLE 18.03

PROBABILITY OF SAYING "YES" TO, "DID YOU SEE ANY BROKEN GLASS?" CONDITIONALIZED ON SPEED ESTIMATES				
VERB CONDITION	**SPEED ESTIMATE (MPH)**			
	1–5	**6–10**	**11–15**	**16–20**
Smashed	.09	.27	.41	.62
Hit	.06	.09	.25	.50

ditions is attenuated, it is by no means eliminated when estimate of speed is controlled for. It thus appears that the verb *smashed* has other effects besides that of simply increasing the estimate of speed. One possibility will be discussed in the next section.

Discussion

To reiterate, we have first of all provided an additional demonstration of something that has been known for some time, namely, that the way a question is asked can enormously influence the answer that is given. In this instance, the question, "About how fast were the cars going when they smashed into each other?" led to higher estimates of speed than the same question asked with the verb *smashed* replaced by *hit*. Furthermore, this seemingly small change had consequences for how questions are answered a week after the original event occurred.

As a framework for discussing these results, we would like to propose that two kinds of information go into one's memory for some complex occurrence. The first is information gleaned during the perception of the original event; the second is external information supplied after the fact. Over time, information from these two sources may be integrated in such a way that we are unable to tell from which source some specific detail is recalled. All we have is one "memory."

Discussing the present experiments in these terms, we propose that the subject first forms some representation of the accident he has witnessed. The experimenter then, while asking, "About how fast were the cars going when they smashed into each other?" supplies a piece of external information, namely, that the cars did indeed smash into each other. When these two pieces of information are integrated, the subject has a memory of an accident that was more severe than in fact it was. Since broken glass is commensurate with a severe accident, the subject is more likely to think that broken glass was present

There is some connection between the present work and earlier work on the influence of verbal labels on memory for visually presented form stimuli. A classic study in psychology showed that when subjects are asked to reproduce a visually presented form, their drawings tend to err in the direction of a more familiar object suggested by a verbal label initially associated with the to-be-remembered form (Carmichael, Hogan, & Walter, 1932). More re-cently, Daniel (1972) showed that recognition memory, as well as reproductive memory, was similarly affected by verbal labels, and he concluded that the verbal label causes a shift in the memory strength of forms which are better representatives of the label.

When the experimenter asks the subject, "About how fast were the cars going when they smashed into each other?", he is effectively labeling the accident a smash. Extrapolating the conclusions of Daniel to this situation, it is natural to conclude that the label, smash, causes a shift in the memory representation of the accident in the direction of being more similar to a representation suggested by the verbal label.

References

1. Bird, C. The influence of the press upon the accuracy of report. *Journal of Abnormal and Social Psychology*, 1927, **22**, 123–129.
2. Block, R. A. Memory and the experience of duration in retrospect. *Memory & Cognition*, 1974, **2**, 153–160.
3. Bransford, J. D., & McCarrell, N. S. A sketch of a cognitive approach to comprehension: Some thoughts about understanding what it means to comprehend. In D. Palermo & W. Weimer (Eds.), *Cognition and the symbolic processes*. Washington, D.C.: V. H. Winston & Co., in press.
4. Carmichael, L., Hogan, H. P., & Walter, A. A. An experimental study of the effect of language on the reproduction of visually perceived form. *Journal of Experimental Psychology*, 1932, **15**, 73–86.
5. Clark, H. H. The language-as-fixed-effect fallacy: A critique of language statistics in psychological research. *Journal of Verbal Learning and Verbal Behavior*, 1973, **12**, 335–359.
6. Daniel, T. C. Nature of the effect of verbal labels on recognition memory for form. *Journal of Experimental Psychology*, 1972, **96**, 152–157.
7. Fillmore, C. J. Types of lexical information. In D. D. Steinberg and L. A. Jakobovits (Eds.), *Semantics: An interdisciplinary reader in philosophy, linguistics, and psychology*. Cambridge: Cambridge University Press, 1971.
8. Gardner, D. S. The perception and memory of witnesses. *Cornell Law Quarterly*, 1933, **8**, 391–409.
9. Marshall, J. *Law and psychology in conflict*. New York: Anchor Books, 1969.
10. Ornstein, R. E. *On the experience of time*. Harmondsworth. Middlesex, England: Penguin, 1969.
11. Whipple, G. M. The observer as reporter: A survey of the psychology of testimony. *Psychological Bulletin*, 1909, **6**, 153–170.
12. *Supreme Court Reporter*, 1973, **3**: Rules of Evidence for United States Courts and Magistrates.

QUESTIONS FOR REFLECTION AND DISCUSSION:

1. Loftus's research suggests that the ways in which lawyers phrase questions may distort the "memories" of eyewitnesses to crimes or accidents. Can you provide an example?

2. Do you believe that you have precise memories of the past? Is your belief likely to be accurate?

3. What was the experimental manipulation in each of the studies reported by Loftus?

4. Have you ever gotten into an argument with someone about what happened on some occasion? Of course it is possible that one of you was not telling the truth, but is it also possible that one or both of you were distorting the memory to meet your own needs?

5. If something important happens, what can we do to increase the likelihood that we will remember it accurately?

SOURCE

Steele, C. M., & Aronson, J. (1995). Stereotype threat and the intellectual test performance of African Americans. *Journal of Personality and Social Psychology, 69*, 797–811. Copyright © 1995 by the American Psychological Association. Reprinted with permission.

As a group, African Americans score some 10 to 15 points lower on standardized intelligence tests than European Americans do. Why? A number of authors have attributed most of the racial difference in IQ scores to genetic factors (nature). This view is fraught with social and political issues because it suggests that the difference in IQ cannot be altered and that many African Americans will be second-class citizens in our high-tech society. Other authors attribute most of the difference to environmental factors (nurture). They argue that nutrition, enriched early childhood experiences, and personal belief in the importance of education can close the gap in IQ. Psychologist Claude Steele has chosen to investigate the ways in which African Americans perform on tests of cognitive ability, and he has found that regardless of ability as shown by tests like the SAT, many African Americans do not perform up to their capabilities because of stereotype threat, *or* stereotype vulnerability.

"His research may shed fresh light on why many [African Americans] do poorly on standardized tests," writes Ethan Watters[1], but "It has done little to improve his standing with one leading [African American] intellectual—his twin brother, Shelby." Claude and Shelby Steele are the sons of a social worker (their mother) and a truck driver (their father) who met while taking part in the civil rights movement. Shelby is probably the better known of the brothers outside the field of psychology. He is a conservative essayist.

In his writing, Shelby has noted how African Americans experience a feeling of racial vulnerability when, for example, they see Band-Aids tinted to match pink skin. Claude's concept of stereotype vulnerability *could be said to describe what African Americans experience when they see standardized tests that seem to be designed to match pink skin. Like other conservative social critics, Shelby has argued that the solution for African Americans is not affirmative action but personal achievement through willpower, despite the odds. Claude argues that the sense of vulnerability is not so easy to overcome and that society as well as individuals must change.*

Claude Steele began developing his ideas in the 1980s when he took a teaching position at the University of Michigan and became aware of the greater dropout rate of African American students. He helped create the 21st Century Program, which maintains racially integrated dormitories and requires that dorm members take some classes with other dorm members. To date, the program has significantly reduced the grade gap between African American and White students at the University of Michigan. It remains to be seen whether the future will reduce the gap between Claude and Shelby Steele.

---

[1] Watters, E. (1995, September 17). Claude Steele has scores to settle. *The New York Times Magazine*, pp. 44–47.

The current article reports the results of a study on stereotype threat that was undertaken by Steele and a colleague, Joshua Aronson.

Stereotype Threat and the Intellectual Test Performance of African Americans

CLAUDE M. STEELE
DEPARTMENT OF PSYCHOLOGY STANFORD UNIVERSITY
JOSHUA ARONSON
SCHOOL OF EDUCATION UNIVERSITY OF TEXAS, AUSTIN

Abstract

Stereotype threat is being at risk of confirming, as self-characteristic, a negative stereotype about one's group. Studies 1 and 2 varied the stereotype vulnerability of Black participants taking a difficult verbal test by varying whether or not their performance was ostensibly diagnostic of ability, and thus, whether or not they were at risk of fulfilling the racial stereotype about their intellectual ability. Reflecting the pressure of this vulnerability, Blacks underperformed in relation to Whites in the ability-diagnostic condition but not in the nondiagnostic condition (with Scholastic Aptitude Tests controlled). Study 3 validated that ability-diagnosticity cognitively activated the racial stereotype in these participants and motivated them not to conform to it, or to be judged by it. Study 4 showed that mere salience of the stereotype could impair Blacks' performance even when the test was not ability diagnostic. The role of stereotype vulnerability in the standardized test performance of ability-stigmatized groups is discussed.

Not long ago, in explaining his career-long preoccupation with the American Jewish experience, the novelist Philip Roth said that it was not Jewish culture or religion per se that fascinated him, it was what he called the Jewish "predicament." This is an apt term for the perspective taken in the present research. It focuses on a social-psychological predicament that can arise from widely-known negative stereotypes about one's group. It is this: the existence of such a stereotype means that anything one does or any of one's features that conform to it make the stereotype more plausible as a self-characterization in the eyes of others, and perhaps even in one's own eyes. We call this predicament *stereotype threat* and argue that it is experienced, essentially, as a self-evaluative threat. In form, it is a predicament that can beset the members of any group about whom negative stereotypes exist. Consider the stereotypes elicited by the terms *yuppie, feminist, liberal,* or *White male.* Their prevalence in society raises the possibility for potential targets that the stereotype is true of them and, also, that other people will see them that way. When the allegations of the stereotype are importantly negative, this predicament may be self-threatening enough to have disruptive effects of its own.

The present research examined the role these processes play in the intellectual test performance of African Americans. Our reasoning is this: whenever African American students perform an explicitly scholastic or intellectual task, they face the threat of confirming or being judged by a negative societal stereotype—a suspicion—about their group's intellectual ability and competence. This threat is not borne by people not stereotyped in this way. And the self-threat it causes—through a variety of mechanisms—may interfere with the intellectual functioning of these students, particularly during standardized tests. This is the principal hypothesis examined in the present research. But as this threat persists over time, it may have the further effect of pressuring these students to protectively disidentify with achievement in school and related intellectual domains. That is, it may pressure the person to define or redefine the self-concept such that school achievement is neither a basis of self-evaluation nor a personal identity. This protects the person against the self-evaluative threat posed by the stereotypes but may have the byproduct of diminishing interest, motivation, and, ultimately, achievement in the domain (Steele, 1992).

The anxiety of knowing that one is a potential target of prejudice and stereotypes has been much discussed: in classic social science (e.g., Allport, 1954; Goffman, 1963), popular books (e.g., Carter,

1991) and essays, as, for example, S. Steele's (1990) treatment of what he called *racial vulnerability*. In this last analysis, S. Steele made a connection between this experience and the school life of African Americans that has similarities to our own. He argued that after a lifetime of exposure to society's negative images of their ability, these students are likely to internalize an "inferiority anxiety"—a state that can be aroused by a variety of race-related cues in the environment. This anxiety, in turn, can lead them to blame others for their troubles (for example, White racism), to underutilize available opportunities, and to generally form a victim's identity. These adaptations, in turn, the argument goes, translate into poor life success.

The present theory and research do not focus on the internalization of inferiority images or their consequences. Instead they focus on the immediate situational threat that derives from the broad dissemination of negative stereotypes about one's group—the threat of possibly being judged and treated stereotypically, or of possibly self-fulfilling such a stereotype. This threat can befall anyone with a group identity about which some negative stereotype exists, and for the person to be threatened in this way, he need not even believe the stereotype. He need only know that it stands as a hypothesis about him in situations where the stereotype is relevant. We focused on the stereotype threat of African Americans in intellectual and scholastic domains to provide a compelling test of the theory and because the theory, should it be supported in this context for this group, would have relevance to an important set of outcomes.

Gaps in school achievement and retention rates between White and Black Americans at all levels of schooling have been strikingly persistent in American society (e.g., Steele, 1992). Well publicized at the kindergarten through 12th grade level, recent statistics show that they persist even at the college level where, for example, the national drop-out rate for Black college students (the percentage who do not complete college within a 6-year window of time) is 70% compared to 42% for White Americans (American Council on Education, 1990). Even among those who graduate, their grades average two thirds of letter grade lower than those of graduating Whites (e.g., Nettles, 1988). It has been most common to understand such problems as stemming largely from the socioeconomic disadvantage, segregation, and discrimination that African Americans have endured and continue to endure in this society, a set of conditions that, among other things, could produce racial gaps in achievement by undermining preparation for school.

Some evidence, however, questions the sufficiency of these explanations. It comes from the sizable literature examining racial bias in standardized testing. This work, involving hundreds of studies over several decades, generally shows that standardized tests predict subsequent school achievement as well for Black students as for White students (e.g., Cleary, Humphreys, Kendrick, & Wesman, 1975; Linn, 1973; Stanley, 1971). The slope of the lines regressing subsequent school achievement on entry-level standardized test scores is essentially the same for both groups. But embedded in this literature is another fact: At every level of preparation as measured by a standardized test—for example, the Scholastic Aptitude Test (SAT)—Black students with that score have poorer subsequent achievement—GPA, retention rates, time to graduation, and so on—than White students with that score (Jensen, 1980). This is variously known as the overprediction or underachievement phenomenon, because it indicates that, relative to Whites with the same score, standardized tests actually overpredict the achievement that Blacks will realize. Most important for our purposes, this evidence suggests that Black-White achievement gaps are not due solely to group differences in preparation. Blacks achieve less well than Whites even when they have the same preparation, and even when that preparation is at a very high level. Could this underachievement, in some part, reflect the stereotype threat that is a chronic feature of these students' schooling environments?

Research from the early 1960s—largely that of Irwin Katz and his colleagues (e.g., Katz, 1964) on how desegregation affected the intellectual performance of Black students—shows the sizable influence on Black intellectual performance of factors that can be interpreted as manipulations of stereotype threat. Katz, Roberts, and Robinson (1965), for example, found that Black participants performed better on an IQ subtest when it was presented as a test of eye-hand coordination—a nonevaluative and thus threat-negating test representation—than when it was said to be a test of intelligence. Katz, Epps, and Axelson (1964) found that Black students performed better on an IQ test when they believed their performance would be compared to other Blacks as opposed to Whites. But as evidence that bears on our hypothesis, this literature has several limitations. Much of the research was conducted in an era when American race relations were different in important ways than they are now. Thus, without their being replicated, the extent to which these findings reflect enduring processes of stereotype threat as opposed to the racial dynamics of a specific historical era is not clear. Also, this research seldomly used White control groups. Thus it is difficult to know the extent to which some of the critical effects were mediated by the stereotype threat of Black students as opposed to processes experienced by any students.

Other research supports the present hypothesis by showing that factors akin to stereotype threat—that is, other factors that add self-evaluative threat to test taking or intellectual performance—are capable of disrupting that performance. The presence of observers or coactors, for example, can interfere with performance on mental tasks (e.g., Geen, 1985; Seta, 1982). Being a "token" member of a group—the sole representative of a social category—can inhibit one's memory for what is said during a group discussion (Lord & Saenz, 1985; Lord, Saenz, & Godfrey, 1987). Conditions that increase the importance of performing well—prizes, competition, and audience approval—have all been shown to impair performance of even motor skills (e.g., Baumeister, 1984). The stereotype threat hypothesis shares with these approaches the assumption that performance suffers when the situation redirects attention needed to perform a task onto some other concern—in the case of stereotype threat, a concern with the significance of one's performance in light of a devaluing stereotype.

For African American students, the act of taking a test purported to measure intellectual ability may be enough to induce this threat. But we assume that this is most likely to happen when the test is also frustrating. It is frustration that makes the stereotype—as an allegation of inability—relevant to their performance and thus raises the possibility that they have an inability linked to their race. This is not to argue that the stereotype is necessarily believed; only that, in the face of frustration with the test, it becomes more plausible as a self-characterization and thereby more threatening to the self. Thus for Black students who care about the skills being tested—that is, those who are identified with these skills in the sense of their self-regard being somewhat tied to having them—the stereotype loads the testing situation with an extra degree of self-threat, a degree not borne by people not stereotyped in this way. This additional threat, in turn, may interfere with their performance in a variety of ways: by causing an arousal that reduces the range of cues participants are able to use (e.g., Easterbrook, 1959), or by diverting attention onto task-irrelevant worries (e.g., Sarason, 1972; Wine, 1971), by causing an interfering self-consciousness (e.g., Baumeister, 1984), or overcautiousness (Geen, 1985). Or, through the ability-indicting interpreta-

tion it poses for test frustration, it could foster low performance expectations that would cause participants to withdraw effort (e.g., Bandura, 1977, 1986). Depending on the situation, several of these processes may be involved simultaneously or in alternation. Through these mechanisms, then, stereotype threat might be expected to undermine the standardized test performance of Black participants relative to White participants who, in this situation, do not suffer this added threat.

Study 1

Accordingly, Black and White college students in this experiment were given a 30-min test composed of items from the verbal Graduate Record Examination (GRE) that were difficult enough to be at the limits of most participants' skills. In the stereotype-threat condition, the test was described as diagnostic of intellectual ability, thus making the racial stereotype about intellectual ability relevant to Black participants' performance and establishing for them the threat of fulfilling it. In the non-stereotype-threat condition, the same test was described simply as a laboratory problem-solving task that was nondiagnostic of ability. Presumably, this would make the racial stereotype about ability irrelevant to Black participants' performance and thus preempt any threat of fulfilling it. Finally, a second nondiagnostic condition was included which exhorted participants to view the difficult test as a challenge. For practical reasons we were interested in whether stressing the challenge inherent in a difficult test might further increase participants' motivation and performance over what would occur in the nondiagnostic condition. The primary dependent measure in this experiment was participants' performance on the test adjusted for the influence of individual differences in skill level (operationalized as participants' verbal SAT scores).

We predicted that Black participants would underperform relative to Whites in the diagnostic condition where there was stereotype threat, but not in the two nondiagnostic conditions—the non-diagnostic-only condition and the non-diagnostic-plus-challenge condition—where this threat was presumably reduced. In the non-diagnostic-challenge condition, we also expected the additional motivation to boost the performance of both Black and White participants above that observed in the non-diagnostic-only condition. Several additional measures were included to assess the effectiveness of the manipulation and possible mediating states.

METHOD DESIGN AND PARTICIPANTS

This experiment took the form of a 2 × 3 factorial design. The factors were race of the participant, Black or White, and a test description factor in which the test was presented as either diagnostic of intellectual ability (the diagnostic condition), as a laboratory tool for studying problem solving (the non-diagnostic-only condition), or as both a problem-solving tool and a challenge (the non-diagnostic-challenge condition). Test performance was the primary dependent measure. We recruited 117 male and female, Black and White Stanford undergraduates through campus advertisements which offered $10.00 for 1 hr of participation. The data from 3 participants were excluded from the analysis because they failed to provide their verbal SAT scores. This left a total of 114 participants randomly assigned to the three experimental conditions with the exception that we ensured an equal number of participants per condition.

PROCEDURE

Participants who signed up for the experiment were contacted by telephone prior to their experimental participation and asked to provide their verbal and quantitative SAT scores, to rate their enjoyment of verbally oriented classes, and to provide background information (e.g., year in school, major, etc.). When participants arrived at the laboratory, the experimenter (a White man) explained that for the next 30 min they would work on a set of verbal problems in a format identical to the SAT exam, and end by answering some questions about their experience.

The participant was then given a page that stated the purpose of the study, described the procedure for answering questions, stressed the importance of indicating guessed answers (by a check), described the test as very difficult and that they should expect not to get many of the questions correct, and told them that they would be given feedback on their performance at the end of the session. We included the information about test difficulty to, as much as possible, equate participants' performance expectations across the conditions. And, by acknowledging the difficulty of the test, we wanted to reduce the possibility that participants would see the test as a miscalculation of their skills and perhaps reduce their effort. This description was the same for all conditions with the exception of several key phrases that comprised the experimental manipulation.

Participants in the diagnostic condition were told that the study was concerned with "various per-sonal factors involved in performance on problems requiring reading and verbal reasoning abilities." They were further informed that after the test, feedback would be provided which "may be helpful to you by familiarizing you with some of your strengths and weaknesses" in verbal problem solving. As noted, participants in all conditions were told that they should not expect to get many items correct, and in the diagnostic condition, this test difficulty was justified as a means of providing a "genuine test of your verbal abilities and limitations so that we might better understand the factors involved in both." Participants were asked to give a strong effort in order to "help us in our analysis of your verbal ability."

In the non-diagnostic-only and non-diagnostic-challenge conditions, the description of the study made no reference to verbal ability. Instead, participants were told that the purpose of the research was to better understand the "psychological factors involved in solving verbal problems. . . . " These participants too were told that they would receive performance feedback, but it was justified as a means of familiarizing them "with the kinds of problems that appear on tests [they] may encounter in the future." In the non-diagnostic-only condition, the difficulty of the test was justified in terms of a research focus on difficult verbal problems and in the non-diagnostic-challenge condition it was justified as an attempt to provide "even highly verbal people with a mental challenge. . . . " Last, participants in both conditions were asked to give a genuine effort in order to "help us in our analysis of the problem solving process." As the experimenter left them to work on the test, to further differentiate the conditions, participants in the non-diagnostic-only condition were asked to try hard "even though we're not going to evaluate your ability." Participants in the non-diagnostic-challenge condition were asked to "please take this challenge seriously even though we will not be evaluating your ability."

DEPENDENT MEASURES

The primary dependent measure was participants' performance on 30 verbal items, 27 of which were difficult items taken from GRE study guides (only 30% of earlier samples had gotten these items correct) and 3 difficult anagram problems. Both the total number correct and an accuracy index of the number correct over the number attempted were analyzed.

Participants next completed an 18-item self-report measure of their current thoughts relating to academic competence and personal worth (e.g., "I feel confident about my abilities," "I feel self-conscious," "I feel as smart as others," etc.). These were measured on 5-point scales anchored by the phrases *not at all* (1) and *extremely* (5). Participants also completed a 12-item measure of cognitive interference frequently used in test anxiety research (Sarason, 1980) on which they indicated the frequency of several distracting thoughts during the exam (e.g., "I wondered what the experimenter would think of me," "I thought about how poorly I was doing," "I thought about the difficulty of the problems," etc.) by putting a number from 1 *(never)* to 5 *(very often)* next to each statement. Participants then rated how difficult and biased they considered the test on 15-point scales anchored by the labels *not at all* (1) and *extremely* (15). Next, participants evaluated their own performance by estimating the number of problems they correctly solved, and by comparing their own performance to that of the average Stanford student on a 15-point scale with the end points *much worse* (1) and *much better* (15). Finally, as a check on the manipulation, participants responded to the question:

> The purpose of this experiment was to: (a) provide a genuine test of my abilities in order to examine personal factors involved in verbal ability; (b) provide a challenging test in order to examine factors involved in solving verbal problems; (c) present you with unfamiliar verbal problems to measure verbal learning.

Participants were asked to circle the appropriate response.

RESULTS

Because there were no main or interactive effects of gender on verbal test performance or the self-report measures, we collapsed over this factor in all analyses.

MANIPULATION CHECK

Chi-square analyses performed on participants' responses to the postexperimental question about the purpose of the study revealed only an effect of condition, $\chi^2{}_2 = 43.18$, $p < .001$. Participants were more likely to believe the purpose of the experiment was to evaluate their abilities in the diagnostic condition (65%) than in the nondiagnostic condition (3%), or the challenge condition (11%).

TEST PERFORMANCE

The ANCOVA on the number of items participants got correct, using their self-reported SAT scores as

the covariate (Black mean = 592, White mean = 632) revealed a significant condition main effect, F (2, 107) = 4.74, $p < .02$, with participants in the non-diagnostic-challenge condition performing higher than participants in the non-diagnostic-only and diagnostic conditions, respectively, and a significant race main effect, F (1, 107) = 5.22, $p < .03$, with White participants performing higher than Black participants. The race-by-condition interaction did not reach conventional significance ($p < .19$). The adjusted condition means are presented in Figure 19.01.

If making the test diagnostic of ability depresses the performance of Black students through stereotype threat, then their performance should be lower in the diagnostic condition than in either the non-diagnostic-only or non-diagnostic-challenge conditions which presumably lessened stereotype threat, and it should be lower than that of Whites in the diagnostic condition. Bonferroni contrasts with SATs as a covariate supported this reasoning by showing that Black participants in the diagnostic condition performed significantly worse than Black participants in either the nondiagnostic condition, t (107)

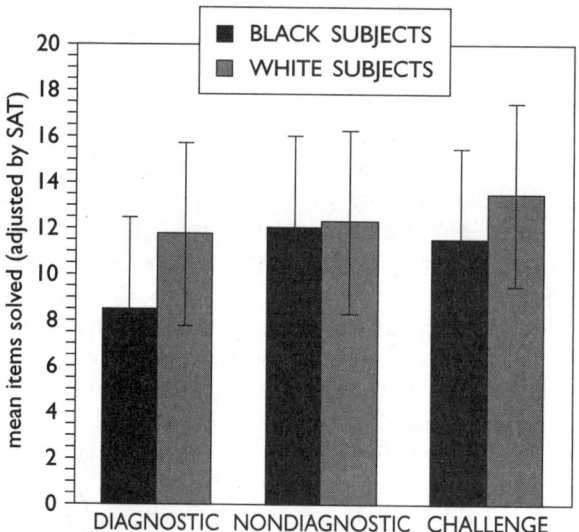

FIGURE 19.01

Because we did not warn participants to avoid guessing in these experiments, we do not report the performance results in terms of the index used by Educational Testing Service, which includes a correction for guessing. This correction involves subtracting from the number correct, the number wrong adjusted for the number of response options for each wrong item and dividing this by the number of items on the test. Because 27 of our 30 items had the same number of response options (5), this correction amounts to adjusting the number correct almost invariably by the same number. All analyses are the same regardless of the index used.

= 2.88, $p < .01$, or the challenge condition, t (107) = 2.63, $p < .01$, as well as significantly worse than White participants in the diagnostic condition t (107) = 2.64, $p < .01$.

But, as noted, the interaction testing the differential effect of test diagnosticity on Black and White participants did not reach significance. This may have happened, however, because an incidental pattern of means—Whites slightly outperforming Blacks in the nondiagnostic-challenge condition—undermined the overall interaction effect. To pursue a more sensitive test, we constructed a weighted contrast that compared the size of the race effect in the diagnostic condition with that in the nondiagnostic condition and assigned weights of zero to the White and Black non-diagnostic-challenge conditions. This analysis (including the use of SATs as a covariate) reached marginal significance, F (1, 107) = 3.27, $p < .08$. In sum, then, the hypothesis was supported by the pattern of contrasts, but when tested over the whole design, reached only marginal significance.

ACCURACY

An ANCOVA on accuracy, the proportion correct of the number attempted, with SATs as the covariate, found that neither condition main effect nor the interaction reached significance, although there was a marginally significant tendency for Black participants to evidence less accuracy, $p < .10$. This tendency was primarily due to Black participants in the diagnostic condition who had the lowest adjusted mean accuracy of any group in the experiment, .420. The adjusted means for the White diagnostic, White non-diagnostic-only, White non-diagnostic-challenge, Black non-diagnostic-only, and Black diagnostic-challenge conditions were, .519, .518, .561, .546, and .490, respectively. Bonferroni tests revealed that Black participants in the diagnostic condition were reliably less accurate than Black participants in the non-diagnostic-only condition and White participants in the diagnostic condition, t (107) = 2.64, $p < .01$, and t (107) = 2.13, $p < .05$, respectively.

No condition or interaction effects reached significance for the number of items completed or the number of guesses participants recorded on the test (all F s < 1). The overall means for these two measures were 22.9 and 4.1, respectively.

SELF-REPORT MEASURES

There were no significant condition effects on the self-report measure of academic competence and personal worth or on the self-report measure of disruptive thoughts and feelings during the test. Analysis of participants' responses to the question about test bias yielded a main effect of race, F (1, 107) = 10.47, $p < .001$. Black participants in all conditions thought the test was more biased than White participants.

PERCEIVED PERFORMANCE

Participants' estimates of how many problems they solved correctly and of how they compared to other participants both showed significant condition main effects, F (2, 106) = 7.91, $p < .001$, and F (2, 107) = 3.17, $p < .05$, respectively. Performance estimates were higher in the non-diagnostic-only condition ($M = 11.81$) than in either the diagnostic ($M = 9.20$) or non-diagnostic-challenge conditions ($M = 8.15$). Bonferroni tests showed that Black participants in the diagnostic condition ($M = 4.89$) saw their relative performance as poorer than Black participants in the non-diagnostic-only condition ($M = 6.54$), t (107) = 2.81, $p < .01$, and than Black participants in the non-diagnostic-challenge condition ($M = 6.30$), t (107) = 2.40, $p < .02$, while test description had no effect on the ratings of White participants. The overall mean was 5.86.

DISCUSSION

With SAT differences statistically controlled, Black participants performed worse that White participants when the test was presented as a measure of their ability, but improved dramatically, matching the performance of Whites, when the test was presented as less reflective of ability. Nonetheless, the race-by-diagnosticity interaction testing this relationship reached only marginal significance, and then, only when participants from the non-diagnostic-challenge condition were excluded from the analysis. Thus there remained some question as to the reliability of this interaction.

We had also reasoned that stereotype threat might undermine performance by increasing interfering thoughts during the test. But the conditions affected neither self-evaluative thoughts nor thoughts about the self in the immediate situation (Sarason, 1980). Thus to further test the reliability of the predicted interaction and explore the mediation of the stereotype threat effect, we conducted a second experiment.

Study 2

We argued that the effect of stereotype threat on performance is mediated by an apprehension over possibly conforming to the negative group stereotype. Could this apprehension be detected as a higher level of general anxiety among stereotype-threatened participants? To test this possibility, participants in all conditions completed a version of the Spielberger State Anxiety Inventory (STAI) immediately after the test. This scale has been successfully used in other research to detect anxiety induced by evaluation apprehension (e.g., Geen, 1985). We also measured the amount of time they spent on each test item to learn whether greater anxiety was associated with more time spent answering items.

METHOD PARTICIPANTS

Twenty Black and 20 White Stanford female undergraduates were randomly assigned (with the exception of attaining equal cell sizes) to either the diagnostic or the nondiagnostic conditions as described in Study 1, yielding 10 participants per condition. Female participants were used in this experiment because, due to other research going on, we had considerably easier access to Black female undergraduates than to Black male undergraduates. This decision was justified by the finding of no gender differences in the first study, or, as it turned out, in any of the subsequent studies reported in this article—all of which used both men and women.

PROCEDURE

This experiment used the same test used in Study 1, with several exceptions; the final three anagram problems were deleted and the test period was reduced from 30 to 25 min. Also, the test was presented on a Macintosh computer (LCII). Participants controlled with the mouse how long each item or item component was on the screen and could, at their own pace, access whatever item material they wanted to see. The computer recorded the amount of time the items, or item components were on the screen as well as the number of referrals between item components (as in the reading comprehension items)—in addition to recording participants' answers.

Following the exam, participants completed the STAI and the cognitive interference measure described for Study 1. Also, on 11-point scales (with end-points *not at all* and *extremely*) participants indicated the extent to which they guessed when having difficulty, expended effort on the test, persisted on problems, limited their time on problems, read problems more than once, became frustrated and gave up, and felt that the test was biased.

RESULTS AND DISCUSSION

The ANCOVA performed on the number of items correctly solved yielded a significant main effect of race, $F(1, 35) = 10.04$, $p < .01$, qualified by a significant Race $\times$ Test Description interaction, $F(1, 35) = 8.07$, $p < .01$. The mean SAT score for Black participants was 603 and for White participants 655. The adjusted means are presented in Figure 19.02. Planned contrasts on the adjusted scores revealed that, as predicted, Blacks in the diagnostic condition performed significantly worse than Blacks in the nondiagnostic condition $t(35) = 2.38$, $p < .02$, than Whites in the diagnostic condition $t(35) = 3.75$, $p < .001$, and than Whites in the nondiagnostic condition $t(35) = 2.34$, $p < .025$.

For accuracy—the number correct over the number attempted—a similar pattern emerged: Blacks in the diagnostic condition had lower accuracy ($M = .392$) than Blacks in the nondiagnostic condition ($M = .490$) or than Whites in either the diagnostic condition ($M = .485$) or the nondiagnostic condition ($M = .435$). The diagnosticity-by-race interaction testing this pattern reached significance, $F(1, 35) = 4.18$, $p < .05$. But the planned contrasts of the Black diagnostic condition against the other conditions did not reach conventional significance, although its contrasts with the Black nondiagnostic and White diagnostic conditions were marginally significant, with p s of .06 and .09 respectively.

Blacks completed fewer items than Whites, $F(1, 35) = 9.35$, $p < .01$, and participants in the diag-

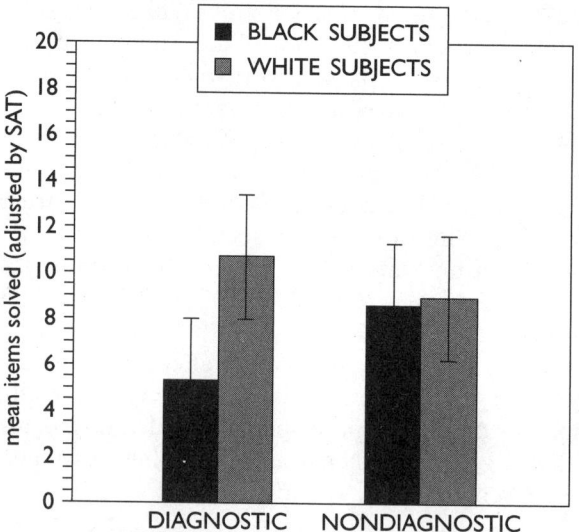

FIGURE 19.02

All comparisons of adjusted means reported hereafter used the Bonferroni procedure.

nostic conditions tended to complete fewer items than those in the nondiagnostic conditions, $F(1, 35) = 3.69$, $p < .07$. The overall interaction did not reach significance. But planned contrasts revealed that Black participants in the diagnostic condition finished fewer items ($M = 12.38$) than Blacks in the nondiagnostic condition ($M = 18.53$), $t(35) = 2.50$, $p < .02$; than Whites in the diagnostic condition ($M = 20.93$), $t(35) = 3.39$, $p < .01$; and than Whites in the nondiagnostic condition ($M = 21.45$), $t(35) = 3.60$, $p < .01$.

These results establish the reliability of the diagnosticity-by-race interaction for test performance that was marginally significant in Study 1. They also reveal another dimension of the effect of stereotype threat. Black participants in the diagnostic condition completed fewer test items than participants in the other conditions. Test diagnosticity impaired the rate, as well as the accuracy of their work. This is precisely the impairment caused by evaluative pressures such as evaluation apprehension, test anxiety, and competitive pressure (e.g., Baumeister, 1984). But one might ask why this did not happen in the near-identical Study 1. Several factors may be relevant. First, the most involved test items—reading comprehension items that took several steps to answer—came first in the test. And second, the test lasted 25 min in the present experiment whereas it lasted 30 min in the first experiment. Assuming, then, that stereotype threat slowed the pace of Black participants in the diagnostic conditions of both experiments, this 5-min difference in test period may have made it harder for these participants in the present experiment to get past the early, involved items and onto the more quickly answered items at the end of the test, a possibility that may also explain the generally lower scores in this experiment.

This view is reinforced by the ANCOVA (with SATs as a covariate) on the average time spent on each of the first five test items—the minimum number of items that all participants in all conditions answered. A marginal effect of test presentation emerged, $F(1, 35) = 3.52$, $p < .07$, but planned comparisons showed that Black participants in the diagnostic condition tended to be slower than participants in the other conditions. On average they spent 94 s answering each of these items in contrast to 71 for Black participants in the nondiagnostic condition, $t(35) = 2.39$, $p < .05$; 73 s for Whites in the diagnostic condition, $t(35) = 2.12$, $p < .05$, and 71 s for Whites in the nondiagnostic condition, $t(35) = 2.37$, $p < .05$. Like other forms of evaluative pressure, stereotype threat causes an impairment of both accuracy and speed of performance.

No differences were found on any of the remaining measures, including self-reported effect, cognitive interference, or anxiety. These measures may have been insensitive, or too delayed. Nonetheless, we lack an important kind of evidence. We have not shown that test diagnosticity causes in Black participants a specific apprehension about fulfilling the negative group stereotype about their ability—the apprehension that we argue disrupts their test performance. To examine this issue we conducted a third experiment.

Study 3

Taking an intellectually diagnostic test and experiencing some frustration with it, we have assumed, is enough to cause stereotype threat for Black participants. In testing this reasoning, the present experiment examines several specific propositions.

First, if taking or expecting to take a difficult, intellectually diagnostic test makes Black participants feel threatened by a specifically racial stereotype, then it might be expected to activate that stereotype in their thinking and information processing. That is, the racial stereotype, and perhaps also the self-doubts associated with it, should be more cognitively activated for these participants than for Black participants in the nondiagnostic condition or for White participants in either condition (e.g., Dovidio, Evans, & Tyler, 1986; Devine, 1989; Higgins, 1989). Accordingly, in testing whether test diagnosticity arouses this state, the present experiment measured the effect of conditions on the activation of this stereotype and of related self-doubts about ability.

Second, if test diagnosticity makes Black participants apprehensive about fulfilling and being judged by the racial stereotype, then these participants, more than participants in the other conditions, might be motivated to disassociate themselves from the stereotype. Brent Staples, an African American editorialist for the *New York Times*, offers an example of this in his recent autobiography, *Parallel Time*. He describes beginning graduate school at the University of Chicago and finding that as he walked the streets of Hyde Park he made people uncomfortable. They grouped more closely when he walked by, and some even crossed the street to avoid him. He eventually realized that in that urban context, dressed as a student, he was being perceived through the lens of a race-class stereotype as a potentially menacing Black man. To deflect this perception he learned a trick; he would whistle Vivaldi. It worked. Upon hearing him do this, people around him visibly relaxed and he felt out of suspicion. If it is apprehension about being judged in light of the racial stereotype that interferes with the performance of Black participants in the diagnostic condition, then these participants, like Staples, might be motivated to deflect such a perception by showing that the broader racial stereotype is not applicable to them. To test this possibility, the present experiment measured the effect of conditions on participants' stated preferences for such things as activities and styles of music, some of which were stereotypic of African Americans.

Third, by adding to the normal evaluative risks of test performance the further risk of self-validating the racial stereotype, the diagnostic condition should also make Black participants more apprehensive about their test performance. The present experiment measured this apprehension as the degree to which participants self-handicapped their expected performance, that is, endorsed excuses for poor performance before the test.

The experiment took the form of a 2 × 3 design in which the race of participants (African American or White) was crossed with diagnostic, nondiagnostic, and control conditions. The diagnostic and nondiagnostic conditions were the same as those described for Study 2, while in the control condition participants completed the critical dependent measures without expecting to take a test of any sort. In the experimental conditions, the dependent measures were administered immediately after the diagnosticity instructions and just before the test was ostensibly to be taken. These included measures of stereotype activation, stereotype avoidance, and, as a measure of general performance apprehension, participants' willingness to self-handicap. Participants in this experiment never took the test. The measures of stereotype activation and stereotype avoidance, we felt, could activate the racial stereotype and stereotype threat among Black participants in both the diagnostic and nondiagnostic conditions, making performance results difficult to interpret.

If test diagnosticity threatens Black participants with a specifically racial stereotype, then Black participants in the diagnostic condition, more than participants in the other conditions, should show greater cognitive activation of the stereotype and ability-related self-doubts, greater motivation to disassociate themselves from the stereotype, and greater performance apprehension as indicated by the endorsement of self-handicapping excuses.

METHOD PARTICIPANTS

Thirty-five Black (9 male, 26 female) and 33 White (20 male, 13 female) Stanford undergraduates were randomly assigned to either a diagnostic, nondiagnostic, or control condition, yielding from 10 to 12 participants per experimental group.

PROCEDURE

A White male experimenter gave a booklet to participants as they arrived that explained that the study was examining the relationship between two types of cognitive processes: lexical access processing (LAP) and higher verbal reasoning (HVR). They were told that they would be asked to complete two tasks, one of which measured LAP—"the visual and recognition processing of words"—and the other of which measured HVR—"abstract reasoning about the meaning of words." Test diagnosticity was manipulated as in Study 1 with the following written instructions to further differentiate the conditions:

> *Diagnostic:* Because we want an accurate measure of your ability in these domains, we want to ask you to try as hard as you can to perform well on these tasks. At the end of the study, we can give you feedback which may be helpful by pointing out your strengths and weaknesses.
> *Nondiagnostic:* Even though we are not evaluating your ability on these tasks, we want to ask you to try as hard as you can to perform well on these tasks. If you want to know more about your LAP and HVR performance, we can give you feedback at the end of the study.

Finally, participants were shown one sample item from the LAP (an item of the same sort as used in the fragment completion task) and three sample items from the HVR-difficult verbal GRE problems. The purpose of the HVR sample items was to alert participants to the difficulty of the test and the possibility of poor performance, thus occasioning the relevance of the racial stereotype in the diagnostic condition.

Participants in the control condition arrived at the laboratory to find a note on the door from the experimenter apologizing for not being present. The note instructed them to complete a set of measures lying on the desk in an envelope with the participant's name on it. The envelope contained the LAP word fragment measure and the stereotype avoidance measure (described below) with detailed instructions. No mention of verbal ability evaluation was made.

Measures Stereotype Activation

Participants first performed a word-fragment completion task, introduced as the "LAP task," versions of which have been shown to measure the cognitive activation of constructs that are either recently primed or self-generated (Gilbert & Hixon, 1991; Tulving, Schacter, & Stark, 1982). The task was made up of 80 word fragments with missing letters specified as blank spaces (e.g., _ _ CE). Twelve of these fragments had as one possible solution a word reflecting either a race-related construct or an image associated with African Americans. The list was generated by having a group of 40 undergraduates (White students from the introductory psychology pool) generate a set of words that reflected the image of African Americans. From these lists, the research team identified the 12 most common constructs (e.g., lower class, minority) and selected single words to represent those constructs on the task. For example, the word "race" was used to represent the construct "concerned with race" on the task. Then, for each of the words placed on the task, at least two letter spaces were omitted and the word was checked again to determine whether other, non-stereotype-related associations to the word stem were possible. Leaving at least two letter spaces blank in each word fragment greatly unconstrains the number of word completions possible for each fragment when compared to leaving only one letter space blank. This reduces the chance of ceiling effects in which virtually all participants would think of the race-related fragment completion. The complete list was as follows: _ _ C E (RACE); L A _ _ (LAZY); _ _ A C K (BLACK); _ _ O R (POOR); C L _ S _ (CLASS); B R _ _ _ _ _ (BROTHER); _ _ _ T E (WHITE); M I _ _ _ _ _ _ (MINORITY); W E L _ _ _ _ (WELFARE); C O _ _ _ (COLOR); T O _ _ _ (TOKEN).

We included a fairly high number (12) of target fragments so that if ceiling or floor effects occurred on some fragments it would be less likely to damage the sensitivity of the overall measure. To reduce the chance that participants would become aware of the racial nature of the target fragments, they were spaced with at least three filler items between them, and there were only two target fragments per page in the task booklet. Participants were instructed to work quickly, spending no more than 15 s on each item.

Self-doubt Activation

Seven word fragments reflecting self-doubts about competence and ability were included in the 80-item LAP task: L O _ _ _ (LOSER); D U _ _ (DUMB); S H A _ _ (SHAME); _ _ _ E R I O R (INFERIOR); F L _ _ _ (FLUNK); _ A R D (HARD); W _ _ K (WEAK). These were generated by the research team, and again included at least two blank letter spaces in each fragment. As with the racial fragments, these were separated from one another (and from the racial fragments) by at least three filler items.

Stereotype Avoidance

This measure asked participants to rate their preferences for a variety of activities and to rate the self-descriptiveness of various personality traits, some of which were associated with images of African Americans and African American life. Participants in the diagnostic and nondiagnostic conditions were told that these ratings were taken to give us a better understanding of the underpinnings of LAP and HVR processes. Control participants were told that these measures were being taken to assess the typical interests and personality traits of Stanford undergraduates. The measure contained 57 items asking participants to rate the extent to which they enjoyed a number of activities (e.g., pleasure reading, socializing, shopping, traveling, etc.), types of music (e.g., jazz, rap music, classical music), sports (e.g., baseball, basketball, boxing), and finally, how they saw themselves standing on various personality dimensions (e.g., extroverted, organized, humorous, etc.). All ratings were made on 7-point Likert scales with 1 indicating the lowest preference or degree of trait descriptiveness. Some of these activities and traits were stereotypic of African Americans. For an item to be selected as stereotypic, 65% of our pretest sample of 40 White participants had to have generated the item when asked to list activities and traits they believed to be stereotypic of African Americans. In the activities category, the stereotype-relevant items were: "How much do you enjoy sports?" and "How much do you enjoy being a lazy 'couch potato'?" The stereotype-relevant music preference item was *rap music*; the stereotype-relevant sports preference item was *basketball*; and the stereotype-relevant trait ratings were *lazy* and *aggressive/belligerent*.

Participants also completed a brief demographic questionnaire (asking their age, gender, major, etc.) just before they expected to begin the test. As another measure of participants' motivation to distance themselves from the stereotype, the second item of this questionnaire gave them the option of recording their race. We reasoned that participants who wanted to avoid having their performance viewed through the lens of a racial stereotype would be less willing to indicate their race.

Self-Handicapping Measure This measure just preceded the demographic questionnaire. The directions stated "as you know, student life is sometimes stressful, and we may not always get enough sleep, etc. Such things can affect cognitive functioning, so it will be necessary to ask how prepared you feel." Participants then indicated the number of hours they slept the night before in addition to responding, on 7-point scales (with 7 being the higher rating on these dimensions) to the following questions: "How able to focus do you feel?;" "How much stress have you been under lately?;" "How tricky/unfair do you typically find standardized tests?"

RESULTS STEREOTYPE ACTIVATION

A 2 (race) × 3 (condition: diagnostic, nondiagnostic, or control) ANCOVA (with verbal SAT as the covariate: Black mean = 581, White mean = 650) was performed on the number of target word fragments filled in with stereotypic completions. This analysis yielded significant main effects for both race, $F(1, 61) = 13.77$, $p < .001$, and for experimental condition, $F(2, 61) = 5.90$, $p < .005$. These main effects, however, were qualified by a significant Race × Condition interaction, $F(2, 61) = 3.30$, $p < .05$. Figure 19.03 shows that as expected, the diagnostic condition significantly increased the number of race-related completions of Black participants but not of White participants. Black participants in the diagnostic condition produced more race-related completions ($M = 3.70$) than Black participants in the nondiagnostic condition ($M = 2.10$), $t(61) = 3.53$, $p < .001$, or for that matter, more than participants in any of other conditions, all p s < .05.

SELF-DOUBT ACTIVATION

It did the same for their self doubts. The number of self-doubt-related completions of self-doubt target fragments were submitted to an ANCOVA (as described above) yielding a main effect of experimental condition, $F(2, 61) = 4.33$, $p < .02$, and a Race × Condition interaction, $F(2, 61) = 3.34$, $p < .05$. As Figure 19.03 shows, Black participants in the diagnostic condition, as predicted, generated the most self-doubt-related completions, significantly more than Black participants in the nondiagnostic condition, $t(61) = 3.52$, $p < .001$, and more than partici-

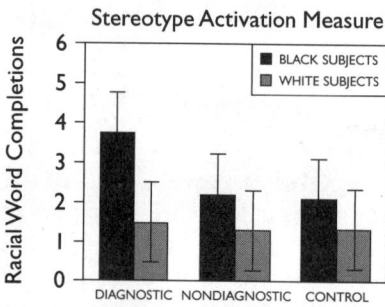

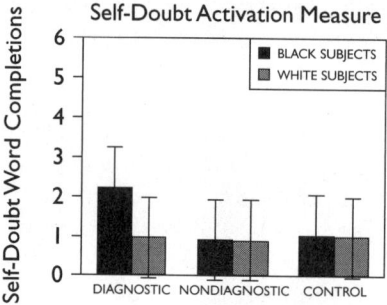

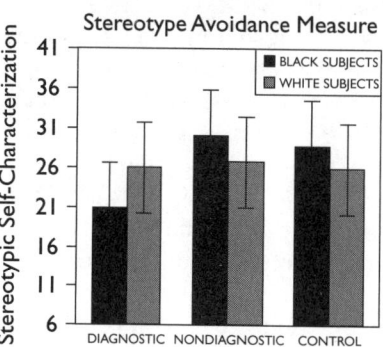

FIGURE 19.03
Mean test performance Study 2.

pants in any of the other conditions as well, all p s < .05.

STEREOTYPE AVOIDANCE

The six preference and stereotype items described above were summed to form an index of stereotype avoidance that ranged from 6 to 42 with 6 indicating high avoidance and 42 indicating low avoidance (Cronbach's alpha = .65). When these scores were submitted to the ANCOVA they yielded a significant effect of condition, $F(2, 61) = 4.73$, $p < .02$, and a significant Race × Condition interaction, $F(2, 61) = 4.14$, $p < .03$. As can be seen in Figure 19.03, Black participants in the diagnostic condition were the most avoidant of conforming to stereotypic images of African Americans ($M = 20.80$), more so than Black participants in the nondiagnostic condition ($M = 29.80$), $t(61) = 3.61$, $p < .001$, and/or White participants in either condition, all p s < .05.

INDICATING RACE

Did the ability diagnosticity of the test affect participants' tendency to indicate their race on the demographic questionnaire? Among Black participants in the diagnostic condition, only 25% would indicate their race on the questionnaire, whereas 100% of the participants in each of the other conditions would do so. Using a 0/1 conversion of the response frequencies (with 0 = refusal to indicate race and 1 = indication of race) the standard ANCOVA performed on this measure revealed a marginally significant effect of race, $F (1, 61) = 3.86, p < .06$, a significant effect of condition, $F (2.61) = 3.40, p < .04$, and a significant Race × Condition interaction, $F (1, 61) = 6.60, p < .01$, all due, of course, to the unique unwillingness of Black participants in the diagnostic condition to indicate their race.

SELF-HANDICAPPING

Four measures assessed participants' desire to claim impediments to performance. Because participants in the control conditions did not complete this measure, these responses were submitted to separate 2 (race) × 2 (diagnosticity) ANCOVAs. Cell means are presented in Table 19.01. Framing the verbal tasks as diagnostic of ability had significant effects on three of the four measures. For the number of hours of sleep, the ANCOVA yielded a significant effect of race, $F (1, 39) = 8.22, p < .01$, and a significant effect of condition, $F (1, 39) = 6.53, p < .02$. These effects were qualified by a significant Race × Condition interaction, $F (1, 39) = 4.1, p < .01$. For participants' ratings of their ability to focus, a similar result emerged: main effects of race, $F (1, 39) =$

$7.26, p < .02$, and condition, $F (1, 39) = 10.67, p < .01$, and a significant qualifying interaction, $F (1, 39) = 5.73, p < .03$. And finally, the same pattern of effects emerged for participants' ratings of how tricky or unfair they generally find standardized tests to be: a race main effect, $F (1, 39) = 13.24, p < .001$, a condition main effect, $F (1, 39) = 13.42, p < .001$, and a marginally significant, qualifying interaction, $F (1, 39) = 3.58, p < .07$. No significant effects emerged on participants' ratings of their current stress.

DISCUSSION

We had assumed that presenting an intellectual test as diagnostic of ability would arouse a sense of stereotype threat in Black participants. The present results dramatically support this assumption. Compared to participants in the other conditions—that is, Blacks in the nondiagnostic condition and Whites in either condition—Black participants expecting to take a difficult, ability-diagnostic test showed significantly greater cognitive activation of stereotypes about Blacks, greater cognitive activation of concerns about their ability, a greater tendency to avoid racially stereotypic preferences, a greater tendency to make advance excuses for their performance, and finally, a greater reluctance to have their racial identity linked to their performance even in the pedestrian way of recording it on their questionnaires. Clearly the diagnostic instructions caused these participants to experience a strong apprehension, a distinct sense of stereotype threat.

So far, then, we have shown that representing a difficult test as diagnostic of ability can undermine

TABLE 19.01				
SELF-HANDICAPPING RESPONSES IN STUDY 3				
	EXPERIMENTAL CONDITION			
	DIAGNOSTIC		**NONDIAGNOSTIC**	
MEASURE	**BLACKS** ($N = 12$)	**WHITES** ($N = 11$)	**BLACKS** ($N = 11$)	**WHITES** ($N = 10$)
Hours of sleep	5.10$_a$	7.48$_b$	7.05$_b$	7.70$_a$
Ability to focus	4.03$_a$	5.88$_b$	5.85$_b$	6.16$_a$
Current stress	5.51$_a$	5.24$_a$	5.00$_a$	5.02$_a$
Tests unfair	5.46$_a$	2.78$_b$	3.14$_b$	2.04$_b$

Note. Means not sharing a common subscript differ at the .01 level according to Bonferroni procedure. Means sharing a common subscript do not differ.

the performance of Black participants, and that it can cause in them a distinct sense of being under threat of judgment by a racial stereotype. This manipulation of stereotype threat—in terms of test diagnosticity—is important because it establishes the generality of the effect to a broad range of real-life situations.

But two questions remain. The first is whether stereotype threat itself—in the absence of the test being explicitly diagnostic of ability—is sufficient to disrupt the performance of these participants on a difficult test. That is, we do not know whether mere activation of the stereotype in the test situation—without the test being explicitly diagnostic of ability—would be enough to cause such effects. A second question is whether the disruptive effect of the diagnosticity manipulation was in fact mediated by the stereotype threat it caused. Showing first that test diagnosticity disrupts Black participants' performance and then, separately, that it causes in these participants to be threatened by the stereotype, does not prove that the effect of test diagnosticity on performance was mediated by the stereotype threat it caused. The performance effect could have been mediated by some other effect of the diagnosticity manipulation. We conducted a fourth experiment to address these questions, and thereby, to test the replicability of the stereotype threat effect under different conditions.

Study 4

This experiment again crossed a manipulation of stereotype threat with the race of participants in a 2×2 design with test performance as the chief dependent measure. We addressed the first question above by representing the test in this experiment as nondiagnostic of ability. If stereotype threat then depressed Black participants' performance, we would know that stereotype threat is sufficient to cause this effect even when the test is not represented as diagnostic of ability. We addressed the second question by taking from Study 3 a dependent measure of stereotype threat that had been significantly affected by the diagnosticity manipulation, and manipulating that variable as an independent variable in the present experiment. If this manipulation then affects Black participants' performance, we would know that at least one aspect of the stereotype threat caused by the diagnosticity manipulation was able to impair performance. This would mean that the effect of that manipulation on performance was, or could have been, mediated by the stereotype threat it caused.

The variable that we manipulated in the present study was whether or not participants were required to list their race before taking the test. Recall that in Study 3, 75% of the Black participants in the diagnostic condition refused to record their race on the questionnaire when given the option, whereas all of the participants in the other conditions did. On the assumption that this was a sign of their stereotype avoidance, we reasoned that having participants record their race just prior to the test should prime the racial stereotype about ability for Black participants, and thus make them stereotype threatened. If this threat alone is sufficient to impair their performance, then, with SATs covaried, these participants should perform worse than White participants in this condition.

In the non-stereotype-threat conditions, the demographic questionnaire simply omitted the item requesting participants' race and, otherwise, followed the nondiagnostic procedures of Studies 1 and 2. Without raising the specters of ability or race-relevant evaluation, we expected Black participants in this condition to experience no stereotype threat and to perform (adjusted for SATs) on par with White participants.

METHOD DESIGN AND PARTICIPANTS

This experiment took the form of a 2×2 design in which participants' race was crossed with whether or not they recorded their ethnicity on a preliminary questionnaire. Twenty-four Black (6 male, 18 female) and 23 White (11 male, 12 female) Stanford undergraduates were randomly assigned to either the race-prime condition or the no-race-prime condition. Data from two Black participants were discarded because they arrived with suspicions about the racial nature of the study. One White student failed to provide her SAT score and was discarded from data analyses. These participants were replaced to bring the number of participants in each of the four conditions to 11.

PROCEDURE

The procedure closely paralleled that of the nondiagnostic conditions in Studies 1 and 2. After explaining the purpose and format of the test, the experimenter (White man) randomly assigned the participant to the race-prime or no-race-prime condition by drawing a brief questionnaire (labeled "personal information") from a shuffled stack. This questionnaire comprised the experimental manipulation. It was identical for all participants—asking them to provide their age, year in school, major, number of siblings, and parents' education—except that in the race-prime condition the final item asked participants to indicate their race. Because this questionnaire was given to the participant immediately prior to the test, the experimenter remained blind to the participant's condition throughout the pretest interaction. After ensuring that the participant had completed the questionnaire, the experimenter started the test and left the room. Twenty-five minutes later he returned, collected the test, and gave the participant a dependent measure questionnaire.

DEPENDENT MEASURES

This experiment used the same 25-min test used in Study 2, but in this experiment it was administered on paper. During the test, participants marked their guesses, and after the test, they indicated on 11-point scales (with end points *not at all* and *extremely*) the extent to which they guessed when they were having difficulty, expended effort on the test, persisted on problems, limited their time on problems, read problems more than once, became frustrated and gave up, and felt that the test was biased.

Participants also completed a questionnaire aimed at measuring their stereotype threat, by expressing their agreement on 7-point scales (with endpoints *strongly disagree* and *strongly agree*) with each of eight statements (e.g., "Some people feel I have less verbal ability because of my race," "The test may have been easier for people of my race," "The experimenter expected me to do poorly because of my race," "In English classes people of my race often face biased evaluations," "My race does not affect people's perception of my verbal ability").

As a measure of academic identification, nine further items explored the effect of conditions on participants' perceptions of the importance of verbal and math skills to their education and intended career (e.g., "verbal skills will be important to my career," "I am a verbally oriented person," "I feel that math is important to me," etc.). Participants responded to these items on 11-point scales with endpoints labeled *not at all* and *extremely*.

RESULTS TEST PERFORMANCE

A 2 (race) × 2 (race prime vs. no race prime) ANCOVA on test performance with self-reported SATs as a covariate (Black mean = 591, White mean = 643) revealed a strong condition interaction in the predicted direction. As Figure 19.04 shows, Blacks in the race-prime condition performed worse than

virtually all of the other groups, yet in the no-race-prime condition their performance equaled that of Whites, $F(1, 39) = 7.82, p < .01$. Planned contrasts on these adjusted scores revealed that, as predicted, Blacks in the race-prime condition performed significantly worse than Blacks in the no-race-prime condition, $t(39) = 2.43, p < .02$, and significantly worse than Whites in the race-prime condition, $t(39) = 2.87, p < .01$. Black participants in the race-prime condition performed worse than Whites in the no-race-prime condition, but not significantly so. Nonetheless, the comparison pitting the Black race-prime condition against the three remaining conditions was highly significant, $F(1, 39) = 8.15, p < .01$.

ACCURACY

The ANCOVA for this index—the percent correct of the items attempted for each participant—with participants' SATs as the covariate revealed a significant tendency for participants in the race-prime condition to have poorer accuracy, $F(1, 39) = 4.07, p = .05$. The adjusted means for the Black and White participants in the race-prime condition were .402 and .438 respectively, while those for the Black and White participants in the no-race-prime condition were .541 and .520 respectively. Condition contrasts did not reach significance, although the difference between the Black participants in the race-prime and no-race-prime conditions was marginally significant, $p < .08$. Again, these data suggest that lessened accuracy is part of the process through which stereotype threat impairs performance.

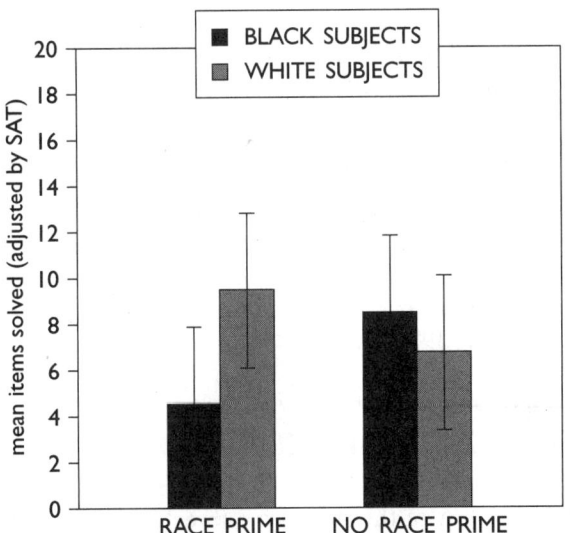

FIGURE 19.04

Indicators of stereotype threat.

NUMBER OF ITEMS COMPLETED

An ANCOVA (again with SATs removed as a covariate) revealed only a significant Race × Race Prime interaction for the number of test items participants completed, $F(1, 39) = 12.13$, $p < .01$. In the race-prime condition Blacks completed fewer items than Whites, $t(39) = 3.83$, $p < .001$. The adjusted means were 11.58 and 20.15 respectively. In the no-race-prime condition, however, Blacks and Whites answered roughly the same number of problems. The adjusted means were 15.32 and 13.03, respectively.

PERFORMANCE-RELEVANT MEASURES

Although participants' postexam ratings revealed no differences in the degree to which they thought they guessed on the test ($F < 1$), the ANCOVA performed on the actual number of guesses participants indicated on their test sheet revealed a Race × Race Prime interaction, $F(1, 39) = 5.56$, $p < .03$. Black participants made fewer guesses when race was primed ($M = 1.99$) than when it was not ($M = 2.74$), whereas White participants tended to guess more when race was primed ($M = 4.23$) than when it was not ($M = 1.58$). No significant condition effects emerged for participants' self-reported effort where, on an 11-point scale with 11 indicating *extremely hard* work, the overall mean was 8.84.

Participants' estimates of how well they had performed, taken after the test, showed no condition effects (the overall mean was 7.4 items). Neither were there condition effects on participants' ratings (made during the postexperimental debriefing) of how much having to indicate their ethnicity bothered them during the test (or *would* have bothered them in the case of participants in the no-race-prime condition). The overall mean was 3.31 on an 11-point scale for which 11 indicated the most distraction. Participants often stated in postexperimental interviews that they found recording their race unnoteworthy because they had to do it so often in everyday life. Of the items bearing on participants' experience taking the test, only one effect emerged: Black participants reported reading test items more than once to a greater degree than did White participants, $F(1, 39) = 8.62$, $p < .01$.

STEREOTYPE THREAT AND ACADEMIC IDENTIFICATION MEASURES

A MANOVA of the stereotype threat scale revealed that Black participants felt more stereotype threat than White participants, $F(9, 31) = 8.80$, $p < .01$. No other effects reached significance. Analyses of participants' responses to questions regarding the personal importance of math, verbal skills, and athletics revealed that Black participants reported valuing sports less than Whites, $F(1, 39) = 4.11$, $p < .05$. As in Study 3, this result may reflect Black participants distancing themselves from the stereotype of the academically untalented Black athlete. Correlations between participants' numerical performance estimates and their ratings of the importance of sports, showed that for Blacks, the worse they believed they performed, the more they devalued sports—in the no-race-prime condition ($r = .56$), and particularly in the race-prime condition ($r = .70$).

DISCUSSION

Priming racial identity depressed Black participants' performance on a difficult verbal test even when the test was not presented as diagnostic of intellectual ability. It did this, we assume, by directly making the stereotype mentally available and thus creating the self-threatening predicament that their performance could prove the stereotype self-characteristic. In Studies 1, 2 and 3, the stereotype was evoked indirectly by describing the test as diagnostic of an ability to which it was relevant. What this experiment shows is that mere cognitive availability of the racial stereotype is enough to depress Black participants' intellectual performance, and that this is so even when the test is presented as not diagnostic of intelligence. Also—because we know from Study 3 that the diagnosticity manipulation strongly affects participants' willingness to record their race—this finding shows that the performance-depressing effect of the diagnosticity manipulation in the earlier experiments was, or could have been, mediated by the effect of that manipulation on stereotype threat—as opposed to some other aspect of the manipulation.

Still, we had expected Black participants in the race-prime condition to show more stereotype threat (as measured by the stereotype threat and stereotype avoidance measures) than Black participants in the no-race-prime condition—reflecting the effect of the manipulation. Instead, while Blacks showed more stereotype threat than Whites, Blacks in the race-prime condition showed no more stereotype threat than Blacks in the no-race-prime condition. Nor did these groups differ on the identification measures. This may have happened for several reasons. These measures came after the test in this experiment, not before it as in Study 3. Thus, after experiencing the difficult, frustrating exam, all Black participants may have been somewhat stereotype threatened and stereotype avoidant (more so than the White participants) regardless of their condition.

Also, the lack of a condition difference between Black participants on the stereotype threat and identification items may have occurred because these items asked participants to respond in reference to settings (e.g., English classes) and attitudes (e.g., about how one's race is generally regarded) that are beyond their immediate experience in the experiment.

Compared to participants in the other conditions, Black participants in the race-prime condition did not report expending less effort on the test; they were not more disturbed at having to list their race; and they did not guess more than other participants. Also, Black participants in both conditions reread the test items more than White participants. Such findings do not fit the idea that these participants underperformed because they withdrew effort from the experiment.

To establish the replicability of the race-prime effect and to explore the possible mediational role of anxiety, we conducted a two-condition experiment which randomly assigned only Black participants to either the race-prime or no-race-prime conditions described in Study 4. We also administered the test on computer to enable a measure of the time participants spent on the items, and gave participants an anxiety measure at the end of the experiment. Replicating Study 4, race-prime participants got significantly fewer items correct ($M = 4.4$) than no-race-prime participants ($M = 7.7$), $t(18) = 2.34$, $p < .04$; they were marginally less accurate ($M = .334$) than no-race-prime participants ($M = .395$), $p = .10$; and they answered fewer items ($M = 13.2$) than no-race-prime participants ($M = 20.1$), $t(18) = 2.89$, $p < .01$. Race-prime participants spent more time on the first five test items (the number which all participants completed) ($M = 79$ s) than no-race-prime participants ($M = 61$ s), $t(18) = 2.27$, $p < .04$, and they were significantly more anxious than no-race-prime participants, $t(18) = 2.34$, $p < .04$. The means on the STAI were 48.5 and 40.5 respectively, on a scale that ranged from 20 (indicating *low anxiety*) to 80 (*extreme anxiety*). These results show that a race prime reliably depresses Black participants' performance on this difficult exam, and that it causes reactions that could be a response to stereotype threat—namely, an anxiety-based perseveration on especially the early test items, items that, as reading comprehension items, required multiple steps.

General Discussion

The existence of a negative stereotype about a group to which one belongs, we have argued, means that in situations where the stereotype is applicable, one is at risk of confirming it as a self-characterization, both to one's self and to others who know the stereotype. This is what is meant by stereotype threat. And when the stereotype involved demeans something as important as intellectual ability, this threat can be disruptive enough, we hypothesize, to impair intellectual performance.

In support of this reasoning, the present experiments show that making African American participants vulnerable to judgment by negative stereotypes about their group's intellectual ability depressed their standardized test performance relative to White participants, while conditions designed to alleviate this threat, improved their performance, equating the two groups once their differences in SATs were controlled. Studies 1 and 2 produced this pattern by varying whether or not the test was represented as diagnostic of intellectual ability—a procedure that varied stereotype threat by varying the relevance of the stereotype about Blacks' ability to their performance. Study 3 provided direct evidence that this manipulation aroused stereotype threat in Black participants by showing that it activated the racial stereotype and stereotype-related self-doubts in their thinking, that it led them to distance themselves from African American stereotypes. Study 4 showed that merely recording their race—presumably by making the stereotype salient—was enough to impair Black participants' performance even when the test was not diagnostic of ability. Taken together these experiments show that stereotype threat—established by quite subtle instructional differences—can impair the intellectual test performance of Black students, and that lifting it can dramatically improve that performance.

MEDIATION: HOW STEREOTYPE THREAT IMPAIRS PERFORMANCE

Study 3 offers clear evidence of what being stereotype threatened is like—as well as demonstrating that the mere prospect of a difficult, ability-diagnostic test was enough to do this to our sample of African American participants. But how precisely did this state of self-threat impair performance, through what mechanism or set of mechanisms did the impairment occur?

There are a number of possibilities: distraction, narrowed attention, anxiety, self-consciousness, withdrawal of effort, over-effort, and so on (e.g., Baumeister, 1984). In fact, several such mechanisms may be involved simultaneously, or different mechanisms may be involved under different conditions. For example, if the test were long enough to solidly engender low performance expectations, then withdrawal of effort might play a bigger mediational role than, say, anxiety, which might be more important with a shorter test. Such complexities notwithstanding, our findings offer some insight into how the present effects were mediated.

Our best assessment is that stereotype threat caused an inefficiency of processing much like that caused by other evaluative pressures. Stereotype-threatened participants spent more time doing fewer items more inaccurately—probably as a result of alternating their attention between trying to answer the items and trying to assess the self-significance of their frustration. This form of debilitation—reduced speed and accuracy—has been shown as a reaction to evaluation apprehension (e.g., Geen, 1985); test anxiety (e.g., Wine, 1971; Sarason, 1972); the presence of an audience (e.g., Bond, 1982); and competition (Baumeister, 1984). Several findings, by suggesting that stereotype-threatened participants were both motivated and inefficient, point in this direction. They reported expending as much effort as other participants. In those studies that included the requisite measures—Study 2 and the replication study reported with Study 4—they actually spent more time per item. They did not guess more than non-stereotype-threatened participants, and, as Black participants did generally, they reported rereading the items more. Also, as noted, these participants were strong students, and almost certainly identified with the material on the test. They may even have been more anxious. Stereotype threat increased Black participants' anxiety in the replication study, although not significantly in Study 2. Together then, these findings suggest that stereotype threat led participants to try hard but with impaired efficiency.

Still, we note that lower expectations may have also been involved, especially in real-life occurrences of stereotype threat. As performance falters under stereotype threat, and as the stereotype frames that faltering as a sign of a group-based inferiority, the individual's expectations about his or her ability and performance may drop—presumably faster than they would if the stereotype were not there to credit the inability interpretation. And lower expectations, as the literature has long emphasized (e.g., Bandura, 1977, 1986; Carver, Blaney, & Scheier, 1979; Pyszczynski & Greenberg, 1983) can further undermine performance by undermining motivation and effort. It is precisely a process of stereotype threat fostering low expectations in a domain that we suggest leads eventually to disidentification with the domain. We assume that this process did not get very far in the present research because the tests were short, and because

our participants, as highly identified students, were unlikely to give up on these tests—as their self-reports tell us. But we do assume that lower expectations can play a role in mediating stereotype threat effects.

There is, however, strong evidence against one kind of expectancy mediation. This is the idea that lowered performance or self-efficacy expectations alone mediated the effects of stereotype threat. Conceivably, the stereotype threat treatments got Black participants to expect that they would perform poorly on the test—presumably by getting them to accept the image of themselves inherent in the racial stereotype. The stereotype threat condition did activate participants' self-doubts. This lower expectation, then, outside of any experience these participants may have had with the test itself, and outside of any apprehension they may have had about self-confirming the stereotype, may have directly weakened their motivation and performance. Of course it would be important to show that stereotype threat effects are mediated in African American students by expectations implicit in the stereotype, expectations powerful enough to more or less automatically cause their underperformance.

But there are several reasons to doubt this view. For one thing, it isn't clear that our stereotype threat manipulations led Black participants to accept lower expectations and then to follow them unrevisedly to lower performance. For example, they resisted the self-applicability of the stereotype. But most important, as noted, it is almost certain that any expectation formed prior to the test would be superseded by the participants' actual experience with the test items; rising with success and falling with frustration. In fact, another experiment in our lab offered direct evidence of this by showing that expectations manipulated before the test had no effect on performance. Its procedure followed, in all conditions, that of the standard diagnostic condition used in Studies 1 and 2—with the exception that it directly manipulated efficacy and performance expectations before participants took the test. After being told that the test was ability diagnostic, and just before taking the test, the experimenter (an Asian woman) asked participants what their SAT scores were. After hearing the score, in the positive expectation condition, she commented that the participant should have little trouble with the test. In the negative expectation condition, this comment indicated that the participant would have trouble with the test, and nothing was said in a no-expectation condition. Both White and Black participants were run in all three expectation conditions. While the experiment replicated the standard effect of

Whites outperforming Blacks under these stereotype threat conditions (participants' SATs were again used as a covariate) $F (1, 32) = 5.12, p < .03$, this personalized expectation manipulation had no effect on the performance of either group. For Blacks, the means were 4.32, 6.38, and 6.55, for the positive, negative and no-expectations conditions, respectively, and for Whites, for the same conditions, they were 8.24, 9.25, and 11.23, respectively. Thus in an experiment that was sensitive enough to replicate the standard stereotype threat effect, expectations explicitly manipulated before the test had no effect on performance. They are unlikely, then, to have been the medium through which stereotype threat affected performance in this research.

Finally, participants in all conditions of these experiments were given low performance expectations by telling them that they should expect to get few items correct due to the difficulty of the test. Importantly, this instruction did not depress the performance of participants in the non-stereotype-threat conditions. Thus it is not likely that a low performance expectation, implied by the stereotype, would have been powerful enough, by itself, to lower performance among these participants when a direct manipulation of the expectation could not.

THE EMERGING PICTURE OF STEREOTYPE THREAT

In the social psychological literature there are other constructs that address the experience of potential victims of stereotypes. For clarity's sake, we briefly compare the construct of stereotype threat to these.

"TOKEN" STATUS AND COGNITIVE FUNCTIONING

Lord & Saenz (1985) have shown that token status in a group—that is, being the token minority in a group that is otherwise homogeneous—can cause deficits in cognitive functioning and memory, presumably as an outgrowth of the self-consciousness it causes. Although probably in the same family of effects as stereotype threat, token status would be expected to disrupt cognitive functioning even when the token individual is not targeted by a performance-relevant stereotype, as with, for example, a White man in a group of women solving math problems. Nor do stereotype threat effects require token status, as was shown in the present experiments. In real life, of course, these two processes may often co-occur, as for the Black in an otherwise non-Black classroom. They are nonetheless, distinct processes.

ATTRIBUTIONAL AMBIGUITY

Another important theory, and now extensive program of research by Crocker and Major (e.g., Crocker & Major, 1989; Crocker, Voelkl, Testa, & Major, 1991) examined how people contend with the self-evaluative implications of having a stigmatized identity. Both their theory and ours focus on the psychology of contending with social devaluation and differ most clearly in which aspect of this psychology they attend to. The work of Crocker and Major focused on the implications of this psychology for self-esteem maintenance (for example, the strategies available for protecting self-esteem against stigmatized status) and we have focused on its implications for intellectual performance. There is also a conceptual difference. Attributional ambiguity refers to the confusion a potential target of prejudice might have over whether or not he is being treated prejudicially. Stereotype threat, of course, refers to his apprehension over confirming, or eliciting the judgment that the stereotype is self-characteristic. Again, the two processes can co-occur—as for the woman who gets cut from the math team, for example—but are distinct.

THE EARLIER RESEARCH OF THE KATZ GROUP

We also note that stereotype threat may explain the earlier findings of Katz and his colleagues. They found in the 1960s that the intellectual performance of Black participants rose and fell with conditions that seemed to vary in stereotype threat—for example, whether the test was represented as a test of intelligence or as one of psychomotor skill. A stereotype threat interpretation of these findings was foiled, however, by the lack of White participant control groups. Thus, the finding that manipulations very similar to Katz's depressed Black participants' performance while not depressing White participants' performance makes stereotype threat a parsimonious account of all these findings.

TEST DIFFICULTY AND RACIAL DIFFERENCES IN STANDARDIZED TEST PERFORMANCE

The test used in these experiments is quite difficult, as the low performance scores indicate. As we argued, it may have to be at least somewhat demanding for stereotype threat to be occasioned. But acknowledging this parameter raises a question: Does stereotype threat significantly undermine the performance of Black students on the SAT? And if it does, is it appropriate to use the SAT as the standard for equating Black and White participants on skill level within our experiments? The answer to the first question has to be that it depends on how much frustration is experienced on the SAT. If the student perceives that a significant portion of the test is within his or her competence, it may preempt or override stereotype threat by proving the stereotype inapplicable. When the student cannot gain this perception, however, the group stereotype becomes relevant as an explanation and may undermine performance. Thus we surmise that over the entire range of Black student test takers, stereotype threat causes a significant depression of scores.

And, of course, this point holds more generally. An important implication of this research is that stereotype threat is an underappreciated source of classic deficits in standardized test performance (e.g., IQ) suffered by Blacks and other stereotype-threatened groups such as those of lower socioeconomic status and women in mathematics (Herrnstein, 1973; Jensen, 1969, 1980; Spencer & Steele, 1994). In addition to whatever environmental or genetic endowments a person brings to the testing situation, this research shows that this situation is not group-neutral—not even, quite possibly, when the tester and test content have been accommodated to the test-taker's background. The problem is that stereotypes afoot in the larger society establish a predicament in the testing situation—aside from test content—that still has the power to undermine standardized test performance, and, we suspect, contribute powerfully to the pattern of group differences that have characterized these tests since their inception.

But, for several reasons, we doubt that this possibility compromises the interpretation of the present findings. First, it is unlikely that stereotype threat had much differential effect on the SATs of our Black and White participants since both groups, as highly selected students, are not likely to have experienced very great frustration on these tests. Second, even if our Black participants' SATs were more depressed in this way, using such depressed scores as a covariate in the present analyses would only adjust Black performance more in the direction of reducing the Black-White difference in the stereotype threat conditions. Thus, while a self-threateningly difficult test is probably a necessary condition for stereotype threat, and while stereotype threat may commonly depress the standardized test performance of Black test takers, these facts are not likely to have compromised the present results.

In conclusion, our focus in this research has been on how social context and group identity come together to mediate an important behavior. This approach is Lewinian; it is also hopeful. Compared to viewing the problem of Black underachievement as rooted in something about the group or its societal conditions, this analysis uncovers a social psychological predicament of race, rife in the standardized testing situation, that is amenable to change—as we hope our manipulations have illustrated.

References

1. Allport, G. (1954). *The nature of prejudice,* New York: Addison-Wesley.
2. American Council on Education. (1990). *Minorities in higher education.* Washington, DC: Office of Minority Concerns.
3. Bandura, A. (1977). Self-efficacy: Toward a unifying theory of behavioral change. *Psychological Review, 84,* 191–215.
4. Bandura, A. (1986). Fearful expectations and avoidant actions as coeffects of perceived self-inefficacy. *American Psychologist, 41,* 1389–1391.
5. Baumeister, R. F. (1984). Choking under pressure: Self-consciousness and paradoxical effects of incentives on skillful performance. *Journal of Personality and Social Psychology, 46,* 610–620.
6. Bond, C. F. (1982). Social facilitation: A self-presentational view. *Journal of Personality and Social Psychology, 42,* 1042–1050.
7. Carter, S. L. (1991). *Reflections of an affirmative action baby.* New York: Basic Books.
8. Carver, C. S., Blaney, P. H. & Scheier, M. F. (1979). Reassertion and giving up: The interactive role of self-directed attention and outcome expectancy. *Journal of Personality and Social Psychology, 37,* 1859–1870.
9. Cleary, T. A., Humphreys, L. G., Kendrick, S. A. & Wesman, A. (1975). Educational uses of tests with disadvantaged students. *American Psychologist, 30,* 15–41.
10. Crocker, J. & Major, B. (1989). Social stigma and self-esteem: The self-protective properties of stigma. *Psychological Review, 96,* 608–630.
11. Crocker, J., Voelkl, K., Testa, M. & Major, B. (1991). Social stigma: The affective consequences of attributional ambiguity. *Journal of Personality and Social Psychology, 60,* 218–228.
12. Devine, P. G. (1989). Stereotypes and prejudice: Their automatic and controlled components. *Journal of Personality and Social Psychology, 56,* 5–18.
13. Dovidio, J. F., Evans, N. & Tyler, R. B. (1986). Racial stereotypes: The contents of their cognitive representations. *Journal of Experimental Social Psychology, 22,* 22–37.
14. Easterbrook, J. A. (1959). The effect of emotion on cue utilization and the organization of behavior. *Psychological Review, 66,* 183–201.
15. Geen, R. G. (1985). Evaluation apprehension and response withholding in solution of anagrams. *Personality and Individual Differences, 6,* 293–298.

16. Geen, R. G. (1991). Social motivation. *Annual Review of Psychology, 42*, 377–399.

17. Gilbert, D. T. & Hixon, J. G. (1991). The trouble of thinking: Activation and application of stereotypic beliefs. *Journal of Personality and Social Psychology, 60*, 509–517.

18. Goffman, I. (1963). *Stigma.* New York: Simon & Shuster, Inc.

19. Herrnstein, R. (1973). *IQ in the meritocracy.* Boston: Little Brown.

20. Higgins, E. T. (1989). Knowledge accessibility and activation: Subjectivity and suffering from unconscious sources. In J. S. Uleman & J. A. Bargh (Eds.), *Unintended Thoughts* (pp. 75–123). New York: Guilford.

21. Jensen, A. R. (1969). How much can we boost IQ and scholastic achievement? *Harvard Educational Review, 39*, 1–123.

22. Jensen, A. R. (1980). *Bias in mental testing.* New York: Free Press.

23. Katz, I. (1964). Review of evidence relating to effects of desegregation on the intellectual performance of Negroes. *American Psychologist, 19*, 381–399.

24. Katz, I., Epps, E. G. & Axelson, L. J. (1964). Effect upon Negro digit symbol performance of comparison with Whites and with other Negroes. *Journal of Abnormal and Social Psychology, 69*, 963–970.

25. Katz, I., Roberts, S. O. & Robinson, J. M. (1965). Effects of task difficulty, race of administrator, and instructions on digit-symbol performance of Negroes. *Journal of Personality and Social Psychology, 2*, 53–59.

26. Linn, R. L. (1973). Fair test use in selection. *Review of Educational Research, 43*, 139–161.

27. Lord, C. G. & Saenz, D. S. (1985). Memory deficits and memory surfeits: Differential cognitive consequences of tokenism for tokens and observers. *Journal of Personality and Social Psychology, 49*, 918–926.

28. Lord, C. G., Saenz, D. S. & Godfrey, D. K. (1987). Effects of perceived scrutiny on participant memory for social interactions. *Journal of Experimental Social Psychology, 23*, 498–517.

29. Nettles, M. T. (1988). *Toward undergraduate student equality in American higher education.* New York: Greenwood.

30. Pyszczynski, T. & Greenberg, J. (1983). Determinants of reduction in effort as a strategy for coping with anticipated failure. *Journal of Research in Personality, 17*, 412–422.

31. Sarason, I. G. (1972). Experimental approaches to test anxiety: Attention and the uses of information. In C. D. Spielberger (Ed.), *Anxiety: Current trends in theory and research* (Vol. 2). New York: Academic Press.

32. Seta, J. J. (1982). The impact of coactors' comparison processes on task performance. *Journal of Personality and Social Psychology, 42*, 281–291.

33. Spencer, S. J. & Steele, C. M. (1994). *Under suspicion of inability: Stereotype vulnerability and women's math performance.* Unpublished manuscript, State University of New York at Buffalo and Stanford University.

34. Stanley, J. C. (1971). Predicting college success of the educationally disadvantaged. *Science, 171*, 640–647.

35. Steele, C. M. (1992, April). Race and the schooling of black Americans. *The Atlantic Monthly.*

36. Steele, S. (1990). *The content of our character.* New York: St. Martin's Press.

37. Tulving, E., Schacter, D. L. & Stark, H. A. (1982). Priming effects in word-fragment completion are independent of recognition memory. *Journal of Experimental Psychology: Learning, Memory, and Cognition, 8*, 336–342.

38. Wine, J. (1971). Test anxiety and direction of attention. *Psychological Bulletin, 76*, 92–104.

QUESTIONS FOR REFLECTION AND DISCUSSION:

1. What is the "predicament" to which the authors refer at the beginning of their article?

2. How did the authors induce stereotype threat in the participants in the study? How does stereotype threat impair performance, according to the authors?

3. Exactly what do IQ tests measure?

4. What kinds of research are undertaken to try to unravel the relative impact of genetic and environmental factors on intelligence?

5. When do environmental influences begin? (Were you about to say "at birth"? Are you sure?)

6. What does the research show about the influences of genetic and environmental factors on intelligence?

7. What does the research show about the attitudes of various ethnic groups toward the importance of education? (Include attitudes of Asian Americans in your discussion.) Where do these attitudes come from? How are they influential?

8. What attitudes toward education were expressed in your home as you were growing up? How did these attitudes influence you?

IV

MOTIVATION AND EMOTION

The psychology of motivation is concerned with the *whys* of behavior. Why do we eat? Why do we dance, strive to get ahead, seek the company of others, or try new things? An emotion can be a response to a situation, as fear is a response to a threat. But emotions can also motivate behavior, as anger can flare into aggression. An emotion can also be a goal in itself, as when we try to experience joy or find love.

The psychology of motivation and emotion deals with matters such as hunger, stimulus motives, achievement motivation, and the expression of emotions. This section includes the following primary sources:

20. Bexton, W. H., Heron, W., & Scott, T. H. (1954). Effects of decreased variation in the sensory environment. *Canadian Journal of Psychology, 8,* 70–76.

    Here is the well-known study on sensory deprivation. Although we might sometimes want to get to sleep so badly that we use masks to block out light and earplugs to block out noise, this classic experiment suggests that sensory isolation from the environment can be more disturbing than relaxing.

21. Rozin, P., & Fallon, A. (1988). Body image, attitudes to weight, and misperceptions of figure preferences of the opposite sex: A comparison of men and women in two generations. *Journal of Abnormal Psychology, 97,* 342–345.

    There is a saying that you can never be too rich or too thin. This study suggests that women are more likely than men to assume that they are not thin enough, even though the other gender would like to see a bit more meat on their bones than they imagine. It also reveals that men, ironically, are more likely to think that their physiques are right where they ought to be, when women might prefer them to be a bit more wiry.

22. Festinger, L., & Carlsmith, J. M. (1959). Cognitive consequences of forced compliance. *Journal of Abnormal and Social Psychology, 58,* 203–210.

It is common knowledge that people resent being forced into doing things they do not want to do, is it not? Perhaps not. Classic research by Leon Festinger and his colleagues suggests that people may actually change their attitudes when they are forced to comply with rules or laws that they initially oppose.

23. Ekman, P., & Friesen, W. V. (1971). Constants across cultures in the face and emotion. *Journal of Personality and Social Psychology, 17,* 124–129.

Imagine that you are walking through a primeval forest and happen upon what looks like a fierce band of natives. Should you smile? What are the odds that they will interpret a smile as a sign of friendliness? Is there a chance that in this culture smiling is viewed as an aggressive challenge? What do you think? Place your bets and read the article.

SOURCE

Bexton, W. H., Heron, W., & Scott, T. H. (1954). Effects of decreased variation in the sensory environment. *Canadian Journal of Psychology, 8,* 70–76. Copyright 1954. Canadian Psychological Association. Reprinted with permission.

So, you say you want to get away from it all? You want to lie on the sand on some foreign beach? You want to sleep and sleep and sleep? You just want peace and quiet, and quiet and peace, and peace and . . . ? The experience could be relaxing. It could also be nerve-wracking!

A classic study from the fabulous 50s seemed to toss sand in the face of the idyllic image of floating away quietly on that beach. It was connected with the quest for determining humans' basic needs or drives, and it contributed to the view that we need a certain amount of sensory stimulation to feel comfortable and function properly. The idea seemed rather radical at the time, because it seemed to fly in the face of psychoanalytic theory and behaviorism, both of which were riding high at the time. Psychoanalytic theory suggested that people were motivated by basic instincts and sought to reduce the tension associated with those instincts. There were various behaviorist views. One of them, drive reductionism, was similar to psychoanalytic theory in that it suggested that behavior was motivated by the desire to reduce drives such as hunger, thirst, and the need for oxygen. Even behaviorists who stayed outside the "black box" and spoke of reinforcement as a stimulus that increased the frequency of behavior suspected that reinforcement had something to do with reduction of tension or drives. But the idea that we need sensory stimulation suggested that at least in some ways we seek to increase "tension." (Anyone who has sought a roller coaster or motorcycle ride or battled monsters in video games would probably agree.)

In any event, sensory stimulation would be one of a number of so-called stimulus motives, all of which appear to increase rather than decrease the amount of stimulation impacting on the individual. These include motives for sensory stimulation, novel stimulation, and activity. The study which follows asks the question, What happens when we remove all sources of external stimulation from humans—that is, when we subject them to "sensory deprivation"? Do they unwind and profit from the experience, or do they want to run for the . . . roller coaster or video game?

Effects of Decreased Variation in the Sensory Environment

W. H. BEXTON, W. HERON, & T. H. SCOTT
MCGILL UNIVERSITY

This study began with a practical problem: the lapses of attention that may occur when a man must give close and prolonged attention to some aspect of an environment in which nothing is happening, or in which the changes are very regular. Watching a radar screen hour after hour is a prime example. As Mackworth (5) and others have shown, when at last something *does* happen in such circumstances the watcher may fail to respond. Such monotonous conditions exist in civilian occupations as well as in military ones (marine pilotage by radar, piloting aircraft on long flights), and here too lapses of attention may have extremely serious consequences. For example, such lapses may explain some otherwise inexplicable railroad and highway accidents.

Besides its practical significance this problem has theoretical implications of great interest. [There is much evidence from recent neurophysiological studies to indicate that the normal functioning of the waking brain depends on its being constantly exposed to sensory bombardment, which produces a continuing "arousal reaction."] Work now being done by S. K. Sharpless at McGill indicates, further, that when stimulation does not change it rapidly loses its power to cause the arousal reaction. Thus, although one function of a stimulus is to evoke or guide a specific bit of behaviour, it also has a nonspecific function, that of maintaining "arousal," probably through the brain-stem reticular formation.

In other words, the maintenance of normal, intelligent, adaptive behaviour probably requires a continually varied sensory input. The brain is not like a calculating machine operated by an electric motor which is able to respond at once to specific cues after lying idle indefinitely. Instead it is like one that must be kept warmed up and working. It seemed, therefore, worth while to examine cognitive functioning during prolonged perceptual isolation, as far as this was practicable. Bremer (2) has achieved such isolation by cutting the brain stem; college students, however, are reluctant to undergo brain operations for experimental purposes, so we had to be satisfied with less extreme isolation from the environment.

Procedure

The subjects, 22 male college students, were paid to lie on a comfortable bed in a lighted cubicle 24 hours a day, with time out for eating and going to the toilet. During the whole experimental period they wore translucent goggles which transmitted diffuse light but prevented pattern vision. Except when eating or at the toilet, the subject wore gloves and cardboard cuffs, the latter extending from below the elbow to beyond the fingertips. These permitted free joint movement but limited tactual perception. Communication between subject and experimenters was provided by a small speaker system, and was kept to a minimum. Auditory stimulation was limited by the partially sound-proof cubicle and by a U-shaped foam-rubber pillow in which the subject

kept his head while in the cubicle. Moreover, the continuous hum provided by fans, air-conditioner, and the amplifier leading to earphones in the pillow produced fairly efficient masking noise.

General Effects

As might be expected from the evidence reviewed by Kleitman (3) for onset of sleep following reduced stimulation in man and other animals, the subjects tended to spend the earlier part of the experimental session in sleep. Later they slept less, became bored, and appeared eager for stimulation. They would sing, whistle, talk to themselves, tap the cuffs together, or explore the cubicle with them. This boredom seemed to be partly due to deterioration in the capacity to think systematically and productively— an effect described below. The subjects also became very restless, displaying constant random movement, and they described the restlessness as unpleasant. Hence it was difficult to keep subjects for more than two or three days, despite the fact that the pay ($20 for a 24-hour day) was more than double what they could normally earn. Some subjects, in fact, left before testing could be completed.

There seemed to be unusual emotional lability during the experimental period. When doing tests, for instance, the subjects would seem very pleased when they did well, and upset if they had difficulty. They commented more freely about test items than when they were tested outside. While many reported that they felt elated during the first part of their stay in the cubicle, there was a marked increase in irritability toward the end of the experimental period.

On coming out of the cubicle after the experimental session, when goggles, cuffs, and gloves had been removed, the subjects seemed at first dazed. There also appeared to be some disturbance in visual perception, usually lasting no longer than one or two minutes. Subjects reported difficulty in focussing; objects appeared fuzzy and did not stand out from their backgrounds. There was a tendency for the environment to appear two-dimensional and colours seemed more saturated than usual. The subjects also reported feelings of confusion, headaches, a mild nausea, and fatigue; these conditions persisted in some cases for 24 hours after the session.

Effects on Cognitive Processes

Our present concern is primarily with cognitive disturbances during the period of isolation and immediately afterwards. The subjects reported that they were unable to concentrate on any topic for long while in the cubicle. Those who tried to review their studies or solve self-initiated intellectual problems found it difficult to do so. As a result they lapsed into day-dreaming, abandoned attempts at organized thinking, and let their thoughts wander. There were also reports of "blank periods," during which they seemed unable to think of anything at all.

In an attempt to measure some of the effects on cognitive processes, various tests were given to the subjects before, during, and after the period of isolation.

First, the tests given during isolation. Twelve subjects were given the following types of problems to do in their heads: multiplying two- and three-digit numbers; arithmetical problems (such as "how many times greater is twice $2\frac{1}{2}$ than one-half $2\frac{1}{2}$?"); completion of number series; making a word from jumbled letters; making as many words as possible from the letters of a given word. Each subject was tested on problems of this type before going into the cubicle, after he had been in for 12,

24, and 48 hours, and three days after coming out of the cubicle. Twelve control subjects were given the same series of tasks at the same intervals. The average performance of the experimental subjects was inferior to that of the controls on all tests performed during the cubicle session. With our present small number of subjects the differences are significant only for the error scores on the second anagram task ($p = .01$, see Figure 20.01). The groups are now being enlarged.

Secondly, tests given before entering the cubicle and immediately after leaving it. On the Kohs Block Test and the Wechsler Digit Symbol Test the experimental subjects were inferior to the controls on leaving the cubicle ($p = .01$). They also tended to be slower in copying a prose paragraph ($p = .10$). Figure 20.02 gives samples of handwriting before and after the experiment. The first is from one of the subjects showing the greatest effect, the second illustrates the average effect. As the third sample shows, some subjects were not affected. This disturbance in handwriting, though perhaps due to some sensori-motor disturbance, might also reflect cognitive or motivational changes.

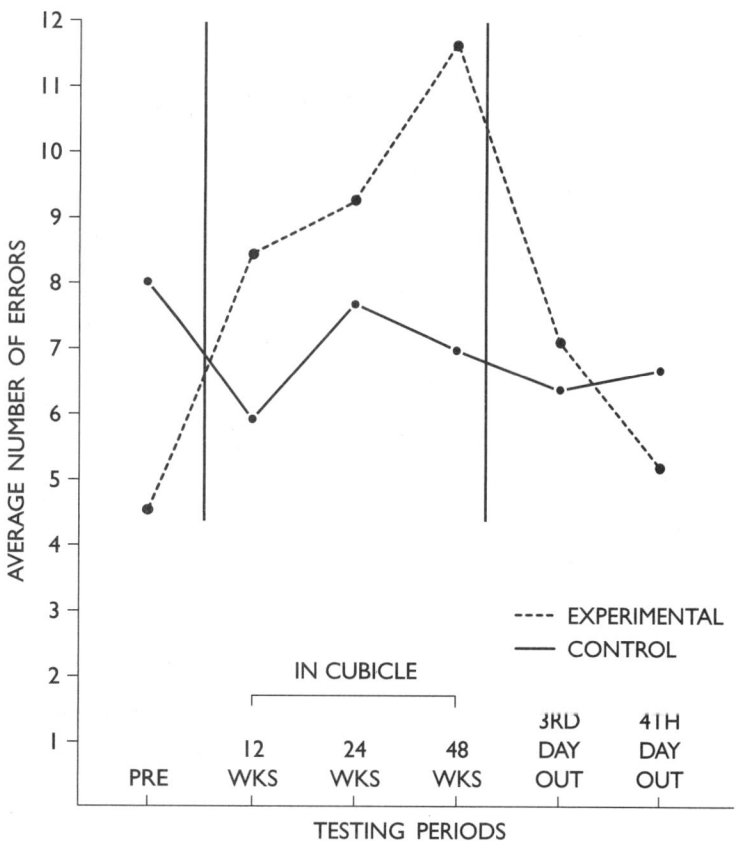

FIGURE 20.01

Mean error scores for experimental and control subjects, before, during, and after the isolation period.

ERRORS IN WORD–MAKING
(WRONG WORDS, MISSPELLINGS, REPEATS)

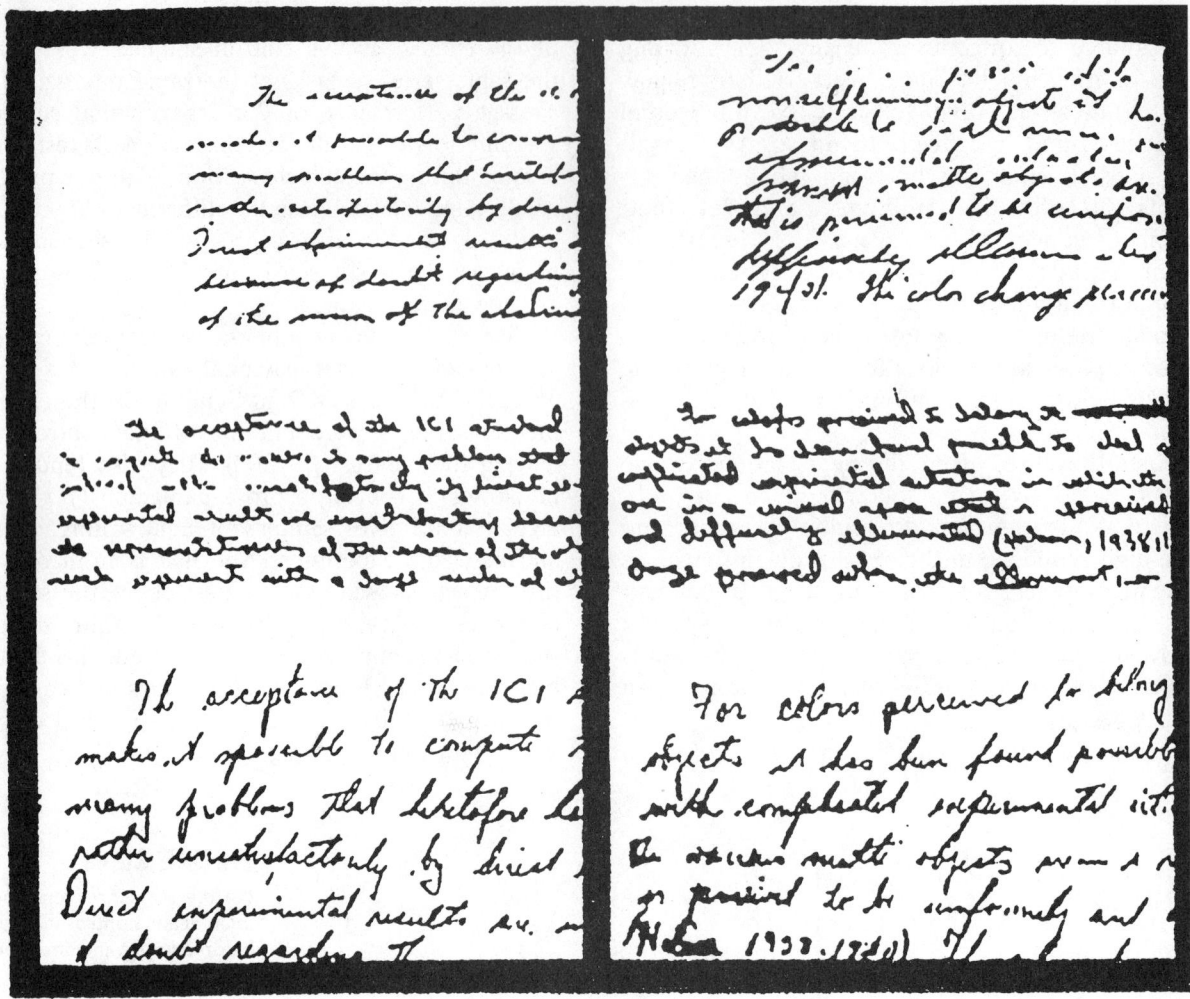

FIGURE 20.02
Specimens of handwriting before and after the isolation period.

Hallucinatory Activity

Finally there were the hallucinations reported by the subjects while in the experimental apparatus. Among our early subjects there were several references, rather puzzling at first, to what one of them called "having a dream while awake." Then one of us, while serving as a subject, observed the phenomenon and realized its peculiarity and extent.

The visual phenomena were actually quite similar to what have been described for mescal intoxication, and to what Grey Walter (6) has recently produced by exposure to flickering light. There have also been rare cases of hallucinations in aged persons without psychosis (1), which, like ours, involved no special chemical or visual stimulation. As we did not ask our first subjects specifically about these phenomena we do not know the frequency among them. The last 14 subjects, however, were asked to report any "visual imagery" they observed, and our report is based on them. In general, where more "formed" (i.e., more complex) hallucinations occurred they were usually preceded by simpler forms of the phenomenon. Levels of complexity could be differentiated as follows: In the simplest form the visual field, with the eyes closed, changed from dark to light colour; next in complexity were dots of light, lines, or simple geometrical patterns. All 14 subjects reported such imagery, and said it was a new experience to them. Still more complex forms consisted in "wall-paper patterns," reported by 11 subjects, and isolated figures or objects, without background (e.g., a row of little yellow men with black caps on and their mouths open; a German helmet), reported by seven subjects. Finally, there were integrated scenes (e.g., a procession of squirrels with sacks over their shoulders marching "purposefully" across a snow field and out of the field of "vision"; prehistoric animals walking about in a jungle). Three of the 14 subjects reported such scenes, frequently including dreamlike distortions, with the figures often being described as "like cartoons." One curious fact is that some of the hallucinations were reported as being inverted or tilted at an angle.

In general, the subjects were first surprised by these phenomena, and then amused or interested, waiting for what they would see next. Later, some subjects found them irritating, and complained that their vividness interfered with sleep. There was some control over content; by "trying," the subject might see certain objects suggested by the experimenter, but not always as he intended. Thus one subject, trying to "get" a pen, saw first an inkblot, then a pencil, a green horse, and finally a pen; trying to "get" a shoe, he saw first a ski boot, then a moccasin. The imagery usually disappeared when the subject was doing a complex task, such as multiplying three-place numbers in his head, but not if he did physical exercises, or talked to the experimenter.

There were also reports of hallucinations involving other senses. One subject could hear the people speaking in his visual hallucinations, and another repeatedly heard the playing of a music box. Four subjects described kinesthetic and somesthetic phenomena. One reported seeing a miniature rocket ship discharging pellets that kept striking his arm, and one reported reaching out to touch a doorknob he saw before him and feeling an electric shock. The other two subjects reported a phenomenon which they found difficult to describe. They said it was as if there were two bodies side by side in the cubicle; in one case the two bodies overlapped, partly occupying the same space. Figure 20.03 shows this subject's subsequent drawing, made in an attempt to show what he meant.

In addition, there were reports of feelings of "otherness" and bodily "strangeness" in which it was hard to know exactly what the subject meant. One subject said "my mind seemed to be a ball of cotton-wool floating above my body"; another reported that his head felt detached from his body. These are familiar phenomena in certain cases of migraine, as described recently by Lippman (4), and earlier by Lewis Carroll in *Alice in Wonderland*. As Lippman points out, Lewis Carroll was a sufferer from migraine, and it is suggested that Alice's bodily distortions are actually descriptions

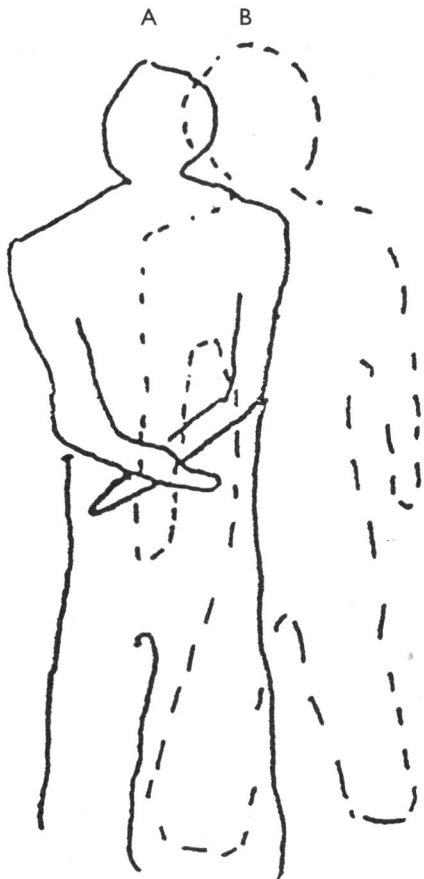

FIGURE 20.03

Drawing made by a subject to show how he felt at one period in the cubicle. He reported that it was as if "there were two of me," and was momentarily unable to decide whether he was A or B.

of Carroll's (i.e., Charles Dodgson's) own experiences.

In summary, both the changes in intelligence-test performance and the hallucinatory activity, induced merely by limiting the variability of sensory input, provide direct evidence of a kind of dependence on the environment that has not been previously recognized. Further experimental study will be needed to elucidate the details of this relationship.

References

1. Bartlet, J. E. A. A case of organized visual hallucinations in an old man with cataract and their relation to the phenomena of the phantom limb. *Brain*, 1951, **74**, 363–373.
2. Bremer, F. & Terzuolo, C. Nouvelles recherches sur le

processus physiologique de réveil. *Arch. internat. de Physiol.,* 1953, **61,** 86–90.

3. Kleitman, N. *Sleep and wakefulness.* Chicago: Univer. of Chicago Press, 1939.

4. Lippman, Caro. Certain hallucinations peculiar to migraine. *J. nerv. ment. Dis.,* 1952, **116,** 346–351.

5. Mackworth, N. H. *Researches on the measurement of human performance.* Med. Res. Council, Spec. Rep. Ser., 1950, No. 268. London.

6. Walter, W. Grey. *The living brain.* New York: Norton, 1953.

QUESTIONS FOR REFLECTION AND DISCUSSION:

1. Why do the authors frame the research issue in terms of "lapses of attention"?

2. At the time this study was conducted, attention was being paid to the reticular activating system (RAS) and "arousal." Where is the RAS? What is meant by arousal?

3. What do the authors mean when they suggest, metaphorically, that the brain must be kept "warmed up and working"?

4. What was the treatment procedure? How did the authors produce sensory deprivation? Was deprivation complete? What were the limits?

5. Subjects were paid $20 a day to participate. How much would that be now? Would it be enough to keep you in the experiment? Are you sure?

6. What were the emotional and cognitive effects of the treatment?

7. Your authors write that the subjects experienced *hallucinations*? What are hallucinations? What kinds of "hallucinations" did the subjects report? What are the usual causes of hallucinations? What seems to have caused the sensory experiences during the experiment?

8. What do your authors conclude about the findings? Does the conclusion seem warranted by the method used and the results?

9. Do you consider the study to be ethical? Why or why not?

SOURCE

Rozin, P., & Fallon, A. (1988). Body image, attitudes to weight, and misperceptions of figure preferences of the opposite sex: A comparison of men and women in two generations. *Journal of Abnormal Psychology, 97,* 342–345. Copyright © 1988 by the American Psychological Association. Reprinted with permission.

Did you know that today the eating habits of the "average" woman in the United States are characterized by dieting? Efforts to restrict the intake of food are now the norm![1] The incidence of the eating disorders of anorexia nervosa and bulimia nervosa, in which people control their weight in unhealthful ways, has reached epidemic proportions.

Anorexia nervosa is a life-threatening disorder that mainly afflicts young women. It is characterized by refusal to maintain a healthful body weight, intense fear of being overweight, a distorted body image, and lack of menstruation. The distorted body image is central. In the typical pattern, girls notice some weight gain after menarche and decide that it must come off. However, dieting often continues at a fever pitch, even after other people have told them that they are losing too much. Whereas others perceive them as "skin and bones," anorexic women frequently sit before the mirror and see themselves as getting where they want to be. Or they focus on nonexistent "remaining" pockets of fat.

Most psychologists connect eating disorders with the (slimming!) Feminine ideal in Western culture. Fashion models, who represent the ideal, are about 9% taller and 16% slimmer than the average woman. Sixteen percent! For most women, that is at least 16 pounds! As the cultural ideal grows slimmer, women with average or heavier-than-average figures feel more pressure to control their weight. Cultural idealization of the (very!) slender female may contribute to distortion of the body image.

The study by Paul Rozin and April Fallon provides some insight into the prevalence of women's concerns about being overweight.

Body Image, Attitudes to Weight, and Misperceptions of Figure Preferences of the Opposite Sex: A Comparison of Men and Women in Two Generations

PAUL ROZIN
UNIVERSITY OF PENNSYLVANIA
AND
APRIL FALLON
MEDICAL COLLEGE OF PENNSYLVANIA

[1] Kassirer, J. P., & Angell, M. (1998). Losing weight—An ill-fated New Year's resolution. *New England Journal of Medicine, 338,* 52–54.

This study explores some possible causes of the recent increase in dieting and eating disorders among American women. Measures on body image, attitudes to eating and weight, and eating behaviors were collected from male (sons) and female (daughters) college students and their biological parents. All groups but the sons considered their current body shape to be heavier than their ideal. Mothers and daughters believed that men (of their own generation) prefer much thinner women than these men actually prefer. Mothers and daughters both showed great concern about weight and eating. Although fathers resembled mothers and daughters in their perception of being overweight, they were more similar to their sons in being relatively unconcerned about weight and eating. Hence, the major factor in concern about weight is sex rather than generation or discrepancy between perception of current and ideal body shape.

Concern about weight and body shape is much more common in women than in men in American society (Cash, Winstead, & Janda, 1986; Dwyer, Feldman, Seltzer, & Mayer, 1969; see Rodin, Silberstein, & Striegel-Moore, 1985, for a review). In this article we examine attitudes to weight or bodies in children (college age) and their parents to see whether there are generational differences that parallel the dramatic rise in eating disorders among women in recent years (Garfinkel & Garner, 1982).

Fallon and Rozin (1985) reported that female college students judged their current appearance to be significantly heavier than their ideal figure, whereas male college students did not. Furthermore, the female students' perception of what male students considered the ideal female figure to be was significantly thinner than the figure that male students actually selected. In contrast, male students believed that women preferred a male figure of the male students' current size, where in fact, female students preferred thinner men. Thus, the female students exaggerated male students' actual preferences in such a direction as to be consistent with or cause dissatisfaction with their current figures. Male students distorted female perceptions so as to be consistent with or cause satisfaction with their current figures. We hypothesize that dissatisfaction with body image, coupled with the belief that thinness is a very important feature, helps to explain the greater female concern with weight control. The greater involvement is manifested in a number of ways, including increased dieting and higher incidences of eating disorders.

In this study we examine these hypotheses, in a cross-generational study. We obtain body-image satisfaction ratings, attitudes to weight, and frequency of weight-related or food restriction practices from college students and their parents. This allows us to evaluate the relative roles of generation and sex. It also allows us to explore the relations among sex, generation, concern about weight, and eating attitudes and behaviors.

Method

SUBJECTS

Questionnaires were distributed to volunteer students in introductory psychology classes, to be taken home over the spring break. Students were eligible to participate if (a) both of their biological parents were alive and still married and (b) the student had spent virtually all of his or her precollege life living with these parents. The student filled out a questionnaire in class, and brought two questionnaires to his or her parents during the spring break. These were mailed back to the investigators. Subjects were instructed not to discuss any of the material in the questionnaires until all were filled out and sealed in the envelope.

Approximately half of the students who were eligible provided a full, usable set of data ($N = 97$ families). The data set contained 55 daughters ($M = 18.6$ years), 42 sons ($M = 19.0$ years), 97 fathers ($M = 50.3$ years) and 97 mothers ($M = 46.5$ years). Ninety-one of the 97 families were white; 31 of the families were Christian, 58 were Jewish and 8 were "other." This represents a vastly higher percentage Jewish families than exists in the American population.

QUESTIONNAIRE

The anonymous questionnaire requested the age, sex, race, ethnic group, height, and weight of each subject. Subjects were presented with nine figure drawings (designed by and illustrated in Stunkard, Sorenson, & Schlusinger, 1980, and identical to those used by Fallon & Rozin, 1985) of each sex, accompanied by numerical values (10 = very thin, 90 = very heavy; see Figure 21.01). Subjects were asked to indicate the value (with encouragement to use intermediate numbers, such as 23 or 49) that best described their current appearance (current), what they would like to look like (ideal), what they thought was most attractive to the opposite sex (attractive) and using the opposite sex set of figures, what figure value they thought was most attractive in the opposite sex (other attractive).

Subjects were also asked the following questions about concern for weight, and weight and feeding-related behaviors:

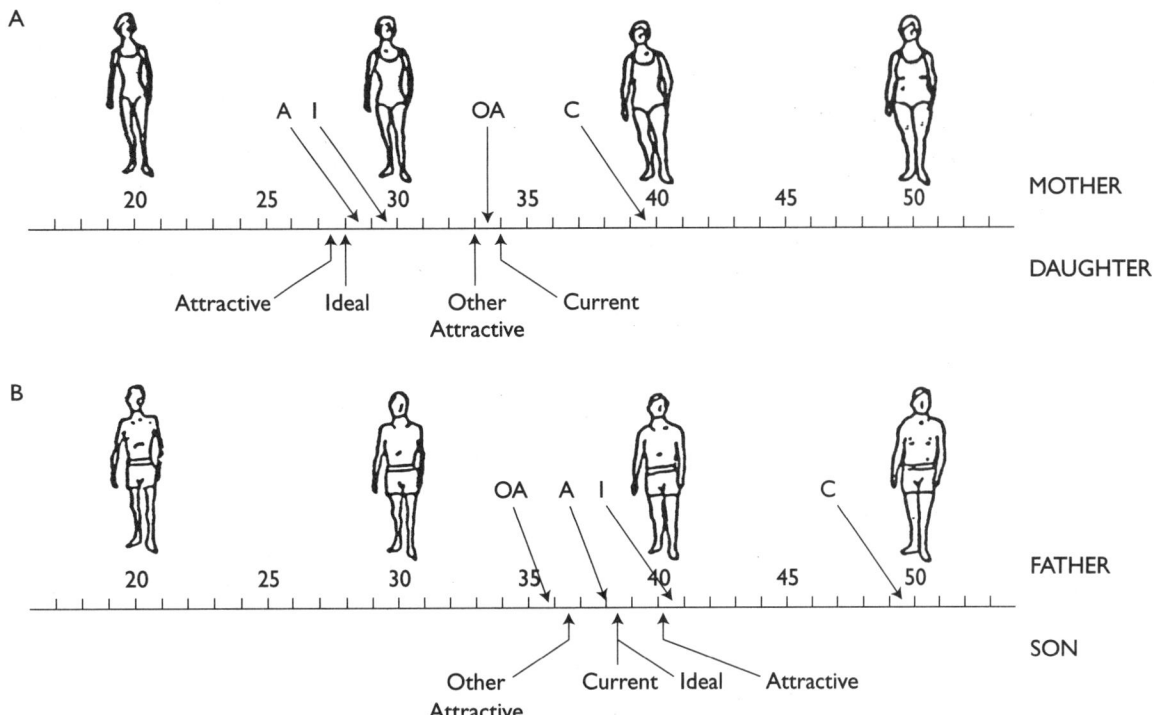

FIGURE 21.01

Mean ratings of current (C), ideal (I), most attractive to opposite sex (A), and most attractive to opposite sex as rated by the opposite sex (other attractive, OA). (The relevant portion of the figure scale shown only includes 4 of the 9 figures. Part A, above top line: Ratings by mothers, except that other attractive rating is by fathers of the most attractive mother figure. Part A, below top line, equivalent ratings by daughters. Part B corresponds exactly to Part A, but presents data from fathers and sons, with other attractive ratings of male figures by mothers and daughters.)

Self-overweight. "I consider myself (a) markedly overweight, (b) slightly overweight, (c) average, (d) slightly underweight, (e) markedly underweight."

Depressed. "When I get depressed, I usually eat: (a) more, (b) about the same, (c) less."

The frequency of *concern about weight, feeling guilty about eating, holding back at meals,* and *dieting* was measured by the following scale: (a) never, (b) rarely, (c) sometimes, (d) often, (e) almost always.

Results

The data from sons and daughters is very similar to the data previously reported from the same population (Fallon & Rozin, 1985). The only notable difference is that although the women's ideal figure was significantly thinner than women's perception of the men's ideal female figure in our previous work, these two values were almost exactly the same in this study (Figure 21.01).

BODY IMAGE

In all statistical analyses, we have adopted the .01 level of significance. This is appropriate because in a number of cases we carried out multiple planned tests between critical groups. For the parametric

body image data, we performed two separate 2 × 2 analyses of variance (ANOVAs) (sex by generation) to examine what we consider the critical variables. One ANOVA dealt with dissatisfaction with current body image (current minus ideal) and the other ANOVA with distortion of opposite sex preferences (attractive minus mean of other attractive score for opposite sex members of the same generation).

The ANOVA on dissatisfaction with current body image indicated that women are more dissatisfied than men in body image (current − ideal; sex effect), $F(1, 287) = 8.39$, $p < .004$, and the old generation is much more dissatisfied than is the young generation (generation effect), $F(1, 287) = 34.64$, $p < .001$, (see Figure 21.01). There is also a significant Sex × Generation interaction, $F(1, 287) = 9.35$, $p < .002$. The interaction arises (see Figure 21.01 and Table 21.01) because there is a substantial current−ideal disparity in all groups except sons[2]

---

[2] The similarity of current and ideal mean ratings by sons could have resulted from high current−ideal disparities in opposite directions in many sons, which would cancel out. However, this is not the case, because 50% of the sons had current and ideal ratings within .5 scale units of one another. The corresponding figure for daughters is 11.3%.

TABLE 21.01

	PERSON				SIGNIFICANCE OF PAIR DIFFERENCES			
ITEM	**SON**	**DAUGHTER**	**FATHER**	**MOTHER**	**SON–DAUGHTER**	**FATHER–MOTHER**	**MOTHER–DAUGHTER**	**FATHER–SON**
N	42	55	97	97				
Body image								
Current–ideal[a]	−0.9	6.2	8.6	9.3	**			**
Attractive–other[b]	3.8	−5.0	1.4	−5.4	**	**		
Weight (% over)[b]	33	60	59	67	*			*
Weight concern (≥ often)[b]	38	65	36	56	*	*		
Dieting (≥ some)[b]	33	62	50	73	**	**		*
Hold back (≥ some)[b]	36	69	40	60	**	*		
Guilt[b]	26	53	34	41	*			
Depression (eat more)[b]	29	62	27	56	*	**		

Note. Statistical tests are described in the Results section.
[a]*Numbers are mean values for body image ratings.* [b]*Numbers are percentages of subjects of each type who reported the answer indicated for the item in question. Thus, for the Weight concern heading, the number 38 in the Son column means that 38% of sons reported weight concern often or almost always.*
*p < .01, two-tailed. **p < .001, two-tailed.

(tests between critical groups are shown in Table 21.01).

The ANOVA that dealt with distortion of opposite sex preferences (attractive−other attractive) showed a strong sex effect, $F(1, 286) = 113.99$, $p < .001$; the women exaggerated men's preferences for thinness, and the men showed the opposite effect. There is not a significant generation effect, $F(1, 286) = 2.63$, $p = .11$, or a significant Sex × Generation interaction, $F(1, 286) = 2.45$, $p = .12$. (See Figure 21.01 and Table 21.01 for specific comparisons.) Hence, sex is the major determinant of body image distortion.

In summary, mothers showed about the same disparity between ideal and current figures, and perceived male preference versus actual male preference as their daughters did. Fathers, unlike their sons, showed a large current-ideal disparity, but both showed a tendency to distort female preferences in judging women to like heavier men than the women actually do.

SEX AND GENERATIONAL DIFFERENCES IN ATTITUDE TO WEIGHT

Fathers, mothers, and daughters showed a notable disparity between current and ideal shape, in contrast to the sons (who showed no disparity). In light of this grouping, it is of interest to look at attitudes to weight and eating in these four groups. For the weight and food attitude questions, the Wilcoxon test was used on each pair except son–daughter, for which a Mann-Whitney U test was used. For the depression item, we used only two categories (eat more when depressed or not), sign tests were used instead of the Wilcoxon, and a chi-square was used instead of the Mann-Whitney. Note that with the exception of the depression and body image items, the significance tests are based on the ordinal 5-point rating scale, although the summary descriptive statistic provided in Table 20.01 (e.g., percentage who consider themselves overweight) dichotomizes the data, for ease in presentation.

As expected from the current–ideal comparison, except for sons, the majority of subjects considered themselves overweight (Table 20.01). The only significant differences on this question involved the sons (Table 20.01). However, if we examine the consequences of feeling (or being) overweight, the fathers' responses were more similar to their sons than to their daughters. Thus, most mothers and daughters reported that concern about weight occurs often or almost always, whereas this is true for a minority of the fathers and sons (the only significant differences are between opposite sex pairs: mother–father and daughter–son; Table 20.01). For frequency of dieting, holding back at meals, or feeling guilty about eating (Table 20.01), fathers exceeded sons significantly only on dieting, whereas fathers were significantly lower than mothers on both dieting and holding back at meals. Finally, although a majority of mothers and daughters said they ate more when depressed, only about 28% of fathers and sons did (Table 20.01).

In summary, except for judgments of degree of overweight, the major differences are between daughter–son and father–mother pairings. That is, the basic attitude differences between the sexes hold across generations even though the departure from ideal weight crosses generations and is present in all groups but sons. Fathers recognize that they are overweight but do not seem to change their eating behaviors or attitudes too much on that account.

Discussion

Sex seems to predict attitudes much better than generation. We compared sex and generation on the five measures of attitudes to weight and eating (weight concern, holding back, guilt, dieting, and depression). The mean generational differences, measured as percentage point differences (see Table 20.01) are small: 6.3 points for father–son and 9.5 points for mother–daughter. In contrast, the sex differences within generation are substantial: 19.8 for mother–father and 29.8 for daughter–son.

Mothers are very much like their daughters in dissatisfaction with body image, concern with weight, and weight or eating-related practices. This finding is inconsistent with the hypothesis that changes in attitudes to weight contribute to the recent rise in incidence of anorexia and bulimia. However, it is possible that mothers' attitudes to weight have themselves changed over the last two decades, such that these mothers were not so preoccupied with weight when they were of college age. Furthermore, even if there has been no transgenerational change in attitudes to weight, there may have been changes in modes of expressing these attitudes. Although this is surely not the whole story, given the major changes in the role of women in society in recent decades, and changes in fashion standards for thinness (Garner, Garfinkel, Schwartz, & Thompson, 1980; Rodin et al., 1985), it seems to be a part of it.

The fact that fathers perceive themselves to be as far from their ideal weight as mothers and daughters allows us to test the importance of disparity from the ideal in generating concern about weight. Strikingly, the fathers showed much lower levels of weight concern and weight-loss related behaviors than did mothers or daughters, though slightly more than did their sons. Although fathers were dissatisfied with their current appearance; this dissatisfaction did not lead to the same concern and discomfort as manifested by their wives or daughters. These results support the idea that dissatisfaction with weight is not a sufficient cause for weight-related concerns and behaviors. For fathers, the issue does not seem to be that important.

Our results come from a single body-image rating technique and a few questions about attitudes to eating. They also come from a very narrow slice of our culture. There are trends in our data that suggest greater weight concern among Jewish subjects, and because these made up somewhat above half of our sample, our data may exaggerate the differences in the American population at large. To be able to interpret the differences we report, it would be necessary to get data from different regions of the country and different socioeconomic classes. Furthermore, to clarify the importance and nature of sociocultural variables, we must obtain information from other countries.

Our principal finding is the importance of sex rather than generation difference with respect to concern about weight. The implication is that the importance of weight, rather than the disparity from the ideal is the more fundamental variable in understanding attitudes to weight, and perhaps, the origins of eating disorders.

References

1. Cash, T. F., Winstead, B. A., & Janda, L. H. (1986, April). The great American shape-up. *Psychology Today*, pp. 30–37.
2. Dwyer, J. T., Feldman, J. J., Seltzer, C. C., & Mayer, J. (1969). Body image in adolescence: Attitudes toward weight and perception of appearance. *American Journal of Clinical Nutrition, 20,* 1045–1056.

3. Fallon, A. E., & Rozin, P. (1985). Sex differences in perceptions of desirable body shape. *Journal of Abnormal Psychology, 94*, 102–105.
4. Garfinkel, P. E., & Garner, D. M. (1982). *Anorexia nervosa: A multidimensional perspective.* New York: Brunner/Mazel.
5. Garner, D. M., Garfinkel, P. E., Schwartz, D., & Thompson, M. (1980). Cultural expectations of thinness in women. *Psychological Reports, 47*, 483–491.
6. Rodin, J., Silberstein, L., & Striegel-Moore, R. (1985). Women and weight: A normative discontent. In T. B. Sonderegger (Ed.), *Psychology and gender: Nebraska Symposium on Motivation* (pp. 267–307). Lincoln: University of Nebraska Press.
7. Stunkard, A. J., Sorenson, T., & Schlusinger, F. (1980). Use of the Danish adoption register for the study of obesity and thinness. In S. Kety (Ed.), *The genetics of neurological and psychiatric disorders* (pp. 115–120). New York: Raven Press.

QUESTIONS FOR REFLECTION AND DISCUSSION:

1. What public figures (models, actors, etc.) do you consider to have excellent figures or physiques? How heavy or slender are they? Do you have different standards for women and men? Explain.

2. What are your attitudes toward your own figure or physique? Are you satisfied with it? Do others share your self-perceptions?

3. A much higher percentage of subjects in the study were Jewish than are found in the general population. Do you believe that this demographic fact prevents us from extending or generalizing the results of the study to the general U.S. population? Explain.

4. The majority of respondents in the study (with the exception of sons) consider themselves to be overweight, yet the current weights of the daughters were not very different from what the sons consider to be most attractive. What inferences can we draw from this finding?

5. Sons by and large saw themselves as currently being at their ideal weight even though daughters viewed the most attractive weight for males as being somewhat lower. What inferences can we draw from this finding?

6. The authors conclude that the gender (sex) of the individual is the most important determinant of attitudes toward one's own weight. Why do you think that women are more concerned about their weight than men are?

SOURCE

Festinger, L., & Carlsmith, J. M. (1959). Cognitive consequences of forced compliance. *Journal of Abnormal and Social Psychology, 58,* 203–210.

Shakespeare wrote an interesting couplet:

> *A man convinced against his will*
> *Is of the same opinion still.*

That is, you may be able to argue a person out of an opinion, but winning the argument is superficial. Underneath it all, the person's attitude will not change. One might even imagine that the person losing the argument might be resentful about it, and thereby his or her initial opinion might even be strengthened.

That's common sense. Or common nonsense. Pick one of the foregoing.

Carry the concept into forcing behavior and not just winning arguments. In the 1950s and 1960s many social commentators argued there was no point to legislating equal rights for African Americans because the laws would only create resentment. They argued that you cannot legislate "morality." Then states passed laws compelling people to recycle items like newspapers and glass bottles rather than toss them into the garbage. Again it was heard that such laws would only cause resentment. Yet there seems to be no evidence for these dire predictions. Attitudes toward equal rights for minority groups have grown more favorable among European Americans, and millions of Americans recycle habitually and express positive attitudes toward recycling.

Enter social psychologists Leon Festinger and James Carlsmith, who undertook a landmark study in the effects of forced compliance. They conceptualized their finding from the perspective of cognitive-dissonance theory.

Cognitive Consequences of Forced Compliance

LEON FESTINGER AND JAMES M. CARLSMITH
STANFORD UNIVERSITY

What happens to a person's private opinion if he is forced to do or say something contrary to that opinion? Only recently has there been any experimental work related to this question. Two studies reported by Janis and King (1954; 1956) clearly showed that, at least under some conditions, the private opinion changes so as to bring it into closer correspondence with the overt behavior the person was forced to perform. Specifically, they showed that if a person is forced to improvise a speech supporting a point of view with which he disagrees, his private opinion moves toward the position advocated in the speech. The observed opinion change is greater than for persons who only hear the speech or for persons who read a prepared speech with emphasis solely on elocution and manner of delivery. The authors of these two studies explain their results mainly in terms of mental rehearsal and thinking up new arguments. In this way, they propose, the person who is forced to improvise a speech convinces himself. They present some evidence, which is not altogether conclusive, in support of this explanation. We will have more to say concerning this explanation in discussing the results of our experiment.

Kelman (1953) tried to pursue the matter further. He reasoned that if the person is induced to make an overt statement contrary to his private opinion by the offer of some reward, then the greater the reward offered, the greater should be the subsequent opinion change. His data, however, did not support this idea. He found, rather, that a large reward produced less subsequent opinion change than did a smaller reward. Actually, this finding by Kelman is consistent with the theory we will outline below but, for a number of reasons, is not conclusive. One of the major weaknesses of the data is that not all subjects in the experiment made an overt statement contrary to their private opinion in order to obtain the offered reward. What is more, as one might expect, the percentage of subjects who complied increased as the size of the offered reward increased. Thus, with self-selection of who did and who did not make the required overt statement and with varying percentages of subjects in the different conditions who did make the required statement, no interpretation of the data can be unequivocal.

Recently, Festinger (1957) proposed a theory concerning cognitive dissonance from which come a number of derivations about opinion change following forced compliance. Since these derivations are stated in detail by Festinger (1957, Ch. 4), we will here give only a brief outline of the reasoning.

Let us consider a person who privately holds opinion "X" but has, as a result of pressure brought to bear on him, publicly stated that he believes "not X."

1. This person has two cognitions which, psychologically, do not fit together: one of these is the knowledge that he believes "X," the other the knowledge that he has publicly stated that he believes "not X." If no factors other than his private opinion are considered, it would follow, at least in our culture, that if he believes "X" he would publicly state "X." Hence, his cognition of his private belief is dissonant with his cognition concerning his actual public statement.

2. Similarly, the knowledge that he has said "not X" is consonant with (does fit together with) those cognitive elements corresponding to the reasons, pressures, promises of rewards and/or threats of punishment which induced him to say "not X."

3. In evaluating the total magnitude of dissonance, one must take account of both dissonances and consonances. Let us think of the sum of all the dissonances involving some particular cognition as "D" and the sum of all the consonances as "C." Then we might think of the total magnitude of dissonance as being a function of "D" divided by "D" plus "C."

Let us then see what can be said about the total magnitude of dissonance in a person created by the knowledge that he said "not X" and really believes "X." With everything else held constant, this total magnitude of dissonance would decrease as the number and importance of the pressures which induced him to say "not X" increased.

Thus, if the overt behavior was brought about by, say, offers of reward or threats of punishment, the magnitude of dissonance is maximal if these promised rewards of threatened punishments were just barely sufficient to induce the person to say "not X." From this point on, as the promised rewards or threatened punishment become larger, the magnitude of dissonance becomes smaller.

4. One way in which the dissonance can be reduced is for the person to change his private opinion so as to bring it into correspondence with what he has said. One would consequently expect to observe such opinion change after a person has been forced or induced to say something contrary to his private opinion. Furthermore, since the pressure to reduce dissonance will be a function of the magnitude of the dissonance, the observed opinion change should be greatest when the pressure used to elicit the overt behavior is just sufficient to do it.

The present experiment was designed to test this derivation under controlled, laboratory conditions. In the experiment we varied the amount of reward used to force persons to make a statement contrary to their private views. The prediction [from 3 and 4 above] is that the larger the reward given to the subject, the smaller will be the subsequent opinion change.

Procedure

Seventy-one male students in the introductory psychology course at Stanford University were used in the experiment. In this course, students are required to spend a certain number of hours as subjects (*Ss*) in experiments. They choose among the available experiments by signing their names on a sheet posted on the bulletin board which states the nature of the experiment. The present experiment was listed as a two-hour experiment dealing with "Measures of Performance."

During the first week of the course, when the requirement of serving in experiments was announced and explained to the students, the instructor also told them about a study that the psychology department was conducting. He explained that, since they were required to serve in experiments, the department was conducting a study to evaluate these experiments in order to be able to improve them in the future. They were told that a sample of students would be interviewed after having served as *Ss*. They were urged to cooperate in these interviews by being completely frank and honest. The importance of this announcement will become clear shortly. It enabled us to measure the opinions of our *Ss* in a context not directly connected with our experiment and in which we could reasonably expect frank and honest expressions of opinion.

When the *S* arrived for the experiment on "Measures of Performance" he had to wait for a few minutes in the secretary's office. The experimenter (*E*) then came in, introduced himself to the *S* and, together, they walked into the laboratory room where the *E* said:

> This experiment usually takes a little over an hour but, of course, we had to schedule it for two hours. Since we have that extra time, the introductory psychology people asked if they could interview some of our subjects. [Offhand and conversationally.] Did they announce that in class? I gather that they're interviewing some people who have been in experiments. I don't know much about it. Anyhow, they may want to interview you when you're through here.

With no further introduction or explanation the *S* was shown the first task, which involved putting 12 spools onto a tray, emptying the tray, refilling it with spools, and so on. He was told to use one hand and to work at his own speed. He did this for one-half hour. The *E* then removed the tray and spools and placed in front of the *S* a board containing 48 square pegs. His task was to turn each peg a quarter turn clockwise, then another quarter turn, and so on. He was told again to use one hand and to work at his own speed. The *S* worked at this task for another half hour.

While the *S* was working on these tasks, the *E* sat, with a stop watch in his hand, busily making notations on a sheet of paper. He did so in order to make it convincing that this was what the *E* was interested in and that these tasks, and how the *S* worked on them, was the total experiment. From our point of view the experiment had hardly started. The hour which the *S* spent working on the repetitive, monotonous tasks was intended to provide, for each *S* uniformly, an experience about which he would have a somewhat negative opinion.

After the half hour on the second task was over, the *E* conspicuously set the stop watch back to zero, put it away, pushed his chair back, lit a cigarette, and said:

O.K. Well, that's all we have in the experiment itself. I'd like to explain what this has been all about so you'll have some idea of why you were doing this. [*E* pauses.] Well, the way the experiment is set up is this. There are actually two groups in the experiment. In one, the group you were in, we bring the subject in and give him essentially no introduction to the experiment. That is, all we tell him is what he needs to know in order to do the tasks, and he has no idea of what the experiment is all about, or what it's going to be like, or anything like that. But in the other group, we have a student that we've hired that works for us regularly, and what I do is take him into the next room where the subject is waiting—the same room you were waiting in before—and I introduce him as if he had just finished being a subject in the experiment. That is, I say: "This is so-and-so, who's just finished the experiment, and I've asked him to tell you a little of what it's about before you start." The fellow who works for us then, in conversation with the next subject, makes these points: [The *E* then produced a sheet headed "For Group B" which had written on it: It was very enjoyable, I had a lot of fun, I enjoyed myself, it was very interesting, it was intriguing, it was exciting. The *E* showed this to the *S* and then proceeded with his false explanation of the purpose of the experiment.] Now, of course, we have this student do this, because if the experimenter does it, it doesn't look as realistic, and what we're interested in doing is comparing how these two groups do on the experiment—the one with this previous expectation about the experiment, and the other, like yourself, with essentially none.

Up to this point the procedure was identical for *Ss* in all conditions. From this point on they diverged somewhat. Three conditions were run, Control, One Dollar, and Twenty Dollars, as follows:

CONTROL CONDITION

The *E* continued:

> Is that fairly clear? [Pause.] Look, that fellow [looks at watch] I was telling you about from the introductory psychology class said he would get here a couple of minutes from now. Would you mind waiting to see if he wants to talk to you? Fine. Why don't we go into the other room to wait? [The *E* left the *S*

in the secretary's office for four minutes. He then returned and said:] O.K. Let's check and see if he does want to talk to you.

ONE AND TWENTY DOLLAR CONDITIONS

The *E* continued:

Is that fairly clear how it is set up and what we're trying to do? [Pause.] Now, I also have a sort of strange thing to ask you. The thing is this. [Long pause, some confusion and uncertainty in the following, with a degree of embarrassment on the part of the *E*. The manner of the *E* contrasted strongly with the preceding unhesitant and assured false explanation of the experiment. The point was to make it seem to the *S* that this was the first time the *E* had done this and that he felt unsure of himself.] The fellow who normally does this for us couldn't do it today—he just phoned in, and something or other came up for him—so we've been looking around for someone that we could hire to do it for us. You see, we've got another subject waiting [looks at watch] who is supposed to be in that other condition. Now Professor ——, who is in charge of this experiment, suggested that perhaps we could take a chance on your doing it for us. I'll tell you what we had in mind: the thing is, if you could do it for us now, then of course you would know how to do it, and if something like this should ever come up again, that is, the regular fellow couldn't make it, and we had a subject scheduled, it would be very reassuring to us to know that we had somebody else we could call on who knew how to do it. So, if you would be willing to do this for us, we'd like to hire you to do it now and then be on call in the future, if something like this should ever happen again. We can pay you a dollar (twenty dollars) for doing this for us, that is, for doing it now and then being on call. Do you think you could do that for us?

If the *S* hesitated, the *E* said things like, "It will only take a few minutes," "The regular person is pretty reliable; this is the first time he has missed," or "If we needed you we could phone you a day or two in advance; if you couldn't make it, of course, we wouldn't expect you to come." After the *S* agreed to do it, the *E* gave him the previously mentioned sheet of paper headed "For Group B" and asked him to read it through again. The *E* then paid

the *S* one dollar (twenty dollars), made out a handwritten receipt form, and asked the *S* to sign it. He then said:

O.K., the way we'll do it is this. As I said, the next subject should be here by now. I think the next one is a girl. I'll take you into the next room and introduce you to her, saying that you've just finished the experiment and that we've asked you to tell her a little about it. And what we want you to do is just sit down and get into a conversation with her and try to get across the points on that sheet of paper. I'll leave you alone and come back after a couple of minutes. O.K.?

The *E* then took the *S* into the secretary's office where he had previously waited and where the next *S* was waiting. (The secretary had left the office.) He introduced the girl and the *S* to one another saying that the *S* had just finished the experiment and would tell her something about it. He then left saying he would return in a couple of minutes. The girl, an undergraduate hired for this role, said little until the *S* made some positive remarks about the experiment and then said that she was surprised because a friend of hers had taken the experiment the week before and had told her that it was boring and that she ought to try to get out of it. Most *S*s responded by saying something like "Oh, no, it's really very interesting. I'm sure you'll enjoy it." The girl, after this listened quietly, accepting and agreeing to everything the *S* told her. The discussion between the *S* and the girl was recorded on a hidden tape recorder.

After two minutes the *E* returned, asked the girl to go into the experimental room, thanked the *S* for talking to the girl, wrote down his phone number to continue the fiction that we might call on him again in the future and then said: "Look, could we check and see if that fellow from introductory psychology wants to talk to you?"

From this point on, the procedure for all three conditions was once more identical. As the *E* and the *S* started to walk to the office where the interviewer was, the *E* said: "Thanks very much for working on those tasks for us. I hope you did enjoy it. Most of our subjects tell us afterward that they found it quite interesting. You get a chance to see how you react to the tasks and so forth." This short persuasive communication was made in all conditions in exactly the same way. The reason for doing it, theoretically, was to make it easier for anyone who wanted to persuade himself that the tasks had been, indeed, enjoyable.

When they arrived at the interviewer's office, the *E* asked the interviewer whether or not he wanted to talk to the *S*. The interviewer said yes, the *E* shook hands with the *S*, said good-bye, and left. The interviewer, of course, was always kept in complete ignorance of which condition the *S* was in. The interview consisted of four questions, on each of which the *S* was first encouraged to talk about the matter and was then asked to rate his opinion or reaction on an 11-point scale. The questions are as follows:

1. Were the tasks interesting and enjoyable? In what way? In what way were they not? Would you rate how you feel about them on a scale from -5 to $+5$ where -5 means they were extremely dull and boring, $+5$ means they were extremely interesting and enjoyable, and zero means they were neutral, neither interesting nor uninteresting.

2. Did the experiment give you an opportunity to learn about your own ability to perform these tasks? In what way? In what way not? Would you rate how you feel about this on a scale from 0 to 10 where 0 means you learned nothing and 10 means you learned a great deal.

3. From what you know about the experiment and the tasks involved in it, would you say the experiment was measuring anything important? That is, do you think the results may have scientific value? In what way? In what way not? Would you rate your opinion on this matter on a scale from 0 to 10 where 0 means the results have no scientific value or importance and 10 means they have a great deal of value and importance.

4. Would you have any desire to participate in another similar experiment? Why? Why not? Would you rate your desire to participate in a similar experiment again on a scale from -5 to $+5$, where -5 means you would definitely dislike to participate, $+5$ means you would definitely like to participate, and 0 means you have no particular feeling about it one way or the other.

As may be seen, the questions varied in how directly relevant they were to what the *S* had told the girl. This point will be discussed further in connection with the results.

At the close of the interview the *S* was asked what he thought the experiment was about and, following this, was asked directly whether or not he was suspicious of anything and, if so, what he was suspicious of. When the interview was over, the interviewer brought the *S* back to the experimental room where the *E* was waiting together with the girl who had posed as the waiting *S*. (In the control condition, of course, the girl was not there.) The true purpose of the experiment was then explained to the *S* in detail, and the reasons for each of the various steps in the experiment were explained carefully in relation to the true purpose. All experimental *S*s in both One Dollar and Twenty Dollar conditions were asked, after this explanation, to return the money they had been given. All *S*s, without exception, were quite willing to return the money.

The data from 11 of the 71 *S*s in the experiment had to be discarded for the following reasons:

1. Five *S*s (three in the One Dollar and two in the Twenty Dollar condition) indicated in the interview that they were suspicious about having been paid to tell the girl the experiment was fun and suspected that that was the real purpose of the experiment.

2. Two *S*s (both in the One Dollar condition) told the girl that they had been hired, that the experiment was really boring but they were supposed to say it was fun.

3. Three *S*s (one in the One Dollar and two in the Twenty Dollar condition) refused to take the money and refused to be hired.

4. One *S* (in the One Dollar condition), immediately after having talked to the girl, demanded her phone number saying he would call her and explain things, and also told the *E* he wanted to wait until she was finished so he could tell her about it.

These 11 *S*s were, of course, run through the total experiment anyhow and the experiment was explained to them afterwards. Their data, however, are not included in the analysis.

SUMMARY OF DESIGN

There remain, for analysis, 20 *S*s in each of the three conditions. Let us review these briefly: 1. *Control condition.* These *S*s were treated identically in all respects to the *S*s in the experimental conditions, except that they were never asked to, and never did, tell the waiting girl that the experimental tasks were enjoyable and lots of fun. 2. *One Dollar condition.* These *S*s were hired for one dollar to tell a waiting *S* that tasks, which were really rather dull and boring, were interesting, enjoyable, and lots of fun. 3. *Twenty-Dollar condition.* These *S*s were hired for twenty dollars to do the same thing.

TABLE 22.01

	EXPERIMENTAL CONDITION		
AVERAGE RATINGS ON INTERVIEW QUESTIONS FOR EACH CONDITION			
QUESTION ON INTERVIEW	CONTROL ($N = 20$)	ONE DOLLAR ($N = 20$)	TWENTY DOLLARS ($N = 20$)
How enjoyable tasks were (rated from -5 to $+5$)	$-.45$	$+1.35$	$-.05$
How much they learned (rated from 0 to 10)	3.08	2.80	3.15
Scientific importance (rated from 0 to 10)	5.60	6.45	5.18
Participate in similar exp. (rated from -5 to $+5$)	$-.62$	$+1.20$	$-.25$

Results

The major results of the experiment are summarized in Table 22.01 which lists, separately for each of the three experimental conditions, the average rating which the Ss gave at the end of each question on the interview. We will discuss each of the questions on the interview separately, because they were intended to measure different things. One other point before we proceed to examine the data. In all the comparisons, the Control condition should be regarded as a baseline from which to evaluate the results in the other two conditions. The Control condition gives us, essentially, the reactions of Ss to the tasks and their opinions about the experiment as falsely explained to them, without the experimental introduction of dissonance. The data from the other conditions may be viewed, in a sense, as changes from this baseline.

HOW ENJOYABLE THE TASKS WERE

The average ratings on this question, presented in the first row of figures in Table 22.01, are the results most important to the experiment. These results are the ones most directly relevant to the specific dissonance which was experimentally created. It will be recalled that the tasks were purposely arranged to be rather boring and monotonous. And, indeed, in the Control condition the average rating was $-.45$, somewhat on the negative side of the neutral point.

In the other two conditions, however, the Ss told someone that these tasks were interesting and enjoyable. The resulting dissonance could, of course,

most directly be reduced by persuading themselves that the tasks were, indeed, interesting and enjoyable. In the One Dollar condition, since the magnitude of dissonance was high, the pressure to reduce this dissonance would also be high. In this condition, the average rating was $+1.35$, considerably on the positive side and significantly different from the Control condition at the .02 level[1] ($t = 2.48$).

In the Twenty Dollar condition, where less dissonance was created experimentally because of the greater importance of the consonant relations, there is correspondingly less evidence of dissonance reduction. The average rating in this condition is only $-.05$, slightly and not significantly higher than the Control condition. The difference between the One Dollar and Twenty Dollar conditions is significant at the .03 level ($t = 2.22$). In short, when an S was induced, by offer of reward, to say something contrary to his private opinion, this private opinion tended to change so as to correspond more closely with what he had said. The greater the reward offered (beyond what was necessary to elicit the behavior) the smaller was the effect.

DESIRE TO PARTICIPATE IN A SIMILAR EXPERIMENT

The results from this question are shown in the last row of Table 22.01. This question is less directly related to the dissonance that was experimentally

---

[1] All statistical tests referred to in this paper are two-tailed.

created for the *Ss*. Certainly, the more interesting and enjoyable they felt the tasks were, the greater would be their desire to participate in a similar experiment. But other factors would enter also. Hence, one would expect the results on this question to be very similar to the results on "how enjoyable the tasks were" but weaker. Actually, the result, as may be seen in the table, are in exactly the same direction, and the magnitude of the mean differences is fully as large as on the first question. The variability is greater, however, and the differences do not yield high levels of statistical significance. The difference between the One Dollar condition (+1.20) and the Control condition (−.62) is significant at the .08 level ($t = 1.78$). The difference between the One Dollar condition and the Twenty Dollar condition (−.25) reaches only the .15 level of significance ($t = 1.46$).

THE SCIENTIFIC IMPORTANCE OF THE EXPERIMENT

This question was included because there was a chance that differences might emerge. There are, after all, other ways in which the experimentally created dissonance could be reduced. For example, one way would be for the *S* to magnify for himself the value of the reward he obtained. This, however, was unlikely in this experiment because money was used for the reward and it is undoubtedly difficult to convince oneself that one dollar is more than it really is. There is another possible way, however. The *Ss* were given a very good reason, in addition to being paid, for saying what they did to the waiting girl. The *Ss* were told it was necessary for the experiment. The dissonance could, consequently, be reduced by magnifying the importance of this cognition. The more scientifically important they considered the experiment to be, the less was the total magnitude of dissonance. It is possible, then, that the results on this question, shown in the third row of figures in Table 22.01, might reflect dissonance reduction.

The results are weakly in line with what one would expect if the dissonance were somewhat reduced in this manner. The One Dollar condition is higher than the other two. The difference between the One and Twenty Dollar conditions reaches the .08 level of significance on a two-tailed test ($t = 1.79$). The difference between the One Dollar and Control conditions is not impressive at all ($t = 1.21$). The result that the Twenty Dollar condition is actually lower than the Control condition is undoubtedly a matter of chance ($t = 0.58$).

HOW MUCH THEY LEARNED FROM THE EXPERIMENT

The results on this question are shown in the second row of figures in Table 22.01. The question was included because, as far as we could see, it had nothing to do with the dissonance that was experimentally created and could not be used for dissonance reduction. One would then expect no differences at all among the three conditions. We felt it was important to show that the effect was not a completely general one but was specific to the content of the dissonance which was created. As can be readily seen in Table 22.01, there are only negligible differences among conditions. The highest *t* value for any of these differences is only 0.48.

Discussion of a Possible Alternative Explanation

We mentioned in the introduction that Janis and King (1954; 1956) in explaining their findings, proposed an explanation in terms of the self-convincing effect of mental rehearsal and thinking up new arguments by the person who had to improvise a speech. Kelman (1953), in the previously mentioned study, in attempting to explain the unexpected finding that the persons who complied in the moderate reward condition changed their opinion more than in the high reward condition, also proposed the same kind of explanation. If the results of our experiment are to be taken as strong corroboration of the theory of cognitive dissonance, this possible alternative explanation must be dealt with.

Specifically, as applied to our results, this alternative explanation would maintain that perhaps, for some reason, the *Ss* in the One Dollar condition worked harder at telling the waiting girl that the tasks were fun and enjoyable. That is, in the One Dollar condition they may have rehearsed it more mentally, thought up more ways of saying it, may have said it more convincingly, and so on. Why this might have been the case is, of course, not immediately apparent. One might expect that, in the Twenty Dollar condition, having been paid more, they would try to do a better job of it than in the One Dollar condition. But nevertheless, the possibility exists that the *Ss* in the One Dollar condition may have improvised more.

Because of the desirability of investigating this possible alternative explanation, we recorded on a tape recorder the conversation between each *S* and the girl. These recordings were transcribed and then rated, by two independent raters, on five

TABLE 22.02

AVERAGE RATINGS OF DISCUSSION BETWEEN SUBJECT AND GIRL			
	CONDITION		
DIMENSION RATED	ONE DOLLAR	TWENTY DOLLARS	VALUE OF *t*
Content before remark by girl (rated from 0 to 5)	2.26	2.62	1.08
Content after remark by girl (rated from 0 to 5)	1.63	1.75	0.11
Over-all content (rated from 0 to 5)	1.89	2.19	1.08
Persuasiveness and conviction (rated from 0 to 10)	4.79	5.50	0.99
Time spent on topic (rated from 0 to 10)	6.74	8.19	1.80

dimensions. The ratings were, of course done in ignorance of which condition each *S* was in. The reliabilities of these ratings, that is, the correlations between the two independent raters, ranged from .61 to .88, with an average reliability of .71. The five ratings were:

1. The content of what the *S* said *before* the girl made the remark that her friend told her it was boring. The stronger the *S*'s positive statements about the tasks, and the more ways in which he said they were interesting and enjoyable, the higher the rating.

2. The content of what the *S* said *after* the girl made the above-mentioned remark. This was rated in the same way as for the content before the remark.

3. A similar rating of the over-all content of what the *S* said.

4. A rating of how persuasive and convincing the *S* was in what he said and the way in which he said it.

5. A rating of the amount of time in the discussion that the *S* spent discussing the tasks as opposed to going off into irrelevant things.

The mean ratings for the One Dollar and Twenty Dollar conditions, averaging the ratings of the two independent raters, are presented in Table 22.02. It is clear from examining the table that, in all cases, the Twenty Dollar condition is slightly higher. The differences are small, however, and only on the rating of "amount of time" does the difference between the two conditions even approach significance. We are certainly justified in concluding that the *Ss* in the One Dollar condition did not improvise more nor act more convincingly. Hence, the alternative explanation discussed above cannot account for the findings.

Summary

Recently, Festinger (1957) has proposed a theory concerning cognitive dissonance. Two derivations from this theory are tested here. These are:

1. If a person is induced to do or say something which is contrary to his private opinion, there will be a tendency for him to change his opinion so as to bring it into correspondence with what he has done or said.

2. The larger the pressure used to elicit the overt behavior (beyond the minimum needed to elicit it) the weaker will be the above-mentioned tendency.

A laboratory experiment was designed to test these derivations. Subjects were subjected to a boring experience and then paid to tell someone that the experience had been interesting and enjoyable. The amount of money paid the subject was varied. The private opinions of the subjects concerning the experiences were then determined.

The results strongly corroborate the theory that was tested.

References

1. Festinger, L. *A theory of cognitive dissonance.* Evanston, Ill: Row Peterson, 1957.
2. Janis, I. L., & King, B. T. The influence of role-playing on opinion change. *J. abnorm. soc. Psychol.,* 1954, **49,** 211–218.
3. Kelman, H. Attitude change as a function of response restriction. *Hum. Relat.,* 1953, **6,** 185–214.
4. King, B. T., & Janis, I. L. Comparison of the effectiveness of improvised versus non-improvised role-playing in producing opinion changes. *Hum. Relat.,* 1956, **9,** 177–186.

QUESTIONS FOR REFLECTION AND DISCUSSION:

1. What is cognitive-dissonance theory? Can you define related concepts such as *attitude-discrepant behavior* and *effort justification*?

2. Consider the theoretical connection between behavior and the size of reward for behavior. How do the predictions of cognitive-dissonance theory differ from behavioral predictions when people are given large versus small rewards for engaging in attitude-discrepant behavior?

3. Who were the subjects in the study? Do you believe that the study's findings would also hold for the general population? Explain.

4. What is the possible alternative explanation, made by Janis and King, for the findings of this kind of study? Does the alternative explanation convince you? Why or why not?

5. Deception was used in the Festinger and Carlsmith study. Can you think of a way in which it could have been carried out without deceiving subjects? Do you have a problem with the ethics of the study? Explain.

Harcourt, Inc.

Ekman, P., & Friesen, W. V. (1971).
Constants across cultures in the face
and emotion. *Journal of Personality
and Social Psychology, 17,*
124–129. Copyright © 1971 by
the American Psychological
Association. Reprinted with
permission.

Nature versus nurture, nature versus nurture—that is the almost universal refrain and question heard among students of human behavior. What are the limits of human heredity? Where does culture enter the picture as a determinant of human behavior. What behaviors are "natural," inborn, innate, instinctive? What behaviors are learned through experience?

The question has been raised in the context of the expression of emotions as in other areas of behavior. Is it natural that the emotion of happiness is accompanied by smiling? Is it natural that surprise is connected with raising of the eyebrows, fear with dilation of the pupils of the eyes, and so on? Charles Darwin suggested the methodology used by Paul Ekman and Wallace Friesen to try to answer this question in The Expression of the Emotions in Man and Animals. *Darwin wrote, "Whenever the same movements of the features or body express the same emotions in several distinct races of man, we may infer with much probability, that such expressions are true ones,—that is, are innate or instinctive. Conventional expressions or gestures, acquired by the individual during early life, would probably have differed in the different races, in the same manner as do their languages. . . . Observations on natives who have had little communication with Europeans would be of course the most valuable. . . . A definite description of the countenance under any emotion or frame of mind, with a statement of the circumstances under which it occurred, would possess much value."*

So it is that many researchers, including Ekman and Friesen, observed "natives who have had little communication with Europeans" or any other outsiders.

Constants Across Cultures in the Face and Emotion

PAUL EKMAN & WALLACE V. FRIESEN
UNIVERSITY OF CALIFORNIA, SAN FRANCISCO   LANGLEY PORTER NEUROPSYCHIATRIC INSTITUTE

This study addresses the question of whether any facial expressions of emotion are universal. Recent studies showing that members of literate cultures associated the same emotion concepts with the same facial behaviors could not demonstrate that at least some facial expressions of emotion are universal; the cultures compared had all been exposed to some of the same mass media presentations of facial expression, and these may have taught the people in each culture to recognize the unique facial expressions of other cultures. To show that members of a preliterate culture who had minimal exposure to literate cultures would associate the same emotion concepts with the same facial behaviors as do members of Western and Eastern literate cultures, data were gathered in New Guinea by telling subjects a story, showing them a set of three faces, and asking them to select the face which showed the emotion appropriate to the story. The results provide evidence in support of the hypothesis that the association between particular facial muscular patterns and discrete emotions is universal.

Prolonged and at times heated controversy has failed to demonstrate whether facial behaviors associated with emotion are universal for man or specific to each culture. Darwin (1872) postulated universals in facial behavior on the basis of his evolutionary theory. Allport (1924), Asch (1952), and Tomkins (1962, 1963) have also postulated universals in emotional facial behavior, although each writer offered a different theoretical basis for his expectation. The culture-specific view, that facial behaviors become associated with emotion through culturally variable learning, received support from Klineberg's (1938) descriptions of how the facial behaviors described in Chinese literature differed from the facial behaviors associated with emotions in the Western world. More recently, Birdwhistell (1963) and LaBarre (1947) have argued against the possibility of any universals in emotional facial behavior, supplying numerous anecdotal examples of variations between cultures.

Ekman (1968) and Ekman and Friesen (1969) considered these contradictory viewpoints within a framework which distinguished between those elements of facial behavior that are universal and those that are culture specific. They hypothesized that the universals are to be found in the relationship between distinctive patterns of the facial muscles and particular emotions (happiness, sadness, anger, fear, surprise, disgust, interest). They suggested that cultural differences would be seen in some of the stimuli, which through learning become established as elicitors of particular emotions, in the rules for controlling facial behavior in particular social settings, and in many of the consequences of emotional arousal.

To demonstrate the hypothesized universal element, Ekman and Friesen (1969) conducted experiments in which they showed still photographs of faces to people from different cultures in order to determine whether the same facial behavior would be judged as the same emotion, regardless of the observers' culture. The faces were selected on the basis of their conformity to Ekman, Friesen, and Tomkins's (in press) a priori descriptions of facial muscles involved in each emotion. College-educated subjects in Brazil, the United States, Argentina, Chile, and Japan were found to identify the same faces with the same emotion words, as were members of two preliterate cultures who had extensive contact with Western cultures (the Sadong of Borneo and the Fore of New Guinea), although the latter results were not as strong (Ekman, Sorenson, & Friesen, 1969). Izard (1968, 1969), working independently with his own set of faces, obtained comparable results across seven other culture-language groups.

While these investigators interpreted their results as evidence of universals in facial behavior, their interpretation was open to argument; because all the cultures they compared had exposure to some of the same mass media portrayals of facial behavior, members of these cultures might have learned to recognize the same set of conventions, or become familiar with each other's different facial behavior.

To overcome this difficulty in the interpretation of previous results, it is necessary to demonstrate that cultures which have had minimal visual contact with literate cultures show similarity to these cultures in their interpretation of facial behavior. The purpose of this paper was to test the hypothesis that members of a preliterate culture who had been selected to insure maximum visual isolation from literate cultures will identify the same emotion concepts with the same faces as do members of literate Western and Eastern cultures.

Method

SUBJECTS

Members of the Fore linguistic-cultural group of the South East Highlands of New Guinea were studied. Until 12 years ago, this was an isolated, Neolithic, material culture (Gajdusek, 1963; Sorenson & Gajdusek, 1966). While many of these people now have had extensive contact with missionaries, government workers, traders, and United States scientists, some have had little such contact. Only subjects who met criteria established to screen out all but those who had minimal opportunity to learn to imitate or recognize uniquely Western facial behaviors were recruited for this experiment. These criteria made it quite unlikely that subjects could have so completely learned some foreign set of facial expressions of emotion that their judgments would be no different from those of members of literate cultures. Those selected had seen no movies, neither spoke nor understood English or Pidgin, had not lived in any of the Western settlement or government towns, and had never worked for a Caucasian (according to their own report). One-hundred and eighty-nine adults and 130 children, male and female, met these criteria. This sample comprises about 3% of the members of this culture.

In addition to data gathered from these more visually isolated members of the South Fore, data were also collected on members of this culture who had had the most contact with Westerners. These subjects all spoke English, had seen movies, lived in a Western settlement or government town, and had attended a missionary or government school for more than 1 year. Twenty-three male adults, but no females, met these criteria.

JUDGMENT TASK

In a pilot study conducted 1 year earlier with members of this same culture, a number of different judgment tasks were tried. The least Westernized subjects could not be asked to select from a printed list of emotion terms the one that was appropriate for a photograph, since they could not read. When the list was repeated to them with each photograph, they seemed to have difficulty remembering the list. Further, doubts remained about whether the meaning of a particular emotion concept was adequately conveyed by translating a single English word into a single South Fore word. Asking the subject to make up his own story about the emotions shown in a picture was not much more successful, although the problems were different. Subjects regarded this as a very difficult task, repeated probes were necessary, and as the procedure became lengthy, subjects became reluctant.

To solve these problems, it was decided to employ a task similar to that developed by Dashiell (1927) for use with young children.[1] Dashiell showed the child a group of three pictures simultaneously, read a story, and told the child to point to the picture in which the person's face showed the emotion described in the story. The advantages of this judgment task in a preliterate culture are that (a) the translator recounts well-rehearsed stories which can be recorded and checked for accurate translation; (b) the task involves no reading; (c) the subject does not have to remember a list of emotion terms; (d) the subject need not speak, but can point to give his answer; and (e) perfect translation of emotion words is not required since the story can help provide connotations.

EMOTION STORIES

With the exception of the stories for fear and surprise, those used in the present study were selected from those which had been most frequently given in the pilot study. Considerable care was taken to insure that each story selected was relevant to only one emotion within the Fore culture, and that members of the culture were agreed on what that emotion was. Since the stories told by the pilot subjects for fear and surprise did not meet these criteria, the authors composed stories for these emotions based on their experience within the culture. The stories used are given below:

> Happiness: His (her) friends have come, and he (she) is happy.
>
> Sadness: His (her) child (mother) has died, and he (she) feels very sad.
>
> Anger: He (she) is angry; or he (she) is angry, about to fight.
>
> Surprise: He (she) is just now looking at something new and unexpected.
>
> Disgust: He (she) is looking at something he (she) dislikes; or He (she) is looking at something which smells bad.
>
> Fear: He (she) is sitting in his (her) house all alone, and there is no one else in the village. There is no knife, axe, or bow and arrow in the house. A wild pig is standing in the door of the house, and the man (woman) is looking at the pig and is very afraid of it. The pig has been standing in the doorway for a few minutes, and the person is looking at it very afraid, and the pig won't move away from the door, and he (she) is afraid the pig will bite him (her).[2]

PICTURES AND EMOTIONS

The six emotions studied were those which had been found by more than one investigator to be discriminable within any one literate culture (cf. Ekman, Friesen, & Ellsworth, in press, for a review of findings). The photographs used to show the facial behavior for each of the six emotions had been judged by more than 70% of the observers in studies of more than one literate culture as showing that emotion. The sample included pictures of both posed and spontaneous behavior used by Ekman

---

[1] Carrol E. Izard brought Dashiell's procedure to our attention. This method has also been used in recent studies of referential communications (e.g., Rosenberg & Gordon, 1968).

[2] The fear story had to be long in order to eliminate possibilities for anger or surprise being associated with the story.

and Friesen (1968), Frijda (1968), Frois-Wittmann (1930), Izard (1968), Engen, Levy, and Schlosberg (1957), and Tomkins and McCarter (1964). A total of 40 pictures were used of 24 different stimulus persons, male and female, adult and child. The photographs were prepared as 3×5 inch prints, cropped to show only the face and neck.

STORY-PHOTOGRAPHS TRIAL

A single item consisted of an emotion story, a correct photograph, in which the facial behavior shown in the photograph was the same as that described in the story, and either one or two incorrect photograph(s). Adult subjects were given two incorrect pictures with each correct picture; children were given only one because of a shortage of copies of the stimuli.

Because of a limitation on the number of available photographs, and upon the subjects' time, not all of the possible pairings of correct and incorrect photographs were tested. Instead, the subjects were presented with some of the presumably more difficult discriminations among emotions. The emotion shown in at least one of the incorrect photographs was an emotion which past studies in literate cultures had found to be most often mistaken for the correct emotion. For example, when *anger* was the emotion described in the story, the incorrect choices included *disgust, fear,* or *sadness,* emotions which have been found to be often mistaken for anger. The age and sex of the stimulus persons shown in the correct and incorrect photographs were held constant within any trial.

No one subject was given all the emotion discriminations, because again the stimuli would have been too few and the task too long. Instead, subjects from different villages were required to make some of the same and some different discriminations. Subjects were shown from 6 to 12 sets of photographs, but no picture appeared in more than 1 of the sets shown to any one particular subject.[3] A subject's task included making at least three different emotion discriminations; the same story was told more than once, with differing correct and incorrect photographs, and often requiring discrimination

among differing sets of emotions. For example, the anger story might have been read once with Anger Picture A, Sadness Picture B, and Fear Picture C; the same anger story might have been read again to the same subject, but now with Anger Picture D, Disgust Picture E, and Surprise Picture F.

PROCEDURE

Two-person teams conducted the experiment. A member of the South Fore tribe recruited subjects, explained the task, and read the translated stories; a Caucasian recorded the subjects' responses. Three such teams operated at once within a village; one team with a male Caucasian worked with male adult subjects; the two others with female Caucasians worked with the female adult subjects and the children. In most instances, almost all members of a village participated in the experiment within less than 3 hours.

Considerable practice and explanation was given to the translators. They were told that there was no correct response and were discouraged from prompting. Repeated practice was given to insure that the translators always repeated the stories in the same way and resisted the temptation to embellish. Spot checks with tape recordings and back translations verified that this was successful. The Caucasians, who did know the correct responses, averted their faces from the view of the subject, looking down at their recording booklet, to reduce the probability of an unwitting experimenter bias effect. Data analysis did not reveal any systematic differences in the responses obtained with different translators.

Results

No differences between male and female subjects were expected, and no such differences had been found in the literate culture data. In this New Guinea group, however, the women were more reluctant to participate in the experiment, and were considered by most outsiders to have had less contact with Caucasians than the men. The number of correct responses for each subject was calculated separately for males and females and for adults and children. The t tests were not significant; the trend was in the direction of better performance by women and girls. The data revealed no systematic differences between male and female subjects in the discrimination of particular emotions, or in relation to the sex of the stimulus person shown on the photographs. In the subsequent analyses, data from males and females were combined.

---

[3] The number of sets of photographs shown varied among villages, because a limited number of photographs were available in this field setting; the need to assure that the three pictures in any one set were comparable (in terms of the configuration of the mouth, the tilt of the head, and the age of the stimulus persons) restricted the number of sets which could be composed for some of the combinations.

TABLE 23.01

	ADULT RESULTS		
EMOTION DESCRIBED IN THE STORY	**EMOTIONS SHOWN IN THE TWO INCORRECT PHOTOGRAPHS**	**NO. Ss**	**% CHOOSING CORRECT FACE**
Happiness	Surprise, disgust	62	90**
	Surprise, sadness	57	93**
	Fear, anger	65	86**
	Disgust, anger	36	100**
Anger	Sadness, surprise	66	82**
	Disgust, surprise	31	87**
	Fear, sadness	31	87**
Sadness	Anger, fear	64	81**
	Anger, surprise	26	81**
	Anger, happiness	31	87**
	Anger, disgust	35	69*
	Disgust, surprise	35	77**
Disgust (smell story)	Sadness, surprise	65	77**
Disgust (dislike story)	Sadness, surprise	36	89**
Surprise	Fear, disgust	31	71*
	Happiness, anger	31	65*
Fear	Anger, disgust	92	64**
	Sadness, disgust	31	87**
	Anger, happiness	35	86**
	Disgust, happiness	26	85**
	Surprise, happiness	65	48
	Surprise, disgust	31	52
	Surprise, sadness	57	28[a]

*p < .05.
**p < .01.
[a]Subjects selected the surprise face (67%) at a significant level (p < .01, two-tailed test).

Table 23.01 shows the results for the least Westernized adults for each emotion discrimination. Within each row, the percentage of subjects who gave the correct response for a particular discrimination between three emotions was calculated across all subjects shown that particular discrimination, regardless of whether the photographs used to represent the three emotions differed for individual subjects. Within each row, each subject contributed only one response, and thus the sum of responses was derived from independent subjects. However, the rows are not independent of each other. Data from a given subject appear in different rows, depending upon the particular discriminations he was asked to make. If a group of subjects was requested to discriminate the same emotion from the same two other emotions more than once, only one randomly chosen response was included in the table.

A binomial test of significance assuming chance performance to be one in three showed that the correct face was chosen at a significant level for all of the discriminations (rows) except that of fear from surprise. Twice, fear was not discriminated from surprise, and once surprise was chosen more often than fear, even though the story had been intended to describe fear. A binomial test assuming chance to be one in two (a more conservative test, justified if it was thought that within a set of three pictures, there may have been one which was obviously wrong) still yielded significant correct choices for all but the fear-from-surprise discriminations.

The results for the most Westernized male adults were almost exactly the same as those reported in Table 23.01 for the least Westernized male and female adults. The number of correct responses for each subject was calculated; the *t* test showed no significant difference between the most and least Westernized subjects. Again, the only failure to select the correct picture occurred when fear was to be distinguished from surprise.

Table 23.02 shows the results for the children, tabulated and tested in similar fashion. The children selected the correct face for all of their discriminations. Through an oversight, the one discrimination which the adults could not make, fear from surprise, was not tried with the children. The percentages reported in Table 23.02 are generally higher than those in Table 23.01, but this is probably due to the fact that the children were given two photographs rather than three, and chance performance would be 50% rather than about 33%. Six- and 7-year-old children were compared with 14- and 15-year-olds, by the same procedures as described for comparing males and females. No significant differences or trends were noted.

Discussion

The results for both adults and children clearly support our hypothesis that particular facial behaviors are universally associated with particular emotions. With but one exception, the faces judged in literate cultures as showing particular emotions were comparably judged by people from a preliterate culture who had minimal opportunity to have learned to recognize uniquely Western facial expressions. Further evidence was obtained in another experiment, in which the facial behavior of these New Guineans was accurately recognized by members of a literate culture. In that study, visually isolated members of the South Fore posed emotions, and college students in the United States accurately judged the emotion intended from their videotaped facial behavior. The evidence from both studies contradicts the view that all facial behavior associated with emotion is culture specific, and that posed facial be-

TABLE 23.02

	RESULTS FOR CHILDREN		
EMOTION DESCRIBED IN THE STORY	EMOTION SHOWN IN THE *ONE* INCORRECT PHOTOGRAPH	NO. Ss	% CHOOSING THE CORRECT FACE
Happiness	Surprise	116	87*
	Sadness	25	96*
	Anger	25	100*
	Disgust	25	88*
Anger	Sadness	69	90*
Sadness	Anger	60	85*
	Surprise	33	76*
	Disgust	27	89*
	Fear	25	76*
Disgust (smell story)	Sadness	19	95*
Disgust (dislike story)	Sadness	27	78*
Surprise	Happiness	14	100*
	Disgust	14	100*
	Fear	19	95*
Fear	Sadness	25	92*
	Anger	25	88*
	Disgust	14	100*

*p ≤ .01.

havior is a unique set of culture-bound conventions not understandable to members of another culture.[4]

The only way to dismiss the evidence from both the judgment and posing studies would be to claim that even these New Guineans who had not seen movies, who did not speak or understand English or Pidgin, who had never worked for a Caucasian, still had *some* contact with Westerners, sufficient contact for them to learn to recognize and simulate culture-specific, uniquely Western facial behaviors associated with each emotion. While these subjects had some contact with Westerners, this argument seems implausible for three reasons. First, the criteria for selecting these subjects makes it highly improbable that they had learned a "foreign" set of facial behaviors to such a degree that they could not only recognize them, but also display them as well as those to whom the behaviors were native. Second, contact with Caucasians did not seem to have much influence on the judgment of emotion, since the most Westernized subjects did no better than the least Westernized and, like the latter, failed to distinguish fear from surprise. Third, the women, who commonly have even less contact with Westerners than the men, did as well in recognizing emotions.

The hypothesis that there are constants across cultures in emotional facial behavior is further supported by Eibl-Eibesfeldt's (1970) films of facial behavior occurring within its natural context in a number of preliterate cultures. Evidence of constants in facial behavior and emotion across cultures is also consistent with early studies which showed many similarities between the facial behavior of blind and sighted children (Fulcher, 1942; Goodenough, 1932; Thompson, 1941). Universals in facial behavior associated with emotion can be explained from a number of nonexclusive viewpoints as being due to evolution, innate neural programs, or learning experiences common to human development regardless of culture (e.g., those of Allport, 1924; Asch, 1952; Darwin, 1872; Huber, 1931; Izard, 1969; Peiper, 1963; Tomkins, 1962, 1963). To evaluate the different viewpoints will require further research, particularly on early development.

The failure of the New Guinean adults to discriminate fear from surprise, while succeeding in discriminating surprise from fear, and fear from other emotions, suggests that cultures may not make *all* of the same distinctions among emotions, but does not detract from the main finding that most of the distinctions were made across cultures. Experience within a culture, the kinds of events which typically elicit particular emotions, may act to influence the ability to discriminate particular pairs of emotions. Fear faces may not have been distinguished from surprise faces, because in this culture fearful events are almost always also surprising; that is, the sudden appearance of a hostile member of another village, the unexpected meeting of a ghost or sorcerer, etc.

The growing body of evidence of a pan-cultural element in emotional facial behavior does not imply the absence of cultural differences in the face and emotion. Ekman (1968) and Ekman and Friesen (1969) have suggested that cultural differences will be manifest in the circumstances which elicit an emotion, in the action consequences of an emotion, and in the display rules which govern the management of facial behavior in particular social settings. Izard (1969) agrees with the view that there are cultural differences in the antecedent and consequent events, and has also found evidence suggesting differences in attitudes about particular emotions.

References

1. Allport, F. H. *Social psychology.* Boston: Houghton Mifflin, 1924.
2. Asch, S. E. *Social psychology.* Englewood Cliffs, N. J.: Prentice-Hall, 1952.
3. Birdwhistell, R. L. The kinesic level in the investigation of the emotions. In P. H. Knapp (Ed.), *Expression of the emotions in man.* New York: International Universities Press, 1963.
4. Darwin, C. *The expression of the emotions in man and animals.* London: Murray, 1872.
5. Dashiell, J. F. A new method of measuring reactions to facial expression of emotion. *Psychological Bulletin,* 1927, **24**, 174–175.
6. Eibl-Eibesfeldt, I. *Ethology, the biology of behavior.* New York: Holt, Rinehart & Winston, 1970.
7. Ekman, P. Research findings on recognition and display of facial behavior in literate and nonliterate cultures. *Proceedings of the 76th Annual Convention of the American Psychological Association,* 1968, **3**, 727. (Summary)
8. Ekman, P., & Friesen, W. V. Nonverbal behavior in psychotherapy research. In J. Shlien (Ed.), *Research in psychotherapy.* Vol. 3. Washington, D. C.: American Psychological Association, 1968.

---

[4] If posed behavior were simply a set of arbitrary conventions, it would be unlikely that the same conventions would be utilized in the cultures discussed here. That does not, however, imply that posed facial behavior is identical with spontaneous behavior. Ekman, Friesen, and Ellsworth (in press) have suggested that most posed behavior is similar in appearance to that spontaneous facial behavior which is of extreme intensity and unmodulated, although it may still differ in onset, duration, and decay time.

9. Ekman, P., & Friesen, W. V. The repertoire of nonverbal behavior—Categories, origins, usage and coding. *Semiotica*, 1969, **1**, 49–98.

10. Ekman, P., Friesen, W. V., & Ellsworth, P. *Emotion in the human face: Guidelines for research and integration of findings.* New York: Pergamon Press, in press.

11. Ekman, P., Friesen, W. V., & Tomkins, S. S. Facial affect scoring technique: A first validity study. *Semiotica*, in press.

12. Ekman, P., Sorenson, E. R., & Friesen, W. V. Pan-cultural elements in facial displays of emotions. *Science*, 1969, **164**, 86–88.

13. Engen, T., Levy, N., & Schlosberg, H. A new series of facial expressions. *American Psychologist*, 1957, **12**, 264–266.

14. Frijda, N. H. Recognition of emotion. In L. Berkowitz (Ed.), *Advances in experimental social psychology.* New York: Academic Press, 1968.

15. Frois-Wittmann, J. The judgment of facial expression. *Journal of Experimental Psychology*, 1930, **13**, 113–151.

16. Fulcher, J. S. "Voluntary" facial expression in blind and seeing children. *Archives of Psychology*, 1942, **38**, 272.

17. Gajdusek, D. C. Kuru. *Transactions of the Royal Society of Tropical Medicine and Hygiene*, 1963, **57**, 151–169.

18. Goodenough, F. L. Expression of the emotions in a blind-deaf child. *Journal of Abnormal and Social Psychology*, 1932, **27**, 328–333.

19. Huber, E. *Evolution of facial musculature and facial expression.* Baltimore: Johns Hopkins Press, 1931.

20. Izard, C. E. Cross-cultural research findings on development in recognition of facial behavior. *Proceedings of the 76th Annual Convention of the American Psychological Association*, 1968, **3**, 727. (Summary)

21. Izard, C. E. The emotions and emotion constructs in personality and culture research. In R. B. Cattell (Ed.), *Handbook of modern personality theory.* Chicago: Aldine Press, 1969.

22. Klineberg, O. Emotional expression in Chinese literature. *Journal of Abnormal and Social Psychology*, 1938, **33**, 517–520.

23. LaBarre, W. The cultural basis of emotions and gestures. *Journal of Personality*, 1947, **16**, 49–68.

24. Peiper, A. *Cerebral function in infancy and childhood.* New York: Consultants Bureau, 1963.

25. Rosenberg, S., & Gordon, A. Identification of facial expressions from affective descriptions: A probabilistic choice analysis of referential ambiguity. *Journal of Personality and Social Psychology*, 1968, **10**, 157–166.

26. Sorenson, E. R., & Gajdusek, D. C. The study of child behavior and development in primitive cultures. A research archive for ethnopediatric film investigations of styles in the patterning of the nervous system. *Pediatrics*, 1966, **37** (1, Pt. 2).

27. Thompson, J. Development of facial expression of emotion in blind and seeing children. *Archives of Psychology*, 1941, **37**, 264.

28. Tomkins, S. S. *Affect, imagery, consciousness.* Vol. 1. *The positive affects.* New York: Springer, 1962.

29. Tomkins, S. S. *Affect, imagery, consciousness.* Vol. 2. *The negative affects.* New York: Springer, 1963.

30. Tomkins, S. S., & McCarter, R. What and where are the primary affects? Some evidence for a theory. *Perceptual and Motor Skills*, 1964, **18**, 119–158.

QUESTIONS FOR REFLECTION AND DISCUSSION:

1. Why is it that studies showing that people in literate cultures link the same concepts of emotion to the same facial expressions do *not* demonstrate the facial expression of many emotions is universal?

2. What facial features are connected with emotions like happiness, sadness, anger, fear, surprise, disgust, and interest?

3. What was the judgment task selected by the researchers? What were its advantages over other methods of connecting emotion with facial expressions?

4. Which emotions did the New Guinean adults fail to discriminate? How would you interpret this "failure"?

5. Why would it be adaptive for the human species for people in various cultures to express the same emotion in the same way?

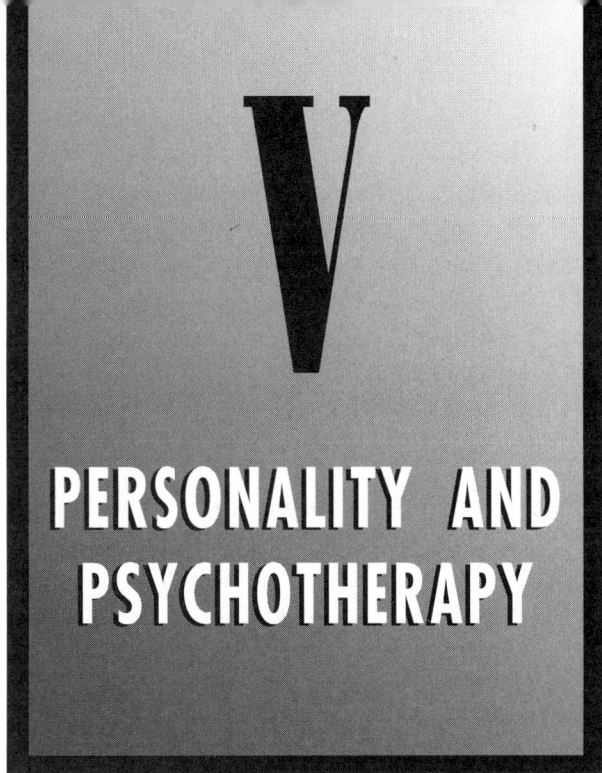

PERSONALITY AND PSYCHOTHERAPY

Personality and psychotherapy are areas of psychology that are usually of high interest to the general public. Personality may be defined as the reasonably stable patterns of emotions, motives, and behavior that distinguish one person from another. Psychologists seek to explain how personality develops and then predict how people with certain personality traits will respond to the demands of life. They also use theories of personality to try to explain the origins of certain psychological problems and disorders, such as anxiety or depression.

Methods of psychotherapy tend to be connected with theories of personality. For example, Sigmund Freud's method of *psychoanalysis* is connected with his personality theory, which goes by the same name. Similarly, Carl Rogers's client-centered therapy is connected with his *self theory* of personality. The following primary sources on personality and psychotherapy are included in this section.

24. Freud, S. (1930/1961). Chapter VII, *Civilization and its discontents*. Trans. by James Strachey. New York: Norton, pp. 70–80.

    Sigmund Freud's psychoanalytic theory sees people as basically selfish and aggressive, and in conflict with social and moral codes and rules. Yet we are unlikely to be conscious of Freud's "truths" about our personalities. Freud's book, *Civilization and its Discontents,* does an excellent job of summarizing his views on people's struggles with civilization and how they come to internalize external rules.

25. Bushman, B. J., Baumeister, R. F., & Stack, A. D. (1999). Catharsis, aggression, and persuasive influence: Self-fulfilling or self-defeating prophecies? *Journal of Personality and Social Psychology, 76*(3), 367–376.157–162.

    Psychoanalytic theory sort of viewed people like tea kettles. When the water is boiling (just like the personality may boil with anger), the lid has to open so some steam can be let off. Otherwise the system will explode. What about people? Does "letting off some steam" (as by watching a prize fight or by insulting someone who is angering us) also prevent us from exploding? The results of this experiment suggest why it is so important that psychology is an *empirical* science.

26. Seligman, M. E. P., & Maier, S. F. (1967). Failure to escape traumatic shock. *Journal of Experimental Psychology, 74,* 1–9.

This experiment with dogs has become a much-cited classic concerning the possible origins of depression in humans. It offers possible insight into why depression may be connected with feelings of hopelessness and helplessness.

27. Richardson, D. C., Bernstein, S., & Taylor, S. P. (1979). The effect of situational contingencies on female retaliative behavior. *Journal of Personality and Social Psychology, 37,* 2044–2048.

Psychologists are concerned about gender differences in personality. For example, it is well known that men are more aggressive than women. The question is whether it is true. This fascinating experiment suggests that women might be less likely than you think to turn the other cheek when they are angry.

28. Ellis, A. (1993). Reflections on rational-emotive therapy. *Journal of Consulting and Clinical Psychology, 61,* 199–201.

Albert Ellis is a towering figure in the field of psychotherapy. He has been a controversial figure because of his R-rated language and his view that it is we, and not unfortunate events, who make ourselves miserable. Here Ellis sets down in his own words some of his basic principles of psychotherapy.

29. Rogers, C. R. (1961). A therapist's view of the good life: The fully functioning person. In *On becoming a person* (pp. 183–196). Boston: Houghton Mifflin.

What should you be like if you have undergone successful psychotherapy? Rogers' answer is that you should be fully functioning. This book chapter by the founder of client-centered therapy explains what that means.

30. Smith, M. L., & Glass, G. V. (1977). Meta-analysis of psychotherapy outcome studies. *American Psychologist, 32,* 752–760.

Psychotherapy sounds wonderful, but let us ask one possibly annoying question: Does it *work*? The answer had been a matter of debate for a generation until meta-analytic studies on the effectiveness of psychotherapy began to appear. This is the study that paved the way.

SOURCE

Freud, S. (1930/1961). Chapter VII,
Civilization and its discontents.
Trans. by James Strachey. New York:
Norton, pp. 70–80. Copyright 1961.

If you ask the general public to name a psychologist, they are most likely to mention the name, "Sigmund Freud." Yet Freud was a medical doctor and not a psychologist. Freud was vitally concerned about bringing scientific methods into the study of the human personality and the formulation of methods of therapy, yet he is widely accused by scientific psychologists of ignoring evidence and creating a world of fantasy rather than reality.

Sigmund Freud (1856–1939) was a mass of contradictions. Some have praised him as the greatest thinker of the 20th century, the most profound of psychologists. Others have considered him overrated, even a "false and faithless prophet." He preached liberal views on sexuality but was himself a model of sexual restraint. He invented a popular form of psychotherapy but experienced lifelong psychologically related problems such as migraine headaches, bowel problems, fainting under stress, hatred of the telephone, and an addiction to cigars. He smoked 20 cigars a day and could not or would not break the habit even after he developed cancer of the jaw.

Freud is said to have seen himself as an outsider. He was born to Jewish parents in a small town in the Austro-Hungarian empire, at a time when Jews were prevented from holding high offices or practicing most professions. His father, a poor merchant, had become a "freethinker." Freud, although he considered himself Jewish, proclaimed himself to be an atheist. He spent nearly all of his adult life in Vienna, fleeing to England to escape the Nazi threat only a year before his death.

Although he was rejected by his fellow students because of his religion, he excelled in medical school at the University of Vienna. His interests lay in neurology and then in psychotherapy. He first practiced hypnotherapy, then developed psychoanalysis, the method that has had such a profound influence in psychology and the arts. He borrowed ideas from others, but his contributions have made him the person that most people think of when asked to name a psychologist.

Freud published Civilization and Its Discontents *late in life, in 1930. The book is highly representative of Freud's ideas because it sums up his views of the conflict between the individual and society. It assumes that people are basically aggressive and that a key function of civilization is to inhibit aggressiveness, to make it possible for people to live together. In the following chapter from Civilization, you will read how people internalize external authority through the development of the superego. The chapter speaks of the power of love and of the "death instinct." It refers to the Oedipus complex—all basic Freudian notions.*

Civilization and its Discontents

SIGMUND FREUD

VII

Why do our relatives, the animals, not exhibit any such cultural struggle? We do not know. Very probably some of them—the bees, the ants, the termites—strove for thousands of years before they arrived at the State institutions, the distribution of functions and the restrictions on the individual, for which we admire them to-day. It is a mark of our present condition that we know from our own feelings that we should not think ourselves happy in any of these animal States or in any of the roles assigned in them to the individual. In the case of other animal species it may be that a temporary balance has been reached between the influences of their environment and the mutually contending instincts within them, and that thus a cessation of development has come about. It may be that in primitive man a fresh access of libido kindled a renewed burst of activity on the part of the destructive instinct. There are a great many questions here to which as yet there is no answer.

Another question concerns us more nearly. What means does civilization employ in order to inhibit the aggressiveness which opposes it, to make it harmless, to get rid of it, perhaps? We have already become acquainted with a few of these methods, but not yet with the one that appears to be the most important. This we can study in the history of the development of the individual. What happens in him to render his desire for aggression innocuous? Something very remarkable, which we should never have guessed and which is nevertheless quite obvious. His aggressiveness is introjected, internalized; it is, in point of fact, sent back to where it came from—that is, it is directed towards his own ego. There it is taken over by a portion of the ego, which sets itself over against the rest of the ego as superego, and which now, in the form of 'conscience', is ready to put into action against the ego the same harsh aggressiveness that the ego would have liked to satisfy upon other, extraneous individuals. The tension between the harsh super-ego and the ego that is subjected to it, is called by us the sense of guilt; it expresses itself as a need for punishment.[1] Civilization, therefore, obtains mastery over the individual's dangerous desire for aggression by weakening and disarming it and by setting up an agency within him to watch over it, like a garrison in a conquered city.

As to the origin of the sense of guilt, the analyst has different views from other psychologists; but even he does not find it easy to give an account of it. To begin with, if we ask how a person comes to have a sense of guilt, we arrive at an answer which cannot be disputed: a person feels guilty (devout people would say 'sinful') when he has done something which he knows to be 'bad'. But then we notice how little this answer tells us. Perhaps, after some hesitation, we shall add that even when a person has not actually *done* the bad thing but has only recognized in himself an *intention* to do it, he may regard himself as guilty; and the question then arises of why the intention is regarded as equal to the deed. Both cases, however, presuppose that one had already recognized that what is bad is reprehensible, is something that must not be carried out. How is this judgment arrived at? We may reject the existence of an original, as it were natural, capacity to distinguish good from bad. What is bad is often not at all what is injurious or dangerous to the ego; on the contrary, it may be something which is desirable and enjoyable to the ego. Here, therefore, there is an extraneous influence at work, and it is this that decides what is to be called good or bad. Since a person's own feelings would not have led him along this path, he must have had a motive for submitting to this extraneous influence. Such a motive is easily discovered in his helplessness and his dependence on other people, and it can best be designated as fear of loss of love. If he loses the love of another person upon whom he is dependent, he also ceases to be protected from a variety of dangers. Above all, he is exposed to the danger that this stronger person will show his superiority in the form of punishment. At the beginning, therefore, what is bad is whatever causes one to be threatened with loss of love. For fear of that loss, one must avoid it. This, too, is the reason why it makes little difference whether one has already done the bad thing or only intends to do it. In either case the danger only sets in if and when the authority discovers it, and in either case the authority would behave in the same way.

This state of mind is called a 'bad conscience'; but actually it does not deserve this name, for at this stage the sense of guilt is clearly only a fear of loss

---

[1] [Cf. 'The Economic Problem of Masochism' (1924c), *Standard Ed.*, **19**, 166–7.]

of love, 'social' anxiety. In small children it can never be anything else, but in many adults, too, it has only changed to the extent that the place of the father or the two parents is taken by the larger human community. Consequently, such people habitually allow themselves to do any bad thing which promises them enjoyment, so long as they are sure that the authority will not know anything about it or cannot blame them for it; they are afraid only of being found out.[2] Present-day society has to reckon in general with this state of mind.

A great change takes place only when the authority is internalized through the establishment of a super-ego. The phenomena of conscience then reach a higher stage. Actually, it is not until now that we should speak of conscience or a sense of guilt.[3] At this point, too, the fear of being found out comes to an end; the distinction, moreover, between doing something bad and wishing to do it disappears entirely, since nothing can be hidden from the super-ego, not even thoughts. It is true that the seriousness of the situation from a real point of view has passed away, for the new authority, the super-ego, has no motive that we know of for ill-treating the ego, with which it is intimately bound up; but genetic influence, which leads to the survival of what is past and has been surmounted, makes itself felt in the fact that fundamentally things remain as they were at the beginning. The super-ego torments the sinful ego with the same feeling of anxiety and is on the watch for opportunities of getting it punished by the external world.

At this second stage of development, the conscience exhibits a peculiarity which was absent from the first stage and which is no longer easy to account for.[4] For the more virtuous a man is, the more severe and distrustful is its behaviour, so that ultimately it is precisely those people who have carried saintliness[5] furthest who reproach themselves with the worst sinfulness. This means that virtue forfeits some part of its promised reward; the docile and continent ego does not enjoy the trust of its mentor, and strives in vain, it would seem, to acquire it. The objection will at once be made that these difficulties are artificial ones, and it will be said that a stricter and more vigilant conscience is precisely the hallmark of a moral man. Moreover, when saints call themselves sinners, they are not so wrong, considering the temptations to instinctual satisfaction to which they are exposed in a specially high degree — since, as is well known, temptations are merely increased by constant frustration, whereas an occasional satisfaction of them causes them to diminish, at least for the time being. The field of ethics, which is so full of problems, presents us with another fact: namely that ill-luck — that is, external frustration — so greatly enhances the power of the conscience in the super-ego. As long as things go well with a man, his conscience is lenient and lets the ego do all sorts of things; but when misfortune befalls him, he searches his soul, acknowledges his sinfulness, heightens the demands of his conscience, imposes abstinences on himself and punishes himself with penances.[6] Whole peoples have behaved in this way, and still do. This, however, is easily explained by the original infantile stage of conscience, which, as we see, is not given up after the introjection into the super-ego, but persists alongside of it and behind it. Fate is regarded as a substitute for the parental agency. If a man is unfortunate it means that he is no longer loved by this highest power; and, threatened by such a loss of love, he once more bows to the parental representative in his super-ego — a representative whom, in his days of good fortune, he was ready to neglect. This becomes especially clear where Fate is looked upon in the strictly religious

---

[2] This reminds one of Rousseau's famous mandarin. [The problem raised by Rousseau had been quoted in full in Freud's paper on 'Our Attitude towards Death' (1915b), *Standard Ed.*, **14**, 298.]

[3] Everyone of discernment will understand and take into account the fact that in this summary description we have sharply delimited events which in reality occur by gradual transitions, and that it is not merely a question of the *existence* of a super-ego but of its relative strength and sphere of influence. All that has been said above about conscience and guilt is, moreover, common knowledge and almost undisputed.

[4] [This paradox had been discussed by Freud earlier. See, for instance, Chapter V of *The Ego and the Id* (1923b), *Standard Ed.*, **19**, 54, where other references are given.]

[5] ['*Heiligkeit.*' The same term, used in the different sense of 'sacredness', is discussed by Freud in some other passages. Cf. the paper on 'civilized' sexual morality (1908d), *Standard Ed.*, **9**, 187.]

[6] This enhancing of morality as a consequence of ill-luck has been illustrated by Mark Twain in a delightful little story, *The First Melon I ever Stole*. This first melon happened to be unripe. I heard Mark Twain tell the story himself in one of his public readings. After he had given out the title, he stopped and asked himself as though he was in doubt: '*Was* it the first?' With this, everything had been said. The first melon was evidently not the only one. [This last sentence was added in 1931. — In a letter to Fliess of February 9th, 1898, Freud reported that he had attended a reading by Mark Twain a few days earlier. (Freud, 1950a, Letter 83.)]

sense of being nothing else than an expression of the Divine Will. The people of Israel had believed themselves to be the favourite child of God, and when the great Father caused misfortune after misfortune to rain down upon this people of his, they were never shaken in their belief in his relationship to them or questioned his power or righteousness. Instead, they produced the prophets, who held up their sinfulness before them; and out of their sense of guilt they created the over-strict commandments of their priestly religion.[7] It is remarkable how differently a primitive man behaves. If he has met with a misfortune, he does not throw the blame on himself but on his fetish, which has obviously not done its duty, and he gives it a thrashing instead of punishing himself.

Thus we know of two origins of the sense of guilt: one arising from fear of an authority, and the other, later on, arising from fear of the super-ego. The first insists upon a renunciation of instinctual satisfactions; the second, as well as doing this, presses for punishment, since the continuance of the forbidden wishes cannot be concealed from the super-ego. We have also learned how the severity of the super-ego—the demands of conscience—is to be understood. It is simply a continuation of the severity of the external authority, to which it has succeeded and which it has in part replaced. We now see in what relationship the renunciation of instinct stands to the sense of guilt. Originally, renunciation of instinct was the result of fear of an external authority: one renounced one's satisfactions in order not to lose its love. If one has carried out this renunciation, one is, as it were, quits with the authority and no sense of guilt should remain. But with fear of the super-ego the case is different. Here, instinctual renunciation is not enough, for the wish persists and cannot be concealed from the super-ego. Thus, in spite of the renunciation that has been made, a sense of guilt comes about. This constitutes a great economic disadvantage in the erection of a super-ego, or, as we may put it, in the formation of a conscience. Instinctual renunciation now no longer has a completely liberating effect; virtuous continence is no longer rewarded with the assurance of love. A threatened external unhappiness—loss of love and punishment on the part of the external authority—has been exchanged for a permanent internal unhappiness, for the tension of the sense of guilt.

These interrelations are so complicated and at the same time so important that, at the risk of repeating myself, I shall approach them from yet another angle. The chronological sequence, then, would be as follows. First comes renunciation of instinct owing to fear of aggression by the *external* authority. (This is, of course, what fear of the loss of love amounts to, for love is a protection against this punitive aggression.) After that comes the erection of an *internal* authority, and renunciation of instinct owing to fear of it—owing to fear of conscience.[8] In this second situation bad intentions are equated with bad actions, and hence come a sense of guilt and a need for punishment. The aggressiveness of conscience keeps up the aggressiveness of the authority. So far things have no doubt been made clear; but where does this leave room for the reinforcing influence of misfortune (of renunciation imposed from without) [p. 73], and for the extraordinary severity of conscience in the best and most tractable people [p. 72 f.]? We have already explained both these peculiarities of conscience, but we probably still have an impression that those explanations do not go to the bottom of the matter, and leave a residue still unexplained. And here at last an idea comes in which belongs entirely to psychoanalysis and which is foreign to people's ordinary way of thinking. This idea is of a sort which enables us to understand why the subject-matter was bound to seem so confused and obscure to us. For it tells us that conscience (or more correctly, the anxiety which later becomes conscience) is indeed the cause of instinctual renunciation to begin with, but that later the relationship is reversed. Every renunciation of instinct now becomes a dynamic source of conscience and every fresh renunciation increases the latter's severity and intolerance. If we could only bring it better into harmony with what we already know about the history of the origin of conscience, we should be tempted to defend the paradoxical statement that conscience is the result of instinctual renunciation, or that instinctual renunciation (imposed on us from without) creates conscience, which then demands further instinctual renunciation.

The contradiction between this statement and what we have previously said about the genesis of conscience is in point of fact not so very great, and we see a way of further reducing it. In order to make our exposition easier, let us take as our example the aggressive instinct, and let us assume that

----

[7] [A very much more extended account of the relations of the people of Israel to their God is to be found in Freud's *Moses and Monotheism* (1939a).]

[8] ['*Gewissensangst.*' Some remarks on this term will be found in an Editor's footnote to Chapter VII of *Inhibitions, Symptoms and Anxiety* (1926d), *Standard Ed.*, **20**, 128.]

the renunciation in question is always a renunciation of aggression. (This, of course, is only to be taken as a temporary assumption.) The effect of instinctual renunciation on the conscience then is that every piece of aggression whose satisfaction the subject gives up is taken over by the super-ego and increases the latter's aggressiveness (against the ego). This does not harmonize well with the view that the original aggressiveness of conscience is a continuance of the severity of the external authority and therefore has nothing to do with renunciation. But the discrepancy is removed if we postulate a different derivation for this first instalment of the super-ego's aggressivity. A considerable amount of aggressiveness must be developed in the child against the authority which prevents him from having his first, but none the less his most important, satisfactions, whatever the kind of instinctual deprivation that is demanded of him may be; but he is obliged to renounce the satisfaction of this revengeful aggressiveness. He finds his way out of this economically difficult situation with the help of familiar mechanisms. By means of identification he takes the unattackable authority into himself. The authority now turns into his super-ego and enters into possession of all the aggressiveness which a child would have liked to exercise against it. The child's ego has to content itself with the unhappy role of the authority—the father—who has been thus degraded. Here, as so often, the [real] situation is reversed: 'If I were the father and you were the child, I should treat you badly.' The relationship between the super-ego and the ego is a return, distorted by a wish, of the real relationships between the ego, as yet undivided, and an external object. That is typical, too. But the essential difference is that the original severity of the super-ego does not—or does not so much—represent the severity which one has experienced from it [the object], or which one attributes to it; it represents rather one's own aggressiveness towards it. If this is correct, we may assert truly that in the beginning conscience arises through the suppression of an aggressive impulse, and that it is subsequently reinforced by fresh suppressions of the same kind.

Which of these two views is correct? The earlier one, which genetically seemed so unassailable, or the newer one, which rounds off the theory in such a welcome fashion? Clearly, and by the evidence, too, of direct observations, both are justified. They do not contradict each other, and they even coincide at one point, for the child's revengeful aggressiveness will be in part determined by the amount of punitive aggression which he expects from his father. Experience shows, however, that the severity of the super-ego which a child develops in no way corresponds to the severity of treatment which he has himself met with.[9] The severity of the former seems to be independent of that of the latter. A child who has been very leniently brought up can acquire a very strict conscience. But it would also be wrong to exaggerate this independence; it is not difficult to convince oneself that severity of upbringing does also exert a strong influence on the formation of the child's super-ego. What it amounts to is that in the formation of the super-ego and the emergence of a conscience innate constitutional factors and influences from the real environment act in combination. This is not at all surprising; on the contrary, it is a universal aetiological condition for all such processes.[10]

It can also be asserted that when a child reacts to his first great instinctual frustrations with excessively strong aggressiveness and with a correspondingly severe super-ego, he is following a phylogenetic model and is going beyond the response that would be currently justified; for the father of prehistoric times was undoubtedly terrible, and an extreme amount of aggressiveness may be attributed to him. Thus, if one shifts over from individual to phylogenetic development, the differences between the two theories of the genesis of conscience are still further diminished. On the other hand, a new and important difference makes its appearance between these two developmental processes. We cannot get away from the assumption that man's sense of guilt springs from the Oedipus complex and was acquired at the killing of the father by the brothers banded together.[11] On that occasion an act of aggression was not suppressed but carried out; but it was the same act of aggression

---

[9] As has rightly been emphasized by Melanie Klein and by other, English, writers.

[10] The two main types of pathogenic methods of upbringing—overstrictness and spoiling—have been accurately assessed by Franz Alexander in his book, *The Psychoanalysis of the Total Personality* (1927) in connection with Aichhorn's study of delinquency [*Wayward Youth*, 1925]. The 'unduly lenient and indulgent father' is the cause of children's forming an over-severe super-ego, because, under the impression of the love that they receive, they have no other outlet for their aggressiveness but turning it inwards. In delinquent children, who have been brought up without love, the tension between ego and super-ego is lacking, and the whole of their aggressiveness can be directed outwards. Apart from a constitutional factor which may be supposed to be present, it can be said, therefore, that a severe conscience arises from the joint operation of two factors: the frustration of instinct, which unleashes aggressiveness, and the experience of being loved, which turns the aggressiveness inwards and hands it over to the super-ego.

[11] [*Totem and Taboo* (1912–13), *Standard Ed.*, **13**, 143.]

whose suppression in the child is supposed to be the source of his sense of guilt. At this point I should not be surprised if the reader were to exclaim angrily: 'So it makes no difference whether one kills one's father or not—one gets a feeling of guilt in either case! We may take leave to raise a few doubts here. Either it is not true that the sense of guilt comes from suppressed aggressiveness, or else the whole story of the killing of the father is a fiction and the children of primaeval man did not kill their fathers any more often than children do nowadays. Besides, if it is not fiction but a plausible piece of history, it would be a case of something happening which everyone expects to happen—namely, of a person feeling guilty because he really has done something which cannot be justified. And of this event, which is after all an everyday occurrence, psycho-analysis has not yet given any explanation.'

That is true, and we must make good the omission. Nor is there any great secret about the matter. When one has a sense of guilt after having committed a misdeed, and because of it, the feeling should more properly be called *remorse*. It relates only to a deed that has been done, and, of course, it presupposes that a *conscience*—the readiness to feel guilty—was already in existence before the deed took place. Remorse of this sort can, therefore, never help us to discover the origin of conscience and of the sense of guilt in general. What happens in these everyday cases is usually this: an instinctual need acquires the strength to achieve satisfaction in spite of the conscience, which is, after all, limited in its strength; and with the natural weakening of the need owing to its having been satisfied, the former balance of power is restored. Psycho-analysis is thus justified in excluding from the present discussion the case of a sense of guilt due to remorse, however frequently such cases occur and however great their practical importance.

But if the human sense of guilt goes back to the killing of the primal father, that was after all a case of 'remorse.' Are we to assume that [at that time] a conscience and a sense of guilt were not, as we have presupposed, in existence before the deed? If not, where, in this case, did the remorse come from? There is no doubt that this case should explain the secret of the sense of guilt to us and put an end to our difficulties. And I believe it does. This remorse was the result of the primordial ambivalence of feeling towards the father. His sons hated him, but they loved him, too. After their hatred had been satisfied by their act of aggression, their love came to the fore in their remorse for the deed. It set up the super-ego by identification with the father; it gave that agency the father's power, as though as a punishment for the deed of aggression they had carried out against him, and it created the restrictions which were intended to pre-

vent a repetition of the deed. And since the inclination to aggressiveness against the father was repeated in the following generations, the sense of guilt, too, persisted, and it was reinforced once more by every piece of aggressiveness that was suppressed and carried over to the super-ego. Now, I think, we can at last grasp two things perfectly clearly: the part played by love in the origin of conscience and the fatal inevitability of the sense of guilt. Whether one has killed one's father or has abstained from doing so is not really the decisive thing. One is bound to feel guilty in either case, for the sense of guilt is an expression of the conflict due to ambivalence, of the eternal struggle between Eros and the instinct of destruction or death. This conflict is set going as soon as men are faced with the task of living together. So long as the community assumes no other form than that of the family, the conflict is bound to express itself in the Oedipus complex, to establish the conscience and to create the first sense of guilt. When an attempt is made to widen the community, the same conflict is continued in forms which are dependent on the past; and it is strengthened and results in a further intensification of the sense of guilt. Since civilization obeys an internal erotic impulsion which causes human beings to unite in a closely-knit group, it can only achieve this aim through an ever-increasing reinforcement of the sense of guilt. What began in relation to the father is completed in relation to the group. If civilization is a necessary course of development from the family to humanity as a whole, then—as a result of the inborn conflict arising from ambivalence, of the eternal struggle between the trends of love and death—there is inextricably bound up with it an increase of the sense of guilt, which will perhaps reach heights that the individual finds hard to tolerate. One is reminded of the great poet's moving arraignment of the 'Heavenly Powers':—

Ihr führt in's Leben uns hinein.
Ihr lasst den Armen schuldig werden,
Dann überlasst Ihr ihn den Pein,
Denn jede Schuld rächt sich auf Erden.[12]

---

[12] One of the Harp-player's songs in Goethe's *Wilhelm Meister*.
[*To earth, this weary earth, ye bring us*
To guilt ye let us heedless go,
Then leave repentance fierce to wring us:
A moment's guilt, an age of woe!

CARLYLE'S TRANSLATION.

The first couplet appears as an association to a dream in Freud's short book *On Dreams* (1901*a*), *Standard Ed.*, **5**, 637 and 639.]

And we may well heave a sigh of relief at the thought that it is nevertheless vouchsafed to a few to salvage without effort from the whirlpool of their own feelings the deepest truths, towards which the rest of us have to find our way through tormenting uncertainty and with restless groping.

QUESTIONS FOR REFLECTION AND DISCUSSION:

1. Does Freud seem to think of people as basically rational or irrational? Why?

2. Why, within Freud's theory, will people feel "discontent" within civilization? What is the source of the discontent?

3. What does Freud mean by the terms "conscience" and "guilt"? How do these develop in the individual?

4. Freud has been accused of arguing that men are more moral than women (even though the research literature suggests that women are more likely to refrain from criminal behavior because of feelings of guilt, whereas men are more likely to refrain because of fear of punishment). What is there is this reading that may explain why Freud held this view?

5. What are the ambivalent feelings that sons are theorized to have toward their fathers?

6. What does Freud say about religion? What role may religion play in his views of the psychological development of the individual?

7. Why would scientific psychologists take issue with Freud's views as they are expressed in *Civilization and its Discontents*?

8. Why do you think that some psychologists say that Freud's place in psychology is only historic? Why do you think that some psychologists go so far as to argue that Freud should not even be mentioned in a course in psychology? What do you think? Explain.

SOURCE

Bushman, B. J., Baumeister, R. F., &
Stack, A. D. (1999). Catharsis,
aggression, and persuasive influence:
Self-fulfilling or self-defeating
prophecies? *Journal of Personality
and Social Psychology, 76*(3),
367–376. 157–162. Copyright
1999 by the American Psychological
Association. Reprinted with
permission.

It is common knowledge that expressing or "ventilating" some feelings of anger helps prevent a greater outburst. Expressing or purging such feelings is known as catharsis. The Greek philosopher Aristotle wrote that catharsis, or emotional release, was responsible for the audience's deep emotional reaction to tragedies on stage. Many observers argue today that watching prize fights or pro football or pro wrestling helps viewers release their own feelings of anger. In the popular film "Analyze This," a psychiatrist (played by Billy Crystal) urges a mobster (Robert DiNiro) to hit a pillow when he is frustrated because he cannot or should not kill another mobster.

As pointed out by Brad Bushman and his colleagues (1999), in the following primary source, Sigmund Freud's psychoanalytic theory is consistent with Aristotle's philosophizing. Freud adopted a so-called hydraulic model of human personality. Freud believed that feelings of frustration and anger could build up in the personality in the same way that pressure builds up in a steam engine when water is heated. The engine must be able to ventilate excess steam, or else it will explode. Thus those who adhere to the catharsis hypothesis believe that people must be able to ventilate some of their feelings of frustration and anger if they are not to "explode"—either through maladaptive behavior, such as physical aggression, or through the development of serious psychological symptoms.

Such common knowledge cannot be wrong, can it? Can common knowledge be common ignorance? Perhaps it can. In "Catharsis, Aggression, and Persuasive Influence," Brad Bushman and his colleagues report experimental evidence that is not in keeping with the catharsis hypothesis. As you read, keep in mind that ANOVA stands for analysis of variance, which is a statistical technique that assesses whether group differences are statistically significant. Also, in order for group differences to be considered statistically significant, the probability that the differences are due to chance fluctuation should be smaller than 5% (i.e., $p < .05$).

Catharsis, Aggression, and Persuasive Influence: Self-Fulfilling or Self-Defeating Prophecies?

BRAD J. BUSHMAN
IOWA STATE UNIVERSITY

ROY F. BAUMEISTER
CASE WESTERN RESERVE UNIVERSITY

ANGELA D. STACK
IOWA STATE UNIVERSITY

Does media endorsement for catharsis produce a self-fulfilling or a self-defeating prophecy? In Study 1, participants who read a procatharsis message (claiming that aggressive action is a good way to relax and reduce anger) subsequently expressed a greater desire to hit a punching bag than did participants who read an anticatharsis message. In

Study 2, participants read the same messages and then actually did hit a punching bag. This exercise was followed by an opportunity to engage in laboratory aggression. Contrary to the catharsis hypothesis and to the self-fulfilling prophecy prediction, people who read the procatharsis message and then hit the punching bag were subsequently more aggressive than were people who read the anticatharsis message.

Punch a pillow or a punching bag. And while you do it, yell and curse and moan and holler. . . . Punch with all the frenzy you can. If you are angry at a particular person, imagine his or her face on the pillow or punching bag, and vent your rage physically and verbally. You will be doing violence to a pillow or punching bag so that you can stop doing violence to yourself by holding in poisonous anger. You are not hitting a person. You are hitting the ghost of that person—a ghost from the past, a ghost alive in you that must be exorcised in a concrete, physical way.

—JOHN LEE, *FACING THE FIRE: EXPRESSING AND EXPERIENCING ANGER APPROPRIATELY*

One of television's greatest contributions is that it brought murder back into the home where it belongs. Seeing a murder on television can be good therapy. It can help work off one's antagonism.

—ALFRED HITCHCOCK

When angry count four; when very angry, swear.

—MARK TWAIN

Popular belief in the catharsis theory remains strong despite the theory's dismal record in research findings. According to the catharsis hypothesis, acting aggressively or even viewing aggression is an effective way to reduce anger and aggressive feelings. One likely reason for the continued widespread belief in catharsis is that the mass media continue to endorse the view that expressing anger or aggressive feelings is healthy, constructive, and relaxing, whereas restraining oneself creates internal tension that is unhealthy and bound to lead to an eventual blowup.

The present research was concerned with a pair of related questions. First, can media support for the catharsis hypothesis cause people to engage in catharsis-seeking activities, such as aggressive ac-

tion? Second, if media messages do persuade people to believe in the effectiveness of catharsis, will their own indulgence in aggressive action produce that effect?

The concept of a self-fulfilling prophecy suggests that people's beliefs can shape their choices and the outcomes of their actions, so that expectations tend to come true by virtue of the changed behaviors resulting directly from the expectations (e.g., Darley & Fazio, 1980). Although researchers have mostly failed to find laboratory evidence of catharsis effects, it is plausible that media endorsement produces such self-fulfilling prophecies, which in turn might be sufficient to sustain popular belief in catharsis. In the present research, we provided people with procatharsis messages telling them that acting aggressively or expressing anger is a good way to reduce inner tensions. Consistent with the self-fulfilling prophecy notion, we investigated whether such messages would increase behavioral choices of aggressive activity following an anger provocation (Study 1) and, more important, would help produce the anticipated benefits of expressing anger (Study 2)—specifically, by reducing aggressive behavior toward another person after the participant was supposedly able to reach catharsis by hitting a punching bag.

Catharsis: Theory and Evidence

The first recorded mention of catharsis occurred over a thousand years ago, in Aristotle's *Poetics*. Aristotle taught that viewing tragic plays gave people emotional catharsis from feelings of fear and pity. This emotional cleansing was believed to be beneficial to both the individual and society. The notion of catharsis was revived by Freud (Wegman, 1985), who believed that repressed emotions could build up in an individual and cause psychological symptoms, such as hysteria or phobias. Freud's therapeutic ideas on emotional catharsis became part of the hydraulic model of anger, which is the basis of the modern theory of anger catharsis (Geen & Quanty, 1977). The hydraulic model suggests that frustrations lead to anger, and that anger, in turn, builds up inside an individual like hydraulic pressure inside a closed environment until it is released in some way.

In general, empirical findings have been inconsistent with the catharsis hypothesis (see reviews by Geen & Quanty, 1977, and Warren & Kurlychek, 1981). Tavris (1988) concluded that "it is time to put a bullet, once and for all, through heart of the catharsis hypothesis. The belief that observing violence (or 'ventilating it') gets rid of hostilities has virtually never been supported by research" (p. 194). Because activities considered to be cathartic also are aggressive, they could lead to the activation of other aggressive thoughts, emotions, and behavioral tendencies, which in turn could lead to greater anger and aggression (Berkowitz, 1984; Tice & Baumeister, 1993).

Catharsis in the Popular Press

False popular belief that there is scientific justification for the catharsis hypothesis makes the hypothesis durable and resistant to change. Unfortunately, few laypeople are likely to consult scientific journal articles to find out if there is empirical evidence to support catharsis. Instead, they consult the popular press, which often reports that catharsis is valid. The pervasiveness of false beliefs about catharsis makes them potentially harmful. People expect that performing cathartic activities will reduce their anger and aggression, when cathartic activities are actually more likely to have the opposite effect (Geen & Quanty, 1977; Warren & Kurlychek, 1981). The quotations with which we began this article illustrate such misinformed views.

Fortunately, most media endorsements of catharsis stop short of advocating that people physically attack those at whom they are angry. The mass media recommend an assortment of ways of satisfying angry impulses without physically causing harm. One popular approach is to suggest displacing aggression away from its human targets and onto inanimate objects. For example, one self-help book recommended that angry people twist a towel, punch a pillow, wallop a punching bag, hit a couch with a plastic baseball bat, throw rocks, or break glass to reduce pent-up anger (Lee, 1995).

Self-Fulfilling and Self-Defeating Prophecies

The current situation may therefore be as follows. The scientific community has largely disconfirmed and abandoned catharsis theory and, if anything, is looking to understand why the opposite effect occurs (i.e., venting anger leads to higher subsequent aggression). Meanwhile, the popular mass media continue to suggest that catharsis theory is true and has scientific support, so the message reaching the general public is that catharsis is an effective, desirable way of handling angry impulses.

Two possible scenarios could follow from the popular belief in a scientifically unsound hypothe-

sis. One is that of self-fulfilling prophecy: People would be persuaded that catharsis effects are real and effective and would act on these beliefs. When angry, they would believe that the best response would be to express this anger, possibly against a surrogate (displaced) target. These beliefs might actually help them perceive beneficial effects that have eluded laboratory researchers. That is, the expectation that catharsis relaxes the person and reduces subsequent aggression might cause people to feel relaxed and to behave less aggressively after they indulge in some form of anger expression.

However, an alternative, darker scenario might be proposed if the self-fulfilling prophecy effect is weaker than the aggression-enhancing effects of expressing anger. In this view, belief in catharsis could cause people to choose to express anger, but these actions would increase, rather than decrease, their feelings of anger and their aggressive inclinations. As a result, people would end up behaving more aggressively than they would have otherwise. The media endorsement of catharsis would thus have the potential for increasing violence through a self-*defeating* prophecy effect: The expectation elicits behavior that produces results opposite of what was expected.

The present investigation was concerned with how people are affected by media messages supporting (vs. questioning) catharsis. Study 1 examined whether people can be persuaded by such messages to choose expressive ways of dealing with anger. Specifically, we hypothesized that exposure to a message advocating catharsis would induce people to choose to hit a punching bag when angry.

Study 2 examined the consequences of this choice. Participants saw a procatharsis message, an anticatharsis message, or a message unrelated to catharsis. Then, all participants were induced to hit the punching bag. Following this, they had the opportunity to aggress against someone who had provoked and angered them—or, in some cases, toward an innocent third person. If the self-fulfilling prophecy effect prevailed, then people who read the procatharsis message would be less aggressive interpersonally after they had "blown off steam" by hitting the punching bag. (One would hope that they would not aggress against the innocent third person in either case.) This would suggest that the popular belief in catharsis may be sustained by self-fulfilling prophecies engendered by the media advocacy of catharsis.

Alternatively, if the self-defeating-prophecy hypothesis is correct, then hitting the punching bag might increase subsequent aggression. In many ways, this would be the worst possible outcome. It would suggest that media endorsements of catharsis can persuade people to choose to express their angry, aggressive feelings toward supposedly safe, non-human targets. However, those actions end up increasing aggressive tendencies, which can result in even higher aggression toward a human target.

Study 1

In Study 1, we tested the first part of the expectancy hypothesis in a persuasion format. If the media advise people that catharsis is a good way to handle anger and achieve a desirable state of relaxation, would people then in fact be more likely to choose cathartic activities? If media messages have self-fulfilling prophecy effects, then procatharsis messages should increase participants' preference for aggressive activities.

In Study 1, the aggressive activity took the form of hitting a punching bag. As noted above, various mass media sources advise people to express aggression toward inanimate objects. These sources say that when people are angry at someone, it would be socially desirable for them to satisfy their aggressive impulses by attacking suitable inanimate objects (such as a pillow or punching bag) instead of directly attacking the (human) target of their anger.

Although we favored the straightforward prediction that procatharsis messages would cause an increase in participants' desire to hit the punching bag, there were reasons to doubt that this would happen. Research has not consistently found displacement to be an effective defense mechanism against aggression (see Baumeister, Dale, & Sommer, 1998, for review), especially if one distinguishes displaced aggression from the simple carry-over of arousal from one situation to another (as in excitation transfer; Zillmann, 1979). Our own prior work failed to find that people chose to displace aggression toward an alternative human target, even among highly aggressive narcissists who were provoked by an esteem threat (Bushman & Baumeister, 1998). Therefore, we felt it was necessary to verify that media messages could induce people to seek catharsis through displaced aggression.

METHOD

Catharsis Messages A separate sample of 100 undergraduate students (50 men and 50 women) enrolled in introductory psychology courses was used to judge the catharsis messages. The judges were drawn from the same population as those who would later participate in the experiment proper. Judges were randomly assigned to read either a pro- or an anticatharsis message, which was constructed to look like a newspaper article. The headline for the procatharsis article was "Research Shows That Hitting Inanimate Objects Is an Effective Way to Vent Anger." In the anticatharsis article, the word "Effective" was replaced with "Ineffective." The procatharsis article purported to describe findings from a 2-year study, recently published in *Science* by a Harvard psychologist, showing that people who were instructed to vent their anger by hitting a punching bag were less aggressive afterward toward other people. The anticatharsis article (which was the same as the text of the procatharsis article but with key words changed) reported opposite findings. The full text of the articles is presented in the Appendix.

Judges rated how credible and authoritative they thought the article was. The procatharsis article was judged to be as authoritative ($M = 5.92$) and credible ($M = 5.63$) as the anticatharsis article ($Ms = 6.00$ and 5.65, respectively). Neither difference approached significance (both $ts < 1$, $ps > .05$). All mean ratings were above the scale midpoint.

Procedure Participants were 360 undergraduate students (180 men and 180 women) enrolled in introductory psychology courses. Students received extra class credit in exchange for their voluntary participation. They were tested individually in the laboratory session, but each was led to believe that he or she would be interacting with someone of the same sex. They were told that the researchers were studying how accurate people's perceptions of others were in different types of interactions. After giving informed consent, participants were randomly assigned to message conditions (i.e., procatharsis, anticatharsis, or control). The control message was a newspaper article unrelated to catharsis. To eliminate suspicion about any connection between the article and the activities to be chosen later in the experiment, participants drew a number from a bag to determine which article they would read. Participants were told that they would discuss the article with the other participant later in the experiment.

Next, each participant wrote a one-paragraph essay on abortion, either pro-choice or pro-life (whichever the participant preferred). After finishing, the participant's essay was taken away to be shown to the other participant (who was, in fact, nonexistent) for evaluation. Meanwhile, the participant was permitted to evaluate the partner's essay, which by random assignment was either a pro-choice or a pro-life essay.

A short time later, the experimenter brought back the participant's own essay with comments ostensibly made by the other participant. These comments constituted the experimental manipulation of anger. By the flip of a coin, half the participants were assigned to the anger condition, and they received bad evaluations consisting of negative ratings on organization, originality, writing style, clarity of expression, persuasiveness of arguments, and overall quality. There was also a handwritten comment stating "This is one of the worst essays I have read!" The other participants received favorable, positive evaluations, consisting of high (positive) numerical ratings and a written comment stating "No suggestions, great essay!" This anger manipulation has been validated in previous research that showed people reported feeling significantly more angry after receiving the negative evaluation than before, $t(9) = 4.00$, $p < .05$, $d = 1.27$, and more angry than those who received the favorable evaluation, $t(18) = 2.21$, $p < .05$, $d = 0.99$ (Bushman & Baumeister, 1998).

After reading the evaluation, the participant ranked a list of 10 activities in the order of his or her preference for doing them later in the experiment. Included in this list of activities was "hitting a punching bag." Some other activities on the list included playing solitaire, reading a short story, watching a comedy, and playing a computer game. After ranking the activities, the study was terminated, and the experimenter probed to see whether the participant was suspicious about the study. Three participants indicated that they were suspicious, but stated that their suspicion had not changed their responses. In addition, these three participants did not correctly guess the true purpose of the study, and excluding their data did not change the results. Hence, all data were included in the analyses. Last, the participant was fully debriefed.

RESULTS

For clarity, we reverse scored the rankings assigned to the punching bag activity, so that higher numbers would reflect higher aggressive intent. The scores were also standardized. A 3 (article: procatharsis, anticatharsis, control) × 2 (angered vs. not angered) × 2 (participant sex) analysis of variance (ANOVA) was used to analyze these data.[1]

Although the simple interaction between article condition and anger was nonsignificant, $F(2, 348) = 1.49$, $p > .05$, planned contrasts were performed to test the effects of article condition on punching bag

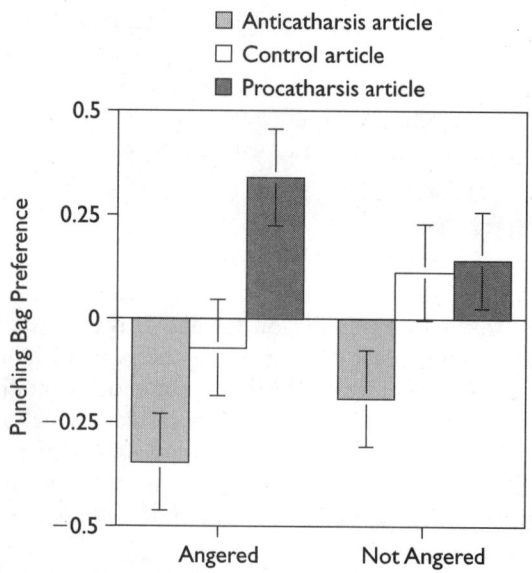

FIGURE 25.01

Preference for hitting a punching bag as a function of anger and article condition. Preferences are standardized scores. Capped vertical bars denote 1 standard error.

preferences among angered participants. As expected, the content of the article had a significant effect on angered participants, $F(2, 348) = 7.91$, $p < .05$. Angered participants who read the procatharsis article wanted to hit the punching bag more than did angered participants who read either the anticatharsis article or the article unrelated to catharsis, $t(348) = 3.91$, $p < .05$, $d = 0.69$, and $t(348) = 2.33$, $p < .05$, $d = 0.42$, respectively (see Figure 25.01). There was no difference between the control and anticatharsis groups, $t(348) = 1.58$, $p > .05$. Among participants who were not angered, there was no effect of the content of the article they read, at least not in terms of producing any differential desire to hit the punching bag, $F(2, 348) = 2.32$, $p > .05$.

There was also a significant main effect for article condition, $F(2, 348) = 8.58$, $p < .05$. Participants who read the anticatharsis article wanted to hit the punching bag less than did participants who read either the procatharsis article or the article unrelated to catharsis, $t(348) = 4.12$, $p < .05$, $d = 0.44$, and $t(348) = 2.39$, $p < .05$, $d = 0.26$, respectively. There was no difference between the latter two groups, $t(348) = 1.73$, $p > .05$, $d = 0.19$. Also, men wanted to hit the punching bag more than women did ($Ms = 0.19$ and -0.19, respectively), $F(1, 348) = 14.62$, $p < .05$, $d = 0.41$.

DISCUSSION

The results of Study 1 confirmed that exposure to media messages in support of catharsis can affect

---

[1] Nonparametric analysis yielded the same pattern of results as parametric analyses.

subsequent behavioral choices. Angry people expressed the highest desire to hit a punching bag when they had been exposed to a (bogus) newspaper article claiming that a good, effective technique for handling anger was to vent it toward an inanimate object. Apparently, people accepted the message and subsequently applied it to their own situation. In contrast, a newspaper article purporting to debunk the catharsis hypothesis and recommending relaxation instead had the opposite effect. Participants exposed to the anticatharsis message were relatively disinclined to hit the punching bag.

It is noteworthy that the procatharsis message was able to increase aggressive inclinations toward the punching bag, as compared with the baseline of people who received a message unrelated to catharsis. We had worried that popular media support for catharsis might have already persuaded most people to try to vent anger against inanimate objects, which would have resulted in no difference between the procatharsis and control conditions. Our results suggest that people's beliefs about how to handle anger are not universally firm and can be altered by media messages.

A potential alternative explanation for these results would be that demand characteristics affected the results. After all, the message advocating catharsis through hitting the punching bag led people to choose the punching bag activity. These effects were only found among angered participants, suggesting that participants did not simply, blindly, and uncritically exhibit whatever behavior the message had advocated. Still, it was possible that participants were simply furnishing the responses that, on the basis of the persuasive message, they believed the researchers wanted, and the design of Study 1 did not offer any easy way to rule that out. However, Study 2 did offer a better opportunity to discern whether behavior was a simple response to demand characteristics or a more complex result of information processing and motivated selection of behaviors.

Study 2

Study 1 showed that people can be persuaded by media messages to seek out catharsis. People presumably came to believe a newspaper article reporting that venting one's anger can produce a desired state of relaxation, and so when they found themselves angry they chose to act out their aggression in the way the article suggested. But would it work? If people were persuaded that venting anger would succeed, they might, in fact, find that they would feel less angry and be less interpersonally aggressive

after venting. Thus, some support might finally be found for the catharsis effect, with a little help from a self-fulfilling prophecy. Alternatively, if aggressive acts produce higher anger and higher aggression, then belief in catharsis might ultimately end up producing more aggression.

Therefore, Study 2 extended the procedure of Study 1 to include an opportunity to actually hit the punching bag followed by an opportunity to aggress toward the person who had insulted the participant or toward an innocent third person. The goal was to see whether people who were led to believe in the catharsis effect would actually feel a reduction in anger after hitting the punching bag and therefore show diminished aggression toward the other person, just as the ostensible newspaper article claimed would happen.

METHOD

Participants Participants were 707 undergraduate students (350 men and 357 women) enrolled in introductory psychology courses. Students received extra class credit in exchange for their voluntary participation. They were randomly assigned among conditions, except that the no-punching-bag condition was run later (in response to editorial suggestion). The no-punching-bag group was recruited in the same way and from the same population as the rest of the participants. The data from 7 women were discarded because they refused to hit the punching bag.

Procedure Experimental participants were tested individually in the laboratory session, but each was led to believe that he or she would be interacting with either 1 or 2 other participants of their same sex. Participants were told that the researchers were studying how accurate people's perceptions of others were in different types of interactions. After giving their consent, participants were randomly assigned to message conditions (i.e., procatharsis, anticatharsis, or control). To eliminate suspicion about any connection between the article and the activities to be chosen later in the experiment, we had participants draw a number from a bag to determine which article they would read. The target article was also the first of three articles in a packet. Participants were told that they would discuss the articles with the other participant(s) later in the experiment.

Next, each participant wrote a one-paragraph essay on abortion, either pro-choice or pro-life (whichever the participant preferred). After finishing, the participant's essay was taken away to be shown to the other participant (who was, in fact, nonexistent) for evaluation. Meanwhile, the participant was permitted to evaluate the partner's essay, which always agreed with the attitudinal position advocated by the participant. This procedural modification allowed us to rule out the possibility that aggression was mediated by perceptions of partner attitude or of similarity between participant and partner.

A short time later, the experimenter brought back the participant's own essay with comments ostensibly made by the other participant. All participants received bad evaluations consisting of negative ratings on organization, originality, writing style, clarity of expression, persuasiveness of arguments, and overall quality. There was also a handwritten comment stating "This is one of the worst essays I have read!" After reading the evaluation, the participant ranked a list of 10 activities in the order of his or her preference for doing them later in the experiment. Included in this list of activities was "hitting a punching bag."

The punching bag manipulation came next. Most participants hit the punching bag. If the participant did not rank the punching bag activity first, the experimenter asked the participant if he or she would be willing to hit the punching bag, explaining that ratings were needed for each activity on the list and that more ratings were needed for the punching bag activity. By requesting the participant to agree, we were able to ensure that the punching bag activity was the result of choice by all participants, including those who had not originally listed it as their top choice. The experimenter gave the participant some boxing gloves and demonstrated how to hit the platform-mounted speed bag (Everlast Model 4213; Everlast, New York, NY).[2] The participant was left alone to hit the punching bag for 2 min. Participants then indicated whether they enjoyed hitting the punching bag (in an answer coded *yes* or *no*).

There was also a condition in which participants did not hit the punching bag. The no-punching-bag condition always included the procatharsis message and the direct, rather than displaced, target (i.e., aggression toward the person who had insulted the participant's essay). Participants in this group ranked the list of activity preferences and then sat still for 2

min rather than hitting the punching bag for 2 min. The justification for the delay was that the experimenter was fixing their partner's computer. No attempt was made to reduce participants' anger during the 2-min delay. Instead, participants in the no-punching-bag group did nothing at all. This allowed us to test whether angry people are better off doing nothing at all than engaging in cathartic activities.

The next part of the procedure was presented as a competitive reaction-time task, based on a paradigm developed by Taylor (1967). Previous studies have established the construct validity of Taylor's paradigm (e.g., Bernstein, Richardson, & Hammock, 1987; Giancola & Zeichner, 1995). The participant was told that he or she and the partner would have to press a button as fast as possible on each trial, and whoever was slower would receive a blast of noise. At the beginning of each trial each participant was permitted to set the intensity of the noise that the other person would receive if he or she lost between 60 dB (Level 1) and 105 dB (Level 10). A nonaggressive no-noise setting (Level 0) was also offered. In addition to deciding the intensity, the winner decided the duration of the loser's suffering, because the duration of the noise depended on how long the winner pressed the button. In effect, each participant controlled a weapon that could be used to blast the other person if the participant won the competition to react faster.

Some participants were led to believe that the other person involved in their competition was the person who had evaluated (and insulted) their essay. Others were led to believe that it was a completely different person. It is important to note that this information was communicated to the participant prior to the punching bag activity. This would allow people to use the punching bag strategically, in case they wanted to preserve their anger for attacking the person who had provoked them or get rid of their anger before competing against an innocent third person.

The reaction time task consisted of 25 trials. Provocation was manipulated by increasing the intensity and duration of noise set by the "other person" across blocks of trials. After the initial (no-provocation) trial, the remaining 24 trials were divided into three blocks with 8 trials in each block. The average noise intensity and duration set by the other person were, respectively, 2.5 and 0.63 s on Block 1, 5.5 and 1.38 s on Block 2, and 8.5 and 2.47 s on Block 3. The participants heard noise on half of the trials within each block (randomly determined). A Macintosh II computer controlled the events in the reaction time task and recorded the noise levels and noise durations the participants set

---

[2] It is interesting to note that the *Everlast Health and Training Guide* that came with the punching bag states that a punching bag is "a great piece of equipment for releasing pent-up frustrations." Instructions are given for individuals of various skill levels, including the individual who wants to "let off steam."

for their partner. The white noise consisted of sound files synthesized by a digital waveform editor (Farallon Soundedit 2.0.5) and reproduced through an Audiomedia 2.0 Digidesign 16-bit DA (digit-to-analog) converter (Digidesign, Inc., Palo Alto, CA). The analog output was amplified by a NAD 3225PE integrated amplifier (NAD Electronics, Buckinghamshire, United Kingdom) and delivered through a pair of Telephonics TDH-39P headphones (Telephonics, Farmingdale, NY). A General Radio 156-B sound-level meter (GenRad Incorporated, Concord, MA) was used to calibrate the noise levels. A full debriefing (with a probe for suspicion) followed.

RESULTS

The analysis strategy featured the original and main design, which was a 3 (article: procatharsis, anticatharsis, control) × 2 (aggression target: direct, displaced) × 2 (participant sex) design. The no-punching-bag group was added on later, and hence we shall report its comparisons separately. Men were more aggressive than women on all measures, but sex did not interact with other variables, so we shall not discuss sex in depth.

Desire to Hit Punching Bag As in Study 1, desire to hit the punching bag was measured by how participants ranked it among the 10 activities. Rankings were reverse scored so that high numbers indicated high desire. The scores were also standardized. An ANOVA with planned contrasts was used to analyze these data. The results were quite similar to what we found in Study 1 (except that Study 2 did not include a no-anger condition). The planned contrasts revealed that angered participants who read the procatharsis article wanted to hit the punching bag more than angered participants who read the anticatharsis article did, $t(588) = 2.02$, $p < .05$, $d = 0.20$ (see Table 25.01). The control group did not differ from the pro- and anticatharsis groups, $ts(588) = -0.67$ and 1.35, respectively (see Table 25.01). The main effect for article condition was not quite significant, however, $F(2, 588) = 2.12$, $p > .05$.

The ANOVA also revealed a trend involving the target of aggression. Participants who anticipated being able to express their aggression toward the person who had angered them wanted to hit the punching bag more than those who could only displace their aggression did ($Ms = 0.08$ and -0.08, respectively), $F(1, 588) = 3.54$, $p < .10$, $d = 0.16$. This clearly rules out any suggestion that people might seek to avoid the punching bag so as to sustain their anger in order to vent it at the person who

TABLE 25.01

PREFERENCE FOR HITTING A PUNCHING BAG AS A FUNCTION OF ARTICLE CONDITION		
ARTICLE CONDITION	*M*	*SE*
Procatharsis	0.09_a	0.07
Control	0.02_{a,b}	0.08
Anticatharsis	−0.11_b	0.07

Note. Means having the same subscript are not significantly different at p < .05.

had provoked them. This effect did not depend on the content of the message the participant had seen (i.e., there was no interaction between aggressive target and message content), so the response apparently should not be interpreted as a consequence of manipulated belief in catharsis.

Interpersonal Aggression The most important goal of Study 2 was to examine aggressive behavior toward the opponent on the reaction time task as indicated by selecting loud or lengthy blasts of noise to deliver to the opponent during the competition. Noise intensity and noise duration were measures of the same construct, namely, aggressive behavior toward another person. The same pattern of results was obtained for both measures, and the two measures were significantly correlated ($r = .34$). The correlation between noise intensity and noise duration did not differ for men and women ($z = 1.35$, $p > .05$). To create a more reliable measure, therefore, we standardized and summed the noise intensity and noise duration data to form a total measure of interpersonally aggressive behavior.

Trial 1. The data from the first trial are the most relevant for testing the hypothesis, because on later trials the participant's aggressive response is influenced (one might say contaminated) by how aggressive the opponent has been on preceding trials. There was a significant main effect of the article content on interpersonal aggression in Trial 1, $F(2, 588) = 6.05$, $p < .05$ (see Table 25.02). Contrary to the self-fulfilling prophecy hypothesis and the demand characteristic explanation, we found participants who had read the procatharsis message to be more aggressive than participants who had read the anticatharsis message, $t(588) = 3.44$, $p < .05$, $d = 0.31$. They were also more aggressive than the participants who had read the irrelevant control

TABLE 25.02

INTERPERSONAL AGGRESSION AS A FUNCTION OF ARTICLE CONDITION

ARTICLE CONDITION	M	SE
Trial I		
Procatharsis	0.26_a	0.14
Control	-0.04_b	0.07
Anticatharsis	-0.22_b	0.08
Remaining trials		
Procatharsis	0.21_a	0.12
Control	$-0.08_{a,b}$	0.10
Anticatharsis	-0.13_b	0.09

Note. *Means having the same subscript are not significantly different at p < .05 (within each category of trials).*

message, $t(588) = 2.14$, $p < .05$, $d = 0.20$. The anticatharsis and control groups did not differ in their aggression, $t(588) = 1.30$, $p > .05$. The target of aggression (direct vs. displaced) had no effect.

Remaining trials. After the first trial, aggression converged on reciprocation of what the partner had ostensibly done. This is consistent with many previous findings suggesting that reciprocation is a powerful norm in determining aggressive responses during an ongoing aggressive exchange. Even on these remaining trials, however, there was a main effect for message content, $F(2, 588) = 3.06$, $p < .05$ (see Table 25.02). Participants who had read the procatharsis article continued to be more aggressive than participants who had read the anticatharsis article, $t(588) = 2.29$, $p < .05$, $d = 0.22$. Participants who had read the procatharsis article also tended to be more aggressive than participants who had read the article unrelated to catharsis, although this difference was not quite significant $t(588) = 1.95$, $p < .10$, $d = 0.17$. There was no difference between the anticatharsis and control groups, $t(588) = 0.35$, $p > .05$. There was also no effect for aggressive target (direct vs. displaced).

Enjoyment of Punching Bag Activity

To shed light on the possible subjective processes relevant to catharsis, we examined whether participants in the procatharsis group enjoyed hitting the punching bag more than those in the anticatharsis group did. Because enjoyment of the punching bag activity was a binary variable (coded *yes* or *no*), these data were analyzed using logistic regression analysis. Most participants (72%) enjoyed hitting

the punching bag regardless of the condition to which they had been randomly assigned. No effects were significant (except sex—men enjoyed hitting the punching bag more than women did). In particular, message condition did not influence whether participants enjoyed hitting the punching bag.

Relation Between Desire to Hit the Punching Bag, Enjoyment of Hitting the Punching Bag, and Interpersonal Aggression

Correlation analysis was performed to determine the relations among the three dependent measures (i.e., desire to hit the punching bag, enjoyment of hitting the punching bag, and interpersonal aggression) for participants who hit the punching bag. As can be seen in Table 25.03, desire to hit the punching bag and enjoyment of hitting the punching bag were positively correlated with interpersonal aggression. In addition, angered participants who wanted to hit the punching bag also enjoyed hitting it more. These results contradict any suggestion that hitting the punching bag would have beneficial effects because one might feel better after doing so (which is what advocates of catharsis often say). People did indeed enjoy hitting the punching bag, but this was related to more rather than less subsequent aggression toward a person.

Is Hitting a Punching Bag Cathartic?

To test whether hitting a punching bag produced a catharsis effect, we compared the level of aggression

TABLE 25.03

RELATION BETWEEN DESIRE TO HIT THE PUNCHING BAG, ENJOYMENT OF HITTING THE PUNCHING BAG, AND INTERPERSONAL AGGRESSION

MEASURE	1	2	3	4
I. Desire to hit punching bag	—	.23*	.08	.19*
2. Enjoyed hitting punching bag		—	.02	.11*
3. Interpersonal aggression (Trial I)			—	.49*
4. Interpersonal aggression (remaining trials)				—

*$p < .05$.

for participants who hit the punching bag with the level of aggression for participants who did not hit the punching bag. For these analyses, we used only participants who read the procatharsis message and who aggressed directly toward the person who had (supposedly) criticized their essay. A 2 (punching bag) × 2 (sex) ANOVA was used.

On Trial 1, participants who hit the punching bag tended to be more (rather than less) aggressive than those who did not hit the punching bag ($Ms = 0.40$ and -0.01, respectively), $F(1, 196) = 2.87$, $p < .10$, $d = 0.24$. Although these results are not quite significant, they are in the direction opposite that predicted by the catharsis hypothesis.

On the remaining trials, participants who did hit the punching bag were significantly more aggressive than those who did not hit the punching bag ($Ms = 0.33$ and -0.17, respectively), $F(1, 196) = 4.96$, $p < .05$, $d = 0.31$. These results directly contradict the catharsis hypothesis.

Because the no-punching-bag group was run later, we were concerned about any possible difference in their sample. The most worrisome possibility was that there would be some baseline difference in desire to hit the punching bag. Analysis of the rank-ordered preferences ruled this out, however: The participants in the two conditions did not differ in their desire to hit the punching bag, $F(1, 196) = 0.43$, $p > .05$.

DISCUSSION

Study 2 accomplished several things. First, we replicated the results from previous research showing that hitting a punching bag does not produce a cathartic effect: It increases rather than decreases subsequent aggression.

Second, we replicated the main finding of Study 1: Exposure to a procatharsis message increased angry people's desire to hit a punching bag. Thus, media messages pertaining to catharsis do seem able to influence behavioral preferences.

Third, we included a manipulation of aggressive target to give participants a possible motivation for reducing their anger. That is, we thought that perhaps people who expected to interact with someone new would want to rid themselves of their anger toward a previous person who had insulted them. If they believed in catharsis, people in this condition might be especially prone to choose the punching bag activity. We did not find this, however. Instead, we found that people who expected to interact with the person who had insulted them were, if anything, more eager to hit the punching bag before that meeting. These results do not fit an affect-regulation

or demand-characteristic explanation. Moreover, this pattern was obtained regardless of which message the participant had read—procatharsis, anticatharsis, or control. A possible explanation is that expecting a further interaction with someone who has insulted you sustains anger, whereas expecting to interact with someone new is already a cue to refocus attention and diminish anger. It is plausible (although direct evidence is lacking) that direct aggression participants were angrier than displaced aggression participants at the point of choosing the activity, and that the anger itself was sufficient to increase preferences for the punching bag.

The major question for Study 2 was how the procatharsis message, followed by the ostensibly cathartic activity of hitting the punching bag, would affect interpersonal aggression. We found that the procatharsis message led to higher levels of interpersonal aggression, even after people might have achieved catharsis by hitting the punching bag. This pattern was found on the first trial (in which the person's aggression could not be influenced by the opponent's ostensible responses on previous trials), and it was sustained through subsequent trials as well, despite the rising situational forces pushing for reciprocal levels of aggression.

Thus, even the people who were led to believe in catharsis failed to show any signs of it. Instead, procatharsis messages led to increased aggression (as compared with people who heard other messages). Moreover, this elevated aggression was found regardless of whether the interpersonal target was the same person who had provoked the participant's anger or was an innocent third person. The most parsimonious conclusion was that the procatharsis message led to increased aggressive behavior across the board, and that people made no meaningful distinction between the punching bag, the person who had provoked them, and an innocent third person as aggressive target.

People who did not hit the punching bag were less, not more, aggressive than people who hit the punching bag. In other words, hitting the punching bag led to subsequently higher levels of aggression, even among participants who had been led to believe in catharsis. These results directly contradict the catharsis hypothesis and suggest that belief in catharsis can generate a self-defeating prophecy effect.

General Discussion

Catharsis has enjoyed a run of support in the popular media that far outstrips its support in the research literature. Scientists have been largely unable to demonstrate that aggressive outbursts reduce subsequent aggressive behavior, whereas the mass media continue to suggest that they do reduce it. Some pop psychology and media sources even propose that restraining angry impulses can result in mental and physical health problems, as well as greater aggression down the road.

The present research was concerned with how people are affected by media messages that tout catharsis as a viable, effective, and socially desirable way of handling one's anger. In two studies, our participants were exposed to a message that either advocated or disputed the catharsis theory, were provoked to be angry at someone, and then had their choices and actions measured. In both studies, people who had been exposed to a procatharsis message were more prone than others to choose the aggressive activity of hitting a punching bag. The procatharsis message seems to have been effective at inducing people to vent their anger aggressively.

Thus, media support for catharsis could induce people to choose cathartic activities—but could it induce the catharsis effect itself? That is, would people who were led to believe in catharsis, and who then engaged in hitting a punching bag after being angered by someone, end up behaving less aggressively toward that person? The answer from Study 2 is a clear "no." In fact, people who had read the procatharsis article behaved more aggressively than participants in the control group, even after they had spent time hitting a punching bag. Hitting the punching bag should have produced catharsis among people who believed in catharsis, but it did not. If anything, it appears to have produced the opposite effect, namely, an increase in subsequent aggression.

One might have hoped that the initial (Trial 1) aggression toward the partner would produce catharsis among people who had been led to believe in it, but even that possibility failed to materialize. The procatharsis message led to elevated levels of aggression right up to the end of the experiment. In other words, the procatharsis message led people to make behavioral choices in favor of increased aggression on three consecutive occasions: on their initial choice to hit a punching bag, on their first competitive trial involving the other person, and on the 24 subsequent trials.

A possible explanation for the persistence of high aggression following the procatharsis message was that people continued to seek cathartic release but failed to find it. Hence, perhaps the procatharsis message persuaded people that acting aggressively was a good way to handle anger, so they chose to hit a punching bag. When they found themselves still angry, they tried again, this time lashing out at their opponents in the first trial of the competitive game. When even that aggression failed to reduce their aggressive feelings, they kept trying on subsequent trials. The failure of the anticipated release to materialize might well cause frustration, creating a vicious circle of continued or even escalating aggression. If so, media messages that promote catharsis could end up contributing to frustration and increased aggression.

The present research extends the long history of empirical failures of the catharsis hypothesis. Even when people were led to believe catharsis worked and they freely chose to seek cathartic release, it did not happen. Put another way, even the added boost of a potentially self-fulfilling prophecy was not enough to create catharsis effects.

The present results suggest that procatharsis media messages may actually generate self-defeating prophecies. Telling people that aggressive activity is a good way to get rid of anger led them to choose aggressive activity, but performing this activity apparently failed to reduce anger. Subsequent interpersonal aggression remained high, in stark contrast to what the procatharsis message led people to believe. We noted that this outcome is the worst of all possible effects that might be predicted for media procatharsis messages. The messages made people seek out aggressive release, but this initial venting then increased their subsequent aggression toward another person.

DIRECT AND DISPLACED AGGRESSION

A possibly surprising feature of the present results is that we found no difference between direct and displaced aggression. This contrasts with many previous findings, including some of our own (Bushman & Baumeister, 1998), indicating that people do aggress differentially toward someone who has provoked them as opposed to an innocent third person. One crucial difference between the present procedure and other, less successful studies of displaced aggression is that the present procatharsis message advocated the effectiveness of displacing anger onto new targets. The failure to distinguish between aggressive targets is consistent with the suggestion we made that people were continuing (unsuccessfully) to seek cathartic release by continued aggression. Indeed, we found the same effects on the punching bag measure as we did on the interpersonal aggression measure, which, in the most parsimonious view, suggests that people did not approach the interpersonal aggression any differently than they approached the punching bag situation. These results raise the possibility that media advocacy of catharsis could have the socially undesirable effect of fostering displacement of aggression onto innocent targets.

LIMITATIONS

Several limitations of the present work must be acknowledged. We did not include a no-anger condition in Study 2, and hence there was no way to assess the effectiveness of the anger manipulation. Probably the best evidence comes from a previous investigation in which we used precisely the same anger induction procedure and had a no-anger control (Bushman & Baumeister, 1998). This anger induction caused a large increase in anger in that study, but we can only infer that it had the same effect in this one. The lack of a no-anger condition likewise precludes us from asserting that anger was a prerequisite for the effects found in Study 2.

We also acknowledge that we do not have evidence regarding the precise intrapsychic process or mechanism that mediated the effects of the persuasive messages. Although we have emphasized anger as a likely factor, we note that the manipulation involved a blow to self-esteem, and concern over self-esteem might have helped mediate the results even apart from the anger that normally ensues from being insulted.

It might be suggested that the procatharsis and anticatharsis messages caused people to experience the punching bag activity differently. Our measures of enjoyment failed to find any such difference, however.

THE ENDURING APPEAL OF CATHARSIS

As we suggested, the present results go beyond prior evidence that disconfirmed the catharsis hypothesis. We could not even find a catharsis effect when we led people to believe in it and to act upon that belief. Surely if the catharsis theory were true at all, under any circumstances, it should have obtained under the highly conducive circumstances we set up. Yet, it did not. If anything, we found the opposite: Aggression remained high throughout the procedure.

Our results thus concur with the calls by Tavris (1988) and others to pronounce the catharsis hypothesis wrong. However, research interest may need to shift to the question of why popular belief in catharsis remains high and people can still be easily persuaded that venting anger is the best way to rid oneself of the aversive inner state (and therefore avoid subsequent interpersonal aggression). We suggest that there are at least three reasons why catharsis techniques for controlling anger retain their popular appeal. First, catharsis techniques are widely advocated by pop psychologists, and they are widely cited in the popular literature. Second, cathartic-type responses may be the most natural (dominant) responses to anger-producing situations. It is possible that procatharsis media messages (such as in our procedure) constitute a kind of permission that people use to justify abandoning their self-control (see Baumeister, 1997; Baumeister, Heatherton, & Tice, 1994). Third, people may think that if the catharsis theory has been around so long, there must be some validity to it. The fact that anger does eventually dissipate, regardless of what one does, may foster the illusion that catharsis is successful. Likewise, we found that people did enjoy hitting the punching bag, so at some level the activity made them feel good, and this may be enough to help sustain popular belief in the benefits of venting. Unfortunately, these good feelings did not translate into reduced interpersonal aggression—if anything, people who enjoyed hitting the punching bag more were also more aggressive toward the opponent in subsequent trials.

CONCLUDING REMARKS

Our findings suggest that media messages advocating catharsis may be worse than useless. They encourage people to vent their anger through aggressive action, and perhaps they even foster the displacement of aggression toward new, innocent third parties. In our research, people who received procatharsis messages first chose to vent their anger by hitting a punching bag, but then they went on to show elevated aggression toward the person at whom they were angry. They even showed increased aggression toward an innocent third person. Pop writers may think they are offering helpful, sage advice on affect regulation, but the effect of advocating catharsis may be to cause a general increase in aggressive behavior. Perhaps media endorsement of cathartic release should come to be regarded as a potential danger to public health, peace, and social harmony.

References

1. Baumeister, R. F. (1997). *Evil: Inside human violence and cruelty.* New York: Freeman.
2. Baumeister, R. F., Dale, K., & Sommer, K. L. (1998). Freudian defense mechanisms and empirical findings in modern social psychology: Reaction formation, projection, displacement, undoing, isolation, sublimation, and denial. *Journal of Personality, 66,* 1081–1124.
3. Baumeister, R. F., Heatherton, T. F., & Tice, D. M. (1994). *Losing control: How and why people fail at self-regulation.* San Diego, CA: Academic Press.

4. Berkowitz, L. (1984). Some effects of thoughts on anti- and prosocial influences of media events: A cognitive-neoassociation analysis. *Psychological Bulletin, 95,* 410–427.

5. Bernstein, S., Richardson, D., & Hammock, G. (1987). Convergent and discriminant validity of the Taylor and Buss measures of physical aggression. *Aggressive Behavior, 13,* 15–24.

6. Bushman, B. J., & Baumeister, R. F. (1998). Threatened egotism, narcissism, self-esteem, and direct and displaced aggression: Does self-love or self-hate lead to violence? *Journal of Personality and Social Psychology, 75,* 219–229.

7. Darley, J. M., & Fazio, R. H. (1980). Expectancy confirmation processes arising in the social interaction sequence. *American Psychologist, 35,* 867–881.

8. Geen, R. G., & Quanty, M. B. (1977). The catharsis of aggression: An evaluation of a hypothesis. In L. Berkowitz (Ed.), *Advances in experimental social psychology* (Vol. 10, pp. 1–37). New York: Academic Press.

9. Giancola, P. R., & Zeichner, A. (1995). Construct validity of a competitive reaction-time aggression paradigm. *Aggressive Behavior, 21,* 199–204.

10. Lee, J. (1995). *Facing the fire: Experiencing and expressing anger appropriately.* New York: Bantam.

11. Tavris, C. (1988). Beyond cartoon killings: Comments on two overlooked effects of television. In S. Oskamp (Ed.), *Television as a social issue* (pp. 189–197). Newbury Park, CA: Sage.

12. Taylor, S. P. (1967). Aggressive behavior and physiological arousal as a function of provocation and the tendency to inhibit aggression. *Journal of Personality, 35,* 297–310.

13. Tice, D. M., & Baumeister, R. F. (1993). Controlling anger: Self-induced emotion change. In D. M. Wegner & J. W. Pennebaker (Eds.), *Handbook of mental control* (pp. 393–409). Englewood Cliffs, NJ: Prentice Hall.

14. Warren, R., & Kurlychek, R. T. (1981). Treatment of maladaptive anger and aggression: Catharsis vs behavior therapy. *Corrective and Social Psychiatry and Journal of Behavior Technology, Methods and Therapy, 27,* 135–139.

15. Wegman, C. (1985). *Psychoanalysis and cognitive psychology.* Orlando, FL: Academic Press.

16. Zillmann, D. (1979). *Hostility and aggression.* Hillsdale, NJ: Erlbaum.

Appendix: Pro- and Anticatharsis Articles

This is the text of the procatharsis article. The anticatharsis article was identical except for the changes noted in brackets.

RESEARCH SHOWS THAT HITTING INANIMATE OBJECTS IS AN EFFECTIVE [INEFFECTIVE] WAY TO VENT ANGER

Cambridge, Mass. (AP) Do you believe that you can vent anger by hitting a punching bag? According to the results of a study published this week in *Science,* you could not be more right [wrong].

The study confirms a long history of research on the effectiveness [ineffectiveness] of displacing anger to inanimate objects. The study was conducted by Dr. Elias Boran, a psychological researcher at Harvard University. Boran says that his results provide direct confirmation of the idea that anger can[not] be vented harmlessly when people can displace their anger to an inanimate object.

The findings are the results of a 2-year study involving 1,000 university students living in the university's residence halls. Participants in the study were randomly divided into one of two groups. One group hit a punching bag (a portable floor model provided by the experimenter) when they were angry. The other group tried to relax when they were angry. Boran found that students who hit a punching bag when angry were 4 times less [more] likely to have complaints filed against them by other students in the residence hall and were 2 times less [more] likely to have been reported to campus police for aggressive incidents than were students who tried to relax.

Boran says that his study is consistent with the results of scores of studies showing that people can[not] effectively vent anger to inanimate objects. According to Boran, "When you are angry, the best [worst] thing that you can do is to find something inanimate to hit or kick to vent your anger."

QUESTIONS FOR REFLECTION AND DISCUSSION:

1. The authors are concerned about the possible role of the self-fulfilling prophecy in connection with the catharsis theory. What is meant by a self-fulfilling prophecy? Can you think of examples of self-fulfilling prophecies in your own experience?

2. What have you heard about the concept of catharsis? Has it followed along with the popular view?

3. The catharsis theory appears to be consistent with Sigmund Freud's psychoanalytic theory. Why might the behaviorist perspective predict quite different outcomes for the effects of "venting" anger through aggressive behavior?

4. What was the operational definition of aggression in the article? In your opinion, does this form of aggression represent "real-life" aggression? Why or why not?

5. What do the authors acknowledge to be the limitations of their study? Can you think of others?

6. What are the reasons that the catharsis theory remains popular, despite research evidence to the contrary?

7. What messages are found in this study for folklore and tradition in explanations of human personality and behavior? (Should one believe an idea just because it has been popular for thousands of years?)

Here is a seemingly little study which turns out to have had a large impact on psychology. It involves dogs. If you read it closely—especially the introduction, results, and discussion sections—you will find that there is no reference to human beings or to human behavior. However, the most significant application of the study has been in the area of abnormal psychology, particularly the nature of depression among humans.

This study is said to provide an "animal model" for depression. So-called animal models are commonly thought to reflect natural processes in humans. Human models would include an overlay of cultural influences and experiences. Depression in humans is said to be characterized by feelings of helplessness and hopelessness. In serious cases of depression, people are overwhelmed by these feelings and believe that there is nothing they can do to change their plights. In the extreme, the feelings may be irrational. You will note the use of the words helplessness *and* hopelessness *in the discussion of the first experiment, even though, again, it is not applied to humans.*

Martin Seligman, the first author, brought the term learned helplessness *into the field of abnormal psychology as an explanation for depression. Psychoanalytic theory had largely viewed depression as anger turned inward because an overbearing superego prevented the socially appropriate expression of anger toward the real objects of the emotion—people who were probably frustrating the depressed person in some important way. Seligman, a learning theorist, preferred to focus on situational variables that lead to depressive behavior—in this case, the apathetic or irritated withdrawn behavior shown by the dogs who could not escape electric shock.*

Failure to Escape Traumatic Shock

MARTIN E. P. SELIGMAN & STEVEN F. MAIER
UNIVERSITY OF PENNSYLVANIA

Dogs which had 1st learned to panel press in a harness in order to escape shock subsequently showed normal acquisition of escape/avoidance behavior in a shuttle box. In contrast, yoked, inescapable shock in the harness produced profound interference with subsequent escape responding in the shuttle box. Initial experience with escape in the shuttle box led to enhanced panel pressing during inescapable shock in the harness and prevented interference with later responding in the shuttle box. Inescapable shock in the harness and failure to escape in the shuttle box produced interference with escape responding after a 7-day rest. These results were interpreted as supporting a learned "helplessness" explanation of interference with escape responding: Ss failed to escape shock in the shuttle box following inescapable shock in the harness because they had learned that shock termination was independent of responding.

Overmier and Seligman (1967) have shown that the prior exposure of dogs to inescapable shock in a Pavlovian harness reliably results in interference with subsequent escape/avoidance learning in a shuttle box. Typically, these dogs do not even escape from shock in the shuttle box. They initially show normal reactivity to shock, but after a few trials, they passively "accept" shock and fail to make escape movements. Moreover, if an escape or avoidance response does occur, it does not reliably predict future escapes or avoidances, as it does in normal dogs.

This pattern of effects is probably not the result of incompatible skeletal responses reinforced during the inescapable shocks, because it can be shown even when the inescapable shocks are delivered while the dogs are paralyzed by curare. This behavior is also probably not the result of adaptation to shock, because it occurs even when escape/avoidance shocks are intensified. However, the fact that interference does not occur if 48 hr. elapse between exposure to inescapable shock in the harness and escape/avoidance training, suggests that the phenomenon may be partially dependent upon some other temporary process.

Overmier and Seligman (1967) suggested that the degree of control over shock allowed to the animal in the harness may be an important determinant of this interference effect. According to this hypothesis, if shock is terminated independently of S's responses during its initial experience with shock, interference with subsequent escape/avoidance responding should occur. If, however, S's responses terminate shock during its initial experience with shock, normal escape/avoidance responding should subsequently occur. Experiment I investigates the effects of escapable as compared with inescapable shock on subsequent escape/avoidance responding.

Experiment I

METHOD

Subjects The Ss were 30 experimentally naive, mongrel dogs, 15–19 in. high at the shoulder, and weighing between 25 and 29 lb. They were maintained on ad lib food and water in individual cages. Three dogs were discarded from the Escape group, two because they failed to learn to escape shock in the harness (see procedure), and one because of a procedural error. Three dogs were discarded from the "Yoked" control group, two because they were too small at the neck to be adequately restrained in the harness; the third died during treatment. This left 24 Ss, eight in each group.

Apparatus The apparatus was the same as that described in Overmier and Seligman (1967). It consisted of two distinctively different units, one for escapable/inescapable shock sessions and the other for escape/avoidance training. The unit in which Ss were exposed to escapable/inescapable shock consisted of a rubberized, cloth hammock located inside a shielded, white, sound-attenuating cubicle. The hammock was constructed so that S's legs hung down below its body through four holes. The S's legs were secured in this position, and S was strapped into the hammock. In addition, S's head was held in position by panels placed on either side and a yoke between the panels across S's neck. The S could press the panels with its head. For the Escape group pressing the panels terminated shock, while for the "Yoked" control group, panel presses did not effect the preprogrammed shock. The shock source for this unit consisted of 500 v. ac transformer and a parallel voltage divider, with the current applied through a fixed resistance of 20,000 ohms. The shock was applied to S through brass plate electrodes coated with commercial electrode paste and taped to the footpads of S's hind feet. The shock intensity was 6.0 ma. Shock presentations were controlled by automatic relay circuitry located outside the cubicle.

Escape/avoidance training was conducted in a two-way shuttle box with two black compartments separated by an adjustable barrier (described in Solomon & Wynne, 1953). The barrier height was adjusted to S's shoulder height. Each shuttle-box compartment was illuminated by two 50-w. and one $7\frac{1}{2}$-w. lamps. The CS consisted of turning off the four 50-w. lamps. The US, electric shock, was administered through the grid floor. A commutator shifted the polarity of the grid bars four times per second. The shock was 550 v. ac applied through a variable current limiting resistor in series with S. The shock was continually regulated by E at 4.5 ma. Whenever S crossed the barrier, photocell beams were interrupted, a response was automatically recorded, and the trial terminated. Latencies of barrier jumping were measured from CS onset to the nearest .01 sec. by an electric clock. Stimulus presentations and temporal contingencies were controlled by automatic relay circuitry in a nearby room.

White masking noise at approximately 70-db. SPL was presented in both units.

TABLE 26.01

GROUP	MEAN LATENCY (IN SEC.)	% Ss FAILING TO ESCAPE SHOCK ON 9 OR MORE OF THE 10 TRIALS	MEAN NO. FAILURES TO ESCAPE SHOCK[a]
Escape	27.00	0	2.63
Normal Control	25.93	12.5	2.25
"Yoked" Control	48.22	75	7.25

INDEXES OF SHUTTLE BOX ESCAPE/AVOIDANCE RESPONDING: EXP. I

[a] Out of 10 trials.

Procedure The Escape group received escape training in the harness. Sixty-four unsignaled 6.0 ma. shocks were presented at a mean interval of 90 sec. (range, 60–120 sec.). If the dog pressed either panel with its head during shock, shock terminated. If the dog failed to press a panel during shock, shock terminated automatically after 30 sec. Two dogs were discarded for failing to escape 18 of the last 20 shocks.[1]

Twenty-four hours later dogs in the Escape group were given 10 trials of escape/avoidance training in the shuttle box: S was placed in the shuttle box and given 5 min. to adapt before any treatment was begun. Presentation of the CS began each trial. The CS-US interval was 10 sec. If S jumped the barrier during this interval, the CS terminated and no shock was presented. Failure to jump the barrier during the CS-US interval led to shock which remained on until S did jump the barrier. If no response occurred within 60 sec. after CS onset, the trial was automatically terminated and a 60-sec. latency recorded. The average intertrial interval was 90 sec. with a range of 60–120 sec. If S failed to cross the barrier on all of the first five trials, it was removed, placed on the other side of the shuttle box, and training then continued. At the end of the tenth trial, S was removed from the shuttle box and returned to its home cage.

The Normal control group received only 10 escape/avoidance trials in the shuttle box as described above.

The "Yoked" control group received the same exposure to shock in the harness as did the Escape group, except that panel pressing did not terminate shock. The duration of shock on any given trial was determined by the mean duration of the corresponding trial in the Escape group. Thus each S in the "Yoked" control group received a series of shocks of decreasing duration totaling to 226 sec.

Twenty-four hours later, Ss in the "Yoked" control group received 10 escape/avoidance trials in the shuttle box as described for the Escape group. Seven days later, those Ss in this group which showed the interference effect received 10 more trials in the shuttle box.

RESULTS[2]

The Escape group learned to panel press to terminate shock in the harness. Each S in this group showed decreasing latencies of panel pressing over the course of the session ($p = .008$, sign test, Trials 1–8 vs. Trials 57–64). Individual records revealed that each S learned to escape shock by emitting a single, discrete panel press following shock onset. The Ss in the "Yoked" control group typically ceased panel pressing altogether after about 30 trials.

Table 26.01 presents the mean latency of shuttle box responding, the mean number of failures to escape shock, and the percentage of Ss which failed to escape nine or more of the 10 trials during escape/avoidance training in the shuttle box for

---

[1] It might be argued that eliminating these two dogs would bias the data. Thus naive dogs which failed to learn the panel-press escape response in the harness might also be expected to be unable to learn shuttle box escape/avoidance. One of these dogs was run 48 hr. later in the shuttle box. It escaped and avoided normally. The other dog was too ill to be run in the shuttle box 48 hr. after it received shock in the harness.

[2] All p values are based upon two-tailed tests.

each group. The "Yoked" control group showed marked interference with escape responding in the shuttle box. It differed significantly from the Escape group and from the Normal control group on mean latency and mean number of failures to escape (in both cases, $p < .05$, Duncan's multiple-range test). The Escape group and the Normal control group did not differ on these indexes.

Six Ss in the "Yoked" control group failed to escape shock on 9 or more of the 10 trials in the shuttle box. Seven days after the first shuttle-box treatment, these six Ss received 10 further trials in the shuttle box. Five of them continued to fail to escape shock on every trial.

DISCUSSION

The degree of control over shock allowed a dog during its initial exposure to shock was a determinant of whether or not interference occurred with subsequent escape/avoidance learning. Dogs which learned to escape shock by panel pressing in the harness did not differ from untreated dogs in subsequent escape/avoidance learning in the shuttle box. Dogs for which shock termination was independent of responding in the harness showed interference with subsequent escape learning.

Because the Escape group differed from the "Yoked" control group during their initial exposure to shock only in their control over shock termination, we suggest that differential learning about their control over shock occurred in these two groups. This learning may have acted in the following way: (a) Shock initially elicited active responding in the harness in both groups. (b) Ss in the "Yoked" control group learned that shock termination was independent of their responding, i.e., that the conditional probability of shock termination in the presence of any given response did not differ from the conditional probability of shock termination in the absence of that response. (c) The incentive for the initiation of active responding in the presence of electric shock is the expectation that responding will increase the probability of shock termination. In the absence of such incentive, the probability that responding will be initiated decreases. (d) Shock in the shuttle box mediated the generalization of b to the new situation for the "Yoked" control group, thus decreasing the probability of escape response initiation in the shuttle box.

Escapable shock in the harness (Escape group) did not produce interference, because Ss learned that their responding was correlated with shock termination. The incentive for the maintenance of re-

sponding was thus present, and escape response initiation occurred normally in the shuttle box.

Learning that shock termination is independent of responding seems related to the concept of learned "helplessness" or "hopelessness" advanced by Richter (1957), Mowrer (1960, p. 197), Cofer and Appley (1964, p. 452), and to the concept of external control of reinforcement discussed by Lefcourt (1966).

In untreated Ss the occurrence of an escape or avoidance response is a reliable predictor of future escape and avoidance responding. Dogs in the "Yoked" control group and in the groups which showed the interference effect in Overmier and Seligman (1967) occasionally made an escape or avoidance response and then reverted to "passively" accepting shock. These dogs did not appear to benefit from the barrier-jumping—shock termination contingency. A possible interpretation of this finding is that the prior learning that shock termination was independent of responding inhibited the formation of the barrier-jumping—shock-termination association.

The Ss in the "Yoked" control group which showed the interference effect 24 hr. after inescapable shock in the harness again failed to escape from shock after a further 7-day interval. In contrast, Overmier and Seligman (1967) found that no interference occurred when 48 hr. elapsed between inescapable shock in the harness and shuttle-box training. This time course could result from a temporary state of emotional depletion (Brush, Myer, & Palmer, 1963), which was produced by experience with inescapable shock, and which could be prolonged by being conditioned to the cues of the shuttle box. Such a state might be related to the parasympathetic death which Richter's (1957) "hopeless" rats died. Further research is needed to clarify the relationship between the learning factor, which appears to cause the initial occurrence of the interference effect, and an emotional factor, which may be responsible for the time course of the effect.

The results of Exp. I provide a further disconfirmation of the adaptation explanation of the interference effect. If Ss in the "Yoked" control group had adapted to shock and, therefore, were not sufficiently motivated to respond in the shuttle box, Ss in the Escape group should also have adapted to shock. Further, the Escape and the "Yoked" control groups were equated for the possibility of adventitious punishment for active responding by shock onset in the harness. Thus it seems unlikely that the "Yoked" control group failed to escape in the shuttle box because it had been adventitiously punished for active responding in the harness.

Experiment II

Experiment I provided support for the hypothesis that *S* learned that shock termination was independent of its responding in the harness and that this learning inhibited subsequent escape responding in the shuttle box. Experiment II investigates whether prior experience with *escapable* shock in the shuttle box will mitigate the effects of inescapable shock in the harness on subsequent escape/avoidance behavior. Such prior experience might be expected (*a*) to inhibit *S*'s learning in the harness that its responding is not correlated with shock termination and (*b*) to allow *S* to discriminate between the escapability of shock in the shuttle box and the inescapability of shock in the harness.

METHOD

Subjects The *S*s were 30 experimentally naive, mongrel dogs, weight, height, and housing as above. Three dogs were discarded: two because of procedural errors and one because of illness. The remaining 27 dogs were randomly assigned to three groups of nine *S*s each.

Apparatus The two units described for Exp. I were used.

Procedure The Preescape group received 3 days of treatment. On Day 1, each *S* received 10 escape/avoidance trials in the shuttle box as described in Exp. I. On Day 2, approximately 24 hr. after the shuttle-box treatment, each *S* in this group received an inescapable shock session in the harness. All inescapable shocks were unsignaled. The inescapable shock session consisted of 64, 5-sec. shocks, each of 6.0 ma. The average intershock interval was 90 sec. with a range of 60–120 sec. On Day 3, approximately 24 hr. after the inescapable shock, *S* was returned to the shuttle box and given 30 more escape/avoidance trials, as described for Day 1.

The No Pregroup received no experience in the shuttle box prior to receiving inescapable shock. On the first treatment day for this group, each *S* was placed in the harness and exposed to an inescapable shock session as described for the Preescape group, Day 2. Approximately 24 hr. later, *S* was placed in the shuttle box and given 40 trials of escape/avoidance training as described above. If *S* failed to respond on all of the first five trials, *S* was moved to the other side of the shuttle box. If *S* continued to fail to respond on all trials, it was put back on the original side after the twenty-fifth trial. Thus, if *S*

failed to escape on every trial, it received a total of 2,000 sec. of shock.

The No Inescapable group was treated exactly as the Preescape group except that it received no shock in the harness. On Day 1, *S* received 10 escape/avoidance trials in the shuttle box. On Day 2, it was strapped in the harness for 90 min., but received no shock. On Day 3, it was returned to the shuttle box and given 30 more escape/avoidance trials.

RESULTS

The No Pregroup showed significant interference with escape/avoidance responding in the shuttle box on Day 3. The Preescape and the No Inescapable groups did not show such interference. Figure 26.01 presents the mean median latency of jumping responses for the three groups (and a posterior control group, see below) over the four blocks of 10 trials. Analysis of variance on the three groups revealed that the effect of groups, $F(2, 24) = 3.55$, $p < .05$, and the effect of trial blocks, $F(3, 72) = 6.84$, $p < .01$, were significant. Duncan's multiple-range test indicated that the No Pregroup differed from the other two groups across all 40 trials both $p < .05$. The Preescape and the No Inescapable groups did not differ from each other. Similar results held for the mean of mean latencies. A small, transitory disruption of improvement in shuttle-box performance following inescapable shock in the harness occurred in the Preescape group relative to the No Inescapable group. Difference scores for latencies between consecutive blocks of trials measure improvement in performance. A comparison of the Preescape group with the No Inescapable group on the difference between the mean latency on Trials 1–10 and the mean latency on Trials 11–20 revealed that the No Inescapable group showed signif-

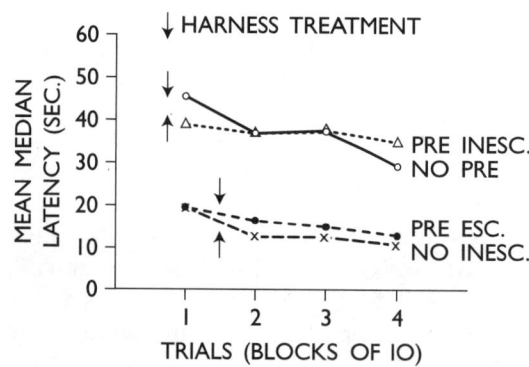

FIGURE 26.01

Mean median latency of escape/avoidance responding. (The position of the arrow denotes whether the harness treatment occurred 24 hr. before the first or second block of trials.)

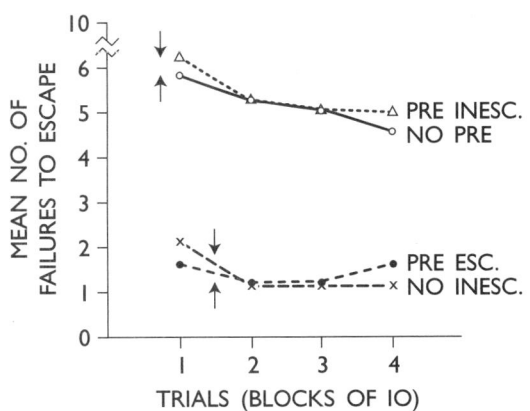

FIGURE 26.02

Mean number of failures to escape shock. (The position of the arrow denotes whether the harness treatment occurred 24 hr. before the first or second block of trials.)

icantly more improvement than the Preescape group, Mann-Whitney U test, $U = 15$, $p < .05$. No significant differences were found on difference scores for any subsequent blocks of trials.

Figure 26.02 presents the mean number of failures to escape shock for the three groups across the four blocks of trials. Analysis of variance revealed a significant overall effect of blocks, $F(3, 72) = 5.94$, $p < .01$, and a significant Groups × Blocks interaction, $F(6, 72) = 17.82$, $p < .01$. Duncan's tests indicated that the No Pregroup showed significantly more failures to escape than the other two groups across the 40 trials, both $p < .05$. The Preescape and the No Inescapable groups did not differ.

Figure 26.03 presents the total number of avoidance responses for the groups across the blocks

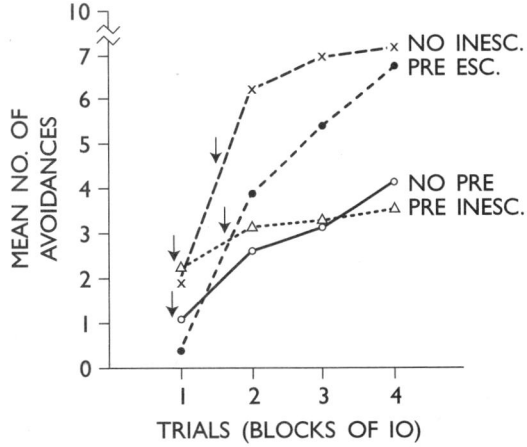

FIGURE 26.03

Mean number of avoidances. (The position of the arrow denotes whether the harness treatment occurred 24 hr. before the first or second block of trials.)

of trials. Only the blocks effect was significant in the overall analysis of variance, $F(3, 72) = 27.90$, $p < .01$. No other effects were significant.

Panel presses made in the harness during the inescapable shock session were counted. On either side of S's head were panels which S could press; panel pressing had no effect on the shock, but merely indicated attempts to respond and/or struggling in the harness. The Preescape group, having received 10 trials with *escapable* shock in the shuttle box the previous day, made more panel presses during the inescapable shock session than did the No Pregroup, the group for which the inescapable shock in the harness was the first experimental treatment, Mann-Whitney U test, $U = 9$, $p < .02$.

Posterior Control Group Subsequent to this experiment, a control group was run to determine if the *escapability* of shock in the shuttle box on Day 1 for the Preescape group was responsible for its enhanced panel pressing in the harness and lack of interference with responding in the shuttle box. Or would the mere occurrence of inescapable shock for a free-moving animal in the shuttle box have produced these results? Nine naive dogs received the following treatment: On Day 1, Ss were placed in shuttle box and given 10 trials as for the Preescape and the No Inescapable groups. Unlike these groups, however, S's barrier jumping did not (except adventitiously) terminate the shock and CS, because trial durations were programmed independently of S's behavior. The duration of each of the 10 trials for this Preinescapable group corresponded to the mean trial duration for the Preescape and the No Inescapable groups on that trial. On Day 2, Ss received 64 trials of inescapable shock in the harness. On Day 3, Ss received 40 escape/avoidance trials in the shuttle box.

Figures 26.01, 26.02, and 26.03 present the escape/avoidance performance of the Preinescapable group on Day 3. In general this group performed like the No Pregroup. This impression was borne out by statistical tests. The Preinescapable group showed significantly slower median latency of barrier jumping than the Preescape and the No Inescapable groups across all 40 trials, both $p < .05$, Duncan's test. The Preinescapable group did not differ from the No Pregroup. Similar results held for the other indexes.

Analysis of the panel press data showed that the Preinescapable group made significantly fewer panel presses in the harness than the Preescape group, Mann-Whitney U test, $U = 14$, $p < .05$. The Preinescapable group did not differ significantly from the No Pregroup, $U = 26$.

DISCUSSION

Three main findings emerged from Exp. II: (*a*) *S*s (Preescape), which first received escapable shock in the shuttle box, then inescapable shock in the harness, did not react passively to subsequent shock in the shuttle box, as did *S*s which either first received inescapable shock in the shuttle box (Preinescapable) or no treatment prior to shock in the harness (No Pre). (*b*) The Preescape group, having received experience with escapable shock in the shuttle box, showed enhanced panel pressing when exposed to inescapable shock in the harness, relative to naive *S*s given inescapable shock in the harness. Such enhanced panel pressing was specifically the result of the *escapability* of shock in the shuttle box: The Preinescapable group did not show enhanced panel pressing. (*c*) The interference effect persisted for 40 trials.

The *S*s which have had prior experience with *escapable* shock in the shuttle box showed more energetic behavior in response to inescapable shock in the harness. This contrasts with the interference effect produced by *inescapable* shock in *S*s which have had no prior experience with shock or in *S*s which have had prior experience with inescapable shock. Thus, if an animal first learns that its responding produces shock termination and then faces a situation in which reinforcement is independent of its responding, it is more persistent in its attempts to escape shock than is a naive animal.

General Discussion

We have proposed that *S* learned as a consequence of inescapable shock that its responding was independent of shock termination, and therefore the probability of response initiation during shock decreased. Alternative explanations might be offered: (*a*) Inactivity, somehow, reduces the aversiveness of shock. Thus *S* failed to escape shock in the shuttle box because it had been reinforced for inactivity in the harness. Since the interference effect occurred in *S*s which had been curarized during inescapable shock, such an aversiveness-reducing mechanism would have to be located inward of the neuro-myal junction. (*b*) *S* failed to escape in the shuttle box because certain responses which facilitate barrier jumping were *extinguished* in the harness during inescapable shock. In conventional extinction procedures, some response is first explicitly reinforced by correlation with shock termination, and then that response is extinguished by removing shock altogether from the situation. Responding during extinction is conventionally not *un*correlated with shock termination; rather, responding is correlated with

the total absence of shock. In our harness situation, no response was first explicitly reinforced, and shock was presented throughout the session. A broader concept of extinction, however, might be tenable. On this view, any procedure which decreases the probability of a response by eliminating the incentive to respond is an extinction procedure. If the independence of shock termination and responding eliminates the incentive to respond (as assumed), then our harness procedure could be thought of as an extinction procedure. Such an explanation seems only semantically different from the one we have advanced, since both entail that the probability of responding during shock has decreased because *S* learned that shock termination was independent of its responses.

Learning that one's own responding and reinforcement are independent might be expected to play a role in appetitive situations. If *S* received extensive pretraining with rewarding brain stimulation delivered independently of its operant responding, would the subsequent acquisition of a bar press to obtain this reward be retarded? Further, might learned "helplessness" transfer from aversive to appetitive situations or vice versa?

If dogs learn in one situation that their active responding is to no avail, and then transfer this training to another shock situation, the opposite type of transfer (avoidance learning sets) might be possible: If a dog first learned a barrier-hurdling response which avoided shock in the shuttle box, would that dog be facilitated in learning to panel press to avoid shock in the harness (to a different CS)? Our finding, that dogs which first successfully escape shock in the shuttle box later showed enhanced panel pressing in the harness, is consonant with this prediction.

Does learning about response–reinforcement contingencies have its analogs in classical conditioning? If *S* experienced two stimuli randomly interspersed with each other (adventitious pairings possible), would it be retarded in forming an association between the two stimuli once true pairing was begun? Conversely, pretraining in which one stimulus is correlated with a US might facilitate the acquisition of the CR to a new CS. Pavlov (1927, p. 75) remarked that the first establishment of a conditioned inhibitor took longer than any succeeding one.

In conclusion, learning theory has stressed that two operations, explicit contiguity between events (acquisition) and explicit noncontiguity (extinction), produce learning. A third operation that is proposed, independence between events, also produces learning, and such learning may have effects upon behavior that differ from the effects of explicit pairing and explicit nonpairing. Such learning may produce an *S* who does not attempt to escape electric shock; an *S* who, even if he does respond, may not benefit from instrumental contingencies.

References

1. Brush, F. R., Myer, J. S., & Palmer, M. E. Effects of kind of prior training and intersession interval upon subsequent avoidance learning. *J. comp. physiol. Psychol.*, 1963, **56**, 539–545.
2. Cofer, C. N., & Appley, M. H. *Motivation: Theory and research.* New York: Wiley, 1964.
3. Lefcourt, H. M. Internal vs. external control of reinforcement: A review. *Psychol. Bull.,* 1966, **65**, 206–221.
4. Mowrer, O. H. *Learning theory and behavior.* New York: Wiley, 1960.
5. Overmier, J. B., & Seligman, M. E. P. Effects of inescapable shock on subsequent escape and avoidance learning. *J. comp. physiol. Psychol.,* 1967, **63**, 28–33.
6. Pavlov, I. P. *Conditioned reflexes.* New York: Dover, 1927.
7. Richter, C. On the phenomenon of sudden death in animals and man. *Psychosom. Med.,* 1957, **19**, 191–198.
8. Solomon, R. L., & Wynne, L. C. Traumatic avoidance learning: Acquisition in normal dogs. *Psychol. Monogr.,* 1953, **67** (4, Whole No. 354).

QUESTIONS FOR REFLECTION AND DISCUSSION:

1. What are some of the alternative explanations for the behavior of the laboratory animals in the experiment? What arguments do the authors present for their own interpretation of the behavior?

2. In recent years animal rights groups have criticized the kinds of procedures used in the experiment by Seligman and Maier. The activities of these groups have led to better housing and maintenance of laboratory animals and to heightened awareness of what they may experience. How did you feel about the treatment to which the animals in this study were exposed? Why? Do you feel that the study was ethical? How would you make that decision?

3. Can we truly say that the behavior displayed by an animal—for example, a rat or a dog—is similar enough to the behavior and mental processes of human that the behavior can serve as a "model" for the human activity?

4. What is your understanding of the range of symptoms that characterize depression in humans? How far do you feel can one go in applying animal models to explain depression or other kinds of psychopathology in humans?

SOURCE

Richardson, D. C., Bernstein, S., & Taylor, S. P. (1979). The effect of situational contingencies on female retaliative behavior. *Journal of Personality and Social Psychology, 37,* 2044–2048. Copyright © 1979 by the American Psychological Association. Reprinted with permission.

Common knowledge, folklore, and psychological research all agree that the human male is more aggressive than the human female. Correct? Well . . . we're really not so sure. Although most psychological, sociological, and anthropological studies have shown that males are more aggressive, there are some fascinating exceptions. For example, there are the classic cross-cultural findings of anthropologist Margaret Mead[1] on New Guinea. She reported that among the Mundugumor, a tribe of headhunters and cannibals, both women and men were warlike and aggressive. Among another tribe, the Tchambuli, the women were more aggressive than the men. The men spent most of their time nurturing the children, primping, and gossiping. Recent research in the United States found that women may be equally involved as aggressors in domestic violence, but they are more likely to be injured because they are (usually) smaller and weaker than men.[2]

Then, too, there is the occasional study like that by Deborah Richardson and her colleagues, presented here. They looked into the "situational contingencies" that affect aggressive behavior in women. That is, they focus not on the "nature" of women, but on the circumstances that elicit aggression in women.

The Effect of Situational Contingencies on Female Retaliative Behavior

DEBORAH CAPASSO RICHARDSON & SANDY BERNSTEIN
UNIVERSITY OF GEORGIA
STUART P. TAYLOR
KENT STATE UNIVERSITY

Most studies that have found sex differences in aggression have reported that males are more aggressive than females. Recent evidence, however, suggests that the expectation of female nonaggressiveness may be unwarranted. The present study attempted to reconcile these differences by considering the contingencies of female aggression.

Thirty females competed in a task designed to measure aggression (a) alone, (b) in the presence of a silent observer, or (c) in the presence of a supportive observer. Results indicated that as provocation increased, women in the private condition responded more aggressively than did women in the public condition. Also, women who responded in the presence of an audience were more aggressive when the observer was supportive than when she was silent. It is concluded that the usual findings of female nonaggressiveness may be attributable to women's expectations of disapproval for aggressive behavior.

---

[1] Mead, M. (1935). *Sex and temperament in three primitive societies.* New York: Dell.

[2] O'Leary, K. D. (1995, July). Assessment and treatment of partner abuse. *Clinician's Research Digest,* Supplemental Bulletin 12, pp. 1–2.

Harcourt, Inc.

Traditionally, women have been viewed as the nonaggressive sex. Most of the studies that have found sex differences in aggression have reported that males are more aggressive than females. These results have been obtained with children (Liebert & Baron, 1972; Pederson & Bell, 1970; Santrock, 1970; Shortell & Biller, 1970) as well as with adult subjects (Buss, 1966; Doob & Gross, 1968; Epstein, 1965; Youssef, 1968), using various methodologies and different aggression paradigms.

It might appear, then, that females are adhering to a "norm of passivity." According to Maccoby and Jacklin (1974):

> Aggression in general is less acceptable for girls, and is more actively discouraged in them, by either direct punishment, withdrawal of affection, or simply cognitive training that "that isn't the way girls act." Girls then build up greater anxieties about aggression, and greater inhibitions against displaying it. (p. 234)

This response inhibition hypothesis proposes that the female's socialization history causes her to inhibit the display of aggression. Maccoby and Jacklin (1974) suggest that sex differences in aggression may arise because females are reinforced for nonaggressive behavior. Since aggression in general is less acceptable for girls and is more actively discouraged in them by socialization agents, girls have greater anxieties about aggression as well as greater inhibitions against displaying it. Frodi, Macaulay, and Thome (1977), in their review of the literature on sex differences in aggression, note that in the course of normal socialization, women learn to respond to provocation with aggression anxiety and that in our culture aggressive behavior from women is not approved of and receives negative evaluations. Thus, they conclude that "through avoidance or anticipatory arousal of aggression anxiety or guilt, women avoid acting aggressively" (p. 654).

Other evidence, however, suggests that the expectation of female nonaggressiveness may be unwarranted. Taylor and Epstein (1967) found that sex differences in aggression disappeared when women were confronted with increasing provocation by a male opponent in a reaction time experiment. Using the same paradigm, Richardson (Note 1) found no sex differences in response to continually high provocation. In addition, Frodi et al. (1977) concluded that evidence indicates that women do *not* show consistently lesser tendencies to physically aggress than do men.

It is apparent that experimental evidence concerning the aggressiveness of women is contradictory. These differences might be reconciled, however, by looking at the environmental contingencies of female aggression. The variability of findings may result from the presence or absence of elements in the experimental situation that evoke conformity to sex role expectations (Frodi et al., 1977). The socialization process that women in our culture undergo has taught them that in many or most situations, aggression will not be approved of and will receive negative sanctions (Costrich, Feinstein, Kidder, Marecek, & Pascale, 1975). Thus women have learned to inhibit their aggressive behavior. At times, however, in spite of childhood socialization and adult sex role restrictions, women do behave aggressively. This negation of traditional sex role requirements can be explained once certain situational factors have been inspected.

Using a competitive reaction time task, Taylor and Epstein (1967) found that when faced with increasing provocation from a male opponent, women would deliver shocks to their opponent at an intensity equivalent to that set by male participants for male opponents. Since the male opponent violated social expectations by delivering relatively high shocks to a woman, the female participants may have felt that they, also, were excused from the usual sex role requirements. Frodi et al. (1977) note that sex differences in aggression seldom appear when aggression is permissible behavior for women. That is, when aggression is justified or when women are acting anonymously—as a deindividuated member of a group—sex differences in aggression are not found.

The contention that women may drop their stereotypical feminine role and behave in a relatively masculine manner also receives support beyond the area of aggression. In a study conducted by Kidder, Bellettirie, and Cohn (1977), reward allocations were made by male and female participants in either a public or a private condition. In the public condition, each sex conformed to its role expectations. When assured of anonymity, however, both sexes abandoned their traditional sex-typed roles.

The present study was designed to investigate the effects of situational contingencies on so-called female nonaggressiveness. Female participants competed against a male opponent in a reaction time task designed to measure aggression. The participants competed in one of three conditions: (a) private—alone in the experimental room; (b) public—in the presence of a silent female observer; or (c) supportive other—in the presence of a female observer who offered social support for retaliating against the opponent.

It was hypothesized that women in the public condition would behave less aggressively in response to provocation than would women in the private condition. The presence of a silent female observer in the public condition was expected to make salient the traditional sex role expectations for *female* nonaggressiveness (e.g., Frodi et al., 1977) and result in behavior that conformed to the participants' perceptions of what the observer expected of them. Women in the supportive other condition, not having to rely on their perceptions of the observer's expectations and knowing that the observer did not expect nonaggressive behavior, were expected to behave more aggressively than would women in the public condition. It was also hypothesized that women in all three conditions would respond more aggressively as provocation by their male opponent increased.

Method

PARTICIPANTS

The participants were 30 female undergraduates enrolled in introductory psychology classes at a large midwestern university. Participation was in partial fulfillment of course requirements. Ten women were randomly assigned to each of the three experimental conditions.

PROCEDURE

Before initiating the procedure, participants were informed that they would be competing in a reaction time task with the person in the next room, that there would be a slight electric shock involved, and that they had the right to leave the experiment at any time without penalty. Participants were then encouraged to ask questions before signing the informed consent statement, which also served as their record of participation.[3]

The female experimenter seated the participant at the task board (described by Taylor, 1967) and attached a concentric shock electrode to her wrist.

In the public and supportive other conditions, a female observer (confederate) arrived at the door of the participant's cubicle and reminded the experimenter that she was a student whose adviser had recommended that she observe an experiment in progress. After obtaining the participant's consent, the experimenter seated the observer slightly behind and to the side of the participant and then left the room for 5 minutes, presumably to attach the opponent's shock electrode.

In the private condition, no observer was present, but the procedure was otherwise identical to the other two conditions.

The participant's "unpleasantness" threshold was then determined. That is, intensity of shock was gradually increased until the participant reported it to be "definitely unpleasant." This was the maximum intensity administered and was designated as Level 5; 90% of the maximum was designated as Level 4; 80% as Level 3; 70% as Level 2; and 60% of the maximum was designated as Level 1. The participant also overheard a tape recording of a male voice telling the experimenter when the shock was unpleasant for him. Thus, she was led to believe that she was to be competing with a male opponent, although no opponent was actually involved in this experiment.

The participant then heard a tape recording of the task instructions. She was told that at the beginning of each trial she should select any one of the five intensities of shock she wished her opponent to receive at the end of the trial if his reaction time was slower than hers and that she would receive the shock her opponent set for her if she was slower than her opponent.

The trials began immediately after the completion of the task instructions. Each trial consisted of four specific events: (a) the onset of the *set* light, which instructed the participant to press one of the five buttons corresponding to the intensity of shock she wished her opponent to receive; (b) the onset of the *press* light, which instructed her to press the reaction time key; (c) the onset of the *release* light, signaling to the participant that she should remove her finger from the reaction time key as quickly as possible; and (d) the onset of one of the five small red lights at the top of the task board, which indicated the intensity of shock that had been set for the participant by her opponent and, if the opponent was faster, the shock as well.

Each participant competed in 25 trials. These consisted of four blocks of 6 trials each plus an extra trial to measure the participant's reaction to Trial 24. The average feedback settings for Blocks 1 through 4 were 1.5, 2.5, 3.5, and 4.5, respectively. Wins and losses and feedback/shock delivered to the participant were programmed by the experimenter. The participant was led to believe that she had won 50% of the trials within each block.

---

[3] This statement indicated that the participant understood (a) the purpose of the experiment, (b) any risks that might be involved, (c) that she could leave the experiment at any time without penalty, and (d) that the details of the experiment would be explained after participation was complete.

In the supportive other condition, the observer initiated conversation with the participant during the first block of trials, speaking in a friendly, spontaneous manner and sympathizing with her whenever she lost a trial. As the attack increased in the later blocks of trials, the observer attempted to encourage the participant to reciprocate by commenting upon the male opponent's behavior ("he went up there a little bit," "he gave a three!"); indicating that if she were competing with the opponent, she would retaliate ("I wouldn't let him get away with that!", "I don't think I'd let him step all over me"); and suggesting that the participant reciprocate ("Another 4! Maybe you should give it back"). At no time did the observer suggest initiating attacks or setting higher intensity shocks than the opponent. The observer in the public condition remained silent throughout the experimental session.

Following the competition task, women in the public and supportive other conditions were asked to rate the observer on a series of 6-point bipolar adjective scales.

Results

Aggression was measured by the magnitude of shock the participants set for administration to their opponent. Participants were required to select a shock intensity on the first trial without any knowledge of the aggressive intentions of the opponent. As expected, there were no significant differences among conditions in the initial trial, $F_{(2, 27)} = .20$, ns.

A 3 (Group) $\times$ 4 (Blocks) analysis of variance was performed on mean shock intensities set during the four blocks of trials in order to examine changes in shock settings over blocks. There was no significant main effect for group, $F_{(2, 27)} = 2.24$, ns. However, the interaction between groups and blocks was significant, $F_{(6, 81)} = 4.66$, $p < .0005$. According to Newman–Keuls analyses, as the trials progressed, women in the private and supportive other conditions responded in an increasingly more aggressive manner than did women in the public condition ($p < .05$). Figure 27.01 demonstrates this relationship and the similarity of the behavior of participants in supportive other and private conditions.

The mean shock intensities set by women in the private condition in Blocks 1 through 4 were 1.52, 1.97, 2.68, and 3.20, respectively. Women in the supportive other condition set mean shock intensities of 1.60, 1.90, 2.79, and 3.57 in Blocks 1 through 4, respectively. However, women in the public condition evidenced less increase by setting

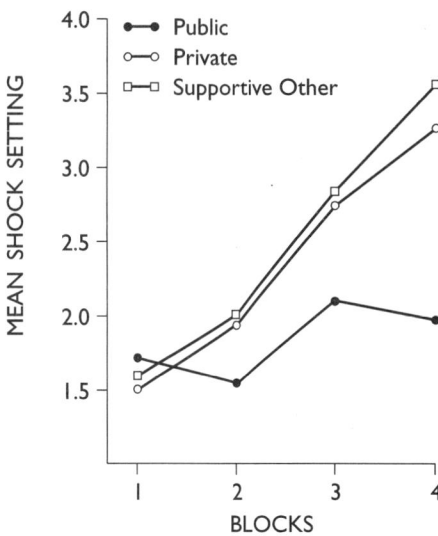

FIGURE 27.01

Mean shock settings as a function of group and block.

mean shock intensities of 1.73, 1.58, 2.12, and 2.03 in Blocks 1 through 4. Further analysis revealed that the differences in mean shock settings were significant only in the final blocks of trials.

As predicted, there was a significant main effect of blocks, $F_{(3, 81)} = 36.22$, $p < .001$, indicating that shock settings, in general, increased over blocks. The mean shock intensities set in Blocks 1 through 4, respectively, were 1.62, 1.85, 2.53, and 2.93.

Following their participation in the competition task, women in supportive other and public conditions were asked to rate the observer on a series of 6-point adjective scales with a midpoint of 3.5. Analysis of this data by t tests indicated that the observer in the supportive other condition was perceived to be significantly more friendly (4.90 vs. 3.90), good-humored (5.50 vs. 4.60), happy (4.40 vs. 3.60), honest (4.60 vs. 3.40), and sociable (4.70 vs. 3.60) than was the observer in the public condition. Also, the observer in the public condition was perceived as being significantly less revengeful (1.40 vs. 3.40), less competitive (2.40 vs. 4.10), less aggressive (2.30 vs. 4.00), and more passive (3.60 vs. 2.00) than was the observer in the supportive other condition (all $ps < .05$).

Discussion

The present study attempted to delineate the effects of situational contingencies on female aggression. It was assumed that women would respond to provocation less aggressively in the presence of a silent audience than when they were either alone or in the presence of a supportive audience. Both hypotheses were supported. Women in the private condition responded to the male opponent's provocation by setting higher shocks than the women who participated in the presence of a silent observer. Similarly, women who were encouraged by the audience retaliated at higher levels than did those who received no such social support.

As predicted, situational contingencies influenced female retaliative behavior, thereby bringing into question the common assumption of female nonaggressiveness. Indeed, it appears that the aggressiveness of women was largely determined by the contingencies present. When reciprocal responding was clearly called for, as in the supportive other condition, women retaliated. When their response was relatively anonymous, as in the private condition, women retaliated. The only situation in which nonaggressiveness was evidenced was in the presence of a silent observer in the public condition. In this case, one might expect that the women were responding to the assumed expectations of the audience.

The relatively low level of aggression in the public condition lends support to the response inhibition hypothesis mentioned earlier. That is, the presence of the silent observer may have increased the participant's concern about the "appropriateness" of her behavior, thereby enhancing the salience of the "norm of passivity." Evidence for this interpretation is provided by Borden (1975), who found that male participants' aggressive behavior was influenced by their expectations of approval from observers. Borden noted that the "generalized expectancy associated with the sex of the observer" could account for his participants' lower levels of aggression when they were observed by a female than when they were observed by a male. Borden concluded, as we might, that the participants' aggressive behavior was "apparently a function of their expectations of approval for such behavior, based on the inferred or explicit values of the observer" (p. 567). Although such values were not explicit in the present study, participants did attribute characteristics consistent with the "norm of passivity" to the silent observer. They perceived her to be relatively nonrevengeful, noncompetitive, nonaggressive, and passive. The participants in the public condition apparently adapted their retaliative responding in accordance with this expectation.

Similarly, behavior of participants in the supportive other condition was consistent with expectations of the observer. The contingencies in that situation reinforced reciprocation of the opponent's behavior. Thus, expectations were no longer for nonaggressive responding and the female participants could reject the "norm of passivity" and still respond in a manner that would conform to the apparent values of the observer. It was not necessary for these women to inhibit their aggressive behavior due to fear of negative sanction for "out-of-role" behavior.

Reference Note

1. Richardson, D. C. *Sex differences in aggression: A new perspective.* Paper presented at the meeting of the Southeastern Psychological Association, Atlanta, March 1978.

References

1. Borden, R. Witnessed aggression: Influence of an observer's sex and values on aggressive responding. *Journal of Personality and Social Psychology,* 1975, *31,* 567–573.
2. Buss, A. H. Instrumentality of aggression, feedback, and frustration as determinants of physical aggression. *Journal of Personality and Social Psychology,* 1966, *3,* 153–162.
3. Costrich, N., Feinstein, J., Kidder, L. H., Marecek, J., & Pascale, L. When stereotypes hurt: Three studies of penalties for sex-role reversals. *Journal of Experimental Social Psychology,* 1975, *11,* 520–530.
4. Doob, A. N., & Gross, A. E. Status of frustrator as an inhibitor of horn-honking responses. *Journal of Social Psychology,* 1968, *76,* 213–218.
5. Epstein, R. Authoritarianism, displaced aggression and social status of the target. *Journal of Personality and Social Psychology,* 1965, *2,* 585–589.
6. Frodi, A., Macaulay, J., & Thome, P. R. Are women always less aggressive than men? A review of the experimental literature. *Psychological Bulletin,* 1977, *84,* 634–660.
7. Kidder, L. H., Bellettirie, G., & Cohn, E. S. Secret ambitions and public performance: The effects of anonymity on reward allocations made by men and women. *Journal of Experimental Social Psychology,* 1977, *13,* 70–80.
8. Liebert, R. N., & Baron, R. A. Some immediate effects of televised violence on children's behavior. *Developmental Psychology,* 1972, *6,* 469–475.
9. Maccoby, E. E., & Jacklin, C. N. *The psychology of sex differences.* Stanford, Calif.: Stanford University Press, 1974.
10. Pederson, F. A., & Bell, R. Q. Sex differences in preschool children without histories of complications of pregnancy and delivery. *Developmental Psychology,* 1970, *3,* 10–15.
11. Santrock, J. W. Paternal absence, sex typing, and identification. *Developmental Psychology,* 1970, *2,* 264–272.

12. Shortell, J. R., & Biller, H. B. Aggression in children as a function of sex of subject and sex of opponent. *Developmental Psychology*, 1970, 3, 143–144.
13. Taylor, S. Aggressive behavior and physiological arousal as a function of provocation and the tendency to inhibit aggression. *Journal of Personality*, 1967, 35, 297–310.
14. Taylor, S., & Epstein, S. Aggression as a function of the interaction of the sex of the aggressor and the sex of the victim. *Journal of Personality*, 1967, 35, 474–486.
15. Youssef, Z. I. The role of race, sex, hostility, and verbal stimulus in inflicting punishment. *Psychonomic Science*, 1968, 12, 285–286.

QUESTIONS FOR REFLECTION AND DISCUSSION:

1. What are some theories as to why women might be less aggressive than men? (Hint: In your discussion, refer to evolutionary psychology and to the *response inhibition hypothesis.*)

2. What is the apparent influence of sex-role (or gender-role) expectations on aggressive behavior in women?

3. Why did the researchers predict that women would behave less aggressively in the presence of a silent female observer?

4. What was the operational definition of aggression in the study? Are you satisfied that the example of aggression can be extended or generalized to aggressive behavior in general? Explain.

5. Who actually received electric shock in the experiment?

6. Do you believe that the Richardson study was ethical? Why or why not?

7. Can you think of a way that this study could have been carried out without deceiving subjects?

8. How can you generalize from this study to the real world? What kinds of conditions apparently stimulate women to act aggressively?

Not very modestly, psychologist Albert Ellis refers to himself as "the father of REBT [rational emotive behavior therapy] and the grandfather of cognitive-behavioral therapy." Trained in psychoanalysis, Ellis found Freud's methods slow and ineffective. He noted that people who were undergoing analysis often felt better, at least for a while, because of talking about their problems and getting attention from the therapist. But he did not believe that they got better. He also was not convinced that it was useful for the therapist to be so passive, so he became more active and began to offer direct advice.

Ellis was a sickly youth, repeatedly hospitalized for nephritis during middle childhood. He was not permitted to participate in sports, and became quite shy. Nevertheless, Ellis resolved to be happy. He earned early degrees in business and accounting and did not become a psychologist until he was in his 30s. He has written many popular as well as professional books on psychology, including How to Stubbornly Refuse to Make Yourself Miserable About Anything—Yes, Anything!, Anger: How to Live With and Without It, *and* Overcoming Procrastination.

The following "Reflections on Rational–Emotive Therapy" appeared in the American Psychologist, *before Ellis changed the name of his form of therapy to rational emotive* behavior *therapy. Ellis takes the opportunity to outline some of the significant aspects of his form of psychotherapy.*

Reflections on Rational–Emotive Therapy

ALBERT ELLIS

This article reflects rational–emotive therapy in 1955 and discusses some of its recent constructivist and humanist theories and practices.

Let me, in a few pages, do the impossible: reflect on the development of rational–emotive therapy (RET), comment on what it is today, and suggest some future directions.

As the first of today's cognitive–behavioral therapies, RET in 1955 was highly cognitive, largely positivist, and very active–directive. Its ABC theory of human disturbance held that people experience undesirable activating events (A), that they have rational and irrational beliefs (B) about these stimuli, and that they create appropriate emotional and behavioral consequences (aC) with their rational beliefs (rB) or they create inappropriate and dysfunctional consequences (iC) with their irrational beliefs (rB). At first, RET largely followed the "scientific" philosophy of logical positivism that was then in vogue, favoring empirical "reality" and data seeking tied in with human observation and sensation. Holding that unrealistic and illogical self-talk about unfortunate life events, and not these events in their own right, created or "caused" emotional disturbance, it heavily espoused rational instead of irrational cognition and actively–directively disputed (D) clients' antiempirical and overgeneralized self-statements while teaching them how to do hypothetical–deductive disputing for themselves (Ellis, 1962).

Early RET, however, had many humanistic existential, emotive–evocative, and holistically oriented theories and practices (Ellis, 1962), so it was far from being rationalist, sensationalist, or strictly positivist, as it has sometimes wrongly been accused of being.

As the years went by, the cognitive revolution in psychology progressed and psychotherapy became increasingly cognitive–behavioral. But my own work with thousands of clients, as well as my familiarity with the subsequent work of Aaron Beck, Donald Meichenbaum, and other cognitive therapists, most of whom were too empirical and not sufficiently philosophical for my taste, pushed me in more constructivist and more affective directions. During the late 1960s, moreover, I somewhat merged RET with the encounter movement, conducted many rational encounter marathons, and began to do considerable group therapy and public workshops that included live affective demonstrations of RET.

As a result of this activity, I began to differentiate general RET, which I see as synonymous with general cognitive–behavioral therapy, from preferential RET, which I see as a unique kind of cognitive therapy that partially overlaps with general cognitive–behavioral therapy but also differs from it in several significant respects. Preferential RET, which I have practiced and written about for the last 15 years, is distinctly constructivist and humanistic. Very briefly, it includes the following points:

1. RET holds that humans largely learn their goals and preferences for success and approval from their families and culture and feel appropriately frustrated and disappointed when they fail and are disapproved. But they mainly construct (because they are innately prone to do so) absolutist "musts" and demands about their desires. Hence, when they are neurotic they do not get disturbed by obnoxious environmental influences but largely make themselves emotionally and behaviorally dysfunctional.

2. When people make irrational (self-defeating) demands on themselves, on others, and on the conditions under which they live, they also tend to construct, as derivatives of their musts, unrealistic misperceptions, inferences, and attributions that make important contributions to their disturbances. Thus, if they insist, "John absolutely *must* like me!" and John actually ignores them, they rashly con-

clude (and devoutly believe) that (a) "He hates me!" (b) "It's *awful* that he hates me!" (c) "I'm worthless because he hates me!" and (d) "No decent person will ever like me!"

3. To help people overcome their dysfunctional beliefs and the disturbances that accompany them, RET not only shows them their unrealistic inferences and attributions and how to dispute them but also shows them their imperative musts and demands that usually unconsciously and tacitly underlie and lead to these dysfunctional imperatives. It teaches them how to look for their necessitizing on their own, and shows them how to try to ultimately arrive at the "elegant" RET solution to neurosis: to arrange, for the rest of their lives, that they rarely (not never) change their preferences to grandiose demands and thereby make themselves significantly less upsettable.

4. RET holds that cognitions, emotions, and behaviors are practically never pure or disparate but integrally and holistically interact with and include each other. Although it is highly philosophical, RET fully recognizes that feelings and behaviors have an important influence on beliefs, that beliefs affect feelings and behaviors, and that feelings affect beliefs and behaviors (Ellis, 1962, 1988, 1991). Thus, RET is always multimodal and uses a good number of cognitive, emotive, and behavioral methods with most clients.

5. RET theorizes that people often are biologically predisposed to strongly, passionately, and rigidly construct and hold on to their disturbance-creating musts and other irrational beliefs. Therefore, RET tries to persuade and teach clients to vigorously, powerfully, and persistently think, feel, and act against their demandingness and to return to their preferences. Consequently, it almost always uses a number of emotive–evocative techniques with individual and group therapy clients. These include unconditional acceptance of the client by the therapist, rational-emotive imagery, shame-attacking exercises, powerful coping statements, role playing, encouragement, humor, and other emotive methods (Ellis, 1988; Ellis & Dryden, 1987; Walen, DiGiuseppe, & Dryden, 1992).

6. RET theorizes that people tend to become habituated to their disturbed thoughts, feel-

ings, and actions and easily and automatically keep repeating them, even when they "know" they bring about poor results. To change, they therefore often have to force themselves, quite uncomfortably, to push themselves to break their dysfunctional habits. But they often have a low frustration tolerance and irrationally believe that "I *shouldn't* have to do the work of changing myself and *must* find comfortable, magical ways to change." They also often have secondary disturbances of "ego-downing" about their primary disturbances, and they consciously or unconsciously insist that "I *must not* upset myself in this foolish manner! I'm a worthless idiot for doing so!" RET looks for and concentrates on uprooting their secondary as well as their primary disturbances; in doing so it uses a number of cognitive and emotive methods. But it also emphasizes behavioral homework, including reinforcements and penalties, in vivo desensitization, implosive counter-phobic procedures, and response prevention. It thereby tends to be more heavily behavioral than some of the other cognitive–behavioral therapies.

7. RET has always been psychoeducational and consequently uses a great deal of bibliotherapy, audiotherapy, courses, workshops, lectures, and other teaching methods. It helps each person in a dysfunctional system (such as a crisis-creating family) to change himself or herself in spite of the system. But it also teaches people problem solving, skill training, and social change methods, so that they can modify the environment and the system in which they live.

8. RET theorizes that virtually all humans, however reared, have two opposing creative tendencies: (a) to damn and to deify themselves and others, as noted earlier, and thereby to make themselves disturbed and dysfunctional, and (b) to change and actualize themselves as healthier and less disturbed. RET tries to show them how to use their self-actualizing to reduce their self-disturbing tendencies, and thus to construct a more enjoyable life.

9. RET is opposed to rigidity, "must-urbation," one-sidedness, and stasis and strongly favors openness, alternative seeking, antidogma, and flexibility. It holds that science intrinsically is knowledge seeking, free of dogma, skeptical, and flexible, and that it uses empiricism and logic *un*rigidly to arrive at better (and still imperfect) solutions to world mysteries and to increased human happiness. This kind of scientific outlook, RET hypothesizes, is closely related to what is often called mental health.

10. Although RET holds that people are innately creative and constructive, and that whenever they needlessly upset themselves they also have the tendency and ability to think about their dysfunctional thinking, feeling, and behaving to reconstruct the self-defeating ways they have largely constructed, it also hypothesizes that once people upset themselves, their emotional reactions—especially their panic, depression, and self-hatred—are often so strong and consuming that these emotions interfere with their curative powers and sabotage some of their constructiveness. Also, as noted earlier, their disturbance about their disturbance often blocks them from changing.

Consequently, if left to their own devices in an existential encounter with their therapists, clients will receive less help and often become more disturbed than if guided and taught by a more active–directive therapist. In addition to strongly upholding an existentialist philosophy that people can fully accept themselves merely because they exist and because they choose to be self-accepting—and not because they perform well or are approved by significant others—RET goes one step further and teaches clients that they do not have to rate or measure their self, their being, or their totality at all but can choose to merely rate their acts, deeds, and performances in relation to their goals and desires. Thus, they can say "*It* is good that I succeed and am loved" or "*It* is bad when I fail and get rejected." But they had better not say "*I* am good for succeeding" and "*I* am bad for getting rejected."

Unlike Carl Rogers and other existential therapists, who believe that unconditional positive regard can be given by the therapist's modeling it and accepting clients unconditionally, RET practitioners try to give this kind of acceptance to all clients but also teach them how to give it to themselves. In this way, RET is both humanistic–existential and didactic and active–directive.

What about RET's directions for the future? These are potentially many; RET is increasingly applied to business, management, politics, economics, marriage and family, and many other fields. The one I would most like to stress, however, is education.

Even if RET and cognitive–behavioral therapy stay on a good track, their future in psychotherapy may always be somewhat limited because psychotherapy itself, in its individual and group applications, has the serious limitation of being available, now and in the foreseeable future, only to limited numbers of paying clients. But RET and cognitive–behavioral therapy, unlike most of the other popular therapies, have the unique potential of being properly introduced to the general public in books, audio- and videocassettes, lectures, workshops, and other mass media presentations, and thus considerably helping vast numbers of people. They are already being, and can continue to be, widely applied in educational settings, from nursery school to graduate school and adult education settings. Therefore, the main future of RET will be, I predict, in its psychoeducational applications, and I hope this kind of usage will be of considerable help to clients who are in therapy as well as those who are in various kinds of self-help groups. Better yet, perhaps, it will help literally millions of people who never have had any form of individual or group treatment to clearly see some of the ways in which they are needlessly disturbing themselves; to work at overcoming their self-constructed emotional, cognitive, and behavioral problems; and to achieve a more self-actualized and self-fulfilled existence.

References

1. Ellis, A. (1962). *Reason and emotion in psychotherapy.* Secaucus, NJ: Citadel.
2. Ellis, A. (1988). *How to stubbornly refuse to make yourself miserable about anything—yes, anything!* Secaucus, NJ: Lyle Stuart.
3. Ellis, A. (1991). The revised ABCs of rational–emotive therapy. *Journal of Rational–Emotive and Cognitive–Behavior Therapy, 9,* 139–192.
4. Ellis, A., & Dryden, W. (1987). *The practice of rational–emotive therapy.* New York: Springer.
5. Walen, S., DiGiuseppe, R., & Dryden, W. (1992). *A practitioner's guide to rational–emotive therapy.* New York: Oxford University Press.

QUESTIONS FOR REFLECTION AND DISCUSSION:

1. Ellis wrote this article for his fellow psychologists. How might he have changed his approach if he had been writing it for the lay audience (nonprofessionals)?

2. What is Ellis's "ABC theory of human disturbance"?

3. Ellis suggests that his views are more philosophical than those of people like Aaron Beck and Donald Meichenbaum. As you read his article, what principles of RET—if any—strike you as being philosophical rather than purely scientific? Why? (Hint: How does Ellis relate a scientific outlook to mental health?)

4. How does Ellis distinguish between so-called general RET and preferential RET?

5. Ellis has a knack for writing in appealing everyday language, even for inventing language to communicate his ideas. For example, what does Ellis mean by his term *must-urbation*? How is this term a play on words? How does must-urbation make people miserable?

6. Would you consider RET to be a form of cognitive therapy? Why or why not?

7. What, if anything, can you learn from this article to improve your own life?

SOURCE

Rogers, C. R. (1961). A therapist's view of the good life: The fully functioning person. In *On becoming a person* (pp. 183–196). Boston: Houghton Mifflin Co. All rights reserved.

Carl Rogers (1902–1987) spent his early years in a wealthy Chicago suburb, where he attended school with Ernest Hemingway and Frank Lloyd Wright's children. His family, with its six children, was religious and close-knit. His father viewed pastimes like smoking, drinking, playing cards, and going to the movies as immoral. His father said that one could be tolerant of such behavior but he discouraged relationships with people who engaged in them. When Carl Rogers was 12, his family moved to a farm farther from the city to protect the children from unwholesome influences.

Rogers took refuge in books and developed an interest in science. His first college major was agriculture. During a student visit to Peking in 1922, he was exposed for the first time to people from different ethnic backgrounds. He wrote his parents to proclaim his independence from their conservative views. Shortly thereafter he developed an ulcer and had to be hospitalized.

Rogers then attended New York's Union Theological Seminary with the goal of becoming a minister. At the same time he took courses in psychology and education literally across the street at Columbia University. After a couple of years he came to believe that psychology might be a better way of helping people, so he transferred to Columbia. Perhaps in response to his parents' efforts to "protect" him from other ways of thinking, Rogers developed a form of therapy—client-centered therapy—that is intended to help people get in touch with their genuine feelings and pursue their own interests, regardless of other people's wishes.

What would such a person be like—that is, someone who was in touch with himself or herself and living life to its fullest? Here is Rogers's view of that person.

A Therapist's View of the Good Life: The Fully Functioning Person

CARL R. ROGERS

My views regarding the meaning of the good life are largely based upon my experience in working with people in the very close and intimate relationship which is called psychotherapy. These views thus have an empirical or experiential foundation, as contrasted perhaps with a scholarly or philosophical foundation. I have learned what the good life seems to be by observing and participating in the struggle of disturbed and troubled people to achieve that life.

I should make it clear from the outset that this experience I have gained comes from the vantage point of a particular orientation to psychotherapy which has developed over the years. Quite possibly all psychotherapy is basically similar, but since I am less sure of that than I once was, I wish to make it clear that my therapeutic experience has been along the lines that seem to me most effective, the type of therapy termed "client-centered."

Let me attempt to give a very brief description of what this therapy would be like if it were in every

Harcourt, Inc.

respect optimal, since I feel I have learned most about the good life from therapeutic experiences in which a great deal of movement occurred. If the therapy were optimal, intensive as well as extensive, then it would mean that the therapist has been able to enter into an intensely personal and subjective relationship with the client—relating not as a scientist to an object of study, not as a physician expecting to diagnose and cure, but as a person to a person. It would mean that the therapist feels this client to be a person of unconditional self-worth: of value no matter what his condition, his behavior, or his feelings. It would mean that the therapist is genuine, hiding behind no defensive façade, but meeting the client with the feelings which organically he is experiencing. It would mean that the therapist is able to let himself go in understanding this client; that no inner barriers keep him from sensing what it feels like to be the client at each moment of the relationship; and that he can convey something of his empathic understanding to the client. It means that the therapist has been comfortable in entering this relationship fully, without knowing cognitively where it will lead, satisfied with providing a climate which will permit the client the utmost freedom to become himself.

For the client, this optimal therapy would mean an exploration of increasingly strange and unknown and dangerous feelings in himself, the exploration proving possible only because he is gradually realizing that he is accepted unconditionally. Thus he becomes acquainted with elements of his experience which have in the past been denied to awareness as too threatening, too damaging to the structure of the self. He finds himself experiencing these feelings fully, completely, in the relationship, so that for the moment he *is* his fear, or his anger, or his tenderness, or his strength. And as he lives these widely varied feelings, in all their degrees of intensity, he discovers that he has experienced *himself*, that he *is* all these feelings. He finds his behavior changing in constructive fashion in accordance with his newly experienced self. He approaches the realization that he no longer needs to fear what experience may hold, but can welcome it freely as a part of his changing and developing self.

This is a thumbnail sketch of what client-centered therapy comes close to, when it is at its optimum. I give it here simply as a brief picture of the context in which I have formed my views of the good life.

A Negative Observation

As I have tried to live understandingly in the experiences of my clients, I have gradually come to one negative conclusion about the good life. It seems to me that the good life is not any fixed state. It is not, in my estimation, a state of virtue, or contentment, or nirvana, or happiness. It is not a condition in which the individual is adjusted, or fulfilled, or actualized. To use psychological terms, it is not a state of drive-reduction, or tension-reduction, or homeostasis.

I believe that all of these terms have been used in ways which imply that if one or several of these states is achieved, then the goal of life has been achieved. Certainly, for many people happiness, or adjustment, are seen as states of being which are synonymous with the good life. And social scientists have frequently spoken of the reduction of tension, or the achievement of homeostasis or equilibrium as if these states constituted the goal of the process of living.

So it is with a certain amount of surprise and concern that I realize that my experience supports none of these definitions. If I focus on the experience of those individuals who seem to have evidenced the greatest degree of movement during the therapeutic relationship, and who, in the years following this relationship, appear to have made and to be making real progress toward the good life, then it seems to me that they are not adequately described at all by any of these terms which refer to fixed states of being. I believe they would consider themselves insulted if they were described as "adjusted," and they would regard it as false if they were described as "happy" or "contented," or even "actualized." As I have known them I would regard it as most inaccurate to say that all their drive tensions have been reduced, or that they are in a state of homeostasis. So I am forced to ask myself whether there is any way in which I can generalize about their situation, any definition which I can give of the good life which would seem to fit the facts as I have observed them. I find this not at all easy, and what follows is stated very tentatively.

A Positive Observation

If I attempt to capture in a few words what seems to me to be true of these people, I believe it will come out something like this:

The good life is a *process*, not a state of being.

It is a direction, not a destination.

The direction which constitutes the good life is that which is selected by the total organism, when there is psychological freedom to move in *any* direction.

This organismically selected direction seems to have certain discernible general qualities which appear to be the same in a wide variety of unique individuals.

So I can integrate these statements into a definition which can at least serve as a basis for consideration and discussion. The good life, from the point of view of my experience, is the process of movement in a direction which the human organism selects when it is inwardly free to move in any direction, and the general qualities of this selected direction appear to have a certain universality.

The Characteristics of the Process

Let me now try to specify what appear to be the characteristic qualities of this process of movement, as they crop up in person after person in therapy.

AN INCREASING OPENNESS TO EXPERIENCE

In the first place, the process seems to involve an increasing openness to experience. This phrase has come to have more and more meaning for me. It is the polar opposite of defensiveness. Defensiveness I have described in the past as being the organism's response to experiences which are perceived or anticipated as threatening, as incongruent with the individual's existing picture of himself, or of himself in relationship to the world. These threatening experiences are temporarily rendered harmless by being distorted in awareness, or being denied to awareness. I quite literally cannot see, with accuracy, those experiences, feelings, reactions in myself which are significantly at variance with the picture of myself which I already possess. A large part of the process of therapy is the continuing discovery by the client that he is experiencing feelings and attitudes which heretofore he has not been able to be aware of, which he has not been able to "own" as being a part of himself.

If a person could be fully open to his experience, however, every stimulus—whether originating within the organism or in the environment—would be freely relayed through the nervous system without being distorted by any defensive mechanism. There would be no need of the mechanism of "subception" whereby the organism is forewarned of any experience threatening to the self. On the contrary, whether the stimulus was the impact of a configuration of form, color, or sound in the environment on the sensory nerves, or a memory trace from the past, or a visceral sensation of fear or pleasure or disgust, the person would be "living" it, would have it completely available to awareness.

Thus, one aspect of this process which I am naming "the good life" appears to be a movement away from the pole of defensiveness toward the pole of openness to experience. The individual is becoming more able to listen to himself, to experience what is going on within himself. He is more open to his feelings of fear and discouragement and pain. He is also more open to his feelings of courage, and tenderness, and awe. He is free to live his feelings subjectively, as they exist in him, and also free to be aware of these feelings. He is more able fully to live the experiences of his organism rather than shutting them out of awareness.

INCREASINGLY EXISTENTIAL LIVING

A second characteristic of the process which for me is the good life, is that it involves an increasing tendency to live fully in each moment. This is a thought which can easily be misunderstood, and which is perhaps somewhat vague in my own thinking. Let me try to explain what I mean.

I believe it would be evident that for the person who was fully open to his new experience, completely without defensiveness, each moment would be new. The complex configuration of inner and outer stimuli which exists in this moment has never existed before in just this fashion. Consequently such a person would realize that "What I will be in the next moment, and what I will do, grows out of that moment, and cannot be predicted in advance either by me or by others." Not infrequently we find clients expressing exactly this sort of feeling.

One way of expressing the fluidity which is present in such existential living is to say that the self and personality emerge *from* experience, rather than experience being translated or twisted to fit preconceived self-structure. It means that one becomes a participant in and an observer of the ongoing process of organismic experience, rather than being in control of it.

Such living in the moment means an absence of rigidity, of tight organization, of the imposition of structure on experience. It means instead a maximum of adaptability, a discovery of structure *in* experience, a flowing, changing organization of self and personality.

It is this tendency toward existential living which appears to me very evident in people who are involved in the process of the good life. One might almost say that it is the most essential quality of it. It involves discovering the structure of experience in the process of living the experience. Most of us, on the other hand, bring a preformed structure and evaluation to our experience and never relinquish it, but cram and twist the experience to fit our preconceptions, annoyed at the fluid qualities which make it so unruly in fitting our carefully constructed pigeonholes. To open one's spirit to what is going on *now,* and to discover in that present process whatever structure it appears to have—this to me is one of the qualities of the good life, the mature life, as I see clients approach it.

AN INCREASING TRUST IN HIS ORGANISM

Still another characteristic of the person who is living the process of the good life appears to be an increasing trust in his organism as a means of arriving at the most satisfying behavior in each existential situation. Again let me try to explain what I mean.

In choosing what course of action to take in any situation, many people rely upon guiding principles, upon a code of action laid down by some group or institution, upon the judgment of others (from wife and friends to Emily Post), or upon the way they have behaved in some similar past situation. Yet as I observe the clients whose experiences in living have taught me so much, I find that increasingly such individuals are able to trust their total organismic reaction to a new situation because they discover to an ever-increasing degree that if they are open to their experience, doing what "feels right" proves to be a competent and trustworthy guide to behavior which is truly satisfying.

As I try to understand the reason for this, I find myself following this line of thought. The person who is fully open to his experience would have access to all of the available data in the situation, on which to base his behavior; the social demands, his own complex and possibly conflicting needs, his memories of similar situations, his perception of the uniqueness of this situation, etc., etc. The data would be very complex indeed. But he could permit his total organism, his consciousness participating, to consider each stimulus, need, and demand, its relative intensity and importance, and out of this complex weighing and balancing, discover that course of action which would come closest to satisfying all his needs in the situation. An analogy which might come close to a description would be to compare this person to a giant electronic computing machine. Since he is open to his experience, all of the data from his sense impressions, from his memory, from previous learning, from his visceral and internal states, is fed into the machine. The machine takes all of these multitudinous pulls and forces which are fed in as data, and quickly computes the course of action which would be the most economical vector of need satisfaction in this exis-

tential situation. This is the behavior of our hypothetical person.

The defects which in most of us make this process untrustworthy are the inclusion of information which does *not* belong to this present situation, or the exclusion of information which *does.* It is when memories and previous learnings are fed into the computations as if they were *this* reality, and not memories and learnings, that erroneous behavioral answers arise. Or when certain threatening experiences are inhibited from awareness, and hence are withheld from the computation or fed into it in distorted form, this too produces error. But our hypothetical person would find his organism thoroughly trustworthy, because all of the available data would be used, and it would be present in accurate rather than distorted form. Hence his behavior would come as close as possible to satisfying all his needs—for enhancement, for affiliation with others, and the like.

In this weighing, balancing, and computation, his organism would not by any means be infallible. It would always give the best possible answer for the available data, but sometimes data would be missing. Because of the element of openness to experience, however, any errors, any following of behavior which was not satisfying, would be quickly corrected. The computations, as it were, would always be in process of being corrected, because they would be continually checked in behavior.

Perhaps you will not like my analogy of an electronic computing machine. Let me return to the clients I know. As they become more open to all of their experiences, they find it increasingly possible to trust their reactions. If they "feel like" expressing anger they do so and find that this comes out satisfactorily, because they are equally alive to all of their other desires for affection, affiliation, and relationship. They are surprised at their own intuitive skill in finding behavioral solutions to complex and troubling human relationships. It is only afterward that they realize how surprisingly trustworthy their inner reactions have been in bringing about satisfactory behavior.

THE PROCESS OF FUNCTIONING MORE FULLY

I should like to draw together these three threads describing the process of the good life into a more coherent picture. It appears that the person who is psychologically free moves in the direction of becoming a more fully functioning person. He is more able to live fully in and with each and all of his feelings and reactions. He makes increasing use of all his organic equipment to sense, as accurately as possible, the existential situation within and without. He makes use of all of the information his nervous system can thus supply, using it in awareness, but recognizing that his total organism may be, and often is, wiser than his awareness. He is more able to permit his total organism to function freely in all its complexity in selecting, from the multitude of possibilities, that behavior which in this moment of time will be most generally and genuinely satisfying. He is able to put more trust in his organism in this functioning, not because it is infallible, but because he can be fully open to the consequences of each of his actions and correct them if they prove to be less than satisfying.

He is more able to experience all of his feelings, and is less afraid of any of his feelings; he is his own sifter of evidence, and is more open to evidence from all sources; he is completely engaged in the process of being and becoming himself, and thus discovers that he is soundly and realistically social; he lives more completely in this moment, but learns that this is the soundest living for all time. He is becoming a more fully functioning organism, and because of the awareness of himself which flows freely in and through his experience, he is becoming a more fully functioning person.

Some Implications

Any view of what constitutes the good life carries with it many implications, and the view I have presented is no exception. I hope that these implications may be food for thought. There are two or three of these about which I would like to comment.

A NEW PERSPECTIVE ON FREEDOM VS DETERMINISM

The first of these implications may not immediately be evident. It has to do with the age-old issue of "free will." Let me endeavor to spell out the way in which this issue now appears to me in a new light.

For some time I have been perplexed over the living paradox which exists in psychotherapy between freedom and determinism. In the therapeutic relationship some of the most compelling subjective experiences are those in which the client feels within himself the power of naked choice. He is *free*—to become himself or to hide behind a façade; to move forward or to retrogress; to behave in ways which are destructive of self and others, or in ways which are enhancing; quite literally free to live or die, in both the physiological and psychological meaning of those terms. Yet as we enter this field

of psychotherapy with objective research methods, we are, like any other scientist, committed to a complete determinism. From this point of view every thought, feeling, and action of the client is determined by what preceded it. There can be no such thing as freedom. The dilemma I am trying to describe is no different than that found in other fields—it is simply brought to sharper focus, and appears more insoluble.

This dilemma can be seen in a fresh perspective, however, when we consider it in terms of the definition I have given of the fully functioning person. We could say that in the optimum of therapy the person rightfully experiences the most complete and absolute freedom. He wills or chooses to follow the course of action which is the most economical vector in relationship to all the internal and external stimuli, because it is that behavior which will be most deeply satisfying. But this is the same course of action which from another vantage point may be said to be determined by all the factors in the existential situation. Let us contrast this with the picture of the person who is defensively organized. He wills or chooses to follow a given course of action, but finds that he *cannot* behave in the fashion that he chooses. He is determined by the factors in the existential situation, but these factors include his defensiveness, his denial or distortion of some of the relevant data. Hence it is certain that his behavior will be less than fully satisfying. His behavior is determined, but he is not free to make an effective choice. The fully functioning person, on the other hand, not only experiences, but utilizes, the most absolute freedom when he spontaneously, freely, and voluntarily chooses and wills that which is also absolutely determined.

I am not so naive as to suppose that this fully resolves the issue between subjective and objective, between freedom and necessity. Nevertheless it has meaning for me that the more the person is living the good life, the more he will experience a freedom of choice, and the more his choices will be effectively implemented in his behavior.

CREATIVITY AS AN ELEMENT OF THE GOOD LIFE

I believe it will be clear that a person who is involved in the directional process which I have termed "the good life" is a creative person. With his sensitive openness to his world, his trust of his own ability to form new relationships with his environment, he would be the type of person from whom creative products and creative living emerge. He would not necessarily be "adjusted" to his culture, and he would almost certainly not be a conformist. But at any time and in any culture he would live constructively, in as much harmony with his culture as a balanced satisfaction of needs demanded. In some cultural situations he might in some ways be very unhappy, but he would continue to move toward becoming himself, and to behave in such a way as to provide the maximum satisfaction of his deepest needs.

Such a person would, I believe, be recognized by the student of evolution as the type most likely to adapt and survive under changing environmental conditions. He would be able creatively to make sound adjustments to new as well as old conditions. He would be a fit vanguard of human evolution.

BASIC TRUSTWORTHINESS OF HUMAN NATURE

It will be evident that another implication of the view I have been presenting is that the basic nature of the human being, when functioning freely, is constructive and trustworthy. For me this is an inescapable conclusion from a quarter-century of experience in psychotherapy. When we are able to free the individual from defensiveness, so that he is open to the wide range of his own needs, as well as the wide range of environmental and social demands, his reactions may be trusted to be positive, forward-moving, constructive. We do not need to ask who will socialize him, for one of his own deepest needs is for affiliation and communication with others. As he becomes more fully himself, he will become more realistically socialized. We do not need to ask who will control his aggressive impulses; for as he becomes more open to all of his impulses, his need to be liked by others and his tendency to give affection will be as strong as his impulses to strike out or to seize for himself. He will be aggressive in situations in which aggression is realistically appropriate, but there will be no runaway need for aggression. His total behavior, in these and other areas, as he moves toward being open to all his experience, will be more balanced and realistic, behavior which is appropriate to the survival and enhancement of a highly social animal.

I have little sympathy with the rather prevalent concept that man is basically irrational, and that his impulses, if not controlled, will lead to destruction of others and self. Man's behavior is exquisitely rational, moving with subtle and ordered complexity toward the goals his organism is endeavoring to achieve. The tragedy for most of us is that our defenses keep us from being aware of this rationality, so that consciously we are moving in one direction, while organismically we are moving in another. But in our person who is living the process of the good life, there would be a decreasing number of such barriers, and he would be increasingly a participant in the rationality of his organism. The only control of impulses which would exist, or which would prove necessary, is the natural and internal balancing of one need against another, and the discovery of behaviors which follow the vector most closely approximating the satisfaction of all needs. The experience of extreme satisfaction of one need (for aggression, or sex, etc.) in such a way as to do violence to the satisfaction of other needs (for companionship, tender relationship, etc.)—an experience very common in the defensively organized person—would be greatly decreased. He would participate in the vastly complex self-regulatory activities of his organism—the psychological as well as physiological thermostatic controls—in such a fashion as to live in increasing harmony with himself and with others.

THE GREATER RICHNESS OF LIFE

One last implication I should like to mention is that this process of living in the good life involves a wider range, a greater richness, than the constricted living in which most of us find ourselves. To be a part of this process means that one is involved in the frequently frightening and frequently satisfying experience of a more sensitive living, with greater range, greater variety, greater richness. It seems to me that clients who have moved significantly in therapy live more intimately with their feelings of pain, but also more vividly with their feelings of ecstasy; that anger is more clearly felt, but so also is love; that fear is an experience they know more deeply, but so is courage. And the reason they can thus live fully in a wider range is that they have this underlying confidence in themselves as trustworthy instruments for encountering life.

I believe it will have become evident why, for me, adjectives such as happy, contented, blissful, enjoyable, do not seem quite appropriate to any general description of this process I have called the good life, even though the person in this process would experience each one of these feelings at appropriate times. But the adjectives which seem more generally fitting are adjectives such as enriching, exciting, rewarding, challenging, meaningful. This process of the good life is not, I am convinced, a life for the faint-hearted. It involves the stretching and growing of becoming more and more of one's potentialities. It involves the courage to be. It means launching oneself fully into the stream of life. Yet the deeply exciting thing about human beings is that when the individual is inwardly free, he chooses as the good life this process of becoming.

QUESTIONS FOR REFLECTION AND DISCUSSION:

1. How did Rogers collect the "data" for his conclusions about the nature of the fully-functioning person? Are there limitations to this method? Explain.

2. Why is unconditional positive regard a key component of Rogers's method of therapy?

3. Why does Rogers say that people who live the good life are not "adjusted, or fulfilled, or actualized"? What does it mean to say that the good life is "a direction, not a destination"? (What role does self-actualization play in Rogers's self theory?)

4. Are you open to new experience? (Are you sure?)

5. What is meant by *existential living*? Are you living "for the moment" or are you always looking to the future?

6. What does it mean to "trust one's organism"? Is it a prescription for selfishness or a means to freedom?

7. What does Rogers mean by *freedom vs. determinism*?

8. Why might behaviorists or behavior therapists object to Rogers's goals of therapy?

SOURCE

Smith, M. L., & Glass, G. V. (1977). Meta-analysis of psychotherapy outcome studies. *American Psychologist, 32,* 752–760. Copyright © 1977 by the American Psychological Association. Reprinted with permission.

Some articles have great impact on a scientific field. The following article by Mary Lee Smith and Gene V. Glass was important in that it provided support for the effectiveness of psychotherapy. It also countered an influential article that had been written by Hans Eysenck 25 years earlier, that stated that it had not been shown that people who receive psychotherapy fare better than those who do not. Eysenck admitted that people who received psychotherapy tended to do better afterward; however, he argued that it had not been shown that they do better than they would have done if they had been left untreated. (People who do better without treatment are said to show "spontaneous remission," and Eysenck was not convinced that the rate of improvement associated with psychotherapy significantly surpassed the spontaneous remission rate.)

Meta-analysis is currently a commonly used technique for combining the results of many studies in a given area of research. When Smith and Glass used it, it was rather new. They combined the results of hundreds of studies in psychotherapy and counseling to arrive at their conclusion that psychotherapy does work.

As you read their study, look for the following: What standards were used to include or exclude studies from the research sample? How is the term "effect size" used. Note briefly that an effect size of 1 refers to a difference of 1 standard deviation. If you picture a normal curve, 34% of the individuals contained in the curve would lie between the mean (the 50th percentile) and plus 1 standard deviation (the 84th percentile). This will help explain the authors' math.

Meta-Analysis of Psychotherapy Outcome Studies

MARY LEE SMITH & GENE V. GLASS
UNIVERSITY OF COLORADO—BOULDER

ABSTRACT: Results of nearly 400 controlled evaluations of psychotherapy and counseling were coded and integrated statistically. The findings provide convincing evidence of the efficacy of psychotherapy. On the average, the typical therapy client is better off than 75% of untreated individuals. Few important differences in effectiveness could be established among many quite different types of psychotherapy. More generally, virtually no difference in effectiveness was observed between the class of all behavioral therapies (systematic desensitization, behavior modification) and the nonbehavioral therapies (Rogerian, psychodynamic, rational-emotive, transactional analysis, etc.).

Scholars and clinicians have argued bitterly for decades about the efficacy of psychotherapy and counseling. Michael Scriven proposed to the American Psychological Association's Ethics Committee that APA-member clinicians be required to present a card to prospective clients on which it would be explained that the procedure they were about to undergo had never been proven superior to a placebo ("Psychotherapy Caveat," 1974). Most academics have read little more than Eysenck's (1952, 1965) tendentious diatribes in which he claimed to prove that 75% of neurotics got better regardless of whether or not they were in therapy—a conclusion based on the interpretation of six controlled studies. The perception that research shows the inefficacy of psychotherapy has become part of conventional wisdom even within the profession. The following testimony was recently presented before the Colorado State Legislature:

> Are they [the legislators] also aware of the relatively primitive state of the art of treatment outcome evaluation which is still, after fifty years, in kind of a virginal state? About all we've been able to prove is that a third of the people get better, a third of the people stay the same, and a third of the people get worse, irregardless of the treatment to which they are subjected. (Quoted by Ellis, 1977, p. 3)

Only close followers of the issue have read Bergin's (1971) astute dismantling of the Eysenck myth in his review of the findings of 23 controlled evaluations of therapy. Bergin found evidence that therapy is effective. Emrick (1975) reviewed 72 studies of the psychological and psychopharmacological treatment of alcoholism and concluded that evidence existed for the efficacy of therapy. Luborsky, Singer, and Luborsky (1975) reviewed about 40 controlled studies and found more evidence. Although these reviews were reassuring, two sources of doubt remained. First, the number of studies in which the effects of counseling and psychotherapy have been tested is closer to 400 than to 40. How representative the 40 are of the 400 is unknown. Second, in these reviews, the "voting method" was used; that is, the number of studies with statistically significant results in favor of one treatment or another was tallied. This method is too weak to answer many important questions and is biased in favor of large-sample studies.

The purpose of the present research has three parts: (1) to identify and collect all studies that tested the effects of counseling and psychotherapy; (2) to determine the magnitude of effect of the therapy in each study; and (3) to compare the effects of different types of therapy and relate the size of effect to the characteristics of the therapy (e.g., diagnosis of patient, training of therapist) and of the study. Meta-analysis, the integration of research through statistical analysis of the analyses of individual studies (Glass, 1976), was used to investigate the problem.

Procedures

Standard search procedures were used to identify 1,000 documents: *Psychological Abstracts, Dissertation Abstracts,* and branching off of bibliographies of the documents themselves. Of those documents located, approximately 500 were selected for inclusion in the study, and 375 were fully analyzed. To be selected, a study had to have at least one therapy treatment group compared to an untreated group or to a different therapy group. The rigor of the research design was not a selection criterion but was one of several features of the individual study to be related to the effect of the treatment in that study. The definition of psychotherapy used to select the studies was presented by Meltzoff and Kornreich (1970):

> Psychotherapy is taken to mean the informed and planful application of techniques derived from established psychological principles, by persons qualified through training and experience to understand these principles and to apply these techniques with the intention of assisting individuals to modify such personal characteristics as feelings, values, attitudes, and behaviors which are judged by the therapist to be maladaptive or maladjustive. (p. 6)

Those studies in which the treatment was labeled "counseling" but whose methods fit the above definition were included. Drug therapies, hypnotherapy, bibliotherapy, occupational therapy, milieu therapy, and peer counseling were excluded. Sensitivity training, marathon encounter groups, consciousness-raising groups, and psychodrama were also excluded. Those studies that Bergin and Luborsky eliminated because they used "analogue" therapy were retained for the present research. Such studies have been designated analogue studies because therapy lasted only a few hours or the therapists were relatively untrained. Rather than arbitrarily eliminating large numbers of studies and losing potentially valuable information, it was deemed preferable to retain these studies and investigate the relationship between length of therapy, training of therapists, and other characteristics of the study and their measured ef-

The research reported here was supported by a grant from the Spencer Foundation, Chicago, Illinois. This paper draws in part from the presidential address of the second author to the American Educational Resesarch Association, San Francisco, April 21, 1976.

Requests for reprints should be sent to Gene V. Glass, Laboratory of Educational Research, University of Colorado, Boulder, Colorado 80302.

fects. The arbitrary elimination of such analogue studies was based on an implicit assumption that they differ not only in their methods but also in their effects and how those effects are achieved. Considering methods, analogue studies fade imperceptibly into "real" therapy, since the latter is often short term, or practiced by relative novices, etc. Furthermore, the magnitude of effects and their relationships with other variables are empirical questions, not to be assumed out of existence. Dissertations and fugitive documents were likewise retained, and the measured effects of the studies compared according to the source of the studies.

The most important feature of an outcome study was the magnitude of the effect of therapy. The definition of the magnitude of effect—or *"effect size"*—was the *mean difference between the treated and control subjects divided by the standard deviation of the control group*, that is, $ES = (\overline{X}_T - \overline{X}_C)/s_C$. Thus, an "effect size" of $+1$ indicates that a person at the mean of the control group would be expected to rise to the 84th percentile of the control group after treatment.

The effect size was calculated on any outcome variable the researcher chose to measure. In many cases, one study yielded more than one effect size, since effects might be measured at more than one time after treatment or on more than one different type of outcome variable. The effect-size measures represent different types of outcomes: self-esteem, anxiety, work/school achievement, physiological stress, etc. Mixing different outcomes together is defensible. First, it is clear that all outcome measures are more or less related to "well-being" and so at a general level are comparable. Second, it is easy to imagine a Senator conducting hearings on the NIMH appropriations or a college president deciding whether to continue funding the counseling center asking, "What kind of effect does therapy produce—on anything?" Third, each primary researcher made value judgments concerning the definition and direction of positive therapeutic effects for the particular clients he or she studied. It is reasonable to adopt these value judgments and aggregate them in the present study. Fourth, since all effect sizes are identified by type of outcome, the magnitude of effect can be compared across type of outcome to determine whether therapy has greater effect on anxiety, for example, than it does on self-esteem.

Calculating effect sizes was straightforward when means and standard deviations were reported. Although this information is thought to be fundamental in reporting research, it was often overlooked by authors and editors. When means and standard deviations were not reported, effect sizes were obtained by the solution of equations from t and F ratios or other inferential test statistics. Probit transformations were used to convert to effect sizes the percentages of patients who improved (Glass, in press). Original data were requested from several authors when effect sizes could not be derived from any reported information. In two instances, effect sizes were impossible to reconstruct: (a) nonparametric statistics irretrievably disguise effect sizes, and (b) the reporting of no data except the alpha level at which a mean difference was significant gives no clue other than that the standardized mean difference must exceed some known value.

Eight hundred thirty-three effect sizes were computed from 375 studies, several studies yielding effects on more than one type of outcome or at more than one time after therapy. Including more than one effect size for each study perhaps introduces dependence in the errors and violates some assumptions of inferential statistics. However, the loss of information that would have resulted from averaging effects across types of outcome or at different follow-up points was too great a price to pay for statistical purity.

The effect sizes of the separate studies became the "dependent variable" in the meta-analysis. The "independent variables" were 16 features of the study described or measured in the following ways:

1. The type of therapy employed, for example, psychodynamic, client centered, rational-emotive, behavior modification, etc. There were 10 types in all; each will be mentioned in the Results section.

2. The duration of therapy in hours.

3. Whether it was group or individual therapy.

4. The number of years' experience of the therapist.

5. Whether clients were neurotics or psychotics.

6. The age of the clients.

7. The IQ of the clients.

8. The source of the subjects—whether solicited for the study, committed to an institution, or sought treatment themselves.

9. Whether the therapists were trained in education, psychology, or psychiatry.

10. The social and ethnic similarity of therapists and clients.

11. The type of outcome measure taken.

12. The number of months after therapy that the outcomes were measured.

13. The reactivity or "fakeability" of the outcome measure.

14. The date of publication of the study.

15. The form of publication.

16. The internal validity of the research design.

Definitions and conventions were developed to increase the reliability of measurement of the features of the studies and to assist the authors in estimating the data when they were not reported. The more important conventions appear in Table 30.01. Variables not mentioned in Table 30.01 were measured in fairly obvious ways. The reliability of measurement was determined by comparing the codings of 20 studies by the two authors and four assistants. Agreement exceeded 90% across all categories.[1]

Analysis of the data comprised four parts: (1) descriptive statistics for the body of data as a whole; (2) descriptive statistics for the comparison of therapy types and outcome types; (3) descriptive statistics for a subset of studies in which behavioral and nonbehavioral therapies were compared *in the same study;* and (4) regression analyses in which effect sizes were regressed onto variables descriptive of the study.

Findings

DATA FROM ALL EXPERIMENTS

Figure 30.01 contains the findings at the highest level of aggregation. The two curves depict the average treated and untreated groups of clients across 375 studies, 833 effect-size measures, representing an evaluation of approximately 25,000 control and experimental subjects each. On the average, clients 22 years of age received 17 hours of therapy from therapists with about $3\frac{1}{2}$ years of experience and were measured on the outcome variables about $3\frac{3}{4}$ months after the therapy.

For ease of representation, the figure is drawn in the form of two normal distributions. No conclusion about the distributions of the scores within studies is intended. In most studies, no information was given about the shape of an individual's scores within treated and untreated groups. We suspect that normality has as much justification as any other form.

The average study showed a .68 standard deviation superiority of the treated group over the con-

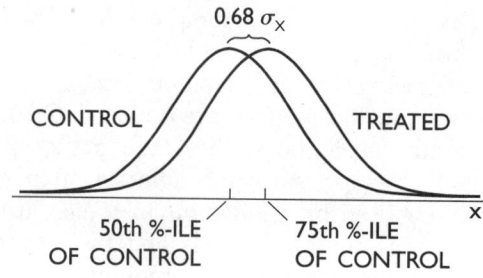

FIGURE 30.01

Effect of therapy on any outcome. (Data based on 375 studies; 833 data points.)

trol group. Thus, the average client receiving therapy was better off than 75% of the untreated controls. Ironically, the 75% figure that Eysenck used repeatedly to embarrass psychotherapy appears in a slightly different context as the most defensible figure on the efficacy of therapy: The therapies represented by the available outcome evaluations move the average client from the 50th to the 75th percentile.

The standard deviation of the effect sizes is *.67.* Their skewness is *+.99.* Only 12% of the 833 effect-size measures from the 375 studies were negative. If therapies of any type were ineffective and design and measurement flaws were immaterial, one would expect half the effect-size measures to be negative.

The 833 effect-size measures were classified into 10 categories descriptive of the type of outcome being assessed, for example, fear and anxiety reduction, self-esteem, adjustment (freedom from debilitating symptoms), achievement in school or on the job, social relations, emotional-somatic problems, physiological stress measures, etc. Effect-size measures for four outcome categories are presented in Table 30.02.

Two hundred sixty-one effect sizes from over 100 studies average about 1 standard deviation on measures of fear and anxiety reduction. Thus, the average treated client is better off than 83% of those untreated with respect to the alleviation of fear and anxiety. The improvement in self-esteem is nearly as large. The effect sizes average .9 of a standard deviation. Improvement on variables in the "adjustment" outcome class averages considerably less, roughly .6 of a standard deviation. These outcome variables are measures of personal functioning and frequently involve indices of hospitalization or incarceration for psychotic, alcoholic, or criminal episodes. The average effect size for school or work

---

[1] The values assigned to the features of the studies, the effect sizes, and all procedures are available in Glass, Smith, and Miller (Note 1).

TABLE 30.01

CONVENTIONS FOR MEASUREMENT OF THE FEATURES OF STUDIES

STUDY FEATURE	VALUE	STUDY FEATURE	VALUE
Experience of therapist (when not given)	Lay counselor (0 years) MA candidate (1 year) MA counselor (2 years) PhD candidate or psychiatric resident (3 years) PhD therapist (4 years) Well-known PhD or psychiatrist (5 years)	Type of outcome measure (*continued*)	Work/school achievement: grade point average, job supervisor ratings, promotions. Personality traits: MMPI or other trait inventories, projective test results. Social behavior: dating, classroom discipline, public speaking, information-seeking behavior, sociometrics. Emotional-somatic disorder: frigidity, impotence.
Diagnosis of client (neurotic or psychotic)	Neurotic unless symptoms or labels clearly indicate otherwise.		
IQ of client (low, average, high)	Average unless identified as otherwise by diagnostic labels (e.g., mentally retarded) or institutional affiliation (college attendance).	Reactivity of measurement	Physiological stress: galvanic skin response, Palmer Sweat Index, blood pressure, heart rate. 1 (low): Physiological measures; grade point average
Source of subjects	Clients solicited for purpose of the study. Clients committed to institution, hence to therapy. Clients recognized existence of problem and sought treatment.		2 Projective device (blind); discharge from hospital (blind) 3 Standardized measures of traits (MMPI, Rotter) 4 Experimenter-constructed questionnaires; client's self-report to experimenter; discharge (nonblind); behavior in presence of therapist
Similarity of therapist and client ("very similar" to "very dissimilar")	College students: very similar Neurotic adults: moderately similar Juveniles, minorities: moderately dissimilar Hospitalized, chronic adults, disturbed children, prisoners: very dissimilar		5 (high): Therapist rating; projective device (nonblind)
Type of outcome measure	Fear, anxiety: Spielberger & Cattell anxiety measures, behavioral approach tests. Self-esteem: inventories, self-ideal correlations, ratings by self and others. Adjustment: adjustment scales, improvement ratings, rehospitalization, time out of hospital, sobriety, symptomatic complaints, disruptive behavior.	Form of publication	Journal Book Thesis Unpublished document
		Internal validity (high, medium, low)	High: Randomization, low mortality Medium: More than one threat to internal validity Low: No matching of pretest information to equate groups

achievement—most frequently "grade point average"—is smallest of the four outcome classes.

The studies in the four outcome measure categories are not comparable in terms of type of therapy, duration, experience of therapists, number of months posttherapy at which outcomes were measured, etc. Nonetheless, the findings in Table 30.02 are fairly consistent with expectations and give the credible impression that fear and self-esteem are more susceptible to change in therapy than are the

TABLE 30.02

EFFECTS OF THERAPY ON FOUR TYPES OF OUTCOME MEASURE				
TYPE OF OUTCOME	AVERAGE EFFECT SIZE	NO. OF EFFECT SIZES	STANDARD ERROR OF MEAN EFFECT SIZE[a]	*MDN* TREATED PERSON'S PERCENTILE STATUS IN CONTROL GROUP
Fear-anxiety reduction	.97	261	.15	83
Self-esteem	.90	53	.13	82
Adjustment	.56	229	.05	71
School/work achievement	.31	145	.03	62

[a]*The standard errors of the mean are calculated by dividing the standard deviation of the effect sizes (not reported) by the square root of the number of them. This method, based on the assumption of independence known to be false, gives a lower bound to the standard errors (Tukey, Note 2). Inferential techniques employing Tukey's jackknife method which take the nonindependence into account are examined in Glass (in press).*

relatively more serious behaviors grouped under the categories "adjustment" and "achievement."

Table 30.03 presents the average effect sizes for 10 types of therapy. Nearly 100 effect-size measures arising from evaluations of psychodynamic therapy, that is, Freudianlike therapy but *not* psychoanalysis, average approximately .6 of a standard deviation. Studies of Adlerian therapy show an average of .7 sigma, but only 16 effect sizes were found. Eclectic therapies, that is, verbal, cognitive, nonbehavioral therapies more similar to psychodynamic therapies than any other type, gave a mean effect size of about .5 of a standard deviation. Although the number of controlled evaluations of Berne's transactional analysis was rather small, it gave a respectable average effect size of .6 sigma, the same as psychodynamic therapies. Albert Ellis's rational-emotive therapy, with a mean effect size of nearly .8 of a standard deviation, finished second among all 10 therapy types. The Gestalt therapies were relatively untested, but 8 studies showed 16 effect sizes averaging only .25 of a standard deviation. Rogerian client-centered therapy showed a .6 sigma effect size averaged across about 60 studies. The average of over 200 effect-size measures from approximately 100 studies of systematic desensitization therapy was .9 sigma, the largest average effect size of all therapy types. Implosive therapy showed a mean effect size of .64 of a standard deviation, about equal to that for Rogerian and psychodynamic therapies. Significantly, the average effect size for implosive therapy is markedly lower than that for systematic desensitization, which was usually

evaluated in studies using similar kinds of clients with similar problems—principally, simple phobias. The final therapy depicted in Table 30.03 is Skinnerian behavior modification, which showed a .75 sigma effect size.

Hay's ω^2, which relates the categorical variable "type of therapy" to the quantitative variable "effect size," has the value of .10 for the data in Table 30.03. Thus, these 10 therapy types account for 10% of the variance in the effect size that studies produce.

The types of therapy depicted in Table 30.03 were clearly not equated for duration, severity of problem, type of outcome, etc. Nonetheless, the differences in average effect sizes are interesting and interpretable. There is probably a tendency for researchers to evaluate the therapy they like best and to pick clients, circumstances, and outcome measures which show that therapy in the best light. Even so, major differences among the therapies appear. Implosive therapy is demonstrably inferior to systematic desensitization. Behavior modification shows the same mean effect size as rational-emotive therapy.

EFFECTS OF CLASSES OF THERAPY

To compare the effect of therapy type after equating for duration of therapy, diagnosis of client, type of outcome, etc., it was necessary to move to a coarser level of analysis in which data could be grouped into more stable composites. The problem was to group the 10 types of therapy into classes, so that

TABLE 30.03

TYPE OF THERAPY	AVERAGE EFFECT SIZE	NO. OF EFFECT SIZES	STANDARD ERROR OF MEAN EFFECT SIZE	*MDN* TREATED PERSON'S PERCENTILE STATUS IN CONTROL GROUP
EFFECTS OF TEN TYPES OF THERAPY ON ANY OUTCOME MEASURE				
Psychodynamic	.59	96	.05	72
Adlerian	.71	16	.19	76
Eclectic	.48	70	.07	68
Transactional analysis	.58	25	.19	72
Rational-emotive	.77	35	.13	78
Gestalt	.26	8	.09	60
Client-centered	.63	94	.08	74
Systematic desensitization	.91	223	.05	82
Implosion	.64	45	.09	74
Behavior modification	.76	132	.06	78

effect sizes could be compared among more general types of therapy. Methods of multidimensional scaling were used to derive a structure from the perceptions of similarities among the 10 therapies by a group of 25 clinicians and counselors. All of the judges in this scaling study were enrolled in a graduate-level seminar. For five weeks, the theory and techniques of the 10 therapies were studied and discussed. Then, each judge performed a multidimensional rank ordering of the therapies, judging similarity among them on whatever basis he or she chose, articulated or unarticulated, conscious or unconscious. The results of the Shepard-Kruskal multidimensional scaling analysis appear as Figure 30.02.

In Figure 30.02 one clearly sees four classes of therapies: the ego therapies (transactional analysis and rational-emotive therapy) in front; the three dynamic therapies low, in the background; the behavioral triad, upper right; and the pair of "humanistic" therapies, Gestalt and Rogerian. The average effect sizes among the four classes of therapies have been compared, but the findings are not reported here. Instead, a higher level of aggregation of the therapies, called "superclasses," was studied. The first superclass was formed from those therapies above the horizontal plane in Figure 30.02, with the exception of Gestalt therapy for which there was an inadequate number of studies. This superclass was then identical with the group of behavioral therapies: implosion, systematic desensitization, and behavior

modification. The second superclass comprises the six therapies below the horizontal plane in Figure 30.02 and is termed the *nonbehavioral superclass*, a composite of psychoanalytic psychotherapy, Adlerian, Rogerian, rational-emotive, eclectic therapy, and transactional analysis.

Figure 30.03 represents the mean effect sizes for studies classified by the two superclasses. On the average, approximately 200 evaluations of behavioral therapies showed a mean effect of about $.8\sigma_x$, standard error of .03, over the control group. Approximately 170 evaluations of nonbehavioral studies gave

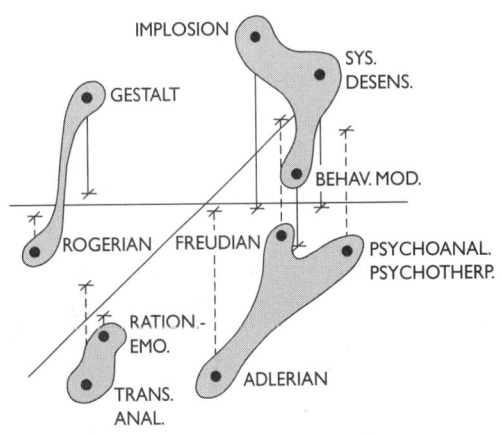

FIGURE 30.02

Multidimensional scaling of 10 therapies by 25 clinicians and counselors.

TREATMENT DESCRIPTION

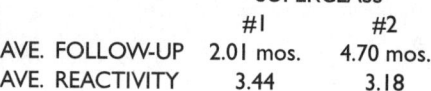

	SUPERCLASS	
	#1	#2
AVE. FOLLOW-UP	2.01 mos.	4.70 mos.
AVE. REACTIVITY	3.44	3.18

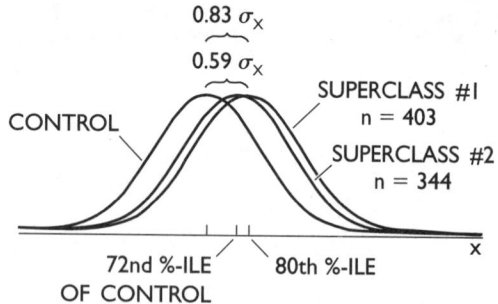

FIGURE 30.03

Effect of Superclass #1 (behavioral) and Superclass #2 (nonbehavioral).

a mean effect size of $.6\sigma_x$, standard error of .04. This small difference ($.2\sigma_x$) between the outcomes of behavioral and nonbehavioral therapies must be considered in light of the circumstances under which these studies were conducted. The evaluators of behavioral superclass therapies waited an average of 2 months after the therapy to measure its effects, whereas the postassessment of the nonbehavioral therapies was made in the vicinity of 5 months, on the average. Furthermore, the reactivity or susceptibility to bias of the outcome measures was higher for the behavioral superclass than for the nonbehavioral superclass; that is, the behavioral researchers showed a slightly greater tendency to rely on more subjective outcome measures. These differences lead one to suspect that the $.2\sigma_x$ difference between the behavioral and nonbehavioral superclasses is somewhat exaggerated in favor of the behavioral superclass. Exactly

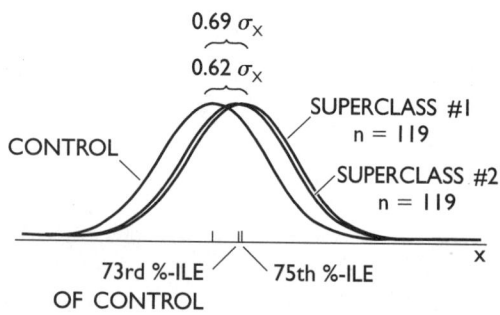

FIGURE 30.04

Effect of Superclass #1 (behavioral) and Superclass #2 (nonbehavioral). (Data drawn only from experiments in which Superclass #1 and Superclass #2 were simultaneously compared with control.)

TABLE 30.04

CORRELATIONS OF SEVERAL DESCRIPTIVE VARIABLES WITH EFFECT SIZE

VARIABLE	CORRELATION WITH EFFECT SIZE
Organization (1 = individual; 2 = group)	− .07
Duration of therapy (in hours)	− .02
Years' experience of therapists	− .01
Diagnosis of clients (1 = psychotic; 2 = neurotic)	.02
IQ of clients (1 = low; 2 = medium; 3 = high)	.15**
Age of clients	.02
Similarity of therapists and clients (1 = very similar; . . . ; 4 = very dissimilar)	− .19**
Internal validity of study (1 = high; 2 = medium; 3 = low)	− .09*
Date of publication	.09*
"Reactivity" of outcome measure (1 = low; . . . ; 5 = high)	.30**
No. of months posttherapy for follow-up	− .10*

*p < .05.
**p < .01.

how much the difference ought to be reduced is a question that can be approached in at least two ways: (a) examine the behavioral versus nonbehavioral difference for only those studies in which one therapy from each superclass was represented, since for those studies the experimental circumstances will be equivalent; (2) regress "effect size" onto variables descriptive of the study and correct statistically for differences in circumstances between behavioral and nonbehavioral studies.

Figure 30.04 represents 120 effect-size measures derived from those studies, approximately 50 in number, in which a behavioral therapy and nonbehavioral therapy were compared simultaneously with an untreated control. Hence, for these studies, the collective behavioral and nonbehavioral therapies are equivalent with respect to all important features of the experimental setting, namely, experience of the therapists, nature of the clients' problems, duration of therapy, type of outcome measure, months after therapy for measuring the outcomes, etc.

TABLE 30.05

	REGRESSION ANALYSES WITHIN THERAPIES		
	UNSTANDARDIZED REGRESSION COEFFICIENTS		
INDEPENDENT VARIABLE	PSYCHODYNAMIC ($n = 94$)	SYSTEMATIC DESENSITIZATION ($n = 212$)	BEHAVIOR MODIFICATION ($n = 129$)
Diagnosis (1 = psychotic; 2 = neurotic)	.174	−.193	.041
Intelligence (1 = low; . . . ; 3 = high)	−.114	.201	.201
Transformed age[a]	.002	−.002	.002
Experience of Therapist × Neurotic	−.011	−.034	−.018
Experience of Therapist × Psychotic	−.015	.004	−.033
Clients self-presented	−.111	.287	−.015
Clients solicited	.182	.088	−.163
Organization (1 = individual; 2 = group)	.108	−.086	−.276
Transformed months posttherapy[b]	−.031	−.047	.007
Transformed reactivity of measure[c]	.003	.025	.021
Additive constant	.757	.489	.453
Multiple R	.423	.512	.509
σ_e	.173	.386	.340

[a]Transformed age $= (Age - 25)(|Age - 25|)^{\frac{1}{2}}$.
[b]Transformed months posttherapy $= (No.\ months)^{\frac{1}{2}}$.
[c]Transformed reactivity of measure $= (Reactivity)^{2.25}$.

The results are provocative. The $.2\sigma_x$ "uncontrolled" difference in Figure 30.03 has shrunk to a $.07\sigma_x$ difference in average effect size. The standard error of the mean of the 119 different scores (behavioral effect size minus nonbehavioral effect size in each study) is $.66/\sqrt{119} = .06$. The behavioral and nonbehavioral therapies show about the same average effect.

The second approach to correcting for measurable differences between behavioral and nonbehavioral therapies is statistical adjustment by regression analysis. By this method, it is possible to quantify and study the natural covariation among the principal outcome variable of studies and the many variables descriptive of the context of the studies.

Eleven features of each study were correlated with the effect size the study produced (Table 30.04). For example, the correlation between the duration of the therapy in hours and the effect size of the study is nearly zero, $-.02$. The correlations are generally low, although several are reliably nonzero. Some of the more interesting correlations show a positive relationship between an estimate of the intelligence of the group of clients and the effect of therapy, and a somewhat larger correlation indicating that therapists who resemble their clients in

ethnic group, age, and social level get better results. The effect sizes diminish across time after therapy as shown by the last correlation in Table 30.04, a correlation of $-.10$ which is closer to $-.20$ when the curvilinearity of the relationship is taken into account. The largest correlation is with the "reactivity" or subjectivity of the outcome measure.

The multiple correlation of these variables with effect size is about .50. Thus, 25% of the variance in the results of studies can be reduced by specification of independent variable values. In several important subsets of the data not reported here, the multiple correlations are over .70, which indicates that in some instances it is possible to reduce more than half of the variability in study findings by regressing the outcome effect onto contextual variables of the study.

The results of three separate multiple regression analyses appear in Table 30.05. Multiple regressions were performed within each of three types of therapy: psychodynamic, systematic desensitization, and behavior modification. Relatively complex forms of the independent variables were used to account for interactions and nonlinear relationships. For example, years' experience of the therapist bore a slight curvilinear relationship with outcome, probably because more experienced therapists worked with more seriously ill clients. This situation was accommodated by entering, as an independent variable, "therapist experience" in interaction with "diagnosis of the client." Age of client and follow-up date were slightly curvilinearly related to outcome in ways most directly handled by changing exponents. These regression equations allow estimation of the effect size a study shows when undertaken with a certain type of client, with a therapist of a certain level of experience, etc. By setting the independent variables at a particular set of values, one can estimate what a study of that type would reveal under each of the three types of therapy. Thus, a statistically controlled comparison of the effects of psychodynamic, systematic desensitization, and behavior modification therapies can be obtained in this case. The three regression equations are clearly not homogeneous; hence, one therapy might be superior under one set of circumstances and a different therapy superior under others. A full description of the nature of this interaction is elusive, though one can illustrate it at various particularly interesting points.

In Figure 30.05, estimates are made of the effect sizes that would be shown for studies in which simple phobias of high-intelligence subjects, 20 years of age, are treated by a therapist with 2 years' experience and evaluated immediately after therapy with highly subjective outcome measures. This verbal description of circumstances can be translated into quantitative values for the independent variables in Table 5 and substituted into each of the three regression equations. In this instance, the two behavioral therapies show effects superior to the psychodynamic therapy.

In Figure 30.06, a second prototypical psychotherapy client and situation are captured in the independent variable values, and the effects of the three types of therapy are estimated. For the typical

ESTIMATED EFFECT SIZES
PSYCHODYNAMIC   0.919
SYSTEMATIC DESENSITIZATION   1.049
BEHAVIORAL MODIFICATION   1.119

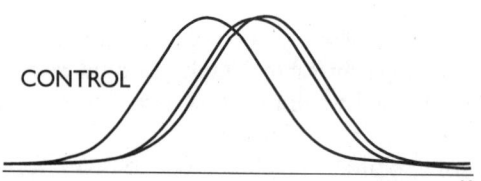

FIGURE 30.05

Three within-therapy regression equations set to describe a prototypic therapy client (phobic) and therapy situation.

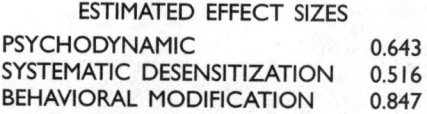

ESTIMATED EFFECT SIZES
PSYCHODYNAMIC   0.643
SYSTEMATIC DESENSITIZATION   0.516
BEHAVIORAL MODIFICATION   0.847

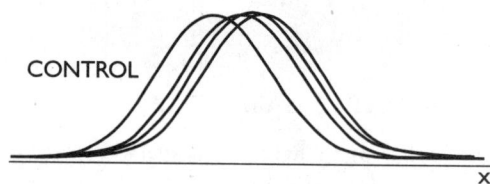

FIGURE 30.06

Three within-therapy regression equations set to describe a prototypic therapy client (neurotic) and therapy situation.

30-year-old neurotic of average IQ seen in circumstances like those that prevail in mental health clinics (individual therapy by a therapist with 5 years' experience), behavior modification is estimated to be superior to psychodynamic therapy, which is in turn superior to systematic desensitization at the 6-month follow-up point.

Besides illuminating the relationships in the data, the quantitative techniques described here can give direction to future research. By fitting regression equations to the relationship between effect size and the independent variables descriptive of the studies and then by placing confidence regions around these hyperplanes, the regions where the input–output relationships are most poorly determined can be identified. By concentrating new studies in these regions, one can avoid the accumulation of redundant studies of convenience that overelaborate small areas.

Conclusions

The results of research demonstrate the beneficial effects of counseling and psychotherapy. Despite volumes devoted to the theoretical differences among different schools of psychotherapy, the results of research demonstrate negligible differences in the effects produced by different therapy types. Unconditional judgments of superiority of one type or another of psychotherapy, and all that these claims imply about treatment and training policy, are unjustified. Scholars and clinicians are in the rather embarrassing position of knowing less than has been proven, because knowledge, atomized and sprayed across a vast landscape of journals, books, and reports, has not been accessible. Extracting knowledge from accumulated studies is a complex and important methodological problem which deserves further attention.

Reference Notes

1. Glass, G. V., Smith, M. L., & Miller, T. I. *The benefits of psychotherapy*. Book in preparation, 1977.
2. Tukey, J. W. Personal communication, November 15, 1976.

References

1. Bergin, A. E. The evaluation of therapeutic outcomes. In A. E. Bergin & S. L. Garfield (Eds.), *Handbook of psychotherapy and behavior change*. New York: Wiley, 1971.
2. Ellis, R. H. Letters. *Colorado Psychological Association Newsletter*, April 1977, p. 3.
3. Emrick, C. D. A review of psychologically oriented treatment of alcoholism. *Journal of Studies on Alcohol*, 1975, *36*, 88–108.
4. Eysenck, H. J. The effects of psychotherapy: An evaluation. *Journal of Consulting Psychology*, 1952, *16*, 319–324.
5. Eysenck, H. J. The effects of psychotherapy. *Journal of Psychology*, 1965, *1*, 97–118.
6. Glass, G. V. Primary, secondary, and meta-analysis of research. *The Educational Researcher*, 1976, *10*, 3–8.
7. Glass, G. V. Integrating findings: The meta-analysis of research. *Review of Research in Education*, in press.
8. Luborsky, L., Singer, B., & Luborsky, L. Comparative studies of psychotherapies. *Archives of General Psychiatry*, 1975, *32*, 995–1008.
9. Meltzoff, J., & Kornreich, M. *Research in psychotherapy*. New York: Atherton, 1970.
10. Psychotherapy caveat. *APA Monitor*, December 1974, p. 7.

QUESTIONS FOR REFLECTION AND DISCUSSION:

1. What standards did Smith and Glass use to include or exclude studies from the research sample?

2. Did Smith and Glass evaluate the validity of each experiment they included in their sample? Why or why not? Does their approach call into question the validity of their meta-analysis?

3. Did the investigators in the studies used by Smith and Glass have a vested interest in the outcome? (That is, might they have been interested in demonstrating that psychotherapy works?) If so, might this vested interest introduce a bias into the results of the meta-analysis?

4. Which forms of therapy were found to have the greatest effect sizes? Which were found to have the smallest?

5. Smith and Glass conclude that there are only "negligible differences in the effects produced by different therapy types" and that claims that one type of psychotherapy is superior to another are therefore "unjustified." This conclusion raises at least two questions: First, which forms of psychotherapy in the meta-analysis were found to have greater effects than others? Second, Smith and Glass's broad conclusion may not consider the types of problems of clients in therapy. On the basis of their meta-analysis, are they justified in claiming that the benefits of the various types of therapy are more or less equivalent for all kinds of psychological problems and disorders?

6. How would you find more recent meta-analyses of the effects of psychotherapy? Do their findings coincide with the conclusions of Smith and Glass?

7. Is the Smith and Glass study of greatest interest because of the accuracy of its results or because of its historic impact on directions for evaluating types of psychotherapy?

VI

DEVELOPMENTAL PSYCHOLOGY

Developmental psychology is all about wonder, about how we develop from an unaware single microscopic cell to self-aware beings composed of trillions of specialized cells. Developmental psychology is concerned with biological development because our biology affects our behavior, our mental processes, and our general well being. But it also addresses our social, cognitive, and personality development. Some developmental psychologists specialize in childhood or adolescence; others take a lifespan approach to development.

The following primary sources are included in this part:

31. Harlow, H. F. (1958). The nature of love. *American Psychologist, 13,* 673–685.

I will confess: This is my favorite primary source in the collection. Not only is the experimental study of infant attachment of interest, but the writing of the author, former American Psychological Association president Harry Harlow, is often hilarious. There is something to offend everyone, and the poems about hippos and rhinoceri are not your standard fare for psychology journals. We can only hope that there will come a day when someone other than an APA president can have this sort of writing published in the professional journals.

32. Cernoch, J., & Porter, R. (1985). Recognition of maternal axillary odors by infants. *Child Development, 56,* 1593–1598.

Here is another enjoyable journal article in infant attachment. Various methods were used to determine just what the infants were smelling, and from whom. I hope that you looking up the meaning of the word *axillary* will not cause you to turn up your nose at this article.

33. Piaget, J. (1997 Edition). Objective responsibility. I. Clumsiness and stealing. In *The moral judgment of the child.* Trans. by Marjorie Gabain. New York: Free Press, pp. 121–138.

Piaget was one of the 20th century's foremost figures in the cognitive development of the child. He saw children as budding scientists who strive to make sense of the world around them. This selection will offer insight into Piaget's investigative method as well as the child's view of objective responsibility versus subjective responsibility for wrongdoing.

34. Steinberg, L., Dornbusch, S. M., & Brown, B. B. (1992). Ethnic differences in adolescent achievement. *American Psychologist, 47,* 723–729. 121–138.

Because we live in a high-tech society, the great majority of people need to achieve as much as they can in school if they are going to be successful later in life. As groups, African American, Asian American, European (White) American, and Hispanic American adolescents show different patterns of academic achievement. This article finds a number of reasons why, and some of them may surprise you.

35. Harvey, E. (1999). Short-term and long-term effects of early parental employment on children of the National Longitudinal Survey of Youth. *Developmental Psychology, 35*(2), 445–459.

In today's society nearly every adult works, not just for the money but also for the intrinsic rewards of working, including self-identity, social status, and the social and intellectual rewards of being out in the adult world. Some parents take brief parental leaves when a child is born and then return to work within weeks or a few short months. Thus developmental psychologists are concerned about the possible effects of early parental employment on children. This article reports psychologist Elizabeth Harvey's findings on this important social and psychological issue.

36. Langer, E. G., & Rodin, J. (1976). The effects of choice and enhanced personal responsibility for the aged: A field experiment in an institutional setting. *Journal of Personality and Social Psychology, 34,* 191–198.

Developmental psychologists study people's psychological development from conception to death. This landmark study shows that older people—even those living in institutional settings—profit from remaining involved in the choices and decisions that determine the courses of their lives.

SOURCE

Harlow, H. F. (1958). The nature of love. *American Psychologist, 13,* 673–685.

Harry Harlow's "The Nature of Love" stands as a classic report of research and also as evidence of the author's wit and his willingness to share his, shall we say, strongly held opinions. It was an oral address to the convention of the American Psychological Association, and as such it has much that is humorous and also much that is antagonistic. Put it this way: It was sure to offend nearly everybody, but presumably in a cute, crotchety way.

Let us note that the title of the piece may be somewhat misleading for many readers. I think when I first came across it, it made me think of romantic love. It turns out that it is about what developmental psychologists refer to as attachment—*the enduring bond between one organism and another, and, in this case, mainly between mother and infant.*

The Nature of Love

HARRY F. HARLOW
UNIVERSITY OF WISCONSIN

Love is a wondrous state, deep, tender, and rewarding. Because of its intimate and personal nature it is regarded by some as an improper topic for experimental research. But, whatever our personal feelings may be, our assigned mission as psychologists is to analyze all facets of human and animal behavior into their component variables. So far as love or affection is concerned, psychologists have failed in this mission. The little we know about love does not transcend simple observation, and the little we write about it has been written better by poets and novelists. But of greater concern is the fact that psychologists tend to give progressively less attention to a motive which pervades our entire lives. Psychologists, at least psychologists who write textbooks, not only show no interest in the origin and development of love or affection, but they seem to be unaware of its very existence.

The apparent repression of love by modern psychologists stands in sharp contrast with the attitude taken by many famous and normal people. The word "love" has the highest reference frequency of any word cited in Bartlett's book of *Familiar Quotations*. It would appear that this emotion has long had a vast interest and fascination for human beings, regardless of the attitude taken by psychologists; but the quotations cited, even by famous and normal people, have a mundane redundancy. These authors and authorities have stolen love from the child and infant and made it the exclusive property of the adolescent and adult.

Thoughtful men, and probably all women, have speculated on the nature of love. From the developmental point of view, the general plan is quite clear: The initial love responses of the human being are those made by the infant to the mother or some mother surrogate. From this intimate attachment of the child to the mother, multiple learned and generalized affectional responses are formed.

Unfortunately, beyond these simple facts we know little about the fundamental variables underlying the formation of affectional responses and little about the mechanisms through which the love of the infant for the mother develops into the multi-faceted response patterns characterizing love or affection in the adult. Because of the dearth of experimentation, theories about the fundamental nature of affection have evolved at the level of observation, intuition, and discerning guesswork, whether these have been proposed by psychologists, sociologists, anthropologists, physicians, or psychoanalysts.

The position commonly held by psychologists and sociologists is quite clear: The basic motives are, for the most part, the primary drives—particularly hunger, thirst, elimination, pain, and sex—and all other motives, including love or affection, are derived or secondary drives. The mother is associated with the reduction of the primary drives—particularly hunger, thirst, and pain—and through learning, affection or love is derived.

It is entirely reasonable to believe that the mother through association with food may become a secondary-reinforcing agent, but this is an inadequate mechanism to account for the persistence of the infant-maternal ties. There is a spate of researches on the formation of secondary reinforcers to hunger and thirst reduction. There can be no question that almost any external stimulus can become a secondary reinforcer if properly associated with tissue-need reduction, but the fact remains that this redundant literature demonstrates unequivocally that such derived drives suffer relatively rapid experimental extinction. Contrariwise, human affection does not extinguish when the mother ceases to have intimate association with the drives in question. Instead, the affectional ties to the mother show a lifelong, unrelenting persistence and, even more surprising, widely expanding generality.

Oddly enough, one of the few psychologists who took a position counter to modern psychological dogma was John B. Watson, who believed that love was an innate emotion elicited by cutaneous stimulation of the erogenous zones. But experimental psychologists, with their peculiar propensity to discover facts that are not true, brushed this theory aside by demonstrating that the human neonate had no differentiable emotions, and they established a fundamental psychological law that prophets are without honor in their own profession.

The psychoanalysts have concerned themselves with the problem of the nature of the development of love in the neonate and infant, using ill and aging human beings as subjects. They have discovered the overwhelming importance of the breast and related this to the oral erotic tendencies developed at an age preceding their subjects' memories. Their theories range from a belief that the infant has an innate need to achieve and suckle at the breast to beliefs not unlike commonly accepted psychological theories. There are exceptions, as seen in the recent writings of John Bowlby, who attributes importance not only to food and thirst satisfaction, but also to "primary object-clinging," a need for intimate physical contact, which is initially associated with the mother.

As far as I know, there exists no direct experimental analysis of the relative importance of the stimulus variables determining the affectional or love responses in the neonatal and infant primate. Unfortunately, the human neonate is a limited experimental subject for such researches because of his inadequate motor capabilities. By the time the human infant's motor responses can be precisely measured, the antecedent determining conditions cannot be defined, having been lost in a jumble and jungle of confounded variables.

Many of these difficulties can be resolved by the use of the neonatal and infant macaque monkey as the subject for the analysis of basic affectional variables. It is possible to make precise measurements in this primate beginning at two to ten days of age, depending upon the maturational status of the individual animal at birth. The macaque infant differs from the human infant in that the monkey is more mature at birth and grows more rapidly; but the basic responses relating to affection, including nursing, contact, clinging, and even visual and auditory exploration, exhibit no fundamental differences in the two species. Even the development of perception, fear, frustration, and learning capability follows very similar sequences in rhesus monkeys and human children.

Three years' experimentation before we started our studies on affection gave us experience with the neonatal monkey. We had separated more than 60 of these animals from their mothers 6 to 12 hours after birth and suckled them on tiny bottles. The infant mortality was only a small fraction of what would have obtained had we let the monkey mothers raise their infants. Our bottle-fed babies were healthier and heavier than monkey-mother-reared infants. We know that we are better monkey mothers than are real monkey mothers thanks to synthetic diets, vitamins, iron extracts, penicillin, chloromycetin, 5% glucose, and constant, tender, loving care.

During the course of these studies we noticed that the laboratory-raised babies showed strong attachment to the cloth pads (folded gauze diapers) which were used to cover the hardware-cloth floors of their cages. The infants clung to these pads and engaged in violent temper tantrums when the pads

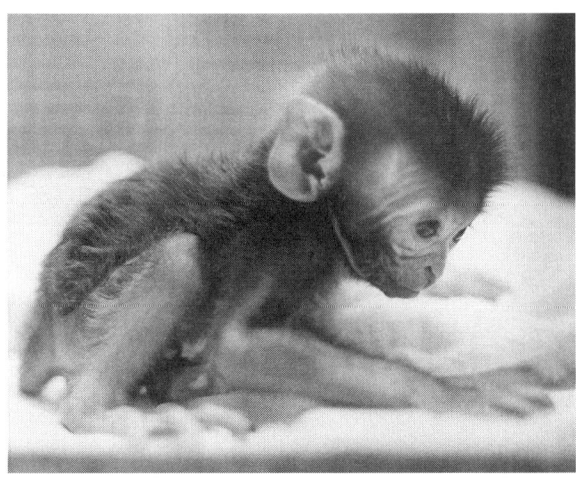

FIGURE 31.01
Response to cloth pad by one-day-old monkey.

were removed and replaced for sanitary reasons. Such contact-need or responsiveness had been reported previously by Gertrude van Wagenen for the monkey and by Thomas McCulloch and George Haslerud for the chimpanzee and is reminiscent of the devotion often exhibited by human infants to their pillows, blankets, and soft, cuddly stuffed toys. Responsiveness by the one-day-old infant monkey to the cloth pad is shown in Figure 31.01, and an unusual and strong attachment of a six-month-old infant to the cloth pad is illustrated in Figure 31.02. The baby, human or monkey, if it is to survive, must clutch at more than a straw.

We had also discovered during some allied observational studies that a baby monkey raised on a

bare wire-mesh cage floor survives with difficulty, if at all, during the first five days of life. If a wire-mesh cone is introduced, the baby does better; and, if the cone is covered with terry cloth, husky, healthy, happy babies evolve. It takes more than a baby and a box to make a normal monkey. We were impressed by the possibility that, above and beyond the bubbling fountain of breast or bottle, contact comfort might be a very important variable in the development of the infant's affection for the mother.

At this point we decided to study the development of affectional responses of neonatal and infant monkeys to an artificial, inanimate mother, and so we built a surrogate mother which we hoped and believed would be a good surrogate mother. In devising this surrogate mother we were dependent neither upon the capriciousness of evolutionary processes nor upon mutations produced by chance radioactive fallout. Instead, we designed the mother surrogate in terms of modern human-engineering principles (Figure 31.03). We produced a perfectly proportioned, streamlined body stripped of unnecessary bulges and appendices. Redundancy in the surrogate mother's system was avoided by reducing the number of breasts from two to one and placing this unibreast in an upper-thoracic, sagittal position, thus maximizing the natural and known perceptual-

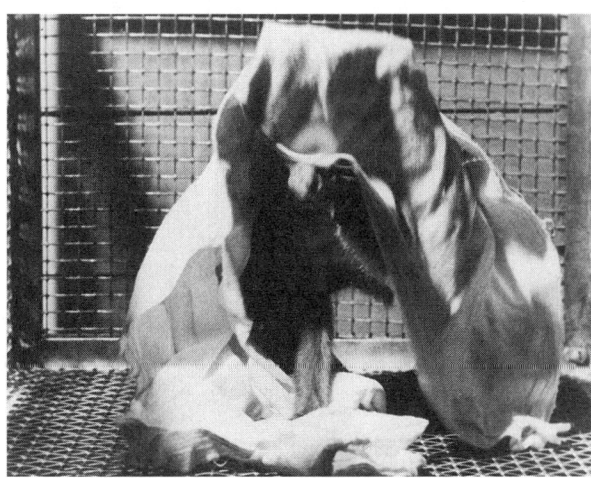

FIGURE 31.02
Response to gauze pad by six-month-old monkey used in earlier study.

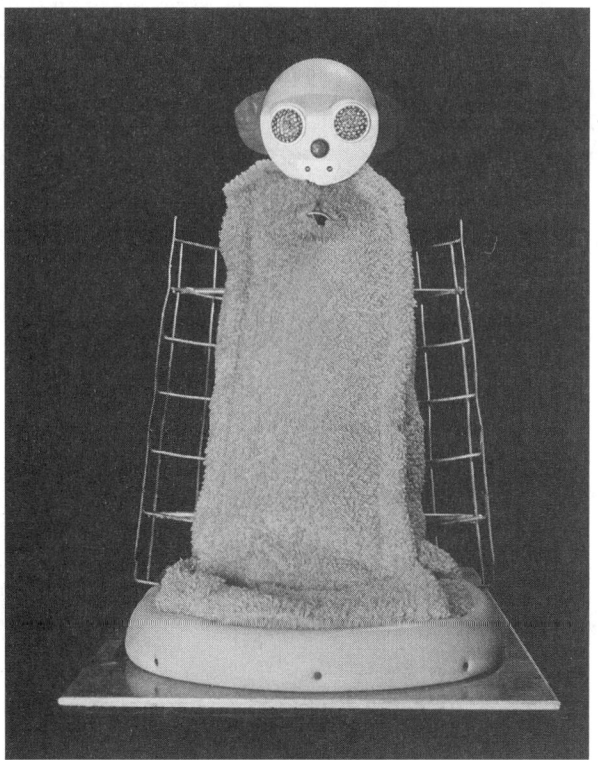

FIGURE 31.03
Cloth mother surrogate.

motor capabilities of the infant operator. The surrogate was made from a block of wood, covered with sponge rubber, and sheathed in tan cotton terry cloth. A light bulb behind her radiated heat. The result was a mother, soft, warm, and tender, a mother with infinite patience, a mother available twenty-four hours a day, a mother that never scolded her infant and never struck or bit her baby in anger. Furthermore, we designed a mother-machine with maximal maintenance efficiency since failure of any system or function could be resolved by the simple substitution of black boxes and new component parts. It is our opinion that we engineered a very superior monkey mother, although this position is not held universally by the monkey fathers.

Before beginning our initial experiment we also designed and constructed a second mother surrogate, a surrogate in which we deliberately built less than the maximal capability for contact comfort. This surrogate mother is illustrated in Figure 31.04. She is made of wire-mesh, a substance entirely adequate to provide postural support and nursing capability, and she is warmed by radiant heat. Her body differs in no essential way from that of the cloth mother surrogate other than in the quality of the contact comfort which she can supply.

In our initial experiment, the dual mother-surrogate condition, a cloth mother and a wire mother were placed in different cubicles attached to the infant's living cage as shown in Figure 31.04. For four newborn monkeys the cloth mother lactated and the

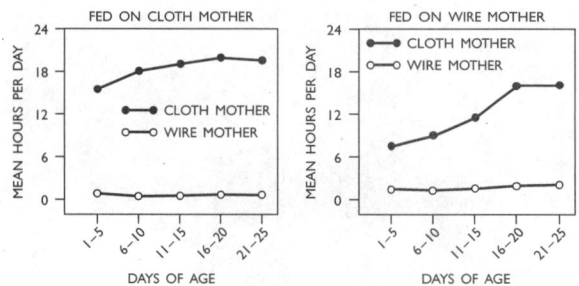

FIGURE 31.05

Time spent on cloth and wire mother surrogates.

wire mother did not; and, for the other four, this condition was reversed. In either condition the infant received all its milk through the mother surrogate as soon as it was able to maintain itself in this way, a capability achieved within two or three days except in the case of very immature infants. Supplementary feedings were given until the milk intake from the mother surrogate was adequate. Thus, the experiment was designed as a test of the relative importance of the variables of contact comfort and nursing comfort. During the first 14 days of life the monkey's cage floor was covered with a heating pad wrapped in a folded gauze diaper, and thereafter the cage floor was bare. The infants were always free to leave the heating pad or cage floor to contact either mother, and the time spent on the surrogate mothers was automatically recorded. Figure 31.05 shows the total time

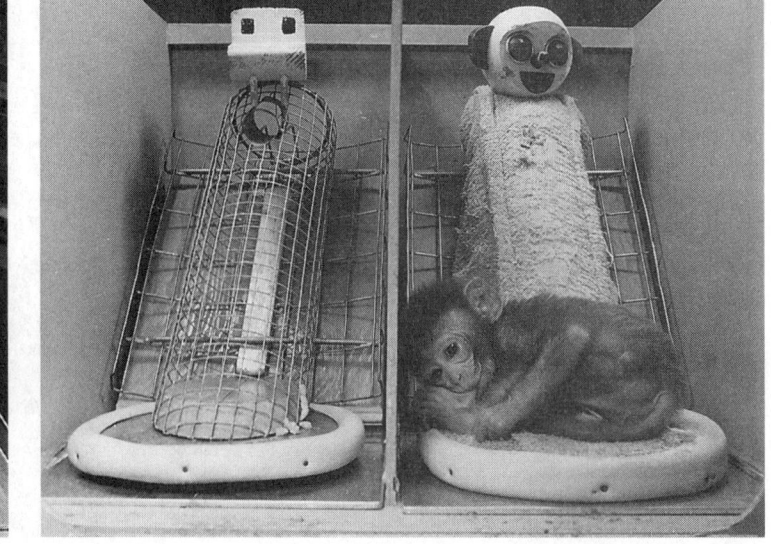

FIGURE 31.04

Wire and cloth mother surrogates.

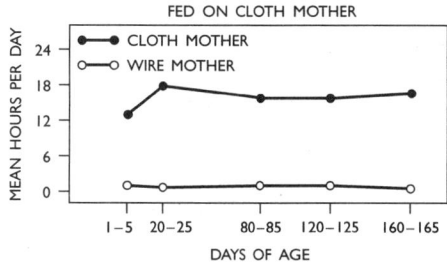

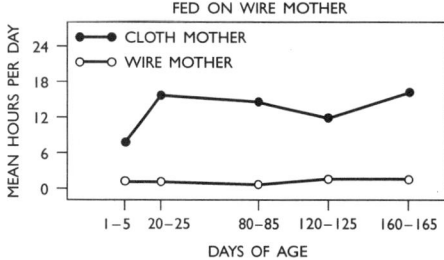

FIGURE 31.06

Long-term contact time on cloth and wire mother surrogates.

spent on the cloth and wire mothers under the two conditions of feeding. These data make it obvious that contact comfort is a variable of overwhelming importance in the development of affectional responses, whereas lactation is a variable of negligible importance. With age and opportunity to learn, subjects with the lactating wire mother showed decreasing responsiveness to her and increasing responsiveness to the nonlactating cloth mother, a finding completely contrary to any interpretation of derived drive in which the mother-form becomes conditioned to hunger-thirst reduction. The persistence of these differential responses throughout 165 consecutive days of testing is evident in Figure 31.06.

One control group of neonatal monkeys was raised on a single wire mother, and a second control group was raised on a single cloth mother. There were no differences between these two groups in amount of milk ingested or in weight gain. The only difference between the groups lay in the composition of the feces, the softer stools of the wire-mother infants suggesting psychosomatic involvement. The wire mother is biologically adequate but psychologically inept.

We were not surprised to discover that contact comfort was an important basic affectional or love variable, but we did not expect it to overshadow so completely the variable of nursing; indeed, the disparity is so great as to suggest that the primary function of nursing as an affectional variable is that of insuring frequent and intimate body contact of the infant with the mother. Certainly, man cannot live by milk alone. Love is an emotion that does not need to be bottle- or

The Hippopotamus

This is the skin some babies feel
Replete with hippo love appeal.
Each contact, cuddle, push, and shove
Elicits tons of baby love.

The Rhinocerus

The rhino's skin is thick and tough,
And yet this skin is soft enough
That baby rhinos always sense,
A love enormous and intense.

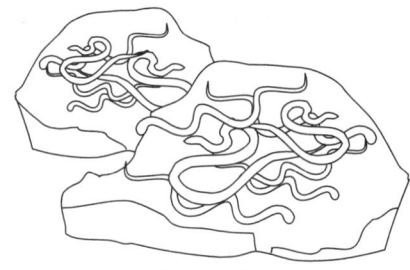

The Snake

To baby vipers, scaly skin
Engenders love 'twixt kith and kin.
Each animal by God is blessed
With kind of skin it loves the best.

The Elephant

Though mother may be short on arms,
Her skin is full of warmth and charms.
And mother's touch on baby's skin
Endears the heart that beats within.

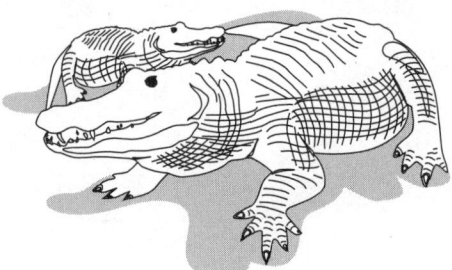

The Crocodile

Here is the skin they love to touch.
It isn't soft and there isn't much,
But its contact comfort will beguile
Love from the infant crocodile.

You see, all God's chillun's got skin.

FIGURE 31.07
Typical fear stimulus.

spoon-fed, and we may be sure that there is nothing to be gained by giving lip service to love.

A charming lady once heard me describe these experiments; and, when I subsequently talked to her, her face brightened with sudden insight: "Now I know what's wrong with me," she said, "I'm just a wire mother." Perhaps she was lucky. She might have been a wire wife.

We believe that contact comfort has long served the animal kingdom as a motivating agent for affectional responses. Since at the present time we have

no experimental data to substantiate this position, we supply information which must be accepted, if at all, on the basis of face validity.

One function of the real mother, human or subhuman, and presumably of a mother surrogate, is to provide a haven of safety for the infant in times of fear and danger. The frightened or ailing child clings to its mother, not its father; and this selective responsiveness in times of distress, disturbance, or danger may be used as a measure of the strength of affectional bonds. We have tested this kind of differential responsiveness by presenting to the infants in their cages, in the presence of the two mothers, various fear-producing stimuli such as the moving toy bear illustrated in Figure 31.07. A typical response to a fear stimulus is shown in Figure 31.08, and the data on differential responsiveness are presented in Figure 31.09. It is apparent that the cloth mother is highly preferred over the wire one, and this differential selectivity is enhanced by age and experience. In this situation, the variable of nursing appears to be of absolutely no importance: the infant consistently seeks the soft mother surrogate regardless of nursing condition.

Similarly, the mother or mother surrogate provides its young with a source of security, and this role or function is seen with special clarity when

FIGURE 31.08

Typical response to cloth mother surrogate in fear test.

mother and child are in a strange situation. At the present time we have completed tests for this relationship on four of our eight baby monkeys assigned to the dual mother-surrogate condition by introducing them for three minutes into the strange environment of a room measuring six feet by six feet by six feet (also called the "open-field test") and containing multiple stimuli known to elicit curiosity-manipulatory responses in baby monkeys. The subjects were placed in this situation twice a week for eight weeks with no mother surrogate present during alternate sessions and the cloth mother present during the others. A cloth diaper

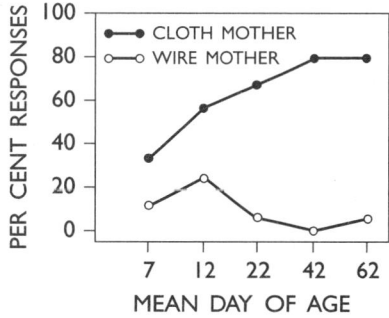

FIGURE 31.09

Differential responsiveness in fear tests.

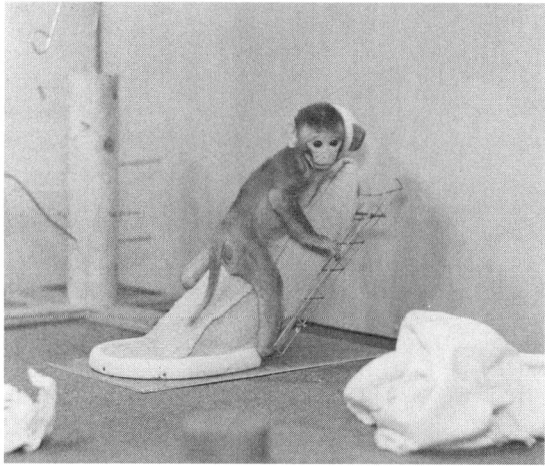

FIGURE 31.10

Response to cloth mother in the open-field test.

was always available as one of the stimuli throughout all sessions. After one or two adaptation sessions, the infants always rushed to the mother surrogate when she was present and clutched her, rubbed their bodies against her, and frequently manipulated her body and face. After a few additional sessions, the infants began to use the mother surrogate as a source of security, a base of operations. As is shown in Figures 31.10 and 31.11, they would explore and manipulate a stimulus and then return to the mother before adventuring again into the strange new world. The behavior of these infants was quite different when the mother was absent from the room. Frequently they would freeze in a crouched position, as is illustrated in Figures 31.12 and 31.13. Emotionality indices such as vocalization, crouch-

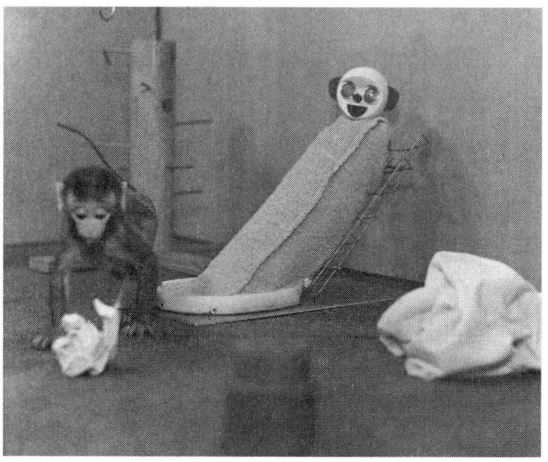

FIGURE 31.11

Object exploration in presence of cloth mother.

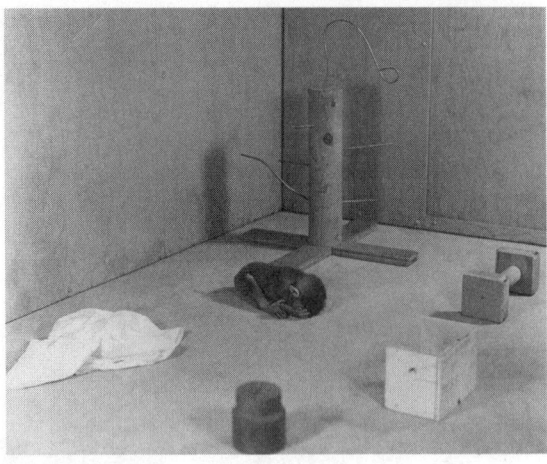

FIGURE 31.12

Response in the open-field test in the absence of the mother surrogate.

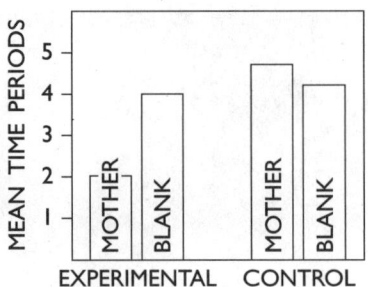

FIGURE 31.14

Emotionality index with and without the presence of the cloth mother.

ing, rocking, and sucking increased sharply, as shown in Figure 31.14. Total emotionality score was cut in half when the mother was present. In the absence of the mother some of the experimental monkeys would rush to the center of the room where the mother was customarily placed and then run rapidly from object to object, screaming and crying all the while. Continuous, frantic clutching of their bodies was very common, even when not in the crouching position. These monkeys frequently contacted and clutched the cloth diaper, but this action never pacified them. The same behavior occurred in the presence of the wire mother. No difference between the cloth-mother-fed and wire-mother-fed infants was demonstrated under either condition. Four

control infants never raised with a mother surrogate showed the same emotionality scores when the mother was absent as the experimental infants showed in the absence of the mother, but the controls' scores were slightly larger in the presence of the mother surrogate than in her absence.

Some years ago Robert Butler demonstrated that mature monkeys enclosed in a dimly lighted box would open and reopen a door hour after hour for no other reward than that of looking outside the box. We now have data indicating that neonatal monkeys show this same compulsive visual curiosity on their first test day in an adaptation of the Butler apparatus which we call the "love machine," an apparatus designed to measure love. Usually these tests are begun when the monkey is 10 days of age, but this same persistent visual exploration has been obtained in a three-day-old monkey during the first half-hour of testing. Butler also demonstrated that rhesus monkeys show selectivity in rate and frequency of door-opening to stimuli of differential attractiveness in the visual field outside the box. We have utilized this principle of response selectivity by the monkey to measure strength of affectional responsiveness in our infants in the baby version of the Butler box. The test sequence involves four repetitions of a test battery in which four stimuli—cloth mother, wire mother, infant monkey, and empty box—are presented for a 30-minute period on successive days. The first four subjects in the dual mother-surrogate group were given a single test sequence at 40 to 50 days of age, depending upon the availability of the apparatus, and only their data are presented. The second set of four subjects is being given repetitive tests to obtain information relating to the development of visual exploration. The apparatus is illustrated in Figure 31.15. The data obtained from the first four infants raised with the two mother surrogates are presented in the middle graph of Figure 31.16 and show approximately equal responding to the cloth mother and another infant monkey, and

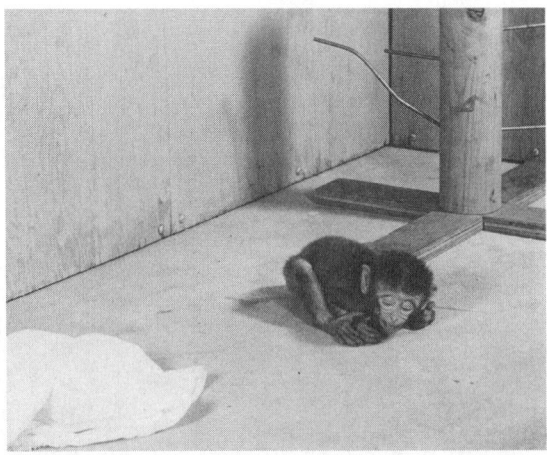

FIGURE 31.13

Response in the open-field test in the absence of the mother surrogate.

FIGURE 31.15
Visual exploration apparatus.

no greater responsiveness to the wire mother than to an empty box. Again, the results are independent of the kind of mother that lactated, cloth or wire. The same results are found for a control group raised, but not fed, on a single cloth mother; these data appear in the graph on the right. Contrariwise, the graph on the left shows no differential responsiveness to cloth and wire mothers by a second control group, which was not raised on any mother surrogate. We can be certain that not all love is blind.

The first four infant monkeys in the dual mother-surrogate group were separated from their mothers

between 165 and 170 days of age and tested for retention during the following 9 days and then at 30-day intervals for six successive months. Affectional retention as measured by the modified Butler box is given in Figure 31.17. In keeping with the data obtained on adult monkeys by Butler, we find a high rate of responding to any stimulus, even the empty box. But throughout the entire 185-day retention period there is a consistent and significant difference in response frequency to the cloth mother contrasted with either the wire mother or the empty box, and no consistent difference between wire mother and empty box.

Affectional retention was also tested in the open field during the first 9 days after separation and then at 30-day intervals, and each test condition was run twice at each retention interval. The infant's behavior differed from that observed during the period preceding separation. When the cloth mother was present in the post-separation period, the babies rushed to her, climbed up, clung tightly to her, and rubbed their heads and faces against her body. After this initial embrace and reunion, they played on the mother, including biting and tearing at her cloth cover; but they rarely made any attempt to leave her during the test period, nor did they manipulate or play with the objects in the room, in contrast with their behavior before maternal separation. The only exception was the occasional monkey that left the mother surrogate momentarily, grasped the folded piece of paper (one of the standard stimuli in the field), and brought it quickly back to the mother. It appeared that deprivation had enhanced the tie to the mother and rendered the contact-comfort need so prepotent that need for the mother overwhelmed the exploratory motives during the brief, three-minute test sessions. No change in these behaviors was observed throughout the 185-day period. When the mother was absent from the open field, the behavior of the infants was similar in the

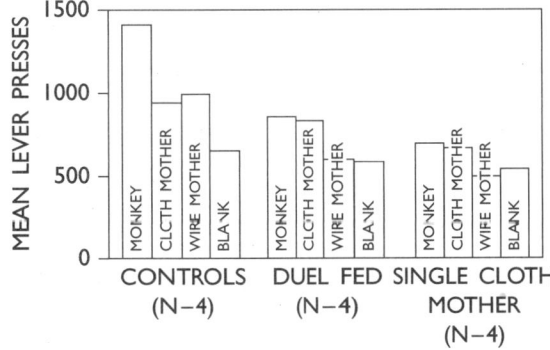

FIGURE 31.16
Differential responses to visual exploration.

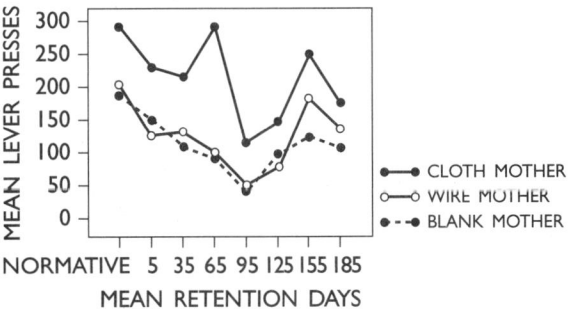

FIGURE 31.17
Retention of differential visual-exploration responses.

initial retention test to that during the preseparation tests; but they tended to show gradual adaptation to the open-field situation with repeated testing and, consequently, a reduction in their emotionality scores.

In the last five retention test periods, an additional test was introduced in which the surrogate mother was placed in the center of the room and covered with a clear Plexiglas box. The monkeys were initially disturbed and frustrated when their explorations and manipulations of the box failed to provide contact with the mother. However, all animals adapted to the situation rather rapidly. Soon they used the box as a place of orientation for exploratory and play behavior, made frequent contacts with the objects in the field, and very often brought these objects to the Plexiglas box. The emotionality index was slightly higher than in the condition of the available cloth mothers, but it in no way approached the emotionality level displayed when the cloth mother was absent. Obviously, the infant monkeys gained emotional security by the presence of the mother even though contact was denied.

Affectional retention has also been measured by tests in which the monkey must unfasten a three-device mechanical puzzle to obtain entrance into a compartment containing the mother surrogate. All the trials are initiated by allowing the infant to go through an unlocked door, and in half the trials it finds the mother present and in half, an empty compartment. The door is then locked and a ten-minute test conducted. In tests given prior to separation from the surrogate mothers, some of the infants had solved this puzzle and others had failed. The data of Figure 31.18 show that on the last test before separation there were no differences in total manipulation under mother-present and mother-absent conditions, but striking differences exist between the two conditions throughout the post-separation test peri-

ods. Again, there is no interaction with conditions of feeding.

The over-all picture obtained from surveying the retention data is unequivocal. There is little, if any, waning of responsiveness to the mother throughout this five-month period as indicated by any measure. It becomes perfectly obvious that this affectional bond is highly resistant to forgetting and that it can be retained for very long periods of time by relatively infrequent contact reinforcement. During the next year, retention tests will be conducted at 90-day intervals, and further plans are dependent upon the results obtained. It would appear that affectional responses may show as much resistance to extinction as has been previously demonstrated for learned fears and learned pain, and such data would be in keeping with those of common human observation.

The infant's responses to the mother surrogate in the fear tests, the open-field situation, and the baby Butler box and the responses on the retention tests cannot be described adequately with words. For supplementary information we turn to the motion picture record. (At this point a 20-minute film was presented illustrating and supplementing the behaviors described thus far in the address.)

We have already described the group of four control infants that had never lived in the presence of any mother surrogate and had demonstrated no sign of affection or security in the presence of the cloth mothers introduced in test sessions. When these infants reached the age of 250 days, cubicles containing both a cloth mother and a wire mother were attached to their cages. There was no lactation in these mothers, for the monkeys were on a solid-food diet. The initial reaction of the monkeys to the alterations was one of extreme disturbance. All the infants screamed violently and made repeated attempts to escape the cage whenever the door was opened. They kept a maximum distance from the mother surrogates and exhibited a considerable amount of rocking and crouching behavior, indicative of emotionality. Our first thought was that the critical period for the development of maternally directed affection had passed and that these macaque children were doomed to live as affectional orphans. Fortunately, these behaviors continued for only 12 to 48 hours and then gradually ebbed, changing from indifference to active contact on, and exploration of, the surrogates. The home-cage behavior of these control monkeys slowly became similar to that of the animals raised with the mother surrogates from birth. Their manipulation and play on the cloth mother became progressively more vigorous to the point of actual mutilation, particularly during the morning after the cloth mother had been given

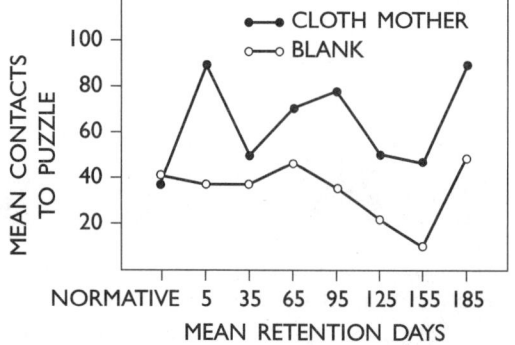

FIGURE 31.18

Retention of puzzle manipulation responsiveness.

her daily change of terry covering. The control subjects were now actively running to the cloth mother when frightened and had to be coaxed from her to be taken from the cage for formal testing.

Objective evidence of these changing behaviors is given in Figure 31.19, which plots the amount of time these infants spent on the mother surrogates. Within 10 days mean contact time is approximately nine hours, and this measure remains relatively constant throughout the next 30 days. Consistent with the results on the subjects reared from birth with dual mothers, these late-adopted infants spent less than one and one-half hours per day in contact with the wire mothers, and this activity level was relatively constant throughout the test sessions. Although the maximum time that the control monkeys spent on the cloth mother was only about half that spent by the original dual mother-surrogate group, we cannot be sure that this discrepancy is a function of differential early experience. The control monkeys were about three months older when the mothers were attached to their cages than the experimental animals had been when their mothers were removed and the retention tests begun. Thus, we do not know what the amount of contact would be for a 250-day-old animal raised from birth with surrogate mothers. Nevertheless, the magnitude of the differences and the fact that the contact-time curves for the mothered-from-birth infants had remained constant for almost 150 days suggest that early experience with the mother is a variable of measurable importance.

The control group has also been tested for differential visual exploration after the introduction of the cloth and wire mothers; these behaviors are plotted in Figure 31.20. By the second test session a high level of exploratory behavior had developed, and the responsiveness to the wire mother and the empty box is significantly greater than that to the cloth mother. This is probably not an artifact since there is every reason to believe that the face of the cloth mother is a fear stimulus to most monkeys that have not had extensive experience with this object during the first 40 to 60 days of life. Within the third test session a sharp change in trend occurs, and the cloth mother is then more frequently viewed than the wire mother or the blank box; this trend continues during the fourth session, producing a significant preference for the cloth mother.

Before the introduction of the mother surrogate into the home-cage situation, only one of the four control monkeys had ever contacted the cloth mother in the open-field tests. In general, the surrogate mother not only gave the infants no security, but instead appeared to serve as a fear stimulus. The emotionality scores of these control subjects were slightly higher during the mother-present test sessions than during the mother-absent test sessions. These behaviors were changed radically by the fourth post-introduction test approximately 60 days later. In the absence of the cloth mothers the emotionality index in this fourth test remains near the earlier level, but the score is reduced by half when the mother is present, a result strikingly similar to that found for infants raised with the dual mother-surrogates from birth. The control infants now show increasing object exploration and play behavior, and they begin to use the mother as a base of operations, as did the infants raised from birth with the

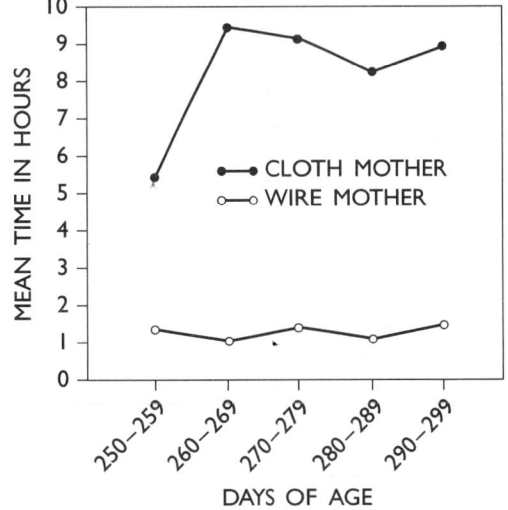

FIGURE 31.19

Differential time spent on cloth and wire mother surrogates by monkeys started at 250 days of age.

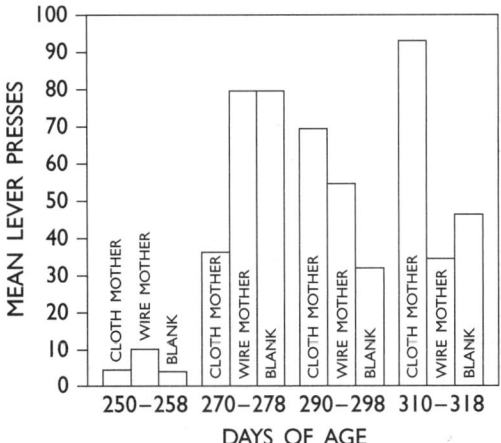

FIGURE 31.20

Differential visual exploration of monkeys started at 250 days of age.

mother surrogates. However, there are still definite differences in the behavior of the two groups. The control infants do not rush directly to the mother and clutch her violently; but instead they go toward, and orient around, her, usually after an initial period during which they frequently show disturbed behavior, exploratory behavior, or both.

That the control monkeys develop affection or love for the cloth mother when she is introduced into the cage at 250 days of age cannot be questioned. There is every reason to believe, however, that this interval of delay depresses the intensity of the affectional response below that of the infant monkeys that were surrogate-mothered from birth onward. In interpreting these data it is well to remember that the control monkeys had had continuous opportunity to observe and hear other monkeys housed in adjacent cages and that they had had limited opportunity to view and contact surrogate mothers in the test situations, even though they did not exploit the opportunities.

During the last two years we have observed the behavior of two infants raised by their own mothers. Love for the real mother and love for the surrogate mother appear to be very similar. The baby macaque spends many hours a day clinging to its real mother. If away from the mother when frightened, it rushes to her and in her presence shows comfort and composure. As far as we can observe, the infant monkey's affection for the real mother is strong, but no stronger than that of the experimental monkey for the surrogate cloth mother, and the security that the infant gains from the presence of the real mother is no greater than the security it gains from a cloth surrogate. Next year we hope to put this problem to final, definitive, experimental test. But, whether the mother is real or a cloth surrogate, there does develop a deep and abiding bond between mother and child. In one case it may be the call of the wild and in the other the McCall of civilization, but in both cases there is "togetherness."

In spite of the importance of contact comfort, there is reason to believe that other variables of measurable importance will be discovered. Postural support may be such a variable, and it has been suggested that, when we build arms into the mother surrogate, 10 is the minimal number required to provide adequate child care. Rocking motion may be such a variable, and we are comparing rocking and stationary mother surrogates and inclined planes. The differential responsiveness to cloth mother and cloth-covered inclined plane suggests that clinging as well as contact is an affectional variable of importance. Sounds, particularly natural,

maternal sounds, may operate as either unlearned or learned affectional variables. Visual responsiveness may be such a variable, and it is possible that some semblance of visual imprinting may develop in the neonatal monkey. There are indications that this becomes a variable of importance during the course of infancy through some maturational process.

John Bowlby has suggested that there is an affectional variable which he calls "primary object following," characterized by visual and oral search of the mother's face. Our surrogate-mother-raised baby monkeys are at first inattentive to her face, as are human neonates to human mother faces. But by 30 days of age ever-increasing responsiveness to the mother's face appears—whether through learning, maturation, or both—and we have reason to believe that the face becomes an object of special attention.

Our first surrogate-mother-raised baby had a mother whose head was just a ball of wood since the baby was a month early and we had not had time to design a more esthetic head and face. This baby had contact with the blank-faced mother for 180 days and was then placed with two cloth mothers, one motionless and one rocking, both being endowed with painted, ornamented faces. To our surprise the animal would compulsively rotate both faces 180 degrees so that it viewed only a round, smooth face and never the painted, ornamented face. Furthermore, it would do this as long as the patience of the experimenter in reorienting the faces persisted. The monkey showed no sign of fear or anxiety, but it showed unlimited persistence. Subsequently it improved its technique, compulsively removing the heads and rolling them into its cage as fast as they were returned. We are intrigued by this observation, and we plan to examine systematically the role of the mother face in the development of infant-monkey affections. Indeed, these observations suggest the need for a series of ethological-type researches on the two-faced female.

Although we have made no attempts thus far to study the generalization of infant-macaque affection or love, the techniques which we have developed offer promise in this uncharted field. Beyond this, there are few if any technical difficulties in studying the affection of the actual, living mother for the child, and the techniques developed can be utilized and expanded for the analysis and developmental study of father-infant and infant-infant affection.

Since we can measure neonatal and infant affectional responses to mother surrogates, and since we know they are strong and persisting, we are in a position to assess the effects of feeding and contactual schedules; consistency and inconsistency in the mother surrogates; and early, intermediate, and late maternal deprivation. Again, we have here a family of problems of fundamental interest and theoretical importance.

If the researches completed and proposed make a contribution, I shall be grateful; but I have also given full thought to possible practical applications. The socioeconomic demands of the present and the threatened socioeconomic demands of the future have led the American woman to displace, or threaten to displace, the American man in science and industry. If this process continues, the problem of proper child-rearing practices faces us with star-tling clarity. It is cheering in view of this trend to realize that the American male is physically endowed with all the really essential equipment to compete with the American female on equal terms in one essential activity: the rearing of infants. We now know that women in the working classes are not needed in the home because of their primary mammalian capabilities; and it is possible that in the foreseeable future neonatal nursing will not be regarded as a necessity, but as a luxury—to use Veblen's term—a form of conspicuous consumption limited perhaps to the upper classes. But whatever course history may take, it is comforting to know that we are now in contact with the nature of love.

QUESTIONS FOR REFLECTION AND DISCUSSION:

1. When we consider research with animals, we are always concerned about whether or not it seems that the findings are likely to extend or generalize to humans. Do you think that Harlow's findings with monkeys are generalizable to humans? Why or why not?

2. Harlow (presumably) has fun saying "The position commonly held by psychologists . . . is quite clear: The basic motives are, for the most part, the primary drives—particularly hunger, thirst, elimination, pain, and sex—and all other motives, including love or affection, are derived or secondary drives. The mother is associated with the reduction of primary drives—particularly hunger, thirst, and pain—and through learning, affection or love is derived." Consider: *Is* this "the position commonly held by psychologists"? What school of psychology might hold this position? What is the reason for the position?

3. What was John B. Watson's position on love? Was it the characteristic behaviorist view? Why or why not?

4. Harlow says that "experimental psychologists [have] their peculiar propensity to discover facts that are not true." How would you describe the tone of this remark? What would be its purpose?

5. How does Harlow describe the psychoanalytic theory of the infant's attachment to its mother? How does he evaluate it?

6. What behaviors did Harlow interpret as attachment behaviors?

7. Harlow says that John Bowlby refers to "primary object-clinging" in his writings on attachment. What does this phrase mean?

8. What does Harlow mean when he says, "Certainly, man cannot live by milk alone. Love is an emotion that does not need to be bottle- or spoon-fed"?

9. In addition to the role of contact comfort, what other variables of "measurable importance" does Harlow say may be found to contribute to infant attachment? For example, what is "primary object following"? How does this view fit in with the findings of ethologists like Konrad Lorenz and Bill Lishman?

SOURCE

Cernoch, J., & Porter, R. (1985). Recognition of maternal axillary odors by infants. *Child Development, 56,* 1593–1598. Copyright © 1985 by the Society for Research and Child Development. Reprinted with permission.

Attachment is the emotional tie between one organism and another specific individual. Attachment keeps organisms together and endures over time. Infants who are attached to their caregivers attempt to maintain contact with them or nearness to them, and they show anxiety when they are separated from them.

Psychologists have discovered many factors in attachment. For example, Harry Harlow (see "The Nature of Love" in this book) found that contact comfort—the sensation of skin against skin—was one such factor. Caregivers may also foster attachment by taking care of infants' needs, although the path to an infant's heart is not primarily through its stomach (that is, a result of feeding). Ethologists have found that some animals (e.g., ducks and geese) become attached after they hatch by following moving objects. Humans, of course, show signs of attachment long before they are capable of locomotion. Contact comfort relies on the sense of touch. However, infants have many more senses than touch, and as we see in the following article by Jennifer Cernoch and Richard Porter, another path to an infant's heart may be through its nose—that is, the sense of smell can also play a role.

Recognition of Maternal Axillary Odors by Infants

JENNIFER M. CERNOCH & RICHARD H. PORTER
GEORGE PEABODY COLLEGE OF VANDERBILT UNIVERSITY

CERNOCH, JENNIFER M., and PORTER, RICHARD H. *Recognition of Maternal Axillary Odors by Infants.* CHILD DEVELOPMENT, 1985, 56, 1593–1598. A series of 5 experiments was conducted to determine whether neonates, at approximately 2 weeks of age, can recognize their parents through axillary odors alone. Breast-feeding infants discriminated between their mother's axillary odor and odors produced by either nonparturient or unfamiliar lactating females. In contrast, breast-feeding infants displayed no evidence of recognizing the axillary odors of their father. Likewise, bottle-feeding infants appeared unable to recognize the odor of their mother when presented along with odors from a nonparturient female or an unfamil-

iar bottle-feeding female. Several hypotheses were presented in an attempt to account for the differential reactions to maternal odors by breast-feeding versus bottle-feeding infants. It was tentatively concluded that, while breast-feeding, infants are exposed to salient maternal odors and thereby rapidly become familiarized with their mother's unique olfactory signature.

The ability of infants to recognize their own mother is an important component in the development of mother-infant social relationships (Bowlby, 1969; Schaffer, 1971). Before they can develop a preference for, or become attached to, their mother, infants must be able to discriminate between her and other individuals; thus, individual recognition is

298

a prerequisite for the establishment of specific social relationships. Neonates' recognition of their mothers may have the additional effect of strengthening mothers' responsiveness and attraction to their infants. According to anecdotal reports, as infants begin to respond selectively to their mother (e.g., display preferential smiling and visual orientation toward their mother and reduced crying when held by her rather than others), mothers experience increasingly positive feelings about their infants (Robson & Moss, 1970).

Although olfaction has long been suspected of playing a role in the social development of children (Brill, 1932; Kalogerakis, 1963; Peto, 1973), it is only within the last decade that the salience of odor cues for mother-infant recognition has been well documented. Several studies have now determined that breast-feeding infants can discriminate between a breast pad worn by their mother and a second pad worn by another nursing female (Macfarlane, 1975; Russell, 1976; Schaal et al., 1980). Likewise, mothers are able to recognize the odors associated with their infants (Porter, Cernoch, & McLaughlin, 1983; Russell, Mendelson, & Peeke, 1983; Schaal et al., 1980). Even mothers who gave birth by cesarean section, and therefore had only limited direct contact with their neonates prior to testing, recognized their 21–42-hour-old infants by odor cues alone (Porter et al., 1983).

The responsiveness of neonates to olfactory cues produced by mothers (and fathers) was investigated further in the present series of experiments. In particular, an attempt was made to ascertain whether breast-feeding infants differ from bottle-feeding infants in their recognition of maternal odors, and to elucidate further the range of biological odors to which infants are responsive.

GENERAL METHODS

Subjects Mothers and fathers were recruited while in the hospital where their subject infant had been born. All infants included in the following experiments were full-term (37–42 weeks gestation) and healthy, with Apgar scores ranging from 6 to 10 at 1 and 5 min after delivery.

Apparatus Each infant was tested individually in a standard hospital bassinet measuring 66 × 36 × 20 cm high. A U-shaped flexible metal hose was attached to the head of the bassinet so that the two ends extended inside. Large clips were fastened to each end of the hose to hold the gauze pads that served as odor stimuli.

Testing Procedures In each of the experiments reported below, infants were tested for their responses to two simultaneously presented 10 × 10-cm gauze pads—one that had been worn in the underarm area of the mother (or father), and a second pad that had been worn by an unfamiliar adult. Individuals who served as sources of odor stimuli were instructed to wear one pad in each armpit for approximately 8 hours during the night preceding testing. They were also asked to follow their daily hygiene routine but to refrain from using deodorant while wearing the pads. Gauze pads were secured in the axillary region by surgical tape supplied to each odor donor and were sealed in zip-lock plastic bags after being removed. Testing followed within 11.5 hours after removal of the stimulus pads. There was no statistically reliable difference in the interval between removal of the stimulus pads and testing for parents versus unfamiliar donors in any of the following experiments.

Odor recognition tests were conducted in the infant's home at 12–18 days after birth. During the test session, the infant was placed in a supine position in the bassinet. Infants who were sleeping were stimulated by the experimenter or mother to an alert state with the eyes open (Stage IV; Prechtl & Beintema, 1964). One of the odor stimuli (gauze pads) was hung to the left and the other to the right of the infant's midline (i.e., alongside each cheek but not in direct contact with the infant). Turning the head to the left or right would bring the infant's nostrils within 1–2 cm of either of the pads. The experimenter held the infant's head centered between the two pads until a timer was activated to signal the start of the test trial. Each infant was presented with the same two odor pads on two successive 1-min trials, with a 2-min interval between the two trials. During the 2-min interval, the positions of the two pads were reversed while the infant remained in the bassinet. For each infant the position of the mother's (or father's) pad on the first trial was randomly determined. The infant's responses to the odor stimuli were videotaped throughout the two 1-min trials with a portable video recorder with the camera mounted on a tripod approximately 2 feet from the top of the bassinet. Videotapes were later analyzed by the experimenter and an observer who was blind in regard to the individuals who had worn the stimulus pads. The amount of time that the infant was oriented to each of the stimulus pads (duration scores) was recorded from the videotapes and summed across the two trials for each pad. Orientation toward a particular pad was defined as any deviation from midline in the direction of that pad. For each stimulus pad a reliability index for the two observers was obtained by dividing the lower of the two duration scores by the greater score for that particular pad (i.e., agreed duration/agreed plus disagreed durations). Mean interobserver reliability indices obtained in this manner ranged from .92 to .97 across the five experiments presented below. The duration measures reported for each experiment are those of the blind observer.

I. Breast-feeding Infants

As mentioned above, previous studies of infant recognition of maternal odors have focused almost exclusively on olfactory cues associated with the breast region of lactating females (Macfarlane, 1975; Russell, 1976; but see Schaal et al., 1980). To determine whether the odor of maternal breast secretions is unique in its attractiveness to breast-feeding infants, a series of experiments was conducted in which breast-feeding neonates were tested for their responses to axillary odors produced by their mothers and fathers. The major question investigated in these studies was whether breast-feeding infants can use axillary odors to recognize their parents.

EXPERIMENT 1: MOTHER VERSUS NONPARTURIENT FEMALE

Methods Thirteen breast-feeding infants were tested as described above for their responsiveness to a gauze pad soiled with their own lactating mother's axillary odors in comparison with an axillary pad from a (unrelated, unfamiliar) nonparturient adult female (i.e., a nonlactating female with no infant of her own at the time of testing) who differed for each subject infant. Birthweights of these seven male and six female infants ranged from 3,132 to 4,040 grams, and their mean age at testing was 15.0 days. Mean ages of the stimulus mothers and nonparturient females were 27.1 and 26.1 years, respectively.

Results The results of Experiment 1 (along with those of the remaining four experiments) are summarized in Table 32.01. As seen on inspection of Table 32.01, infants spent significantly longer oriented toward their mother's axillary pad than to the pad worn by a nonparturient female. In addition, 11 of the 13 infants oriented more toward their mother's pad as compared to the nonparturient female's pad, while the remaining two infants spent equal amounts of time turned toward each of the two pads. Thus, all 11 infants who displayed a preference (as defined by more time oriented toward one odor stimulus than the other) responded preferentially to their own mother's stimulus pad ($p <$ .001; two-tailed binomial test).

EXPERIMENT 2: MOTHER VERSUS UNFAMILIAR LACTATING FEMALE

The results of the first experiment indicate that breast-feeding infants can discriminate between the axillary odors of their mother and an unfamiliar nonparturient female. These data, however, do not allow one to ascertain whether the mother's unique axillary odors are recognized by her infant, or, alternatively, whether breast-feeding infants simply prefer odors of any lactating female over those of nonparturient females. In an attempt to elucidate this issue, breast-feeding neonates were tested with olfactory cues from their mother and an unfamiliar lactating female.

Methods Sixteen breast-feeding mothers and infants (mean age = 15.0 days) participated in this experiment. Two infants (e.g., A and B) who had been born within 72 hours of one another were tested on a given day, allowing each of these infants to be tested with odor stimuli from the same two females. Thus, the mother of infant A would serve as the unfamiliar lactating female for infant B, and infant B's mother, in turn, would be the unfamiliar breast-feeding female for infant A. Each stimulus female wore two odor pads so that a separate set of pads (mother's and unfamiliar female's) was used for each subject infant. Stimulus mothers ranged in age from 22 to 34 years, and the eight male and eight female infants weighed 2,951–4,086 grams at birth.

Results Overall, the infants oriented to their mother's axillary pad for a significantly longer time than to the unfamiliar lactating female's odor pad (see Table 32.01). Such preferential orientation is taken as evidence that the breast-feeding infants recognized the axillary odors of their own mother. Thirteen of the 16 infants preferred their mother's pad, while three infants oriented for a longer period to the pad soiled by the unfamiliar female ($p <$ .01; one-tailed binomial test).

EXPERIMENT 3: FATHER VERSUS UNFAMILIAR ADULT MALE

Experiment 3 was conducted in an attempt to determine whether breast-feeding infants can recognize the axillary odors of family members other than their mother. Since fathers may interact frequently with their neonates, and the degree of genetic relatedness between fathers and offspring is the same as

TABLE 32.01

MEAN DURATIONS OF ORIENTATION TO THE SIMULTANEOUSLY PRESENTED OLFACTORY STIMULI IN EXPERIMENTS 1–5		
EXPERIMENT AND OLFACTORY STIMULI	MEAN SECONDS ORIENTED TOWARD EACH ODOR STIMULUS	*t* TEST FOR CORRELATED SAMPLES
1 (*N* = 13 breast-feeding infants): Mother's axillary odor . . . . vs. Nonparturient female's axillary odor	62.5 42.0	2.65, *df* = 12, *p* < .05
2 (*N* = 16 breast-feeding infants): Mother's axillary odor . . . . vs. Unfamiliar lactating female's axillary odor	72.9 37.1	3.16, *df* = 15, *p* < .01
3 (*N* = 15 breast-feeding infants): Father's axillary odor . . . . vs. Axillary odor of unrelated adult male	48.7 55.7	.82, *df* = 14, N.S.
4 (*N* = 15 bottle-feeding infants): Mother's axillary odor . . . . vs. Axillary odor of unfamiliar bottle-feeding female	53.5 57.4	.26, *df* = 14, N.S.
5 (*N* = 15 bottle-feeding infants): Mother's axillary odor . . . . vs. Nonparturient female's axillary odor	49.3 51.3	.26, *df* = 14, N.S.

that of mothers and offspring (i.e., .50 in each instance), it was hypothesized that fathers might be the most likely class of kin (aside from the mother) to elicit an odor-based response from their neonates.

Methods Breast-feeding infants (*N* = 15; eight males, seven females) were tested at a mean age of 14.6 days for their responses to simultaneously presented olfactory cues from their father and from an unfamiliar, unrelated adult male. The unfamiliar comparison males were 24–42 years of age and the birthweights of the subject infants between 2,497 and 4,812 grams. Fathers, whose ages ranged from 25 to 38 years, and comparison males were given the same set of instructions as the mothers in the previous experiment. In addition, fathers were asked to keep a daily log of the duration of direct physical contact that they had with their infant prior to the test session. Further details of the testing procedures are otherwise identical to those of the previous experiments.

Results As seen in Table 32.01, infants did not differ reliably in the amount of time that they oriented toward the odor pads worn by their father versus an unfamiliar adult male. Seven of the infants oriented preferentially to their father's odor, while eight infants spent longer oriented to the pad worn by an unfamiliar male. Thus, breast-feeding infants displayed no evidence of recognizing their father's axillary odor.

The fathers' logs revealed that the total amount of physical contact between father and infant prior to testing ranged from .5 through 59 hours across the 15 participating fathers. The amount of father-infant contact did not correlate significantly with the time that the infants spent oriented toward their father's odor during the olfactory preference test (*r* = .03). Likewise, there was no significant correlation between the difference in time oriented toward the father's pad versus the comparison male's pad and the amount of physical contact that the infants had with their fathers (*r* = − .05).

II. Bottle-feeding Infants

In the previous experiments, only breast-feeding infants were tested for recognition of olfactory cues produced by their mothers and fathers. The question arises, therefore, whether bottle-feeding infants would respond in a similar manner as breast-feeding infants to parental odors. In particular, will bottle-feeding infants also display evidence of recognizing their mother's axillary odors? The final two experiments (4 and 5) were designed to address this question.

EXPERIMENT 4: MOTHERS VERSUS UNFAMILIAR BOTTLE-FEEDING FEMALES

Methods A total of 15 infants (seven males and eight females) participated in Experiment 4. These bottle-feeding infants were individually tested for their responses to an odor pad worn by their own mother and a second pad soiled by an unfamiliar female who was also bottle-feeding her own infant. Two infants who had been born within 72 hours of one another were scheduled for testing on a given day. As for Experiment 2, this allowed each of the paired infants to be tested with odor stimuli from the mothers of those same two infants. Each stimulus female wore two odor pads so that a separate set of pads was used for each subject infant.

The stimulus mothers ranged in age from 17 to 37 years and the birthweights of infants from 2,769 to 4,540 grams. The mean age of infants at the time of testing was 15.2 days. Further procedural details are otherwise identical to those presented above for the experiments with breast-feeding infants.

Results The mean duration of orientation to the mother's odor pad (across all 15 infants) did not differ reliably from the mean time oriented to the pad worn by an unfamiliar bottle-feeding female (see Table 32.01). Likewise, the number of infants who preferred the mother's pad was not significantly different from the number who preferred the comparison female's pad; nine of the infants spent more time oriented toward their mother's pad than to the unfamiliar female's pad, while the remaining six infants oriented preferentially to the odor pad of the unfamiliar female.

EXPERIMENT 5: BOTTLE-FEEDING MOTHERS VERSUS NONPARTURIENT FEMALES

It is possible (albeit unlikely) that recently parturient females who do not breast-feed their infants and therefore cease lactating nevertheless produce somewhat similar odor cues as a function of physiological changes (metabolic or endocrinal) associated with birth-giving. Accordingly, the lack of differential responsiveness by the infants in Experiment 4 to

odor cues from their mother as compared to an unfamiliar bottle-feeding female may reflect, in part, the difficulty of this discrimination task. In an attempt to test this hypothesis, bottle-feeding infants were tested for their responses to olfactory cues from their own mother and from an unfamiliar *nonparturient* female.

Methods Fifteen bottle-feeding infants (eight males and seven females) were each tested with two odor pads, one soiled by their own mother and a second that had been soiled by an unfamiliar nonparturient female. Birthweights of infants ranged from 2,270 to 3,949 grams, and mean ages of mothers and comparison females were 24.5 and 27.0 years, respectively. The mean age of infants at the time of testing was 14.7 days.

Results No reliable differences were found between the mean durations of orientation to olfactory cues from the bottle-feeding infant's mother versus an unfamiliar nonparturient female (Table 32.01). Preferences for the mother's odor pad over the unfamiliar female's pad were displayed by eight infants; however, the remaining seven infants oriented preferentially to the pad soiled by an unfamiliar female.

DISCUSSION

Maternal odors emanating from the breast region are not unique in their attractiveness to breast-feeding infants. Rather (as seen in Experiments 1 and 2), at 12–18 days after birth, breast-feeding infants also orient preferentially to axillary odors produced by their mother in comparison to such odors from either unfamiliar nonparturient females or unfamiliar breast-feeding females. These latter data indicate that breast-feeding infants do not simply respond indiscriminately to axillary odors from lactating females but can recognize the characteristic olfactory signature of their own mother.

In contrast with the breast-feeding infants, bottle-feeding infants displayed no evidence of recognizing their mother's axillary odors; that is, they did not differ in their responses to maternal axillary odors and odors from unfamiliar bottle-feeding females (Experiment 4) or from nonparturient females (Experiment 5). It should be pointed out that lack of an overt preference for the maternal odor does not necessarily imply that these infants were unable to recognize that stimulus. Although discriminative responsiveness is an indication of recognition, stimulus preferences and recognition cannot be equated. There are several logically possible explanations for the differences in responsiveness to maternal axillary odors observed between breast-feeding and bottle-feeding infants. Although unlikely, the perceptual capabilities of bottle- and breast-feeding infants may differ. Accordingly, breast-feeding infants may be more sensitive to olfactory cues (i.e., have a lower detection threshold than bottle-feeding infants for odor stimuli) and therefore better able to discern or recognize their mother's characteristic body odor. Alternatively, chemical signals emitted by breast-feeding females may differ, either qualitatively or quantitatively, from those produced by nonlactating (e.g., bottle-feeding) females. Therefore, discrimination between pads soiled by lactating versus nonlactating females could be based on stimulus strength alone. The difference in odors among lactating females might also be greater than that among nonlactating females. In several nonhuman species, lactating females are known to produce chemical signals (maternal pheromone) that are uniquely attractive to suckling young (Breen & Leshner, 1977; Leon, 1974; Porter & Doane, 1976). Human infants may similarly be responsive to odors that are specifically associated with lactation and learn rapidly to recognize such signals produced by their own mother.

Perhaps the most parsimonious hypothesis to explain the discrimination of maternal axillary odors by breast-feeding, but not bottle-feeding, infants concerns the differential mother-infant interactions between these two groups of infants. During the recurring bouts of breast-feeding, infants' nostrils are maintained within close physical proximity of the mother's bare skin for prolonged periods of time. Bottle-feeding infants, in comparison, are not necessarily routinely exposed to their mother's bare skin to the same extent as are breast-feeding infants. These two groups of infants, therefore, are quite likely to differ markedly in their degree of exposure to body odors produced by their mothers, especially if such olfactory signals are best perceived when in close contact with the mother's body surface. Such differential exposure to salient maternal odors might be sufficient to account for the pattern of results reported above. In addition, fathers would be somewhat similar to bottle-feeding mothers in having relatively limited direct skin-to-skin (or skin-to-nostril) contact with their infants. Therefore, as seen in Experiment 3, even breast-feeding infants show no evidence of recognizing paternal axillary odors.

The current emphasis on olfactory recognition does not imply that other sensory modalities are of minimal importance for maternal recognition by neonates. As early as the third day after birth, infants respond discriminatively to their mother's voice (DeCasper & Fifer, 1980; see also Mehler, Bertoncini, Barriere, & Jassik-Gerschenfeld, 1978, and Mills & Melhuish, 1974). Similar to the above results with odor stimuli, however, neonates displayed no evidence of discriminating between the voices of their father and another male within the first 3 days postpartum (DeCasper & Prescott, 1984).

The developmental time course of visual recognition of the mother's face is somewhat ambiguous. When tested with photographs of females' faces, 3-month-old infants recognize their mother's face (Barrera & Maurer, 1981). More recent experiments revealed that 22–93-hour-old infants respond preferentially to the silent live face of their mother over faces of unfamiliar nonparturient women (Field, Cohen, Garcia, & Greenberg, 1984). As pointed out by the authors, however, the testing procedures did not rule out the possibility that the infants were actually responding to odors associated with the stimulus faces rather than their visual appearance. The results of the present series of experiments offer further support for the conclusion that the infants tested by Field et al. may have discriminated their mother's face by olfactory cues.

Given the importance of mutual mother-infant recognition for the development of early social relationships, it would be adaptive for infants to be able to discriminate their mother by cues across several sensory modalities. Breast-feeding infants have been found to recognize their mother by her breast odor or, as seen above, her axillary odor alone. As research on human olfaction progresses, the potential influence of biological odors on the mediation of social behavior in our own species becomes increasingly evident.

References

1. Barrera, M. E., & Maurer, D. (1981). Recognition of mother's photographed face by the three-month-old infant. *Child Development, 52,* 714–718.
2. Bowlby, J. (1969). *Attachment and loss: Vol. 1. Attachment.* New York: Basic.
3. Breen, M. F., & Leshner, A. I. (1977). Maternal pheromone: A demonstration of its existence in the mouse (*Mus musculus*). *Physiology and Behavior, 18,* 527–529.
4. Brill, A. A. (1932). The sense of smell in the neuroses and psychoses. *Psychoanalytic Quarterly, 1,* 7–42.
5. DeCasper, A. J., & Fifer, W. P. (1980). Of human bonding: Newborns prefer their mothers' voices. *Science, 208,* 1174–1176.
6. DeCasper, A. J., & Prescott, P. A. (1984). Human newborns' perception of male voices: Preference, discrim-

ination, and reinforcing value. *Developmental Psychobiology,* **17,** 481–491.

7. Field, T. M., Cohen, D., Garcia, R., & Greenberg, R. (1984). Mother-stranger face discrimination by the newborn. *Infant Behavior and Development,* **7,** 19–25.

8. Kalogerakis, M. G. (1963). The role of olfaction in sexual development. *Psychosomatic Medicine,* **25,** 420–432.

9. Leon, M. (1974). Maternal pheromone. *Physiology and Behavior,* **13,** 441–453.

10. Macfarlane, A. (1975). Olfaction in the development of social preferences in the human neonate. *Parent-infant interaction* (Ciba Foundation Symposium 33) (pp. 103–113). New York: Elsevier.

11. Mehler, J., Bertoncini, J., Barriere, M., & Jassik-Gerschenfeld, D. (1978). Infant recognition of mother's voice. *Perception,* **7,** 491–497.

12. Mills, M., & Melhuish, E. (1974). Recognition of mother's voice in early infancy. *Nature* (London), **252,** 123–124.

13. Peto, A. (1973). The olfactory forerunner of the superego: Its role in normalcy, neurosis and fetishism. *International Journal of Psycho-Analysis,* **54,** 323–330.

14. Porter, R. H., Cernoch, J. M., & McLaughlin, F. J. (1983). Maternal recognition of neonates through olfactory cues. *Physiology and Behavior,* **30,** 151–154.

15. Porter, R. H., & Doane, H. M. (1976). Maternal pheromone in the spiny mouse (*Acomys cahirinus*). *Physiology and Behavior,* **16,** 75–78.

16. Prechtl, H., & Beintema, D. (1964). *The neurological examination of the full term infant* (Clinics in Developmental Medicine No. 12). London: Heinemann.

17. Robson, K. S., & Moss, H. A. (1970). Patterns and determinants of maternal attachment. *Journal of Pediatrics,* **77,** 976–985.

18. Russell, M. J. (1976). Human olfactory communication. *Nature,* **260,** 520–522.

19. Russell, M. J., Mendelson, T., & Peeke, H. V. S. (1983). Mother's identification of their infant's odors. *Ethology and Sociobiology,* **4,** 29–31.

20. Schaal, B., Montagner, H., Hertling, E., Bolzoni, D., Moyse, A., & Quichon, R. (1980). Les stimulations olfactives dans les relations entre l'enfant et la mere. *Reproduction, Nutrition et Development,* **20,** 843–858.

21. Schaffer, H. R. (1971). *The growth of sociability.* Harmondsworth, Middlesex: Penguin.

QUESTIONS FOR REFLECTION AND DISCUSSION:

1. What is the effect of infants' recognizing their mothers on the mothers' feelings about the infants?

2. What is "axillary odor"? How was the "olfactory sample" collected from adults?

3. How did the experimenters determine which of two gauze pads an infant "preferred"? Do you accept their method as a valid indicator of preference? Explain.

4. Why did the experimenters reverse the positions of the gauze pads between trials?

5. Why did the experimenters compare the responses of infants who were breast-fed with their responses toward other lactating (milk-producing) women?

6. What were the differences in the "preferences" of infants who were breast-fed versus infants who were bottle-fed? What explanation for this difference is suggested by the authors?

7. Do you see implications in this study for parents? Explain.

8. What other sensory modalities play a role in infant-mother recognition and attachment?

SOURCE

Piaget, J. (1997 Edition). Objective responsibility. I. Clumsiness and stealing. In *The moral judgment of the child*. Trans. By Marjorie Gabain. New York: Free Press, a division of Simon & Schuster, Inc., pp. 121–138. Copyright © 1965 by The Free Press.

Jean Piaget (1896–1980) is a towering figure in the annals of child development. His writings have inspired thousands of research studies, and his theory of development is a key target for critics. Piaget was once offered the curatorship of a museum in Geneva, but he had to turn it down. It turns out that he was only 11 at the time. Piaget's first intellectual love was biology, and he published his first scientific article at the age of 10. He then became a laboratory assistant to the director of a museum of natural history and engaged in research on mollusks (oysters, clams, snails, and such). The director soon died, and Piaget published the research findings himself. On the basis of these papers, he was offered the curatorship.

During adolescence Piaget studied philosophy, logic, and mathematics, but he earned his Ph.D. in biology. In 1920 he obtained a job at the Binet Institute in Paris, where work on intelligence tests was being conducted. His first task was to adapt English verbal reasoning items for use with French children. To do so, he had to try out the items on children in various age groups and see whether they could arrive at correct answers. The task was boring until Piaget became intrigued by the children's wrong *answers. Another investigator might have shrugged them off and forgotten them, but young Piaget realized that there were methods in the children's madness. The wrong answers seemed to reflect consistent, if illogical, cognitive processes. Piaget investigated these "wrong" answers by probing the children's responses to discover the underlying patterns of thought that led to them. These early probings eventually resulted in Piaget's influential theory of cognitive development.*

Many of Piaget's original texts can be difficult to read—even when translated into English. In fact, Piaget once remarked that as he undertook the study of child development he had the distinct advantage of not *having to read Piaget! However, the following section from* The Moral Judgment of the Child *goes down relatively smoothly. It compares* objective responsibility *with* subjective responsibility. *We are not talking of objective versus subjective responsibility in terms of social, philosophical, or legal codes; rather, we are referring to how children judge right and wrong. That is, do they focus primarily on the amount of damage done (objective responsibility) or on the intentions of the wrongdoer (subjective responsibility)?*

Objective Responsibility. I. Clumsiness and Stealing

JEAN PIAGET

We noted, in connection with the rules of a game, that the child seems to go through a stage when rules constitute an obligatory and untouchable reality. We must now see how far this moral realism goes, and in particular whether adult constraint, which is probably its cause, is sufficient to give rise to the phenomenon of objective responsibility. For all that we have been saying about the difficulties of interpretation in the study of the moral judgments of children need not put a stop to our enquiry in this matter. It is immaterial whether the objective responsibility of which we are about to give examples is connected with the whole of the child's life or only with the most external and verbal aspects of his moral thought. The problem still remains as to where this responsibility comes from and why it develops.

The questions put to the children on this point are those whose results we shall study first, but they were actually the last that we thought of. We began, by way of introduction, with the problem of judgments relating to telling lies. In making this analysis, of which we shall speak in the following sections, we immediately noticed that the younger children often measured the gravity of a lie not in terms of the motives which dictated it, but in terms of the falseness of its statements. It was in order to verify the existence and the generality of this tendency to objective responsibility that we devised the following questions.

The first set of questions deals with the consequences of clumsiness. Clumsiness plays, however unjustly, an enormously important part in a child's life, as he comes into conflict with his adult surrounding. At every moment, the child arouses the anger of those around him by breaking, soiling, or spoiling some object or other. Most of the time such anger is unjustifiable, but the child is naturally led to attach a meaning to it. On other occasions, his clumsiness is more or less due to carelessness or disobedience, and an idea of some mysterious and immanent justice comes to be grafted on to the emotions experienced at the time. We therefore tried to make the children compare the stories of two kinds of clumsiness, one, entirely fortuitous or even the result of a well-intentioned act, but involving considerable material damage, the other, negligible as regards the damage done but happening as the result of an ill-intentioned act.

Here are the stories:

I. A. A little boy who is called John is in his room. He is called to dinner. He goes into the dining room. But behind the door there was a chair, and on the chair there was a tray with fifteen cups on it. John couldn't have known that there was all this behind the door. He goes in, the door knocks against the tray, bang go the fifteen cups and they all get broken!

B. Once there was a little boy whose name was Henry. One day when his mother was out he tried to get some jam out of the cupboard. He climbed up on to a chair and stretched out his arm. But the jam was too high up and he couldn't reach it and have any. But while he was trying to get it he knocked over a cup. The cup fell down and broke.

II. A. There was a little boy called Julian. His father had gone out and Julian thought it would be fun to play with his father's ink-pot. First he played with the pen, and then he made a little blot on the table cloth.

B. A little boy who was called Augustus once noticed that his father's ink-pot was empty. One day that his father was away he thought of filling the ink-pot so as to help his father, and so that he should find it full when he came home. But while he was opening the ink-bottle he made a big blot on the table cloth.

III. A. There was once a little girl who was called Marie. She wanted to give her mother a nice surprise, and cut out a piece of sewing for her. But she didn't know how to use the scissors properly and cut a big hole in her dress.

B. A little girl called Margaret went and took her mother's scissors one day that her mother was out. She played with them for a bit. Then as she didn't know how to use them properly she made a little hole in her dress.

When we have analysed the answers obtained by means of these pairs of stories, we shall study two problems relating to stealing. As our aim is for the moment to find out whether the child pays more attention to motive or to material results, we have confined ourselves to the comparison of selfishly motivated acts of stealing with those that are well-intentioned.

IV. A. Alfred meets a little friend of his who is very poor. This friend tells him that he has had no dinner that day because there was nothing to eat in his home. Then Alfred goes into a baker's shop, and as he has no money, he waits till the baker's back is turned and steals a roll. Then he runs out and gives the roll to his friend.

B. Henriette goes into a shop. She sees a pretty piece of ribbon on a table and thinks to herself that it would look very nice on her dress. So while the shop lady's back is turned (while the shop lady is not looking), she steals the ribbon and runs away at once.

V. A. Albertine had a little friend who kept a bird in a cage. Albertine thought the bird was very unhappy, and she was always asking her friend to let him out. But the friend wouldn't. So one day when her friend wasn't there, Albertine went and stole the bird. She let it fly away and hid the cage in the attic so that the bird should never be shut up in it again.

B. Juliet stole some sweeties from her mother one day that her mother was not there, and she hid and ate them up.

About each of these pairs of stories we ask two questions: 1) Are these children equally guilty (or as the young Genevese say "la même chose vilain")? 2) Which of the two is the naughtiest, and why? It goes without saying that each of these questions is the occasion for a conversation more or less elaborate according to the child's reaction. It is also as well to make the subjects repeat the stories before questioning them. The way the child reproduces the story is enough to show whether he has understood it.

We obtained the following result. Up to the age of 10, two types of answer exist side by side. In one type actions are evaluated in terms of the material result and independently of motives; according to the other type of answer motives alone are what counts. It may even happen that one and the same child judges sometimes one way, sometimes the other. Besides, some stories point more definitely to objective responsibility than others. In detail, therefore, the material cannot be said to embody stages properly so called. Broadly speaking, however, it cannot be denied that the notion of objective responsibility diminishes as the child grows older. We did not come across a single definite case of it after the age of 10. In addition, by placing the answers obtained under 10 into two groups defined respectively by objective and by subjective responsibility (reckoning by answers given to each story and not by children, since each child is apt to vary from one story to another) we obtained 7 as the average age for objective responsibility, and 9 as the average age for subjective responsibility. Now, we were unable to question children under 6 with any profit because of the intellectual difficulties of comparison. The average of 7 years therefore represents the youngest of the children. If the two attitudes simply represented individual types or types of family education, the two age averages ought to coincide. But since this is not so, there must be some degree of development present. We can at least venture to submit that even if the objective and the subjective conceptions of responsibility are not, properly speaking, features of two successive stages, they do at least define two distinct processes, one of which on the average precedes the other in the moral development of the child, although the two partially synchronize.

Having made this point clear, let us now turn to the facts, beginning with the stories about clumsiness. Here are typical answers showing a purely objective notion of responsibility.

I. Stories of the Broken Cups

GEO (6): "Have you understood these stories? — *Yes.* — What did the first boy do? — *He broke eleven cups.* — And the second one? — *He broke a cup by moving roughly.* — Why did the first one break the cups? — *Because the door knocked them.* — And the second? — *He was clumsy. When he was getting the jam the cup fell down.* — Is one of the boys naughtier than the other? — *The first is because he knocked over twelve cups.* — If you were the daddy, which one would you punish most? — *The one who broke twelve cups.* — Why did he break them? — *The door shut too hard and knocked them. He didn't do it on purpose.* — And why did the other boy break a cup? — *He wanted to get the jam. He moved too far. The cup got broken.* — Why did he want to get the jam? — *Because he was all alone. Because his mother wasn't there.* — Have you got a brother? — *No, a little sister.* — Well, if it was you who had broken the twelve cups when you went into the room and your little sister who had broken one cup while she was trying to get the jam, which of you would be punished most severely? — *Me, because I broke more than one cup.*"

SCHMA (6): "Have you understood the stories? Let's hear you tell them. — *A little child was called in to dinner. There were fifteen plates on a tray. He didn't know. He opens the door and he breaks the fifteen plates.* — That's very good. And now the second story? — *There was a child. And then this child wanted to go and get some jam. He gets on to a chair, his arm catches on to a cup, and it gets broken.*—Are those children both naughty, or is one not so naughty as the other?—*No. The one who broke fifteen plates.*—And would you punish the other one more, or less?—*The first broke lots of things, the other one fewer.*—How would you punish them?—*The one who broke the fifteen cups: two slaps. The other one, one slap.*"

CONST (7) G.: "Tell me those two stories.—*There was a chair in the dining room with cups on it. A boy opens the door, and all the cups are broken.*—And now the other story?—*A little boys wants to take some jam. He tried to take hold of a cup and it broke.*—If you were their mother, which one would you punish most severely?—*The one who broke the cups.*—Is he the naughtiest?—*Yes.*—Why did he break them?—*Because he wanted to get into the room.*—And the other?—*Because he wanted to take the jam.*—Let's pretend that you are the mummy. You have two little girls. One of them breaks fifteen cups as she is coming into the dining room, the other breaks one cup as she is trying to get some jam while you are not there. Which of them would you punish most severely?—*The one who broke the fifteen cups.*" But Const who is so decided about our stories goes on to tell us some personal reminiscences in which it is obviously subjective responsibility that is at work. "Have you ever broken anything?—*A cup.*—How?—*I wanted to wipe it, and I let it drop.*—What else have you broken?—*Another time, a plate.*—How?—*I took it to play with.*—Which was the naughtiest thing to do?—*The plate, because I oughtn't to have taken it.*—And how about the cup?—*That was less naughty because I wanted to wipe it.*—Which were you punished most for, for the cup or for the plate?—*For the plate.* Listen, I am going to tell you two more stories. A little girl was wiping the cups. She was putting them away, wiping them with the cloth, and she broke five cups. Another little girl is playing with some plates. She breaks a plate. Which of them is the naughtiest?—*The one who broke the five cups.*" This shows that in the case of her own personal recollections (where, incidentally, the number of objects broken does not come in) subjective responsibility alone is taken into account. As soon as we go back to the stories, even basing them on the child's recollections, objective responsibility reappears in all its purity!

II. The Stories of the Ink-Stains

CONST (7) G., whose answers we have just been examining repeats correctly the story of the blot of ink: "*A little boy sees that his father's ink-pot is empty. He takes the ink-bottle, but he is clumsy and makes a big blot.*—And the other one?—*There was a boy who was always touching things. He takes the ink and makes a little blot.*—Are they both equally naughty or not?—*No.*—Which is the most naughty?—*The one who made the big blot.*—Why?—*Because it was big.*—Why did he make a big blot?—*To be helpful.*—And why did the other one make a little blot?—*Because he was always touching things. He made a little blot.*—Then which of them is the naughtiest?—*The one who made a big blot.*"

GEO (6) also understands the stories and knows that the two children's intentions were quite different. But he regards as the naughtiest "*the one who made the big blot.*—Why?—*Because that blot is bigger than the other one.*"

III. The Story of the Holes

GEO (6) is equally successful in understanding these two stories. "*The first wanted to help her mother and she made a big hole in her frock. The other one was playing and made a little hole.*—Is one of these little girls naughtier than the others?—*The one who wanted to help her mother a little is the naughtiest because she made a big hole. She got scolded.*"

CONST (7) G. repeats the stories as follows: "*A little girl wanted to make a handkerchief for her mother. She was clumsy, and made a big hole in her frock.*—And the other one?—*There was a little girl who was always touching things. She took some scissors to play and made a little hole in her frock.*—Which of them is naughtiest?—*The one who made the big hole.*—Why did she make this hole?—*She wanted to give her mother a surprise.*—That's right. And the other one?—*She took the scissors because she was always touching things and made a little hole.*—That's right. Then which of the little girls was nicest?— . . . (hesitation).— Say what you think.—*The one who made the little hole is the nicest.*—If you were the mother you would have seen everything they did. Which would you have punished most?—*The one who made a big hole.*— And which one would you have punished least?—*The one who made the little hole.*— And what would the one who made the big hole say when you punished her most?—*She would say, I wanted to give a surprise.*— And the other one?—*She was playing.*— Which one ought to be punished most?— *The one who made the big hole.*—Let's pretend that it was you who made the big hole so as to give your mother a surprise. Your sister is playing and makes the little hole. Which ought to be punished most?— *Me.*—Are you quite sure, or not quite sure?—*Quite sure.*—Have you ever made holes?—*Never.*—Is what I am asking you quite easy?—*Yes.*—Are you quite sure you meant what you said?—*Yes.*"

These answers reveal the strength of the resistance offered to the counter-suggestions we attempted to make, and they also show what store the children set by material results, in spite of the fact that they have perfectly well understood the story and consequently the intentions of its characters, and what little account they take of the intentions which have indirectly caused these material happenings.

Such facts as these taken by themselves of course prove nothing. Before speaking about objective responsibility, we must ask ourselves whether the child does not draw a distinction analogous to that which the adult makes in the case of ethics and of certain legal punishments. One can without any loss of honour be run in for having broken police regulations. One can be the object of a legal sentence devoid of any penal element (cf. Durkheim's restitutive and retributive punishment). In the same way, then, when a child pronounces a little girl to be "naughty" because she has made a big hole in her dress, although he knows that her intentions were not only innocent but admirable, does he not simply mean that she has damaged her parents materially and therefore deserves a purely legal punishment devoid of any moral significance?

The question arises in the same form in connection with stealing, as we shall see presently. But with regard to lying, since all question of material damage can be disregarded, we shall endeavour to prove that the child's judgments really do imply objective responsibility. An analogous conclusion may therefore be formulated concerning the present examples. Here preoccupation about material damage certainly outweighs any question of obedience or disobedience to rules. But this is a form of objective responsibility only in so far as the child fails to distinguish the element of civic responsibility, as it were, from the penal element. Now, on the verbal plane where we have taken up our stand it seems to us that this differentiation is one that hardly enters into the subject's mind. Responsibility is thus still held to be objective, even from the moral point of view.

Before carrying our analysis any further and in order to place the previous attitudes in their true perspective, let us examine the answers that contradict those which we have just dealt with and which relate to the same pairs of stories.

I. Story of the Broken Cups

Here, to begin with, is a rather exceptional case of a 6-year-old child. (Most of the children of 6 gave us answers which corresponded to the type of objective responsibility.)

SCHMA ($6\frac{1}{2}$, G., forward intellectually and looking more like a girl of 8) begins by telling us that the two boys of the story are *"equally naughty,"* and that they must be punished *"Both just the same."* "Well, I think one of them is naughtier than the other. Which one do you think?—*Both the same.*—Have you never broken anything?—*No, I never have. My brother has.*—What did he break?—*A cup and a pail.*—How?—*He wanted to fish. He broke half my pail, and then afterwards he broke it again on purpose to annoy me.*— Did he also break a cup?—*He had wiped it and was putting it on the edge of the table and it fell.*—What day was he naughtiest, the day he broke the pail or the day he broke the cup?—*The pail.*—Why?—*He broke my pail on purpose.*—And the cup?—*He didn't do that on purpose. He put it right on the edge and it broke.*—And in the stories I told you, which boy is naughtiest, the one who broke the fifteen cups or the one who broke one cup?—*The one who wanted to take the jam because he wanted to eat it.*" Thus by appealing to her personal memories one sees that Schma can be led to judge according to subjective responsibility.

MOL (7): "Which is naughtiest?—*The second, the one who wanted to take the jam-pot, because he wanted to take something without asking.*—Did he catch it?—*No.*—Was he the naughtiest all the same?—*Yes.*—And the first?—*It wasn't his fault. He didn't do it on purpose.*"

CORM (9): "*Well, the one who broke them as he was coming isn't naughty, 'cos he didn't know there was any cups. The other one wanted to take the jam and caught his arm on a cup.*—Which one is the naughtiest?—*The one who wanted to take the jam.*—How many cups did he break?—*One.*—And the other boy?—*Fifteen.*—Which one would you punish most?—*The boy who wanted to take the jam. He knew, he did it on purpose.*"

GROS (9): "What did the first one do?—*He broke fifteen cups as he was opening a door.*—And the second one?—*He broke one cup as he was taking some jam.*—Which of these two silly things was naughtiest, do you think?—*The one where he tried to take hold of a cup was* [the silliest] *because the other boy didn't see* [that there were some cups behind the door]. *He saw what he was doing.*—How many did he break?—*One cup.*—And the other one?—*Fifteen.*—Then which one would you punish most?—*The one who broke one cup.*—Why?—*He did it on purpose. If he hadn't taken the jam, it wouldn't have happened.*"

NUSS (10): The naughtiest is "*the one who wanted to take the jam.*—Does it make any difference the other one having broken more cups?—*No, because the one who broke fifteen cups didn't do it on purpose.*"

II. Story of the Ink-Stains

SCI (6): "What did the first one do?—*He wanted to please his daddy. He saw that the ink-pot was empty and thought he would fill it. He made a big spot on his suit.*—And the second one?—*He wanted to play with his daddy's ink, and he made a little spot.*—Which is the naughtiest?—*The one who played with the ink pot. He was playing with it. The other wanted to be kind.*—Did the one who wanted to be kind make a big spot or a little one?—*He made a big spot, the other boy made a little one.*—Does it not matter the first one having made a big

spot?—*All the same, the other wanted more to do something wrong. The one who made a little spot wanted to do something more wrong than the other.*"

GROS (9): "*The one who wanted to be helpful, even if the stain is bigger, mustn't be punished.*"

NUSS (10): The naughtiest is "*the one who made the little stain, because the other one wanted to help.*"

III. The Story of the Holes

SCI (6) repeats the stories as follows: "*The first one wanted to give her mother a surprise. She pricked herself and made a big hole in her frock. The second one liked touching everything. She took the scissors and made a little hole in her dress.*—Which one is naughtiest?—*The one who wanted to take the scissors. She made a little hole in her frock. She is the naughtiest.*—Which one would you punish most, the one who made a little hole, or the other one?—*Not the one who made a big hole; she wanted to give her mother a surprise.*"

CORM (9): The naughtiest is "*the second. She oughtn't to have taken the scissors to play with. The first one didn't do it on purpose. You can't say that she was naughty.*"

These answers show what fine shades even some of the youngest children we questioned could distinguish and how well able they were to take intentions into account. The hypothesis may therefore be advanced that evaluations based on material damage alone are the result of adult constraint refracted through childish respect far rather than a spontaneous manifestation of the child mind. Generally speaking, adults deal very harshly with clumsiness. In so far as parents fail to grasp the situation and lose their tempers in proportion to the amount of damage done, in so far will the child begin by adopting this way of looking at things and apply literally the rules thus imposed, even if they were only implicit. And in so far as the parents are just, and, above all, in so far as the growing child sets up his own feelings as against the adult's reactions, objective responsibility will diminish in importance.

With regard to stealing we also found two groups of answers, and here again, while both objective and subjective responsibility are to be found at all ages between 6 and 10, it is the latter that predominates as the child develops.

Here are examples of objective responsibility:

IV. The Story of the Roll and of the Ribbon

SCI (6) who showed signs of a subjective conception of responsibility in regard to clumsiness, changes his attitude here. He repeats the stories as follows: *"A boy was with his friend. He stole a roll and gave it to his friend. A little girl wanted a ribbon, and put it round her frock to look pretty.*—Is one of them naughtier than the other?—*Yes. . . . No. They're just the same.*—Why did the first one steal the roll?—*Because his friend liked it.*—Why did the little girl steal the ribbon?—*Because she was longing for it.*—Which one would you punish most?—*The boy who stole the roll and gave it to his brother instead of keeping it for himself.*—Was it naughty to give it?—*No. He was kind. He gave it to his brother.*—Must one of them be punished more than the other?—*Yes. The little boy stole the roll to give to his brother. He must be punished more. Rolls cost more."*

SCHMA (6) repeats the stories as follows: *"There was a boy. As his friend had had no dinner, he took a roll and put in his pocket and gave it to his friend. A little girl went into a shop. She saw a ribbon. She says, it would be nice to put on my dress, she says. She took it.*—Is one of these children naughtier than the other?—*The boy is, because he took a roll. It's bigger.*—Ought they to be punished?—*Yes. Four slaps for the first.*—And the girl?—*Two slaps.*—Why did he take the roll?—*Because his friend had had no dinner.*—And the other child?—*To make herself pretty."*

GEO (6): "Which of them is the naughtiest?—*The one with the roll, because the roll is bigger than the ribbon."* And yet Geo is like the other children perfectly well aware of the motives involved.

V. The Story of the Cage and of the Sweets

DESA (6): *"The little girl had a friend who had a cage and a bird. She thought this was too unkind. So she took the cage and let the bird out.*—And the other one?—*A little girl stole a sweet and ate it.*—Are they both equally naughty or is one of them naughtier than the other?—*The one who stole the*

cage is naughtiest.—Why?—*Because she stole the cage.*—And the other one?—*She stole a sweet.*—Is that one more or less naughty than the first?—*Less. The sweet is smaller than the cage.*—If you were the daddy, which one would you punish most?—*The one who stole the cage.*—Why did she steal it?—*Because the bird was unhappy.*—And why did the other one steal the sweet?—*To eat it."*

These cases of objective responsibility are thus all three of 6-year-olds. We found none above 7 years in the case of this kind of story. Here are some definite cases of subjective responsibility found in connection with the same stories. They are nearly all children of 9 and 10. The types are therefore better dissociated with regard to age than in the case of the stories about clumsiness.

IV. Story of the Roll and the Ribbon

CORM (9) tells the two stories correctly. "What do you think about it?—*Well, the little boy oughtn't to have stolen. He oughtn't to have stolen it, but to have paid for it. And the other one, she oughtn't to have stolen the ribbon either.*—Which of them is the naughtiest?—*The little girl took the ribbon for herself. The little boy took the roll too, but to give it to his friend who had had no dinner.*—If you were the school teacher, which one would you punish most?—*The little girl."*

NUSS (10): "Which one is the naughtiest?—*The little girl is because she took it for herself."*

V. Story of the Cage and the Sweets

SCI (6): "Which one is naughtiest?—*The one who steals the sweet. The first one took the cage so as to set the little bird free."*

CORM (9), G.: *"It was good of the little girl who wanted to set the little bird free. The other one oughtn't to have eaten the sweet."*

GROS (9): *"The one who stole the sweet, that was naughtier.*—Why?—*Because the other let the little bird go free again."*

Thus these answers present us with two distinct moral attitudes—one that judges actions according to their material consequences, and one that only takes intentions into account. These two attitudes may co-exist at the same age and even in the same child, but broadly speaking, they do not synchronize. Objective responsibility diminishes on the average as the child grows older, and subjective responsibility gains correlatively in importance. We have therefore two processes partially overlapping, but of which the second gradually succeeds in dominating the first.

What explanation can we give of these facts? The objective conception of responsibility arises, without any doubt, as a result of the constraint exercised by the adult. But the exact meaning of this constraint has still to be established, because in cases of theft and clumsiness it is exercised in a rather different form from what appears in cases of lying. For in some of the cases we have been examining it is quite certain that adults, or some adults, apply their own sanctions, whether "diffused" (blame) or "organized" (punishment), in conformity with the rules of objective responsibility. The average housewife (most of the children we examined came from very poor districts) will be more angry over fifteen cups than over one, and independently, up to a point, of the offender's intentions. Broadly speaking, then, one may say that it is not only the externality of the adult command in relation to the child's mind that produces the effects we are discussing, it is the example of the adult himself. In cases of lying, on the other hand, we shall find that it is almost entirely in spite of the adult's intention that objective responsibility imposes itself upon the child's mind.

Restricted though the question under discussion may appear, it has a very distinct interest. When the adult allows himself to evaluate acts of clumsiness and pilfering in terms of their material result, there can be no doubt that in most people's eyes he is unjust. On the other hand, those parents who try to give their children a moral education based on intention, achieve very early results as is shown by current observation and the few examples of subjective responsibility we were able to note at 6 or 7. How is it, then, that in most of the cases under 9–10 years the child accepts so completely the criterion of objective responsibility and even outdoes the average adult on this point? The child is much more of an objectivist, so to speak, than the least intelligent parent. Also, most parents draw a distinction which the children precisely neglect to make: they scold, that is, according to the extent of the material damage caused by the clumsy act, but they do not regard the act itself exactly as a moral fault. The child on the contrary seems, as we have noted before, not to differentiate the legal or, as it were,

the purely police aspect from the moral aspect of the question. It is "naughtier" to make a big spot on your coat than a small one, and this in spite of the fact that the child knows perfectly well that the intentions involved may have been good. To commit certain acts is therefore, in a sense, wrong in itself, independently of the psychological context. With regard to stealing, which is unanimously held up to children as a grave moral offence, this phenomenon appears even more clearly. Nearly all the children under 9–10, while paying full tribute to the thief's intentions, consider the theft of the roll and the cage a more culpable act both from a police and from a moral point of view than that of the ribbon or the sweet. Now, we can understand anyone condemning a theft regardless of the object pursued, but it is rather curious to see little children adopting an exclusively material criterion when they are asked to compare two such dissimilar acts as are described in our stories.

The problem involved in all this is the following. What is the origin of this initial predominance of judgments of objective responsibility, surpassing in scope and intensity what may have been done or said to the children by adults? Only one answer seems to us to be possible. The rules imposed by the adult, whether verbally (not to steal, not to handle breakable objects carelessly, etc.) or materially (anger, punishments) constitute categorical obligations for the child, before his mind has properly assimilated them, and no matter whether he puts them into practice or not. They thus acquire the value of ritual necessities, and the forbidden things take on the significance of taboos. Moral realism would thus seem to be the fruit of constraint and of the primitive forms of unilateral respect. Is this an inevitable product or an accidental result? This is the point we shall try to settle in connection with lying.

But before going too far in our generalizations, let us remember that the child's answers are given in answer to stories that are told to him and do not arise out of really experienced facts. As in the case of method we may therefore ask ourselves whether these verbal evaluations do or do not correspond with the child's real thoughts. These evaluations certainly change as the child grows older, and they also seem to be the result of some systematic influence. But are they a mere derivative, a verbal and therefore ineffectual deduction from the words spoken by adults, or do they correspond with a genuine attitude, moulded by unilateral respect and conditioning the child's behaviour before they inspire his sayings?

As we noticed in certain cases, the child pays far more attention to intentions where his own memories are concerned than when he is being questioned about one or other of our little stories. Such a fact as this surely shows us that if the child's objectivist attitude (unmistakable enough in his theoretical thought) corresponds to anything in his concrete and active thought, there must have been a time-lag taking place between one of these manifestations and the other, for the theoretical attitude is certainly a later-comer as compared to the practical. But the problem goes deeper than this, and the question may be raised whether at any moment in the immediate experiences of his moral life, or at any rate in those connected with clumsiness and lying, the child has ever been dominated by the notion of objective responsibility.

Immediate observation—the only judge in the matter—is sufficiently explicit on this point. It is very easy to notice—especially in very young children, under 6–7 years of age—how frequently the sense of guilt on the occasion of clumsiness is proportional to the extent of the material disaster instead of remaining subordinate to the intentions in question. I have often noticed in the case of my own children, who have never been blamed for involuntary clumsiness, how difficult it was to take away from them all sense of responsibility when they chanced to break an article or soil some linen. Which of us cannot recall the accusing character which such a minor accident would take on as soon as it had happened, rising, with all the suddenness of a shock and overwhelming us with a sense of guilt that was the more burning, the more unexpected and the more irreparable the disaster. To be sure, all sorts of factors come into play (the sense of "immanent" justice, affective associations with previous carelessness, fear of punishment, etc.). But how could the material damage be felt as a fault if the child were not applying in a literal and realistic manner a whole set of rules, implicit and explicit, for which he feels respect?

We can therefore put forward the hypothesis that judgments of objective responsibility occurring in the course of our interrogatory were based upon a residue left by experiences that had really been lived through. Although new material may since have enriched the child's moral consciousness and enabled him to discern the nature of subjective responsibility, these earlier experiences are sufficient, it would seem, to constitute a permanent foundation of moral realism which reappears on each fresh occasion. Now, since thought in the child always lags behind action, it is quite natural that the solution of theoretical problems such as we made use of should be formed by means of the older and more habitual schemas rather than the more subtle and less robust schemas that are in process of formation. Thus an adult who may be in the midst of reviewing all his values and experiencing feelings of which the novelty surprises him, will, if he is suddenly faced with the necessity of solving someone else's problems, very probably appeal to moral principles which he has discarded for himself. For example, he will, if he is not given time to reflect, judge his neighbour's actions with a severity which would be incomprehensible in view of his present deeper tendencies, but which effectively corresponds to his previous system of values. In the same way, our children may perfectly well take account of intentions in appraising their own conduct, and yet confine themselves to considerations of the material consequences of actions in the case of the characters involved in our stories, who are indifferent to them.

How, then, does subjective responsibility appear and develop within the limited domain we are analysing at present? There is no doubt that by adopting a certain technique with their children, parents can succeed in making them attach more importance to intentions than to rules conceived as a system of ritual interdictions. Only the question is, whether this technique does not involve perpetually taking care not to impose on their children any duties properly so called, and placing mutual sympathy above everything else? It is when the child is accustomed to act from the point of view of those around him, when he tries to please rather than to obey, that he will judge in terms of intentions. So that taking intentions into account presupposes cooperation and mutual respect. Only those who have children of their own know how difficult it is to put this into practice. Such is the prestige of parents in the eyes of the very young child, that even if they lay down nothing in the form of general duties, their wishes act as law and thus give rise automatically to moral realism (independently, of course, of the manner in which the child eventually carries out these desires). In order to remove all traces of moral realism, one must place oneself on the child's own level, and give him a feeling of equality by laying stress on one's own obligations and one's own deficiencies. In the sphere of clumsiness and of untidiness in general (putting away toys, personal cleanliness, etc.), in short in all the multifarious obligations that are so secondary for moral theory but so all-important in daily life (perhaps nine-tenths of the commands given to children relate to these material questions) it is quite easy to draw attention to one's own needs, one's own difficulties, even one's own blunders, and to point out their consequences, thus creating an atmosphere of mutual help and understanding. In this way the child will find himself in the presence, not of a system of commands requiring ritualistic and external obedience, but of a system of social relations such that everyone does his best to obey the same obligations, and does so out of mutual respect. The passage from obedience to cooperation thus marks a progress analogous to that of which we saw the effects in the evolution of the game of marbles: only in the final stage does the morality of intention triumph over the morality of objective responsibility.

When parents do not trouble about such considerations as these, when they issue contradictory commands and are inconsistent in the punishments they inflict, then, obviously, it is not because of moral constraint but in spite of and as a reaction against it that the concern with intentions develops in the child. Here is a child, who, in his desire to please, happens to break something and is snubbed for his pains, or who in general sees his actions judged otherwise than he judges them himself. It is obvious that after more or less brief periods of submission, during which he accepts every verdict, even those that are wrong, he will begin to feel the injustice of it all. Such situations can lead to revolt. But if, on the contrary, the child finds in his brothers and sisters or in his playmates a form of society which develops his desire for cooperation and mutual sympathy, then a new type of morality will be created in him, a morality of reciprocity and not of obedience. This is the true morality of intention and of subjective responsibility.

In short, whether parents succeed in embodying it in family life or whether it takes root in spite of and in opposition to them, it is always cooperation that gives intention precedence over literalism, just as it was unilateral respect that inevitably provoked moral realism. Actually, of course, there are innumerable intermediate stages between these two attitudes of obedience and collaboration, but it is useful for the purposes of analysis to emphasize the real opposition that exists between them.

QUESTIONS FOR REFLECTION AND DISCUSSION:

1. Piaget has been said to use the "clinical method" in his study of child development. Can you describe his method, as shown in the extract from *The Moral Judgment of the Child*?

2. Piaget's cognitive developmental theory tends to put maturation (nature) at the core of development, yet it also acknowledges the role of experience (nurture). In the reading, what references do you find to (1) the idea that the child's view of morality unfolds due to maturation, and (2) the recognition that experience plays a role?

3. Piaget's work has been replicated and some researchers have found that children may develop intellectually somewhat faster than Piaget thought. More specifically, Piaget's critics suggest that Piaget sometimes misinterpreted children's limited memory ability as a lower level of intellectual development. What precautions did Piaget take to make certain that the children in his research remembered the stories he told them?

4. If you were going to replicate (repeat) Piaget's research on clumsiness and stealing, can you think of ways in which you would more tightly "control" the research? (Hints: Would you limit the questioning to one interviewer? Would your interviewers know what they were looking for? Would you tell stories or show videos?)

5. Consider your own attitudes toward immoral behavior and crime. Although you are an adult, can you think of circumstances under which your moral judgments are based on, or at least influenced by, objective responsibility?

SOURCE

Steinberg, L., Dornbusch, S. M., & Brown, B. B. (1992). Ethnic differences in adolescent achievement. *American Psychologist, 47,* 723–729. 121–138. Copyright © 1992 by the American Psychological Association. Reprinted with permission.

Adolescents from different ethnic backgrounds tend to perform differently in high school, as measured by grade point averages, drop out rates, teacher ratings, achievement test scores, and the like. Overall, Asian American adolescents tend to outperform other groups, and African and Hispanic American students tend to perform less well than the average.[1] How do we account for these differences? Some psychologists and educators suggest that different outcomes in school reflect inborn ethnic differences in academic ability. This interpretation is troubling to many psychologists because it is degrading to the groups who fare less well and because it suggests that there is no point in trying to change the situation. Other psychologists have found that students' attitudes toward their own academic achievement, peer support (or the lack of it), and parental involvement in their children's education play key roles in adolescent achievement. Consider these examples offered by psychologist Laurence Steinberg and his colleagues[2]:

- *Many White students report just trying to get by in high school,*

- *African and Hispanic American students often say they recognize the value of good grades and college education, but generally do not fear getting poor grades, and*

- *Asian American students tend to spend twice as much time doing their homework as students in other ethnic groups and are also the most fearful of getting poor grades.*

The following article by Steinberg and his colleagues summarizes many of their findings from a survey of a large sample of U.S. high school students.

Ethnic Differences in Adolescent Achievement: An Ecological Perspective

LAURENCE STEINBERG TEMPLE UNIVERSITY
SANFORD M. DORNBUSCH STANFORD UNIVERSITY
B. BRADFORD BROWN UNIVERSITY OF WISCONSIN—MADISON

Using data collected from a large sample of high school students, the authors challenge three widely held explanations for the supe- rior school performance of Asian American adolescents, and the inferior performance of African- and Hispanic-American adolescents: group differences in (a) parenting practices, (b) familial values about education, and (c) youngsters' beliefs about the occupational rewards of academic success. They found that White youngsters benefit from the combina-

[1] Steinberg, L., Brown, B. B., & Dornbusch, S. M. (1996). Ethnicity and adolescent achievement. *American Educator, 20*(2), 28–35.

[2] Ibid.

tion of authoritative parenting and peer support for achievement, whereas Hispanic youngsters suffer from a combination of parental authoritarianism and low peer support. Among Asian-American students, peer support for academic excellence offsets the negative consequences of authoritarian parenting. Among African-American youngsters, the absence of peer support for achievement undermines the positive influence of authoritative parenting.

One of the most consistent and disturbing findings in studies of adolescent achievement concerns ethnic differences in school performance. Many studies indicate that African-American students "generally earn lower grades, drop out more often, and attain less education than do whites" (Mickelson, 1990, p. 44). Although less research has focused on direct comparisons between other ethnic groups, recent reports on adolescent achievement in America suggest that the performance of Hispanic adolescents also lags behind that of their White counterparts, but that the performance of Asian-American students exceeds that of White, African-American, and Hispanic students (see Sue & Okazaki, 1990). Despite the widely held assumption that ethnic differences in achievement are accounted for by group differences on other variables, such as socioeconomic status and family structure, research indicates quite clearly that these patterns of ethnic differences in achievement persist even after important third variables are taken into account.

Although there is considerable agreement that these ethnic differences in school performance are genuine, there is little consensus about the causes of these differences, and a variety of explanations for the pattern have been offered. Among the most familiar are that (a) there are inherited differences between ethnic groups in intellectual abilities, which are reflected in differences in school performance (e.g., Lynn, 1977; Rushton, 1985); (b) that ethnic differences in achievement-related socialization practices in the family lead youngsters from some ethnic groups to develop more positive achievement-related attitudes and behaviors (e.g., Mordkowitz & Ginsburg, 1987); (c) that there are ethnic differences in cultural values, and especially in the value placed on educational success (see Sue & Okazaki, 1990, for a discussion); and (d) that there are ethnic differences in perceived and actual discrimination within educational and occupational institutions (e.g., Mickelson, 1990; Ogbu, 1978).

This article focuses on ethnic differences in school achievement, a phenomenon that, as a recent article in this journal put it, is "in search of an explanation" (Sue & Okazaki, 1990, p. 913). Because the genetic hypothesis has received so little support in studies of school achievement (see Sue & Okazaki, 1990; Thompson, Detterman, & Plomin, 1991), we focus instead on the various environmental accounts of the phenomenon. To do so, we present and integrate several sets of findings from the first wave of data collected as part of a program of research on a large, multiethnic sample of high school students. The research is aimed at understanding how different contexts in youngsters' lives affect their behavior, schooling, and development.

Overview of the Research Program

During the 1987–1988 school year, we administered a 30-page, two-part questionnaire with a series of standardized psychological inventories, attitudinal indices, and demographic questions to approximately 15,000 students at nine different high schools. The schools were selected to provide a window on the contrasting social ecologies of contemporary American adolescents. They included an inner-city school in Milwaukee, Wisconsin, serving a substantially Black population; a San Jose, California, school serving a large number of Hispanic students; a small rural Wisconsin school in a farming community; a semirural California school with youngsters from farm families, migrant workers, and recently arrived Asian refugees; and several suburban schools serving mixtures of working-class and middle-class adolescents from a variety of ethnic backgrounds. All told, our sample was approximately one third non-White, with nearly equal proportions of African-American, Hispanic, and Asian-American youngsters—much like the adolescent population in the United States today (Wetzel, 1987). The sample was quite diverse with respect to socioeconomic status and household composition.

The questionnaires, which were administered schoolwide, contained numerous measures of psychosocial development and functioning, as well as several measures of social relations in and outside of school. The outcome variables fell into four general categories: *psychosocial adjustment* (including measures of self-reliance, work orientation, self-esteem, and personal and social competence); *schooling* (including measures of school performance, school engagement, time spent on school activities, educational expectations and aspirations, and school-related attitudes and beliefs); *behavior problems* (including measures of drug and alcohol use, delinquency, susceptibility to antisocial peer pressure, and school misconduct); and *psychological distress* (including measures of anxiety, depression, and psychosomatic complaints).

This outcome battery is more or less standard fare in the field of adolescent social and personality development. What makes our database different, however, is that it is equally rich in measures of the contexts in which our adolescents live. We have tried to move beyond the simple "social address" models that are pervasive in survey research, in which measures of the environment do not go beyond checklists designed to register the number of persons present in the setting and their relationship to the respondent (see Bronfenbrenner, 1986, for a critique of such models). Accordingly, our measures of family relationships include a number of scales tapping such dimensions as parental warmth, control, communication style, decision making, monitoring, and autonomy granting. Our peer measures include affiliation patterns, peer crowd membership, perceptions of peer group norms, and time spent in various peer activities. Our measures of extracurricular and work settings provide information on the activities the adolescents engage in outside of school. Our measures of the school environment concern the classes the adolescents are taking and the classroom environments they encounter. For each student, we also have information on the family's ethnicity, composition, socioeconomic status, marital history, immigration history, and patterns of language use. For some of these variables, the questionnaire data was supplemented with interviews with both students and parents from a cross section of the schools.

Our large and heterogeneous sample permits us to examine a number of questions about the importance of contextual variations in shaping and structuring youngsters' lives and behavior during the high school years. Because the youngsters in our sample are growing up under markedly different circumstances, we can ask whether and how patterns of development and adjustment differ across these social addresses. Because we have detailed information on processes of influence within these social addresses, we can look more specifically at mechanisms of influence, both across and within contexts. And because we have information on more than one context in youngsters' lives, we can look at the interactions between contexts and how variations in the way in which contexts are themselves linked affect youngsters' development. Indeed, as we shall argue, ethnic differences in school performance can be explained more persuasively by examining the interplay between the major contexts in which youngsters develop—the family, the peer group,

and the school—than by examining any one of these contexts alone.

Socialization of Achievement in the Family

According to familial socialization explanations of ethnic group differences of achievement discussed above, we should be able to account for achievement differences among ethnic groups by taking into account the extent to which they use different sorts of parenting practices. Although psychologists have only recently begun examining ethnic differences in adolescent development (Spencer & Dornbusch, 1990), interest among developmentalists in the relation between parenting practices and youngsters' school performance has quite a lengthy history (see Maccoby & Martin, 1983). This literature indicates that adolescent competence, virtually however indexed, is higher among youngsters raised in *authoritative* homes—homes in which parents are responsive and demanding (see Baumrind, 1989)—than in other familial environments (Steinberg, 1990). Presumably, better performance in school is just one of many possible manifestations of psychosocial competence. Researchers writing in this tradition have hypothesized that parental authoritativeness contributes to the child's psychosocial development, which in turn facilitates his or her school success (e.g., Steinberg, Elmen, & Mounts, 1989).

Recently, it has been suggested that three specific components of authoritativeness contribute to healthy psychological development and school success during adolescence: parental acceptance or warmth, behavioral supervision and strictness, and psychological autonomy granting or democracy (Steinberg, 1990; Steinberg et al., 1989; Steinberg, Mounts, Lamborn, & Dornbusch, 1991). This trinity—warmth, control, and democracy—parallel the three central dimensions of parenting identified by Schaefer (1965) in his pioneering work on the assessment of parenting practices through children's reports. These components are also conceptually similar to dimensions of parental control proposed by Baumrind (1991a, 1991b) in her recent reports: supportive control (similar to warmth), assertive control (similar to behavioral supervision and strictness), and directive/conventional control (similar to the antithesis of psychological autonomy granting).

The parenting inventory embedded in our questionnaire contained scales designed to assess parental warmth, behavioral control, and psychological autonomy granting. In our model, authoritative parents were defined as those who scored high in acceptance, behavioral control, and psychological autonomy granting. Not surprisingly, these parenting dimensions are moderately intercorrelated with each other and with other aspects of the parent–child relationship. For example, authoritative parents not only are warmer, firmer, and more democratic than other parents, but they are also more involved in their children's schooling, are more likely to engage in joint decision making, and are more likely to maintain an organized household with predictable routines. In view of this, we have used a categorical approach to the study of parenting, in which we used scores on each of our three dimensions to assign families to one of several categories. Using this general model of authoritative parenting, we have documented in several different studies that adolescents who are raised in authoritative homes do indeed perform better in school than do their peers (Dornbusch, Ritter, Leiderman, Roberts, & Fraleigh, 1987; Lamborn, Mounts, Steinberg, & Dornbusch, 1991; Steinberg et al., 1989; Steinberg et al., 1991).

Can ethnic differences in school performance be explained by ethnic differences in the use of authoritative parenting? According to Dornbusch's earlier work (Dornbusch et al., 1987; Ritter & Dornbusch, 1989), the answer is no. For example, although Asian-American students have the highest school performance, their parents are among the least authoritative. Although African-American and Hispanic parents are considerably more authoritative than Asian-American parents, their children perform far worse in school on average. Given the strong support for the power of authoritative parenting in the socialization literature, these findings present somewhat of a paradox.

One explanation for this paradox is that the effects of authoritative parenting may differ as a function of the ecology in which the adolescent lives. Some writers have speculated that parental authoritarianism may be more beneficial than authoritativeness for poor minority youth (e.g., Baldwin & Baldwin, 1989; Baumrind, 1972). To examine this possibility, we used three demographic variables to partition our sample into 16 ecological niches, defined by ethnicity (four categories: African-American, Asian-American, Hispanic, and White), socioeconomic status (two categories: working class and below versus middle class and above), and family structure (two categories: biological two-parent and nonintact; for details, see Steinberg et al., 1991).

After ensuring that the reliability of each of our three parenting scales was adequate in every ecological niche, we categorized families as authorita-

tive or nonauthoritative. Families who scored above the entire sample median on warmth, behavioral control, and psychological autonomy granting were categorized as authoritative. Families who had scored below the entire sample median on any of the three dimensions were categorized as nonauthoritative. Consistent with previous research (e.g., Dornbusch et al., 1987), we found that authoritativeness is more prevalent among White households than minority households. Also consistent with previous work, we found that Asian-American youngsters are least likely to come from authoritative homes. Again, in light of the superior performance of Asian-American students, this finding runs counter to the family socialization hypothesis.

We contrasted the adolescents from authoritative and nonauthoritative homes within each niche on several outcome variables, including our indices of school performance. Across the outcome variables that are not related to school (psychosocial development, psychological distress, and behavior problems), we found that youngsters from authoritative homes fared better than their counterparts from nonauthoritative homes, in all ethnic groups. When we looked at youngsters' school performance, however, we found that White and Hispanic youngsters were more likely to benefit from authoritative parenting than were African-American or Asian-American youngsters. Within the African-American and Asian-American groups, youngsters whose parents were authoritative did not perform better than youngsters whose parents were nonauthoritative. Virtually regardless of their parents' practices, the Asian-American students in our sample were receiving higher grades in school than other students, and the African-American students were receiving relatively lower grades than other students. Indeed, we found that African-American students' school performance was even unrelated to their parents' level of education (Dornbusch, Ritter, & Steinberg, in press)—a finding that is quite surprising, given the strong association between parental social class and scholastic success reported in the sociological literature on status attainment (e.g., Featherman, 1980).

Glass Ceiling Effect

Why would authoritativeness benefit Asian-American and African-American youngsters when it comes to psychological development and mental health, but not academic performance? One possibility we explored derives from the work of urban anthropologist John Ogbu and his colleagues (e.g., Fordham & Ogbu, 1986; Ogbu, 1978). Ogbu has argued that African-American and Hispanic youngsters perceive the opportunity structure differently than White and Asian-American youngsters do. Because adolescents from what he has called "caste-like" minorities believe that they will face a job ceiling that prohibits them from "receiving occupational rewards commensurate with their educational credentials" (Mickelson, 1990, p. 45), they put less effort into their schoolwork. According to this view, the lower school performance of African-American and Hispanic youngsters is a rational response to their belief that, for them, educational effort does not pay off.

Although Ogbu's (1978) thesis has received a great deal of popular attention, it has been subjected to very little empirical scrutiny. The main tests of his hypothesis have come from ethnographic studies focusing on single peer groups of Black adolescents. Although important in their own right, these studies have not permitted the crucial cross-ethnic comparisons that are at the heart of Ogbu's thesis, because it is impossible to determine from these studies whether the beliefs expressed by the students in these samples are unique to minority adolescents. As several commentators (e.g., Steinberg, 1987) have pointed out, the notion that it is admirable to work hard in school is not widespread among contemporary American adolescents, whatever their color.

On one of our questionnaires, students responded to two questions designed to tap their beliefs about the likelihood of school success: (a) "Suppose you *do* get a good education in high school. How likely is it that you will end up with the kind of job you hope to get?"; and (b), "Suppose you *don't* get a good education in high school. How likely is it that you will still end up with the kind of job you hope to get?" Interestingly, responses to these two questions were only modestly correlated.

When we examined the correlations between our two measures of beliefs about the value of school success and our indices of school performance and school engagement, we found results that are generally consistent with one of the central assumptions of Ogbu's (1978) theory—namely, that the more students believe that doing well in school pays off, the more effort they exert in school and the better they perform there. Of particular interest, however, is the finding that the extent to which students believe that there are *negative* consequences of school failure is a better predictor of their school performance and engagement than the extent to which they believe that there are positive consequences of school success. That is, across ethnic groups, the more youngsters believe that not getting a good education hurts their chances, the better they do in school.

We then looked at ethnic differences in the extent to which youngsters endorse these beliefs. The results were quite surprising. We found no ethnic differences in the extent to which youngsters believe that getting a good education pays off. From the point of view of educators, the news is good: Virtually all students in our sample, regardless of their ethnicity, endorsed the view that getting a good education would enhance their labor market success. However, on the second of these questions—concerning students' beliefs about the consequences of not getting a good education—we found significant variability and significant ethnic differences. Much more than other groups, Asian-American adolescents believe that it is unlikely that a good job can follow a bad education. Hispanic and African-American students are the most optimistic. In other words, what distinguishes Asian-American students from others is not so much their stronger belief that educational success pays off, but their stronger fear that educational failure will have negative consequences. Conversely, unwarranted optimism, rather than excessive pessimism, may be limiting African-American and Hispanic students' school performance.

We noted earlier that academic success and school engagement are more strongly correlated with the belief that doing poorly in school will have negative repercussions than with the belief that doing well will have positive ones. The pattern of ethnic differences on our measures of school performance and engagement is generally consistent with this general principle. In general, Asian-American students, who in our sample were the most successful in school and were most likely to believe that doing poorly in school has negative repercussions, devote relatively more time to their studies, are more likely to attribute their success to hard work, and are more likely to report that their parents have high standards for school performance. Asian-American students spend twice as much time each week on homework as do other students and report that their parents would be angry if they came home with less than an A−. In contrast, African-American and Hispanic students, who do less well in school, are more cavalier about the consequences of poor school performance, devote less time to their studies, are less likely than others to attribute their success to hard work, and report that their parents have relatively lower standards.

In sum, we found that students' beliefs about the relation between education and life success influence their performance and engagement in school. However, it may be students' beliefs about the negative consequences of doing poorly in school, rather than their beliefs about the positive consequences of doing well, that matter. Youngsters who believe that they can succeed without doing well in school devote less energy to academic pursuits, whereas those who believe that academic failure will have negative repercussions are more engaged in their schooling. Although African-American and Hispanic youth earn lower grades in school than their Asian-American and White counterparts, they are just as likely as their peers to believe that doing well in school will benefit them occupationally.

In essence, our findings point to an important discrepancy between African-American and Hispanic students' values and their behavior. In contrast to the differential cultural values hypothesis outlined earlier—which suggests that ethnic differences in achievement can be explained in terms of ethnic differences in the value placed on education—we found that African-American and Hispanic students are just as likely as other students to value education. Their parents are just as likely as other parents to value education as well. Yet, on average, African-American and Hispanic youth devote less time to homework, perceive their parents as having lower performance standards, and are less likely to believe that academic success comes from working hard.

These ethnic differences in student behaviors have important implications for how students are perceived by their teachers and may help illuminate the relation between ethnicity and student performance. A recent paper by George Farkas and his colleagues (Farkas, Grobe, & Shuan, 1990) helps to make this link more understandable. In a large-scale study of Dallas students, they found that teachers assigned grades to students in part on the basis of such noncognitive factors as their work habits. The lower relative performance of African-American and Hispanic students and the higher relative performance of Asian-American students may be in large measure due to differences in these groups' work habits, which affect performance both directly, through their influence on mastery, and indirectly, through their effects on teachers' judgments.

We noted earlier that our analysis of the influence of authoritative parenting on psychosocial development, including youngsters' work orientation, indicated similar effects across all ethnic groups. Because earlier work had indicated that work orientation is a very strong predictor of school performance, and authoritative parenting a strong predictor of work orientation (Patterson, 1986;

Steinberg et al. 1991), we were left with somewhat of a mystery. Why should youngsters who say they value school success, who believe in the occupational payoff of school success, and whose parents rear them in ways known to facilitate a positive work orientation, perform less well in school than we would expect? For African-American students in particular, where was the slippage in the processes linking authoritative parenting, work orientation, and school success? To understand this puzzle, we turned to yet another context—the peer group—and examined how it interacts with that of the family.

Peers and Parents as Influences on Achievement

Many of the items on our questionnaire asked students directly about the extent to which their friends and parents encouraged them to perform well in school. We used a number of these items to calculate the degree to which a student felt he or she received support for academic accomplishment from parents and, independently, from peers. We then used these indices of support to predict various aspects of students' attitudes and behaviors toward school.

We found, as have others (e.g., Brittain, 1963), that although parents are the most salient influence on youngsters' long-term educational plans, peers are the most potent influence on their day-to-day behaviors in school (e.g., how much time they spend on homework, whether they enjoy coming to school each day, and how they behave in the classroom). There are interesting ethnic differences in the relative influence of parents and peers on student achievement, however. These differences help to shed light on some of the inconsistencies and paradoxes in the school performance of minority youngsters.

For reasons that we do not yet understand, at least in the domain of schooling, parents are relatively more potent sources of influence on White and Hispanic youngsters than they are on Asian-American or African-American youngsters (Brown, Steinberg, Mounts, & Philipp, 1990). This is not to say that the mean levels of parental encouragement are necessarily lower in minority homes than in majority homes. Rather, the relative magnitude of the correlations between parental encouragement and academic success and between peer encouragement and academic success is different for minority than for majority youth. In comparison with White youngsters, minority youngsters are more influenced by their peers, and less by their parents, in matters of academic achievement.

Understanding the nature of peer group norms and peer influence processes among minority youth holds the key to unlocking the puzzle about the lack of relation between authoritative parenting and academic achievement among Asian-American and African-American youth. To fully understand the nature of peer crowds and peer influence for minority youth, it is essential to recognize the tremendous level of ethnic segregation that characterizes the social structure of most ethnically mixed high schools. We discovered this quite serendipitously. To map the social structure of each school, we interviewed students from each ethnic group in each grade level about the crowds characteristic of their school and their classmates' positions in the crowd structure (Schwendinger & Schwendinger, 1985).

For the most part, students from one ethnic group did not know their classmates from other ethnic groups. When presented with the name of a White classmate, for instance, a White student could usually assign that classmate to one of several differentiated peer crowds—"jocks," "populars," "brains," "nerds," and so forth. When presented with the name of an African-American classmate, however, a White student would typically not know the group that this student associated with, or might simply say that the student was a part of the "Black" crowd. The same was true for Hispanic and Asian-American students. In other words, within ethnic groups, youngsters have a very differentiated view of their classmates; across ethnic groups, however, they see their classmates as members of an ethnic group first, and members of a more differentiated crowd second, if at all.

The location of an adolescent within the school's social structure is very important, because peer crowd membership exerts an effect on school achievement above and beyond that of the family (Steinberg & Brown, 1989). Across all ethnic groups, youngsters whose friends and parents both support achievement perform better than those who receive support only from one source but not the other, who in turn perform better than those who receive no support from either. Thus, an important predictor of academic success for an adolescent is having support for academics from both parents and peers. This congruence of parent and peer support is greater for White and Asian-American youngsters than for African-American and Hispanic adolescents.

For White students, especially those in the middle class, the forces of parents and peers tend to converge around an ethic that supports success in school. Working with our data set, Durbin, Stein-berg, Darling, and Brown (1991) found that, among White youth, youngsters from authoritative homes are more likely to belong to peer crowds that encourage academic achievement and school engagement—the "jocks" and the "populars." For these youngsters, authoritative parenting is related to academic achievement not only because of the direct effect it has on the individual adolescent's work habits, but because of the effect it has on the adolescent's crowd affiliation. Among White youngsters, authoritatively raised adolescents are more likely to associate with other youngsters who value school and behave in ways that earn them good grades.

The situation is more complicated for youngsters from minority backgrounds, because the ethnic segregation characteristic of most high schools limits their choices for peer crowd membership. We recently replicated Durbin et al.'s (1991) analyses on the relation between parenting practices and peer crowd affiliation separately within each ethnic group. Surprisingly, among African-American and Asian-American students, we found no relation between parenting practices and peer crowd membership. In other words, authoritatively raised minority youngsters do not necessarily belong to peer groups that encourage academic success. Those whose peers and parents do push them in the same direction perform quite well in school, but among authoritatively reared minority youth who are not part of a peer crowd that emphasizes achievement, the influence of peers offsets the influence of their parents.

In ethnically mixed high schools, Asian-American, African-American, and, to a lesser extent, Hispanic students find their choices of peer groups more restricted than do White students. But the nature, and consequently, the outcome of the restriction vary across ethnic groups. More often than not, Asian-American students belong to a peer group that encourages and rewards academic excellence. We have found, through student interviews, that social supports for help with academics—studying together, explaining difficult assignments, and so on—are quite pervasive among Asian-American students. Consistent with this, on our surveys, Asian-American youngsters reported the highest level of peer support for academic achievement. Interestingly, and in contrast to popular belief, our survey data indicate that Asian-American parents are less involved in their children's schooling than any other group of parents.

African-American students face quite a different situation. Although their parents are supportive of academic success, these youngsters, we learned from our interviews, find it much more difficult to join a peer group that encourages the same goal.

Our interviews with high-achieving African-American students indicated that peer support for academic success is so limited that many successful African-American students eschew contact with other African-American students and affiliate primarily with students from other ethnic groups (Liederman, Landsman, & Clark, 1990). As Fordham and Ogbu (1986) reported in their ethnographic studies of African-American teenagers, African-American students are more likely than others to be caught in a bind between performing well in school and being popular among their peers.

Understanding African-American and Asian-American students' experiences in their peer groups helps to account for the finding that authoritative parenting practices, although predictive of psychological adjustment, appear almost unrelated to school performance among these youngsters. For Asian-American students, the costs to schooling of nonauthoritative parenting practices are offset by the homogeneity of influence in favor of academic success that these youngsters encounter in their peer groups. For African-American youngsters, the benefits to schooling of authoritative parenting are offset by the lack of support for academic excellence that they enjoy among their peers. Faced with this conflict between academic achievement and peer popularity, and the cognitive dissonance it must surely produce, African-American youngsters diminish the implications of doing poorly in school and maintain the belief that their occupational futures will not be harmed by school failure. This, we believe, is one explanation for the apparent paradox between African-American students' espoused values and their actual school behavior.

The situation of Hispanic students is different still. Among these youngsters, as among White youngsters, the family exerts a very strong influence on school performance and the relative influence of the peer group is weaker. Yet Hispanic students report grades and school behaviors comparable with those of African-American students. This illustrates why the influence of the family must be evaluated in terms of the other contexts in which youngsters are expected to perform. Although Hispanic youngsters may be influenced strongly by what goes on at home (at least as much as White youngsters), what goes on in many Hispanic households may not be conducive to success in school, at least as schools are presently structured. As is the case in Asian-American homes, in Hispanic homes, the prevalence of authoritative parenting is relatively lower, and the prevalence of authoritarian parenting relatively higher. In a school system that emphasizes autonomy and self-direction, authoritarian parenting,

with its emphasis on obedience and conformity and its adverse effects on self-reliance and self-confidence, may place youngsters at a disadvantage. Without the same degree of support for academics enjoyed by Asian-American students in their peer group, the level of parental authoritarianism experienced by Hispanic students may diminish their performance in school.

Conclusion

These findings illustrate the complex mechanisms through which the contexts in which adolescents live influence their lives and their achievement. We began by looking at one process occurring in one context: the relation between authoritative parenting and adolescent adjustment. We found, in general, that adolescents whose parents are warm, firm, and democratic achieve more in school than their peers. At the same time, however, our findings suggest that the effects of authoritative parenting must be examined without the broader context in which the family lives and in which youngsters develop. Our findings suggest that the effect of parenting practices on youngsters' academic performance and behavior is moderated to large extent by the social milieu they encounter among their peers at school.

The nature of this moderating effect depends on the nature of the peers' values and norms: Strong peer support for academics offsets what might otherwise be the ill effects of growing up in a nonauthoritative home, whereas the absence of peer support for academics may offset some of the benefits of authoritativeness. Whether such offsetting and compensatory effects operate in other outcome domains is a question we hope to investigate in further analyses of these data.

We do not believe that we have explained the phenomenon of ethnic differences in achievement in any final sense. We do believe that the ecological approach, with its focus on the multiple contexts in which youngsters live, offers promise as a foundation for future research on this important social issue. Any explanation of the phenomenon of ethnic differences in adolescent achievement must take into account multiple, interactive processes of influence that operate across multiple interrelated contexts.

References

1. Baldwin, C., & Baldwin, A. (1989, April). *The role of family interaction in the prediction of adolescent competence.* Symposium presented at the meeting of

the Society for Research in Child Development, Kansas City, MO.

2. Baumrind, D. (1972). An exploratory study of socialization effects on Black children: Some Black–White comparisons. *Child Development, 43,* 261–267.

3. Baumrind, D. (1989). Rearing competent children. In W. Damon (Ed.), *Child development today and tomorrow* (pp. 349–378). San Francisco: Jossey-Bass.

4. Baumrind, D. (1991a). Parenting styles and adolescent development. In J. Brooks-Gunn, R. Lerner, and A. C. Petersen (Eds.), *The encyclopedia of adolescence* (pp. 746–758). New York: Garland.

5. Baumrind, D. (1991b). Effective parenting during the early adolescent transition. In P. A. Cowan & E. M. Hetherington (Eds.), *Advances in family research* (Vol. 2, pp. 111–163). Hillsdale, NJ: Erlbaum.

6. Brittain, C. V. (1963). Adolescent choices and parent–peer cross-pressures. *American Sociological Review, 28,* 385–391.

7. Bronfenbrenner, U. (1986). Ecology of the family as a context for human development: Research perspectives. *Developmental Psychology, 22,* 723–742.

8. Brown, B., Steinberg, L., Mounts, N., & Philipp, M. (1990, March). The comparative influence of peers and parents on high school achievement: Ethnic differences. In S. Lamborn (Chair), *Ethnic variations in adolescent experience.* Symposium conducted at the biennial meetings of the Society for Research on Adolescence, Atlanta.

9. Dornbusch, S. M., Ritter, P. L., Liederman, P., Roberts, D., & Fraleigh, M. (1987). The relation of parenting style to adolescent school performance. *Child Development, 58,* 1244–1257.

10. Dornbusch, S., Ritter, P., & Steinberg, L. (in press). Differences between African Americans and non-Hispanic Whites in the relation of family statuses to adolescent school performance. *American Journal of Education.*

11. Durbin, D., Steinberg, L., Darling, N., & Brown, B. (1991). *Parenting style and peer group membership in adolescence.* Manuscript submitted for publication.

12. Farkas, G., Grobe, R., & Shuan, Y. (1990). Cultural differences and school success: Gender, ethnicity, and poverty groups within an urban school district. *American Sociological Review, 55,* 127–142.

13. Featherman, D. L. (1980). Schooling and occupational careers: Constancy and change in worldly success. In O. Brim, Jr., & J. Kagan (Eds.), *Constancy and change in human development* (pp. 675–738). Cambridge, MA: Harvard University Press.

14. Fordham, S., & Ogbu, J. U. (1986). Black students' school success: Coping with the burden of "acting White." *Urban Review, 18,* 176–206.

15. Lamborn, S. D., Mounts, N. S., Steinberg, L., & Dornbusch, S. M. (1991). Patterns of competence and adjustment among adolescents from authoritative, authoritarian, indulgent, and neglectful families. *Child Development, 62,* 1049–1065.

16. Liederman, P. H., Landsman, M., & Clark, C. (1990, March). *Making it or blowing it: Coping strategies and academic performance in a multiethnic high school population.* Paper presented at the biennial meetings of the Society for Research on Adolescence, Atlanta.

17. Lynn, R. (1977). The intelligence of the Japanese. *Bulletin of the British Psychological Society, 40,* 464–468.

18. Maccoby, E., & Martin, J. (1983). Socialization in the context of the family: Parent–child interaction. In E. M. Hetherington (Ed.), *Handbook of child psychology: Vol. 4. Socialization, personality, and social development.* (pp. 1–101). New York: Wiley.

19. Mickelson, R. (1990). The attitude–achievement paradox among Black adolescents. *Sociology of Education, 63,* 44–61.

20. Mordkowitz, E., & Ginsberg, H. (1987). Early academic socialization of successful Asian-American college students. *Quarterly Newsletter of the Laboratory of Comparative Human Cognition, 9,* 85–91.

21. Ogbu, J. (1978). *Minority education and caste.* San Diego, CA: Academic Press.

22. Patterson, G. (1986). Performance models for antisocial boys. *American Psychologist, 41,* 432–444.

23. Ritter, P., & Dornbusch, S. (1989, March). *Ethnic variation in family influences on academic achievement.* Paper presented at the American Education Research Association Meeting, San Francisco.

24. Rushton, J. (1985). Differential K theory: The sociobiology of individual and group differences. *Personality and Individual Differences, 6,* 441–452.

25. Schaefer, E. (1965). Children's reports of parental behavior: An inventory. *Child Development, 36,* 413–424.

26. Schwendinger, H., & Schwendinger, J. (1985). *Adolescent subcultures and delinquency.* New York: Prager.

27. Spencer, M., & Dornbusch, S. (1990). Challenges in studying minority youth. In S. Feldman & G. Elliot (Eds.), *At the threshold: The developing adolescent* (pp. 123–146). Cambridge, MA: Harvard University Press.

28. Steinberg, L. (1987, April 25). Why Japan's students outdo ours. *The New York Times,* p. 15.

29. Steinberg, L. (1990). Autonomy, conflict, and harmony in the family relationship. In S. Feldman & G. Elliot (Eds.), *At the threshold: The developing adolescent.* (pp. 255–276). Cambridge, MA: Harvard University Press.

30. Steinberg, L., & Brown, B. (1989, March). *Beyond the classroom: Family and peer influences on high school achievement.* Paper presented to the Families as Educators special interest group at the annual meetings of the American Educational Research Association, San Francisco.

31. Steinberg, L., Elmen, J., & Mounts, N. (1989). Authoritative parenting, psychosocial maturity, and academic success among adolescents. *Child Development, 60,* 1424–1436.

32. Steinberg, L., Mounts, N., Lamborn, S., & Dornbusch, S. (1991). Authoritative parenting and adolescent adjustment across various ecological niches. *Journal of Research on Adolescence, 1,* 19–36.

33. Sue, S., & Okazaki, S. (1990). Asian-American educational achievements: A Phenomenon in search of an explanation. *American Psychologist, 45,* 913–920.
34. Thompson, L., Detterman, D., & Plomin, R. (1991). Association between cognitive abilities and scholastic achievement: Genetic overlap but environmental differences. *Psychological Science, 2,* 158–165.
35. Wetzel, J. (1987). *American youth: A statistical snapshot.* New York: William T. Grant Foundation Commission on Work, Family, and Citizenship.

QUESTIONS FOR REFLECTION AND DISCUSSION:

1. What are the various kinds of explanations offered for differences in academic achievement among various ethnic groups?

2. How did the researchers select the schools for their study? Do the wide variety of locations and the imbalance in ethnic mix in the various locations pose problems for the validity of the study? Explain.

3. How did the researchers assess the family relationships of the students' families?

4. What are the differences between *authoritative parenting* and *authoritarian parenting*? Which parenting style is most strongly associated with academic achievement among students? Does this finding hold for all ethnic groups? Explain.

5. What is the "glass ceiling effect," and how does it affect students' motivation to excel academically?

6. How may African and Hispanic American students be suffering from what your authors term "unwarranted optimism" about the consequences of not getting a good education?

7. How do peers affect academic success? For which ethnic groups do peer groups exert the most influence? Are there ethnic differences in peer support for academic success? Explain.

8. What are the implications of the study for parents? For educators?

SOURCE

Harvey, E. (1999). Short-term and long-term effects of early parental employment on children of the National Longitudinal Survey of Youth. *Developmental Psychology, 35*(2), 445–459. Copyright © 1999 by the American Psychological Association. Reprinted with permission.

Have you seen re-runs of the black-and-white situation comedies of the 1950s and 1960s? Shows like "Father Knows Best" and "Ozzie and Harriet"? Did you see the movie "Pleasantville"? In these shows and films, Dad was the breadwinner and Mom was the housewife. Today we speak of homemakers and not housewives, because homemakers can be male or female. But 50 years ago or so most women in the United States remained in the home, cooking, cleaning, and rearing the kids.

No more. In these early years of the new millennium, only a small percentage of families in the United States fit the traditional model in which the husband is the sole breadwinner and the wife is a full-time homemaker. Most mothers, including more than half of mothers of children younger than 1 year of age, work outside the home. A generation ago, many social commentators attributed problems with America's youth to women's being out of the home. Logic would dictate, of course, that if a parent is needed full-time in the home, it can be the father as well as the mother (even breast milk can be kept in the refrigerator). But "logic" aside, empirical research evidence does not indicate that a full-time parent is needed in the home. Research into the effects of parental employment during children's early years has yielded a complex, mixed picture. Clearly the horror stories of old have been shown to be nonsense. However, as noted in the article by psychologist Elizabeth Harvey, there are some legitimate concerns.

Short-Term and Long-Term Effects of Early Parental Employment on Children of the National Longitudinal Survey of Youth

ELIZABETH HARVEY
UNIVERSITY OF CONNECTICUT

This study examined the effects of early parental employment on children in the National Longitudinal Survey of Youth. Minimal effects on children's later functioning were found. Early maternal employment status and the timing and continuity of early maternal employment were not consistently related to children's development. Working more hours was associated with slightly lower cognitive development through age 9 and slightly lower academic achievement scores before age 7 but had no significant re- lation to children's behavior problems, compliance, or self-esteem. Early parental employment appeared to be somewhat more beneficial for single mothers and lower income families. There was some support for the hypothesis that early parental employment positively affects children's development by increasing family income.

The past several decades have seen an increase in the number of employed mothers, with a particularly large increase in the frequency with which mothers of young children are employed (Bureau of the Census, 1994). Researchers who have reviewed the literature on the effects of maternal employment on children's development have agreed that there is little evidence of negative effects when children are older (Belsky, 1988, 1990; Hoffman, 1961, 1974, 1989). However, there remains debate about the effects of *early* maternal employment on children. After reviewing the literature, Belsky (1988) concluded that maternal employment during infancy had ill effects on children's well-being. Specifically, he concluded that infants who were in nonmaternal care for more than 20 hr per week were at elevated risk for being insecurely attached at age 1 and were more disobedient and aggressive between ages 3 and 8. However, his conclusions have been criticized on several counts. For example, it has been argued that the studies Belsky reviewed failed to take into account background variables that may have been confounded with maternal employment and children's well-being (e.g., Clarke-Stewart, 1988, 1989). In addition, Clarke-Stewart noted that many of these studies were based on nonrepresentative samples. Finally, she argued that the measures of attachment used in these studies may not have predictive validity for children of working mothers and that more longitudinal studies are needed to determine effects on children's later functioning.

In recent years, several studies have addressed some of these criticisms using the National Longitudinal Survey of Youth (NLSY). The NLSY is a survey of women who have been interviewed annually since 1979 when they were 14 to 22 years old. Beginning in 1986, children of these women were also assessed. Six published studies have used this sample to examine the longitudinal effects of early maternal employment on children's development, controlling for various family background variables. The results of these studies have been surprisingly mixed considering they used the same data set. The sample size and longitudinal design of the NLSY make it potentially valuable for illuminating the effects of early maternal employment. However, rather than shedding light on this issue, conflicting results of studies based on these data have added further confusion.

Although these six studies all used the same data set, they each used quite different methodological approaches with respect to sample selection, construction of independent and dependent variables, and selection of control variables. The present study sought to resolve some of these differences through a reanalysis using an updated version of the NLSY that contained a much larger and more representative sample. In this article, I examined the six studies, explored how their methodological differences might have yielded discrepant results, evaluated their methodological strengths and limitations, and reanalyzed the effects of early parental employment by drawing on the strengths and addressing the limitations of these six previous studies.

A Comparison of Methodological Approaches and Findings[1]

Of the six previous studies, none used the exact same sample. Slightly different age ranges were selected, and three studies did not include all races. Four studies included the Peabody Picture Vocabulary Test—Revised (PPVT–R) as a dependent variable, and four studies used the Behavior Problems Index (BPI). Vandell and Ramanan (1992) conducted the only study that examined school achievement. There was surprisingly little overlap across studies in the construction of maternal employment variables. There was also considerable variation in the background variables used as controls. The number of control variables varied from 4 to over 25. Mother's IQ, race, and family income or poverty status were the only variables that were controlled across all six studies. Child gender was the only moderating variable examined in all six studies. Only one study directly evaluated potential mediators of early maternal employment.

It is therefore less surprising that these studies yielded very different findings. In general, the Vandell and Ramanan (1992), Parcel and Menaghan (1994), and Greenstein (1995) studies found no adverse effects of early maternal employment on PPVT–R or behavior problems, and Vandell and Ramanan (1992) found some positive effects on children's Peabody Individual Achievement Test (PIAT) scores. Desai, Chase-Lansdale, and Michael (1989) found negative effects on PPVT–R scores only for boys from high-income families, and Bayder and Brooks-Gunn (1991) found negative effects on PPVT–R and behavior problems for White families only. Belsky and Eggebeen (1991) found adverse effects on their variable called ADJUST, a composite of BPI scores and temperament variables, but when they examined BPI scores alone, they did not find significant effects.

Because the studies were based on the same data set, the conflicting results must be due to one or more of the methodological variations, although

---

[1] A table summarizing these six studies is available from the author.

it is not clear which. Possible ways in which these methodological differences could have caused these discrepancies and affected results are explored next.

AN EXAMINATION OF VARIOUS METHODOLOGICAL APPROACHES AND THEIR POSSIBLE EFFECTS ON FINDINGS

Sample Selection Differences in sample selection might be one possible reason for the discrepancies. The children studied by Vandell and Ramanan (1992) were much older and their mothers were much younger than in any other study. Thus, it is possible that any negative effects of early maternal employment disappear by second grade or that maternal employment is not harmful for younger, lower income mothers. Similarly, as Bayder and Brooks-Gunn (1991) pointed out, the discrepancy between their results and those reported by Desai et al. (1989) may have been because the former study included only White children.

There are theoretical reasons why the effects of early maternal employment might vary depending on the age of the child. The effects might fade over time as more proximal factors play a larger role in a child's development. On the other hand, sleeper effects might be observed as minor, early negative effects spiral into larger problems. A cross-study comparison of these six studies supports the former hypothesis. However, a within-study comparison of children across a wide age range would better address this issue. This was not feasible using the 1986 NLSY but is an option with the more recent version.

Each of the studies recognized the importance of addressing race but did so in different ways. Some limited their sample to certain racial groups, arguing that other racial groups were not adequately represented and that the assessments were conducted in English. Others included all children but controlled for race. Using the former approach limits the generalizability of the results, whereas using the latter approach may mask important racial differences. Greenstein (1995) included all races and performed separate analyses by race. This avoids both of these problems, but it does not directly test whether race moderates the effects of early employment, and it increases the number of analyses and the chance of Type I error. A modification of the approach used by Vandell and Ramanan (1992) would avoid these problems: include all races and evaluate the moderating effect of race. In the updated NLSY, adequate sample size for each racial group is no longer an issue. In addition, beginning in 1988 the PPVT–R was administered in

Spanish to those children who so preferred, decreasing somewhat the cultural bias of the assessment. It is important to note that results would still need to be interpreted with caution given questions regarding the validity of standardized cognitive assessments in non-White children.

Constructing Maternal Employment Variables

The different approaches to maternal employment variable construction could be another reason for the discrepancies. For example, Parcel and Menaghan (1994), who found no effects, examined the number of hours worked among employed mothers, whereas each of the other studies involved comparisons between employed mothers and non-employed mothers. It may be that employment status rather than the intensity of employment is related to child development. Consistent with this hypothesis, Desai et al. (1989) found no effects on PPVT–R scores when they compared mothers working full time during the first year with mothers who did not, whereas Bayder and Brooks-Gunn (1991) found an effect on PPVT–R scores when they compared mothers who worked at least 1 hr per week during the first year with mothers who did not work during the first year.

In each study, the primary approach to constructing maternal employment variables was to create categories of early employment characteristics and dummy-code variables to examine each category. Creating categorical maternal employment variables can be useful in interpreting results because it is sometimes easier to use categories to organize information. Researchers have also justified using categories to detect nonlinear effects (Parcel & Menaghan, 1994). However, this approach has been criticized (Scarr, 1991) and presents the following problems. For the most part, these categories were formed from continuous variables, so there are infinite ways one could form categories. This approach can also exclude some participants if the categories do not include every employment pattern. For example, Belsky and Eggebeen's (1991) approach to variable construction excluded almost half of the children in their study. This approach also results in arbitrary boundaries between categories. Participants with similar employment patterns will often be assigned to two different categories. Furthermore, using continuous variables does not preclude one from examining nonlinear effects of early employment and in fact provides more sensitivity in detecting such relationships. Another problem with previous studies' use of categories is that they often combined different dimensions. For example, comparing mothers who worked full time during the first year with mothers who did not combines information about the timing and intensity of early employment. It is not clear whether results reflect one or both employment dimension.

Selecting Control Variables

The six studies varied in their approaches to selection of control variables, with some studies controlling for many more variables than others did. Some studies used theory to guide variable selection, others used empirical methods, and others used a combination. In addition, some studies controlled for family variables assessed at the same time that the dependent variables were measured (in 1986), whereas others did not. Three of the studies that used theory only used a larger number of control variables and tended to control for 1986 variables. These three studies were also the only ones that failed to find any adverse effects of maternal employment.

Controlling for relevant background family characteristics reduces third-variable effects and removes error from the dependent variable. However, if a background variable does not correlate with child outcome, then it cannot act as a third variable and including it will not remove error. In fact, including irrelevant variables in regression models will on average increase standard errors and make it more likely that Type II error will occur. Therefore, the three studies may have failed to find adverse effects because they included irrelevant variables. Thus, in addition to using theory in control variable selection, it is important to empirically evaluate whether each background variable should be included in the regression equations.

In selecting control variables, one must distinguish between selection factors and mediators of the effect of early employment on children. Selection factors are variables that might affect, but are not affected by, early employment. These might include parents' education and mothers' IQ. Mediators are variables that are affected by patterns of early employment and in turn affect children. Thus, many variables assessed in 1986 should not be considered selection factors. Selection factors and mediating effects must be examined using different analytic approaches. For example, each of the six studies controlled for family income or poverty status measured *after* the birth of the child. One of the ways in which early maternal employment may positively affect children may be through its financial benefits. Controlling for income after the child is born involves controlling for an important benefit of maternal employment. It is not surprising, then, that

some of these studies found detrimental effects of maternal employment when they statistically removed its positive effects. Family income *before* the birth of the child should be controlled, because the wealth of the family is likely to affect whether a mother chooses to be employed. However, income after the child's birth should be examined as a mediating variable of positive effects of early employment.

IMPROVEMENTS IN THE SAMPLE

The sample available in the more recent NLSY is stronger than the 1986 sample used by five of the six studies in several ways. First, the 1986 NLSY data on which these studies were based were from unusually young, low-socioeconomic status (SES) mothers. The NLSY has continued to follow these women and their children, and the data set now contains more older, higher SES mothers. Thus, the most recent version of the NLSY allows for an examination of the effects of early maternal employment in a more representative sample. Whereas the children in the 1986 data were estimated to represent the first 40% of the offspring that these women would bear, the recent data set is estimated to represent the first 70% to 75% of these women's offspring (Center for Human Resource Research, 1997). In addition, the sample size is now much larger. This should allow for more stable, robust results and should provide more confidence that null effects truly represent no or negligible effects rather than Type II error. Furthermore, the more recent data allow for an examination of much longer term effects, because there are now a sizable number of elementary school age children in the sample. This also means that two additional outcome variables specific to older children are available: self-esteem and academic achievement.

PATERNAL EMPLOYMENT

In contrast to the focus on the effects of maternal employment on child development, few studies have examined early paternal employment. McHale and Huston (1984) found that fathers' time in paid work affected the amount but not the quality of interaction with their infants. However, Parcel and Menaghan's (1994) analysis of the NLSY indicated that fathers working fewer hours during their children's first few years was associated with more behavior problems in children. The small body of literature on fathers' employment focuses on job quality or unemployment rather than on how the time demands of fathers' jobs affect the family (e.g., Barling, 1986).

THE PRESENT STUDY

The more recent NLSY provides the opportunity to reexamine the effects of early parental employment on children's development, addressing a number of important limitations of these six previous studies as follows: (a) A larger, more representative sample was used that should significantly increase the generalizability of results; (b) selection factors were distinguished from mediating variables; (c) control variables were selected using both theory and empirical decision rules; (d) the sample contained a wider age range of children allowing for an evaluation of short-term and long-term effects of early employment; (e) children from all races were included; and (f) whenever possible, continuous variables of early parental employment were used rather than artificially creating categorical variables. Thus, by drawing on the methodological strengths and addressing the methodological weaknesses of previous studies of early parental employment, it is hoped that this study will more fully realize the potential of the NLSY to address this topic.

Past research and theory have been conflicting regarding the effects of early parental employment, making it difficult to make specific predictions regarding the presence or direction of effects. Although previous inconsistent results are likely caused by methodological differences, the studies differ in too many ways to determine which findings are correct. Thus, the goal of this study is to examine whether and when early parental employment affects children's emotional, cognitive, and academic development.

Method

THE NLSY SAMPLE

The NLSY is a survey of approximately 12,600 individuals who have been interviewed annually since 1979 when they were 14 to 22 years old. This survey oversampled African American, Hispanic, and economically disadvantaged White individuals. The economically disadvantaged White oversample was dropped in 1990 for financial reasons. In 1986, 1988, 1990, 1992, and 1994, the survey conducted child assessments on offspring of the female participants.

Children of all races who were between 3 and 12 years of age at any of the five child assessment dates and who were born in 1980 or later (several background variables were unavailable for children born before 1980) were included. To assess possible developmental differences in the effects of early employment, I examined four different age groups sep-arately: 3- to 4-year-olds, 5- to 6-year-olds, 7- to 9-year-olds, and 10- to 12-year-olds. See Table 35.01 for descriptive statistics on this sample.

It should be noted that there is partial overlap of participants across these four age groups; each age group contains some participants who were also included in another age group. Of the 4,924 children who were 3- to 4-year-olds, 3,371 were also in the 5- to 6-year-old group. There were 4,486 children in the 5- to 6-year-old group, 3,203 of whom were also in the 7- to 9-year-old group. There were 3,711 children in the 7- to 9-year-old group, 1,951 of whom were also in the 10- to 12-year-old group. There were 2,095 children in the 10- to 12-year-old group. Thus, some of the data in this study are longitudinal and some are cross-sectional. (These figures are based on the number of children in each age group who had scores on at least one of the child outcome measures. The actual number of participants for each analysis varies because not all children were administered all measures.) In addition, although this sample is more representative than samples used in previous studies of early maternal employment (Bayder & Brooks-Gunn, 1991; Belsky & Eggebeen, 1991), it still does not represent women who bear children after age 34 and is still somewhat socioeconomically disadvantaged.

MEASUREMENT OF VARIABLES

Early maternal employment variables. Five indexes of early maternal employment were used. They were constructed on the basis of mothers' reports of how many weeks after their children's birth they returned to work and their estimates of the average number of hours they worked per week during each quarter-year of the first 3 years of their children's lives.

For an evaluation of whether early employment status affects children, the first variable indicated whether or not the mother was employed at some time during the child's first 3 years (*employment during the first 3 years*); mothers who reported returning to work by the 156th week after their child's birth were coded 1 and mothers who did not return to work in the first 3 years were coded 0. The second, third, and fourth variables were applicable only for women who were employed at some point during the first 3 years. The second variable was the number of weeks after the child's birth before the mother returned to work (*timing of early employment*), the third variable was the average number of hours per week that she worked when she returned to work (*early employment hours*), and the fourth variable was the number of quarters the mother did

TABLE 35.01

		DESCRIPTIVE STATISTICS										
				AGE OF CHILD								
	3–4 YEARS			**5–6 YEARS**			**7–9 YEARS**			**10–12 YEARS**		
VARIABLE	%	M	SD	%	M	SD	%	M	SD	%	M	SD
Timing[a]		31.88	40.00		34.35	40.45		36.50	41.26		40.32	42.62
Hours[b]		33.64	11.28		33.43	11.20		33.30	11.02		32.76	11.02
Fathers' hours[c]		43.24	10.13		43.07	9.96		42.90	9.65		42.92	9.37
Discontinuity[d]		2.03	2.82		2.21	2.84		2.30	2.87		2.48	2.94
BPI		105.24	14.78		105.57	14.77		107.36	14.20		108.06	14.34
SPPC								202.20	33.60		205.04	32.47
PPVT–R		87.77	18.82		89.50	17.48		90.47	17.79		98.89	12.56
PIAT					101.36	11.86		101.09	11.70		98.89	12.56
Family income ($)		23,697.72	19,766.25		20,085.91	16,152.10		17,647.86	14,208.02		15,168.42	11,989.10
Mothers' education (years)		12.06	2.30		11.75	2.19		11.53	2.09		11.21	1.99
Mothers' age at child's birth (years)		24.61	3.51		23.34	3.29		22.33	2.93		21.09	2.45
Mothers' AFQT		77.32	26.57		75.38	26.47		73.96	26.18		71.75	25.94
Child's birth order		1.97	1.05		1.87	0.99		1.79	0.95		1.69	0.89
Fathers' education (years)		12.84	2.26		12.60	2.13		12.38	2.07		12.09	1.94
Fathers' age at child's birth (years)		27.67	4.76		26.90	4.53		25.90	4.27		24.90	4.14
Employed during child's first 3 years	75			74			74			73		
Employed during child's first year	36			33			29			26		
Married at first interview after child's birth	66			62			58			55		
African American	28			29			31			34		
Hispanic	20			21			21			25		

Note. BPI = Behavior Problems Index; SPPC = Self-Perception Profile for Children; PPVT–R = Peabody Picture Vocabulary Test—Revised; PIAT = Peabody Individual Achievement Test; AFQT = Armed Forces Qualification Test.
[a]*Timing of early employment.*   [b]*Early employment hours.*   [c]*Early paternal employment hours.*   [d]*Discontinuity of early employment.*

not work after she had returned to work (*discontinuous employment*). Early employment hours was constructed by identifying the quarter-year during which the mother returned to work and calculating the average number of hours per week she worked from this quarter-year until the child's third birthday (not including quarters during which she reported working 0 hr). Many of the previous studies on the NLSY have included a variable representing whether or not mothers worked during the first year of the child's life. Although the timing of early maternal employment should capture the effects of employment during the first year, a variable *employment during the first year* was also included to facilitate comparison of the results of this study with the findings of previous studies.

Note that employment during the first 3 years and early employment hours could have been combined into one variable by assigning mothers who were never employed during the first 3 years a score of 0 hr. However, doing so assumes that the difference between not being employed and being employed 5 hr per week is the same as the difference between working 35 hr per week and working 40 hr per week. That is, it could not be assumed that not being employed is simply one end of the employment intensity dimension. Early employment status (comparing being employed with not being employed) might have a different effect on children than the intensity of employment and was therefore examined separately.

Early Parental Employment Variable
Mothers reported the average number of hours per week that their spouses spent at their jobs every year from 1979 to 1994. The variable for *early paternal employment hours* consisted of an average of the spouse's job hours over the first 3 yearly assessments following the birth of the child.

Child Outcome Measures
Five child outcome variables were examined: compliance, behavior problems, cognitive development, self-esteem, and academic achievement. For children who were in one of the four specified age ranges at more than one assessment date, their multiple scores were averaged to obtain the best possible estimate of their functioning.

Compliance was assessed using a six-item subscale from the Temperament scale, which was developed for the NLSY. The scale correlates modestly but significantly with later behavior problems (Center for Human Resource Research, 1995). Higher scores indicate greater compliance.

Children's behavior problems were assessed using the BPI, which was developed to measure behavior problems in children age 4 and older. Many items were derived from the Child Behavior Checklist (Achenbach & Edelbrock, 1981) and other child behavior scales (Graham & Rutter, 1968; Kellam, Branch, Agrawal, & Ensminger, 1975; Peterson & Zill, 1986; Rutter, 1970). The parent reports the frequency with which the child exhibited each of 28 specific problems (1 = *often true*, 2 = *sometimes true*, 3 = *not true*). Standard scores (based on all children, not same sex) were used, with higher scores indicating more behavior problems. This scale

has demonstrated good construct validity (Center for Human Resource Research, 1993).

Children's self-esteem was measured using the global self-worth subscale of the Self-Perception Profile for Children. This is a self-report measure that assesses children's sense of self-competence in the domain of academic skills and general self-worth (Harter, 1985). It correlates highly with teacher ratings and has good reliability (Harter, 1985). This measure was administered to children age 8 years and older.

Children's cognitive development was assessed using the PPVT–R (Dunn & Dunn, 1981), a widely used test of receptive language. This measure was administered to all children age 3 years and older. It was administered to all children in 1986 and 1992, and only to children without a previous valid score in 1988, 1990, and 1994. Children's academic achievement was measured using the PIAT. Three subtests from the PIAT were administered to children age 5 years and older: mathematics, reading recognition, and reading comprehension. Standard scores were used for both the PPVT–R and PIAT. Both cognitive measures have good reliability and validity (Dunn & Dunn, 1981; Dunn & Markwardt, 1970).

Selection Factors
Theory and previous research suggested a number of family background variables that might act as selection factors for early employment. The following background variables were created for examining the effects of early maternal employment: family income, mother's education, mother's age at the child's birth, child gender, mother's IQ, child's race, birth order of the child, and marital status. For the effects of parental employment, the following background characteristics were used: family income, father's education, father's age at the child's birth, child's gender, child's race, and birth order of the child. Fathers' IQs were not assessed in the NLSY. Mother's reports of these variables at the first assessment following the birth of the child were used, except for income, which was based on reports regarding the year before the child's birth. Mother's intelligence was assessed using the Armed Forces Qualification Test (AFQT), which was administered to all NLSY participants in 1980. The AFQT consists of the sum of scores on four subtests of the Armed Services Vocational Aptitude Battery: word knowledge, numeric operations, paragraph comprehension, and arithmetic reasoning.

Moderating Variables
On the basis of theory and research, the following variables were examined as possible moderators of the effects of

TABLE 35.02

INTERCORRELATIONS AMONG EARLY PARENTAL EMPLOYMENT VARIABLES AND CHILD OUTCOME VARIABLES

EMPLOYMENT OR CHILD OUTCOME VARIABLE	EMPLOYMENT VARIABLE					
	EMP3	TIMING[a]	HOURS[b]	DISCONTINUITY[c]	EMP1	FATHERS' HOURS[d]
Timing[a]						
Hours[b]		−.17***				
Discontinuity[c]		−.03	−.11***			
EMP1	.43***	−.70***	.17***	−.03		
Fathers' hours[d]	.02	−.01	.02	.02	.01	
Compliance						
3–4 years	−.00	−.01	−.04*	.01	.01	.04*
5–6 years	.04**	−.03	−.05**	−.00	.04*	.05**
BPI						
3–4 years	−.05*	.03	.03	.08**	−.04*	−.03
5–6 years	−.02	.06***	.05**	.05**	−.07***	−.04*
7–9 years	−.03	.05*	.04	.04*	−.06***	−.06**
10–12 years	−.07**	.02	−.01	.08**	−.07**	−.04
SPPC						
7–9 years	.05*	−.03	−.02	.04	.04*	.08***
10–12 years	.07**	−.06*	−.05	−.03	.07**	.00
PPVT–R						
3–4 years	.13***	−.12***	−.14***	−.09***	.14***	.10***
5–6 years	.13***	−.10***	−.17***	−.06*	.14***	.10***
7–9 years	.18***	−.08**	−.13***	−.02	.13***	.15***
10–12 years	.19***	−.12***	−.13***	−.09**	.14***	.06
PIAT						
5–6 years	.14***	−.08***	−.09***	−.05**	.14***	.07***
7–9 years	.17***	−.12***	−.09***	−.05*	.15***	.12***
10–12 years	.18***	−.12***	−.06*	−.06*	.13***	.08**

Note. EMP3 = early employment during the first 3 years; EMP1 = early employment during the first year; BPI = Behavior Problems Index; SPPC = Self-Perception Profile for Children; PPVT–R = Peabody Picture Vocabulary Test—Revised; PIAT = Peabody Individual Achievement Test.
[a]Timing of early employment. [b]Early employment hours. [c]Discontinuity of early employment. [d]Early paternal employment hours.
*p < .05. **p < .01. ***p < .001.

early parental employment: marital status, race, gender, family income, and job satisfaction. The six NLSY studies yielded conflicting findings regarding the moderating effects of these variables, but each variable was supported by at least one study. Job satisfaction was assessed by asking individuals to indicate how they felt about their current jobs on a 4-point scale from 1 = *like it very much* to 4 = *dislike it very much*. Previous studies have suggested that job satisfaction predicts child functioning (Brody, Stoneman, & MacKinnon, 1986; Gold & Andres, 1978), and it was thought that this would more directly assess the moderating effects of occupational complexity reported by Parcel and Menaghan (1994).

Results

Descriptive statistics for the entire sample and separately for each age group are presented in Table 35.01. Correlations among the early parental employment variables and child outcome variables are presented in Table 35.02. These simple correlations suggest that before controlling for selection factors, mothers' working early in the child's life is generally associated with more positive child outcome; however, more intense maternal employment (working more hours) is associated with less positive child outcome. Early parental employment tended to be associated with more positive child outcomes.

ANALYTIC APPROACH

Testing for Nonlinearity and Interactions

Because main effects are meaningful only in the absence of interaction or nonlinear effects, the effects of each parental employment variable on each dependent variable were initially tested for nonlinearity and for interactions with moderating variables. First, the relationships between each dependent variable and early maternal employment hours, timing of early maternal employment, discontinuity, and father's employment hours were tested for nonlinearity using quadratic terms of each employment variable. For each child outcome variable, regression equations were created for each of these parental employment variables. The following variables were entered simultaneously: each of the chosen selection factors, one of the early employment variables, product terms for each moderator by the parental employment variable (see below), and a quadratic term of the employment variable.

Interactions between each potential moderator variable and early parental employment variable were evaluated using regression analyses with product terms (Jaccard, Turrisi, & Wan, 1990). For each child outcome variable, regression equations were created for each of the parental employment variables as the principal main-effect predictor. The following variables were entered simultaneously in the prototypic equation: one of the parental employment variables, all chosen selection factors (see below), one moderating variable, and the product term created by multiplying the moderator variable by the parental employment variable. To reduce multicollinearity, I centered the independent variables before forming the product terms (Jaccard et al., 1990). Job satisfaction was examined as a moderator only of early maternal employment hours, timing of early maternal employment, and discontinuity.

Examination of Background Variables

Each of the background variables for maternal employment was examined to determine whether it was associated with at least one early maternal employment variable and at least one child outcome variable (using an alpha of .05). Gender was the only variable that did not meet this criterion; it was not associated with the early maternal employment variables. Therefore, it was not entered as a control variable. (However, it was included as a potential moderating variable.) Each of the background variables for parental employment was also examined to determine whether it was associated with father employment hours and at least one child outcome variable. Gender, birth order, and father's age were not associated with father's employment hours and were therefore not included as control variables. Race, income before the child's birth, and father's education were all associated with father's employment hours and at least one child outcome variable and were included as background controls.

Determining Significance

Previous studies using the NLSY have used an alpha of .05. Because the large sample size in this study protects against Type II error and because a large number of analyses were conducted, a more conservative alpha of .01 was used to protect against Type I error, except where indicated. Although one could argue that an even more conservative alpha should be used in this study, doing so would make comparison with previous studies very difficult. However, examining potential moderator variables does involve a particularly large number of analyses, because many moderator variables and many age groups were examined. One could collapse across some of these dimensions or focus on only some of these variables; however, this would result in losing important information and again would limit comparisons with previous studies. Instead, for protection against Type I error, statistically significant interactions were only interpreted if there was converging evidence supporting them. Thus, interactions that were significant at the .01 level were interpreted only if there was some evidence that the interaction also at least approached significance ($p < .05$) in at least one other age group. Although there are theoretical reasons why effects might vary depending on the age of the child (either fading over time or sleeper effects), one would not expect effects to disappear or emerge suddenly. One would expect to see at least weak effects at other ages.

Interpreting Significant Interactions

Interactions with converging support were interpreted by examining the relation between the employment variable and the child outcome variable at different levels of the moderating variable (see Jaccard et al., 1990, for a description of the

TABLE 35.03

SIGNIFICANT INTERACTION COEFFICIENTS (STANDARDIZED) BETWEEN EARLY EMPLOYMENT VARIABLES AND MODERATOR VARIABLES

AGE OF CHILD	COMPLIANCE	BPI	SPPC	PPVT–R	PIAT
		Marital Status × EMP3		Marital Status × EMP3	
3–4 years		−.02		.04**	
5–6 years		−.05**		−.01	
7–9 years		−.04*		.06*	
10–12 years		−.03		.06*	
		Income × EMP3			
3–4 years		.06*			
5–6 years		.001			
7–9 years		.07**			
10–12 years		.06			
				Gender × Timing[a]	
3–4 years				−.02	
5–6 years				.02	
7–9 years				−.08**	
10–12 years				−.04	
				Marital Status × Discontinuity[b]	
3–4 years				−.03	
5–6 years				−.07**	
7–9 years				−.02	
10–12 years				−.03	
	African American × EMP1		Hispanic × EMP1	Gender × EMP1	
3–4 years	−.06*			−.00	
5–6 years	−.02			.00	
7–9 years			.06	.07**	
10–12 years			.09**	.04*	
				Income × Fathers' Hours[c]	Income × Fathers' Hours[c]
3–4 years				−.07**	
5–6 years				−.04	−.06*
7–9 years				−.10**	−.06*
10–12 years				−.04	−.13***
				African American × Fathers' Hours	African American × Fathers' Hours
3–4 years				.10**	
5–6 years				.01	.04
7–9 years				.11*	.11**
10–12 years				.06	.09

Note. BPI = Behavior Problems Index; SPPC = Self-Perception Profile for Children; PPVT–R = Peabody Picture Vocabulary Test—Revised; PIAT = Peabody Individual Achievement Test; EMP3 = employment during the first 3 years; EMP1 = early employment during the first year.
[a]Timing of early employment. [b]Discontinuity of early employment. [c]Early paternal employment hours.
*p < .05. **p < .01. ***p < .001.

Harcourt, Inc.

procedure). For categorical variables, the relation was examined separately for each category. For continuous variables, the relation was examined at the mean and one standard deviation above and below the mean of the moderator variable.

EMPLOYMENT DURING THE FIRST 3 YEARS

Nonlinear and Interaction Effects Marital status interacted with employment during the first 3 years in predicting behavior problems at ages 5 to 6, and the interaction approached significance for behavior problems at ages 7 to 9 (see Table 35.03 for all significant interactions). The direction of the interaction indicated that the relation between being employed during the first 3 years and behavior problems was significantly more positive for married mothers than for single mothers. The relation between employment during the first 3 years and behavior problems was not significant when married and single mothers were examined separately; however, for married mothers, employment during the first 3 years was associated with somewhat more behavior problems at ages 5 to 6 at a probability level that approached significance (see Table 35.04 for interpretations of all significant interactions with converging evidence).

Employment during the first 3 years interacted with marital status in predicting PPVT–R scores in 3- to 4-year-olds. There was also evidence of weak interactions for PPVT–R scores in 7- to 9-year-olds and 10- to 12-year-olds. These interactions indicate that the relation between employment during the first 3 years and PPVT–R scores at these ages was significantly more positive for single than for married mothers. For single mothers but not for married mothers, being employed during the first 3 years was associated with higher PPVT–R scores at each age group except in 5- to 6-year-olds.

Income interacted with employment during the first 3 years in predicting behavior problems at ages 7 to 9, and this interaction approached significance for behavior problems at ages 3 to 4. For high-income families, employment during the first 3 years was associated with significantly more behavior problems at ages 7 to 9. In contrast, for low-income families, employment during the first 3 years was associated with fewer behavior problems at ages 7 to 9 at probability levels that approached significance. However, these effects were not observed in any other age group.

Main Effects Table 35.05 presents the relations between early maternal employment and child outcome controlling for background variables. No effects were significant for employment during the first 3 years.

TIMING OF EARLY EMPLOYMENT

Nonlinear and Interaction Effects There was no evidence of a quadratic effect of timing of early employment on any of the child outcome variables. Gender interacted with timing of early employment in predicting PPVT–R scores in 7- to 9-year-olds; however, there was no converging evidence for this interaction.

Main Effects Table 35.05 presents the relations between timing of early employment and child outcome. The only significant main effect was for compliance in 3- to 4-year-olds. Returning to work later was associated with more compliance; however, this effect was small.

EARLY EMPLOYMENT HOURS

Nonlinear and Interaction Effects There was no evidence of a quadratic effect of early employment hours on any of the child outcome variables. There were no significant interactions involving early employment hours.

Main Effects More early employment hours was associated with significantly lower PPVT–R scores at ages 3 to 4, 5 to 6, and 7 to 9, and with significantly lower PIAT scores for 5- to 6-year-olds (see Table 35.05). More early employment hours was associated with somewhat lower PPVT–R scores in 10- to 12-year-olds and more behavior problems for 5- to 6-year-olds and 7- to 9-year-olds all at probability levels that approached significance. However, these effects were quite small. The largest effect on PPVT–R scores indicated that working 10 hr more per week was associated with a 1.5-point decrease in PPVT–R scores. Working 10 hr more per week was associated with only a 0.6-point decrease in PIAT scores in 5- to 6-year-olds.

DISCONTINUOUS EMPLOYMENT

The effects of discontinuous employment were examined controlling for timing of early employment, because women who returned to work earlier would have more opportunity for greater discontinuity compared with women who returned later.

Nonlinear and Interaction Effects There was no evidence of a quadratic effect of dis-

TABLE 35.04

RELATIONS BETWEEN EARLY EMPLOYMENT AND CHILD OUTCOME AT MULTIPLE LEVELS OF MODERATOR VARIABLES

EMPLOYMENT VARIABLE	MODERATING VARIABLE	CHILD OUTCOME	AGE (YEARS)	INTERACTION COEFFICIENT	β AT VARIOUS LEVELS OF MODERATING VARIABLE		
EMP3	Marital status	BPI			Married	Single	
			3–4	−.02	.00	−.04	
			5–6	−.05**	.05*	−.05	
			7–9	.04*	.05	−.03	
			10–12	.03	.01	−.06	
EMP3	Marital status	PPVT–R			Married	Single	
			3–4	.04**	−.03	.07**	
			5–6	−.01	.02	−.01	
			7–9	.06*	−.03	.12**	
			10–12	.06*	−.03	.09*	
EMP3	Income	BPI			Low	Medium	High
			3–4	.06*	−.06	−.00	.05
			5–6	.00	.01	.01	.01
			7–9	.07**	−.06*	.02	.11***
			10–12	.06	−.06	−.01	.04
EMP1	Gender	PPVT–R			Boys	Girls	
			3–4	−.00	−.00	−.00	
			5–6	.00	−.00	.00	
			7–9	.07**	−.09[a]	.04	
			10–12	.04*	−.04	.04	
Fathers' hours[a]	Income	PPVT–R			Low	Medium	High
			3–4	−.07**	.07**	.02	−.04*
			5–6	−.04	.02	−.01	−.04
			7–9	−.10**	.13**	.06	−.01
			10–12	−.04	−.02	−.05	−.08**
Fathers' hours[a]	Income	PIAT			Low	Medium	High
			5–6	−.06*	.03	−.02	−.07***
			7–9	−.06*	.07*	.02	−.02
			10–12	−.13***	.06	−.03	−.12***
Fathers' hours[a]	Race	PPVT–R			African American	Non-African American	
			3–4	.10**	.18**	−.01	
			5–6	.01	.02	.01	
			7–9	.11*	.24*	.01	
			10–12	.06	.02	−.10	

Note. EMP3 = early employment during the first 3 years; BPI = Behavior Problems Index; PPVT–R = Peabody Picture Vocabulary Test—Revised; EMP1 = early employment during the first year; PIAT = Peabody Individual Achievement Test.
[a]Early paternal employment hours.
*p < .05.   **p < .01.   ***p < .001.

continuous employment on any of the child outcome variables. Marital status interacted with discontinuous employment in predicting PPVT–R scores in 5- to 6-year-olds. However, there was not converging evidence for this effect at any other age range.

Main Effects Greater discontinuity was associated with significantly more compliance in 3- to 4-year-olds. Greater discontinuity was associated with somewhat higher self-esteem and PPVT–R scores in 7- to 9-year-olds at probability levels that approached significance.

TABLE 35.05

RELATIONS BETWEEN EARLY PARENTAL EMPLOYMENT VARIABLES AND CHILD OUTCOME VARIABLES CONTROLLING FOR BACKGROUND VARIABLES: STANDARDIZED REGRESSION COEFFICIENTS (βs)

PARENTAL EMPLOYMENT	CHILD OUTCOME					PARENTAL EMPLOYMENT	CHILD OUTCOME				
	COMPLIANCE	BPI	SPPC	PPVT–R	PIAT		COMPLIANCE	BPI	SPPC	PPVT–R	PIAT
EMP3						Discontinuity[c]					
3–4-year-olds						3–4-year-olds					
β	−.03	−.02		.01		β	.06**	.03		−.02	
n	3,640	1,850		2,718		n	2,707	1,417		2,126	
5–6-year-olds						5–6-year-olds					
β	−.02	.01		.01	−.00	β	.02	.01		−.01	.01
n	3,219	3,177		1,489	3,214	n	2,480	2,453		1,127	2,471
7–9-year-olds						7–9-year-olds					
β		.02	−.01	.03	.02	β		−.00	.07*	.06*	−.01
n		2,650	2,086	1,120	2,614	n		2,024	1,589	865	1,995
10–12-year-olds						10–12-year-olds					
β		−.03	.04	.03	.03	β		.03	.01	−.02	−.01
n		1,409	1,387	1,356	1,439	n		1,072	1,052	1,037	1,091
Timing[a]						EMP1					
3–4-year-olds						3–4-year-olds					
β	.05**	−.02		.01		β	−.04*	.03		−.00	
n	2,825	1,421		2,132		n	3,640	1,850		2,718	
5–6-year-olds						5–6-year-olds					
β	.01	.01		.02	.02	β	.00	−.03		−.00	.00
n	2,484	2,457		1,130	2,475	n	3,219	3,177		1,489	3,214
7–9-year-olds						7–9-year-olds					
β		.01	.01	.05	−.03	β		−.02	−.00	−.02	.02
n		2,028	1,593	866	1,999	n		2,650	2,086	1,120	2,614
10–12-year-olds						10–12-year-olds					
β		−.03	−.03	−.01	−.02	β		−.04	.02	.00	.01
n		1,073	1,053	1,038	1,092	n		1,409	1,387	1,356	1,439
Hours[b]						Fathers' hours[d]					
3–4-year-olds						3–4-year-olds					
β	−.00	.04		−.07**		β	.04	−.04		.02	
n	2,803	1,410		2,116		n	2,288	1,203		1,680	
5–6-year-olds						5–6-year-olds					
β	−.02	.04*		−.10***	−.06***	β	.03	−.03		−.01	−.02
n	2,466	2,439		1,120	2,459	n	1,886	1,873		774	1,867
7–9-year-olds						7–9-year-olds					
β		.05*	−.02	−.08**	−.03	β		−.06*	.05	.05	.02
n		2,010	1,578	860	1,980	n		1,434	1,051	650	1,386
10–12-year-olds						10–12-year-olds					
β		.00	−.05	−.05*	−.01	β		.01	−.04	−.05	−.03
n		1,062	1,041	1,027	1,080	n		629	603	595	634

Note. BPI = Behavior Problems Index; SPPC = Self-Perception Profile for Children; PPVT–R = Peabody Picture Vocabulary Test—Revised; PIAT = Peabody Individual Achievement Test; EMP3 = early employment during the first 3 years; EMP1 = early employment during the first year.
[a]Timing of early employment.   [b]Early employment hours.   [c]Discontinuity of early employment.   [d]Early paternal employment hours.
*p < .05.   **p < .01.   ***p < .001.

EMPLOYMENT DURING THE FIRST YEAR

Nonlinear and Interaction Effects Race interacted with employment during the first year in predicting self-esteem at ages 10 to 12 and compliance at ages 3 to 4. However, there was no converging evidence for either of the interactions at the other age ranges for self-esteem and compliance.

Gender interacted with employment during the first year in predicting PPVT–R scores at ages 7 to 9. This interaction approached significance for 10- to 12-year-olds. These interactions indicate that the relations between employment during the first year and PPVT–R scores in these age ranges were more positive for girls than for boys. Examination of the relation between employment during the first year and PPVT–R scores separately for boys and girls revealed no significant effects, although for 7- to 9-year-old boys, employment during the first year was associated with lower PPVT–R scores at a probability level that approached significance.

Main Effects No significant main effects emerged for employment during the first year.

EARLY PARENTAL EMPLOYMENT HOURS

Nonlinear and Interaction Effects There was a significant quadratic effect of early paternal employment hours on compliance at ages 3 to 4. Further evaluation of this nonlinear relationship (the maximum of the obtained quadratic regression equation was identified by setting the first derivative equal to zero) indicated that compliance scores peaked when fathers were employed about 50 hr per week.

Income interacted with early parental employment hours in predicting PPVT–R scores at ages 3 to 4 and 7 to 9. The direction of the interaction suggested that fathers' working more hours was significantly more beneficial for lower income families than for higher income families. For fathers from families whose income fell one standard deviation below the mean, working more hours was associated with significantly higher PPVT–R scores in 3- to 4-year-olds and 7- to 9-year-olds; for fathers from families whose income fell one standard deviation above the mean, working more hours was associated with significantly lower PPVT–R scores in 10- to 12-year-olds and somewhat lower PPVT–R scores in 3- to 4-year-olds.

Income also interacted with early parental employment hours in predicting PIAT scores in 10- to 12-year-olds. This interaction approached significance for 5- to 6-year-olds and 7- to 9-year-olds. For fathers in high-income families, working more hours was associated with significantly lower PIAT scores at ages 5- to 6-year-olds and 10- to 12-year-olds. For fathers in low-income families, working more hours was associated with higher PIAT scores in 7- to 9-year-olds at a probability level that approached significance.

Race interacted with early paternal employment hours in predicting PPVT–R scores in 3- to 4-year-olds. This interaction approached significance for 7- to 9-year-olds. For African American children, fathers' working more hours was associated with significantly higher PPVT–R scores in 3- to 4-year-olds and with higher PPVT–R scores in 7- to 9-year-olds at a probability level that approached significance.

Race interacted with early paternal employment hours in predicting PIAT scores in 7- to 9-year-olds; however, there was no converging evidence for this interaction.

Main Effects There were no significant main effects of early paternal employment hours.

INTERACTIONS AMONG INDEPENDENT VARIABLES

Regression analyses were conducted to determine whether timing of maternal employment and early maternal employment hours interacted with each other in predicting child development. This interaction term was not significant for any of the child outcome variables. The interaction between early paternal employment hours and each of the early maternal employment hours was also examined. None of the interaction terms was significant.

EXAMINING INCOME AS A MEDIATING VARIABLE

Previous studies on the NLSY have examined the effect of early parental employment on children controlling for income after the child's birth. As noted earlier, income after the child's birth is a potential mediating variable rather than a selection factor. It has been suggested that early parental employment may positively affect mothers' mental health by increasing family income (Repetti, Matthews, & Waldron, 1989). Similarly, income generated from maternal employment may benefit children. Using path-analytic regression analyses, I tested the following hypothesis: Greater early parental employment would be associated with higher family income during the child's early years,

TABLE 35.06

	STANDARDIZED PATH COEFFICIENTS FOR THE EFFECTS OF EARLY EMPLOYMENT VARIABLES ON CHILD OUTCOME MEDIATED BY INCOME			
EMPLOYMENT VARIABLE/ AGE OF CHILD	EMPLOYMENT VARIABLE ON INCOME	INCOME ON BPI	EMPLOYMENT VARIABLE ON INCOME	INCOME ON PIAT
Hours[a]				
3–4 years	.05**	−.16***		
5–6 years	.05***	−.11***	.05***	.10**
7–9 years	.05**	−.13***	.05***	.08*
10–12 years	.06*	−.07	.06*	.04
Timing[b]				
3–4 years	−.10***	−.16***		
5–6 years	−.06***	−.10**	−.06***	.09**
7–9 years	−.09***	−.12***	−.08***	.06*
10–12 years	−.09***	−.07	−.08***	.03
Discontinuity[c]				
3–4 years	−.07***	−.16***		
5–6 years	−.09***	−.10**	−.08***	.10**
7–9 years	−.09***	−.12***	−.09***	.06*
10–12 years	−.08**	−.07	−.07**	.03
EMP1				
3–4 years	.07***	−.11**		
5–6 years	.08***	−.10***	.08***	.07**
7–9 years	.11***	−.11***	.11***	.09**
10–12 years	.10***	−.07*	.11***	.04
Fathers' hours[d]				
3–4 years	.07***	−.12*		
5–6 years	.06***	−.08*	.07***	.10**
7–9 years	.08***	−.13***	.08***	.11**
10–12 years	.08**	−.14*	.08*	.08

Note. BPI = Behavior Problems Index; PIAT = Peabody Individual Achievement Test; EMP1 = early maternal employment during the first year.
[a]Early employment hours. [b]Timing of early employment. [c]Discontinuity of early employment. [d]Early paternal employment hours.
*p < .05. **p < .01. ***p < .001.

which in turn would positively affect children's development. Note that this hypothesis does not necessarily assume a simple relation between early parental employment and child outcome; it is possible that this positive pathway is offset by other negative pathways, resulting in a null total relation. Following the procedure suggested by Pedhazur (1982), each child outcome variable was first regressed on income after the child's birth, one of the employment variables, and each of the background variables (including family income before the child's birth) to calculate the path coefficient representing

the effect of income after the child's birth on the child outcome variable. Next, income after the child's birth was regressed on the employment variable and each of the background variables to calculate the effect of the employment variable on income after birth.

Analyses supported this hypothesis for four of the five maternal employment variables and paternal employment hours for behavior problems and the PIAT but not for the PPVT—R, compliance, or self-esteem. Table 35.06 presents the path coefficients for behavior problems and the PIAT with each of the four maternal employment variables and early paternal employment hours. The benefits of early employment on child development by means of income appear to weaken over time.

EXAMINATION OF COHORT EFFECTS

Because this study combined children of the same age who were born as much as 8 years apart, the moderating effects of children's year of birth on each of the early parental employment variables were examined, using regression analyses with product terms as described earlier. There was no evidence of any cohort effects.

COMPARISONS WITH NLSY STUDIES

Several analyses were conducted to facilitate comparison between the present study and previous studies on the NLSY. Desai et al. (1989) found that income interacted with discontinuous employment and employment during the first year in predicting PPVT–R scores for boys only. Therefore, the interactions between income and discontinuous employment and employment during the first year in predicting PPVT–R scores were examined separately for boys. These interactions were not significant.

Vandell and Ramanan (1992) examined PIAT mathematics and reading achievement separately rather than combining them as was done in the present study. They found a positive correlation between early maternal employment hours and mathematics but not reading achievement. In the present study, the analyses involving early maternal employment hours were conducted again using PIAT mathematics scores, rather than total scores, as dependent variables. The results were similar to those using the total PIAT scores. Thus, the fact that the present study combined PIAT mathematics and reading achievement whereas Vandell and Ramanan examined them separately does not appear to explain the discrepant results between the two studies.

Discussion

This study examined the effects of early parental employment on children's later cognitive, academic, behavioral, and emotional functioning using the 1994 NLSY. It sought to clarify conflicting results from previous NLSY studies by addressing several previous methodological limitations. Consistent with previous studies, family characteristics including family income, parents' education, mothers' IQ and age, and child race and birth order were related to both early parental employment variables and child outcome variables. Therefore, the effects of early parental employment were examined controlling for these background characteristics.

The results of this study revealed few simple effects of early parental employment. There were no significant main effects of early maternal employment status. Among mothers who were employed during the first 3 years, the only significant effects of the timing of the return to employment and discontinuity of early employment were on compliance in 3- to 4-year-olds and these effects were small; returning to work later and greater discontinuity were associated with somewhat higher compliance. Among mothers who were employed during the first 3 years, working more hours was associated with significantly lower PPVT–R scores up through age 9 and with somewhat lower PPVT–R scores through age 12. However, the effect was small; an increase of 10 hr per week was associated with a 1- to 1.5-point decrease in PPVT–R standard scores. Working more hours was also associated with significantly lower achievement scores in 5- to 6-year-olds. However, this effect was also small; a 10 hr per week increase in employment hours was associated with a 0.6-point decrease in PIAT standard scores. Furthermore, this effect was not maintained beyond age 6. Early maternal employment hours was associated with children's behavior problems only at probability levels that approached significance and was not associated with children's compliance or self-esteem. There were no significant main, linear effects of fathers' employment hours on children's development. There was a significant quadratic effect of fathers' employment hours on children's compliance at age 3 to 4, with fathers' working about 50 hr per week associated with the highest level of compliance.

There was no evidence that race or job satisfaction moderated the effects of early maternal employment and no consistent evidence that income and gender acted as moderators. Modest support was found for the moderating effects of marital status on early maternal employment. It appeared that for single but not married mothers, being employed during the child's first 3 years was associated with significantly, but only slightly, higher PPVT–R scores. Income and race appeared to moderate some of the effects of early paternal employment. For low-income families, fathers' working more hours tended to be associated with children's higher PPVT–R scores, whereas for high-income families, fathers' working more hours tended to be associated with lower PPVT–R and PIAT scores. There was also some evidence that for African American children, fathers' working more hour hours was associated with higher PPVT–R scores.

The few significant findings in the present study were only somewhat supported by previous NLSY studies. The finding that the timing and continuity of employment were associated with children's compliance was consistent with Belsky and Eggebeen's (1991) finding that full-time employment during the first and second year was associated with less compliance in children. The present study's finding that maternal employment hours was associated with PPVT–R scores was consistent with Bayder and Brooks-Gunn's (1991) results, but not with Vandell and Ramanan's (1992), Parcel and Menaghan's (1994), and Greenstein's (1995) findings. The finding that greater early maternal employment hours was associated with lower PIAT scores in 5- to 6-year-olds stands in contrast to Vandell and Ramanan's (1992) finding that early maternal employment hours was associated with higher achievement in second-grade children. Finally, the finding that for low-income fathers, working more hours was associated with higher PPVT–R scores stands somewhat in contrast to Parcel and Menaghan's (1994) finding that fathers working more hours was associated with fewer behavior problems but not with higher PPVT–R scores.

Likewise, the present study failed to replicate the significant results of the previous NLSY studies. In contrast to findings presented by Desai et al. (1989), but consistent with Greenstein's (1995) findings, income did not moderate the effects of maternal employment during the first year and discontinuous employment on boys' PPVT–R scores. In contrast to findings presented by Belsky and Eggebeen (1991), early maternal employment hours and employment during the first year were not associated with children's compliance.

Thus, the results of the present study generally conflicted with the six previous NLSY studies, just as the six studies conflicted with each other. It is possible that differences between the present study and previous studies are due to differences in the characteristics of the samples used. The samples used in the previous studies were more homogeneous than the samples used in the present study. It may be that some of the effects found in previous studies are true for only specific, homogeneous groups. However, the examination of moderating variables such as ethnic group should identify the subgroups for which early employment affects children. The few moderating effects that were found in the present study do not seem to account for any of the previous findings.

Another possible reason why previous findings were not replicated in the present study may be that previous significant findings are simply not robust and were sample specific. Examination of the specific discrepancies provides some support for this explanation. For example, when the effect of employment during the first year on PPVT–R scores was replicated using the same methodology used by Bayder and Brooks-Gunn (1991), the effect approached significance[2] in the 1986 sample they used but not in the 3- to 4-year-olds taken from the sample used in the present study. There is no evidence that this failure to replicate is due to the moderating influence of variables on which the two samples differ. A more likely possibility, therefore, is that these effects were sample specific. A number of other factors also support this possibility. For most of the studies, nonsignificant relations between maternal employment and child outcome outnumbered the significant relations reported. None of the studies corrected for familywise error, and a relatively liberal alpha of .05 was used. Furthermore, in many of the studies the ultimate sample size on which the significant findings were based was relatively small considering the number of variables entered in each regression equation.

Inconsistencies may also be due to differences in the formation of maternal employment variables. The six previous NLSY studies created categorical variables from continuous variables. This can create inconsistent results in at least two ways. First, maternal employment variables from previous studies frequently combined employment dimensions. For example, Belsky and Eggebeen's (1991) maternal employment variable, which they found to be related to children's compliance, combined information about the timing, intensity, and continuity of early maternal employment. Thus, the present study's finding that early maternal employment hours was not related to children's compliance appears inconsistent with Belsky and Eggebeen's finding; however, if it was the timing and continuity component of Belsky and Eggebeen's variable that accounted for the effect, then the two studies are consistent.

---

[2] I was unable to replicate either finding exactly, although the results were quite similar. McCartney and Rosenthal (1991) reported a similar experience when attempting to replicate Belsky and Eggebeen's (1991) findings using an updated version of the NLSY and attributed it to corrections that were made in later versions. Consistent with this possibility, the sample sizes were somewhat different in my analyses (i.e., there were somewhat more 3- and 4-year-olds in the 1986 data available on the recent version of the NLSY).

Categorical variables may also cause inconsistent results because the results may vary depending on where the boundaries are drawn. For example, when Bayder and Brooks-Gunn (1991) examined maternal employment hours, they contrasted mothers who worked 10–19 hr and mothers who worked more than 20 hr with mothers who worked less than 10 hr. Parcel and Menaghan (1994) on the other hand contrasted mothers who worked 1–20 hr, mothers who worked 21–34 hours, and mothers who worked more than 40 hr with mothers who worked 35–40 hr. To examine whether inconsistent results may have been due to such arbitrarily formed groups, I used these two different categorical systems in the present study to predict PPVT–R scores in 3- to 4-year-olds. With Bayder and Brooks-Gunn's (1991) system, early employment hours was unrelated to PPVT–R scores, whereas, with Parcel and Menaghan's (1994) system, there was a relation (which is in fact opposite to each of their own findings).

Another possible reason for discrepant results between the present study and past NLSY studies may be differences in controlling for selection variables. For example, Parcel and Menaghan's (1994) and Greenstein's (1995) failure to find effects of early maternal employment hours may have been due to the number and nature of control variables they used. First, they controlled for a number of variables (such as the 1986 Home Observation for Measurement of the Environment) that might be more aptly termed mediating variables rather than selection variables. Second, they controlled for a number of variables that did not appear to be significantly related to child outcome and did not present an evaluation of whether these variables were related to early parental employment. This may also explain the discrepancies between these two studies and the other NLSY studies.

The fact that the few small effects that emerged in the present study were generally not found in previous NLSY studies may be due to the greater power of the present study. The effect of early maternal employment hours was very small and not likely detectable with the sample sizes used in previous NLSY studies. This may also explain conflicting results from previous studies to some extent. Power varied across the six studies because of differences with sample sizes ranging from 189 to 2,040.

Thus, although the NLSY provides a potentially ideal vehicle for examining the effects of early parental employment on children's development, methodological variation in using this data set has been an obstacle in addressing this question. This article examined various methodological approaches and selected and applied those approaches that were thought to maximize the internal and external validity of the results and that could increase the potential for cross-study comparison. That is not to say that the methodological approaches selected in this study are not open to criticism; future studies may select alternative methods. What appears to be critical is recognition of the powerful influence that methodology can have on the results of these studies and that greater consideration is given to choosing methodological approaches.

It is important to compare the results of this study not only with previous NLSY studies, but also with other studies examining the effects of early parental employment on children's development. Although earlier reviews examining the effects of early maternal employment reported detrimental effects on children's adjustment (e.g., Belsky, 1988), there is a growing number of more recent studies that have failed to find negative effects of the quantity of early nonmaternal care on children's development (NICHD Early Child Care Research Network, 1997a, 1997b; Roggman, Langlois, Hubbs-Tait, & Rieser-Danner, 1994). Several possible explanations have been suggested for this discrepancy between earlier and recent reports (NICHD Early Child Care Research Network, 1997a). First, it has been suggested that the effects of early nonmaternal care are changing as more and more women are engaging in early employment. However, the absence of a cohort effect in the present study does not support this possibility. Second, it may be that recent studies have more systematically controlled for selection factors. However, recent studies have failed to find effects even when selection factors were not controlled (NICHD Early Child Care Research Network, 1997a). In fact, in the present study, positive effects of several early maternal employment variables were observed in the absence of controls. A third proposed explanation is that previous studies with null findings were less likely to be published. Another possibility is that these discrepancies are also due to some of the methodological factors that seem to have caused discrepancies in NLSY studies. It is also important to note that the NLSY studies examined the effects of early maternal employment, whereas many previous studies examined the effects of early nonmaternal or nonparental child care. This difference could also lead to discrepant results, although these two constructs should be highly related.

This is one of the few studies to examine the effects of early paternal employment on children's later development. These results are consistent with

McHale and Huston's (1984) finding that early paternal employment hours did not have substantial effects on children's later cognitive and emotional development, but stand in contrast to Parcel and Menaghan's (1994) finding based on the NLSY that fathers' working more hours was associated with fewer behavior problems. In addition to some of the methodological reasons described earlier, this discrepancy may be because the Parcel and Menaghan (1994) sample had lower incomes. The results of the present study suggest that greater early parental hours may be more beneficial for low-income families than for high-income families. However, this study found this moderating effect for PPVT–R and PIAT but not for behavior problems.

The results partially supported the hypothesis that early parental employment has a positive effect on children's development by increasing family income. This positive pathway seemed to affect children's behavior problems and academic achievement but not children's compliance, self-esteem, or language–cognitive development. All of these indirect effects existed largely in the absence of any total effects of early parental employment on behavior problems and academic achievement. This suggests that early parental employment may have both positive and negative effects on children's development that counteract each other. This study has identified one potential positive effect. Future studies are needed to explore other positive and negative pathways. This mediating effect of family income also highlights the importance of distinguishing between selection factors and mediating variables. Controlling for income after birth may yield misleading results; one should not control for a benefit of early employment in examining its effects.

In a comparison of the results of the present study to previous studies of the NLSY, it is important to note that the samples used in previous NLSY studies were subsets of the samples used in the present study. The degree of overlap ranged from study to study. Of the studies using the 1986 NLSY, the greatest sample overlap occurred with the Parcel and Menaghan (1994) sample. Using PPVT–R scores as an example, the percentage of participants in the present sample who were also included in the past study was calculated. The overlap ranged from 24% to 32% for 3- to 4-, 5- to 6-, and 7- to 9-year-olds. The overlap was 68% for 10- to 12-year-olds. The least overlap based on PPVT–R scores occurred with the Bayder and Brooks-Gunn (1991) study with a range of 2% (5- to 6-year-old) to 18% overlap (10- to 12-year-old). Note that this represents participant overlap; data overlap is even less than

these figures suggest. For example, the PPVT–R 7- to 9-year-olds' scores used in the present study have not been analyzed in any previous study. In addition, the data overlap pertains primarily to the BPI and PPVT–R data rather than to the other three child outcome variables. Greenstein (1995) used a more recent version of the NLSY (1990) so his sample overlapped more with that used in the present study. For example, 50% to 60% of the data from 3- to 4-year-olds and 5- to 6-year-olds PPVT–R scores in this study were included in Greenstein's analyses. In sum, the present study is based largely on data that have not previously been analyzed. However, the results based on the older children in this study should to some degree be considered follow-up results of children analyzed in previous NLSY studies.

It should also be noted that the analyses in this study are partly based on longitudinal data and partly on cross-sectional data. That is, some of the participants in each age group were also included in another age group. Thus, the analyses conducted on each age group are not independent from analyses conducted on other age groups. The findings at each age range should therefore not be considered independent replications.

These results should be interpreted within the context of the limitations of the study. Although the sample in the present study was more representative of the general population of mothers than previous studies, the sample is still younger and of lower SES than average; these results may not be generalized to older, higher SES parents. In addition, this study addressed ethnicity in only a limited way. Finer distinctions within each of the racial groups should be made in future studies. Of course, this study was also limited by its correlational design. Although attempts were made to statistically control for third variables, other important background variables may have been omitted; the few significant results that were found may have been due to unmeasured third variables. Finally, data regarding the quality of child care were not available in this data set. Previous research indicates that this is an important contextual variable (Belsky, 1990; NICHD Early Child Care Research Network, 1997b). Although maternal employment appeared to have little effect on these children's development, quality of early child care may have a much larger impact. Further study is needed in this area.

Nonetheless, this study adds to the existing literature in several ways. This study had an unusually large sample size, providing more power to detect effects, particularly interaction effects that are notoriously difficult to detect (McClelland & Judd, 1993). This greater power allows more confidence that nonsignificant effects represent no or negligible effects. In addition, the sample was more representative than previous studies. Also, continuous parental employment variables were examined whenever possible rather than artificially created groups formed by categorizing continuous variables. This study used a longitudinal design to examine the long-term effects of early parental employment; previous longitudinal studies have only examined the relatively short-term effects on children. Finally, this is one of the few studies to examine both early maternal and paternal employment variables, recognizing the importance of examining the role of fathers in children's development.

In sum, findings reported by previous NLSY studies may have been somewhat sample and method specific. When methodological limitations were addressed in the present study, few of the previous findings were replicated, and no consistent evidence of substantial effects of early parental employment on children's later development was found.

References

1. Achenbach, T. S., & Edelbrock, C. (1981). Behavioral problems and competencies reported by parents of normal and disturbed children aged four through sixteen. *Monographs of the Society for Research in Child Development, 46*(1, Serial No. 188).
2. Barling, J. (1986). Fathers' work experiences, the father–child relationship and children's behaviour. *Journal of Occupational Behaviour, 7*, 61–66.
3. Bayder, N., & Brooks-Gunn, J. (1991). Effects of maternal employment and child-care arrangements on preschoolers' cognitive and behavioral outcomes: Evidence from the children of the National Longitudinal Survey of Youth. *Developmental Psychology, 27*, 932–945.
4. Belsky, J. (1988). The "effects" of infant day care reconsidered. *Early Childhood Research Quarterly, 3*, 235–272.
5. Belsky, J. (1990). Parental and nonparental care and children's socioemotional development: A decade in review. *Journal of Marriage and the Family, 52*, 885–903.
6. Belsky, J., & Eggebeen, D. (1991). Early and extensive maternal employment and young children's socioemotional development: Children of the National Longitudinal Survey of Youth. *Journal of Marriage and the Family, 53*, 1083–1110.
7. Brody, G. H., Stoneman, Z., & MacKinnon, C. E. (1986). Contributions of maternal child rearing practices and play contexts to sibling interactions. *Journal of Applied Developmental Psychology, 7*, 225–236.
8. Bureau of the Census. (1994). *Statistical abstract of the United States* (114th ed.). Lanham, MD: Bernan Press.
9. Center for Human Resource Research. (1993). *NLSY child handbook: A guide to the 1986–1990 National Longitudinal Survey of Youth child data.* Columbus, OH: Author.
10. Center for Human Resource Research. (1995). *NLSY 1992 child assessment data users guide.* Columbus, OH: Author.
11. Center for Human Resource Research. (1997). *NLSY/79 1994 child and young adult data users guide.* Columbus, OH: Author.
12. Clarke-Stewart, K. A. (1988). "The 'effects' of infant day care reconsidered" reconsidered: Risks for parents, children, and researchers. *Early Childhood Research Quarterly, 3*, 293–318.
13. Clarke-Stewart, K. A. (1989). Infant day care: Maligned or malignant? *American Psychologist, 44*, 266–273.
14. Desai, S., Chase-Lansdale, P. L., & Michael, R. T. (1989). Mother or market? Effects of maternal employment on the intellectual ability of 4-year-old children. *Demography, 26*, 545–561.
15. Dunn, L. M., & Dunn, L. M. (1981). *PPVT–Revised manual.* Circle Pines, MN: American Guidance Service.
16. Dunn, L. M., & Markwardt, F. C., Jr. (1970). *Peabody Individual Achievement Test.* Circle Pines, MN: American Guidance Service.
17. Gold, D., & Andres, D. (1978). Development comparisons between ten-year-old children with employed and nonemployed mothers. *Child Development, 49*, 75–84.
18. Graham, P. J., & Rutter, M. (1968). The reliability and validity of the psychiatric assessment of the child: II. Interview with the parent. *British Journal of Psychiatry, 114*, 581–592.
19. Greenstein, T. N. (1995). Are the "most advantaged" children truly disadvantaged by early maternal employment? *Journal of Family Issues, 16*, 149–169.
20. Harter, S. (1985). *Manual for the Self-Perception Profile for Children.* Unpublished manuscript, University of Denver.
21. Hoffman, L. W. (1961). Effects of maternal employment on the child. *Child Development, 32*, 187–197.
22. Hoffman, L. W. (1974). Effects of maternal employment on the child: A review of the research. *Developmental Psychology, 10*, 204–228.
23. Hoffman, L. W. (1989). Effects of maternal employment in the two-parent family. *American Psychologist, 44*, 283–292.
24. Jaccard, J., Turrisi, R., & Wan, C. K. (1990). *Interaction effects in multiple regression.* Newbury Park, CA: Sage.
25. Kellam, S., Branch, J. D., Agrawal, K. C., & Ensminger, M. E. (1975). *Mental health and going to school.* Chicago: University of Chicago Press.
26. McCartney, K., & Rosenthal, S. (1991). Maternal employment should be studied within social ecologies. *Journal of Marriage and the Family, 53*, 1103–1107.

27. McClelland, G. H., & Judd, C. M. (1993). Statistical difficulties of detecting interactions and moderator effects. *Psychological Bulletin, 114,* 376–390.

28. McHale, S. M., & Huston, T. L. (1984). Men and women as parents: Sex role orientation, employment, and parental roles with infants. *Child Development, 55,* 1349–1361.

29. NICHD Early Child Care Research Network. (1997a). The effects of infant child care on infant–mother attachment security: Results of the NICHD study of early child care. *Child Development, 68,* 860–879.

30. NICHD Early Child Care Research Network. (1997b). *Mother–child interaction and cognitive outcomes associated with early child care: Results of the NICHD study* (Tech. Rep.). Bethesda, MD: NICHD.

31. Parcel, T. L., & Menaghan, E. G. (1994). Early parental work, family social capital, and early childhood outcomes. *American Journal of Sociology, 99,* 972–1009.

32. Pedhazur, E. J. (1982). *Multiple regression in behavioral research: Explanation and prediction.* New York: Holt, Rinehart & Winston.

33. Peterson, J. L., & Zill, N. (1986). Marital disruption, parent–child relationships, and behavior problems in children. *Journal of Marriage and the Family, 48,* 295–307.

34. Repetti, R. L., Matthews, K. A., & Waldron, I. (1989). Employment and women's health: Effects of paid employment on women's mental and physical health. *American Psychologist, 44,* 1394–1401.

35. Roggman, L., Langlois, J., Hubbs-Tait, L., & Rieser-Danner, L. (1994). Infant day-care, attachment, and the "file drawer problem." *Child Development, 65,* 1429–1443.

36. Rutter, M. (1970). Sex differences in children's responses to family stress. In E. J. Anthony & C. Koupernik (Eds.), *The child in his family* (pp. 165–196). New York: Wiley.

37. Scarr, S. (1991). On comparing apples and oranges and making inferences about bananas. *Journal of Marriage and the Family, 53,* 1099–1100.

38. Vandell, D., & Ramanan, J. (1992). Effects of early and recent maternal employment on children from low-income families. *Child Development, 63,* 938–949.

QUESTIONS FOR REFLECTION AND DISCUSSION:

1. Why do traditionalists argue that "a woman's place is in the home"? What historic fears have been expressed concerning the effects of being in the workplace on women?

2. Why do you think that most social commentators talk about the possible effects of maternal employment but not of paternal employment?

3. Harvey takes issue with the Belsky (1988) review of the literature on the grounds that he may have confused "background variables" with the effects of maternal employment on young children. What might some of these background variables be? (Hint: Consider the issue of the *selection factor.* That is, why do mothers choose to work or to remain in the home, and how might this choice—this self-selection—affect the outcomes of such studies?)

4. The issue of the selection factor comes about in the previous question because the NLSY data refers to parents who have chosen to work during the early years of their children's lives. Psychologists agree that the experiment provides more accurate information about cause and effect than the survey. What factors make it impractical to perform experiments on the effects of early parental employment?

5. How did Harvey obtain the data she analyzes in her study?

6. Why did Harvey obtain different results than were obtained by previous investigators who had used the same set of data?

7. If you were a parent, how could you make use of the information in the Harvey study in your own life?

SOURCE

Langer, E. G., & Rodin, J. (1976). The effects of choice and enhanced personal responsibility for the aged: A field experiment in an institutional setting. *Journal of Personality and Social Psychology, 34,* 191–198. Copyright © 1976 by the American Psychological Association. Reprinted with permission.

An "agequake" is coming. So many people in the United States are living longer that the age of the population is shifting radically. Consider:

- *In 1900 only 1 person in 25 was over the age of 65. Today, that figure has more than tripled, to 1 in 8. By the year 2030, about one in four of us will be in the 65+ age group, more than 66 million people.*

- *Children born in the 1990s can expect to live 76 years, as compared to 47 years for children born in 1900.*

- *In 1790, only half of the population of the newly formed United States was over 16 years of age or older. By 1990, half of the population was 33 years of age or older. By the year 2030, half of the population will be over the age of 40.*

- *The fasting growing segment of the elderly population consists of people in the advanced elderly range, age 85 and above. The 85+ age group is 25 times larger today than 100 years ago.*

- *The number of centenarians—people who live to be 100 years or more—is also increasing rapidly. In 1900, only one out of 400 persons in the United States had surpassed the century mark. In the year 2000, centenarians numbered nearly 1 out of every 80 people in the nation.*

The aging of the population is expected to accelerate even more rapidly early in the new millennium as the so-called baby boomers, who were born during the population explosion that followed World War II, approach late adulthood.

Developmental psychologists are therefore more concerned than ever about the quality of life for older people. Once upon a time it was assumed that the golden years were a time for relaxing, for taking it easy, for transferring responsibility to the younger generations, and for avoiding taxing an aging body so that one could extend one's years as long as possible. Yet nowadays the motto seems to be more like "Use it or lose it."

Older people today differ in many ways from their counterparts of a generation or two ago. Chronological age has become less likely to determine behavior and lifestyle. Older people today are more likely to engage in regular exercise, to continue to have sexual activity, to work in some meaningful manner (even if they are "retired"), and to maintain responsibility for themselves and perhaps others. All this activity—selecting and maintaining a commitment to key concerns and causes, the seeking of new challenges, even exercise programs—are a part of what we refer to as successful aging.

A variety of social forces have contributed to the vastly changing expectations of older people. Psychological research has also made its contribution, as we see in the following classic experiment by Ellen Langer and Judith Rodin.

The Effects of Choice and Enhanced Personal Responsibility for the Aged: A Field Experiment in an Institutional Setting

ELLEN J. LANGER
GRADUATE CENTER, CITY UNIVERSITY
OF NEW YORK

JUDITH RODIN
YALE UNIVERSITY

A field experiment was conducted to assess the effects of enhanced personal responsibility and choice on a group of nursing home residents. It was expected that the debilitated condition of many of the aged residing in institutional settings is, at least in part, a result of living in a virtually decision-free environment and consequently is potentially reversible. Residents who were in the experimental group were given a communication emphasizing their responsibility for themselves, whereas the communication given to a second group stressed the staff's responsibility for them. In addition, to bolster the communication, the former group was given the freedom to make choices and the responsibility of caring for a plant rather than having decisions made and the plant taken care of for them by the staff, as was the case for the latter group. Questionnaire ratings and behavioral measures showed a significant improvement for the experimental group over the comparison group on alertness, active participation, and a general sense of well-being.

The transition from adulthood to old age is often perceived as a process of loss, physiologically and psychologically (Birren, 1958; Gould, 1972). However, it is as yet unclear just how much of this change is biologically determined and how much is a function of the environment. The ability to sustain a sense of personal control in old age may be greatly influenced by societal factors, and this in turn may affect one's physical well-being.

Typically the life situation does change in old age. There is some loss of roles, norms, and reference groups, events that negatively influence one's perceived competence and feeling of responsibility (Bengston, 1973). Perception of these changes in addition to actual physical decrements may enhance a sense of aging and lower self-esteem (Lehr & Puschner, Note 1). In response to internal developmental changes, the aging individual may come to see himself in a position of lessened mastery relative to the rest of the world, as a passive object manipulated by the environment (Neugarten & Gutman, 1958). Questioning whether these factors can

be counteracted, some studies have suggested that more successful aging—measured by decreased mortality, morbidity, and psychological disability—occurs when an individual feels a sense of usefulness and purpose (Bengston, 1973; Butler, 1967; Leaf, 1973; Lieberman, 1965).

The notion of competence is indeed central to much of human behavior. Adler (1930) has described the need to control one's personal environment as "an intrinsic necessity of life itself" (p. 398). deCharms (1968) has stated that "man's primary motivation propensity is to be effective in producing changes in his environment. Man strives to be a causal agent, to be the primary locus of, causation for, or the origin of, his behavior; he strives for personal causation" (p. 269).

Several laboratory studies have demonstrated that reduced control over aversive outcomes increases physiological distress and anxiety (Geer, Davison, & Gatchel, 1970; Pervin, 1963) and even a nonveridical perception of control over an impending event reduces the aversiveness of that event (Bowers, 1968; Glass & Singer, 1972; Kanfer & Seidner, 1973). Langer, Janis, and Wolfer (1975) found that by inducing the perception of control over stress in hospital patients by means of a communication that emphasized potential cognitive control, subjects requested fewer pain relievers and sedatives and were seen by nurses as evidencing less anxiety.

Choice is also a crucial variable in enhancing an induced sense of control. Stotland and Blumenthal (1964) studied the effects of choice on anxiety reduction. They told subjects that they were going to take a number of important ability tests. Half of the subjects were allowed to choose the order in which they wanted to take the tests, and half were told that the order was fixed. All subjects were informed that the order of the tests would have no bearing on their scores. They found that subjects not given the choice were more anxious, as measured by palmar sweating. In another study of the effects of choice, Corah and Boffa (1970) told their subjects that there were two conditions in the experiment, each of which would be signaled by a different light. In one condition they were given the choice of whether or not to press a button to escape from an aversive noise, and in the other one they were not given the option of escaping. They found that the choice instructions decreased the aversiveness of the threatening stimulus, apparently by increasing perceived control. Although using a very different paradigm, Langer (1975) also demonstrated the importance of choice. In that study it was found that the exercise of choice in a chance situation, where choice was objectively inconsequential, nevertheless had psychological consequences manifested in increased confidence and risk taking.

Lefcourt (1973) best summed up the essence of this research in a brief review article dealing with the perception of control in man and animals when he concluded that "the sense of control, the illusion that one can exercise personal choice, has a definite and a positive role in sustaining life" (p. 424). It is not surprising, then, that these important psychological factors should be linked to health and survival. In a series of retrospective studies, Schmale and his associates (Adamson & Schmale, 1965; Schmale, 1958; Schmale & Iker, 1966) found that ulcerative colitis, leukemia, cervical cancer, and heart disease were linked with a feeling of helplessness and loss of hope experienced by the patient prior to the onset of the disease. Seligman and his co-workers have systemmatically investigated the learning of helplessness and related it to the clinical syndrome of depression (see Seligman, 1975). Even death is apparently related to control-relevant variables. McMahon and Rhudick (1964) found a relationship between depression or hopelessness and death. The most graphic description of this association comes from Bettelheim (1943), who in his analysis of the "Muselmanner," the walking corpses in the concentration camps, described them as:

> Prisoners who came to believe the repeated statements of the guards—that there was no hope for them, that they would never leave the camp except as a corpse—who came to feel that their environment was one over which they could exercise no influence whatsoever. . . . Once his own life and the environment were viewed as totally beyond his ability to influence them, the only logical conclusion was to pay no attention to them whatsoever. Only then, all conscious awareness of stimuli coming from the outside was blocked out, and with it all response to anything but inner stimuli.

Death swiftly followed and, according to Bettelheim,

> [survival] depended on one's ability to arrange to preserve some areas of indepen-

dent action, to keep control of some important aspects of one's life despite an environment that seemed overwhelming and total.

Bettelheim's description reminds us of Richter's (1957) rats, who also "gave up hope" of controlling their environment and subsequently died.

The implications of these studies for research in the area of aging are clear. Objective helplessness as well as feelings of helplessness and hopelessness—both enhanced by the environment and by intrinsic changes that occur with increasing old age—may contribute to psychological withdrawal, physical disease, and death. In contrast, objective control and feelings of mastery may very well contribute to physical health and personal efficacy.

In a study conceived to explore the effects of dissonance, Ferrare (1962; cited in Seligman, 1975; Zimbardo & Ruch, 1975) presented data concerning the effects of the ability of geriatric patients to control their place of residence. Of 17 subjects who answered that they did not have any other alternative but to move to a specific old age home, 8 died after 4 weeks of residence and 16 after 10 weeks of residence. By comparison, among the residents who died during the initial period, only one person had answered that she had the freedom to choose other alternatives. All of these deaths were classified as unexpected because "not even insignificant disturbances had actually given warning of the impending disaster."

As Zimbardo (Zimbardo & Ruch, 1975) suggested, the implications of Ferrare's data are striking and merit further study of old age home settings. There is already evidence that perceived personal control in one's residential environment is important for younger and noninstitutional populations. Rodin (in press), using children as subjects, demonstrated that diminished feelings of control produced by chronic crowding at home led to fewer attempts to control self-reinforcement in the laboratory and to greater likelihood of giving up in the face of failure.

The present study attempted to assess directly the effects of enhanced personal responsibility and choice in a group of nursing home patients. In addition to examining previous results from the control-helplessness literature in a field setting, the present study extended the domain of this conception by considering new response variables. Specifically, if increased control has generalized beneficial effects, then physical and mental alertness, activity, general level of satisfaction, and sociability should all be affected. Also, the manipulation of the independent variables, assigning greater responsibility and decision freedom for relevant behavior, allowed subjects real choices that were not directed toward a single behavior or stimulus condition. This manipulation tested the ability of the subjects to generalize from specific choices enumerated for them to other aspects of their lives, and thus tested the generalizability of feelings of control over certain elements of the situation to more broadly based behavior and attitudes.

Method

SUBJECTS

The study was conducted in a nursing home, which was rated by the state of Connecticut as being among the finest care units and offering quality medical, recreational, and residential facilities. The home was large and modern in design, appearing cheerful and comfortable as well as clean and efficient. Of the four floors in the home, two were selected for study because of similarity in the residents' physical and psychological health and prior socioeconomic status, as determined from evaluations made by the home's director, head nurses, and social worker. Residents were assigned to a particular floor and room simply on the basis of availability, and on the average, residents on the two floors had been at the home about the same length of time. Rather than randomly assigning subjects to experimental treatment, a different floor was randomly selected for each treatment. Since there was not a great deal of communication between floors, this procedure was followed in order to decrease the likelihood that the treatment effects would be contaminated. There were 8 males and 39 females in the responsibility-induced condition (all fourth-floor residents) and 9 males and 35 females in the comparison group (all second-floor residents). Residents who were either completely bedridden or judged by the nursing home staff to be completely noncommunicative (11 on the experimental floor and 9 on the comparison floor) were omitted from the sample. Also omitted was one woman on each floor, one 40 years old and the other 26 years old, due to their age. Thus, 91 ambulatory adults, ranging in age from 65 to 90, served as subjects.

PROCEDURE

To introduce the experimental treatment, the nursing home administrator, an outgoing and friendly 33-year-old male who interacts with the residents daily, called a meeting in the lounge of each floor. He delivered one of the following two communications at that time:

[*Responsibility-induced group*] I brought you together today to give you some information about Arden House. I was surprised to learn that many of you don't know about the things that are available to you and more important, that many of you don't realize the influence you have over your own lives here. Take a minute to think of the decisions you can and should be making. For example, you have the responsibility of caring for yourselves, of deciding whether or not you want to make this a home you can be proud of and happy in. You should be deciding how you want your rooms to be arranged—whether you want it to be as it is or whether you want the staff to help you rearrange the furniture. You should be deciding how you want to spend your time, for example, whether you want to be visiting your friends who live on this floor or on other floors, whether you want to visit in your room or your friends' room, in the lounge, the dining room, etc., or whether you want to be watching television, listening to the radio, writing, reading, or planning social events. In other words, it's your life and you can make of it whatever you want.

This brings me to another point. If you are unsatisfied with anything here, you have the influence to change it. It's your responsibility to make your complaints known, to tell us what you would like to change, to tell us what you would like. These are just a few of the things you could and should be deciding and thinking about now and from time to time everyday. You made these decisions before you came here and you can and should be making them now.

We're thinking of instituting some way for airing complaints, suggestions, etc. Let [nurse's name] know if you think this is a good idea and how you think we should go about doing it. In any case let her know what your complaints or suggestions are.

Also, I wanted to take this opportunity to give you each a present from the Arden House. [A box of small plants was passed around, and patients were given two decisions to make: first, whether or not they wanted a plant at all, and second, to choose which one they wanted. All residents did select a plant.] The plants are yours to keep and take care of as you'd like.

One last thing, I wanted to tell you that we're showing a movie two nights next week,

Thursday and Friday. You should decide which night you'd like to go, if you choose to see it at all.

[*Comparison group*] I brought you together today to give you some information about the Arden House. I was surprised to learn that many of you don't know about the things that are available to you; that many of you don't realize all you're allowed to do here. Take a minute to think of all the options that we've provided for you in order for your life to be fuller and more interesting. For example, you're permitted to visit people on the other floors and to use the lounge on this floor for visiting as well as the dining room or your own rooms. We want your rooms to be as nice as they can be, and we've tried to make them that way for you. We want you to be happy here. We feel that it's our responsibility to make this a home you can be proud of and happy in, and we want to do all we can to help you.

This brings me to another point. If you have any complaints or suggestions about anything, let [nurse's name] know what they are. Let us know how we can best help you. You should feel that you have free access to anyone on the staff, and we will do the best we can to provide individualized attention and time for you.

Also, I wanted to take this opportunity to give you each a present from the Arden House. [The nurse walked around with a box of plants and each patient was handed one.] The plants are yours to keep. The nurses will water and care for them for you.

One last thing, I wanted to tell you that we're showing a movie next week on Thursday and Friday. We'll let you know later which day you're scheduled to see it.

The major difference between the two communications was that on one floor, the emphasis was on the residents' responsibility for themselves, whereas on the other floor, the communication stressed the staff's responsibility for them. In addition, several other differences bolstered this treatment: Residents in the responsibility-induced group were asked to give their opinion of the means by which complaints were handled rather than just being told that any complaints would be handled by staff members; they were given the opportunity to select their own plant and to care for it themselves, rather than being given a plant to be taken care of by someone else; and they were given their choice of a movie night, rather than being assigned a particular night, as was typically the case in the old age home. However, there was no difference in the amount of attention paid to the two groups.

Three days after these communications had been delivered, the director visited all of the residents in their rooms or in the corridor and reiterated part of the previous message. To those in the responsibility-induced group he said, "Remember what I said last Thursday. We want you to be happy. Treat this like your own home and make all the decisions you used to make. How's your plant coming along?" To the residents of the comparison floor, he said the same thing omitting the statement about decision making.

DEPENDENT VARIABLES

Questionnaires Two types of questionnaires were designed to assess the effects of induced responsibility. Each was administered 1 week prior to and 3 weeks after the communication. The first was administered directly to the residents by a female research assistant who was unaware of the experimental hypotheses or of the specific experimental treatment. The questions dealt with how much control they felt over general events in their lives and how happy and active they felt. Questions were responded to along 8-point scales ranging from 0 (none) to 8 (total). After completing each interview, the research assistant rated the resident on an 8-point scale for alertness.

The second questionnaire was responded to by the nurses, who staffed the experimental and comparison floors and who were unaware of the experimental treatments. Nurses on two different shifts completed the questionnaires in order to obtain two ratings for each subject. There were nine 10-point scales that asked for ratings of how happy, alert, dependent, sociable, and active the residents were as well as questions about their eating and sleeping habits. There were also questions evaluating the proportion of weekly time the patient spent engaged in a variety of activities. These included reading, watching television, visiting other patients, visiting outside guests, watching the staff, talking to the staff, sitting alone doing nothing, and others.

Behavioral Measures Since perceived personal control is enhanced by a sense of choice over relevant behaviors, the option to choose which night the experimental group wished to see the movie was expected to have measurable effects on active participation. Attendance records were kept by the occupational therapist, who was unaware that an experiment was being conducted.

Another measure of involvement was obtained by holding a competition in which all participants had to guess the number of jelly beans in a large jar. Each patient wishing to enter the contest simply wrote his or her name and estimate on a piece of paper and deposited it in a box that was next to the jar.[1]

Finally, an unobtrusive measure of activity was taken. The tenth night after the experimental treatment, the right wheels of the wheelchairs belonging to a randomly selected subsample of each patient group were covered with 2 inches (.05 m) of white adhesive tape. The following night, the tape was removed from the chairs and placed on index cards for later evaluation of amount of activity, as indicated by the amount of discoloration.

Results

QUESTIONNAIRES

Before examining whether or not the experimental treatment was effective, the pretest ratings made by the subjects, the nurses, and the interviewer were compared for both groups. None of the differences approached significance, which indicates comparability between groups prior to the start of the investigation.

The means for responses to the various questionnaires are summarized in Table 36.01. Statistical tests compared the posttest minus pretest scores of the experimental and comparison groups.

In response to direct questions about how happy they currently were, residents in the responsibility-induced group reported significantly greater increases in happiness after the experimental treatment than did the comparison group, $t(43) = 1.96$, $p < .05$.[2] Although the comparison group heard a communication that had specifically stressed the home's commitment to making them happy, only 25% of them reported feeling happier by the time of the second interview, whereas 48% of the experimental group did so.

The responsibility-induced group reported themselves to be significantly more active on the second interview than the comparison group, $t(43) = 2.67$, $p < .01$. This interviewer's ratings of alertness also showed significantly greater increase for the experimental group, $t(43) = 2.40$, $p < .025$. However, the questions that were relevant to perceived control showed no significant changes for the experimental group. Since over 20% of the patients indicated that they were unable to understand what we meant by control, these questions were obviously not adequate to discriminate between groups.

The second questionnaire measured nurses' ratings of each patient. The correlation between the two nurses' ratings of the same patient was .68 and .61 ($ps < .005$) on the comparison and responsibility-induced floors, respectively.[3] For each patient, a score was calculated by averaging the two nurses' ratings for each question, summing across questions, and subtracting the total pretreatment score from the total posttreatment score.[4] This yielded a positive average total change score of 3.97 for the responsibility-induced group as compared with an average negative total change of −2.37 for the comparison group. The difference between these means is highly significant, $t(50) = 5.18$, $p < .005$. If one looks at the percentage of people who were judged improved rather than at the amount of judged improvement, the same pattern emerges: 93% of the experimental group (all but one subject) were considered improved, whereas only 21% (six subjects) of the comparison group showed this positive change ($\chi^2 = 19.23$, $p < .005$).

The nurses' evaluation of the proportion of time subjects spent engaged in various interactive and noninteractive activities was analyzed by comparing the average change scores (post−precommunication) for all of the nurses for both groups of subjects on each activity. Several significant differences were found. The experimental group showed increases in the proportion of time spent visiting with other patients (for the experimental group, $\overline{X} = 12.86$ vs. −6.61 for the comparison group), $t(50) = 3.83$, $p < .005$; visiting people from outside of the nursing home (for the experimental group, $\overline{X} = 4.28$

---

[1] We also intended to measure the number of complaints that patients voiced. Since one often does not complain after becoming psychologically helpless, complaints in this context were expected to be a positive indication of perceived personal control. This measure was discarded, however, since the nurses failed to keep a systematic written record.

[2] All of the statistics for the self-report data and the interviewers' ratings are based on 45 subjects (25 in the responsibility-induced group and 20 in the comparison group), since these were the only subjects available at the time of the interview.

---

[3] There was also significant agreement between the interviewer's and nurses' ratings of alertness ($r = .65$).

[4] Since one nurse on the day shift and one nurse on the night shift gave the ratings, responses to the questions regarding sleeping and eating habits were not included in the total score. Also, in order to reduce rater bias, patients for whom there were ratings by a nurse on only one shift were excluded from this calculation. This left 24 residents from the experimental group and 28 from the comparison group.

TABLE 36.01

MEAN SCORES FOR SELF-REPORT, INTERVIEWER RATINGS, AND NURSES' RATINGS FOR EXPERIMENTAL AND COMPARISON GROUPS

QUESTIONNAIRE RESPONSES	RESPONSIBILITY INDUCED ($N = 24$)			COMPARISON ($N = 28$)			COMPARISON OF CHANGE SCORES ($P <$)
	PRE	POST	CHANGE: POST-PRE	PRE	POST	CHANGE: POST-PRE	
Self-report							
Happy	5.16	5.44	.28	4.90	4.78	− .12	.05
Active	4.07	4.27	.20	3.90	2.62	− 1.28	.01
Perceived Control							
Have	3.26	3.42	.16	3.62	4.03	.41	—
Want	3.85	3.80	− .05	4.40	4.57	.17	—
Interviewer rating							
Alertness	5.02	5.31	.29	5.75	5.38	− .37	.025
Nurses' ratings							
General improvement	41.67	45.64	3.97	42.69	40.32	− 2.39	.005
Time spent							
Visiting patients	13.03	19.81	6.78	7.94	4.65	− 3.30	.005
Visiting others	11.50	13.75	2.14	12.38	8.21	− 4.16	.05
Talking to staff	8.21	16.43	8.21	9.11	10.71	1.61	.01
Watching staff	6.78	4.64	− 2.14	6.96	11.60	4.64	.05

vs. − 7.61 for the comparison group, $t(50) = 2.30$, $p < .05$; and talking to the staff (for the experimental group, $\overline{X} = 8.21$ vs. 1.61 for the comparison group), $t(50) = 2.98$, $p < .05$.[5] In addition, they spent less time passively watching the staff (for the experimental group, $\overline{X} = -4.28$ vs. 9.68 for the comparison group), $t(50) = 2.60$, $p < .05$. Thus, it appears that the treatment increased active, interpersonal activity but not passive activity such as watching television or reading.

BEHAVIORAL MEASURES

As in the case of the questionnaires, the behavioral measures showed a pattern of differences between groups that was generally consistent with the predicted effects of increased responsibility. The movie attendance was significantly higher in the responsibility-induced group than in the control group after the experimental treatment ($z = 1.71$, $p < .05$, one-tailed), although a similar attendance check taken one month before the communications revealed no group differences.[6]

In the jelly-bean-guessing contest, 10 subjects (21%) in the responsibility-induced group and only 1 subject (2%) from the comparison group participated ($\chi^2 = 7.72$, $p < .01$). Finally, very little dirt was found on the tape taken from any of the patients' wheelchairs, and there was no significant difference between the two groups.

Discussion

It appears that inducing a greater sense of personal responsibility in people who may have virtually relinquished decision making, either by choice or necessity, produces improvement. In the present investigation, patients in the comparison group were given a communication stressing the staff's desire to make them happy and were otherwise treated in the

---

[5] This statistic is based only on the responses of nurse on duty in the evening.

[6] Frequencies were transformed into arc sines and analyzed using the method that is essentially the same as that described by Langer and Abelson (1972).

sympathetic manner characteristic of this high-quality nursing home. Despite the care provided for these people, 71% were rated as having become more debilitated over a period of time as short as 3 weeks. In contrast with this group, 93% of the people who were encouraged to make decisions for themselves, given decisions to make, and given responsibility for something outside of themselves, actually showed overall improvement. Based on their own judgments and by the judgments of the nurses with whom they interacted on a daily basis, they became more active and felt happier. Perhaps more important was the judged improvement in their mental alertness and increased behavioral involvement in many different kinds of activities.

The behavioral measures showed greater active participation and involvement for the experimental group. Whether this directly resulted from an increase in perceived choice and decision-making responsibility or from the increase in general activity and happiness occurring after the treatment cannot be assessed from the present results. It should also be clearly noted that although there were significant differences in active involvement, the overall level of participation in the activities that comprised the behavioral measures was low. Perhaps a much more powerful treatment would be one that is individually administered and repeated on several occasions. That so weak a manipulation had any effect suggests how important increased control is for these people, for whom decision making is virtually nonexistent.

The practical implications of this experimental demonstration are straightforward. Mechanisms can and should be established for changing situational factors that reduce real or perceived responsibility in the elderly. Furthermore, this study adds to the body of literature (Bengston, 1973; Butler, 1967; Leaf, 1973; Lieberman, 1965) suggesting that senility and diminished alertness are not an almost inevitable result of aging. In fact, it suggests that some of the negative consequences of aging may be retarded, reversed, or possibly prevented by returning to the aged the right to make decisions and a feeling of competence.

Reference Note

1. Lehr, K., & Puschner, I. *Studies in the awareness of aging.* Paper presented at the 6th International Congress on Gerontology, Copenhagen, 1963.

References

1. Adamson, J., & Schmale, A. Object loss, giving up, and the onset of psychiatric disease. *Psychosomatic Medicine*, 1965, *27*, 557–576.

2. Adler, A. Individual psychology. In C. Murchinson (Ed.), *Psychologies of 1930*. Worcester, Mass.: Clark University Press, 1930.

3. Bengston, V. L. Self determination: A social and psychological perspective on helping the aged. *Geriatrics*, 1973.

4. Bettelheim, B. Individual and mass behavior in extreme situations. *Journal of Abnormal and Social Psychology*, 1943, *38*, 417–452.

5. Birren, J. Aging and psychological adjustment. *Review of Educational Research*, 1958, *28*, 475–490.

6. Bowers, K. Pain, anxiety, and perceived control. *Journal of Consulting and Clinical Psychology*, 1968, *32*, 596–602.

7. Butler, R. Aspects of survival and adaptation in human aging. *American Journal of Psychiatry*, 1967, *123*, 1233–1243.

8. Corah, N., & Boffa, J. Perceived control, self-observation, and response to aversive stimulation. *Journal of Personality and Social Psychology*, 1970, *16*, 1–4.

9. deCharms, R. *Personal causation.* New York: Academic Press, 1968.

10. Geer, J., Davison, G., & Gatchel, R. Reduction of stress in humans through nonveridical perceived control of aversive stimulation. *Journal of Personality and Social Psychology*, 1970, *16*, 731–738.

11. Glass, D., & Singer, J. *Urban stress.* New York: Academic Press, 1972.

12. Gould, R. The phases of adult life: A study in developmental psychology. *American Journal of Psychiatry*, 1972, *129*, 521–531.

13. Kanfer, R., & Seidner, M. Self-Control: Factors enhancing tolerance of noxious stimulation. *Journal of Personality and Social Psychology*, 1973, *25*, 381–389.

14. Langer, E. J. The illusion of control. *Journal of Personality and Social Psychology*, 1975, *32*, 311–328.

15. Langer, E. J., & Abelson, R. P. The semantics of asking a favor: How to succeed in getting help without really dying. *Journal of Personality and Social Psychology*, 1972, *24*, 26–32.

16. Langer, E. J., Janis, I. L., & Wolfer, J. A. Reduction of psychological stress in surgical patients. *Journal of Experimental Social Psychology*, 1975, *11*, 155–165.

17. Leaf, A. Threescore and forty. *Hospital Practice*, 1973, *34*, 70–71.

18. Lefcourt, H. The function of the illusion of control and freedom. *American Psychologist*, 1973, *28*, 417–425.

19. Lieberman, M. Psychological correlates of impending death: Some preliminary observations. *Journal of Gerontology*, 1965, *20*, 181–190.

20. McMahon, A., & Rhudick, P. Reminiscing, adaptational significance in the aged. *Archives of General Psychiatry*, 1964, *10*, 292–298.

21. Neugarten, B., & Gutman, D. Age-sex roles and personality in middle age: A thematic apperception study. *Psychological Monographs*, 1958, *72*(17, Whole No. 470).

22. Pervin, L. The need to predict and control under conditions of threat. *Journal of Personality*, 1963, *31*, 570–585.

23. Richter, C. On the phenomenon of sudden death in animals and man. *Psychosomatic Medicine,* 1957, *19,* 191–198.
24. Rodin, J. Crowding, perceived choice, and response to controllable and uncontrollable outcomes. *Journal of Experimental Social Psychology,* in press.
25. Schmale, A. Relationships of separation and depression to disease. I.: A report on a hospitalized medical population. *Psychosomatic Medicine,* 1958, *20,* 259–277.
26. Schmale, A., & Iker, H. The psychological setting of uterine cervical cancer. *Annals of the New York Academy of Sciences,* 1966, *125,* 807–813.
27. Seligman, M. E. P. *Helplessness.* San Francisco: Freeman, 1975.
28. Stotland, E., & Blumenthal, A. The reduction of anxiety as a result of the expectation of making a choice. *Canadian Review of Psychology,* 1964, *18,* 139–145.
29. Zimbardo, P. G., & Ruch, F. L. *Psychology and life* (9th ed.). Glenview, Ill.: Scott, Foresman, 1975.

QUESTIONS FOR REFLECTION AND DISCUSSION:

1. The authors note that "more successful aging—measured by decreased mortality, morbidity, and psychological disability—occurs when an individual feels a sense of usefulness and purpose." What kinds of activities are connected with a sense of usefulness and purpose?

2. What do you envision for your own later years as you look into the future?

3. The authors note that some aspects of aging which have been considered physical may actually be psychological. Can you give an example?

4. Why do the authors refer to Bettelheim's description of prisoners in the Nazi death camps? What can be the possible connection with older people in the United States?

5. What do the authors mean when they write that they conducted a "field experiment"? Who were the subjects in the study? How were they selected? Are you satisfied that the results of the study can be generalized to older people in general? Why or why not?

6. How did the researchers induce a sense of personal responsibility in the subjects?

7. What kinds of measures did the researchers use to determine whether subjects improved as a result of treatment? Can you think of others?

8. Did reading this study change your attitudes toward older people or your expectation of older people? Explain.

VII

SOCIAL AND ENVIRONMENTAL PSYCHOLOGY

Humans are social creatures. Even those who choose to live alone were reared by others and highly dependent on others during the early years. Perhaps because of our early dependence on others, we come to be strongly influenced by other people's opinions of us.

Social psychology studies the nature and causes of our behavior in social situations. The topics of interest to social psychologists include attitudes, social perception, social influence, interpersonal attraction, and group behavior. The closely related field of environmental psychology considers the ways in which we influence, and are influenced by, the physical environment. The primary sources in this part include the following:

37. Freedman, J. L., & Fraser, S. C. (1966). Compliance without pressure: The foot-in-the-door technique. *Journal of Personality and Social Psychology, 4,* 195–202.

   When you give people an inch do they take a yard, or is enough . . . enough? The findings of this study suggest that once you let people get their foot in the door, it may be too late to close the door.

38. Asch, S. E. (1953). Opinions and social pressure. *Scientific American, 193,* 31–35.

   How strong is the felt need to conform to social pressure? Are we a nation of rugged individualists, or are we kidding ourselves? This classic study suggests that most of us tend to bow to social pressure, at least occasionally.

39. Milgram, S. (1963). Behavioral study of obedience. *Journal of Abnormal and Social Psychology, 67,* 371–378.

   The results of this classic study into social influence are some of the more frightening findings in the entire literature of psychology. Who are the people who kill innocents in Nazi Germany, in Ruanda, or in Bosnia and

Kosovo? Are they the demented few, or could they be almost any one of us? Are you sure?

40. Benson, P. L., Karabenick, S. A., & Lerner, R. M. (1976). Pretty pleases: The effects of physical attractiveness, race, and sex on receiving help. *Journal of Experimental Social Psychology, 12,* 409–415.

We are too intelligent and sophisticated to be influenced by a pretty face, aren't we? Actually, the findings of this study and others like it suggest that when we are in need of help, it helps to be good-looking.

41. Darley, J. M., & Latané, B. (1968). Bystander intervention in emergencies: Diffusion of responsibility. *Journal of Personality and Social Psychology, 8,* 377–383.

This study grew out of the disturbing case of Kitty Genovese, the woman who was stabbed to death in New York City while at least 38 people were aware of her plight. Why did no one come to her aid? Is it because nobody cared what happened to her or precisely because there were so many people available to come to her aid? If you are in dire need, will you be better off if there are many people available to help, or just one? Why?

42. Calhoun, J. B. (1962). Population density and social pathology. *Scientific American, 206,* 139–148.

Here is a classic study on the effects of crowding. As you read it, consider whether the behavior of the animals in the study (rats) serve as acceptable "models" for human behavior.

43. Donnerstein, E. I., & Wilson, D. W. (1976). Effects of noise and perceived control on ongoing and subsequent aggressive behavior. *Journal of Personality and Social Psychology, 34,* 774–781.

Environmental psychologists look at the effects of noise, air pollution, ambient temperatures and the like on behavior and mental processes. Here is a representative study on the effects of noise. Are the findings relevant for your next visit to the disco?

SOURCE

Freedman, J. L., & Fraser, S. C. (1966). Compliance without pressure: The foot-in-the-door technique. *Journal of Personality and Social Psychology, 4,* 195–202. Copyright © 1966 by the American Psychological Association. Reprinted with permission.

Have you found yourself on a list of people who give willingly to charity, to political causes, or who help out in the children's school? Has it seemed that you are called on all the time? You might think, "How did I wind up here? Haven't I given enough? Haven't I done enough?" You might even think, "They're pushing it. Don't they know that if they ask for more and more, they'll push me into saying no?"

Sounds logical, doesn't it? After all, don't we have our limits? Yet psychological theory and research often does not follow or support common sense. The following experiment by Jonathan Freedman and Scott Fraser suggests that when we give once, we are more likely to give again. That is, if we at first give them an inch, we are later likely to give them the entire yard.

Compliance Without Pressure: The Foot-In-The-Door Technique

JONATHAN L. FREEDMAN AND SCOTT C. FRASER
STANFORD UNIVERSITY

2 experiments were conducted to test the proposition that once someone has agreed to a small request he is more likely to comply with a larger request. The 1st study demonstrated this effect when the same person made both requests. The 2nd study extended this to the situation in which different people made the 2 requests. Several experimental groups were run in an effort to explain these results, and possible explanations are discussed.

How can a person be induced to do something he would rather not do? This question is relevant to practically every phase of social life, from stopping at a traffic light to stopping smoking, from buying Brand X to buying savings bonds, from supporting the March of Dimes to supporting the Civil Rights Act.

One common way of attacking the problem is to exert as much pressure as possible on the reluctant individual in an effort to force him to comply. This technique has been the focus of a considerable amount of experimental research. Work on attitude change, conformity, imitation, and obedience has all tended to stress the importance of the degree of external pressure. The prestige of the communicator (Kelman & Hovland, 1953), degree of discrepancy of the communication (Hovland & Pritzker, 1957), size of the group disagreeing with the subject (Asch, 1951), perceived power of the model (Bandura, Ross, & Ross, 1963), etc., are the kinds of variables that have been studied. This impressive body of work, added to the research on rewards and punishments in learning, has produced convincing evidence that greater external pressure generally leads to greater compliance with the wishes of the experimenter. The one exception appears to be situations involving the arousal of cognitive dissonance in which, once discrepant behavior has been elicited from the subject, the greater the pressure that was used to elicit the behavior, the less subsequent change occurs (Festinger & Carlsmith, 1959). But even in this situation one critical element is the amount of external pressure exerted.

Clearly, then, under most circumstances the more pressure that can be applied, the more likely it is that the individual will comply. There are, however, many times when for ethical, moral, or practical reasons it is difficult to apply much pressure when the goal is to produce compliance with a minimum of apparent pressure, as in the forced-compliance studies involving dissonance arousal. And even when a great deal of pressure is possible, it is still important to maximize the compliance it produces. Thus, factors other than external pressure are often quite critical in determining degree of compliance. What are these factors?

Although rigorous research on the problem is rather sparse, the fields of advertising, propaganda, politics, etc., are by no means devoid of techniques designed to produce compliance in the absence of external pressure (or to maximize the effectiveness of the pressure that is used, which is really the same problem). One assumption about compliance that has often been made either explicitly or implicitly is that once a person has been induced to comply with a small request he is more likely to comply with a larger demand. This is the principle that is commonly referred to as the foot-in-the-door or gradation technique and is reflected in the saying that if you "give them an inch, they'll take a mile." It was, for example, supposed to be one of the basic techniques upon which the Korean brainwashing tactics were based (Schein, Schneier, & Barker, 1961), and, in a somewhat different sense, one basis for Nazi propaganda during 1940 (Bruner, 1941). It also appears to be implicit in many advertising campaigns which attempt to induce the consumer to do anything relating to the product involved, even sending back a card saying he does not want the product.

The most relevant piece of experimental evidence comes from a study of conformity done by Deutsch and Gerard (1955). Some subjects were faced with incorrect group judgments first in a series in which the stimuli were not present during the actual judging and then in a series in which they were present, while the order of the memory and visual series was reversed for other subjects. For both groups the memory series produced more conformity, and when the memory series came first there was more total conformity to the group judgments. It seems likely that this order effect occurred because, as the authors suggest, once conformity is elicited at all it is more likely to occur in the future. Although this kind of conformity is probably somewhat different from compliance as described above, this finding certainly lends some support to the foot-in-the-door idea. The present research attempted to provide a rigorous, more direct test of this notion as it applies to compliance and to provide data relevant to several alternative ways of explaining the effect.

Experiment I

The basic paradigm was to ask some subjects (Performance condition) to comply first with a small request and then 3 days later with a larger, related request. Other subjects (One-Contact condition) were asked to comply only with the large request. The hypothesis was that more subjects in the Performance condition than in the One-Contact condition would comply with the larger request.

Two additional conditions were included in an attempt to specify the essential difference between these two major conditions. The Performance subjects were asked to perform a small favor, and, if they agreed, they did it. The question arises whether the act of agreeing itself is critical or whether actually carrying it out was necessary. To assess this a third group of subjects (Agree-Only) was asked the first request, but, even if they agreed, they did not carry it out. Thus, they were identical to the Performance group except that they were not given the opportunity of performing the request.

Another difference between the two main conditions was that at the time of the larger request the subjects in the Performance condition were more familiar with the experimenter than were the other subjects. The Performance subjects had been contacted twice, heard his voice more, discovered that the questions were not dangerous, and so on. It is possible that this increased familiarity would serve to decrease the fear and suspicion of a strange voice on the phone and might accordingly increase the likelihood of the subjects agreeing to the larger request. To control for this a fourth condition was run (Familiarization) which attempted to give the subjects as much familiarity with the experimenter as in the Performance and Agree-Only conditions with the only difference being that no request was made.

The major prediction was that more subjects in the Performance condition would agree to the large request than in any of the other conditions, and that the One-Contact condition would produce the least compliance. Since the importance of agreement and familiarity was essentially unknown, the expectation was that the Agree-Only and Familiarization conditions would produce intermediate amounts of compliance.

Method

The prediction stated above was tested in a field experiment in which housewives were asked to allow a survey team of five or six men to come into their homes for 2 hours to classify the household products they used. This large request was made under four different conditions: after an initial contact in which the subject had been asked to answer a few questions about the kinds of soaps she used, and the questions were actually asked (Performance condition); after an identical contact in which the questions were not actually asked (Agree-Only condition); after an initial contact in which no request was made (Familiarization condition); or after no initial contact (One-Contact condition). The dependent measure was simply whether or not the subject agreed to the large request.

PROCEDURE

The subjects were 156 Palo Alto, California, housewives, 36 in each condition, who were selected at random from the telephone directory. An additional 12 subjects distributed about equally among the three two-contact conditions could not be reached for the second contact and are not included in the data analysis. Subjects were assigned randomly to the various conditions, except that the Familiarization condition was added to the design after the other three conditions had been completed. All contacts were by telephone by the same experimenter who identified himself as the same person each time. Calls were made only in the morning. For the three groups that were contacted twice, the first call was made on either Monday or Tuesday and the second always 3 days later. All large requests were made on either Thursday or Friday.

At the first contact, the experimenter introduced himself by name and said that he was from the California Consumers' Group. In the Performance condition he then proceeded:

> We are calling you this morning to ask if you would answer a number of questions about what household products you use so that we could have this information for our public service publication, "The Guide." Would you be willing to give us this information for our survey?

If the subject agreed, she was asked a series of eight innocuous questions dealing with household soaps (e.g., "What brand of soap do you use in your kitchen sink?") She was then thanked for her cooperation, and the contact terminated.

Another condition (Agree-Only) was run to assess the importance of actually carrying out the request as opposed to merely agreeing to it. The only difference between this and the Performance condition was that, if the subject agreed to answer the questions, the experimenter thanked her, but said that he was just lining up respondents for the survey and would contact her if needed.

A third condition was included to check on the importance of the subject's greater familiarity with the experimenter in the two-contact conditions. In this condition the experimenter introduced himself, described the organization he worked for and the survey it was conducting, listed the questions he was asking, and then said that he was calling merely to acquaint the subject with the existence of his organization. In other words, these subjects were contacted, spent as much time on the phone with the experimenter as the Performance subjects did, heard all the questions, but neither agreed to answer them nor answered them.

In all of these two-contact conditions some subjects did not agree to the requests or even hung up before the requests were made. Every subject who answered the phone was included in the analysis of the results and was contacted for the second request regardless of her extent of cooperativeness during the first contact. In other words, no subject who could be contacted the appropriate number of times was discarded from any of the four conditions.

The large request was essentially identical for all subjects. The experimenter called, identified himself, and said either that his group was expanding its survey (in the case of the two-contact conditions) or that it was conducting a survey (in the One-Contact condition). In all four conditions he then continued:

> The survey will involve five or six men from our staff coming into your home some morning for about 2 hours to enumerate and classify all the household products that you have. They will have to have full freedom in your house to go through the cupboards and storage places. Then all this information will be used in the writing of the reports for our public service publication, "The Guide."

If the subject agreed to the request, she was thanked and told that at the present time the experimenter was merely collecting names of people who were willing to take part and that she would be contacted if it were decided to use her in the survey. If she did not agree, she was thanked for her time. This terminated the experiment.

TABLE 37.01

PERCENTAGE OF SUBJECTS COMPLYING WITH LARGE REQUEST IN EXPERIMENT I	
CONDITION	**%**
Performance	52.8
Agree-Only	33.3
Familiarization	27.8*
One-Contact	22.2**

Note.—N = 36 for each group. Significance levels represent differences from the Performance condition.
*p < .07.
**p < .02.

Results

Apparently even the small request was not considered trivial by some of the subjects. Only about two thirds of the subjects in the Performance and Agree-Only conditions agreed to answer the questions about household soaps. It might be noted that none of those who refused the first request later agreed to the large request, although as stated previously all subjects who were contacted for the small request are included in the data for those groups.

Our major prediction was that subjects who had agreed to and carried out a small request (Performance condition) would subsequently be more likely to comply with a larger request than would subjects who were asked only the larger request (One-Contact condition). As may be seen in Table 37.01, the results support the prediction. Over 50% of the subjects in the Performance condition agreed to the larger request, while less than 25% of the One-Contact condition agreed to it. Thus it appears that obtaining compliance with a small request does tend to increase subsequent compliance. The question is what aspect of the initial contact produces this effect.

One possibility is that the effect was produced merely by increased familiarity with the experimenter. The Familiarization control was included to assess the effect on compliance of two contacts with the same person. The group had as much contact with the experimenter as the Performance group, but no request was made during the first contact. As the table indicates, the Familiarization group did not differ appreciably in amount of compliance from the One-Contact group, but was different from the Performance group ($\chi^2 = 3.70$, $p < .07$). Thus, although increased familiarity may well lead to in-

creased compliance, in the present situation the differences in amount of familiarity apparently were not great enough to produce any such increase; the effect that was obtained seems not to be due to this factor.

Another possibility is that the critical factor producing increased compliance is simply agreeing to the small request (i.e., carrying it out may not be necessary). The Agree-Only condition was identical to the Performance condition except that in the former the subjects were not asked the questions. The amount of compliance in this Agree-Only condition fell between the Performance and One-Contact conditions and was not significantly different from either of them. This leaves the effect of merely agreeing somewhat ambiguous, but it suggests that the agreement alone may produce part of the effect.

Unfortunately, it must be admitted that neither of these control conditions is an entirely adequate test of the possibility it was designed to assess. Both conditions are in some way quite peculiar and may have made a very different and extraneous impression on the subject than did the Performance condition. In one case, a housewife is asked to answer some questions and then is not asked them; in the other, some man calls to tell her about some organization she has never heard of. Now, by themselves neither of these events might produce very much suspicion. But, several days later, the same man calls and asks a very large favor. At this point it is not at all unlikely that many subjects think they are being manipulated, or in any case that something strange is going on. Any such reaction on the part of the subjects would naturally tend to reduce the amount of compliance in these conditions.

Thus, although this first study demonstrates that an initial contact in which a request is made and carried out increases compliance with a second request, the question of why and how the initial request produces this effect remains unanswered. In an attempt to begin answering this question and to extend the results of the first study, a second experiment was conducted.

There seemed to be several quite plausible ways in which the increase in compliance might have been produced. The first was simply some kind of commitment to or involvement with the particular person making the request. This might work, for example, as follows: The subject has agreed to the first request and perceives that the experimenter therefore expects him also to agree to the second request. The subject thus feels obligated and does not want to disappoint the experimenter; he also feels that he needs a good reason for saying "no"—a better reason than he would need if he had never said "yes." This is just one line of causality—the particular process by which involvement with the experimenter operates might be quite different, but the basic idea would be similar. The commitment is to the particular person. This implies that the increase in compliance due to the first contact should occur primarily when both requests are made by the same person.

Another explanation in terms of involvement centers around the particular issue with which the requests are concerned. Once the subject has taken some action in connection with an area of concern, be it surveys, political activity, or highway safety, there is probably a tendency to become somewhat more concerned with the area. The subject begins thinking about it, considering its importance and relevance to him, and so on. This tends to make him more likely to agree to take further action in the same area when he is later asked to. To the extent that this is the critical factor, the initial contact should increase compliance only when both requests are related to the same issue or area of concern.

Another way of looking at the situation is that the subject needs a reason to say "no." In our society it is somewhat difficult to refuse a reasonable request, particularly when it is made by an organization that is not trying to make money. In order to refuse, many people feel that they need a reason—simply not wanting to do it is often not in itself sufficient. The person can say to the requester or simply to himself that he does not believe in giving to charities or tipping or working for political parties or answering questions or posting signs, or whatever he is asked to do. Once he has performed a particular task, however, this excuse is no longer valid for not agreeing to perform a similar task. Even if the first thing he did was trivial compared to the present request, he cannot say he never does this sort of thing, and thus one good reason for refusing is removed. This line of reasoning suggests that the similarity of the first and second requests in terms of the type of action required is an important factor. The more similar they are, the more the "matter of principle" argument is eliminated by agreeing to the first request, and the greater should be the increase in compliance.

There are probably many other mechanisms by which the initial request might produce an increase in compliance. The second experiment was designed in part to test the notions described above, but its major purpose was to demonstrate the effect unequivocally. To this latter end it eliminated one of the important problems with the first study which was that when the experimenter made the second request he was not blind as to which condition the subjects were in. In this study the second request was always made by someone other than the person who made the first request, and the second experimenter was blind as to what condition the subject was in. This eliminates the possibility that the experimenter exerted systematically different amounts of pressure in different experimental conditions. If the effect of the first study were replicated, it would also rule out the relatively uninteresting possibility that the effect is due primarily to greater familiarity or involvement with the particular person making the first request.

Experiment II

The basic paradigm was quite similar to that of the first study. Experimental subjects were asked to comply with a small request and were later asked a considerably larger request, while controls were asked only the larger request. The first request varied along two dimensions. Subjects were asked either to put up a small sign or to sign a petition, and the issue was either safe driving or keeping California beautiful. Thus, there were four first requests: a small sign for safe driving or for beauty, and a petition for the two issues. The second request for all subjects was to install in their front lawn a very large sign which said "Drive Carefully." The four experimental conditions may be defined in terms of the similarity of the small and large requests along the dimensions of issue and task. The two requests were similar in both issue and task for the small-sign, safe-driving group, similar only in issue for the safe-driving-petition group, similar only in task for the small "Keep California Beautiful" sign group, and similar in neither issue nor task for the "Keep California Beautiful" petition group.

The major expectation was that the three groups for which either the task or the issue were similar would show more compliance than the controls, and it was also felt that when both were similar there would probably be the most compliance. The fourth condition (Different Issue-Different Task) was included primarily to assess the effect simply of the initial contact which, although it was not identical to the second one on either issue or task, was in many ways quite similar (e.g., a young student asking for cooperation on a noncontroversial issue). There were no clear expectations as to how this condition would compare to the controls.

Method

The subjects were 114 women and 13 men living in Palo Alto, California. Of these, 9 women and 6 men could not be contacted for the second request and are not included in the data analysis. The remaining 112 subjects were divided about equally among the five conditions (see Table 37.02). All subjects were contacted between 1:30 and 4:30 on weekday afternoons.

Two experimenters, one male and one female, were employed, and a different one always made the second contact. Unlike the first study, the experimenters actually went to the homes of the subjects and interviewed them on a face-to-face basis. An effort was made to select subjects from blocks and neighborhoods that were as homogeneous as possible. On each block every third or fourth house was approached, and all subjects on that block were in one experimental condition. This was necessary because of the likelihood that neighbors would talk to each other about the contact. In addition, for every four subjects contacted, a fifth house was chosen as a control but was, of course, not contacted. Throughout this phase of the experiment, and in fact throughout the whole experiment, the two experimenters did not communicate to each other what conditions had been run on a given block nor what condition a particular house was in.

The small-sign, safe-driving group was told that the experimenter was from the Community Committee for Traffic Safety, that he was visiting a number of homes in an attempt to make the citizens more aware of the need to drive carefully all the time, and that he would like the subject to take a small sign and put it in a window or in the car so that it would serve as a reminder of the need to drive carefully. The sign was 3 inches square, said "Be a safe driver," was on thin paper without a gummed backing, and in general looked rather amateurish and unattractive. If the subject agreed, he was given the sign and thanked; if he disagreed, he was simply thanked for his time.

The three other experimental conditions were quite similar with appropriate changes. The other organization was identified as the Keep California Beautiful Committee and its sign said, appropriately enough, "Keep California Beautiful." Both signs were simply black block letters on a white background. The two petition groups were asked to sign a petition which was being sent to California's United States Senators. The petition advocated support for any legislation which would promote either safer driving or keeping California beautiful. The subject was shown a petition, typed on heavy bond paper, with at least 20 signatures already affixed. If she agreed, she signed and was thanked. If she did not agree, she was merely thanked.

The second contact was made about 2 weeks after the initial one. Each experimenter was armed with a list of houses which had been compiled by the other experimenter. This list contained all four experimental conditions and the controls, and, of course, there was no way for the second experimenter to know which condition the subject had been in. At this second contact, all subjects were asked the same thing: Would they put a large sign concerning safe driving in their front yard? The experimenter identified himself as being from the Citizens for Safe Driving, a different group from the original safe-driving group (although it is likely that most subjects who had been in the safe-driving conditions did not notice the difference). The subject was shown a picture of a very large sign reading "Drive Carefully" placed in front of an attractive house. The picture was taken so that the sign obscured much of the front of the house and completely concealed the doorway. It was rather poorly lettered. The subject was told that: "Our men will come out and install it and later come and remove it. It makes just a small hole in your lawn, but if this is unacceptable to you we have a special mount which will make no hole." She was asked to put the sign up for a week or a week and a half. If the subject agreed, she was told that more names than necessary were being gathered and if her home were to be used she would be contacted in a few weeks. The experimenter recorded the subject's response and this ended the experiment.

Results

First, it should be noted that there were no large differences among the experimental conditions in the percentages of subjects agreeing to the first request. Although somewhat more subjects agreed to post the "Keep California Beautiful" sign and somewhat fewer to sign the beauty petition, none of these differences approach significance.

The important figures are the number of subjects in each group who agreed to the large request. These are presented in Table 37.02. The figures for the four experimental groups include all subjects who were approached the first time, regardless of whether or not they agreed to the small request. As noted above, a few subjects were lost because they could not be reached for the second request, and, of course, these are not included in the table.

It is immediately apparent that the first request tended to increase the degree of compliance with the second request. Whereas fewer than 20% of the controls agreed to put the large sign on their lawn, over 55% of the experimental subjects agreed, with over 45% being the lowest degree of compliance for

TABLE 37.02

ISSUE[a]	TASK[a]			
	SIMILAR	*N*	DIFFERENT	*N*
Similar	76.0**	25	47.8*	23
Different	47.6*	21	47.4*	19
	One-Contact 16.7 (*N* = 24)			

PERCENTAGE OF SUBJECTS COMPLYING WITH LARGE REQUEST IN EXPERIMENT II

Note.— *Significance levels represent differences from the One-Contact condition.*
[a]*Denotes relationship between first and second requests.*
*$p < .08$.
**$p < .01$.

any experimental condition. As expected, those conditions in which the two requests were similar in terms of either issue or task produced significantly more compliance than did the controls (χ^2's range from 3.67, $p < .07$ to 15.01, $p < .001$). A somewhat unexpected result is that the fourth condition, in which the first request had relatively little in common with the second request, also produced more compliance than the controls ($\chi^2 = 3.40$, $p < .08$). In other words, regardless of whether or not the two requests are similar in either issue or task, simply having the first request tends to increase the likelihood that the subject will comply with a subsequent, larger request. And this holds even when the two requests are made by different people several weeks apart.

A second point of interest is a comparison among the four experimental conditions. As expected, the Same Issue-Same Task condition produced more compliance than any of the other two-contact conditions, but the difference is not significant (χ^2's range from 2.7 to 2.9). If only those subjects who agreed to the first request are considered, the same pattern holds.

Discussion

To summarize the results, the first study indicated that carrying out a small request increased the likelihood that the subject would agree to a similar larger request made by the same person. The second study showed that this effect was quite strong even when a different person made the larger request, and the two requests were quite dissimilar. How may these results be explained?

Two possibilities were outlined previously. The matter-of-principle idea which centered on the particular type of action was not supported by the data, since the similarity of the tasks did not make an appreciable difference in degree of compliance. The notion of involvement, as described previously, also has difficulty accounting for some of the findings. The basic idea was that once someone has agreed to any action, no matter how small, he tends to feel more involved than he did before. This involvement may center around the particular person making the first request or the particular issue. This is quite consistent with the results of the first study (with the exception of the two control groups which as discussed previously were rather ambiguous) and with the Similar-Issue groups in the second experiment. This idea of involvement does not, however, explain the increase in compliance found in the two groups in which the first and second request did not deal with the same issue.

It is possible that in addition to or instead of this process a more general and diffuse mechanism underlies the increase in compliance. What may occur is a change in the person's feelings about getting involved or about taking action. Once he has agreed to a request, his attitude may change. He may become, in his own eyes, the kind of person who does this sort of thing, who agrees to requests made by strangers, who takes action on things he believes in, who cooperates with good causes. The change in attitude could be toward any aspect of the situation or toward the whole business of saying "yes." The basic idea is that the change in attitude need not be toward any particular issue or person or activity, but may be toward activity or compliance in general. This would imply that an increase in compliance would not depend upon the two contacts being made by the same person, or concerning the same issue or involving the same kind of action. The similarity could be much more general, such as both concerning good causes, or requiring a similar kind of action, or being made by pleasant, attractive individuals.

It is not being suggested that this is the only mechanism operating here. The idea of involvement continues to be extremely plausible, and there are probably a number of other possibilities. Unfortunately, the present studies offer no additional data with which to support or refute any of the possible explanations of the effect. These explanations thus remain simply descriptions of mechanisms which might produce an increase in compliance after agreement with a first request. Hopefully, additional research will test these ideas more fully and perhaps also specify other manipulations which produce an increase in compliance without an increase in external pressure.

It should be pointed out that the present studies employed what is perhaps a very special type of situation. In all cases the requests were made by presumably nonprofit service organizations. The issues in the second study were deliberately noncontroversial, and it may be assumed that virtually all subjects initially sympathized with the objectives of safe driving and a beautiful California. This is in strong contrast to campaigns which are designed to sell a particular product, political candidate, or dogma. Whether the technique employed in this study would be successful in these other situations remains to be shown.

References

1. Asch, S. E. Effects of group pressure upon the modification and distortion of judgments. In H. Guetzkow (Ed.), *Groups, leadership and men; research in human relations.* Pittsburgh: Carnegie Press, 1951. Pp. 177–190.

2. Bandura, A., Ross, D., & Ross, S. A. A comparative test of the status envy, social power, and secondary reinforcement theories of identificatory learning. *Journal of Abnormal and Social Psychology,* 1963, **67,** 527–534.

3. Bruner, J. The dimensions of propaganda: German short-wave broadcasts to America. *Journal of Abnormal and Social Psychology,* 1941, **36,** 311–337.

4. Deutsch, M., & Gerard, H. B. A study of normative and informational social influences upon individual judgment. *Journal of Abnormal and Social Psychology,* 1955, **51,** 629–636.

5. Festinger, L., & Carlsmith, J. Cognitive consequences of forced compliance. *Journal of Abnormal and Social Psychology,* 1959, **58,** 203–210.

6. Hovland, C. I., & Pritzker, H. A. Extent of opinion change as a function of amount of change advocated. *Journal of Abnormal and Social Psychology,* 1957, **54,** 257–261.

7. Kelman, H. C., & Hovland, C. I. "Reinstatement" of the communicator in delayed measurement of opinion change. *Journal of Abnormal and Social Psychology,* 1953, **48,** 327–335.

8. Schein, E. H., Schneier, I., & Barker, C. H. *Coercive pressure.* New York: Norton, 1961.

QUESTIONS FOR REFLECTION AND DISCUSSION:

1. How did the researchers define and measure compliance? Does their operational definition of compliance fit with situations such as giving to charity or giving of one's time to help out in school?

2. The researchers say that the compliance they found does not appear to be explained by the "matter-of-principle" idea or the notion of "involvement." What evidence do they offer for their views?

3. How do the researchers use the concept of change in attitude to explain the "foot-in-the-door" technique?

4. Have people ever gotten their "foot in the door" with you? How so?

5. Can you apply the foot-in-the-door concept of compliance to everyday events such as why some individuals become the ones who always change the bedsheets or do the cooking and the cleaning?

6. According to cognitive-dissonance theory, as outlined by Leon Festinger, awareness that two cognitions are dissonant, or that our attitudes are incompatible with our behavior, is unpleasant and motivates us to reduce the discrepancy. Can you explain the results of the Freedman and Fraser study by means of cognitive-dissonance theory? In your explanation, try to use the concept of "attitude-discrepant behavior."

SOURCE

Asch, S. E. (1955). Opinions and social pressure. *Scientific American, 193,* 31–35. Estate of Sara Love.

Social psychology studies the nature and causes of behavior and mental processes in social situations. Social psychologists have noted that people and lower animals often behave differently when they are by themselves or in the presence of others.

When people alter the thoughts, feelings, and behavior of other people, they are said to exert social influence. Two of the key topics in the psychology of social influence are obedience and conformity. *We are said to conform when we change our behavior in order to adhere to social norms. For example, we tend to conform to social norms by facing front in elevators and whispering in libraries.*

Conformity is often a good thing because many social norms promote comfort and survival. But conformity to social norms can also promote maladaptive or dangerous behavior, as when teenagers engage in risky behavior because of the belief that "everyone's doing it."

The following experiment reported by Solomon Asch is a classic in the literature of social psychology. It is about conformity—about nearly blind conformity. Its results were astounding in their day, nearly half a century ago. You might still find them surprising and believe that you would never fall prey to social influence in the same way as subjects in the study did. But can you be so sure? Do you dress like other members of your group? Do you listen to the same music and speak the same slang? Are you absolutely sure that you would resist the tendency to conform?

Opinions and Social Pressure

SOLOMON E. ASCH

Exactly what is the effect of the opinions of others on our own? In other words, how strong is the urge toward social conformity? The question is approached by means of some unusual experiments.

That social influences shape every person's practices, judgments and beliefs is a truism to which anyone will readily assent. A child masters his "native" dialect down to the finest nuances; a member of a tribe of cannibals accepts cannibalism as altogether fitting and proper. All the social sciences take their departure from the observation of the profound effects that groups exert on their members. For psychologists, group pressure upon the minds of individuals raises a host of questions they would like to investigate in detail.

How, and to what extent, do social forces constrain people's opinions and attitudes? This question is especially pertinent in our day. The same epoch that has witnessed the unprecedented technical extension of communication has also brought into existence the deliberate manipulation of opinion and the "engineering of consent." There are many good reasons why, as citizens and as scientists, we should be concerned with studying the ways in which human beings form their opinions and the role that social conditions play.

Studies of these questions began with the interest in hypnosis aroused by the French physician Jean Martin Charcot (a teacher of Sigmund Freud) toward the end of the 19th century. Charcot believed that only hysterical patients could be fully hypnotized, but this view was soon challenged by two other physicians, Hyppolyte Bernheim and A. A. Liébault, who demonstrated that they could put most people under the hypnotic spell. Bernheim proposed that hypnosis was but an extreme form of a normal psychological process which became known as "suggestibility." It was shown that monotonous reiteration of instructions could induce in normal persons in the waking state involuntary bodily changes such as swaying or rigidity of the arms, and sensations such as warmth and odor.

It was not long before social thinkers seized upon these discoveries as a basis for explaining numerous social phenomena, from the spread of opinion to the formation of crowds and the following of leaders. The sociologist Gabriel Tarde summed it all up in the aphorism: "Social man is a somnambulist."

When the new discipline of social psychology was born at the beginning of this century, its first experiments were essentially adaptations of the suggestion demonstration. The technique generally followed a simple plan. The subjects, usually college students, were asked to give their opinions or preferences concerning various matters; some time later they were again asked to state their choices, but now they were also informed of the opinions held by authorities or large groups of their peers on the same matters. (Often the alleged consensus was fictitious.) Most of these studies had substantially the same result: confronted with opinions contrary to their own, many subjects apparently shifted their

FIGURE 38.01

Experiment is repeated in the Laboratory of Social Relations at Harvard University. Seven student subjects are asked by the experimenter (*right*) to compare the length of lines (*see Fig. 38.02*). Six of the subjects have been coached beforehand to give unanimously wrong answers. The seventh (*second from the right*) has merely been told that it is an experiment in perception.

judgments in the direction of the views of the majorities or the experts. The late psychologist Edward L. Thorndike reported that he had succeeded in modifying the esthetic preferences of adults by this procedure. Other psychologists reported that people's evaluations of the merit of a literary passage could be raised or lowered by ascribing the passage to different authors. Apparently the sheer weight of numbers or authority sufficed to change opinions, even when no arguments for the opinions themselves were provided.

Now the very ease of success in these experiments arouses suspicion. Did the subjects actually change their opinions, or were the experimental victories scored only on paper? On grounds of common sense, one must question whether opinions are generally as watery as these studies indicate. There is some reason to wonder whether it was not the investigators who, in their enthusiasm for a theory, were suggestible, and whether the ostensibly gullible subjects were not providing answers which they thought good subjects were expected to give.

The investigations were guided by certain underlying assumptions, which today are common currency and account for much that is thought and said about the operations of propaganda and public opinion. The assumptions are that people submit uncritically and painlessly to external manipulation by suggestion or prestige, and that any given idea or value can be "sold" or "unsold" without reference to its merits. We should be skeptical, however, of the supposition that the power of social pressure necessarily implies uncritical submission to it: independence and the capacity to rise above group passion are also open to human beings. Further, one may question on psychological grounds whether it is possible as a rule to change a person's judgment of a situation or an object without first changing his knowledge or assumptions about it.

In what follows I shall describe some experiments in an investigation of the effects of group pressure which was carried out recently with the help of a number of my associates. The tests not only demonstrate the operations of group pressure upon individuals but also illustrate a new kind of attack on the problem and some of the more subtle questions that it raises.

A group of seven to nine young men, all college students, are assembled in a classroom for a "psychological experiment" in visual judgment. The experimenter informs them that they will be comparing the lengths of lines. He shows two large white cards. On one is a single vertical black line—the standard whose length is to be matched. On the other card are three vertical lines of various lengths.

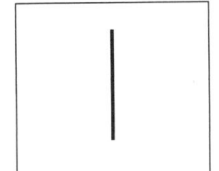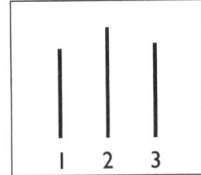

FIGURE 38.02

Subjects were shown two cards. One bore a standard line. The other bore three lines, one of which was the same length as the standard. The subjects were asked to choose this line.

The subjects are to choose the one that is of the same length as the line on the other card. One of the three actually is of the same length; the other two are substantially different, the difference ranging from three quarters of an inch to an inch and three quarters.

The experiment opens uneventfully. The subjects announce their answers in the order in which they have been seated in the room, and on the first round every person chooses the same matching line. Then a second set of cards is exposed, again the group is unanimous. The members appear ready to endure politely another boring experiment. On the third trial there is an unexpected disturbance. One person near the end of the group disagrees with all the others in his selection of the matching line. He looks surprised, indeed incredulous, about the disagreement. On the following trial he disagrees again, while the others remain unanimous in their choice. The dissenter becomes more and more worried and hesitant as the disagreement continues in succeeding trials; he may pause before announcing his answer and speak in a low voice, or he may smile in an embarrassed way.

What the dissenter does not know is that all the other members of the group were instructed by the experimenter beforehand to give incorrect answers in unanimity at certain points. The single individual who is not a party to this prearrangement is the focal subject of our experiment. He is placed in a position in which, while he is actually giving the correct answers, he finds himself unexpectedly in a minority of one, opposed by a unanimous and arbitrary majority with respect to a clear and simple fact. Upon him we have brought to bear two opposed forces: the evidence of his senses and the unanimous opinion of a group of his peers. Also, he must declare his judgments in public, before a majority which has also stated its position publicly.

The instructed majority occasionally reports correctly in order to reduce the possibility that the naive subject will suspect collusion against him. (In only a few cases did the subject actually show suspicion; when this happened, the experiment was stopped and the results were not counted.) There are 18 trials in each series, and on 12 of these the majority responds erroneously.

How do people respond to group pressure in this situation? I shall report first the statistical results of a series in which a total of 123 subjects from three institutions of higher learning (not including my own, Swarthmore College) were placed in the minority situation described above.

Two alternatives were open to the subject: he could act independently, repudiating the majority, or he could go along with the majority, repudiating the evidence of his senses. Of the 123 put to the test, a considerable percentage yielded to the majority. Whereas in ordinary circumstances individuals matching the lines will make mistakes less than 1 per cent of the time, under group pressure the minority subjects swung to acceptance of the misleading majority's wrong judgments in 36.8 per cent of the selections.

Of course individuals differed in response. At one extreme, about one quarter of the subjects were completely independent and never agreed with the erroneous judgments of the majority. At the other extreme, some individuals went with the majority nearly all the time. The performances of individuals in this experiment tend to be highly consistent. Those who strike out on the path of independence do not, as a rule, succumb to the majority even over an extended series of trials, while those who choose the path of compliance are unable to free themselves as the ordeal is prolonged.

The reasons for the startling individual differences have not yet been investigated in detail. At this point we can only report some tentative generalizations from talks with the subjects, each of whom was interviewed at the end of the experiment. Among the independent individuals were many who held fast because of staunch confidence in their own judgment. The most significant fact about them was not absence of responsiveness to the majority but a capacity to recover from doubt and to reestablish their equilibrium. Others who acted independently came to believe that the majority was correct in its answers, but they continued their dissent on the simple ground that it was their obligation to call the play as they saw it.

Among the extremely yielding persons we found a group who quickly reached the conclusion: "I am wrong, they are right." Others yielded in order "not to spoil your results." Many of the individuals who went along suspected that the majority were "sheep" following the first responder, or that the majority were victims of an optical illusion; never-

theless, these suspicions failed to free them at the moment of decision. More disquieting were the reactions of subjects who construed their difference from the majority as a sign of some general deficiency in themselves, which at all costs they must hide. On this basis they desperately tried to merge with the majority, not realizing the longer-range consequences to themselves. All the yielding subjects underestimated the frequency with which they conformed.

Which aspect of the influence of a majority is more important—the size of the majority or its unanimity? The experiment was modified to examine this question. In one series the size of the opposition was varied from one to 15 persons. The results showed a clear trend. When a subject was confronted with only a single individual who contradicted his answers, he was swayed little: he continued to answer independently and correctly in nearly all trials. When the opposition was increased to two, the pressure became substantial: minority subjects now accepted the wrong answer 13.6 per cent of the time. Under the pressure of a majority of three, the subjects' errors jumped to 31.8 per cent. But further increases in the size of the majority apparently did not increase the weight of the pressure substantially. Clearly the size of the opposition is important only up to a point.

Disturbance of the majority's unanimity had a striking effect. In this experiment the subject was given the support of a truthful partner—either another individual who did not know of the prearranged agreement among the rest of the group, or a person who was instructed to give correct answers throughout.

The presence of a supporting partner depleted the majority of much of its power. Its pressure on the dissenting individual was reduced to one fourth: that is, subjects answered incorrectly only one fourth as often as under the pressure of a unanimous majority [*see Fig. 38.05*]. The weakest persons did not yield as readily. Most interesting were the reactions to the partner. Generally the feeling toward him was one of warmth and closeness; he was credited with inspiring confidence. However, the subjects repudiated the suggestion that the partner decided them to be independent.

Was the partner's effect a consequence of his dissent, or was it related to his accuracy? We now introduced into the experimental group a person who was instructed to dissent from the majority but also to disagree with the subject. In some experiments the majority was always to choose the worst of the comparison lines and the instructed dissenter to pick the line that was closer to the length of the standard

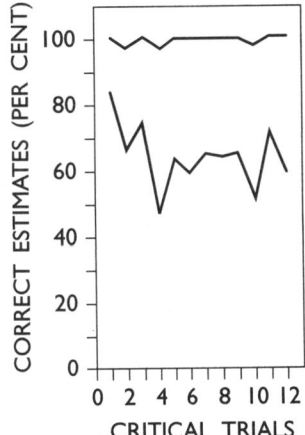

FIGURE 38.03

Error of 123 subjects, each of whom compared lines in the presence of six to eight opponents, is plotted in the colored curve. The accuracy of judgments not under pressure is indicated in black.

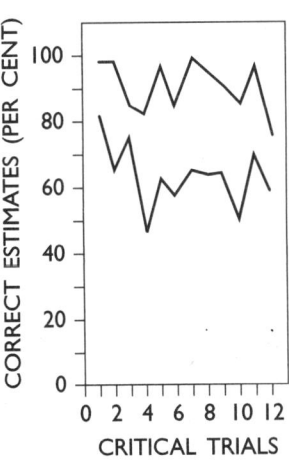

FIGURE 38.05

Two subjects supporting each other against a majority made fewer errors (*colored curve*) than one subject did against a majority (*black curve*).

one; in others the majority was consistently intermediate and the dissenter most in error. In this manner we were able to study the relative influence of "compromising" and "extremist" dissenters.

Again the results are clear. When a moderate dissenter is present, the effect of the majority on the subject decreases by approximately one third, and extremes of yielding disappear. Moreover, most of the errors the subjects do make are moderate, rather than flagrant. In short, the dissenter largely controls

the choice of errors. To this extent the subjects broke away from the majority even while bending to it.

On the other hand, when the dissenter always chose the line that was more flagrantly different from the standard, the results were of quite a different kind. The extremist dissenter produced a remarkable freeing of the subjects; their errors dropped to only 9 per cent. Furthermore, all the errors were of the moderate variety. We were able to conclude that dissent *per se* increased independence and moderated the errors that occurred, and that the direction of dissent exerted consistent effects.

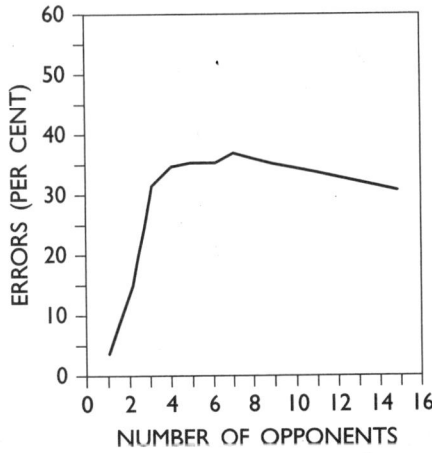

FIGURE 38.04

Size of majority which opposed them had an effect on the subjects. With a single opponent the subject erred only 3.6 per cent of the time; with two opponents he erred 13.6 per cent; three, 31.8 per cent; four, 35.1 per cent; six, 35.2 per cent; seven, 37.1 per cent; nine, 35.1 per cent; 15, 31.2 per cent.

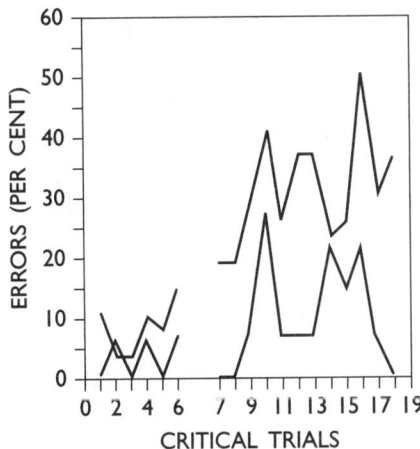

FIGURE 38.06

Partner left subject after six trials in a single experiment. The colored curve shows the error of the subject when the partner "deserted" to the majority. Black curve shows error when partner merely left the room.

In all the foregoing experiments each subject was observed only in a single setting. We now turned to studying the effects upon a given individual of a change in the situation to which he was exposed. The first experiment examined the consequences of losing or gaining a partner. The instructed partner began by answering correctly on the first six trials. With his support the subject usually resisted pressure from the majority: 18 of 27 subjects were completely independent. But after six trials the partner joined the majority. As soon as he did so, there was an abrupt rise in the subjects' errors. Their submission to the majority was just about as frequent as when the minority subject was opposed by a unanimous majority throughout.

It was surprising to find that the experience of having had a partner and of having braved the majority opposition with him had failed to strengthen the individuals' independence. Questioning at the conclusion of the experiment suggested that we had overlooked an important circumstance; namely, the strong specific effect of "desertion" by the partner to the other side. We therefore changed the conditions so that the partner would simply leave the group at the proper point. (To allay suspicion it was announced in advance that he had an appointment with the dean.) In this form of the experiment, the partner's effect outlasted his presence. The errors increased after his departure, but less markedly than after a partner switched to the majority.

In a variant of this procedure the trials began with the majority unanimously giving correct answers. Then they gradually broke away until on the sixth trial the naive subject was alone and the group unanimously against him. As long as the subject had anyone on his side, he was almost invariably independent, but as soon as he found himself alone, the tendency to conform to the majority rose abruptly.

As might be expected, an individual's resistance to group pressure in these experiments depends to a considerable degree on how wrong the majority is. We varied the discrepancy between the standard line and the other lines systematically, with the hope of reaching a point where the error of the majority would be so glaring that every subject would repudiate it and choose independently. In this we regretfully did not succeed. Even when the difference between the lines was seven inches, there were still some who yielded to the error of the majority.

The study provides clear answers to a few relatively simple questions, and it raises many others that await investigation. We would like to know the degree of consistency of persons in situations which differ in content and structure. If consistency of independence or conformity in behavior is shown to be a fact, how is it functionally related to qualities of character and personality? In what ways is independence related to sociological or cultural conditions? Are leaders more independent than other people, or are they adept at following their followers? These and many other questions may perhaps be answerable by investigations of the type described here.

Life in society requires consensus as an indispensable condition. But consensus, to be productive, requires that each individual contribute independently out of his experience and insight. When consensus comes under the dominance of conformity, the social process is polluted and the individual at the same time surrenders the powers on which his functioning as a feeling and thinking being depends. That we have found the tendency to conformity in our society so strong that reasonably intelligent and well-meaning young people are willing to call white black is a matter of concern. It raises questions about our ways of education and about the values that guide our conduct.

Yet anyone inclined to draw too pessimistic conclusions from this report would do well to remind himself that the capacities for independence are not to be underestimated. He may also draw some consolation from a further observation: those who participated in this challenging experiment agreed nearly without exception that independence was preferable to conformity.

QUESTIONS FOR REFLECTION AND DISCUSSION:

1. Asch's research made the subjects uncomfortable. Do you believe that it was ethical? Why or why not?

2. Asch interviewed subjects in the study. What reasons did they give for either going along with the crowd and reporting the wrong lines, or for sticking to their own judgment and reporting what they saw?

Harcourt, Inc.

3. How do you believe that you would have behaved if you had been a subject in Asch's study? Why?

4. Can you tell where the influences of other people leave off and your "real self" begins? Why or why not?

5. Do you believe that people are aware of the areas of their lives in which they conform? Why or why not? Can you provide examples to support your view?

6. Outline areas in your life in which you conform to social norms. Can you find some instances in which conformity is helpful and good? Can you find others in which conformity may potentially be harmful?

7. Why is Asch's research considered so important in the history of psychology? Is it as important today? Why or why not?

SOURCE

Milgram, S. (1963). Behavioral study
of obedience. *Journal of Abnormal
and Social Psychology, 67,*
371–378. Permission granted by
Alexandra Milgram.

Throughout history soldiers have followed orders—even when the orders have been to slaughter innocent civilians. Examples include the Turkish slaughter of Armenians, the Nazi slaughter of Jews, the Serbian slaughters of Bosnian and Kosovar Muslims, and the mutual slaughter of Hutus and Tutsis in Rwanda. We may say that we are horrified by these crimes and cannot imagine why people would engage in them. But how many of us would refuse to follow orders issued by authority figures?

The study of obedience is an important topic in the psychology of social influence. Social influence is the area of social psychology that studies the ways in which people alter the thoughts, feelings, and behavior of other people. There are circumstances under which obedience is useful and helpful, as in obeying sirens so that ambulances may pass your car in an emergency, or as in children obeying the reasonable demands of their parents. But human experience and psychological research suggests that there is a dark side to obedience—the tendency of many, perhaps most, people to obey authority figures, even when the authority figures make immoral demands.

Stanley Milgram's classic research into obedience was in large part inspired by the World War II crimes of the Nazis and those who obeyed them. As you will see in the opening paragraph of his article, his experiment was part of a body of research that was conducted to try to answer the question, Who were the people who assisted in the construction and operation of the Nazi gas chambers that accounted for the deaths of millions of innocents? Who were these people who placed obedience ahead of life and humanity? Is their psychology different from yours or mine? Is their psychology foreign to you and me? Or could these people be you and me?

Behavioral Study of Obedience

STANLEY MILGRAM
YALE UNIVERSITY

This article describes a procedure for the study of destructive obedience in the laboratory. It consists of ordering a naive S to administer increasingly more severe punishment to a victim in the context of a learning experiment. Punishment is administered by means of a shock generator with 30 graded switches ranging from Slight Shock to Danger: Severe Shock. The victim is a confederate of the E. The primary dependent variable is the maximum shock the S is willing to administer before he refuses to continue further. 26 Ss obeyed the experimental commands fully, and administered the highest shock on the

Harcourt, Inc.

generator. 14 Ss broke off the experiment at some point after the victim protested and refused to provide further answers. The procedure created extreme levels of nervous tension in some Ss. Profuse sweating, trembling, and stuttering were typical expressions of this emotional disturbance. One unexpected sign of tension—yet to be explained—was the regular occurrence of nervous laughter, which in some Ss developed into uncontrollable seizures. The variety of interesting behavioral dynamics observed in the experiment, the reality of the situation for the S, and the possibility of parametric variation within the framework of the procedure, point to the fruitfulness of further study.

Obedience is as basic an element in the structure of social life as one can point to. Some system of authority is a requirement of all communal living, and it is only the man dwelling in isolation who is not forced to respond, through defiance or submission, to the commands of others. Obedience, as a determinant of behavior, is of particular relevance to our time. It has been reliably established that from 1933–45 millions of innocent persons were systematically slaughtered on command. Gas chambers were built, death camps were guarded; daily quotas of corpses were produced with the same efficiency as the manufacture of appliances. These inhumane policies may have originated in the mind of a single person, but they could only be carried out on a massive scale if a very large number of persons obeyed orders.

Obedience is the psychological mechanism that links individual action to political purpose. It is the dispositional cement that binds men to systems of authority. Facts of recent history and observation in daily life suggest that for many persons obedience may be a deeply ingrained behavior tendency, indeed a prepotent impulse overriding training in ethics, sympathy, and moral conduct. C. P. Snow (1961) points to its importance when he writes:

> When you think of the long and gloomy history of man, you will find more hideous crimes have been committed in the name of obedience than have ever been committed in the name of rebellion. If you doubt that, read William Shirer's "Rise and Fall of the Third Reich." The German Officer Corps were brought up in the most rigorous code of obedience . . . in the name of obedience they were party to, and assisted in, the most wicked large scale actions in the history of the world [p. 24].

While the particular form of obedience dealt with in the present study has its antecedents in these episodes, it must not be thought all obedience entails acts of aggression against others. Obedience serves numerous productive functions. Indeed, the very life of society is predicated on its existence. Obedience may be ennobling and educative and refer to acts of charity and kindness as well as to destruction.

General Procedure

A procedure was devised which seems useful as a tool for studying obedience (Milgram, 1961). It consists of ordering a naive subject to administer electric shock to a victim. A simulated shock generator is used, with 30 clearly marked voltage levels that range from 15 to 450 volts. The instrument bears verbal designations that range from Slight Shock to Danger: Severe Shock. The responses of the victim, who is a trained confederate of the experimenter, are standardized. The orders to administer shocks are given to the naive subject in the context of a "learning experiment" ostensibly set up to study the effects of punishment on memory. As the experiment proceeds the naive subject is commanded to administer increasingly more intense shocks to the victim, even to the point of reaching the level marked Danger: Severe Shock. Internal resistances become stronger, and at a certain point the subject refuses to go on with the experiment. Behavior prior to this rupture is considered "obedience," in that the subject complies with the commands of the experimenter. The point of rupture is the act of disobedience. A quantitative value is assigned to the subject's performance based on the maximum intensity shock he is willing to administer before he refuses to participate further. Thus for any particular subject and for any particular experimental condition the degree of obedience may be specified with a numerical value. The crux of the study is to systematically vary the factors believed to alter the degree of obedience to the experimental commands.

The technique allows important variables to be manipulated at several points in the experiment. One may vary aspects of the source of command, content and form of command, instrumentalities for its execution, target object, general social setting, etc. The problem, therefore, is not one of designing increasingly more numerous experimental conditions, but of selecting those that best illuminate the *process* of obedience from the sociopsychological standpoint.

TABLE 39.01

	20–29 YEARS *n*	30–39 YEARS *n*	40–50 YEARS *n*	PERCENTAGE OF TOTAL (OCCUPATIONS)
DISTRIBUTION OF AGE AND OCCUPATIONAL TYPES IN THE EXPERIMENT				
OCCUPATIONS				
Workers, skilled and unskilled	4	5	6	37.5
Sales, business, and white-collar	3	6	7	40.0
Professional	1	5	3	22.5
Percentage of total (Age)	20	40	40	

Note.— *Total* N = 40.

Related Studies

The inquiry bears an important relation to philosophic analyses of obedience and authority (Arendt, 1958; Friedrich, 1958; Weber, 1947), an early experimental study of obedience by Frank (1944), studies in "authoritarianism" (Adorno, Frenkel-Brunswik, Levinson, & Sanford, 1950; Rokeach, 1961), and a recent series of analytic and empirical studies in social power (Cartwright, 1959). It owes much to the long concern with *suggestion* in social psychology, both in its normal forms (e.g., Binet, 1900) and in its clinical manifestations (Charcot, 1881). But it derives, in the first instance, from direct observation of a social fact; the individual who is commanded by a legitimate authority ordinarily obeys. Obedience comes easily and often. It is a ubiquitous and indispensable feature of social life.

Method

SUBJECTS

The subjects were 40 males between the ages of 20 and 50, drawn from New Haven and the surrounding communities. Subjects were obtained by a newspaper advertisement and direct mail solicitation. Those who responded to the appeal believed they were to participate in a study of memory and learning at Yale University. A wide range of occupations is represented in the sample. Typical subjects were postal clerks, high school teachers, salesmen, engineers, and laborers. Subjects ranged in educational level from one who had not finished elementary school, to those who had doctorate and other professional degrees. They were paid $4.50 for their participation in the experiment. However, subjects were told that payment was simply for coming to the laboratory, and that the money was theirs no matter what happened after they arrived. Table 39.01 shows the proportion of age and occupational types assigned to the experimental condition.

PERSONNEL AND LOCALE

The experiment was conducted on the grounds of Yale University in the elegant interaction laboratory. (This detail is relevant to the perceived legitimacy of the experiment. In further variations, the experiment was dissociated from the university, with consequences for performance.) The role of experimenter was played by a 31-year-old high school teacher of biology. His manner was impassive, and his appearance somewhat stern throughout the experiment. He was dressed in a gray technician's coat. The victim was played by a 47-year-old accountant, trained for the role; he was of Irish-American stock, whom most observers found mild-mannered and likable.

PROCEDURE

One naive subject and one victim (an accomplice) performed in each experiment. A pretext had to be devised that would justify the administration of electric shock by the naive subject. This was effectively accomplished by the cover story. After a general introduction on the presumed relation between punishment and learning, subjects were told:

> But actually, we know *very little* about the effect of punishment on learning, because almost no truly scientific studies have been made of it in human beings.

For instance, we don't know how *much* punishment is best for learning—and we don't know how much difference it makes as to who is giving the punishment, whether an adult learns best from a younger or an older person than himself—or many things of that sort.

So in this study we are bringing together a number of adults of different occupations and ages. And we're asking some of them to be teachers and some of them to be learners.

We want to find out just what effect different people have on each other as teachers and learners, and also what effect *punishment* will have on learning in this situation.

Therefore, I'm going to ask one of you to be the teacher here tonight and the other one to be the learner.

Does either of you have a preference?

Subjects then drew slips of paper from a hat to determine who would be the teacher and who would be the learner in the experiment. The drawing was rigged so that the naive subject was always the teacher and the accomplice always the learner. (Both slips contained the word "Teacher.") Immediately after the drawing, the teacher and learner were taken to an adjacent room and the learner was strapped into an "electric chair" apparatus.

The experimenter explained that the straps were to prevent excessive movement while the learner was being shocked. The effect was to make it impossible for him to escape from the situation. An electrode was attached to the learner's wrist, and electrode paste was applied "to avoid blisters and burns." Subjects were told that the electrode was attached to the shock generator in the adjoining room.

In order to improve credibility the experimenter declared, in response to a question by the learner: "Although the shocks can be extremely painful, they cause no permanent tissue damage."

Learning Task The lesson administered by the subject was a paired-associate learning task. The subject read a series of word pairs to the learner, and then read the first word of the pair along with four terms. The learner was to indicate which of the four terms had originally been paired with the first word. He communicated his answer by pressing one of four switches in front of him, which in turn lit up one of four numbered quadrants in an answer-box located atop the shock generator.

Shock Generator The instrument panel consists of 30 lever switches set in a horizontal line.

Each switch is clearly labeled with a voltage designation that ranges from 15 to 450 volts. There is a 15-volt increment from one switch to the next going from left to right. In addition, the following verbal designations are clearly indicated for groups of four switches going from left to right: Slight Shock, Moderate Shock, Strong Shock, Very Strong Shock, Intense Shock, Extreme Intensity Shock, Danger: Severe Shock. (Two switches after this last designation are simply marked XXX.)

Upon depressing a switch: a pilot light corresponding to each switch is illuminated in bright red; an electric buzzing is heard; an electric blue light, labeled "voltage energizer," flashes; the dial on the voltage meter swings to the right; various relay clicks are sounded.

The upper left-hand corner of the generator is labeled Shock Generator, Type ZLB, Dyson Instrument Company, Waltham, Mass. Output 15 Volts–450 Volts.

Details of the instrument were carefully handled to insure an appearance of authenticity. The panel was engraved by precision industrial engravers, and all components were of high quality. No subject in the experiment suspected that the instrument was merely a simulated shock generator.[1]

Sample Shock Each naive subject is given a sample shock on the shock generator, prior to beginning his run as teacher. This shock is always 45 volts, and is applied by pressing the third switch of the generator. The shock is applied to the wrist of the naive subject, and has its source in a 45-volt battery wired into the generator. This further convinces the subject of the authenticity of the generator.

Shock Instructions The subject is told to administer a shock to the learner each time he gives a

---

[1] A related technique, making use of a shock generator, was reported by Buss (1961) for the study of aggression in the laboratory. Despite the considerable similarity of technical detail in the experimental procedures, both investigators proceeded in ignorance of the other's work. Milgram provided plans and photographs of his shock generator, experimental procedure, and first results in a report to the National Science Foundation in January 1961. This report received only limited circulation. Buss reported his procedure 6 months later, but to a wider audience. Subsequently, technical information and reports were exchanged. The present article was first received in the Editor's office on December 27, 1961; it was resubmitted with deletions on July 27, 1962.

wrong response. Moreover—and this is the key command—the subject is instructed to "move one level higher on the shock generator each time the learner flashes a wrong answer." He is also instructed to announce the voltage level before administering a shock. This serves to continually remind subjects of the increasing intensity of shocks administered to the learner.

Preliminary and Regular Run

Pretests revealed that the procedure of reading words and administering shocks requires some practice before it can be handled smoothly. Therefore, immediately preceding the regular run, the teacher is given a preliminary series of 10 words to read to the learner. There are 3 neutral words in the practice series (i.e., words that the learner answers correctly), so that shocks are administered for 7 of the words, with the maximum shock at 105 volts (moderate shock). Almost all subjects master the procedure by the time the preliminary run is over.

Subjects are then presented with a second list, and are told that the procedure is the same as for the first list; the experimenter adds, however:

> When you get to the bottom of the list, repeat it over again, and continue giving shocks, until the learner has learned all the pairs correctly.

The experimenter instructs the subject to,

> start from 15 volts and increase the shock level one step each time the learner gives a wrong answer.

Feedback from the Victim

In all conditions the learner gives a predetermined set of responses to the word pair test, based on a schedule of approximately three wrong answers to one correct answer. In the present experimental condition no vocal response or other sign of protest is heard from the learner until Shock Level 300 is reached. When the 300-volt shock is administered, the learner pounds on the wall of the room in which he is bound to the electric chair. The pounding can be heard by the subject. From this point on, the learner's answers no longer appear on the four-way panel.

At this juncture, subjects ordinarily turn to the experimenter for guidance. The experimenter instructs the subject to treat the absence of a response as a wrong answer, and to shock the subject according to the usual schedule. He advises the subjects to allow 5–10 seconds before considering no response as a wrong answer, and to increase the shock level

one step each time the learner fails to respond correctly. The learner's pounding is repeated after the 315-volt shock is administered; afterwards he is not heard from, nor do his answers reappear on the four-way signal box.

Experimenter Feedback

At various points in the experiment the subject may turn to the experimenter for advice on whether he should continue to administer shocks. Or he may indicate that he does not wish to go on. It was important to standardize the experimenter's responses to these inquiries and reactions.

If the subject indicated his unwillingness to go on, the experimenter responded with a sequence of "prods," using as many as necessary to bring the subject into line.

> Prod 1: Please continue. *or* Please go on.
>
> Prod 2: The experiment requires that you continue.
>
> Prod 3: It is absolutely essential that you continue.
>
> Prod 4: You have no other choice, you *must* go on.

The prods were always made in sequence: Only if Prod 1 had been unsuccessful, could Prod 2 be used. If the subject refused to obey the experimenter after Prod 4, the experiment was terminated. The experimenter's tone of voice was at all times firm, but not impolite. The sequence was begun anew on each occasion that the subject balked or showed reluctance to follow orders.

Special prods. If the subject asked if the learner was liable to suffer permanent physical injury, the experimenter said:

> Although the shocks may be painful, there is no permanent tissue damage, so please go on. [Followed by Prods 2, 3, and 4 if necessary.]

If the subject said that the learner did not want to go on, the experimenter replied:

> Whether the learner likes it or not, you must go on until he has learned all the word pairs correctly. So please go on. [Followed by Prods 2, 3, and 4 if necessary.]

DEPENDENT MEASURES

The primary dependent measure for any subject is the maximum shock he administers before he refuses to go any further. In principle this may vary from 0 (for a subject who refuses to administer even the first shock) to 30 (for a subject who administers the highest shock on the generator). A subject who breaks off the experiment at any point prior to administering the thirtieth shock level is termed a *defiant* subject. One who complies with experimental commands fully, and proceeds to administer all shock levels commanded, is termed an *obedient* subject.

Further Records With few exceptions, experimental sessions were recorded on magnetic tape. Occasional photographs were taken through one-way mirrors. Notes were kept on any unusual behavior occurring during the course of the experiments. On occasion, additional observers were directed to write objective descriptions of the subjects' behavior. The latency and duration of shocks were measured by accurate timing devices.

Interview and Dehoax Following the experiment, subjects were interviewed; open-ended questions, projective measures, and attitude scales were employed. After the interview, procedures were undertaken to assure that the subject would leave the laboratory in a state of well being. A friendly reconciliation was arranged between the subject and the victim, and an effort was made to reduce any tensions that arose as a result of the experiment.

Results

PRELIMINARY NOTIONS

Before giving an account of the experimental results, it is instructive to consider how persons predict others will perform when commanded to administer powerful shocks to another person. Fourteen Yale seniors, all psychology majors, were provided with a detailed description of the experimental situation. They were asked to reflect carefully on it, and to predict the behavior of 100 hypothetical subjects. More specifically, they were instructed to plot the distribution of obedience of "100 Americans of diverse occupations, and ranging in age from 20 to 50 years," who were placed in the experimental situation.

There was considerable agreement among the respondents on the expected behavior of hypothetical subjects. All respondents predicted that only an insignificant minority would go through to the end of the shock series. (The estimates ranged from 0 to 3%; i.e., the most "pessimistic" member of the class

predicted that of 100 persons, 3 would continue through to the most potent shock available on the shock generator—450 volts.) The class mean was 1.2%. The question was also posed informally to colleagues of the author, and the most general feeling was that few if any subjects would go beyond the designation Very Strong Shock.

RESULT OF EXPERIMENT I

Subjects Accept Situation With few exceptions subjects were convinced of the reality of the experimental situation, that they were administering shocks to another person, and the most potent shocks were extremely painful. In the post-experimental interview subjects were asked: "How painful to the learner were the last few shocks that you administered to him?" Subjects were instructed to indicate their answers on a printed 14-point scale ranging from "Not at all painful" to "Extremely painful." The modal response was 14 (Extremely painful) with the mean at 13.42.

Signs of Extreme Tension Many subjects showed signs of nervousness in the experimental situation, and especially upon administering the more powerful shocks. In a large number of cases the degree of tension reached extremes that are rarely seen in sociopsychological laboratory studies. Subjects were observed to sweat, tremble, stutter, bite their lips, groan, and dig their fingernails into their flesh. These were characteristic rather than exceptional responses to the experiment.

One sign of tension was the regular occurrence of nervous laughing fits. Fourteen of the 40 subjects showed definite signs of nervous laughter and smiling. The laughter seemed entirely out of place, even bizarre. Full-blown, uncontrollable seizures were observed for 3 subjects. On one occasion we observed a seizure so violently convulsive that it was necessary to call a halt to the experiment. The subject, a 46-year-old encyclopedia salesman, was seriously embarrassed by his untoward and uncontrollable behavior. In the post-experimental interviews subjects took pains to point out that they were not sadistic types, and that the laughter did not mean they enjoyed shocking the victim.

Distribution of Scores It had been conjectured that persons would not, in general, agree to administer shocks beyond the level designated as Very Strong Shock. The distribution of maximum shocks for this experiment is shown in Table 39.02.

TABLE 39.02

DISTRIBUTION OF BREAKOFF POINTS	
VERBAL DESIGNATION AND VOLTAGE INDICATION	**NUMBER OF SUBJECTS FOR WHOM THIS WAS MAXIMUM SHOCK**
Slight Shock	
15	0
30	0
45	0
60	0
Moderate Shock	
75	0
90	0
105	0
120	0
Strong Shock	
135	0
150	0
165	0
180	0
Very Strong Shock	
195	0
210	0
225	0
240	0
Intense Shock	
255	0
270	0
285	0
300	5
Extreme Intensity Shock	
315	4
330	2
345	1
360	1
Danger: Severe Shock	
375	1
390	0
405	0
420	0
XXX	
435	0
450	26

off point. No subject stopped prior to administering Shock Level 20. (At this level—300 volts—the victim kicks on the wall and no longer provides answers to the teacher's multiple-choice questions.)

Of the 40 subjects, 5 refused to obey the experimental commands beyond the 300-volt level. Four more subjects administered one further shock, and then refused to go on. Two broke off at the 330-volt level, and 1 each at 345, 360, and 375 volts. Thus a total of 14 subjects defied the experimenter. It is instructive to reprint their remarks at the point of defiance, as transcribed from the tape recordings:

[0124] I think he's trying to communicate, he's knocking. . . . Well it's not fair to shock the guy . . . these are terrific volts. I don't think this is very humane. . . . Oh, I can't go on with this; no, this isn't right. It's a hell of an experiment. The guy is suffering in there. No, I don't want to go on. This is crazy. [Subject refused to administer more shocks.]

[0123] He's banging in there. I'm gonna chicken out. I'd like to continue, but I can't do that to a man. . . . I'm sorry I can't do that to a man. I'll hurt his heart. You take your check. . . . No really, I couldn't do it.

These subjects were frequently in a highly agitated and even angered state. Sometimes, verbal protest was at a minimum, and the subject simply got up from his chair in front of the shock generator, and indicated that he wished to leave the laboratory.

Of the 40 subjects, 26 obeyed the orders of the experimenter to the end, proceeding to punish the victim until they reached the most potent shock available on the shock generator. At that point, the experimenter called a halt to the session. (The maximum shock is labeled 450 volts, and is two steps beyond the designation: Danger: Severe Shock.) Although obedient subjects continued to administer shocks, they often did so under extreme stress. Some expressed reluctance to administer shocks beyond the 300-volt level, and displayed fears similar to those who defied the experimenter; yet they obeyed.

After the maximum shocks had been delivered, and the experimenter called a halt to the proceedings, many obedient subjects heaved sighs of relief, mopped their brows, rubbed their fingers over their eyes, or nervously fumbled cigarettes. Some shook their heads, apparently in regret. Some subjects had remained calm throughout the experiment, and displayed only minimal signs of tension from beginning to end.

The obtained distribution of scores deviates radically from the prediction.

Upon command of the experimenter, each of the 40 subjects went beyond the expected break-

Discussion

The experiment yielded two findings that were surprising. The first finding concerns the sheer strength of obedient tendencies manifested in this situation. Subjects have learned from childhood that it is a fundamental breach of moral conduct to hurt another person against his will. Yet, 26 subjects abandon this tenet in following the instructions of an authority who has no special powers to enforce his commands. To disobey would bring no material loss to the subject; no punishment would ensue. It is clear from the remarks and outward behavior of many participants that in punishing the victim they are often acting against their own values. Subjects often expressed deep disapproval of shocking a man in the face of his objections, and others denounced it as stupid and senseless. Yet the majority complied with the experimental commands. This outcome was surprising from two perspectives: first, from the standpoint of predictions made in the questionnaire described earlier. (Here, however, it is possible that the remoteness of the respondents from the actual situation, and the difficulty of conveying to them the concrete details of the experiment, could account for the serious underestimation of obedience.)

But the results were also unexpected to persons who observed the experiment in progress, through one-way mirrors. Observers often uttered expressions of disbelief upon seeing a subject administer more powerful shocks to the victim. These persons had a full acquaintance with the details of the situation, and yet systematically underestimated the amount of obedience that subjects would display.

The second unanticipated effect was the extraordinary tension generated by the procedures. One might suppose that a subject would simply break off or continue as his conscience dictated. Yet, this is very far from what happened. There were striking reactions of tension and emotional strain. One observer related:

> I observed a mature and initially poised businessman enter the laboratory smiling and confident. Within 20 minutes he was reduced to a twitching, stuttering wreck, who was rapidly approaching a point of nervous collapse. He constantly pulled on his earlobe, and twisted his hands. At one point he pushed his fist into his forehead and muttered: "Oh God, let's stop it." And yet he continued to respond to every word of the experimenter, and obeyed to the end.

Any understanding of the phenomenon of obedience must rest on an analysis of the particular conditions in which it occurs. The following features of the experiment go some distance in explaining the high amount of obedience observed in the situation.

1. The experiment is sponsored by and takes place on the grounds of an institution of unimpeachable reputation, Yale University. It may be reasonably presumed that the personnel are competent and reputable. The importance of this background authority is now being studied by conducting a series of experiments outside of New Haven, and without any visible ties to the university.

2. The experiment is, on the face of it, designed to attain a worthy purpose—advancement of knowledge about learning and memory. Obedience occurs not as an end in itself, but as an instrumental element in a situation that the subject construes as significant, and meaningful. He may not be able to see its full significance, but he may properly assume that the experimenter does.

3. The subject perceives that the victim has voluntarily submitted to the authority system of the experimenter. He is not (at first) an unwilling captive impressed for involuntary service. He has taken the trouble to come to the laboratory presumably to aid the experimental research. That he later becomes an involuntary subject does not alter the fact that, initially, he consented to participate without qualification. Thus he has in some degree incurred an obligation toward the experimenter.

4. The subject, too, has entered the experiment voluntarily, and perceives himself under obligation to aid the experimenter. He has made a commitment, and to disrupt the experiment is a repudiation of this initial promise of aid.

5. Certain features of the procedure strengthen the subject's sense of obligation to the experimenter. For one, he has been paid for coming to the laboratory. In part this is canceled out by the experimenter's statement that:

Of course, as in all experiments, the money is yours simply for coming to the laboratory. From this point on, no matter what happens, the money is yours.[2]

---

[2] Forty-three subjects, undergraduates at Yale University, were run in the experiment without payment. The results are very similar to those obtained with paid subjects.

6. From the subject's standpoint, the fact that he is the teacher and the other man the learner is purely a chance consequence (it is determined by drawing lots) and he, the subject, ran the same risk as the other man in being assigned the role of learner. Since the assignment of positions in the experiment was achieved by fair means, the learner is deprived of any basis of complaint on this count. (A similar situation obtains in Army units, in which—in the absence of volunteers—a particularly dangerous mission may be assigned by drawing lots, and the unlucky soldier is expected to bear his misfortune with sportsmanship.)

7. There is, at best, ambiguity with regard to the prerogatives of a psychologist and the corresponding rights of his subject. There is a vagueness of expectation concerning what a psychologist may require of his subject, and when he is overstepping acceptable limits. Moreover, the experiment occurs in a closed setting, and thus provides no opportunity for the subject to remove these ambiguities by discussion with others. There are few standards that seem directly applicable to the situation, which is a novel one for most subjects.

8. The subjects are assured that the shocks administered to the subject are "painful but not dangerous." Thus they assume that the discomfort caused the victim is momentary, while the scientific gains resulting from the experiment are enduring.

9. Through Shock Level 20 the victim continues to provide answers on the signal box. The subject may construe this as a sign that the victim is still willing to "play the game." It is only after Shock Level 20 that the victim repudiates the rules completely, refusing to answer further.

These features help to explain the high amount of obedience obtained in this experiment. Many of the arguments raised need not remain matters of speculation, but can be reduced to testable propositions to be confirmed or disproved by further experiments.[3]

The following features of the experiment concern the nature of the conflict which the subject faces.

10. The subject is placed in a position in which he must respond to the competing demands of two persons: the experimenter and the victim. The conflict must be resolved by meeting the demands of one or the other; satisfaction of the victim and the experimenter are mutually exclusive. Moreover, the resolution must take the form of a highly visible action, that of continuing to shock the victim or breaking off the experiment. Thus the subject is forced into a public conflict that does not permit any completely satisfactory solution.

11. While the demands of the experimenter carry the weight of scientific authority, the demands of the victim spring from his personal experience of pain and suffering. The two claims need not be regarded as equally pressing and legitimate. The experimenter seeks an abstract scientific datum; the victim cries out for relief from physical suffering caused by the subject's actions.

12. The experiment gives the subject little time for reflection. The conflict comes on rapidly. It is only minutes after the subject has been seated before the shock generator that the victim begins his protests. Moreover, the subject perceives that he has gone through but two-thirds of the shock levels at the time the subject's first protests are heard. Thus he understands that the conflict will have a persistent aspect to it, and may well become more intense as increasingly more powerful shocks are required. The rapidity with which the conflict descends on the subject, and his realization that it is predictably recurrent may well be sources of tension to him.

13. At a more general level, the conflict stems from the opposition of two deeply ingrained behavior dispositions: first, the disposition not to harm other people, and second, the tendency to obey those whom we perceive to be legitimate authorities.

References

1. Adorno, T., Frenkel-Brunswik, Else, Levinson, D. J., & Sanford, R. N. *The authoritarian personality.* New York: Harper, 1950.
2. Arendt, H. What was authority? In C. J. Friedrich (Ed.), *Authority.* Cambridge: Harvard Univer. Press, 1958. Pp. 81–112.
3. Binet, A. *La suggestibilité.* Paris: Schleicher, 1900.
4. Buss, A. H. *The psychology of aggression.* New York: Wiley, 1961.

---

[3] A series of recently completed experiments employing the obedience paradigm is reported in Milgram (1964).

5. Cartwright, S. (Ed.) *Studies in social power.* Ann Arbor: University of Michigan Institute for Social Research, 1959.
6. Charcot, J. M. *Oeuvres complètes.* Paris: Bureaux du Progrès Médical, 1881.
7. Frank, J. D. Experimental studies of personal pressure and resistance. *J. gen. Psychol.,* 1944, **30**, 23–64.
8. Friedrich, C. J. (Ed.) *Authority.* Cambridge: Harvard Univer. Press, 1958.
9. Milgram, S. Dynamics of obedience. Washington: National Science Foundation, 25 January 1961. (Mimeo)
10 Milgram, S. Some conditions of obedience and disobedience to authority. *Hum. Relat.,* 1964, in press.
11. Rokeach, M. Authority, authoritarianism, and conformity. In I. A. Berg & B. M. Bass (Eds.), *Conformity and deviation.* New York: Harper, 1961. Pp. 230–257.
12. Snow, C. P. Either-or. *Progressive,* 1961 (Feb.), 24.
13. Weber, M. *The theory of social and economic organization.* Oxford: Oxford Univer. Press, 1947.

QUESTIONS FOR REFLECTION AND DISCUSSION:

Note that several of the questions are similar to those asked in conjunction with Solomon Asch's study on "Opinions and Social Pressure."

1. Do you see subjects' willingness to administer shock in the Milgram study as the behavioral or moral equivalent of the Nazis' extermination of people in the death camps? Why or why not?

2. Milgram's methods made the subjects extremely uncomfortable. Do you believe that his research was ethical? Why or why not?

3. Milgram undertook his research in the late 1950s and early 1960s, before Ethics Review Committees were established. These committees weigh the value of proposed research against its potential harm. If you were proposing the research to such a committee, what arguments could you make in its favor? If you were a member of such a committee, what arguments might you make to block the research?

4. Can you think of a way in which Milgram's research might have been conducted without deceiving the subjects?

5. Milgram "debriefed" subjects after they participated in the study. That is, he explained that they did not really shock anyone. Debriefing is intended to protect subjects from harm. If you had participated in the study, which would you have found more stressful: belief that you had or had not shocked anyone? Why?

6. How do you believe that you would have behaved if you had been a subject in Milgram's study? Would you have obeyed the experimenter or refused to do so? Are you sure?

7. Why is Milgram's research considered so important in the history of psychology? Is it as important today? Why or why not?

8. What do you see as the message of Milgram's study?

SOURCE

Benson, P. L., Karabenick, S. A., &
Lerner, R. M. (1976). Pretty
pleases: The effects of physical
attractiveness, race, and sex on
receiving help. *Journal of
Experimental Social Psychology, 12,*
409–415. Reprinted by permission
of Academic Press.

Beauty may only be skin deep, but oh! how important skin can be. One of the topics in social psychology is interpersonal attraction. The research literature shows that physical attractiveness plays a key role in choice of dates and mates. We also tend to assume that good things come in pretty packages—that is, we expect physically attractive people to be more poised, sociable, popular, intelligent, mentally healthy, fulfilled, persuasive, and successful in their jobs and marriages than unattractive people are. Attractive people are more likely to be judged innocent of crimes in jury experiments, and when they are found guilty, they are typically handed down less severe sentences.

Even though we are told not to judge a book by its cover, it also seems to help to be good-looking when you are in need of a favor. Classic research by Peter Benson and his colleagues testifies to that simple truth.

Pretty Pleases: The Effects of Physical Attractiveness, Race, and Sex on Receiving Help

PETER L. BENSON
EARLHAM COLLEGE
STUART A. KARABENICK
EASTERN MICHIGAN UNIVERSITY
RICHARD M. LERNER
THE PENNSYLVANIA STATE UNIVERSITY

The major purpose of this study was to investigate whether favoritism for the physically attractive, a phenomenon demonstrated almost exclusively on the basis of rating scales, generalizes to nonreactive, behavioral helping responses. Four hundred and forty-two males and 162 female white adult callers in public phone booths in a large metropolitan airport found a completed graduate school application form, a photograph of the applicant, and an addressed, stamped envelope. The picture was used to convey information as to the physical attractiveness (attractive vs. unattractive), race (black vs. white), and sex of the applicant. As predicted, delivery of the application was facilitated more for attractive than unattractive persons. There was also a significant race effect, with whites receiving more help than blacks. Implications of these findings for the physical attractiveness literature are discussed.

A rapidly increasing body of literature indicates that physical attractiveness cues generate specific evaluations and impressions. The physically attractive benefit from this process. In comparison to the less attractive, persons with good looks are liked more (Byrne, London, & Reeves, 1968; Kleck &

Rubenstein, 1975; Walster, Aronson, Abrahams, & Rottman, 1966), are desired more as dates (Brislin & Lewis, 1968; Huston, 1973), are attributed more socially desirable characteristics (Dion, Berscheid, & Walster, 1972; Miller, 1970), are expected to achieve more in educational settings (Clifford & Walster, 1973), and receive more favorable task performance ratings (Landy & Sigall, 1974). This preference for the physically attractive appears to be of such strength that even those who associate with beautiful persons gain in stature (Sigall & Landy, 1973).

These findings, however, are based almost exclusively on studies which ask subjects to rate persons of varying attractiveness levels on paper and pencil measures. For two reasons, this procedure limits the generalizability of these findings. First, such measures are potentially reactive (Webb, Campbell, Schwartz, & Sechrest, 1966); that is, subjects are aware that their behavior is being observed and thus demand characteristics and cooperative motives in subjects become problematic (Orne, 1962). Hence, it is not known if physical attractiveness effects generalize to nonreactive situations as would obtain in naturalistic settings where subjects are not aware of their roles. This issue has recently been raised by Kleck and Rubenstein (1975) and Krebs and Adinolfi (1975).

Second, ratings are measures of attitudinal domains, and it remains to be demonstrated in which areas, if any, these attitudes will translate into overt behavioral responses that will favor the physically attractive. Dion, Berscheid, and Walster (1972) argue that although it appears there is a stereotyped preference for the physically attractive, we do not know "the extent to which it determines the pattern of social interactions that develops with a person of a particular attractiveness level. Nevertheless, it would seem odd if people did not behave toward others in accordance with this stereotype" (p. 289). If preferential attitudes translate into preferential behaviors as Dion, *et al.* suggest, then we might expect, for example, that the physically attractive will receive more lucrative court settlements, receive better jobs, receive higher grades, receive more votes in an election, and be helped more in comparison to the unattractive.

To address these two issues, this study investigated the effects of physical attractiveness on helping behavior in a nonreactive field setting. The specific task was that of helping to deliver a graduate school application lost by a traveler at an airport. A picture attached to the application varied the attractiveness of the person needing help (target). It is predicted that the physically attractive will receive more help than the unattractive. Target sex, target race, and subject sex were also varied to determine the generality of physical attractiveness cues across these dimensions as well as their potential interactive influence on the physical attractiveness–helping relationship.

Method

SUBJECTS AND DESIGN

The subjects were 604 white adults (442 males and 162 females), judged to be between 18 and 70 yr of age, who used a public telephone at a large Midwestern metropolitan airport between 10:00 AM and 7:00 PM on 7 days in the fall of 1974. Stimulus materials in the study were placed in a phone booth located in the large center lobby area that contained many booths. Upon entering the booth, the subject encountered a completed graduate school application form which included a picture of the applicant. The type of picture represented one of eight categories in accordance with a 2 (Attractive vs. Unattractive) × 2 (Male vs. Female) × 2 (Black vs. White) design. There were two pictures in each of the eight conditions, and the order of stimulus presentation, as well as the pictures in each category, was determined randomly. Sex of subject constituted the fourth design dimension. There were many more males than females present in the airport population. To obtain an acceptable number of female subjects, the study was conducted until there were at least 20 subjects in each stimulus condition which accounts for the unequal cell frequencies.

STIMULUS MATERIALS

In order to select the 16 pictures, 29 male and 29 female white undergraduates rated the physical attractiveness of 78 monochrome facial portraits of 39 black and 39 white college seniors taken from five large state university yearbooks (three from midwestern schools and one each from a southern and an eastern school). The original 78 pictures were chosen by two persons (one male, one female) who were blind to how these pictures would eventually be used, and who were simply instructed to choose black and white, male and female pictures, without facial hair and glasses, which either were high, medium, or low in physical attractiveness. The 58 judges rated each picture on a 7-point physical attractiveness scale with 7 representing "extremely attractive" and 1 representing "extremely unattractive." The judges were given no information about the subsequent use of the ratings or pictures.

In seven of the eight stimulus categories, the two most extremely rated pictures were selected. In the eighth category (attractive white female), three pictures received considerably higher ratings than the highest-rated picture in any other category. To keep this category similar to the others, the two pictures were chosen which were rated closest to the mean (5.8) of the six pictures in the other three attractive categories. The eight attractive pictures selected had a mean range of 5.3 to 6.1 with an overall mean of 5.77 and a standard deviation range of .79 to 1.19. The eight selected unattractive pictures had a mean range of 1.9 to 2.6 with an overall mean of 2.3 and a standard deviation range of .90 to 1.21. The difference between the means of all unattractive vs. attractive pictures was highly significant, $F(1,56) = 694.40$, $p < .001$. None of the unattractive pictures had any facial deformities. Additional analyses indicated that there were no attractiveness differences between the black and white pictures ($F < 1.00$).

The completed application form found by each subject was to a local graduate program in psychology. It was completed in the name of either Linda or Robert Smith and contained standardized information regarding home address (Manhattan, Kansas), educational background, the names of three personal references, grade point average and Graduate Record Examination scores. The application was filled out in pen. The distant home address was used to prevent subjects from contacting the person by phone, a possibility if a local address had been used. At the bottom of the application was a request for the applicant to include a picture. The wallet-size picture was affixed to the top right-hand corner of the form and in clear view. The form and the picture were paper-clipped to the outside of a 17×25 cm stamped envelope addressed to the psychology department applied to.

The stimulus materials were placed on a small shelf in the phone booth in such a way as to be unavoidable to anyone entering the booth. The experimenter was stationed approximately 10 m from the booth at a vantage point that permitted observation of the subject. A person was used as a subject if he or she entered the phone booth, handled the materials, and read the personal note (the note was assumed to be read if the person looked directly at it for a 5-sec period or more). Only five persons who entered the phone booth did not meet these criteria and thus were not used as subjects: in each case, the person spent less than 2 sec in the booth. It appeared that each of these persons assumed that the booth was taken, and left before they had any opportunity to study the stimulus materials. Thus, all subjects included in the analysis are known to have thoroughly studied the stimulus materials.

It was important that subjects ascertain that helping would consist of mailing the application (or turning it over to an official to mail) and that leaving it in the phone booth would be unhelpful. However, if the subject thought that the applicant might return to retrieve the forgotten application, he or she could infer that leaving it would be one way to provide assistance. In order to remove this ambiguity, the following note was appended to the form: "Dear Dad, Have a nice trip. Please remember to mail this application before you leave Detroit on your (*time of departure*) flight to New York. Love, Linda (Bob)." The time of departure was constantly altered so that all subjects were informed that the father's flight had departed 45 min earlier. Thus, there could be no doubt that, unless the applicant's father had missed the plane, the application would not be retrieved and help would consist of facilitating its delivery.

HELPING MEASURE

Ignoring the application by leaving it in the booth, destroying it, or taking it but doing nothing further was coded as nonhelping behavior. Since the envelope was already stamped and addressed, helping consisted of either mailing the application (a mailbox was situated approximately 40 m from the phone booth although not in view) or taking the application to one of the airport ticket counters. Subjects who eventually mailed the application (not observed by the experimenter) were discovered by its being received in the psychology department. Suitable coding enabled identification of the sex of subject having facilitated the delivery of the application.

Results

For analysis, helping scores were collapsed across the two pictures in each of the eight stimulus conditions. Table 40.01 shows the percentage of subjects providing assistance in each stimulus condition. Considerable variation in helping occurred: The highest rate was exhibited by male subjects helping attractive white females (56%) and the lowest by female subjects who aided unattractive black males in only 25% of the interactions. The overall helping rate was 41%. Data were analyzed using the multidimensional contingency procedure suggested by Winer (1971, pp. 855–859), which permits tests of both main and interaction effects. Dimensions of the analysis consisted of attractiveness, sex, and race of the stimulus person and sex of subject.

TABLE 40.01

	CHARACTERISTICS OF TARGET							
	ATTRACTIVE				UNATTRACTIVE			
	MALE		FEMALE		MALE		FEMALE	
SEX OF SUBJECT	BLACK	WHITE	BLACK	WHITE	BLACK	WHITE	BLACK	WHITE
Male	42.4	49.0	44.8	55.8	37.1	41.4	29.4	36.4
	(59)[a]	(55)	(58)	(52)	(54)	(58)	(51)	(55)
Female	38.1	55.0	35.0	47.6	25.0	40.0	30.0	30.0
	(21)	(20)	(20)	(21)	(20)	(20)	(20)	(20)

PERCENTAGE HELPING AS A FUNCTION OF SEX OF SUBJECT AND THE ATTRACTIVENESS, RACE, AND SEX OF THE TARGET

[a]Numbers in parentheses indicate the number of subjects in each group.

Two significant effects were found, both involving characteristics of the stimulus person. First, as expected, there is a significant main effect of physical attractiveness, χ^2 (1) = 8.75, $p < .005$: attractive stimulus persons received help at a rate of 47% as opposed to 35% for unattractive persons. There is also a significant main effect of target race, χ^2 (1) = 3.88, $p < .05$: whites received help 45% and blacks only 37% of the time. The other main effects were not significant. Males and females gave (42 vs. 38%, respectively) and received help (42 vs. 40%, respectively) almost equally.

None of the interactions between variables were significant, all χ^2 values being less than 1.0. Therefore it should be noted that physical attractiveness and race provide independent influences on whether persons received help in the present study. The combined effects of being black and unattractive resulted in receiving help at a rate 20% less often (32%) than being white and attractive (52%).

Discussion

As predicted, the target's physical attractiveness influenced helping behavior. This effect occurred independently of sex of subject and sex and race of target. The attractive, then, appear to receive the benefits of assistance regardless of these other major stimulus characteristics. The present results thus demonstrate that favoritism for the physically attractive, previously found with rating scale measures, generalizes to overt helping behavior in a nonreactive, naturalistic setting. Since no significant interactions were found, the findings do not corrob-

orate studies which show that the effect of physical attractiveness is modified by the sex of the subject and/or the sex of the target (Byrne, London, & Reeves, 1968; Coombs & Kenkel, 1966; Miller, 1970).

Explanations for why physical attractiveness influences interpersonal processes have focused largely on the specific area of dating and marriage choices. In that context, it has been argued that the physically attractive are preferred because cultural conditioning has taught that they are the most appropriate targets for romantic involvement (Berscheid & Walster, 1974), that people expect to gain prestige by being linked with attractive others (Sigall & Landy, 1973), and that the attractive provide more rewards than the unattractive (Byrne, London, & Reeves, 1968). While such explanations may be germane for understanding heterosexual, romantic choices, they provide little insight into our findings. Since the influence of physical attractiveness on helping occurred independently of target sex and race, and in a setting where subjects do not interact with the target nor have opportunities for future interaction, explanations based on concepts of romantic appeal and/or the externally mediated rewards that come from associating with the attractive are inappropriate.

Three possible explanations for why physical attractiveness information influences helping responses are as follows: First, person perception processes may mediate relationships between appearance and helping. Several studies show that attractiveness cues elicit stereotyped inferences such that "what is beautiful is good" (Dion, Berscheid, & Walster, 1972) and "what is ugly is bad" (Dermer

& Thiel, 1975). In the present study the target persons are applying to graduate school. Accordingly, inferences about the academic competence and potential of the candidate could mediate the differential helping rates. Studies have shown that the physically attractive, in comparison with the unattractive, are perceived to have higher IQs and educational potential (Clifford & Walster, 1973), and be better writers (Landy & Sigall, 1974). From these studies, one might conclude that attractive applicants were considered more qualified and, therefore, more deserving of help in pursuing their vocational goals. Thus, subjects in the unattractive stimulus condition may feel less blameworthy, in comparison to persons in the attractive condition, for neglecting to give help.

Second, studies dealing with liking may also provide clues for explaining appearance–helping relationships. Several authors have found that helping is positively associated with the degree of liking for the target (Daniels & Berkowitz, 1963; Hornstein, Masor, Sole, & Heilman, 1971; Staub & Sherk, 1970). Also, it has been consistently shown that the attractive are liked more than the unattractive (Byrne, London, & Reeves, 1968; Kleck & Rubenstein, 1975). Thus it may be that liking mediates the attractiveness–helping relationship.

Finally, even though all subjects handled the stimulus materials and read the note to the father, those who saw physically attractive pictures may have been led to pay *more* attention to the stimulus materials than those who saw the unattractive pictures. Such a difference in attention may have produced an increased sensitivity to the plight of the "victim" and/or an increased activation of internalized norms to give help in those who saw the attractive picture.

The race main effect appears to demonstrate a racial bias in helping, a finding which is consistent with other studies where white subjects and black or white "victims" do not confront each other directly (Gaertner, 1973; Gaertner & Bickman, 1971). In studies where the interaction between subject and victim is face-to-face and low in cost, no race effect is found (Lerner, Solomon, & Brody, 1971; Wispé & Freshley, 1971). This suggests, then, that the influence of race may depend on the nature of the interaction. Perhaps prejudicial behaviors such as nonhelping are too costly when the interaction is face-to-face—the target and/or bystanders may provide negative feedback for failing to provide assistance. The cloak of anonymity, as found in the present study, may provide some immunity from such costs, thereby making it safer to make a prejudicial response in the form of *not* helping.

References

1. Berscheid, E., & Walster, E. H. Physical attractiveness. *In* L. Berkowitz (Ed.), *Advances in experimental social psychology.* New York: Academic Press, 1974, Vol. 7.
2. Brislin, R. W., & Lewis, S. A. Dating and physical attractiveness: Replication. *Psychological Reports,* 1968, **22**, 976.
3. Byrne, D., London, O., & Reeves, K. The effects of physical attractiveness, sex, and attitude similarity on interpersonal attraction. *Journal of Personality,* 1968, **36**, 259–271.
4. Clifford, M. M., & Walster, E. The effect of physical attractiveness on teacher expectation. *Sociology of Education,* 1973, **46**, 248–258.
5. Coombs, R. H., & Kenkel, W. F. Sex differences in dating aspirations and satisfaction with computer-selected partners. *Journal of Marriage and the Family,* 1966, **28**(1), 62–66.
6. Daniels, L. R., & Berkowitz, L. Liking and response to dependency relationships. *Human Relations,* 1963, **16**, 141–148.
7. Dermer, M., & Thiel, D. L. When beauty may fail. *Journal of Personality and Social Psychology,* 1975, **31**, 1168–1176.
8. Dion, K. K., Berscheid, E., & Walster, E. What is beautiful is good. *Journal of Personality and Social Psychology,* 1972, **24**, 285–290.
9. Gaertner, S. L. Helping behavior and racial discrimination among liberals and conservatives. *Journal of Personality and Social Psychology,* 1973, **25**, 335–341.
10. Gaertner, S., & Bickman, L. Effects of race on the elicitation of helping behavior: The wrong number technique. *Journal of Personality and Social Psychology,* 1971, **20**, 218–222.
11. Hornstein, H. A., Masor, H. N., Sole, K., & Heilman, M. Effects of sentiment and completion of a helping act on observer helping: A case for socially mediated Zeigarnik effects. *Journal of Personality and Social Psychology,* 1971, **17**, 107–112.
12. Huston, T. L. Ambiguity of acceptance, social desirability, and dating choice. *Journal of Experimental Social Psychology,* 1973, **9**, 32–42.
13. Kleck, R. E., & Rubenstein, C. Physical attractiveness, perceived attitude similarity, and interpersonal attraction in an opposite-sex encounter. *Journal of Personality and Social Psychology,* **31**, 107–114.
14. Krebs, D., & Adinolfi, A. A. Physical attractiveness, social relations, and personality style. *Journal of Personality and Social Psychology,* 1975, **31**, 245–253.
15. Landy, D., & Sigall, H. Beauty is talent: Task evaluation as a function of the performer's physical attractiveness. *Journal of Personality and Social Psychology,* 1974, **29**, 299–304.
16. Lerner, R. M., Solomon, H., & Brody, S. Helping behavior at a busstop. *Psychological Reports,* 1971, **28**, 200.

17. Miller, A. G. Role of physical attractiveness in impression formation. *Psychonomic Science,* 1970, **19,** 241–243.

18. Orne, M. T. On the social psychology of the psychological experiment: With particular reference to demand characteristics and their implications. *American Psychologist,* 1962, **17,** 776–783.

19. Sigall, H., & Landy, D. Radiating beauty: Effects of having a physically attractive partner on person perception. *Journal of Personality and Social Psychology,* 1973, **28,** 218–224.

20. Staub, E., & Sherk, L. Need for approval, children's sharing behavior and reciprocity in sharing. *Child Development,* 1970, **41,** 243–252.

21. Walster, E., Aronson, V., Abrahams, D., & Rottman, L. Importance of physical attractiveness in dating behavior. *Journal of Personality and Social Psychology,* 1966, **4,** 508–516.

22. Webb, E. J., Campbell, D. T., Schwartz, R. D., & Sechrest, L. *Unobtrusive measures: Nonreactive research in the social sciences.* Chicago: Rand McNally, 1966.

23. Winer, B. J. *Statistical principles in experimental design.* New York: McGraw-Hill, 1971, 2nd ed.

24. Wispé, L., & Freshley, H. B. Race, sex, and sympathetic helping behavior: The broken bag caper. *Journal of Personality and Social Psychology,* 1971, **17,** 59–65.

QUESTIONS FOR REFLECTION AND DISCUSSION:

1. How did Benson and his colleagues operationally define helping behavior in their experiment? Are you satisfied that it is a good example of helping? Explain.

2. How did Benson and his colleagues determine that one person was more physically attractive than another? Is their methodology convincing? Explain.

3. The Benson study appears to show that people who are physically attractive are more likely to receive help when they are in need. But not everyone helped attractive individuals, and unattractive individuals also received help on many occasions. What would be a most accurate way to phrase the results of the study? (Clearly we cannot just say that attractive people were helped and unattractive people were not helped.)

4. How do you explain racial and gender differences in who was helped and who was not helped?

5. How important a role does your own level of physical attractiveness play in your life? How does it seem to affect the way people respond to you?

6. How important is physical attractiveness in your choice of friends, dates, and mates? Are you satisfied with the importance of the role played by physical attractiveness in your life? Why or why not?

SOURCE

Darley, J. M., & Latané, B. (1968). Bystander intervention in emergencies: Diffusion of responsibility. *Journal of Personality and Social Psychology, 8,* 377–383. Copyright © 1968 by the American Psychological Association. Reprinted with permission.

People throughout the nation were shocked by the murder of 28-year-old Kitty Genovese in New York City. The facts of the case seemed to tear at our very social fabric as a nation. Kitty had screamed repeatedly for help as her killer had stalked her for more than half an hour and stabbed her in three separate attacks. Thirty-eight neighbors are known to have heard the commotion. Their voices and bedroom lights interrupted the assault twice. Yet nobody came to Kitty's aid. No one even called the police. How could this happen? Some witnesses admitted that they had not wanted to get involved. One said that he was tired. Some simply said, "I don't know."

Are these the reasons that no one came to the aid of Kitty Genovese? As a nation, are we a callous bunch who would rather watch than help when other people are in need? News commentators spoke about the alienation and dehumanization of city dwellers, particularly New Yorkers. But John Darley and Bibb Latané, two social psychologists, were not convinced that these were the most important reasons. The two met at a party shortly after the crime and mused about it for hours. They then had a joint flash of inspiration: Perhaps nobody helped precisely because they knew so many other people were watching. Late that evening they began to design an experiment to test what would become known as the bystander effect. *Like so many others of its kind, this classic experiment relied on deceiving the subjects as to the true purpose of the study.*

Bystander Intervention in Emergencies: Diffusion of Responsibility

JOHN M. DARLEY
NEW YORK UNIVERSITY

BIBB LATANÉ
COLUMBIA UNIVERSITY

Ss overheard an epileptic seizure. They believed either that they alone heard the emergency, or that 1 or 4 unseen others were also present. As predicted the presence of other bystanders reduced the individual's feelings of personal responsibility and lowered his speed of reporting ($p < .01$). In groups of size 3, males reported no faster than females, and females reported no slower when the 1 other bystander was a male rather than a female. In general, personality and background measures were not predictive of helping. Bystander inaction in real-life emergencies is often explained by "apathy," "alienation," and "anomie." This experiment suggests that the explanation may lie more in the bystander's response to other observers than in his indifference to the victim.

Several years ago, a young woman was stabbed to death in the middle of a street in a residential section of New York City. Although such murders are not entirely routine, the incident received little public attention until several weeks later when the

New York Times disclosed another side to the case: at least 38 witnesses had observed the attack—and none had even attempted to intervene. Although the attacker took more than half an hour to kill Kitty Genovese, not one of the 38 people who watched from the safety of their own apartments came out to assist her. Not one even lifted the telephone to call the police (Rosenthal, 1964).

Preachers, professors, and news commentators sought the reasons for such apparently conscience-less and inhumane lack of intervention. Their conclusions ranged from "moral decay," to "dehuman-ization produced by the urban environment," to "alienation," "anomie," and "existential despair." An analysis of the situation, however, suggests that factors other than apathy and indifference were involved.

A person witnessing an emergency situation, particularly such a frightening and dangerous one as a stabbing, is in conflict. There are obvious humani-tarian norms about helping the victim, but there are also rational and irrational fears about what might happen to a person who does intervene (Milgram & Hollander, 1964). "I didn't want to get involved," is a familiar comment, and behind it lies fears of phys-ical harm, public embarrassment, involvement with police procedures, lost work days and jobs, and other unknown dangers.

In certain circumstances, the norms favoring intervention may be weakened, leading bystanders to resolve the conflict in the direction of noninterven-tion. One of these circumstances may be the presence of other onlookers. For example, in the case above, each observer, by seeing lights and figures in other apartment house windows, knew that others were also watching. However, there was no way to tell how the other observers were reacting. These two facts provide several reasons why any individual may have delayed or failed to help. The responsibility for helping was diffused among the observers; there was also diffusion of any potential blame for not taking action; and finally, it was possible that somebody, unperceived, had already initiated helping action.

When only one bystander is present in an emergency, if help is to come, it must come from him. Although he may choose to ignore it (out of concern for his personal safety, or desires "not to get involved"), any pressure to intervene focuses uniquely on him. When there are several observers present, however, the pressures to intervene do not focus on any one of the observers; instead the responsibility for intervention is shared among all the onlookers and is not unique to any one. As a result, no one helps.

A second possibility is that potential blame may be diffused. However much we may wish to think that an individual's moral behavior is divorced from considerations of personal punishment or reward, there is both theory and evidence to the contrary (Aronfreed, 1964; Miller & Dollard, 1941, Whiting & Child, 1953). It is perfectly reasonable to assume that, under circumstances of group responsibility for a punishable act, the punishment or blame that accrues to any one individual is often slight or nonex-istent.

Finally, if others are known to be present, but their behavior cannot be closely observed, any one bystander can assume that one of the other observers is already taking action to end the emergency. Therefore, his own intervention would be only redundant—perhaps harmfully or confusingly so. Thus, given the presence of other onlookers whose behavior cannot be observed, any given bystander can rationalize his own inaction by convinc-ing himself that "somebody else must be doing something."

These considerations lead to the hypothesis that the more bystanders to an emergency, the less likely, or the more slowly, any one bystander will intervene to provide aid. To test this proposition it would be necessary to create a situation in which a realistic "emergency" could plausibly occur. Each subject should also be blocked from communicating with others to prevent his getting information about their behavior during the emergency. Finally, the experimental situation should allow for the assessment of the speed and frequency of the subjects' reaction to the emergency. The experiment reported below attempted to fulfill these conditions.

Procedure

OVERVIEW

A college student arrived in the laboratory and was ushered into an individual room from which a communication system would enable him to talk to the other participants. It was explained to him that he was to take part in a discussion about personal problems associated with college life and that the discussion would be held over the intercom system, rather than face-to-face, in order to avoid embar-rassment by preserving the anonymity of the subjects. During the course of the discussion, one of the other subjects underwent what appeared to be a very serious nervous seizure similar to epilepsy. During the fit it was impossible for the subject to talk to the other discussants or to find out what, if anything, they were doing about the emergency. The dependent variable was the speed with which the subjects reported the emergency to the experimenter. The major independent variable was the number of people the subject thought to be in the discussion group.

SUBJECTS

Fifty-nine female and thirteen male students in introductory psychology courses at New York University were contacted to take part in an unspecified experiment as part of a class requirement.

METHOD

Upon arriving for the experiment, the subject found himself in a long corridor with doors opening off it to several small rooms. An experimental assistant met him, took him to one of the rooms, and seated him at a table. After filling out a background information form, the subject was given a pair of headphones with an attached microphone and was told to listen for instructions.

Over the intercom, the experimenter explained that he was interested in learning about the kinds of personal problems faced by normal college students in a high pressure, urban environment. He said that to avoid possible embarrassment about discussing personal problems with strangers several precautions had been taken. First, subjects would remain anonymous, which was why they had been placed in individual rooms rather than face-to-face. (The actual reason for this was to allow tape recorder simulation of the other subjects and the emergency.) Second, since the discussion might be inhibited by the presence of outside listeners, the experimenter would not listen to the initial discussion, but would get the subject's reactions later, by questionnaire. (The real purpose of this was to remove the obviously responsible experimenter from the scene of the emergency.)

The subjects were told that since the experimenter was not present, it was necessary to impose some organization. Each person would talk in turn, presenting his problems to the group. Next, each person in turn would comment on what the others had said, and finally, there would be a free discussion. A mechanical switching device would regulate this discussion sequence and each subject's microphone would be on for about 2 minutes. While any microphone was on, all other microphones would be off. Only one subject, therefore, could be heard over the network at any given time. The subjects were thus led to realize when they later heard the seizure that only the victim's microphone was on and that there was no way of determining what any of the other witnesses were doing, nor of discussing the event and its possible solution with the others. When these instructions had been given, the discussion began.

In the discussion, the future victim spoke first, saying that he found it difficult to get adjusted to New York City and to his studies. Very hesitantly, and with obvious embarrassment, he mentioned that he was prone to seizures, particularly when studying hard or taking exams. The other people, including the real subject, took their turns and discussed similar problems (minus, of course, the proneness to seizures). The naive subject talked last in the series, after the last prerecorded voice was played.[1]

When it was again the victim's turn to talk, he made a few relatively calm comments, and then, growing increasingly louder and incoherent, he continued:

> I-er-um-I think I-I need-er-if-if could-er-er-somebody er-er-er-er-er-er-er give me a little-er-give me a little help here because-er-I-er-I'm-er-er-h-h-having a-a-a real problem-er-right now and I-er-if somebody could help me out it would-it would-er-er s-s-sure be-sure be good . . . because-er-there-er-er-a cause I-er-I-uh-I've got a-a one of the-er-sei—er-er-things coming on and-and-and I could really-er-use some help so if somebody would-er-give me a little h-help-uh-er-er-er-er-er c-could somebody-er-er-help-er-uh-uh-uh (choking sounds). . . . I'm gonna die-er-er-I'm . . . gonna die-er-help-er-er-seizure-er-[chokes, then quiet].

The experimenter began timing the speed of the real subject's response at the beginning of the victim's speech. Informed judges listening to the tape have estimated that the victim's increasingly louder and more disconnected ramblings clearly represented a breakdown about 70 seconds after the signal for the victim's second speech. The victim's speech was abruptly cut off 125 seconds after this signal, which could be interpreted by the subject as indicating that the time allotted for that speaker had elapsed and the switching circuits had switched away from him. Times reported in the results are measured from the start of the fit.

---

[1] To test whether the order in which the subjects spoke in the first discussion round significantly affected the subjects' speed of report, the order in which the subjects spoke was varied (in the six-person group). This had no significant or noticeable effect on the speed of the subjects' reports.

TABLE 41.01

		% RESPONDING		
GROUP SIZE	N	BY END OF FIT	TIME IN SEC.	SPEED SCORE
2 (S & victim)	13	85	52	.87
3 (S, victim, & 1 other)	26	62	93	.72
6 (S, victim, & 4 others)	13	31	166	.51

EFFECTS OF GROUPS SIZE ON LIKELIHOOD AND SPEED OF RESPONSE

Note.—p *value of differences:* $\chi^2 = 7.91$, p $< .02$; F $= 8.09$, p $< .01$, *for speed scores.*

GROUP SIZE VARIABLE

The major independent variable of the study was the number of other people that the subject believed also heard the fit. By the assistant's comments before the experiment, and also by the number of voices heard to speak in the first round of the group discussion, the subject was led to believe that the discussion group was one of three sizes: either a two-person group (consisting of a person who would later have a fit and the real subject), a three-person group (consisting of the victim, the real subject, and one confederate voice), or a six-person group (consisting of the victim, the real subject, and four confederate voices). All the confederates' voices were tape-recorded.

VARIATIONS IN GROUP COMPOSITION

Varying the kind as well as the number of bystanders present at an emergency should also vary the amount of responsibility felt by any single bystander. To test this, several variations of the three-person group were run. In one three-person condition, the taped bystander voice was that of a female, in another a male, and in the third a male who said that he was a premedical student who occasionally worked in the emergency wards at Bellevue hospital.

In the above conditions, the subjects were female college students. In a final condition males drawn from the same introductory psychology subject pool were tested in a three-person female-bystander condition.

TIME TO HELP

The major dependent variable was the time elapsed from the start of the victim's fit until the subject left her experimental cubicle. When the subject left her room, she saw the experimental assistant seated at the end of the hall, and invariably went to the assistant. If 6 minutes elapsed without the subject having emerged from her room, the experiment was terminated.

As soon as the subject reported the emergency, or after 6 minutes had elapsed, the experimental assistant disclosed the true nature of the experiment, and dealt with any emotions aroused in the subject. Finally the subject filled out a questionnaire concerning her thoughts and feelings during the emergency, and completed scales of Machiavellianism, anomie, and authoritarianism (Christie, 1964), a social desirability scale (Crowne & Marlowe, 1964), a social responsibility scale (Daniels & Berkowitz, 1964), and reported vital statistics and socioeconomic data.

Results

PLAUSIBILITY OF MANIPULATION

Judging by the subjects' nervousness when they reported the fit to the experimenter, by their surprise when they discovered that the fit was simulated, and by comments they made during the fit (when they thought their microphones were off), one can conclude that almost all of the subjects perceived the fit as real. There were two exceptions in different experimental conditions, and the data for these subjects were dropped from the analysis.

EFFECT OF GROUP SIZE ON HELPING

The number of bystanders that the subject perceived to be present had a major effect on the likelihood with which she would report the emergency (Table 41.01). Eighty-five percent of the subjects who thought they alone knew of the victim's plight reported the seizure before the victim was cut off, only 31% of those who thought four other bystanders were present did so.

Every one of the subjects in the two-person groups, but only 62% of the subjects in the six-

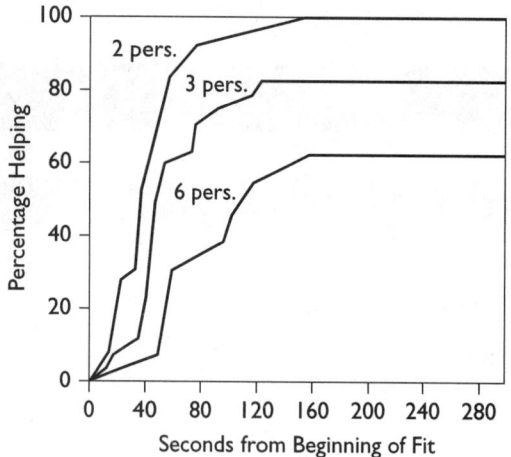

FIGURE 41.01

Cumulative distributions of helping responses.

person groups, ever reported the emergency. The cumulative distributions of response times for groups of different perceived size (Figure 41.01) indicates that, by any point in time, more subjects from the two-person groups had responded than from the three-person groups, and more from the three-person groups than from the six-person groups.

Ninety-five percent of all the subjects who ever responded did so within the first half of the time available to them. No subject who had not reported within 3 minutes after the fit ever did so. The shape of these distributions suggest that had the experiment been allowed to run for a considerably longer time, few additional subjects would have responded.

SPEED OF RESPONSE

To achieve a more detailed analysis of the results, each subject's time score was transformed into a "speed" score by taking the reciprocal of the response time in seconds and multiplying by 100. The effect of this transformation was to deemphasize differences between longer time scores, thus reducing the contribution to the results of the arbitrary 6-minute limit on scores. A high speed score indicates a fast response.

An analysis of variance indicates that the effect of group size is highly significant ($p < .01$). Duncan multiple-range tests indicate that all but the two- and three-person groups differ significantly from one another ($p < .05$).

VICTIM'S LIKELIHOOD OF BEING HELPED

An individual subject is less likely to respond if he thinks that others are present. But what of the vic-

tim? Is the inhibition of the response of each individual strong enough to counteract the fact that with five onlookers there are five times as many people available to help? From the data of this experiment, it is possible mathematically to create hypothetical groups with one, two, or five observers.[2] The calculations indicate that the victim is about equally likely to get help from one bystander as from two. The victim is considerably more likely to have gotten help from one or two observers than from five during the first minute of the fit. For instance, by 45 seconds after the start of the fit, the victim's chances of having been helped by the single bystanders were about 50%, compared to none in the five observer condition. After the first minute, the likelihood of getting help from at least one person is high in all three conditions.

EFFECT OF GROUP COMPOSITION ON HELPING THE VICTIM

Several variations of the three-person group were run. In one pair of variations, the female subject thought the other bystander was either male or female; in another, she thought the other bystander was a premedical student who worked in an emergency ward at Bellevue hospital. As Table 41.02 shows, the variations in sex and medical competence of the other bystander had no important or detectable affect on speed of response. Subjects responded equally frequently and fast whether the other bystander was female, male, or medically experienced.

SEX OF THE SUBJECT AND SPEED OF RESPONSE

Coping with emergencies is often thought to be the duty of males, especially when females are present, but there was no evidence that this was the case in this study. Male subjects responded to the emergency with almost exactly the same speed as did females (Table 41.02).

REASONS FOR INTERVENTION OR NONINTERVENTION

After the debriefing at the end of the experiment each subject was given a 15-item checklist and asked to check those thoughts which had "crossed your

---

[2] The formula for the probability that at least one person will help by a given time is $1 - (1 - P)^n$ where n is the number of observers and P is the probability of a single individual (who thinks he is one of n observers) helping by that time.

TABLE 41.02

		% RESPONDING		
GROUP SIZE	N	BY END OF FIT	TIME IN SEC.	SPEED SCORE
Female S, male other	13	62	94	74
Female S, female other	13	62	92	71
Female S, male medic other	5	100	60	77
Male S, female other	13	69	110	68

EFFECTS OF GROUP COMPOSITION ON LIKELIHOOD AND SPEED OF RESPONSE[a]

[a]*Three-person group, male victim.*

mind when you heard Subject 1 calling for help." Whatever the condition, each subject checked very few thoughts, and there were no significant differences in number or kind of thoughts in the different experimental groups. The only thoughts checked by more than a few subjects were "I didn't know what to do" (18 out of 65 subjects), "I thought it must be some sort of fake" (20 out of 65), and "I didn't know exactly what was happening" (26 out of 65).

It is possible that subjects were ashamed to report socially undesirable rationalizations, or, since the subjects checked the list *after* the true nature of the experiment had been explained to them, their memories might have been blurred. It is our impression, however, that most subjects checked few reasons because they had few coherent thoughts during the fit.

We asked all subjects whether the presence or absence of other bystanders had entered their minds during the time that they were hearing the fit. Subjects in the three- and six-person groups reported that they were aware that other people were present, but they felt that this made no difference to their own behavior.

INDIVIDUAL DIFFERENCE CORRELATES OF SPEED OF REPORT

The correlations between speed of report and various individual differences on the personality and background measures were obtained by normalizing the distribution of report speeds within each experimental condition and pooling these scores across all conditions ($n = 62-65$). Personality measures showed no important or significant correlations with speed of reporting the emergency. In fact, only one of the 16 individual difference measures, the size of the community in which the subject grew up, correlated ($r = -.26$, $p < .05$) with the speed of helping.

Discussion

Subjects, whether or not they intervened, believed the fit to be genuine and serious. "My God, he's having a fit," many subjects said to themselves (and were overheard via their microphones) at the onset of the fit. Others gasped or simply said "Oh." Several of the male subjects swore. One subject said to herself, "It's just my kind of luck, something has to happen to me!" Several subjects spoke aloud of their confusion about what course of action to take, "Oh God, what should I do?"

When those subjects who intervened stepped out of their rooms, they found the experimental assistant down the hall. With some uncertainty, but without panic, they reported the situation. "Hey, I think Number 1 is very sick. He's having a fit or something." After ostensibly checking on the situation, the experimenter returned to report that "everything is under control." The subjects accepted these assurances with obvious relief.

Subjects who failed to report the emergency showed few signs of the apathy and indifference thought to characterize "unresponsive bystanders." When the experimenter entered her room to terminate the situation, the subject often asked if the victim was "all right." "Is he being taken care of?" "He's all right isn't he?" Many of these subjects showed physical signs of nervousness; they often had trembling hands and sweating palms. If anything, they seemed more emotionally aroused than did the subjects who reported the emergency.

Why, then, didn't they respond? It is our impression that nonintervening subjects had not decided *not* to respond. Rather they were still in a state of indecision and conflict concerning whether to respond or not. The emotional behavior of these nonresponding subjects was a sign of their continuing conflict, a conflict that other subjects resolved by responding.

The fit created a conflict situation of the avoidance-avoidance type. On the one hand, subjects worried about the guilt and shame they would feel if they did not help the person in distress. On the other hand, they were concerned not to make fools of themselves by overreacting, not to ruin the ongoing experiment by leaving their intercom, and not to destroy the anonymous nature of the situation which the experimenter had earlier stressed as important. For subjects in the two-person condition, the obvious distress of the victim and his need for help were so important that their conflict was easily resolved. For the subjects who knew there were other bystanders present, the cost of not helping was reduced and the conflict they were in more acute. Caught between the two negative alternatives of letting the victim continue to suffer or the costs of rushing in to help, the nonresponding bystanders vacillated between them rather than choosing not to respond. This distinction may be academic for the victim, since he got no help in either case, but it is an extremely important one for arriving at an understanding of the causes of bystanders' failures to help.

Although the subjects experienced stress and conflict during the experiment, their general reactions to it were highly positive. On a questionnaire administered after the experimenter had discussed the nature and purpose of the experiment, every single subject found the experiment either "interesting" or "very interesting" and was willing to participate in similar experiments in the future. All subjects felt they understood what the experiment was about and indicated that they thought the deceptions were necessary and justified. All but one felt they were better informed about the nature of psychological research in general.

Male subjects reported the emergency no faster than did females. These results (or lack of them) seem to conflict with the Berkowitz, Klanderman, and Harris (1964) finding that males tend to assume more responsibility and take more initiative than females in giving help to dependent others. Also, females reacted equally fast when the other bystander was another female, a male, or even a person practiced in dealing with medical emergencies. The ineffectiveness of these manipulations of group composition cannot be explained by general insensitivity of the speed measure, since the group-size variable had a marked effect on report speed.

It might be helpful in understanding this lack of difference to distinguish two general classes of intervention in emergency situations: direct and reporto-

rial. Direct intervention (breaking up a fight, extinguishing a fire, swimming out to save a drowner) often requires skill, knowledge, or physical power. It may involve danger. American cultural norms and Berkowitz's results seem to suggest that males are more responsible than females for this kind of direct intervention.

A second way of dealing with an emergency is to report it to someone qualified to handle it, such as the police. For this kind of intervention, there seem to be no norms requiring male action. In the present study, subjects clearly intended to report the emergency rather than take direct action. For such indirect intervention, sex or medical competence does not appear to affect one's qualifications or responsibilities. Anybody, male or female, medically trained or not, can find the experimenter.

In this study, no subject was able to tell how the other subjects reacted to the fit. (Indeed, there were no other subjects actually present.) The effects of group size on speed of helping, therefore, are due simply to the perceived presence of others rather than to the influence of their actions. This means that the experimental situation is unlike emergencies, such as a fire, in which bystanders interact with each other. It is, however, similar to emergencies, such as the Genovese murder, in which spectators knew others were also watching but were prevented by walls between them from communication that might have counteracted the diffusion of responsibility.

The present results create serious difficulties for one class of commonly given explanations for the failure of bystanders to intervene in actual emergencies, those involving apathy or indifference. These explanations generally assert that people who fail to intervene are somehow different in kind from the rest of us, that they are "alienated by industrialization," "dehumanized by urbanization," "depersonalized by living in the cold society," or "psychopaths." These explanations serve a dual function for people who adopt them. First, they explain (if only in a nominal way) the puzzling and frightening problem of why people watch others die. Second, they give individuals reason to deny that they too might fail to help in a similar situation.

The results of this experiment seem to indicate that such personality variables may not be as important as these explanations suggest. Alienation, Machiavellianism, acceptance of social responsibility, need for approval, and authoritarianism are often cited in these explanations. Yet they did not predict the speed or likelihood of help. In sharp contrast, the perceived number of bystanders did. The explanation of bystander "apathy" may lie more in the bystander's response to other observers than in presumed personality deficiencies of "apathetic" individuals. Although this realization may force us to face the guilt-provoking possibility that we too might fail to intervene, it also suggests that individuals are not, of necessity, "noninterveners" because of their personalities. If people understand the situational forces that can make them hesitate to intervene, they may better overcome them.

References

1. Aronfreed, J. The origin of self-criticism. *Psychological Review,* 1964, **71,** 193–219.
2. Berkowitz, L., Klanderman, S., & Harris, R. Effects of experimenter awareness and sex of subject on reactions to dependency relationships. *Sociometry,* 1964, **27,** 327–329.
3. Christie, R. The prevalence of machiavellian orientations. Paper presented at the meeting of the American Psychological Association, Los Angeles, 1964.
4. Crowne, D., & Marlowe, D. *The approval motive.* New York: Wiley, 1964.
5. Daniels, L., & Berkowitz, L. Liking and response to dependency relationships. *Human Relations,* 1963, **16,** 141–148.
6. Milgram, S., & Hollander, P. Murder they heard. *Nation,* 1964, **198,** 602–604.
7. Miller, N., & Dollard, J. *Social learning and imitation.* New Haven: Yale University Press, 1941.
8. Rosenthal, A. M. *Thirty-eight witnesses.* New York: McGraw-Hill, 1964.
9. Whiting, J. W. M., & Child, I. *Child training and personality.* New Haven: Yale University Press, 1953.

QUESTIONS FOR REFLECTION AND DISCUSSION:

1. What kind of emergency situation did Darley and Latané construct to study the bystander effect?

2. How did the researchers determine that subjects in their experiment believed that the emergency (the fit) was real and not feigned?

3. Reporting the (apparent) emergency to an experimental assistant was the operational definition of helping in the Darley and Latané study. Do you believe that this behavior is comparable to calling the police to report the attack on Kitty Genovese? Why or why not?

4. What reasons were given by "bystanders"—that is, by people who did not try to help the person apparently having the fit? Do they sound believable? How do they fit in with the researchers' conclusions?

5. Have you ever passed somebody lying in the street or in a doorway without seeing if you could offer help? Why?

6. Do you behave differently when you are on a crowded city street or in a small town or village? How so? Why?

SOURCE

Calhoun, J. B. (1962). Population density and social pathology. *Scientific American, 206,* 139–148. Reprinted by permission of Ikuyo Tagawa Garber. Copyright © 1962 by Scientific American, Inc. All rights reserved.

Sometimes you do everything you can for laboratory rats. You give them all they can eat, sex partners, a comfortable temperature, and protection from predators such as owls and pussycats. And how do they reward you. By acting like, well, rats.

But let us avoid stereotyping rodents and turn to the literature. In the 1950s and 1960s, researchers were concerned about the effects of the population explosion in the nation's cities. They were concerned that social ills like rape, murder, and child abuse might all stem from crowding. They observed the apparent effects of city life among humans, but the most accurate source of information about cause and effect is the experiment. Experiments require that researchers manipulate the variables they are studying. Researchers cannot manipulate the growth of cities, so some have instead manipulated animal populations and studied the effects. In classic research, John Calhoun allowed rats to reproduce with no constraints but for space, as might occur in a human city. At first, all was normal. Males scurried about, gathered females into harems, and defended territories. Monogamous, they did not covet their neighbors' wives. They rarely fought. Females, unliberated, built nests and nursed their young. They resisted the occasional advance of the passing male.

But unchecked population growth proved to be the snake in rat paradise. Beyond a critical population, the mortality rate rose. Family structure broke down. Packs of delinquent males assaulted inadequately defended females. Other males shunned all social contact. Some females avoided sexual advances and huddled with the fearsome males. There were instances of cannibalism. Upon dissection, many rats showed biological changes characteristic of stress.

Population Density and Social Pathology

JOHN B. CALHOUN

When a population of laboratory rats is allowed to increase in a confined space, the rats develop acutely abnormal patterns of behavior that can even lead to the extinction of the population.

In the celebrated thesis of Thomas Malthus, vice and misery impose the ultimate natural limit on the growth of populations. Students of the subject have given most of their attention to misery, that is, to predation, disease and food supply as forces that operate to adjust the size of a population to its environment. But what of vice? Setting aside the moral burden of this word, what are the effects of the social behavior of a species on population growth—and of population density on social behavior?

Some years ago I attempted to submit this question to experimental inquiry. I confined a population of wild Norway rats in a quarter-acre enclosure. With an abundance of food and places to live and with predation and disease eliminated or minimized, only the animals' behavior with respect to one another remained as a factor that might affect the increase in their number. There could be no escape from the behavioral consequences of rising population density. By the end of 27 months the population had become stabilized at 150 adults. Yet adult mortality was so low that 5,000 adults might have been expected from the observed reproductive rate. The reason this larger population did not materialize was that infant mortality was extremely high. Even with only 150 adults in the enclosure, stress from social interaction led to such disruption of maternal behavior that few young survived.

With this background in mind I turned to observation of a domesticated albino strain of the Norway rat under more controlled circumstances indoors. The data for the present discussion come from the histories of six different populations. Each was permitted to increase to approximately twice the number that my experience had indicated could occupy the available space with only moderate stress from social interaction. In each case my associates and I maintained close surveillance of the colonies for 16 months in order to obtain detailed records of the modifications of behavior induced by population density.

The consequences of the behavioral pathology we observed were most apparent among the females. Many were unable to carry pregnancy to full term or to survive delivery of their litters if they did. An even greater number, after successfully giving birth, fell short in their maternal functions. Among the males the behavior disturbances ranged from sexual deviation to cannibalism and from frenetic overactivity to a pathological withdrawal from which individuals would emerge to eat, drink and move about only when other members of the community were asleep. The social organization of the animals showed equal disruption. Each of the experimental populations divided itself into several groups, in each of which the sex ratios were drastically modified. One group might consist of six or seven females and one male, whereas another would have 20 males and only 10 females.

The common source of these disturbances became most dramatically apparent in the populations of our first series of three experiments, in which we observed the development of what we called a behavioral sink. The animals would crowd together in greatest number in one of the four interconnecting pens in which the colony was maintained. As many as 60 of the 80 rats in each experimental population

would assemble in one pen during periods of feeding. Individual rats would rarely eat except in the company of other rats. As a result extreme population densities developed in the pen adopted for eating, leaving the others with sparse populations.

Eating and other biological activities were thereby transformed into social activities in which the principal satisfaction was interaction with other rats. In the case of eating, this transformation of behavior did not keep the animals from securing adequate nutrition. But the same pathological "togetherness" tended to disrupt the ordered sequences of activity involved in other vital modes of behavior such as the courting of sex partners, the building of nests and the nursing and care of the young. In the experiments in which the behavioral sink developed, infant mortality ran as high as 96 per cent among the most disoriented groups in the population. Even in the absence of the behavioral sink, in the second series of three experiments, infant mortality reached 80 per cent among the corresponding members of the experimental populations.

The design of the experiments was relatively simple. The three populations of the first series each began with 32 rats; each population of the second series began with 56 rats. In all cases the animals were just past weaning and were evenly divided between males and females. By the 12th month all the populations had multiplied and each comprised 80 adults. Thereafter removal of the infants that survived birth and weaning held the populations steady. Although the destructive effects of population density increased during the course of the experiments, and the mortality rate among the females and among the young was much higher in the 16th month than it was earlier, the number of young that survived to weaning was always large enough to offset the effects of adult mortality and actually to increase the population. The evidence indicates, however, that in time failures of reproductive function would have caused the colonies to die out. At the end of the first series of experiments eight rats—the four healthiest males and the four healthiest females in each of two populations—were permitted to survive. These animals were six months old at the time, in the prime of life. Yet in spite of the fact that they no longer lived in overpopulated environments, they produced fewer litters in the next six months than would normally have been expected. Nor did any of the offspring that were born survive to maturity.

The males and females that initiated each experiment were placed, in groups of the same size and sex composition, in each of the four pens that partitioned a 10-by-14-foot observation room. The pens

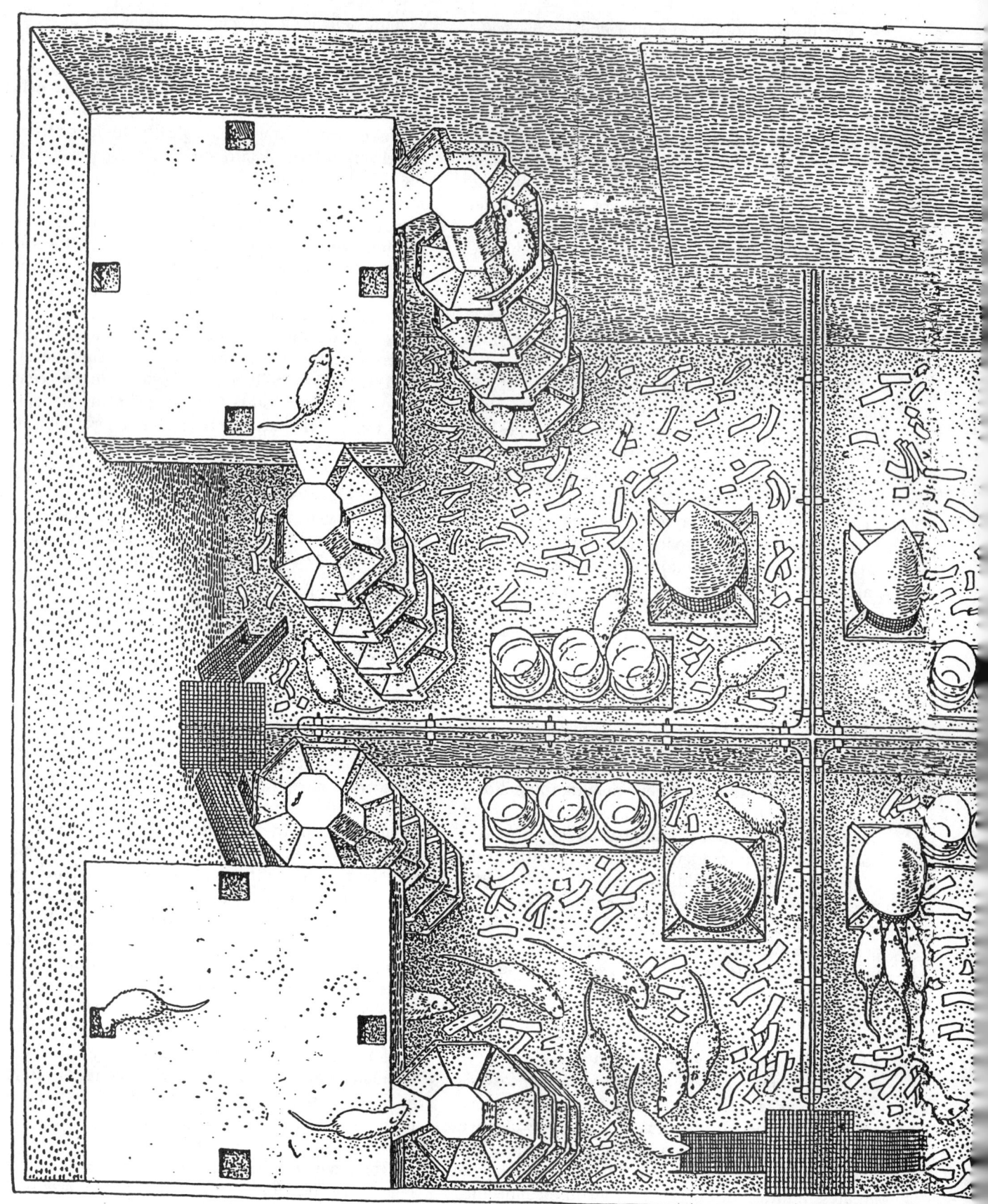

FIGURE 42.01

Effect of population density on the behavior and social organization of rats was studied by confining groups of 80 animals in a 10-by-14-foot room divided into four pens by an electrified fence. All pens (numbered 1, 2, 3 and 4 clockwise from door) were complete dwelling units. Conical objects are food hoppers; trays with three bottles are drinking troughs. Elevated burrows, reached by winding staircases, each had five nest boxes, seen in pen 1, where top of burrow has been removed. Ramps connected all pens but 1 and 4. Rats therefore tended to concentrate in pens 2 and 3. Development of a "behavioral sink," which further increased population in one pen, is reflected in pen 2, where three rats are eating simultaneously. Rat approaching ramp in pen 3 is an estrous female pursued by a pack of males. In pens 2 and 3, where population density was highest, males outnumbered females. In pens 1 and 4 a dominant male was usually able to expel all other males and possess a harem of females. Dominant males are sleeping at the base of the ramps in pens 1 and 4. They wake when other males approach, preventing incursions into their territories. The three rats peering down from a ramp are probers, one of the deviant behavioral types produced by the pressures of a high population density.

Harcourt, Inc.

were complete dwelling units; each contained a drinking fountain, a food hopper and an elevated artificial burrow, reached by a winding staircase and holding five nest boxes. A window in the ceiling of the room permitted observation, and there was a door in one wall. With space for a colony of 12 adults in each pen—the size of the groups in which rats are normally found—this setup should have been able to support 48 rats comfortably. At the stabilized number of 80, an equal distribution of the animals would have found 20 adult rats in each pen. But the animals did not dispose themselves in this way.

Biasing factors were introduced in the physical design of the environment to encourage differential use of the four pens. The partitions separating the pens were electrified so that the rats could not climb them. Ramps across three of the partitions enabled the animals to get from one pen to another and so traverse the entire room. With no ramps to permit crossing of the fourth partition, however, the pens on each side of it became the end pens of what was topologically a row of four. The rats had to make a complete circuit of the room to go from the pen we designated 1 to the pen designated 4 on the other side of the partition separating the two. This arrangement of ramps immediately skewed the mathematical probabilities in favor of a higher population density in pens 2 and 3 than in pens 1 and 4. Pens 2 and 3 could be reached by two ramps, whereas pens 1 and 4 had only one each.

The use of pen 4 was further discouraged by the elevation of its burrow to a height greater than that of the burrow in the other end pen. The two middle pens were similarly distinguished from each other, the burrow in pen 3 being higher than that in pen 2. But here the differential appears to have played a smaller role, although pen 2 was used somewhat more often than pen 3.

With the distribution of the rats biased by these physical arrangements, the sizes of the groups in each pen could have been expected to range from as few as 13 to as many as 27. With the passage of time, however, changes in behavior tended to skew the distribution of the rats among the pens even more. Of the 100 distinct sleeping groups counted in the 10th to 12th month of each experiment, only 37 fell within the expected size range. In 33 groups there were fewer than 13 rats, and in 30 groups the count exceeded 27. The sex ratio approximated equality only in those groups that fell within the expected size range. In the smaller groups, generally composed of eight adults, there were seldom more than two males. In the larger groups, on the other hand, there were many more males than females. As

might be expected, the smaller groups established themselves in the end pens, whereas the larger groups were usually observed to form in the middle pens. The female members of the population distributed themselves about equally in the four pens, but the male population was concentrated almost overwhelmingly in the middle pens.

One major factor in the creation of this state of affairs was the struggle for status that took place among the males. Shortly after male rats reach maturity, at about six months of age, they enter into a round robin of fights that eventually fixes their position in the social hierarchy. In our experiments such fights took place among the males in all the pens, both middle and end. In the end pens, however, it became possible for a single dominant male to take over the area as his territory. During the period when the social hierarchy was being established, the subordinate males in all pens adopted the habit of arising early. This enabled them to eat and drink in peace. Since rats generally eat in the course of their normal wanderings, the subordinate residents of the end pens were likely to feed in one of the middle pens. When, after feeding, they wanted to return to their original quarters, they would find it very difficult. By this time the most dominant male in the pen would probably have awakened, and he would engage the subordinates in fights as they tried to come down the one ramp to the pen. For a while the subordinate would continue its efforts to return to what had been its home pen, but after a succession of defeats it would become so conditioned that it would not even make the attempt. In essence the dominant male established his territorial dominion and his control over a harem of females not by driving the other males out but by preventing their return.

Once a male had established his dominion over an end pen and the harem it contained, he was usually able to maintain it. Although he slept a good deal of the time, he made his sleeping quarters at the base of the ramp. He was, therefore, on perpetual guard. Awakening as soon as another male appeared at the head of the ramp, he had only to open his eyes for the invader to wheel around and return to the adjoining pen. On the other hand, he would sleep calmly through all the comings and goings of his harem; seemingly he did not even hear their clatterings up and down the wire ramp. His conduct during his waking hours reflected his dominant status. He would move about in a casual and deliberate fashion, occasionally inspecting the burrow and nests of his harem. But he would rarely enter a burrow, as some other males did, merely to ferret out the females.

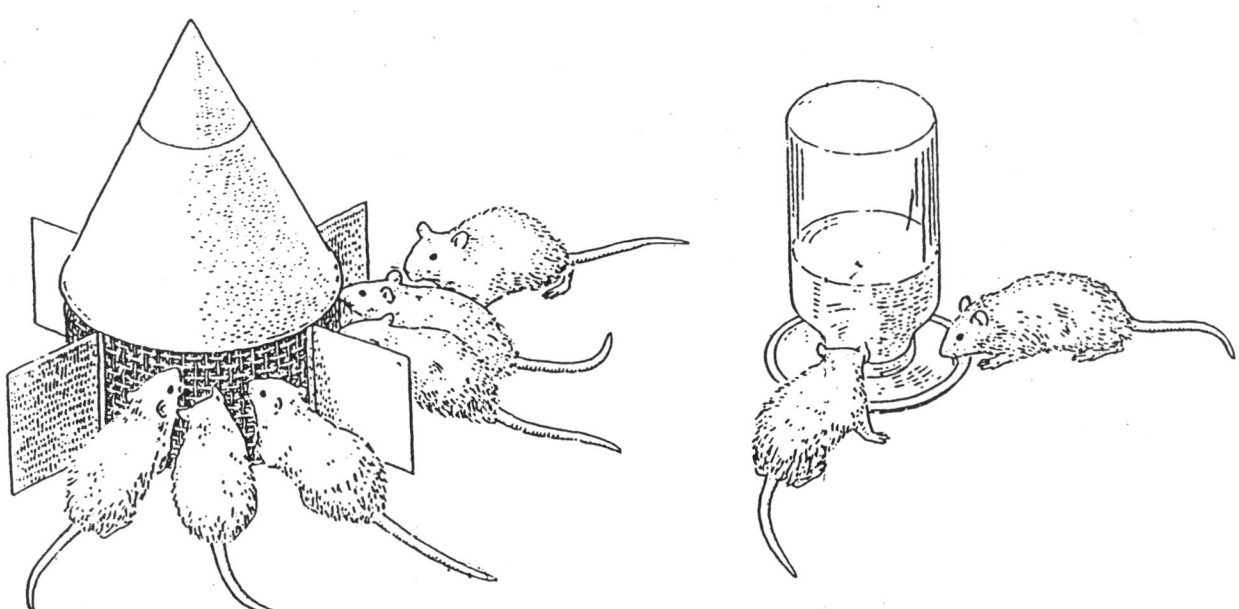

Food hopper used in first series of experiments is seen at the left in this drawing. Water tray is at the right. The hopper, covered with wire grating and holding hard pellets of food, made eating a lengthy activity during which one rat was likely to meet another. Thus it fostered the development of a behavioral sink: the animals would eat only in the presence of others, and they preferred one of the four hoppers in the room to all the others. In time 75 per cent of the animals crowded into the pen containing this hopper to eat.

Water fountain used in second series of experiments is seen at the right in this drawing. Food hopper is at the left. The fountain was operated by pressing a lever. Thus it made drinking a lengthy activity, associated with the presence of others. But it did not create a behavioral sink. Although the rats would drink only if other animals were present, they engaged in this activity in their home pens immediately after awakening. The fountain therefore acted to produce an even distribution of the population.

FIGURE 42.02

A territorial male might tolerate other males in his domain provided they respected his status. Such subordinate males inhabited the end pens in several of the experiments. Phlegmatic animals, they spent most of their time hidden in the burrow with the adult females, and their excursions to the floor lasted only as long as it took them to obtain food and water. Although they never attempted to engage in sexual activity with any of the females, they were likely, on those rare occasions when they encountered the dominant male, to make repeated attempts to mount him. Generally the dominant male tolerated these advances.

In these end pens, where population density was lowest, the mortality rate among infants and females was also low. Of the various social environments that developed during the course of the experiments, the brood pens, as we called them, appeared to be the only healthy ones, at least in terms of the survival of the group. The harem females generally made good mothers. They nursed their young, built nests for them and protected them from harm. If any situation arose that a mother considered a danger to her pups, she would pick the infants up one at a time and carry them in her mouth to a safer place. Nothing would distract her from this task until the entire litter had been moved. Half the infants born in the brood pens survived.

The pregnancy rates recorded among the females in the middle pens were no lower than those recorded in the end pens. But a smaller percentage of these pregnancies terminated in live births. In the second series of experiments 80 per cent of the infants born in the middle pens died before weaning. In the first series 96 per cent perished before this time. The males in the middle pens were no less affected than the females by the pressures of population density. In both series of experiments the social pathology among the males was high. In the first series, however, it was more aggravated than it was in the second.

This increase in disturbance among the middle-pen occupants of the first series of experiments was directly related to the development of the phenomenon of the behavioral sink—the outcome of any behavioral process that collects animals together in unusually great numbers. The unhealthy connotations of the term are not accidental: a behavioral sink does act to aggravate all forms of pathology that can be found within a group.

The emergence of a behavioral sink was fostered by the arrangements that were made for feeding the animals. In these experiments the food consisted of small, hard pellets that were kept in a circular hopper formed by wire-mesh. In consequence satisfaction of hunger required a continuous effort lasting several minutes. The chances therefore were good that while one rat was eating another would join it at the hopper. As was mentioned earlier, rats usually eat intermittently throughout their waking hours, whenever they are hungry and food is available. Since the arrangement of the ramps drew more rats into the middle pens than into the end ones, it was in these pens that individuals were most likely to find other individuals eating. As the population increased, the association of eating with the presence of other animals was further reinforced. Gradually the social aspect of the activity became determinant: the rats would rarely eat except at hoppers already in use by other animals.

At this point the process became a vicious circle. As more and more of the rats tended to collect at the hopper in one of the middle pens, the other hoppers became less desirable as eating places. The rats that were eating at these undesirable locations, finding themselves deserted by their groupmates, would transfer their feeding to the more crowded pen. By the time the three experiments in the first series drew to a close half or more of the populations were sleeping as well as eating in that pen. As a result there was a decided increase in the number of social adjustments each rat had to make every day. Regardless of which pen a rat slept in, it would go to one particular middle pen several times a day to eat. Therefore it was compelled daily to make some sort of adjustment to virtually every other rat in the experimental population.

No behavioral sinks developed in the second series of experiments, because we offered the rats their diet in a different way. A powdered food was set out in an open hopper. Since it took the animals only a little while to eat, the probability that two animals would be eating simultaneously was considerably reduced. In order to foster the emergence of a behavioral sink I supplied the pens with drinking fountains designed to prolong the drinking activity. The effect of this arrangement was unquestionably to make the animals social drinkers; they used the fountain mainly when other animals lined up at it. But the effect was also to discourage them from wandering and to prevent the development of a behavioral sink. Since rats generally drink immediately on arising, drinking and the social interaction it occasioned tended to keep them in the pens in which they slept. For this reason all social pathology in the second series of experiments, although severe, was less extreme than it was in the first series.

Females that lived in the densely populated middle pens became progressively less adept at building adequate nests and eventually stopped building nests at all. Normally rats of both sexes build nests, but females do so most vigorously around the time of parturition. It is an undertaking that involves repeated periods of sustained activity, searching out appropriate materials (in our experiments strips of paper supplied an abundance), transporting them bit by bit to the nest and there arranging them to form a cuplike depression, frequently sheltered by a hood. In a crowded middle pen, however, the ability of females to persist in this biologically essential activity became markedly impaired. The first sign of disruption was a failure to build the nest to normal specifications. These females simply piled the strips of paper in a heap, sometimes trampling them into a pad that showed little sign of cup formation. Later in the experiment they would bring fewer and fewer strips to the nesting site. In the midst of transporting a bit of material they would drop it to engage in some other activity occasioned by contact and

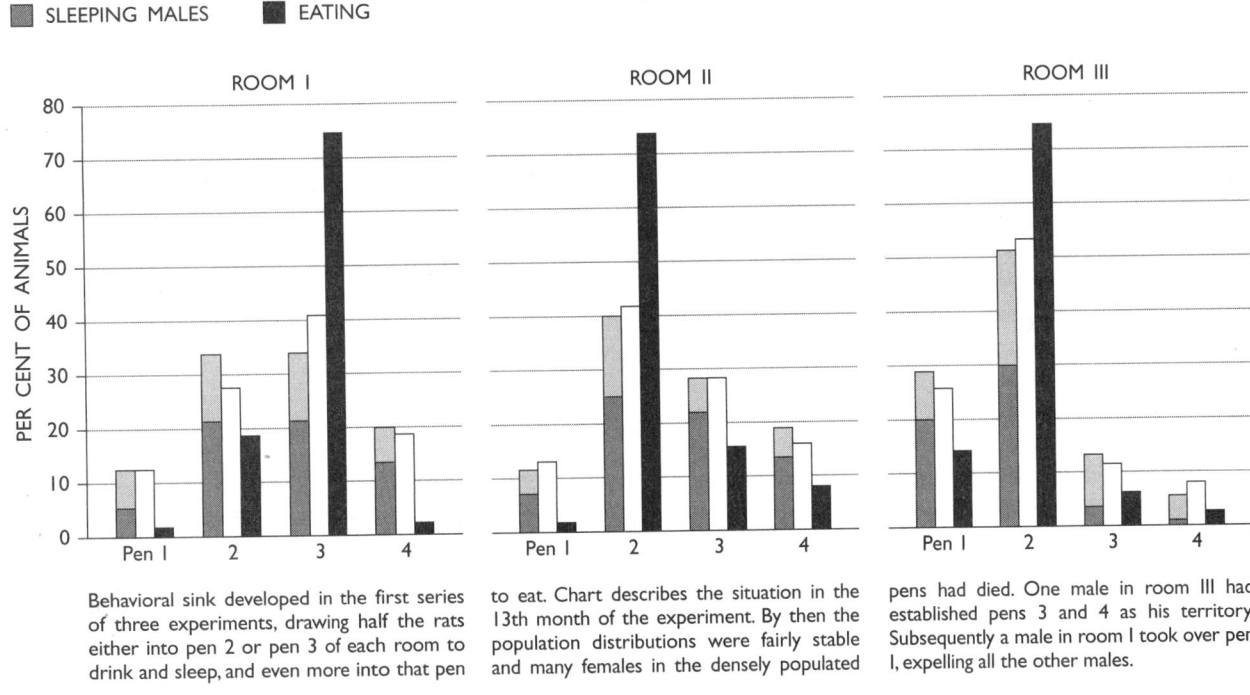

SLEEPING FEMALES   DRINKING
SLEEPING MALES   EATING

Behavioral sink developed in the first series of three experiments, drawing half the rats either into pen 2 or pen 3 of each room to drink and sleep, and even more into that pen

to eat. Chart describes the situation in the 13th month of the experiment. By then the population distributions were fairly stable and many females in the densely populated

pens had died. One male in room III had established pens 3 and 4 as his territory. Subsequently a male in room I took over pen I, expelling all the other males.

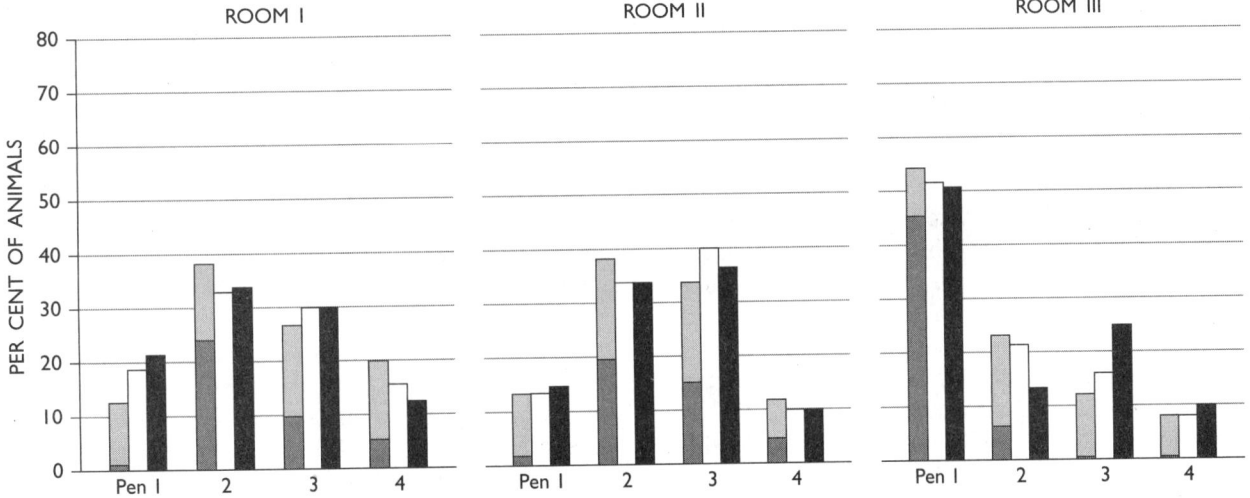

Population distributions in the second series of three experiments, in which no behavioral sink developed, were more even than they were in the first series, and the death rate

among females and infants was lower. Chart shows the situation in the 13th month, when one male had established pens 3 and 4 of room III as his territory, and another was

taking over pen 2, thus forcing most of the males into pen I. Pen I in rooms I and II had also become territories; later pen 4 in room II became a territory.

FIGURE 42.03

interaction with other individuals met on the way. In the extreme disruption of their behavior during the later months of the population's history they would build no nests at all but would bear their litters on the sawdust in the burrow box.

The middle-pen females similarly lost the ability to transport their litters from one place to another. They would move only part of their litters and would scatter them by depositing the infants in different places or simply dropping them on the floor of the pen. The infants thus abandoned throughout the pen were seldom nursed. They would die where they were dropped and were thereupon generally eaten by the adults.

The social stresses that brought about this disorganization in the behavior of the middle-pen females were imposed with special weight on them when they came into heat. An estrous female would be pursued relentlessly by a pack of males, unable to escape from their soon unwanted attentions. Even when she retired to a burrow, some males would follow her. Among these females there was a correspondingly high rate of mortality from disorders in pregnancy and parturition. Nearly half of the first- and second-generation females that lived in the behavioral-sink situation had died of these causes by the end of the 16th month. Even in the absence of the extreme stresses of the behavioral sink, 25 per cent of the females died. In contrast, only 15 per cent of the adult males in both series of experiments died.

A female that lived in a brood pen was sheltered from these stresses even though during her periods of estrus she would leave her pen to mate with males in the other pens of the room. Once she was satiated, however, she could return to the brood pen. There she was protected from the excessive attention of other males by the territorial male.

For the effect of population density on the males there is no index as explicit and objective as the infant and maternal mortality rates. We have attempted a first approximation of such an index, however, by scoring the behavior of the males on two scales: that of dominance and that of physical activity. The first index proved particularly effective in the early period of the experiments, when the males were approaching adulthood and beginning the fights that eventually fixed their status in the social hierarchy. The more fights a male initiated and the more fights he won, the more likely he was to establish a position of dominance. More than half the animals in each experiment gave up the struggle for status after a while, but among those that persisted a clear-cut hierarchy developed.

In the crowded middle pens no one individual occupied the top position in this hierarchy permanently. In every group of 12 or more males one was the most aggressive and most often the victor in fights. Nevertheless, this rat was periodically ousted from his position. At regular intervals during the course of their waking hours the top-ranking males engaged in free-for-alls that culminated in the transfer of dominance from one male to another. In between these tumultuous changings of the guard relative calm prevailed.

The aggressive, dominant animals were the most normal males in our populations. They seldom bothered either the females or the juveniles. Yet even they exhibited occasional signs of pathology, going berserk, attacking females, juveniles and the less active males, and showing a particular predilection—

which rats do not normally display—for biting other animals on the tail.

Below the dominant males both on the status scale and in their level of activity were the homosexuals—a group perhaps better described as pansexual. These animals apparently could not discriminate between appropriate and inappropriate sex partners. They made sexual advances to males, juveniles and females that were not in estrus. The males, including the dominants as well as the others of the pansexuals' own group, usually accepted their attentions. The general level of activity of these animals was only moderate. They were frequently attacked by their dominant associates, but they very rarely contended for status.

Two other types of male emerged, both of which had resigned entirely from the struggle for dominance. They were, however, at exactly opposite poles as far as their levels of activity were concerned. The first were completely passive and moved through the community like somnambulists. They ignored all the other rats of both sexes, and all the other rats ignored them. Even when the females were in estrus, these passive animals made no advances to them. And only very rarely did other males attack them or approach them for any kind of play. To the casual observer the passive animals would have appeared to be the healthiest and most attractive members of the community. They were fat and sleek, and their fur showed none of the breaks and bare spots left by the fighting in which males usually engage. But their social disorientation was nearly complete.

Perhaps the strangest of all the types that emerged among the males was the group I have called the probers. These animals, which always lived in the middle pens, took no part at all in the status struggle. Nevertheless, they were the most active of all the males in the experimental populations, and they persisted in their activity in spite of attacks by the dominant animals. In addition to being hyperactive, the probers were both hypersexual and homosexual, and in time many of them became cannibalistic. They were always on the alert for estrous females. If there were none in their own pens, they would lie in wait for long periods at the tops of the ramps that gave on the brood pens and peer down into them. They always turned and fled as soon as the territorial rat caught sight of them. Even if they did not manage to escape unhurt, they would soon return to their vantage point.

The probers conducted their pursuit of estrous females in an abnormal manner. Mating among rats usually involves a distinct courtship ritual. In the first phase of this ritual the male pursues the

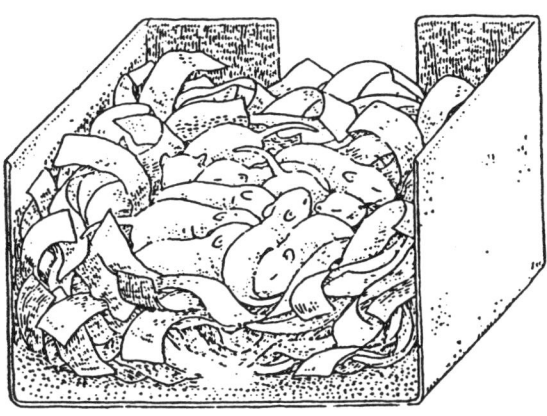

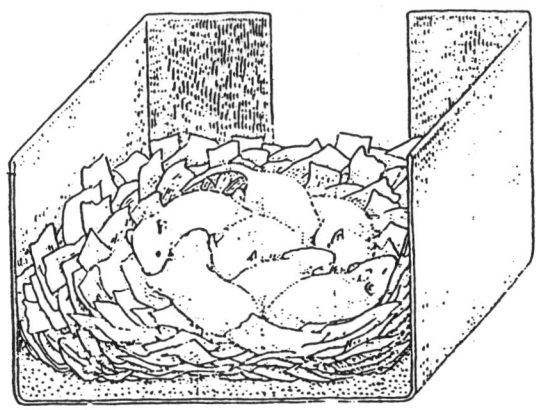

Normal maternal behavior among rats includes building a fluffy, well-shaped nest for the young. The drawing at the left shows such a nest, holding a recently born litter. The drawing at the right shows this same nest about two weeks later. It has been flattened by the weight of the animals' bodies but it still offers ample protection and warmth, and the remaining pups can still rest comfortably. In these experiments half the offspring of normal mothers survived infancy and were successfully weaned.

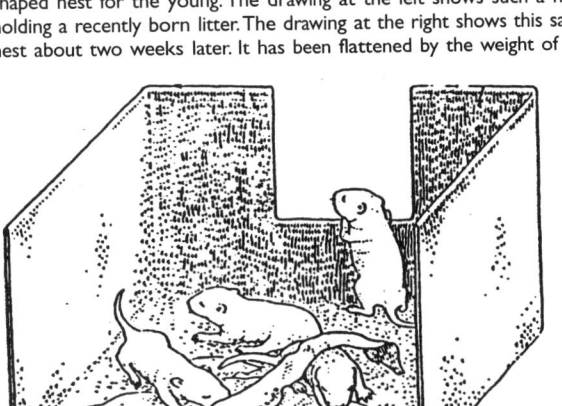

Abnormal maternal behavior, shown by females exposed to the pressures of population density, includes failure to build adequate nests. The drawing at the left shows the recently born young of a disturbed female. She started to make a nest but never finished it. The drawing at the right shows her young about two weeks later. One pup has already left and another is leaving. Neither can survive alone. In these experiments the mortality rate among infants of disturbed mothers was as high as 96 per cent.

FIGURE 42.04

female. She thereupon retires for a while into the burrow, and the male lies quietly in wait outside, occasionally poking his head into the burrow for a moment but never entering it. (In the wild forms of the Norway rat this phase usually involves a courtship dance on the mound at the mouth of the burrow.) The female at last emerges from the burrow and accepts the male's advances. Even in the disordered community of the middle pens this pattern was observed by all the males who engaged in normal heterosexual behavior. But the probers would not tolerate even a short period of waiting at the burrows in the pens where accessible females lived. As soon as a female retired to a burrow, a prober would follow her inside. On these expeditions the probers often found dead young lying in the nests; as a result they tended to become cannibalistic in the later months of a population's history.

Although the behavioral sink did not develop in the second series of experiments, the pathology exhibited by the populations in both sets of experiments, and in all pens, was severe. Even in the brood pens females could raise only half their young to weaning. Nor does the difference in infant mortality between the middle pens of the first and second series—96 per cent in the first as opposed to 80 per cent in the second—represent a biologically significant improvement. It is obvious that the behavioral repertory with which the Norway rat has emerged from the trials of evolution and domestication must break down under the social pressures generated by population density. In time, refinement of experimental procedures and of the interpretation of these studies may advance our understanding to the point where they may contribute to the making of value judgments about analogous problems confronting the human species.

QUESTIONS FOR REFLECTION AND DISCUSSION:

1. Environmental psychologists distinguish between high density (which simply means a large number of people in a relatively small area) and crowding (which refers to uncomfortable closeness). People crowded into prisons, hospitals, even college dormitories, may share some of the problems encountered by Calhoun's rats, such as increased blood pressure. Have you experienced high density and crowding? What accounted for the difference between the two?

2. How did the population of adult rats in Calhoun's enclosure come to stabilize at about 150? How were the numbers contained?

3. What does Calhoun mean by the term "behavioral sink"? What conditions in his experiment created a behavioral sink?

4. Can you generalize from rats to humans? In what ways are the rats in Calhoun's research similar to humans? How are they different? Do you believe that the results of the Calhoun study can be generalized to humans? (That is, does Calhoun's research show that high density in human cities causes social pathology?) If so, how? If not, why not?

5. Have you had the experience of adjusting to crowding? What did you do to cope with the situation?

6. Calhoun's rats had very little control over their crowding. What can people do to reduce the aversiveness of crowding?

SOURCE

Donnerstein, E. I., & Wilson, D. W. (1976). Effects of noise and perceived control on ongoing and subsequent aggressive behavior. *Journal of Personality and Social Psychology, 34,* 774–781. Copyright © 1976 by the American Psychological Association. Reprinted with permission.

Environmental psychologists study the ways in which humans and the physical environment influence each other. Topics of interest include the effects of noise (and noise pollution), high and low ambient temperatures, air pollution, and the presence of other people (as in the issues of crowding and personal space).

Many classic experiments were carried out by environmental psychologists in the 1960s and 1970s. The article by Edward Donnerstein and David Wilson refers to having subjects write essays on whether Richard Nixon (who resigned as President in 1974) should have been pardoned (by President Gerald Ford). The article also shows that there is a tendency for high levels of noise, which are aversive stimuli, to increase aggressive behavior among people who are angry. However, not all noise is the same. We might be upset by noisy snoring or by a neighbor's TV set, although we may enjoy noise that is louder yet when we are cheering at a football game or dancing at the disco. The quality of the noise is obviously of interest, but so is our sense of whether or not we are in control of it. We may perceive ourselves to be victimized by the neighbor's TV, but we choose to go to the disco.

Effects of Noise and Perceived Control on Ongoing and Subsequent Aggressive Behavior

EDWARD DONNERSTEIN AND DONALD W. WILSON
IOWA STATE UNIVERSITY

Two experiments examined the effects of high-intensity (95 dB [A]) noise on ongoing and postnoise aggressive behavior. In Experiment 1, subjects were angered or treated in a neutral manner and given an opportunity to aggress against another subject while being exposed to high-intensity (95 dB) or low-intensity (55 dB) noise. Results indicated that high-intensity noise facilitated aggression for previously angered individuals. Experiment 2 examined postnoise aggression in which subjects completed a math task under high-intensity noise with or without perceived control over the noise. In comparison to a no-noise control, it was found that angered subjects with no control revealed an increase in aggression, whereas perceived-control subjects were no different from no-noise subjects. Results are discussed in terms of the recent Glass and Singer work on noise and task performance and the effects of perceived control on mediating the effects of stressful conditions.

Recently there has been increasing concern with the effects of various environmental stimuli (e.g., noise, pollution, overcrowding) on the quality of human life. While much of this research has focused on health- or task-performance-related problems, recent studies have begun to deal with interpersonal behaviors such as aggression (Baron & Bell, 1975), attraction (Griffitt, 1970), and altruism (Sherrod & Downs, 1974). The effects of noise, in particular, have received much attention. In a significant and systematic investigation of high-intensity noise on physiological responses and task performance, Glass and Singer (1972) have indicated that "unpredictable and uncontrollable noise should affect aggressiveness, exploitative behavior, liking for others, and general irritability in interpersonal relations" (p. 159). While there has been some evidence of noise effects on prosocial responses such as helping behavior (Sherrod & Downs, 1974), except for studies on low-intensity noise (Geen & O'Neal, 1969) and field research (Ward & Suedfeld, 1974), there has been to date no systematic attempt to examine the effects of high-intensity noise on more negative interpersonal behaviors such as aggression. It was the purpose, therefore, of the present studies to examine within the framework of the Glass and Singer research the varying effects of high-intensity noise on interpersonal aggression.

In their research, Glass and Singer investigated the effects of differing forms of noise (i.e., high or low intensity, predictable or unpredictable, controllable or uncontrollable) on both ongoing and subsequent task performance and physiological responses. Since their results indicated markedly different patterns for ongoing and subsequent performance, the present authors conducted two separate studies in which noise effects were examined with respect to ongoing aggressive behavior (Experiment 1) and aggressive behavior following exposure to high-intensity noise (Experiment 2). In addition, another important variable in the Glass and Singer research, that of perceived control, was also examined in light of its potential consequences on aggressive behavior.

Experiment 1: Ongoing Aggressive Behavior

An interesting finding of the Glass and Singer (1972) work was the somewhat rapid adaptation, both physiologically and behaviorally, to high-intensity unpredictable noise. Thus, in terms of ongoing simple task performance, high-intensity noise did not impair performance. In addition, while there was an initial increase in physiological arousal, after a few minutes individuals returned to a base level indicative of an adaptation to the noise. The intent of the present study, then, was to examine ongoing aggressive behavior under noise conditions similar to those of Glass and Singer. In the present study,

male subjects were either angered or treated in a neutral manner by a confederate and subsequently given an opportunity to aggress against the confederate via the administration of electric shock. While delivering shock, subjects were subjected to either a low-intensity (52 dB [A]) or high-intensity (95 dB) unpredictable and uncontrollable noise. Unpredictable and uncontrollable types of noise were employed because they were the forms most conducive to potential effects in the Glass and Singer work. Based on the Glass and Singer research and recent work in the aggression area, one of three possible predictions could be made with regard to the effects of high-intensity noise on ongoing aggressive behavior.

First, given the results of the Glass and Singer work, it might be predicted that there would be an initial increase in aggressive responding under high-intensity noise due to a general increase in the level of arousal. This should occur for both angered and nonangered subjects since Glass and Singer indicate that noise produces a general irritability in interpersonal relations. As subjects became more adapted to the noise, however, there would be a decrease in arousal and subsequent aggression. If this is the case, then higher shock levels should be exhibited in the early shock trials of the present study, with later trials revealing a gradual decrease in intensity level.

A second possible prediction is that aggression will be facilitated by exposure to high-intensity noise for previously angered subjects. This is based on the notion that any source of emotional arousal will tend to facilitate aggression in individuals who are predisposed (i.e., angered) to aggress (Bandura, 1973). Research in which individuals have been angered and subsequently exposed to arousal via strenuous exercise (Zillmann, Katcher, & Milavsky, 1972), erotic stimuli (Donnerstein, Donnerstein, & Evans, 1975; Zillmann, 1971) or drugs (O'Neal & Kaufman, 1972) have lent support to this position. Recent research in this area suggests that subjects come to label their general arousal level from previous anger and external sources (e.g., erotic films) as heightened anger (Konečni, 1975b). This is, of course, analogous to the Schachter–Singer two-factor theory of emotion (Schachter & Singer, 1962) and the recent work of Zillmann on excitation transfer (Zillmann, 1971; Zillmann et al., 1972).[1] Given that subjects are in constant contact with the

---

[1] Recently, Harris and Huang (1974) have shown that when subjects can attribute their arousal to the noise, there is not an increase in aggressive behavior. This, of course, would support the interpretation give above.

source of their anger, it would be expected that their level of anger should remain constant or even increase. In addition, based on research utilizing the shock paradigm as a means of aggressing (e.g., Buss, 1961), it would even be expected that shock levels should increase over trials due to a disinhibition of aggression (Goldstein, Davis, & Herman, 1975).

A third possible prediction is an inhibition of aggression for angered subjects due to the added aversiveness of the high-intensity noise. Baron and Bell (1975) recently found that high ambient temperature served to reduce aggression in previously angered individuals. They speculated that rather than aggression, escape from the aversive situation was the dominant response in the subject's hierarchy. In order to avoid delays such as victim protests or experimenter censure from the use of high shocks, subjects reduced their shock levels to terminate the experiment more rapidly. If this is the case in the present study, it would be expected that shock levels would remain low over trials, or even reveal a decrease, for angered subjects exposed to the aversive high-intensity noise.

In summary, the first experiment investigated the effects of high-intensity noise on ongoing aggressive behavior. Given recent research and theorizing in the area, aggression was expected to either (a) increase and then gradually decrease, (b) be facilitated in angered individuals, or (c) reveal an inhibition due to the aversiveness of the situation.

Method

SUBJECTS

The subjects were 40 male undergraduates who volunteered for extra course credit in introductory psychology.

APPARATUS

Shock was ostensibly administered via a modified Buss (1961) "aggression machine." There were eight shock buttons to be used for shock administration plus one additional button that ostensibly signaled a correct response via a light. A voltage meter above the buttons was calibrated to indicate that higher numbered shock buttons delivered stronger shocks. A set of four lights in the upper right corner was used for communication between the subject and learner. Noise was transcribed from a standard white-noise generator onto a tape recording. Decibel readings were taken at earphone level with two settings, 55 dB and 95 dB, having been selected for

experimental conditions. Noise was administered via a stereo tape recorder and headphone system.

PROCEDURE

Upon arriving for the experiment, the subject was taken to an experimental room where the aggression machine and a number of pieces of bogus physiological equipment were located. Soon a confederate of the experimenter arrived posing as another subject. Both subjects were told that the experiment dealt with the effects of various forms of stress on learning. They were further informed that they would both be asked to take some form of a learning task under stress. The subjects were then given an "informed consent form" to sign, which noted, in addition to the above, that they would be asked both to administer and receive electric shock during the experiment and possibly be exposed to high-intensity white noise. After subjects signed the form, the experimenter supposedly randomly chose the subject to take the first task and took the confederate to another room where he would presumably begin studying for the second task. The subject was told that he would be asked to write a short essay on a recent social issue under the stress that the essay would be evaluated by the other subject through the use of electric shock. It was noted that the evaluation would range from 0 to 10 shocks, with higher shocks indicating a poorer rating. In addition, a written evaluation would be given. This type of anger manipulation is similar to that employed in other studies (e.g., Baron, 1974; Berkowitz & Geen, 1966).

Anger Manipulation The subject was then given 5 minutes to write a short essay on the topic, "whether Richard Nixon should have been pardoned." After the elapsed time, the experimenter returned and took the essay to the other subject, supposedly for him to read. He then returned and attached two electrodes to the subject's fingers. The subject was told that when the four lights on the aggression machine panel were lighted, the evaluation would take place. The experimenter then left the room and shortly thereafter signaled the onset of the evaluation. Subjects in the anger condition were given nine shocks of .5-second duration. Nonangered subjects received only one shock. The experimenter returned to the subject's room with a questionnaire, supposedly completed by the other subject, that evaluated the essay and the subject on a number of bipolar scales. Subjects under anger conditions received negative ratings, whereas nonangered subjects were given positive evaluations.

Exposure to Noise and Administration of Aggression After receiving the two forms of evaluation, the subject was informed that the other subject (who is now referred to as the learner) would now take his task under stress. He was told that the learner would be taking a paired-associate learning task under the stress of electric shock for incorrect responses. Since the experimenter would be involved in monitoring some physiological measures, the subject was informed that he would administer the task and the stressor. The subject was told to call out the stimulus word over the intercom and wait for the learner's answer, which would be signaled by lighting one of the four answer lights on the shock apparatus. The subject was further told that if the response was correct, he was to signal the learner by pushing the button labeled "light," which would ostensibly inform the learner that he made a correct response. The subject was then told that when the learner made an incorrect response, he was to deliver an electric shock. It was noted that any arbitrarily determined intensity could be delivered but that each button on the shock apparatus represented a different shock intensity of increasing magnitude. The subject was then handed a list of 30 consonant-vowel-consonant nonsense syllables of medium M' value (Noble, 1961) and a list of correct responses.

At this point the experimenter indicated that he was interested in trying out a new form of stressor on physiological reactions while an individual was performing a relatively simple task. The subject was informed that while he was administering the learning task, he was to wear a set of headphones over which blasts of white noise would be delivered periodically. It was further explained that his galvanic skin response would be monitored during this time. The subject was presumably chosen for this supposed pilot test because the administration of the learning task was a relatively simple procedure. The experimenter then attached two electrodes from a bogus galvanometer to the subject, instructed him to put on the headphones, and noted that he would be signaled when to begin the learning task.

Shortly thereafter, the subject was signaled to begin the learning task. The subject verbally administered the 30 nonsense syllables and received back from the learner 20 incorrect and 10 correct responses randomly distributed over five blocks of six trials each. Since the experimenter controlled the learner's signaled responses, the task took approximately 8 minutes. During this time the subject was subjected to unpredictable aperiodic 1-second noise bursts. The bursts occurred on the average every 4 seconds, with half the subjects exposed to high-

intensity (95 dB) noise and the remainder to low-intensity (55 dB) noise.

Following the administration of aggression and exposure to noise, the subject was given a brief questionnaire to complete. The questionnaire asked him to rate on a 7-point scale his reactions to the noise and the ratings he received from the other subject. These scores served as manipulation checks for the various conditions. Finally the subject was completely debriefed as to the true nature of the experiment and thanked for his participation.[2]

The experiment was conducted by two experimenters and two confederates who were balanced across all conditions. Since neither of these factors had any significant effects on the results, only the data for the Anger and Noise factors are reported in the subsequent analyses.

Results and Discussion

MANIPULATION CHECKS

Subjects were asked to rate on 7-point scales the quality of rating they received for their essay and how angry they felt after having received the rating. Analyses revealed that angered subjects perceived their rating as poorer, $F(1, 36) = 361.25$, $p < .001$; $Ms = 6.9$ and 1.1, and indicated more anger, $F(1, 36) = 34.42$, $p < .001$; $Ms = 3.8$ and 1.0, than their nonangered counterparts. Additional questions asked subjects to evaluate the noise they had been exposed to during the learning task. Subjects exposed to high-intensity noise rated the noise as louder, $F(1, 36) = 43.18$, $p < .001$; $Ms = 4.9$ and 2.4, more annoying, $F(1, 36) = 18.54$, $p < .001$; $Ms = 4.7$ and 2.5, more aversive, $F(1, 36) = 35.40$, $p < .001$; $Ms = 4.4$ and 2.0, and were more anxious for the experiment to end, $F(1, 36) = 5.12$, $p < .05$; $Ms = 4.5$ and 3.3. The preceding data, then, would tend to support the effectiveness of the anger and noise manipulations.

AGGRESSION DATA

A $2 \times 2 \times 5$ (Anger $\times$ Noise Intensity $\times$ Trials) analysis of variance (ANOVA) was conducted on the shock-intensity data. Significant sources of variation were obtained for anger, $F(1, 36) = 132.63$,

---

[2] During the debriefing, subjects were questioned as to any suspicion regarding the experiment. In both Experiments 1 and 2 no subjects expressed suspicion concerning any of the manipulations or hypotheses under investigation.

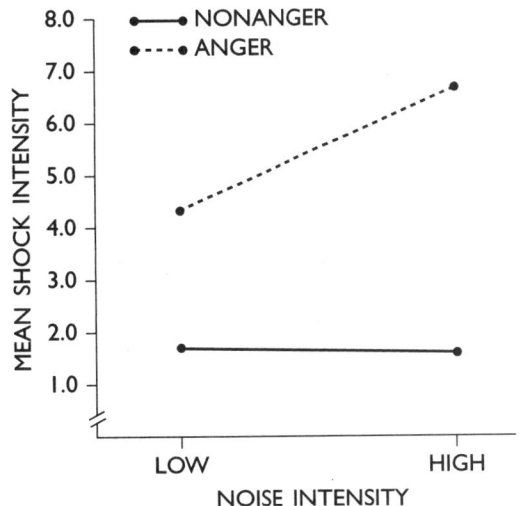

FIGURE 43.01

Mean shock intensity as a function of noise and anger.

$p < .001$, noise intensity, $F(1, 36) = 12.59$, $p < .01$, the Anger $\times$ Noise Intensity interaction, $F(1, 36) = 14.01$, $p < .01$, and trials, $F(4, 144) = 2.64$, $p < .05$. The trials effect indicated that subjects increased their shock levels from the first to the last block of trials. The Anger $\times$ Noise Intensity interaction, which is presented in Figure 43.01, indicated that while nonangered subjects were not affected by differential noise, angered subjects did reveal different patterns of responding. More specifically, angered subjects exposed to high-intensity noise displayed more aggression than their counterparts exposed to low-intensity noise, $F(1, 36) = 5.29$, $p < .05$.

These results would tend to support the facilitation and cognitive labeling hypothesis noted in the introduction. Without some prior aggressive instigation, high-intensity noise had no effect on ongoing aggressive behavior in the present experiment. That some form of cognitive guidance is needed, in this case anger, to produce an aggressive facilitation is analogous to research employing other modes of arousal (e.g., Konečni, 1975b; Zillmann et al., 1972). Though it is possible that subjects did adapt to the noise, as would be suggested by the Glass and Singer (1972) work, the facilitation for angered subjects and the trials effect suggest that this may not have an effect on aggressive responding. The results seem more supportive of the disinhibition hypothesis of Goldstein et al. (1975), in that once subjects begin a somewhat high aggressive response they tend to become more extreme in their behavior over time. It is possible, however, that the length of time (8 minutes) employed in the present study did not allow for complete physiological and behavioral adaptation. This could be examined in future research by systematically varying the time of exposure to high-intensity noise. For the present, however, the results indicate that aversive noise can be a facilitator of ongoing aggressive behavior in individuals who are predisposed to aggression.

Experiment 2: Subsequent Behavior and Control

The first experiment demonstrated that aversive noise could affect ongoing aggressive behavior; however, the work of Glass and Singer (1972) has indicated that the most negative consequences should occur in postnoise conditions. Glass and Singer's research showed impaired task performance and intolerance for frustration following aversive-noise exposure. Although it was initially believed that postnoise impairments were a function of the "psychic costs" of adaptation, more recent theorizing indicates that the effects are a product of "behavioral residues"—a function of exposure to noise independent of adaptation. The behavioral consequences are seen as a function of the intensity of the stressor, in which cognitive factors such as predictability and controllability interact with the physical aspects of the stressor to determine its aversiveness. Thus, one purpose of the present experiment was to determine whether prior noise exposure would affect subsequent aggressive behavior. In addition, it was of interest to examine the effects of perceived control in regard to such behavior. Based on the research of Glass and Singer and others, a number of tentative hypotheses can be suggested.

First, given that subjects are less tolerable of frustration after noise exposure, it would be predicted that subjects exposed to high-intensity noise and later angered should display, in comparison with a no-noise control, increased aggressive behavior against their instigator. One important question might be whether nonangered subjects who are also exposed to aversive noise might also display an increase in aggressive responding when compared with a no-noise control. In a recent study by Sherrod and Downs (1974), subjects exposed to "distracting" background noise during task performance showed decreased postnoise altruism. In their own research, Glass and Singer suggest that a general irritability in interpersonal relations might occur following exposure to aversive events such as high-intensity noise. In order to examine this possibility, subjects in the present experiment were either angered or treated in a neutral manner following noise exposure.

A second prediction in the present study is that perceived control over high-intensity noise should reduce the behavioral aftereffects. Glass and Singer found that control over noise exposure did not impair subsequent task performance. In addition, Sherrod and Downs, in the study noted above, observed that perceived control over noise exposure did not inhibit altruistic behavior. As noted earlier, the behavioral aftereffects observed in the Glass and Singer work were a function of the aversiveness of the stressor. Perception of some control over aversive events seems to reduce the feeling of helplessness during noise exposure and to reduce the magnitude of the stress response. Thus, a sense of control over noise termination, even though not actually exercised, tends to reduce the aversiveness of the noise and the subsequent behavioral impairments. Lefcourt (1973) has also stressed the fact that control and predictability ameliorate the effects of stressful events in both humans and nonhumans. In order to examine the possibility that perceived control might also affect subsequent aggressiveness, subjects in the present experiment were exposed to varying noise conditions while performing a math task. One third of the subjects were exposed to high-intensity (95 dB) noise that was both unpredictable and uncontrollable. This is the type of condition that should produce the most behavioral after-effects. Another third of the subjects were exposed to the same noise but were given additional information that led them to perceive that they had control over terminating the noise. The final group of subjects served as a no-noise control against which to evaluate experimental differences.

METHOD

Subjects The subjects were 60 male undergraduates in introductory psychology who volunteered for extra credit. None of these subjects had participated in Experiment 1.

Procedure The initial portion of the experiment was similar to that of Experiment 1. The subject, along with the confederate, was informed that the experiment involved the effects of stress on learning, signed the informed consent form, and was chosen to take the first task. After taking the confederate to another room, the subject was given instructions concerning the writing of the essay and how the other subject would evaluate its merit. The subject was then given 5 minutes to complete this task. Thus, up to this point, the procedure was identical to that in Experiment 1.

Noise exposure and manipulation of control. Upon returning to the subject's room to collect the essay, the experimenter informed the subject that he would be given a second task to complete while the other subject read the essay and also performed a short task under stress. The subject was told that the task he would be given was a math test, which he would try to complete under the stress of high-intensity noise. The subject was then handed a sheet of 41 math problems (addition, multiplication, etc.) and given further information on the noise. Subjects under high-noise/no-control conditions were instructed to put on the headphones and wait for the experimenter to signal when to begin the task. Subjects under the high-noise/control condition were given additional information, similar to that employed by Glass and Singer (1972), which led them to perceive that they had control over noise termination. Subjects were told that any time they wanted the noise terminated while working on the math problems, they needed only to say the word *terminate* over the intercom. At that point the noise would stop and they could continue with the remainder of the task without noise exposure. It was further noted, however, that a number of subjects had previously used this option and the experimenters were currently interested in obtaining more subjects who maintained noise exposure throughout the entire task. The experimenter noted that he would appreciate it if the subject kept the noise on but that the choice to do so was entirely up to the subject. None of the subjects elected to terminate the noise. In the no-noise condition, subjects were informed that they were to take the task under no stress but were instructed to wear the headphones to block out any background noise. After a signal from the experimenter, the subjects were given 7 minutes to work on the task. During this time, subjects under noise conditions were given unpredictable, aperiodic 1-second white-noise bursts of 95 dB at the average rate of every 4 seconds.

Anger manipulation and administration of aggression. After the elapsed time for the task, the experimenter returned and indicated that it was time for the subject to receive his evaluation from the other subject for the essay. The procedure was the same as in Experiment 1, with angered subjects receiving nine shocks and a poor written evaluation and nonangered subjects receiving one shock and a positive evaluation. Following the evaluation, the subject was given the information regarding the administration of the nonsense-syllable task and use of the aggression machine as done in the previous study. The remaining procedure was the same as before except that the learning task involved 24 trials in which the learner made 18 incorrect and 8 correct responses. Following completion of the task, the subject completed a brief questionnaire in which he rated on 7-point scales his reactions to the noise, the essay rating, the other subject, and his freedom in terminating that noise. The subject was then completely debriefed as to the true nature of the study and thanked for his participation.

The experiment was conducted by three experimenters and three confederates who were balanced across conditions. None of these factors affected the results and are thus eliminated in future analyses.

RESULTS AND DISCUSSION

Manipulation Checks Analyses on ratings of the noise by the two noise-exposure groups indicated that they did not differ from each other on the measures of loudness or annoyance. However, subjects under the noise/with-control condition found the noise less aversive than noise/no-control subjects, $t(38) = 2.28$, $p < .05$; $Ms = 3.6$ and 4.3, respectively. This would tend to support the contention of Glass and Singer (1972) that a feeling of control over stressful events lessens their aversiveness. An additional question with regard to the experimental groups was their feeling of freedom to terminate the noise. Noise/with-control subjects indicated a higher degree of freedom than noise/no-control subjects, $t(38) = 4.05$, $p < .01$; $Ms = 6.2$ and 4.0, respectively.

Additional analyses were conducted on the subjects' reactions to the essay rating. Results indicated that anger subjects perceived their rating as poorer, $F(1, 54) = 862.05$, $p < .001$; $Ms = 6.7$ and 1.3, were angrier, $F(1, 54) = 23.01$, $p < .001$; $Ms = 2.9$ and 1.2, and did not feel as good toward the confederate, $F(1, 54) = 45.85$, $p < .001$; $Ms = 6.5$ and 4.4, compared with their nonangered counterparts.

Math Test A one-way ANOVA with the three noise levels as groups was conducted on the number of problems completed, the number of problems correct, and the percentage of correct problems. There were no significant effects. The results suggest that subjects **were** able to adapt to the noise during ongoing task performance. Such data are analogous to those obtained by Glass and Singer (1972) and others (e.g., Sherrod & Downs, 1974).

Aggression Data A 2 × 3 (Anger × Noise) ANOVA was conducted on the shock intensity data.

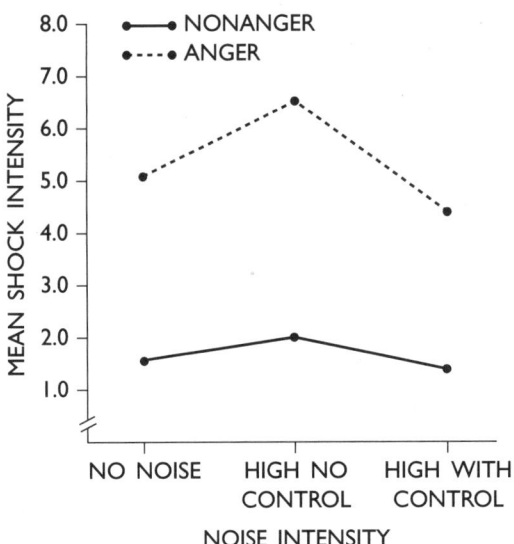

FIGURE 43.02

Mean shock intensity as a function of noise, control, and anger.

Significant sources of variation were obtained for anger, $F(1, 54) = 260.10$, $p < .001$, noise, $F(2, 54) = 12.47$, $p < .01$, and the Anger × Noise interaction, $F(2, 54) = 3.96$, $p < .025$. The interaction is presented in Figure 43.02. As can be seen, although noise did not affect nonangered subjects, it did produce differential responding for angered individuals. More specifically, subjects under noise/no-control were more aggressive than no-noise, $F(1, 54) = 11.97$, $p < .01$, and noise/with-control, $F(1, 54) = 29.70$, $p < .001$, subjects, with the latter two groups not significantly different from each other.

These results suggest that postnoise aggression is not a function of a general irritability in interpersonal relations but is dependent on some form of aggressive instigation. One possible explanation is that subjects under no-control conditions were less tolerable of the essay rating received from the confederate. This notion would be supported by the task performance data of Glass and Singer (1972) and would seem to accord well with the obtained results of the present experiment. Another possibility is that subjects under no-control conditions, who found the noise more aversive, maintained some form of residual arousal when they were receiving their essay evaluation. In terms of the recent work by Zillmann (Zillmann, 1971; Zillmann et al., 1972) on excitation transfer and the cognitive-labeling hypothesis referred to earlier (i.e., Konečni, 1975a), it is possible that subjects came to label their composite emotion as a heightened form of anger. While the self-report data do not lend support to this interpretation, perhaps due to problems of the scale, it would be of interest for future research to examine this possibility through the use of physiological measures of subjects at various times during a similar experiment. Whatever the final explanation, the more significant finding is that perceived control over the noise eliminated any negative consequences due to noise exposure. These results are similar to those found for altruistic behavior (Sherrod & Downs, 1974) and further support the importance of some form of control over stressful events noted by Glass and Singer (1972) and Lefcourt (1973).

General Conclusions

It was the interest of the present two experiments to examine the relationship between exposure to aversive noise and aggressive behavior. The model chosen as a context for this investigation was the research of Glass and Singer (1972) on task performance. The results for an interpersonal behavior (in this case, aggression) seem to parallel those of Glass and Singer for postnoise behavior, though differing somewhat for ongoing responses. An important additional factor in the present studies is the necessity of aggressive provocation for enhancing aggression from exposure to high-intensity noise. Recently, Konečni (1975a) has indicated that prior anger arousal should be considered when one examines the effect of aversive stimulation on interpersonal behavior. The present results seem to support this contention.

The findings concerning the effects of perceived control as a cognitive factor in noise exposure should direct researchers in the future to examine other variables that might mediate the noise–aggression relation. Factors such as expectation, relative deprivation, necessity, choice, and others examined in the Glass and Singer research program would be of obvious interest. As noted earlier, the underlying mechanism for the effects of these factors should also be given further consideration.

In general, the results of the present experiments suggest that high-intensity noise can have negative effects on interpersonal interactions. While these effects seem to depend on a number of mediating factors (i.e., anger, perceived control), there now seems to be evidence for reductions in prosocial (Sherrod & Downs, 1974) and increases in antisocial behaviors. Given the research on other environmental stressors (i.e., overcrowding, high temperatures) and their effects on interpersonal behaviors, it would seem that research should now direct itself toward the examination of variables that might mediate and

consequently reduce the negative consequences of various environmental stimuli on human behavior.

References

1. Bandura, A. *Aggression: A social learning analysis.* Englewood Cliffs, N.J.: Prentice-Hall, 1973.
2. Baron, R. A. The aggression-inhibiting influence of heightened sexual arousal. *Journal of Personality and Social Psychology,* 1974, *30,* 318–322.
3. Baron, R. A., & Bell, P. A. Aggression and heat: Mediating effects of prior provocation and exposure to an aggressive model. *Journal of Personality and Social Psychology,* 1975, *31,* 825–832.
4. Berkowitz, L., & Geen, R. G. Film violence and the cue properties of available targets. *Journal of Personality and Social Psychology,* 1966, *3,* 525–530.
5. Buss, A. H. *The psychology of aggression.* New York: Wiley, 1961.
6. Donnerstein, E., Donnerstein, M., & Evans, R. Erotic stimuli and aggression: Facilitation or inhibition. *Journal of Personality and Social Psychology,* 1975, *32,* 237–244.
7. Geen, R., & O'Neal, E. Activation of cue-elicited aggression by general arousal. *Journal of Personality and Social Psychology,* 1969, *11,* 289–292.
8. Glass, D., & Singer, J. *Urban stress.* New York: Academic Press, 1972.
9. Goldstein, J. H., Davis, R. W., & Herman, D. Escalation of aggression: Experimental studies. *Journal of Personality and Social Psychology,* 1975, *31,* 162–170.
10. Griffitt, W. Environmental effects on interpersonal affective behavior: Ambient effective temperature and attraction. *Journal of Personality and Social Psychology,* 1970, *15,* 240–244.
11. Harris, M., & Huang, L. Aggression and the attribution process. *Journal of Social Psychology,* 1974, *92,* 209–216.
12. Konečni, V. J. The mediation of aggressive behavior: Arousal level versus anger and cognitive labeling. *Journal of Personality and Social Psychology,* 1975, *32,* 706–712. (a)
13. Konečni, V. J. Annoyance, type and duration of postannoyance activity, and aggression: The cathartic effect. *Journal of Experimental Psychology: General,* 1975, *104,* 76–102. (b)
14. Lefcourt, H. The function of the illusions of freedom and control. *American Psychologist,* 1973, *28,* 417–425.
15. Noble, C. E. Measurement of association value (a), rated associations (a′), and scaled meaningfulness (m′) for the 2100 CVC combinations of the English alphabet. *Psychological Reports,* 1961, *8,* 487–521.
16. O'Neal, E., & Kaufman, L. The influence of attack, arousal, and information about one's arousal upon interpersonal aggression. *Psychonomic Science,* 1972, *26,* 211–214.
17. Schachter, S., & Singer, J. E. Cognitive, social and physiological determinants of emotional state. *Psychological Review,* 1962, *69,* 379–399.

18. Sherrod, D. R., & Downs, R. Environmental determinants of altruism: The effects of stimulus overload and perceived control on helping. *Journal of Experimental Social Psychology,* 1974, *10,* 468–479.

19. Ward, L. M., & Suedfeld, R. Human responses to highway noise. *Environmental Research,* 1974, *6,* 306–326.

20. Zillmann, D. Excitation transfer in communication-mediated aggressive behavior. *Journal of Experimental Social Psychology,* 1971, *7,* 419–434.

21. Zillmann, D., Katcher, A., & Milavsky, B. Excitation transfer from physical exercise to subsequent aggressive behavior. *Journal of Experimental Social Psychology,* 1972, *8,* 247–259.

QUESTIONS FOR REFLECTION AND DISCUSSION:

1. How did Donnerstein and Wilson make subjects angry? What was the operational definition of low-intensity and high-intensity uncontrollable noises? How did they measure subjects aggressive behavior?

2. How does Figure 43.01 show that (1) angry subjects were more aggressive than nonangry subjects, and that exposure to high-intensity noise affected the aggressiveness of only the angry subjects?

3. What are the implications of the Donnerstein and Wilson study for the workplace environment, for entertainment, and so forth?

4. Have you ever been exposed to a high-intensity, uncontrollable noise? What were the effects? How did you handle it? Are you satisfied with how you handled it? Why or why not?